# STUDY GUIDE FOR USE V

# Fundamentals of
# CORPORATE FINANCE

## FOURTH CANADIAN EDITION

**STEPHEN A. ROSS**
Massachusetts Institute of Technology

**RANDOLPH W. WESTERFIELD**
University of Southern California

**BRADFORD D. JORDAN**
University of Kentucky

**GORDON S. ROBERTS**
York University

PREPARED BY
**JEANNETTE A. SWITZER**
Dalhousie University

Toronto Montréal Boston Burr Ridge, IL Dubuque, IA Madison, WI New York San Francisco
St. Louis Bangkok Bogotá Caracas Kuala Lumpur Lisbon London Madrid
Mexico City Milan New Delhi Santiago Seoul Singapore Sydney Taipei

**McGraw-Hill**
**Ryerson Limited**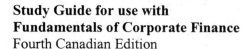
*A Subsidiary of The McGraw·Hill Companies*

**Study Guide for use with**
**Fundamentals of Corporate Finance**
Fourth Canadian Edition

ISBN: 007-088719-5

3 4 5 6 7 8 9 0 CP 0 9 8 7 6 5 4 3

Printed and bound in Canada

Care has been taken to trace ownership of copyright material contained in this text; however, the publisher will welcome any information that enables them to rectify any reference or credit for subsequent editions.

Vice President and Editorial Director: Pat Ferrier
Senior Sponsoring Editor: Lynn Fisher
Associate Sponsoring Editor: Jason Stanley
Developmental Editor: Maria Chu
Supervising Editor: Julie van Veen
Marketing Manager: Kelly Smyth
Production Coordinator: Emily Hickey
Printer: Canadian Printco, Ltd.

# PREFACE

Many business students find the first course in corporate finance to be one of the most challenging, as well as one of the most rewarding, courses in the undergraduate business curriculum. The underlying goal in writing this **Study Guide** is to supplement the preeminent text in its field, **Fundamentals of Corporate Finance**, by Stephen A. Ross, Randolph W. Westerfield, Bradford D. Jordan, and Gordon S. Roberts. I hope you will use this **Study Guide** in conjunction with **Fundamentals of Corporate Finance** in every phase of your introduction to corporate finance.

## ORGANIZATION OF THE STUDY GUIDE

The Study Guide to accompany the text is designed to accomplish one major objective. It will augment and reinforce a sound grasp of modern fundamentals of finance and its underlying principles. The Study Guide contains a comprehensive treatment of each chapter from the text, providing you with **Chapter Highlights**, **Concept Tests**, and **Problems with Solutions**. To accomplish this objective, the **Study Guide** has been organized as discussed below.

## APPROACH

**Chapter Highlights:** These cover all the essential concepts and subjects in an easily understandable narrative form. The goal of the Chapter Highlights is to reinforce the major concepts presented in the text by including summaries of the material, extensive use of numerical examples and, where appropriate, discussion of alternative perspectives designed to provide additional insight.

**Concept Test:** The Concept Test for each chapter is a "do-it-yourself" summary of the chapter. Completing this test will help you to create a summary of the chapter, while also testing your understanding of the material. You will be able to identify your strengths and weaknesses by comparing your answers to those provided at the end of the Concept Test.

**Problems and Solutions:** Problems, with solutions, are provided for each chapter. To obtain the greatest benefit, **work the problems by yourself first**. Then, look at the solutions given in the Study Guide. This is the best way to prepare for an exam on the subject.

## TIPS FOR THE STUDENT

The **Study Guide** is designed to enhance your understanding of corporate finance. It is essential to understand a concept before it can be properly applied to the analysis of a specific problem. Keep this goal in mind as you read and study both the text and this guide. Since much of corporate finance is mathematical in nature, you should have your calculator, as well as pencil and paper, handy as you read. This will allow you to verify your understanding of the calculations used to solve the numerous examples for each chapter.

The **Problems and Solutions** at the end of each chapter will be most helpful to you if you first try to completely solve the problem before reading the solution we have provided. You'll get a lot more out of the problem if you try to solve it yourself and **then** compare your results to our solutions. Remember that the best way to actually learn how to solve finance problems is to do them yourself.

Most of the examples in the Study Guide and the end-of-chapter Problems and Solutions were solved using a financial calculator. If you use the financial tables in the Appendix to your text, your answer may differ slightly from ours; this is a result of rounding in the tables. In addition, you should be aware of the rounding error which can arise in problems which require a sequence of calculations. That is, if you round off an immediate result, you lose accuracy in your final answer. This problem can generally be avoided by working with the most accurate figures possible, until you have completed your solution. We have tried to take this approach throughout this guide. Therefore, for the sake of consistency with our solutions, it is important that you take the same approach. Otherwise, you may find your answers differ from ours, which may cause unnecessary confusion.

I have greatly enjoyed preparing this **Study Guide** for you. However you use it, I hope it makes the study of corporate finance more productive and enjoyable and, of course, a little easier!

## ACKNOWLEDGEMENTS

I am grateful to McGraw-Hill Ryerson, Limited for the opportunity to write this **Study Guide**. In my opinion, **Fundamentals of Corporate Finance** is an excellent text. Preparing a supplement to this outstanding text has been an enlightening and gratifying experience.

I would like to thank Patrick Gill and Jeff Healy who were responsible for proofreading the text and verifying solutions to problems. Finally, many thanks to my husband Abol and daughter Anahita. Without their patience and support, this project would not have been possible.

Jeannette A. Switzer

# CONTENTS

# 1        Introduction to Corporate Finance

## CHAPTER HIGHLIGHTS

The two major issues addressed in this chapter are: (1) What is corporate finance?  (2) What is the goal of the financial manager?  The answers  require an understanding of the forms of business organization.  We also explore the agency problem as it relates to both control of the firm and to Canadian financial markets.

## WHAT IS CORPORATE FINANCE?

The major decisions faced by financial managers are:

1.    What long-term investments should the firm undertake?

2.    What is the best way to raise long-term financing for these investments?

3.    How should the firm manage its short-term assets and liabilities?

The first question represents the firm's **capital budgeting** decision.  The process of making capital budgeting decisions is described in detail in Part Four of the text.

The second question represents the firm's **capital structure** decision.  Capital structure refers to the mix of long-term debt and equity that the firm chooses in order to finance its investments.  Capital structure decisions are discussed in Parts Six and Seven of the text.

The third question relates to the firm's **working capital** decision.  Since cash inflows and outflows do not occur simultaneously, gaps in cash flows must be managed by appropriate adjustments of current assets and current liabilities.  The topic of short-term finance is discussed in Part Eight.

## THE FINANCIAL MANAGER

The owners of a firm are its shareholders.  However, the shareholders of large corporations are not usually involved in the day-to-day operations of the firm.  Managers are employed as agents of the shareholders to make decisions on their behalf.

The financial functions of the firm are usually shared by the treasurer and controller.  They typically report to a top officer of the firm (vice president of finance or chief financial officer).  Financial accounting, tax payments, and management information systems are the responsibility of the controller. The treasurer is responsible for activities related to the three major decisions identified earlier.  Our emphasis is on the treasurer's functions.

# FINANCIAL MANAGEMENT DECISIONS

**Capital Budgeting:** With regard to the firm's long-term investments, the job of the financial manager is to create value for the firm's shareholders by acquiring assets with a value greater than their cost. The financial manager must forecast the cash inflows and outflows generated by an asset. This information is used to determine the asset's value. Then, the manager compares the asset's value with its cost to the firm. Any analysis of cash flows must consider three things: (1) the size of the cash flows, (2) the timing of the cash flows, and (3) the riskiness of the cash flows. These topics are thoroughly discussed in later chapters.

**Capital Structure:** A firm's capital structure is the specific mixture of equity and long-term debt used to finance the acquisition of fixed assets. The financial manager must decide on the best combination of debt and equity. In addition he/she must determine the least expensive sources of funds. Then, if funds need to be raised, the financial manager must decide how and when to raise the money.

**Working Capital Management:** The concept of working capital management deals with the firm's receipt and disbursement of cash. Typically, these decisions involve management of current assets and current liabilities.

# FORMS OF BUSINESS ORGANIZATION

Businesses can be organized in three different legal forms. Differences among these forms are related to the life of the business, the ability of the business to obtain financing, and the way in which the business is taxed.

**Sole Proprietorship:** One person owns the entire business and keeps all the profits from the business, but has *unlimited liability* for business debts. Therefore, the proprietor's personal assets can be seized in payment for outstanding debts. For tax purposes, all business profits are taxed as personal income. This is the simplest and least regulated form of business organization. The life of the business is limited to the owner's life and available equity financing is limited to the owner's personal wealth. Transfer of ownership may be difficult because it requires selling the entire business to a new owner.

**Partnership:** A partnership has two or more owners (partners). In a *general partnership*, all partners share in any gains or losses from the business. They have unlimited liability for any debts incurred by the partnership. In a *limited partnership*, one or more general partners run the business; the limited partners do not actively participate. General partners have unlimited liability for the business debts; the liability of limited partners is restricted to the amount that that partner contributes to the business. Partnerships are easy to form and all profits are taxed as personal income. The major disadvantages are: (1) unlimited liability of general partners, (2) limited life of the business, and (3) difficulty in transferring ownership. These disadvantages may make it difficult for the business to raise the funds needed for investment opportunities.

**Corporation:** The corporation is the most important form of business organization in Canada. A corporation is a legal entity, separate and distinct from its owners. This means a corporation can incur debts in its own name, can sue or be sued, and can enter into legal contracts. The liability of the corporation's owners is therefore limited to the amount of money they have invested in the business.

Corporations are formed according to the development of *articles of incorporation* and the firm's *bylaws*. The articles of incorporation contain information about the corporation's name, its intended life (usually indefinite), its business purpose, and the number of shares that can be issued. The bylaws describe how the corporation regulates its own existence. Canadian firms can be incorporated under either the federal Canada Business Corporation Act or under provincial law.

The owners of a corporation are its shareholders. Ownership interest is represented by shares of common stock.

These shares can be easily transferred, or sold, from one shareholder to another. This means the life of the corporation is not limited to the life of its owners (as with sole proprietorships and partnerships). In addition, the shareholders elect the corporation's board of directors. These directors then decide on the managers for the corporation. This separates the functions of ownership and management. The advantages arising from this are: (1) ownership is easily transferrable, (2) owners' liability is limited to the amount invested in the firm, and (3) the business has an unlimited life span. These advantages make it easier for a corporation to raise large amounts of financing.

The major disadvantage of the corporate form is double taxation. Corporate profits are subject to corporate income taxes. Then, dividends paid to the firm's owners (shareholders) are taxed as personal income for the shareholder.

## THE GOAL OF FINANCIAL MANAGEMENT

Corporate finance is essentially the study of financial decision making within a corporation. The goal of these decisions is to make money for the firm's owners, the shareholders. Shareholders measure financial benefit in terms of changes in the firm's stock price. Decisions which are in the best interest of the shareholders are those which increase the value of the stock. Therefore, the goal of financial management should be to maximize the current price per share of the firm's existing stock. If the firm is privately owned and has no traded stock, the goal should be to maximize the value of the owners' equity. For firms with publicly traded stock, maximizing shareholders' equity translates into maximizing the stock price.

The major factors that financial managers should consider are profitability and risk. Both factors affect the value of the firm's stock. To make decisions consistent with maximizing owners' wealth, financial managers must assess the impact of these factors on the value of the firm's stock.

## THE AGENCY PROBLEM AND CONTROL OF THE CORPORATION

Although the goal of financial managers should be to maximize the current stock price (the owners' wealth), managers may not always act in a manner consistent with shareholders' best interests. Conflicts between the manager's personal interests and those of the firm's owners are referred to as agency problems.

**Agency Relationships:** The relationship between shareholders and managers is an *agency relationship*. The principals (shareholders) contract with agents (managers) to perform the task of managing the firm. When the goals of managers differ from those of shareholders, an agency problem exists.

**Management Goals:** Evidence indicates that managers are sometimes motivated by considerations such as organizational survival, managerial independence, and corporate self-sufficiency. These factors are related to the maximization of corporate wealth, typically related to corporate size or growth. However, decisions that increase the firm's size do not necessarily increase the value of the firm's stock.

**Do Managers Act in the Shareholders' Interests?**

In general, the extent to which managers' actions are consistent with shareholders' goals depends on the nature of managerial compensation and the control of the firm.

1.  *Managerial compensation* plays a major role in determining the extent to which managers act in shareholders' interests. Compensation may be linked either directly or indirectly to the firm's performance. For example, managers may have an option to purchase shares of the firm's stock at a pre-determined price. The value of the option increases with the value of the firm's stock. In addition, both promotions and the manager's value in the labour market are often directly related to the manager's success in achieving the goals of shareholders.

2.  *Control of the firm* rests with the firm's owners (shareholders). They elect the firm's directors, who, in turn, hire (and fire) the firm's managers. This gives shareholders the ability to remove directors or managers who do not act in their interests. Also, poorly-managed firms may be taken over by another firm, in which case the existing management team is usually replaced.

3.  *Stakeholders* are any parties who have an interest in the firm's decisions. Stakeholders include shareholders, creditors, employees, customers, suppliers, and the federal and provincial governments. Well-managed firms pay close attention to the needs and expectations of all stakeholders.

## FINANCIAL MARKETS AND THE CORPORATION

Debt and equity securities issued by firms are bought and sold in the financial markets. The financial markets are simply a way of bringing together the buyers and the sellers of financial securities.

**Money versus Capital Markets:** Financial market transactions are classified according to the maturity of the financial instruments bought and sold. *Money markets* are financial markets where short-term debt securities (maturity is usually one year or less) are bought and sold. Long-term debt and shares of stock are traded in the *capital market*. The money market is a dealer market in which the dealers (brokers and agents) match buyers and sellers, but do not personally own the financial security. The money market has no physical location; trading facilities and market participants are linked via telephone and computers.

**Primary versus Secondary Markets:** The original sale, or issue, of a security by a government or corporation is referred to as a *primary market* transaction. Any subsequent sale or purchase of a security is referred to as a *secondary market* transaction.

**Primary Markets:** When a firm first issues a security, the sale takes place in the primary market. These transactions may be either public offerings or private placements. Most public offerings are *underwritten* by investment dealers or groups of dealers (a *syndicate*) who purchase the securities from the issuing firm and then resell them to the public (hopefully at a higher price). New public offerings must be registered with provincial authorities. The most important is the Ontario Securities Commission (OSC). Private placements do not need to be registered with the OSC and do not require an underwriter's involvement.

**Secondary Markets:** Subsequent trades of a security (after the initial public issue) take place in the secondary markets. These are either *auction markets* or *dealer markets*. Unlike dealer markets, auction markets have a physical location (an *exchange*) where trading takes place on the floor of the exchange. The largest auction market in Canada is the Toronto Stock Exchange (TSE), where the common shares of most large Canadian corporations are traded. Debt securities (bonds) usually trade in dealer markets. Shares of smaller firms often trade in the over-the-counter market (OTC), which is also a dealer market.

**Listing:** Any stock trading on an organized exchange is said to be *listed* on the exchange. Listed firms must apply to the exchange and meet certain minimum requirements regarding asset size and number of shareholders. Listing criteria differ across the various exchanges in Canada.

## FINANCIAL INSTITUTIONS

Financial institutions act as intermediaries between investors (suppliers of funds) and firms that need to raise funds (demanders of funds). These institutions provide a variety of services which promote the efficient allocation of funds. Examples of financial institutions include chartered banks, trust companies, credit unions, investment dealers, insurance companies, pension funds, and mutual funds.

Chartered banks operate under federal regulation. They accept deposits and make loans, earning their income on the spread between the interest paid on deposits and the higher rates charged for loans to both businesses and individuals. Trust companies also accept deposits and make loans. In addition, they engage in fiduciary activities including managing assets for estates, registered retirement savings plans, etc. Credit unions also accept deposits and make loans.

Investment dealers are non-depository institutions. They assist firms in issuing new securities and work with investors to buy or sell securities. Their income is based on transaction fees. Insurance companies include both property and casualty, and health and life insurance. They accept funds in a form similar to deposits and also make loans. Pension funds invest contributions from employers and employees in securities offered by financial markets. Mutual funds pool individual investments to purchase a diversified portfolio of securities.

Recent deregulation affecting Canadian financial institutions now allows the above institutions to engage in most of the above activities, with one exception: chartered banks are not allowed to sell life insurance through their branch networks.

## TRENDS IN FINANCIAL MARKETS AND FINANCIAL MANAGEMENT

*Financial engineering* refers to the design of new securities and processes which can reduce and control risk and minimize taxes. In addition to the use of securitized financial instruments, financial engineering makes use of *derivative securities*, including options and futures. Financial engineering also tries to reduce the costs of issuing securities and compliance with government regulations. For example, the *Prompt Offering Prospectus* (POP) allows firms that frequently issue new equity to bypass most of the OSC regulation requirements.

In addition, advances in technology have created opportunities to combine different types of financial institutions to take advantage of economies of scale and scope. Current regulations allow almost unlimited scope for financial institutions to enter each others' traditional businesses.

## CONCEPT TEST

1.  Corporate finance is the study of ways to answer three major questions.  These three subjects are referred to as _____, _____, and _____ decisions.

2.  The _____ of large corporations are generally not involved in day-to-day operations of the firm.  Consequently, _____ are employed to make decisions on behalf of the owners.

3.  The financial functions of the firm are generally shared by the _____ and the _____ .

4.  The three different legal forms of business organization are the _____, the _____, and the _____ .

5.  In a sole proprietorship, the profits are kept by the _____ . Unlimited liability for all business debts falls on the _____ .

6.  A _____ is a business owned by two or more persons.  In a _____, everyone shares in gains or losses and has unlimited liability for all debts.  In a _____, one or more persons runs the business and has unlimited liability; the others have only limited liability.

7.  The primary disadvantages of the forms of business referred to in questions 5 and 6 are _____, _____, and _____ .

8.  The rules and procedures by which a corporation governs itself are contained in the _____ . All corporations must prepare a document called the _____ , describing the number of shares which may be issued, the business purpose, the intended life, and other details.

9.  The major advantages of the corporate form of organization are _____ , _____ , and _____ . The primary disadvantage of the corporate form of organization is the _____ of corporate income.

10.  The primary goal of the corporation is maximization of _____ . Because management goals may conflict with shareholders' goals, an _____ problem is said to exist. _____ are the costs associated with aligning shareholders' goals with managers' goals.

11.  Chartered banks and investment dealers are examples of institutions which act as _____ . These institutions promote the efficient _____ of funds and _____ of securities.

12.  Banks earn their income from the _____ between interest paid on deposits and the higher rate earned on _____ .

13.  _____ are non-depository financial institutions which assist firms in issuing new securities. Recent _____ allows financial institutions to engage in most of the activities of other financial institutions.

14.  When financial markets are classified according to the maturity of the financial instruments, the two types of markets are the _____ and the _____ . Short-term debt instruments are traded in the _____ , which is a _____ market.  Long-term debt instruments and equities are traded in the _____ .

15.  Financial markets can also be classified as either primary markets or secondary markets.  The original sale, or _____ , of a security takes place in the _____ of a security.

16.     The Toronto Stock Exchange is an example of a secondary market which functions as a(n) _____ market.  A stock that trades on the TSE is said to be _____ on the exchange.

17.     The creation of new securities or financial processes is referred to as _____ .  This has resulted in the reduction and control of _____ and the minimization of _____ .

## ANSWERS TO CONCEPT TEST

1.      capital budgeting; capital structure; working capital

2.      shareholders; managers

3.      treasurer; controller

4.      sole proprietorship; partnership; corporation

5.      owner; owner

6.      partnership; general partnership; limited partnership

7.      unlimited liability; limited life; difficulty of transferring ownership

8.      bylaws; articles of incorporation

9.      ease of transferring ownership; limited liability; unlimited life; double taxation

10.     current price of existing stock;  agency;  agency costs

11.     financial intermediaries; allocation; pricing

12.     spread; loans

13.     investment dealers; deregulation

14.     money market; capital market; money market; dealer; capital market

15.     issue; primary market

16.     auction;  listed

17.     financial engineering; risk; taxes

# 2        Financial Statements, Taxes, and Cash Flow

## CHAPTER HIGHLIGHTS

This chapter examines financial statements, cash flow concepts, and important tax considerations in the Canadian setting. The chapter emphasizes the *use* of accounting statements in corporate finance, rather than the actual preparation of the financial statements. Keep in mind two important distinctions as you work through the chapter: (1) the difference between accounting (book) value and market value, and (2) the difference between accounting income and actual cash flows.

## THE BALANCE SHEET

The *balance sheet* is a snapshot of a firm's accounting value at a particular date. The firm's assets are listed on the left-hand side; the liabilities and shareholders' equity on the right-hand side. By definition, the value of the firm's assets is equal to the sum of its liabilities and shareholders' equity:

$$\text{Assets} = \text{Liabilities} + \text{Shareholders' Equity}$$

Note that the book value of equity is the difference between the values of the firm's assets and its liabilities.

**An Example:** Abbreviated balance sheets for Tin Can, Inc. are given below.

### TIN CAN, INC.
### Balance Sheets as of December 31, 1999 and 2000 ($ in millions)

| Assets | 1999 | 2000 | Liabilities & Owners' Equity | 1999 | 2000 |
|---|---|---|---|---|---|
| Current assets | | | Current liabilities | | |
| Cash | $ 200 | $ 503 | Accounts payable | $ 500 | $ 530 |
| Accounts receivable | 650 | 688 | Notes payable | 543 | 460 |
| Inventory | 1,045 | 700 | Other | 214 | 183 |
| Total | $1,895 | $1,891 | Total | $1,257 | $1,173 |
| | | | Long-term debt | $1,097 | $1,184 |
| Fixed assets | | | Owners' equity | | |
| Net plant | | | Common stock | 590 | 720 |
| and equipment | $1,490 | $1,689 | Retained earnings | 441 | 503 |
| | | | Total | 1,031 | 1,223 |
| Total assets | $3,385 | $3,580 | Total liabilities & Owners' Equity | $3,385 | $3,580 |

The financial manager must be especially aware of the following three aspects of the balance sheet: liquidity, debt versus equity, and market versus book value. These are discussed below.

**Liquidity:**  *Liquidity* refers to the speed and ease with which assets can be converted to cash without significant loss in value.  On the balance sheets, assets are listed in order of decreasing liquidity.  Current assets (cash, marketable securities, accounts receivable, inventory) are relatively liquid.  Fixed assets are, in comparison, relatively illiquid.  Liquidity is valuable because it increases the firm's ability to meet short-term obligations.  However, rates of return are usually lower for liquid assets than for fixed assets, so there is a tradeoff between liquidity and the foregone potential of higher returns on fixed assets.  Managers must consider this tradeoff in deciding on the mix of short- and long-term assets.

**Debt versus Equity:** Debt is a liability that obligates the firm to repay principal and interest to creditors at specified times.  The firm's creditors have the first claim on any cash flows generated.  Equity holders are entitled to the firm's residual value once all claims to creditors have been paid.  This residual value is expressed by the equation:

Shareholders' Equity    =    Assets   -   Liabilities

From an economic standpoint, if the firm sells all of its assets and pays off all of its debts, any remaining cash belongs to the firm's shareholders.  The use of debt financing is referred to as *financial leverage* because it magnifies both the firm's gains and losses that accrue to the shareholders.

**Market Value versus Book Value:** Values shown on the firm's balance sheet show the book value of the firm's assets, rather than the market value.  These values are based on *historical cost*, as determined by Generally Accepted Accounting Principles (GAAP).  Most often, an asset's *market value* (the price at which it could be sold today) is not the same as the book value.  The difference between market and book values is usually higher for fixed assets than for current assets.  Financial managers must consider the difference between market and book values when making capital budgeting decisions.  For financial decisions, the value of an asset, the value of a firm, or the value of a firm's common stock depends on *market* value.  The goal of the financial manager is to maximize the market value of the firm's existing share price.

**An Example:**   The December 31, 2000 balance sheets of the KMS Corporation are presented below in both accounting (book value) and economic (market value) terms:

### KMS CORPORATION
### Balance Sheet

| *Assets* | **Book** | **Market** | *Liabilities & Equity* | **Book** | **Market** |
|---|---|---|---|---|---|
| Net working capital | $ 3,000 | $ 4,000 | Long-term debt | $ 5,000 | $ 5,000 |
| Fixed assets | 8,000 | 12,000 | Shareholders' equity | 6,000 | 11,000 |
| | $11,000 | $16,000 | | $11,000 | $16,000 |

Using market values, the firm would realize $4,000 if it liquidated all current assets and used the proceeds to pay off its current liabilities.  The book value of net working capital, though, is only $3,000.  The $1,000 difference reflects the difference between the market and book values of the firm's current assets.  Similarly, there is a $4,000 difference between the market and book values of the firm's fixed assets.  These differences result in the market value of the shareholders' equity exceeding the book value by $5,000 ($4,000 + $1,000).

## THE INCOME STATEMENT

The firm's *income statement* measures its performance over a period of time, usually one year.  The basic income statement equation is:  Revenues  -  Expenses  =  Income

Income statements report (1) revenues and expenses related to the firm's principal operations, (2) financing expenses, and (3) income taxes.  The last item on the income statement is the firm's *net income*.  The firm's *earnings per share* (EPS) is the net income divided by the number of common shares outstanding.

**An Example:**  An abbreviated 2000 income statement for Tin Can, Inc. is below:

**TIN CAN, INC.**
**2000 Income Statement**

| | | |
|---|---:|---:|
| Net sales | | $ 1,400 |
| Cost of goods sold | | 700 |
| Depreciation | | 200 |
| EBIT | | $   500 |
| Interest paid | | 150 |
| Taxable income | $   350 | |
| Taxes (34%) | | 119 |
| Net income | | $   231 |
| Addition to retained earnings | $    62 | |
| Dividends | 169 | |

According to the income statement, $169 in dividends were paid in 2000.  The remaining $62 of net income was added to the firm's retained earnings.  If you go back to the earlier example, you will notice that the increase in accumulated retained earnings from 1999 to 2000 is the same amount, $62.

**An Example:**  Tin Can has 150 shares of stock outstanding.  What are earnings and dividends per share?

EPS  =  Net income / Shares outstanding  =  $231 / 150  =  $1.54

Dividends per share  =  Dividends / Shares outstanding  =  $169 / 150  =  $1.13

**GAAP and the Income Statement:** Generally Accepted Accounting Principles (GAAP) require revenues to be recorded when they are earned (accrued), even if the cash inflow from payment has not been received. This means revenues are recognized at the time of sale.  Costs are recognized based on the matching principle: they are recorded when the associated revenues are recorded.  Revenues and costs recorded for a particular time period may therefore be very different from the actual cash flows during the same period.

**Non-Cash Items:** Non-cash items appear on the income statement as expenses deducted from income.  Although these items affect the firm's net income, *they do not affect the actual cash flow*.  This is the major reason for the difference between accounting income and the firm's cash flows.

The major non-cash expense is *depreciation*.  If a firm pays $20,000 cash for an asset, the actual cash outflow is $20,000 at the time of purchase.  However, firms may depreciate assets over time, allocating a portion of the cost to each year.  The portion deducted each year is recorded as an expense on the income statement.  Although the expense of the asset is divided over the period during which the firms receive benefit from the asset, these annual deductions are non-cash items.  The actual cash outflow occurred when the asset was purchased.

**Time and Costs:** For financial decision-making, we can distinguish between variable and fixed costs. However, this distinction changes with the time period under consideration. In the long run, all costs are variable, because, given a sufficiently long period of time, even fixed assets can be bought or sold and long-term debts can be paid. In the short run though, costs such as rent or property taxes are considered to be fixed; other costs, including wages and payments to suppliers, are variable. The distinction between fixed and variable costs can be important to financial managers. Accountants, however, classify costs as either product costs or period costs, so the distinction between fixed and variable costs may be blurred. This is another reason for the difference between reported accounting net income and the firm's actual cash flows.

## CASH FLOW

The cash flow a firm generates from the use of its assets is equal to the sum of the cash flows to creditors and shareholders:

> Cash flow from assets   =   Cash flow to creditors   +   Cash flow to shareholders

The three components of cash flow from assets are: operating cash flow, capital spending, and additions to net working capital.

*Operating cash flow* is the cash flow resulting from a firm's day-to-day operations. Operating cash flow is equal to revenues minus costs, excluding depreciation and interest. Depreciation expense is excluded because it does not represent an actual cash flow; interest expense is excluded because it represents a financing expense.

Look back at the information for Tin Can, Inc. The firm's EBIT for 2000 was $500, after deducting $200 depreciation. Adding back the non-cash deduction for depreciation, and subtracting the $80 in current taxes, the firm's operating cash flow is:

| | |
|---|---:|
| Earnings before interest and taxes (EBIT) | $ 500 |
| Depreciation | 200 |
| Current taxes | (119) |
| Operating cash flow | $ 581 |

The accounting definition of operating cash flows is net income plus depreciation. For Tin Can, Inc., this is $231 + $200 = $431. The difference in the two figures is the year's interest expense. This is because the accounting definition treats interest expense as an operating, rather than a financial, expense.

*Capital spending* is the net amount spent on fixed assets, that is, the difference between the acquisition and sale prices of fixed assets. For 1999, Tin Can, Inc. listed fixed assets of $1,490. These assets were depreciated by $200 over the next year. Their value at the end of 2000 would have been $1,490 - $200 = $1,290. However, the 2000 balance sheet reports $1,689 in fixed assets. This means the firm acquired assets worth $1,689 - $1,290 = $399 during the year. The firm's net capital spending for 2000 was, therefore, $399. Note that net capital spending can be negative if the firm sold more assets than it purchased.

Firms invest in both current and fixed assets. For Tin Can, Inc., the investment in current assets decreased by $1,895 - $1,891 = $4 from 1999 to 2000. Current liabilities decreased by $1,257 - $1,173 = $84. The *change in the firm's net working capital* is computed as the change in the level of current assets minus the change in the level of current liabilities: [-$4 - (-$84)] = $80.

Alternatively, the change in the firm's net working capital can be computed as the difference between the 2000 and 1999 levels of net working capital: Net working capital in 1999 is $1,895 - $1,257 = $638; for 2000 it is $1,891 - $1,173 = $718. The addition to net working capital is, therefore, $718 - $638 = $80.

The *total cash flow from assets* can be calculated as operating cash, less net capital spending, less any additions to net working capital. For Tin Can, cash flow from assets equals: $581 - $399 - $80 = $102.

**Cash Flow to Creditors and Shareholders:** The cash flow to investors in a firm consists of net payments to creditors and net payments to shareholders. The net *cash flow to creditors* is the sum of any interest paid, plus any repayment of long-term debt, minus any new long-term borrowing (or, interest paid less net new borrowing). For Tin Can, interest paid during 2000 was $150, and long-term debt increased by $1,184 - $1,097 = $87. The net cash flow to creditors is $150 - $87 = $63.

The *cash flow to shareholders* consists of dividends paid plus the dollar value of stock repurchased by the firm, minus the proceeds from the sale of new equity (or, dividends less net new equity financing). For Tin Can, Inc., 2000 dividends are $169 and net new equity financing is $720 - $590 = $130. The cash flow to shareholders is $169 - $130 = $39. Note that the total cash flow to investors is $63 + $39 = $102, which is the total cash flow generated by the firm's assets.

# TAXES

Taxes are extremely important because the firm's cash flows are measured after taxes. The size of the tax bill is determined through tax laws and regulations and the annual budgets of the federal government (administered by Canada Customs and Revenue Agency) and provincial governments.

**Individual Tax Rates:** Individual federal tax rates and selected provincial rates for the year 2000 are below. These rates apply to income from employment (wages and salary) and from unincorporated businesses. Investment income includes interest income (taxed at individual rates) and dividend and capital gain income (taxed at special rates).

| **Federal** | | | | **Provincial** | |
|---|---|---|---|---|---|
| Taxable Income | Tax | Rate on Excess | | Resident of | Basic Federal Tax |
| $      1 | $ _____ | 17% | | Alberta | 44.0% |
| 32,000 | 5,440 | 25 | | Newfoundland | 62.0 |
| 64,000 | 13,120 | 29 | | Prince Edward Island | 57.5 |
| | | | | Saskatchewan | 48.0 |
| | | | | Northwest Territories | 45.0 |
| | | | | Yukon Territory | 50.0 |
| | | | | Nunavut | 45.0 |

In computing your tax bill, first calculate the federal tax and then the provincial tax as a percentage of the federal tax (with the exception of Quebec residents, who must file two tax returns; those numbers are not given here). If, for example, you are a resident of Yukon Territory with a taxable income of $40,000, your total tax rate on the next dollar earned is: federal rate x (1 + provincial rate)  =  0.25 x (1 + 0.50) = 37.5%. This rate is referred to as the *marginal tax rate*. Your *average tax rate* is the actual percentage of your income spent on taxes: total taxes paid divided by total taxable income.

**An Example:** You live in Newfoundland and have a taxable income of $75,000. Find your total tax bill, your average tax rate, and your marginal tax rate.

Federal tax  =  $13,120 plus 29% of ($75,000 - $64,000)  =  $13,120 + $3,190  =  $16,310

Provincial tax  =  Federal tax x 62%  =  $16,310 x 0.62  =  $10,112.20

Total tax bill  =  Federal tax + Provincial tax  =  $16,310  +  $10,112.20  =  $26,422.20

Average tax rate  =  Total tax / Taxable income  =  $26,422.20 / $75,000  =  35.23%

Marginal tax rate  =  Federal rate x (1 + Provincial rate)  =  0.29 x (1 + 0.62)  =  46.98%

Taxes on individual income in Canada are *progressive*, with higher incomes taxed at higher rates. For financial decisions, the marginal tax rate is the relevant rate because any new cash flows are taxed at the marginal rate.

**Taxes on Investment Income:** Below is an example of the way in which dividend income is taxed for a resident of Yukon. Note that the *dividend tax credit* reduces the effective tax rate on dividends for investors in each of the three federal tax brackets. Actual dividends are 'grossed up' by 25% and federal tax is calculated on the grossed up figure. A dividend tax credit of 16 2/3% of the *actual dividend* is subtracted from the federal tax to get the net federal tax payable. The provincial tax is then added.

|  | Tax bracket | | |
| --- | --- | --- | --- |
|  | 17% | 25% | 29% |
| Actual dividends | $ 5,000.00 | $ 5,000.00 | $ 5,000.00 |
| Gross up at 25% | 1,250.00 | 1,250.00 | 1,250.00 |
| Grossed up dividends | $ 6,250.00 | $ 6,250.00 | $ 6,250.00 |
| Federal tax | 1,062.50 | 1,562.50 | 1,812.50 |
| Less dividend tax credit (0.1667 x $5,000) | ( 833.50) | ( 833.50) | ( 833.50 ) |
| Federal tax payable | $    229.00 | $ 729.00 | $    979.00 |
| Provincial tax at 50% of federal tax | 114.50 | 364.50 | 489.50 |
| Total tax | 343.50 | 1,093.50 | 1,468.50 |

Note: The effective tax rate on dividends can also be computed with the following formula: 1.25 (Federal tax rate − .1333) (1 + Provincial tax rate). As you can see, dividends are taxed more favourably than ordinary income for investors in all tax brackets.

*Capital gains* result when the selling price of an asset exceeds its original cost. Taxes on capital gains are 75% of the applicable marginal rate. For example, an Alberta individual in the highest tax bracket above would pay taxes on capital gains at a rate of 44% x 0.75 = 33%.

In practice, income from capital gains is more attractive than either interest or dividend income because individuals pay taxes on *realized capital gains* only when the asset sale actually takes place. And, as you will see in Chapter 5, the time value of money dramatically reduces the effective tax rate on capital gains.

**An Example:**  Your parents have $50,000 in a chartered bank earning an effective annual interest rate of 6%. As residents of Saskatchewan, they are in the top tax bracket of 48%. They are considering an investment in common shares which will pay dividends of 5%. If you ignore the added risk of investing in stocks as well as the possibility of capital gains or losses, which investment would you recommend to your parents on the basis of after-tax cash flow?

After-tax interest income = $50,000 × .06 (1 − .48) = $1,560.

Effective tax rate on dividends = 1.25 (.29 − .1333) (1 + .48) = 28.99%

After tax dividends = $50,000 × .05 × (1 − .2899) = $1,775.25

Your parents should invest in common shares, rather than leaving their funds in a chartered bank account, because the after-tax cash flows are larger.

**Corporate Taxes:** Canadian corporations must also pay taxes to both the federal and provincial governments. In general, small corporations and some manufacturing and processing companies receive tax breaks in the form of lower rates. Although corporate tax rates appear to be lower than individual tax rates, you must remember that corporate income is subject to double taxation because individuals must pay personal income tax on any dividends received.

Since interest is a tax deductible expense for corporations, debt financing has a tax advantage over financing with common stock. To illustrate, if a firm's tax rate is 40% then it must increase EBIT by [$1 / (1 − 0.40)] = $1.67 to pay $1 in dividends since $0.67 goes to taxes. On the other hand, because interest is tax-deductible, firms need to earn only $1 more to pay $1 of additional interest.

For interest and dividend income *earned* by the firm, however, just the opposite is true. Interest is fully taxable, but dividends received from other Canadian corporations are tax-exempt.

Capital gains received by corporations are taxed at 50% of the marginal rate. When calculating capital gains for tax purposes, a firm nets out all allowable capital losses in the same year. *Capital losses* are recognized on non-depreciable assets only, such as land and securities, and occur when the selling price is lower than the original cost. If capital losses exceed capital gains, the net capital loss may be *carried back* to reduce capital gains in three prior years. Under the carry-back feature, a firm files a revised tax return and receives a refund of prior taxes. Any additional losses may be carried forward indefinitely to reduce future capital gains taxes.

**An Example:** Acme Enterprises experienced a net capital loss of $2 million in 2000 and had net capital gains of $600,000 in 1999, $400,000 in 1998, $300,000 in 1997, and $150,000 in 1996. What is the maximum carry-back, and how much can be carried forward indefinitely?

Maximum carry-back = $600,000 + $400,000 + $300,000 = $1,300,000

Carry-forward amount = $2,000,000 - $1,300,000 = $700,000

**An Example:** A firm sells a building for $500,000 (its original cost five years ago was $200,000), and a tract of land for $250,000 (its original cost 10 years ago was $300,000). If the tax rate is 40%, what are the net capital gains and tax, if any?

Capital gain (building)  =  $500,000 - $200,000  =  $300,000
Capital loss (land)  =  $250,000 - $300,000  =  - $50,000
Net capital gain  =  $300,000  -  $50,000  =  $250,000
Taxes  =  $250,000 x (0.50 x 0.40)  =  $50,000

Carry-back and carry-forward provisions also apply to *operating* losses.  The carry-back period is three years, and carry-forward is allowed for up to seven years.

## CAPITAL COST ALLOWANCE  (CCA)

For tax purposes, CCA depreciation is used to determine taxable income.  Canada Customs and Revenue Agency (CCRA) requires that all firms calculate CCA instead of accounting depreciation computed under GAAP.  CCA calculation begins by assigning every asset to a particular class ('pool') which establishes its maximum CCA rate.  Except for leasehold improvements that follow straight-line depreciation for CCA, all other assets follow the declining balance method.

For a given year, the CCA is computed by multiplying the beginning balance of the asset pool, the *undepreciated capital cost* (UCC), by the appropriate rate.  However, the half-year rule allows us to figure CCA on only one-half of the asset's installed cost of the first year it is put in use.

As a firm buys and sells assets from a given class of assets during the year, the following scenarios are possible:
1.  The firm buys assets (the half-year rule is applied).
2.  The firm buys and sells assets; however, total acquisitions exceed the lower of selling price(s) and original cost(s).  The half-year rule is applied to the net acquisitions.
3.  The firm sells assets.  Any gain or loss is applied to net income.
4.  The firm buys and sells assets. However, total acquisitions are less than the lower of selling price(s) and original cost(s).  The loss is deducted from income.
5.  The firm does not buy or sell assets during the year.

Note, in the last three scenarios, the half-year rule does not apply.

**An Example:**  A firm will acquire class 10 assets to be depreciated at a CCA rate of 30% with a beginning UCC balance of $50,000. Calculate the maximum CCA for each of the next five years.

| Year | Activity |
|---|---|
| 1 | Buy one truck for $100,000 |
| 2 | Buy two vans for $50,000 and $150,000; and sell the truck bought in year 1 for $108,000 |
| 3 | Sell a truck for $15,000 that originally cost $45,000 |
| 4 | Buy one van for $10,000; sell the $50,000 van bought in year 2 for $40,000 |
| 5 | No asset purchases or sales during the year |

|  |  |
|---|---|
| Year 1  UCC beginning | $ 50,000 |
| Acquisition (½ of $100,000) | 50,000 |
| UCC balance | 100,000 |
| CCA @ 30% | 30,000 |
| Add ½ of net acquisition | 50,000 |
| UCC ending | 120,000 |

| Year 2 | UCC beginning | | $120,000 |
|---|---|---|---|
| | Net acquisition ($50,000 + $150,000 − $100,000*)(½) | | 50,000 |
| | UCC balance | | 170,000 |
| | CCA @ 30% | | 51,000 |
| | Add ½ of net acquisition | | 50,000 |
| | UCC ending | | 169,000 |

| Year 3 | UCC beginning | $169,000 | |
|---|---|---|---|
| | Sale* | | 15,000 |
| | UCC balance | | 154,000 |
| | CCA @ 30% | | 46,200 |
| | UCC ending | | 107,800 |

| Year 4 | UCC beginning | $107,800 | |
|---|---|---|---|
| | Acquisition | | 10,000 |
| | Sale* | | 40,000 |
| | UCC balance | | 77,800 |
| | CCA @ 30% | | 23,340 |
| | UCC ending | | 54,460 |

| Year 5 | UCC beginning | $ 54,460 | |
|---|---|---|---|
| | CCA @ 30% | | 16,338 |
| | UCC ending | | 38,122 |

*Note: The lesser of original cost or selling price reduces acquisitions.

As can be seen from the above example, the half-year rule applies to the acquisition of assets and to situations where net acquisitions are positive.   In all other cases, including negative net acquisitions, the rule is not applied.

The procedure illustrated above is repeated in subsequent periods for each asset class until either a "recapture" or a "terminal loss" occurs. A *recapture* occurs when the UCC balance is negative, resulting from over-depreciating the asset class. This amount is added back (recaptured) as ordinary taxable income and taxed at the corporate tax rate. A *terminal loss* occurs when both (1) the UCC class has a positive balance, and (2) there are no assets left in the class. A terminal loss reflects under-depreciation of the asset class because nothing is left in the asset pool. Firms may claim the full terminal loss as an ordinary expense for the year in which it occurs.

**An Example:** Simple, Inc. has five asset classes. We will assume the original cost of one asset sold in each pool is $25,000. Before the sale, asset classes B and C have only one asset left. Simple also sold securities for $100,000, which originally cost $90,000. They also sold a tract of land for a $5,000 loss. All sales are in 2000; the applicable tax rate is 30%. Calculate Simple's taxes payable assuming a before-tax operating income of $30,000.

| Asset Class | UCC Beginning | Sale Proceeds | Terminal Loss | Recaptured Income | Capital Gain |
|---|---|---|---|---|---|
| A | $15,000 | $ 7,500 | | | |
| B | 15,000 | 7,500 | $ 7,500 | | |
| C | 27,500 | 30,000 | 2,500 | | $ 5,000 |
| D | 15,000 | 17,500 | | $ 2,500 | |
| E | 15,000 | 30,000 | | 10,000 | 5,000 |

Note that, for classes D and E there is recaptured income because the UCC balance is reduced by the lower of sales proceeds and original cost ($25,000). For class D, $15,000 - $17,500 = -$2,500; for class E, $15,000 - $25,000 = -$10,000. These amounts must be added to taxable income. For asset classes C and E, sale proceeds are greater than the original cost, so capital gains must be recognized. For classes B and C, the UCC balance after the sale is positive with no assets remaining in the class; this results in terminal losses of $7,500 and $2,500.

Taxes for Simple, Inc. are calculated as follows:

|  |  |  |
|---|---|---|
| Operating income | | $ 30,000 |
| + Recapture of Depreciation ($2,500 + $10,000) | 12,500 | |
| + Net Capital Gains ($5,000 + $5,000 + $10,000* - $5,000**) ( 0.75) | | 11,250 |
| - Terminal losses ($7,500 + $2,500) | | 10,000 |
| Total taxable income | | 43,750 |
| Taxes payable (30%) | | $13,125 |

\*      Capital gains from sale of securities
\*\*    Capital loss on non-depreciable asset (land). Note that capital losses cannot exceed capital gains in any given year. Deferral provisions allow capital losses to be carried back three years to reduce capital gains and carried forward indefinitely.

## CONCEPT TEST

1.  A _____ can be thought of as a snapshot of a firm's accounting value as of a particular date. By definition, the value of a firm's assets is equal to _____ + _____ . Alternately, this definition can be thought of as _____ = assets - _____ .

2.  An asset that can be converted to cash quickly and easily, without significant loss in value, is said to be a _____ asset.

3.  Assets are listed on the balance sheet in the order of decreasing _____ . _____ generally earn lower rates of return than do fixed assets.

4.  If a firm raises funds from investors, the first claim on cash flows is given to the _____ . The residual cash flows belong to the firm's _____ .

5.  The use of debt financing is referred to as _____ because it magnifies both the _____ and the _____ accruing to the firm's shareholders.

6.  The fixed asset values shown on a firm's balance sheet are not current market values. Instead, they are

shown at _____ . The difference between market value and _____ is generally fairly small for the firm's _____ assets, but can be extremely large for _____ assets.

7.  The income statement equation is _____ - _____ = _____ . Net income divided by the number of shares outstanding is called _____ .

8.  For accounting purposes, revenue is shown on the income statement when it _____ , not necessarily when payment is received. For financial decision-making purposes, accounting income must be distinguished from _____ .

9.  One of the reasons that net income is not the same as cash from operations is that some deductions are _____ deductions. The most common of these expenses is _____ .

10. Operating cash flow is calculated as _____ + _____ - _____ . Total cash flow from assets is calculated as _____ - _____ - _____ .

11. Cash flow to creditors is calculated as _____ - _____ . Cash flow to shareholders is calculated as _____ - _____ .

12. The _____ tax rate is computed by dividing total taxes paid by the total taxable income. The _____ tax rate is the tax rate applied to the last dollar earned. A _____ tax is a tax rate which is a constant percentage of income, regardless of income level.

13. The three different types of Canadian investment income, _____, _____, and _____ , are taxed differently.

14. Corporate income taxes create a tax advantage for _____ over _____ financing because interest paid is tax deductible while dividends paid are not.

15. _____ is depreciation for tax purposes in Canada. CCA rates are found by determining the _____ in which an asset belongs.

16. The _____ rule mandates that only _____ of the net acquisition be added to the beginning _____ of the asset class.

17. If an asset is sold from a depreciable class, the lower of _____ or _____ must be deducted from the UCC.

18. Although the _____ reduces the firm's taxes payable dollar for dollar, CCA cannot be claimed on that amount.

19. If a particular class of assets are over depreciated, then the firm must pay taxes on the full amount of the _____ . On the other hand, if there are no assets left in the class and the UCC balance is positive, then a _____ occurs. Terminal losses reduce _____ in the year in which they occur.

20. Capital gains for corporations are taxed at _____ of the _____ .

21. _____ are recognized on non-depreciable assets only and must be netted against capital gains. If _____ exceed _____ , then they may be _____ to reduce capital gains in prior years.

22.    Generally, income from capital gains is more attractive than _____ which is fully taxed or _____ which must be grossed up by _____ . The _____ is then calculated on the grossed-up figure.

23.    A dividend tax credit of _____ of the actual dividend is subtracted from the federal tax to get the net federal tax payable.


## ANSWERS TO CONCEPT TEST

1.     balance sheet; total liabilities; shareholders' equity; shareholders' equity; total liabilities

2.     liquid

3.     liquidity; liquid (or current) assets

4.     creditors; shareholders

5.     financial leverage; gains; losses

6.     book value (or historical cost); book value; current; fixed

7.     revenues; expenses; income; earnings per share (EPS)

8.     accrues; cash flow

9.     non-cash; depreciation

10.    earnings before interest and taxes (EBIT); depreciation; taxes; operating cash flow; capital spending; additions to net working capital

11.    interest; net new borrowing; dividends; net new equity raised

12.    average; marginal; flat rate

13.    interest; dividends; capital gains

14.    debt; equity

15.    capital cost allowance (CCA); class

16.    half-year; half; undepreciated capital cost (UCC)

17.    selling price; original cost

18.    investment tax credit

19.     recaptured depreciation; terminal loss; taxable income

20.     50%; marginal tax rate

21.     Capital losses; capital losses; capital gains; carried back

22.     interest income, dividend income; 25%; federal tax

23.     16 2/3%

## PROBLEMS AND SOLUTIONS

### Problem 1

During the year 2000, the B.C. Company had sales of $1,000, cost of goods sold of $400, depreciation of $100, and interest paid of $150.   Using a 34% corporate tax rate, and assuming all taxes are paid the year they are due, construct B.C.'s income statement for 2000.

**Solution:** Net income can be calculated as follows:

B.C. COMPANY, INC.
2000 Income Statement

| | | |
|---|---|---:|
| Net sales | | $ 1,000 |
| Cost of goods sold | | 400 |
| Depreciation | | 100 |
| Earnings before interest and taxes | | $  500 |
| Interest paid | | 150 |
| Taxable income | $  350 | |
| Taxes (34%) | | 119 |
| Net income | | $   231 |

### Problem 2

The B.C. Company had 100 shares of common stock outstanding at the end of 2000.  Total dividends paid for 2000 were $120.  Compute earnings per share (EPS) and dividends per share for the year.

**Solution:**     EPS  =   Net income / Number of shares outstanding   = $231 / 100  =  $2.31
                 Dividends per share   =   Total dividends / Number of shares  =  $120 / 100  =  $1.20

### Problem 3

At the end of 1999, B.C. had notes payable of $1,200, accounts payable of $2,400, and long-term debt of $3,000. For 2000, those amounts are $1,600, $2,000, and $2,800, respectively.  Asset values for 1999 and 2000, respectively, are $800 and $500 in cash; $400 and $300 in marketable securities; $900 and $800 in accounts receivable; $1,800 and $2,000 in inventory; $6,000 and $8,000 in net plant and equipment. Prepare balance sheets for 1999 and 2000.

**Solution:**

## B.C. COMPANY
### Balance Sheets as of December 31, 1999 and 2000

| | 1999 | 2000 | | 1999 | 2000 |
|---|---|---|---|---|---|
| *Assets* | | | *Liabilities & Owners' Equity* | | |
| Current assets | | | Current liabilities | | |
| Cash | $ 800 | $ 500 | Accounts payable | $ 2,400 | $ 2,000 |
| Marketable securities | 400 | 300 | Notes payable | 1,200 | 1,600 |
| Accounts receivable | 900 | 800 | Total | $ 3,600 | $ 3,600 |
| Inventory | 1,800 | 2,000 | | | |
| Total | $ 3,900 | $ 3,600 | | | |
| | | | Long-term debt | $ 3,000 | $ 2,800 |
| | | | Owners' equity | 3,300 | 5,200 |
| Fixed assets | | | | | |
| Net plant & equipment | $ 6,000 | $ 8,000 | | | |
| Total assets | $ 9,900 | $11,600 | Total liabilities & equity | $ 9,900 | $11,600 |

## Problem 4

Based on the information from Problem 1, calculate B.C.'s operating cash flow for 2000.

**Solution:** Operating cash flow is calculated as:

| | |
|---|---|
| Earnings before interest and taxes | $ 500 |
| + Depreciation | 100 |
| - Taxes | 119 |
| Cash flow from operations | $ 481 |

## Problem 5

During 2000, B.C. sold $300 in net fixed assets. They also issued $2,400 worth of new stock and used the proceeds to buy new fixed assets. What was net capital spending for that year?

**Solution:** Depreciation expense of $100 (from the income statement) means the value of the fixed assets remaining from 1999, not including any asset purchases sales, is $6,000 - $100 = $5,900. The net capital spending, then is $8,000 - $5,900 = $2,100. Alternately, we can compute net capital spending as the difference between the amount of funds raised and used on fixed assets and the funds received from the sales of fixed assets: $2,400 - $300 = $2,100.

## Problem 6

Based on the balance sheets above for B. C. Company, what was net working capital in each year? What were the additions to net working capital in 2000?

**Solution:**

Net working capital   =   Current assets  -  Current liabilities

For 1999:  ($800 + $400 + $900 + $1,800) - ($1,200 + $2,400)   =   $3,900 - $3,600  =   $300

For 2000:  ($500 + $300 + $800 + $2,000)  - ($1,600 + $2,000)   =   $3,600  - $3,600  =  $0

Addition to net working capital   =   $NWC_{2000}$ - $NWC_{1999}$  =  $0 - $300  =  -$300

This is actually a reduction of $300 in net working capital.  Alternatively, the addition in net working capital can be computed as:

Addition to net working capital   =   Change in current assets   -   Change in current liabilities

= - ($3,900 - $3,600) - ($3,600 - $3,600) = -$300

## Problem 7

Using the information from the above problems, what was B.C.'s total cash flow from assets in 2000?

**Solution:**   Total cash flow is computed as follows:

| | | |
|---|---|---|
| Operating cash flow | $   481 | (Problem 4) |
| - Net capital spending | 2,100 | (Problem 5) |
| - Additions to NWC | (300) | (Problem 6) |
| Cash flow from assets | ($1,319) | |

Note: The firm has a positive net income but negative cash flow.  This is because capital expenditures are not included in net income, but are included in actual cash flow.  In general, net income is not equal to cash flow.

## Problem 8

What was B.C.'s cash flow to long-term creditors in 2000?

**Solution:**

| | | |
|---|---|---|
| Interest paid | $  150 | (1998 income statement) |
| - Net new borrowing | (   200) | (long-term debt$_{2000}$ - long-term debt$_{1999}$) |
| Cash flow to creditors | $  350 | |

## Problem 9

Now assume that, in addition to issuing $2,400 in new common shares, B.C. also repurchased $611 in common shares.  What was the firm's cash flow to shareholders in 2000?

**Solution:**      Dividends paid                          $   120   (Problem 2)
                   - Net new equity                         1,789   (Common stock$_{2000}$ - common stock$_{1999}$)
                   Cash flow to shareholders             ($1,669)

Note: You can't compute the net new equity from the owner's equity in the balance sheets because the owner's equity section includes both common stock and retained earnings. (The items were not listed separately.) Net new equity is computed using the value of common stock.  Also note the total cash flow to creditors and shareholders, $350 +  (-$1,669) =  -$1,319, is the same as the total cash flow from assets.

## Problem 10

Based on the following information for Pascucci Corporation, calculate total cash flow from assets, cash flow to creditors, and cash flow to shareholders for 2000.  Use a 34% corporate tax rate.

|                    | 1999    | 2000    |
|--------------------|---------|---------|
| Sales              | $2,230  | $2,890  |
| Costs              | 1,050   | 1,437   |
| Depreciation       | 418     | 418     |
| Interest           | 225     | 276     |
| Dividends          | 350     | 400     |
| Current assets     | 1,140   | 1,335   |
| Fixed assets       | 5,670   | 5,877   |
| Current liabilities| 884     | 1,006   |
| Long-term debt     | 2,349   | 2,666   |

**Solution:**  First you need to calculate the cash flow from operations:   $1,195

Total cash flow from assets   =   $497

Cash flow to long-term creditors   =   $(41)

Cash flow to shareholders   =   $497  - ($41)   =   $538

Note: You can find the cash flow to shareholders directly because the sum of cash flows paid to both creditors and shareholders must equal the total cash flow from assets.

## Problem 11

Having invested $50,000 in the common stock of Garden Enterprises, you receive $0.10 in cash dividends for every $1 invested.  Compute the effective tax rate on dividend income.  Then compute your total marginal tax rate on any interest income you receive.  Assume your federal marginal tax rate is 29% and the provincial tax rate is 50% of the federal tax.

**Solution:**                    Dividends received ($50,000 x 0.10)        $5,000
                                 Grossed up at 25%                           1,250
                                 Grossed up dividend                         6,250

|  |  |
|---|---|
| Federal tax @ 29% | 1,812.50 |
| Dividend tax credit (0.1667 x $5,000) | 833.50 |
| Net federal tax | 979.00 |
| Provincial tax @ 50% | 489.50 |
| Total tax | $1,468.50 |

|  |  |  |  |  |
|---|---|---|---|---|
| Effective tax rate | = Total tax / Total dividends | = $1,468.50 / $5,000 | = | 29.37% |
| OR:   Effective tax rate | = 1.25 x (Federal rate  - 0.1333) x (1 + Provincial rate) | | = | 29.38% |
| Marginal tax rate | = Federal rate x (1 + Provincial rate) = 43.50% | | | |

## Problem 12

Emma Movers, Inc. is purchasing a $50,000 machine to replace an existing one which cost $12,000 five years ago but can be sold for $10,500 today.  The new machine will have a CCA rate of 20%.  If Emma's tax rate is 35%, what is the tax saving from claiming CCA in year 3, if the beginning UCC balance in the asset class is $70,000?

**Solution:**

| Year 1 | UCC beginning Yr 1 | $70,000 |
|---|---|---|
|  | ½ of Net acquisition | 19,750 |
|  | UCC balance | 89,750 |
|  | CCA Yr 1 @ 20 % | 17,950 |
|  | UCC ending | 71,800 |
|  |  |  |
| Year 2 | UCC beginning | 71,800 |
|  | Add ½ of net acquisition | 19,750 |
|  | UCC balance | 91,550 |
|  | CCA Yr 2 @ 20 % | 18,310 |
|  | UCC ending | 73,240 |
|  |  |  |
| Year 3 | UCC beginning | 73,240 |
|  | CCA Yr 2 @ 20 % | 14,648 |
|  |  |  |
|  | Year 3 tax savings at 35% | $ 5,126.80 |

Note that the net acquisition in year 1 is the purchase price, less the lower of original cost or selling price,  taking into consideration the half-year rule.

## Problem 13

The current undepreciated capital cost of a specific pool of assets is $250,000.  The company has decided to sell one of the six assets in the pool.  The original capital cost of that asset was $360,000.  Calculate the amount (if any) of recaptured depreciation, capital gains, and terminal loss resulting from the sale of that asset at the following sale prices: $400,000; $250,000; $170,000.  Also give the new opening UCC balance for each case.  The CCA rate is 20%.

**Solution:**

| | Case I | Case II | Case III |
|---|---|---|---|
| UCC beginning | $ 250,000 | $ 250,000 | $ 250,000 |
| Sale | 400,000 | 250,000 | 170,000 |
| Recapture | 150,000 | 0 | 0 |
| UCC (new) | 0 | 0 | 80,000 |
| Capital gain | 40,000 | 0 | 0 |
| Terminal loss | 0 | 0 | 0 |

Note: There is no terminal loss because, in each case, there were assets remaining in the pool.

## Problem 14

A firm has three asset pools and is subject to a 35% tax rate. The acquisition in asset pool C is eligible for a 10% investment tax credit. Given the information below, please compute amounts of recapture, capital gains, terminal losses, capital losses, and the CCA charge based on a rate of 20%. For asset pool B, no assets remain after the sale.

| Asset Pool | A | B | C |
|---|---|---|---|
| UCC beginning | $ 120,000 | $ 240,000 | $ 100,000 |
| Acquisitions | 50,000 | 0 | 150,000 |
| Assets sold | | | |
| Original cost | 400,000 | 80,000 | 80,000 |
| Proceeds of sale | 450,000 | 120,000 | 60,000 |

**Solution:**

| Asset Pool | A | B | C |
|---|---|---|---|
| Recapture | $ 200,000 | | |
| Terminal loss | 0 | $160,000 | |
| Capital gain | 50,000 | 40,000 | |
| Capital loss | | | |
| CCA charge @ 20% | | | $27,500 |

## Problem 15

Refer to the information in Problem 14. Assume the corporate tax rate is 35% and that the firm's earned net income (after-tax) *excluding* depreciation is $91,000. Compute the firm's tax liability.

**Solution:**

| | |
|---|---|
| Earnings before tax [$91,000 / (1 - 0.35)] | $140,000 |
| Recapture | 200,000 |
| Capital gains ($50,000 + $40,000) x 0.75 | 67,500 |
| Terminal loss | (160,000) |
| CCA | ( 27,500) |
| Total taxable | $220,000 |
| Taxes payable @ 35% | 77,000 |
| Less investment tax credit | 15,000 |
| Net taxes payable | $ 62,000 |

## Problem 16

FYE Company has the following asset pool eligible for CCA @ 20% and is subject to a 40% tax rate.   The acquisition in asset pool A is eligible for a 10% investment tax credit.

| Asset Pool | A |
|---|---|
| UCC beginning | $100,000 |
| Acquisitions | 150,000 |
| Assets sold | |
| Original cost | 80,000 |
| Proceeds of sale | 100,000 |
| Book value | 60,000 |

Assume that FYE has two other assets pools.  Pool B will have a positive UCC balance of $40,000 at the beginning of year 2, from which the *last* asset will be sold for $20,000 (original cost was $15,000).  Pool C will have a positive UCC balance of $30,000 at the beginning of year 2, from which one asset will be sold for $65,000 (original cost was $55,000).  If FYE's earnings before taxes is projected to be $80,000 in year 2, calculate the taxes payable for that year.  Be sure to incorporate the impact of acquisitions and sales from all three asset pools.

**Solution:**

| | | | |
|---|---|---|---|
| Pool A | UCC beginning Yr 1 | | $ 100,000 |
| | Net acquisition ($150,000 x 0.90 - 80,000) x 0.50 | | 27,500 |
| | Balance | 127,500 | |
| | Year 1 CCA @ 20% | | 25,500 |
| | UCC beginning Yr 2 | | 102,000 |
| | Year 2 CCA @ 20% | | 20,400 |
| | | | |
| Pool B | UCC beginning Yr 2 | | $ 40,000 |
| | Sale | | 15,000 |
| | Balance | 25,000 | |
| | Year 2 CCA @ 20% | | 5000 |
| | | | |
| Pool C | UCC beginning Yr 2 | | $ 30,000 |
| | Sale | | 55,000 |
| | Balance | $( 25,000) | |
| | Earnings before taxes | | $ 80,000 |
| | | | |
| Pool A | | | |
| | Taxable capital gain   ($100,000 - $80,000) x 0.50 | | 10,000 |
| Pool B | | | |
| | Taxable capital gain ($20,000 - $15,000) x 0.50 | | 2,500 |
| | Terminal loss | | 25,000 |
| Pool C | | | |
| | Taxable capital gain ($65,000 - $55,000) x 0.50 | | 5,000 |
| | Recapture | | 25,000 |
| | Taxable income | 97,500 | |
| | Taxes @ 40% | | 39,000 |

## Problem 17

Upon their arrival in Quebec in 1998, Marco and Polo decided to form the Marco Polo Pasta Company. At that time they purchased a small industrial pasta mixer for $6,000 and a spaghetti machine for $5,000. Due to rapidly expanding business, in 2000 they bought a larger pasta mixer for $10,000 and a new spaghetti machine for $12,500. They sold the old machines for $4,500 and $7,000, respectively. Their equipment is depreciated at a CCA rate of 20%, and they have a 40% tax rate. The firm has $200,000 of taxable income before considering CCA. Calculate their tax bill for 2000.

**Solution:**

| | |
|---|---:|
| UCC beginning 1998 | $       0 |
| Acquisitions ($11,000) x 0.50 | 5,500 |
| CCA @ 20% | 1,100 |
| UCC balance | 4,400 |
| Add ½ of acquisitions | 5,500 |
| | |
| UCC beginning 1999 | 9,900 |
| CCA @ 20% | 1,980 |
| UCC balance | 7,920 |
| | |
| UCC beginning 2000 | 7,920 |
| Net acquisitions ($10,000 + $12,500 - $4,500 - $5,000) x 0.50 | 5,500 |
| Balance | 13,420 |
| CCA @ 20% | 2,684 |
| Balance | 10,736 |
| | |
| Taxable income before CCA | $ 200,000 |
| Taxable capital gain ($2,000 on spaghetti machine) x 0.50 | 1,000 |
| CCA deduction | ( 2,684) |
| Taxable amount | 198,316 |
| Tax @ 40% | $   79,326.40 |

## Problem 18

Your federal marginal tax rate is 29%. In addition, your provincial rate is 45% of the federal rate. If you invest $50,000 for one year, which alternative would generate the highest after-tax income?

1)      Common stock with a 10% dividend yield
2)      Bonds paying a rate of 12.75%
3)      Investing in common stock that pays no dividends but is worth $55,250 at year end.

**Solution:**

1)

| | |
|---|---:|
| Dividend income | $ 5,000.00 |
| Gross up at @ 25% | 1,250.00 |
| Grossed-up dividend | 6,250.00 |
| Federal tax @ 29% | 1,812.50 |
| Dividend tax credit | 833.50 |
| Net federal tax | 979.00 |
| Provincial tax @45% | 440.55 |
| Total tax | 1,419.55 |
| After-tax income | $ 3,580.45 |

2)      Interest income                                    $ 6,375.00
        After-tax income $6375 x (1 - 0.4205)   $ 3,694.31
        Note: The combined federal-provincial tax rate is 0.29 x (1 + 0.45) = 42.05%

3)      Capital gains income

        Capital gain                                       $ 5,250.00
        Tax ($5,250 x 0.75 x 0.4205)                          1,655.72
        After-tax income                                   $ 3,594.28

The highest after-tax income comes from buying a bond. Therefore, that is your best alternative.

# 3     <u>Working With Financial Statements</u>

## CHAPTER HIGHLIGHTS

In this chapter, we continue to examine the financial statements discussed in Chapter 2. Again, our emphasis is on the use of financial statements as a source of information for financial decisions. Remember that under ideal circumstances, financial decisions are based on market value information, rather than accounting data. However, managers rarely have full market value information about all of a firm's assets. So they (and we) must rely on accounting figures for much of our financial information. And, for privately held corporations, not-for-profit businesses, and smaller firms, accounting statements may provide the only information available.

## CASH FLOW AND FINANCIAL STATEMENTS: A CLOSER LOOK

Remember the firm's cash flow equation: Cash flow from assets = Cash flow to creditors + Cash flow to owners. In Chapter 3, we analyze more closely the impact of various transactions on the firm's cash flows.

**Sources and Uses of Cash**: The transactions which create cash inflows for the firm are referred to as sources of cash, and transactions which create cash outflows are uses of cash. We can create a statement detailing the sources and uses of cash by analyzing the firm's financial statements. First, we examine successive year-end balance sheets to identify those changes in balance sheet accounts which represent sources or uses of cash.

For example, a firm whose inventory increases from $100 to $120 over a given year must have a $20 net expenditure on inventory during the year. This expenditure is considered a net *use* of cash. A decrease in inventory $100 to $70 would represent a $30 net *source* of cash (because the funds were not tied up in inventory, they were available for other purposes). An increase in an asset account represents a use of cash. A decrease represents a source of cash.

A decrease in a liability or equity account represents a net use of cash. For example, a firm with long-term debt of $200 could reduce the debt to $175 by repaying $25 of the debt. The $25 is therefore a net use of cash. Alternatively, suppose the firm's equity accounts increased from $300 to $350 during the year. The additional $50 represents cash coming into the firm, or a source of cash. An increase in a liability or equity account thus represents a source of cash.

**An example:** Balance sheets for the K-Bec Company, for 1999 and 2000 and the 2000 income statement are below:

### K-BEC CO., INC.
### Balance Sheets as of December 31, 1999 and 2000

|  | 1999 | 2000 | Change |
|---|---|---|---|
| *Assets* | | | |
| Current assets | | | |
| Cash | $ 500 | $ 550 | + $ 50 |
| Accounts receivable | 1,000 | 975 | - 25 |
| Inventory | 2,000 | 2,225 | + 225 |
| Total | $ 3,500 | $ 3,750 | + $ 250 |
| | | | |
| Fixed assets | | | |

| | | | |
|---|---|---|---|
| Net plant and equipment | 6,500 | 6,750 | +    250 |
| Total assets | $10,000 | $10,500 | + $   500 |

*Liabilities and Owners' Equity*

| | | | |
|---|---|---|---|
| Current liabilities | | | |
|    Accounts payable | $  1,000 | $  1,200 | + $   200 |
|    Notes payable | 500 | 350 | -    150 |
|      Total | $  1,500 | $  1,550 | +     50 |
| Long-term debt | $  2,500 | $  2,586 | + $    86 |
| Owners' equity | | | |
|    Common stock and paid-in surplus | 3,500 | 3,600 | +    100 |
|    Retained earnings | 2,500 | 2,764 | +    264 |
|      Total | $  6,000 | $  6,364 | + $   364 |
| Total liabilities and owners' equity | $10,000 | $10,500 | + $   500 |

### K-BEC CO., INC.   2000 Income Statement

| | | |
|---|---|---|
| Sales | | $ 5,000 |
| Cost of goods sold | | 3,000 |
| Depreciation | | 600 |
| Earnings before interest and taxes | | $ 1,400 |
| Interest paid | | 400 |
| Taxable income | $ 1,000 | |
| Taxes (34%) | | 340 |
| Net income | | $   660 |
|    Retained earnings | | $   264 |
|    Dividends | | $   396 |

The last column of the balance sheet statement shows the change in each account from the end of 1999 to the end of 2000. For example, the decrease in accounts receivable from $1,000 to $975, is a $25 source of cash; the $225 increase in inventory is a use of cash. The sources and uses of cash for K-Bec are as follows:

| | |
|---|---|
| Sources of cash | |
|    Decrease in accounts receivable | $  25 |
|    Increase in accounts payable | 200 |
|    Increase in long-term debt | 86 |
|    Increase in owners' equity | 100 |
|    Increase in retained earnings | 264 |
|      Total sources | $ 675 |

|                                              |         |
| -------------------------------------------- | ------- |
| Uses of cash                                 |         |
|     Increase in inventory | $225    |
|     Increase in net plant and equipment | 250 |
|     Decrease in notes payable | 150  |
|        Total uses | $ 625 |
|   Net addition to cash             | $  50   |

Note that the net addition to cash, $50, is the difference between total sources and total uses. It agrees with the $50 increase in the cash account from 1999 to 2000, as shown on the balance sheet.

**The Statement of Changes in Financial Position**:  Further detail regarding the firm's sources and uses of cash can be derived by using income statement data and the sources and uses of cash summarized above to create the Statement of Changes in Financial Position.  This statement organizes the sources and uses of cash into three categories: operating, financing, and investment activities.

Comparing the two balance sheets, there is a $250 increase in fixed assets, from $6,500 to $6,750. However, the $600 depreciation expense on the income statement indicates that, had K-Bec not purchased additional fixed assets, the fixed asset account would have decreased by $600, to ($6,500 – $600) = $5,900. Since fixed assets increased to $6,750, the firm actually invested = ($6,750 – $5,900) = $850 in the acquisition of fixed assets.  Note this amount is the same as depreciation plus change in fixed assets: $600 + $250  =  $850.

Depreciation is deducted as an expense in computing net income; since depreciation is not a cash expense, however, it is added to net income as a source of cash on the statement of cash flows. Under the category of financing activities, dividends are deducted as a use of cash; clearly, the payment of dividends requires the expenditure of cash.

**An example:**  The statement of cash flows for K-Bec Co., Inc. is below:

2000 Statement of Changes in Financial Position

|                                              |          |
| -------------------------------------------- | -------- |
| Operating activities                         |          |
|   Net income                       | $   660  |
| Plus:                                        |          |
|   Depreciation                     | 600      |
|   Increase in accounts payable     | 200      |
|   Decrease in accounts receivable  | 25       |
| Less:                                        |          |
|   Increase in inventory            | -   225  |
|   Net cash from operating activity | $ 1,260  |
| Investment activities:                       |          |
|   Fixed asset acquisitions         | - $  850 |
|   Net cash from investment activities | - $  850 |
| Financing activities:                        |          |
|   Decrease in notes payable        | - $  150 |
|   Increase in long-term debt       | 86       |
|   Dividends paid                   | -    396 |
|   Increase in common stock         | 100      |
|   Net cash from financing activity | - $  360 |
| Net increase in cash                         | $   50   |

## STANDARDIZED FINANCIAL STATEMENTS

In making financial decisions, it is often helpful to compare a firm's financial statements with those of companies in the same industry. However, companies in the same industry can differ substantially in size, making comparisons of financial statement data difficult. A similar problem arises when a firm chooses to compare its current financial statements to those of preceding years; if the company has grown significantly, comparisons based on dollar values may not be meaningful. Two approaches to standardizing financial statements, in order to make comparisons more useful, are described in this section.

**Common-size statements:**   These financial statements are standardized by presenting balance sheet accounts as a percentage of total assets and income statements as a percentage of sales.

**An example:**   The common-size balance sheets and income statement for K-Bec are shown here:

K-BEC CO., INC.
Common-Size Balance Sheets
December 31, 1999 and 2000

| | 1999 | 2000 | Change |
|---|---|---|---|
| *Assets* | | | |
| Current assets | | | |
|   Cash | 5.0% | 5.2% | + 0.2% |
|   Accounts receivable | 10.0 | 9.3 | − 0.7 |
|   Inventory | 20.0 | 21.2 | + 1.2 |
|     Total | 35.0 | 35.7 | + 0.7 |
| | | | |
| Fixed assets | | | |
|   Net plant and equipment | 65.0 | 64.3 | − 0.7 |
| | | | |
| Total assets | 100.0% | 100.0% | 0% |
| | | | |
| *Liabilities and Owners' Equity* | | | |
| | | | |
| Current liabilities | | | |
|   Accounts payable | 10.0% | 11.4% | + 1.4% |
|   Notes payable | 5.0 | 3.3 | − 1.7 |
|     Total | 15.0 | 14.8 | − 0.2 |
| | | | |
| Long-term debt | 25.0 | 24.6 | − 0.4 |
| Owners' equity | | | |
|   Common stock and paid-in surplus | 35.0 | 34.3 | − 0.7 |
|   Retained earnings | 25.0 | 26.3 | + 1.3 |
|     Total | 60.0 | 60.6 | + 0.6 |
| | | | |
| Total liabilities and owners' equity | 100.0% | 100.0% | + 0.0 |

K-BEC CO., INC. 2000 Income Statement

| | | |
|---|---|---|
| Sales | | 100.0% |
| Cost of goods sold | | 60.0 |
| Depreciation | | 12.0 |
| Earnings before interest and taxes | | 28.0 |
| Interest paid | | 8.0 |
| Taxable income | 20.0 | |
| Taxes (34%) | | 6.8 |
| Net income | | 13.2% |
| Retained earnings | | 5.3 |
| Dividends | | 7.9 |

**Common-Base-Year Financial Statements: Trend Analysis.**  A second approach to standardizing financial statements is the use of *common-base-year financial statements*. For these statements, a base year is selected; each financial statement item for the base year is assigned a value of 1.00. Then, for subsequent years, each item is assigned a value reflecting the change in the item. For example, suppose that 1999 is selected as the base year, and the firm's inventory level at the end of 1999 is $200.  For the 1999 common-base-year balance sheet, inventory is assigned a value of 1.00. If inventory increases to $210 at the end of 2000, reflecting a 5% increase in inventory, then the 2000 common-base-year balance sheet displays an inventory value of ($210/$200) = 1.05.

## RATIO ANALYSIS

In order to make comparisons over time, or with similar businesses, the analysis of financial statements is often based on ratios of various balance sheet and income statement items, rather than on dollar values. This allows us to compare performance for firms of vastly different size, or for a firm which grows over time. Further, large Canadian companies usually span two or more industries, making comparisons extremely difficult.

The major categories of financial ratios used for financial analysis are:

1.      Short-term solvency or liquidity ratios.
2.      Long-term solvency or financial leverage ratios.
3.      Asset management or turnover ratios.
4.      Profitability ratios.
5.      Market value ratios.

The financial ratios defined in this section are illustrated using the 2000 financial statements for K-Bec Co., Inc.

**Short-Term Solvency or Liquidity Measures**:  This group of ratios measures the firm's short-term liquidity; that is, the firm's ability to meet short-term obligations. The most commonly used measures in this category are the current ratio and the quick, or acid-test, ratio.   The values of these ratios for K-Bec in 2000 are below.

$$\text{Current ratio} = \frac{\text{Current assets}}{\text{Current liabilities}} = \frac{\$3,750}{\$1,550} = 2.42$$

$$\text{Quick ratio} = \frac{\text{Current assets} - \text{Inventory}}{\text{Current liabilities}} = \frac{\$3,750 - \$2,225}{\$1,550} = 0.98$$

The current ratio for K-Bec indicates that the firm has $2.42 of current assets for each $1 of current liabilities. The quick ratio, or acid-test ratio, is similar to the current ratio except that inventory is not included in the numerator. The quick ratio is a more stringent indicator of a firm's liquidity because it only incorporates assets which are most quickly converted into cash.

Caution must be used in interpreting financial ratios such as the current ratio. For short-term creditors, a high ratio is better because it indicates liquidity. However, it may also indicate that the firm is using cash and other short-term assets inefficiently. Under ordinary circumstances, we should expect a current ratio of at least 1, indicating a positive net working capital. However, healthy current ratios vary from industry to industry.

Three additional measures of liquidity are:

$$\text{Cash ratio} \quad = \quad \frac{\text{Cash}}{\text{Current liabilities}} \quad = \quad \frac{\$550}{\$1,550} \quad = \quad 0.35$$

$$\text{NWC to Total assets ratio} \quad = \quad \frac{\text{Net working capital}}{\text{Total assets}} \quad = \quad \frac{\$3,750 - \$1,550}{\$10,500} \quad = \quad 0.21$$

$$\text{Interval measure} \quad = \quad \frac{\text{Current assets}}{\text{Average daily operating cost}} \quad = \quad \frac{\$3,750}{\$3,000 / 365} \quad = \quad 456 \text{ days}$$

Average daily operating cost is computed as total costs, exclusive of depreciation and interest, divided by 365 days: ($3,000/365) = $8.22. The interval measure gives an indication of how long the business could continue to operate if cash inflows were drastically reduced (in this case 456 days).

**Long-Term Solvency Measures**: These are used to gauge the extent to which a firm uses debt rather than equity financing. An increase in the level of debt increases the probability of default. The ratios in this section are also referred to as *financial leverage ratios* or *leverage ratios*. They are illustrated below using the K-Bec example.

$$\text{Total debt ratio} \quad = \quad \frac{\text{Total assets} - \text{Total equity}}{\text{Total assets}} \quad = \quad \frac{\$10,500 - \$6,364}{\$10,500} \quad = \quad 0.39$$

For K-Bec, 39% of its financing is obtained from debt; the remaining 61% is equity financing.

$$\text{Debt / equity ratio} \quad = \quad \frac{\text{Total debt}}{\text{Total equity}} \quad = \quad \frac{\$4,136}{\$6,364} \quad = \quad 0.65$$

The debt/equity ratio can also be computed from the total debt ratio. The total debt ratio indicates that K-Bec has $0.39 of debt for each dollar of assets. Consequently, the firm has $0.39 of debt and ($1.00 − $0.39) = $0.61 of equity financing for each dollar of assets, and a debt/equity ratio of ($0.39 / $0.61) = 0.64. (This result differs slightly from the result of the direct calculation of the ratio above due to rounding in this calculation.)

$$\text{Equity multiplier} \quad = \quad \frac{\text{Total assets}}{\text{Total equity}} \quad = \quad \frac{\$10,500}{\$6,364} \quad = \quad 1.65$$

The equity multiplier can be computed from the debt/equity ratio, using the fact that K-Bec has $0.61 of equity for each $1 of assets. The equity multiplier is equal to ($1 / $.61) = 1.64.

The relationship between the equity multiplier and the debt/equity ratio is further clarified by substituting (Total equity + Total debt) for Total assets in the numerator of the above equation:

$$\text{Equity multiplier} = \frac{\text{Total equity} + \text{Total debt}}{\text{Total equity}} = 1 + \frac{\text{Total debt}}{\text{Total equity}} = 1 + \text{Debt/equity ratio} = 1.65$$

$$\text{Long-term debt ratio} = \frac{\text{Long-term debt}}{\text{Long-term debt} + \text{Total equity}} = \frac{\$2,586}{\$2,586 + \$6,364} = 0.29$$

$$\text{Times interest earned ratio} = \frac{\text{Earnings before interest and taxes}}{\text{Interest}} = \frac{\$1,400}{\$\ 400} = 3.50 \text{ times}$$

The times interest earned ratio provides an indication of the firm's ability to meet its interest obligations. Deterioration in this ratio over time may be a signal that the firm is likely to encounter financial distress.

$$\text{Cash coverage ratio} = \frac{\text{EBIT} + \text{Depreciation}}{\text{Interest}} = \frac{\$1,400 + \$600}{\$400} = 5.00 \text{ times}$$

The cash coverage ratio is often considered more meaningful than the times interest earned ratio because the firm's ability to meet its interest obligations is more closely related to its cash flow than its earnings.

**Asset Management or Turnover Measures**: These ratios measure how effectively the firm uses its assets, and are sometimes referred to as *asset utilization ratios*. For any given category of assets, the appropriate level of investment is analyzed by comparison with the firm's sales. Values of these ratios for K-Bec are below.

$$\text{Inventory turnover} = \frac{\text{Cost of goods sold}}{\text{Inventory}} = \frac{\$3,000}{\$2,225} = 1.35 \text{ times}$$

The inventory turnover ratio measures how quickly inventory is produced and sold. A high turnover ratio, relative to that of similar firms, may indicate that the firm is efficient in its inventory management. Alternatively, a high turnover ratio may mean that the firm is low on inventory and actually foregoing sales.

$$\text{Days' sales in inventory} = \frac{365 \text{ days}}{\text{Inventory turnover}} = \frac{365}{1.35} = 270 \text{ days}$$

This means that, on average, the firm holds its inventory for 270 days before it is sold.

The *receivables turnover* and *days' sales in receivables* measure the firm's ability to manage collections of accounts from customers:

$$\text{Receivables turnover} = \frac{\text{Sales}}{\text{Accounts receivable}} = \frac{\$5,000}{\$975} = 5.13 \text{ times}$$

$$\text{Days' sales in receivables} = \frac{365 \text{ days}}{\text{Receivables turnover}} = \frac{365}{5.13} = 71 \text{ days}$$

Days' sales in receivables is also referred to as the *average collection period* (ACP).

Consider a variation of the receivables collection period. How long, on average, does it take K-Bec Co., Inc. to pay its bills in 2000? We use the following ratios based on the firm's accounts payable and cost of goods sold.

$$\text{Payables turnover} = \frac{\text{Cost of goods sold}}{\text{Accounts payable}} = \frac{\$3,000}{\$1,200} = 2.5 \text{ times}$$

$$\text{Average payables period} = \frac{365}{\text{Payables turnover}} = \frac{365}{2.5} = 146 \text{ days}$$

Three additional turnover ratios are:

$$\text{Net Working Capital (NWC) turnover} = \frac{\text{Sales}}{\text{NWC}} = \frac{\$5,000}{\$3,750 - \$1,550} = 2.27 \text{ times}$$

$$\text{Fixed asset turnover} = \frac{\text{Sales}}{\text{Net fixed assets}} = \frac{\$5,000}{\$6,750} = 0.74 \text{ times}$$

$$\text{Total asset turnover} = \frac{\text{Sales}}{\text{Total assets}} = \frac{\$5,000}{\$10,500} = 0.48 \text{ times}$$

The total asset turnover indicates how effectively the firm uses its total assets to generate revenues. K-Bec generates $0.48 of sales for each $1 of total assets. A low value for this ratio, in comparison with other firms in the same industry, may indicate that assets are not being used as efficiently as possible.

If the total asset turnover is low, the firm should examine the inventory turnover, receivables turnover, etc., to determine the source of inefficiency.

**Profitability Measures**: These ratios are designed to measure a firm's profitability using accounting statement data. However, since accounting data ignore both future profitability and risk, the profitability ratios may not provide a complete indication of a firm's performance. The ratios for K-Bec are given below.

$$\text{Profit margin} = \frac{\text{Net income}}{\text{Sales}} = \frac{\$660}{\$5,000} = 13.2\%$$

K-Bec generates approximately $0.13 of profit for each $1 of sales. It might seem reasonable to conclude that a higher profit margin is preferable. However, a firm may elect a marketing strategy which emphasizes relatively low prices, and, consequently, low profit margins, in order to increase sales and total profits.

$$\text{Return on assets (ROA)} = \frac{\text{Net income}}{\text{Total assets}} = \frac{\$660}{\$10,500} = 6.29\%$$

$$\text{Return on equity (ROE)} = \frac{\text{Net Income}}{\text{Total equity}} = \frac{\$660}{\$6,364} = 10.37\%$$

Although both ROA and ROE are often cited as important measures of a firm's profitability, it is important to recall that both the numerator and denominator in these ratios are book values rather than market values. So, it is unlikely that either of these figures accurately reflects the market return earned by the firm, or by its shareholders, on investments.

**Market Value Measures:** Financial statements provide relatively little information about market values. Analysis of financial statements usually combines market value information with accounting information. The market price of a share of stock is the price paid when an investor buys or sells a share. The total market value of the firm's equity is the price per share multiplied by the number of shares. Rather than comparing market values directly across firms, analysts frequently use ratios to make such comparisons. Three commonly used ratios are the EPS ratio, the P/E ratio, and the market-to-book ratio. These values are given below for K-Bec.

Assume that K-Bec has 330 shares of common stock outstanding. The stock's market price is $25 per share.

$$\text{Earnings per share (EPS)} = \frac{\text{Net income}}{\text{Number of shares}} = \frac{\$660}{330} = \$2$$

$$\text{Price earnings (P/E) ratio} = \frac{\text{Price per share}}{\text{Earnings per share}} = \frac{\$25}{\$2.00} = 12.5$$

$$\text{Market-to-book ratio} = \frac{\text{Market value per share}}{\text{Book value per share}} = \frac{\$25.00}{\$19.28} = 1.30 \text{ times}$$

## THE DU PONT IDENTITY

The use of the Du Pont identity in analyzing financial statements is based on the presumption that return on equity is a primary measure of the firm's performance. Although ROE is based on accounting data, rather than market values, some insight into the firm's performance can be gained by analyzing the firm's ROE using the Du Pont method.

First, ROA can be written as the product of profit margin and total asset turnover as follows:

$$\text{ROA} = \frac{\text{Net income}}{\text{Total assets}} = \frac{\text{Net income}}{\text{Sales}} \times \frac{\text{Sales}}{\text{Total assets}} = \text{Profit margin} \times \text{Total asset turnover}$$

This decomposition of ROA makes it clear that return on assets depends on operating efficiency (as measured by the profit margin) and asset use efficiency (as measured by total asset turnover).

For K-Bec Co., Inc., ROA equals (0.132 x 0.48) = 6.34%. This differs slightly from the value of ROA computed earlier (6.29%) due to rounding. The point of this analysis is that the firm's return on assets can be increased by increasing either its operating or asset use efficiency. A firm can be profitable with a low profit margin, if low prices increase turnover, or with a high profit margin, even if high prices reduce turnover.

Return on equity (ROE) can be re-written as the product of ROA and the equity multiplier:

$$\text{ROE} = \text{ROA} \times \text{Equity multiplier} = \frac{\text{Net income}}{\text{Total assets}} \times \frac{\text{Total assets}}{\text{Total equity}}$$

Substituting for the definition of ROA developed above,

ROE = Profit margin x Total asset turnover x Equity multiplier

$$\text{ROE} = \frac{\text{Net income}}{\text{Sales}} \times \frac{\text{Sales}}{\text{Total assets}} \times \frac{\text{Total assets}}{\text{Total equity}}$$

This equation highlights the fact that the firm's return on equity depends on its operating efficiency (as measured by profit margin), the efficiency of its asset management (measured by total asset turnover), and its financial leverage (measured by the equity multiplier). Alternatively, the equation for ROE can also be rewritten as:

$$\text{ROE} = \frac{\text{ROA}}{1 - \text{Debt ratio}}$$

## USING FINANCIAL STATEMENT INFORMATION

There are three issues associated with using financial statement information: the reasons for evaluating financial statements; the sources of benchmarks for financial statement analysis; and, some problems encountered in the analysis of financial statements.

**Why evaluate financial statements?**  Financial statement analysis has both internal and external uses. Internal uses include performance evaluation and planning for the future. External uses include analysis performed by creditors and potential investors, evaluation of competitors, and assessment of a potential acquisition opportunity.

**Choosing a Benchmark:** The two major types of analysis are time-trend analysis and peer group analysis. Time-trend analysis compares current data with historical data for a given firm to determine changes in the firm's performance and profitability over time. Peer group analysis compares financial information from other firms with similar characteristics to the firm under analysis. Similarity is determined by factors such as the industry and the nature of the firm's assets. Financial statement information to use in comparison to your firm are provided by Statistics Canada, Dun & Bradstreet Canada, the Financial Post, and InfoGlobe.

**Problems with Financial Statement Analysis:** The major problem is that there is no unifying financial or economic theory which can be applied to this analysis. Consequently, there are no clear guidelines regarding the optimal values for the ratios presented here. In fact, it is often not even clear which ratios should be analyzed when performing an analysis. Other problems include: (1) identification of comparable peer groups; (2) differences in accounting procedures; (3) differences in fiscal years for financial statements; and (4) unusual events which have an impact on reported financial results.

## CONCEPT TEST

1.  Transactions which bring in cash are referred to as _____ of cash, and transactions which involve spending cash are _____ of cash.

2.  An increase in an asset account on the balance sheet represents a _____ of cash, and a decrease in an asset account represents a _____ of cash.

3.     A decrease in a liability or equity account is a _____ of cash, while an increase in a liability or equity account is a _____ of cash.

4.     The Statement of Changes in Financial Position organizes the sources and uses of cash into three categories: _____ activities, _____ activities, and _____ activities. Since depreciation is not a cash expense, it is added to net income as a _____ of cash on the Statement of Changes in Financial Position. Under the category of financing activities, dividends are a _____ of cash.

5.     Two approaches to standardizing financial statements are commonly used. Common-size statements are standardized by presenting balance sheet accounts as a percentage of _____ and income statement data as a percentage of _____.

6.     Common-base-year financial statements are standardized by comparing each statement item to its corresponding value during a _____ year. Each financial statement item for the base year is assigned a value of _____. Then, for subsequent years, each item is assigned a value which reflects the increase in the item. For example, suppose that 1998 is selected as the base year, and that the firm's accounts receivable are $500 and $550 at the end of 1998 and 1999, respectively; then, for the 1998 and 1999 common-base-year balance sheets, accounts receivable are assigned a value of _____ and _____, respectively. If accounts receivable increase to $600 at the end of 2000, then the 2000 common-base-year balance sheet displays a value of _____.

7.     Ratios intended to measure the firm's short-term liquidity are referred to as _____ ratios or _____ ratios. Some important ratios in this category are: Current ratio = _____/_____ ; Quick ratio = _____/_____ ; Cash ratio = _____/_____ ; Net working capital to total assets = _____/_____ ; Interval measure = _____/_____ .

8.     Ratios which gauge the extent to which a firm uses debt financing rather than equity financing are called _____ ratios. These ratios are also referred to as _____ ratios. Some important ratios in this category are: Total debt ratio = _____/_____ ; Debt/equity ratio = _____/_____ ; Equity multiplier = _____/_____ . The equity multiplier can also be computed as follows: Equity multiplier = 1 + _____ . Long-term debt ratio = _____/_____ ; Times interest earned ratio = _____/_____ ; Cash coverage ratio = _____/_____

9.     Ratios designed to measure how effectively the firm uses its assets are called _____ ratios or _____ measures. These ratios are also referred to as _____ ratios. For any given category of assets, the appropriate level of investment is analyzed by comparison with the firm's _____. Some important ratios in this category are: Inventory turnover = _____/_____ ; Days' sales in inventory = _____/_____ ; Receivables turnover = _____/_____ ; Days' sales in receivables = _____/_____ ; NWC turnover = _____/_____ ; Fixed asset turnover = _____/_____ ; Total asset turnover = _____/_____ .

10.    Ratios designed to measure a firm's profitability using accounting statement data are _____ ratios. Some important ratios in this category are: Profit margin = _____/_____ ; Return on assets = _____/_____ ; Return on equity = _____/_____ .

11.    Ratios based on market value data are called _____ ratios.  Important ratios in this category are: P/E
       ratio = _____/_____ ; Market-to-book ratio = _____/_____ .

12.    The use of the Du Pont identity in analyzing financial statements is based on the presumption that
       _____ is a primary measure of the firm's performance.  The importance of this ratio is diminished
       by the fact that it is based on _____ data, rather than _____.

13.    The Du Pont identity can be derived by first expressing return on assets as: Return on assets = _____
       × _____ .  This decomposition of ROA makes it clear that return on assets depends on
       _____ efficiency and _____ efficiency.  Return on equity can be written as: Return on
       equity = _____ × _____ .  ROE can be further decomposed by substituting for ROA: ROE =
       _____ × _____ × _____ .  This last equation highlights the fact that the firm's
       return on equity depends on _____ efficiency, _____ efficiency, and _____.

14.    Two basic forms of comparison are used when evaluating financial statement information. Analysis based
       on comparison of current data with historical data is referred to as _____ analysis. Analysis based
       on comparison of data for one firm with corresponding data for similar firms is called _____
       analysis.


# ANSWERS TO CONCEPT TEST

1.     sources; uses

2.     use; source

3.     use; source

4.     operating; financing; investment; source; use

5.     total assets; sales

6.     base; 1.00; 1.00; 1.10; 1.20

7.     short-term solvency;   liquidity; current assets; current liabilities; current assets less inventory; current
       liabilities; cash; current liabilities; net working capital; total assets; current assets; average daily operating
       cost

8.     long-term solvency; financial leverage; total assets less total equity; total assets; total debt; total equity; total
       assets; total equity; debt/equity ratio; long-term debt; long-term debt plus total equity; earnings before
       interest and taxes; interest; EBIT plus depreciation; interest

9.     asset management; turnover; asset utilization; sales; cost of goods sold; inventory; 365 days; inventory
       turnover; sales; accounts receivable; 365 days; receivables turnover; sales; net working capital; sales; net
       fixed assets; sales; total assets

10.    profitability; net income; sales; net income; total assets; net income; total equity

11.     market value; price per share; earnings per share; market value per share; book value per share

12.     return on equity; accounting; market values

13.     profit margin; total asset turnover; operating; asset use; return on assets; equity multiplier; profit margin; total
        asset turnover; equity multiplier; operating; asset use; financial leverage

14.     time-trend; peer group


## PROBLEMS AND SOLUTIONS

Use the following financial statements for Coogan Development Co., Inc., to solve Problems 1 through 14:

**COOGAN DEVELOPMENT CO., INC.**
2000 Income Statement

| | |
|---|---|
| Sales | $ 25,000 |
| Cost of goods sold | 16,000 |
| Depreciation | 3,000 |
| Earnings before interest and taxes | $ 6,000 |
| Interest paid | 2,000 |
| Taxable income | $ 4,000 |
| Taxes (34%) | 1,360 |
| Net income | $ 2,640 |
| | |
| Retained earnings | $ 1,584 |
| Dividends | 1,056 |

**COOGAN DEVELOPMENT CO., INC.**
Balance Sheets as of December 31, 1999 and 2000

| | 1999 | 2000 |
|---|---|---|
| *Assets* | | |
| Current assets | | |
| Cash | $ 4,000 | $ 3,000 |
| Accounts receivable | 9,000 | 11,000 |
| Inventory | 5,000 | 4,500 |
| Total | $ 18,000 | $ 18,500 |
| | | |
| Fixed assets | | |
| Net plant and equipment | 30,000 | 31,500 |
| | | |
| Total assets | $ 48,000 | $ 50,000 |

### Liabilities and Owners' Equity

| | | |
|---|---:|---:|
| Current liabilities | | |
| Accounts payable | $ 3,000 | $ 2,500 |
| Notes payable | 6,000 | 6,416 |
| Total | $ 9,000 | $ 8,916 |
| | | |
| Long-term debt | 15,000 | 13,000 |
| Owners' equity | | |
| Common stock and paid-in surplus | 14,000 | 16,500 |
| Retained earnings | 10,000 | 11,584 |
| Total | $ 24,000 | $ 28,084 |
| | | |
| Total liabilities and owners' equity | $ 48,000 | $ 50,000 |

## Problem 1

Compute the changes in the balance sheet accounts for Coogan Development Co., and summarize the firm's sources and uses of cash as indicated by these changes.

## Solution:

### COOGAN DEVELOPMENT CO., INC.
#### Balance Sheets as of December 31, 1999 and 2000 (Changes)

| | Change |
|---|---:|
| *Assets* | |
| Current assets | |
| Cash | - $ 1,000 |
| Accounts receivable | + 2,000 |
| Inventory | - 500 |
| Total | + $ 500 |
| | |
| Fixed assets | + 1,500 |
| Net plant and equipment | |
| | |
| Total assets | + $ 2,000 |

### Liabilities and Owners' Equity

| | Change |
|---|---:|
| Current liabilities | |
| Accounts payable | - $ 500 |
| Notes payable | + 416 |
| Total | - $ 84 |
| | |
| Long-term debt | - 2,000 |
| Owners' equity | |
| Common stock and paid-in surplus | + 2,500 |
| Retained earnings | + 1,584 |
| Total liabilities and owners' equity | + $ 2,000 |

The sources and uses of cash are summarized as follows:

| Sources of cash | | |
|---|---|---|
| Decrease in inventory | $ | 500 |
| Increase in notes payable | | 416 |
| Increase in common stock | | 2,500 |
| Increase in retained earnings | | 1,584 |
| Total sources | | $ 5,000 |

| Uses of cash | | |
|---|---|---|
| Increase in accounts receivable | | $ 2,000 |
| Decrease in accounts payable | 500 | |
| Decrease in long-term debt | | 2,000 |
| Net fixed asset acquisitions | | 1,500 |
| Total uses | | $ 6,000 |

| Net decrease in cash | | $ 1,000 |
|---|---|---|

## Problem 2

Prepare a statement of changes in financial position for Coogan Development Co., Inc.

**Solution:**   The financial statements for Coogan indicate a $1,500 increase in fixed assets and a $3,000 depreciation expense on the income statement. Therefore, Coogan actually invested ($1,500 + $3,000) = $4,500 in the acquisition of fixed assets.  The statement of changes in financial position for Coogan is below:

COOGAN DEVELOPMENT CO., INC.
2000 Statement of Cash Flows

| Operating activities | | |
|---|---|---|
| Net income | | $ 2,640 |
| Plus: | | |
| Depreciation | 3,000 | |
| Decrease in inventory | | 500 |
| Less: | | |
| Increase in accounts receivable | - | 2,000 |
| Decrease in accounts payable | - 500 | |
| | | |
| Net cash from operating activities | | $ 3,640 |
| | | |
| Investment activities | | |
| Fixed asset acquisitions | | -$ 4,500 |
| | | |
| Net cash from investment activities | | -$ 4,500 |

Financing activities
| | |
|---|---|
| Increase in notes payable | +$   416 |
| Decrease in long-term debt | -   2,000 |
| Dividends paid | -   1,056 |
| Increase in common stock | +   2,500 |
| | |
| Net increase from financing activities | - $   140 |
| | |
| Net decrease in cash | $  1,000 |

## Problem 3

Prepare common-size balance sheets for Coogan Development Co., Inc. for both 1999 and 2000.

**Solution:**  The common-size balance sheets present each balance sheet item as a percentage of total assets. The common-size balance sheets for Coogan Development Co. are below:

### COOGAN DEVELOPMENT CO., INC.
Common-Size Balance Sheets  December 31, 1999 and 2000

| | 1999 | 2000 | Change |
|---|---|---|---|
| *Assets* | | | |
| Current assets | | | |
| Cash | 8.3% | 6.0% | -  2.3% |
| Accounts receivable | 18.8 | 22.0 | +  3.2 |
| Inventory | 10.4 | 9.0 | -  1.4 |
| Total | 37.5 | 37.0-  0.5 | |
| | | | |
| Fixed assets | | | |
| Net plant and equipment | 62.5 | 63.0 | +  0.5 |
| | | | |
| Total assets | 100.0 | 100.0 | 0.0 |
| | | | |
| *Liabilities and Owners' Equity* | | | |
| | | | |
| Current liabilities | | | |
| Accounts payable | 6.3% | 5.0% | -  1.3% |
| Notes payable | 12.5 | 12.8 | +  0.3 |
| Total | 18.8 | 17.8 | -  1.0 |
| | | | |
| Long-term debt | 31.3 | 26.0 | -  5.3 |
| Owners' equity | | | |
| Common stock | 29.2 | 33.0 | +  3.8 |
| Retained earnings | 20.8 | 23.2 | +  2.4 |
| Total | 50.0 | 56.2 | +  6.2 |
| | | | |
| Total liabilities and owners' equity | 100.00 | 100.0 | +  0.0 |

**Problem 4**

Prepare a common-size income statement for Coogan Development Co.

**Solution:** The common-size income statement represents each income statement item as a percentage of sales. The common-size income statement for Coogan is:

COOGAN DEVELOPMENT CO., INC.
Common-Size Income Statement, 2000

| | | |
|---|---|---|
| Sales | | 100.0% |
| Cost of goods sold | | 64.0 |
| Depreciation | | 12.0 |
| Earnings before interest and taxes | | 24.0 |
| Interest paid | | 8.0 |
| Taxable income | 16.0 | |
| Taxes (34%) | | 5.4 |
| Net income | | 10.6 |
| | | |
| Retained earnings | | 6.3 |
| Dividends | | 4.3 |

**Problem 5**

Prepare common base year balance sheets for Coogan Development Co., using 1999 as the base year.

**Solution:** Since 1999 is the base year, the common-base-year balance sheet for 1999 has the value 1.00 for each balance sheet item. The entries for the 2000 common-base-year balance sheet indicate the increase or decrease for each item relative to the 1999 base year. For example, the value for cash is ($3,000/$4,000) = 0.75, reflecting a 25% decrease in the cash balance from 1999 to 2000. The value for accounts receivable is ($11,000/$9,000) = 1.22, indicating a 22% increase in accounts receivable. The common base year balance sheets are:

COOGAN DEVELOPMENT CO., INC.
Common Base Year Balance Sheets
as of December 31, 1999 and 2000

| | 1999 | 2000 |
|---|---|---|
| *Assets* | | |
| Current assets | | |
| Cash | 1.00 | 0.75 |
| Accounts receivable | 1.00 | 1.22 |
| Inventory | 1.00 | 0.90 |
| Total | 1.00 | 1.03 |
| | | |
| Fixed assets | | |
| Net plant and equipment | 1.00 | 1.05 |
| | | |
| Total assets | 1.00 | 1.04 |

*Liabilities and Owners' Equity*

Current liabilities
| | | |
|---|---|---|
| Accounts payable | 1.00 | 0.83 |
| Notes payable | 1.00 | 1.07 |
| Total | 1.00 | 0.99 |

| | | |
|---|---|---|
| Long-term debt | 1.00 | 0.87 |

Owners' equity
| | | |
|---|---|---|
| Common stock and paid-in surplus | 1.00 | 1.18 |
| Retained earnings | 1.00 | 1.16 |
| Total | 1.00 | 1.17 |

| | | |
|---|---|---|
| Total liabilities and owners' equity | 1.00 | 1.04 |

## Problem 6

For Coogan Development Co., compute the five measures of short-term solvency discussed in the chapter. Use the 2000 balance sheet and income statement data.

**Solution:**

Current ratio = Current assets / Current liabilities = $18,500 / $8,916 = 2.07
Quick ratio = (Current assets - inventory ) / Current liabilities = ($18,500 - $4,500) / $8,916 = 1.57
Cash ratio = Cash / Current liabilities = $3,000 / $8,916 = 0.34
Net working capital to total assets = NWC / Total assets = ($18,500 - $8,916)/ $50,000 = 0.19
Interval measure = Current assets / Average daily operating cost = $18,500 / $43.84 = 422 days
Note: Average daily operating cost: ($16,000/365) = $43.84

## Problem 7

For Coogan Development Co., compute the six measures of long-term solvency discussed in the chapter. Use the 2000 balance sheet and income statement data.

**Solution:**

Total debt ratio = (Total assets - Total equity) / Total assets = ($50,000 - $28,084) / $50,000 = .44
Debt/equity ratio = Total debt / Total equity = $21,916 / $28,084 = 0.78
Equity multiplier = Total assets / Total equity = $50,000 / $28,084 = 1.78
Long-term debt ratio = LT debt / (LT debt + Total equity) = $13,000 / ($13,000 + $28,084) = 0.32
Times interest earned ratio = EBIT / Interest = $6,000 / $2,000 = 3.00 times
Cash coverage ratio = (EBIT + Depreciation) / Interest = ($6,000 + $3,000) / $2,000 = 4.5 times

## Problem 8

For Coogan Development Co., compute the seven asset management measures discussed in the chapter. Use the 2000 balance sheet and income statement data.

**Solution:**

Inventory turnover = Cost of goods sold / Inventory = $16,000 / $4,500 = 3.56 times
Days' sales in inventory = 365 days / Inventory turnover = 365 / 3.56 = 103 days
Receivables turnover = Sales / Accounts receivable = $25,000 / $11,000 = 2.27 times
Days' sales in receivables = 365 days / Receivables turnover = 365 / 2.27 = 161 days
NWC turnover = Sales / NWC = $25,000 / ($18,500 - $8,916) = 2.61 times
Fixed asset turnover = Sales / Net fixed assets = $25,000 / $31,500 = 0.79 times
Total asset turnover = Sales / Total assets = $25,000 / $50,000 = 0.50 times

## Problem 9

For Coogan Development Co., compute the three profitability measures discussed in the chapter. Use the 2000 balance sheet and income statement data.

**Solution:**

Profit margin = Net income / Sales = $2,640 / $25,000 = 10.56%
Return on assets = Net income / Total assets = $2,640 / $50,000 = 5.28%
Return on equity = Net income / Total equity = $2,640 / $28,084 = 9.40%

## Problem 10

Use the Du Pont identity to compute return on equity and return on assets for Coogan Development Co. for the year 2000.

**Solution:** Return on assets can be written as follows:

Return on assets = Net income / Total assets = (Net income / Sales) x (Sales / Total assets )
Return on assets = Profit margin x Total asset turnover

For Coogan, profit margin is 10.56% (as computed in the solution to Problem 9) and total asset turnover is 0.50 (as computed in the solution to Problem 8). Therefore, return on assets can be computed:

Return on assets = Profit margin x Total asset turnover = .1056 x .50 = .0528 = 5.28%

Return on equity can be written as the product of ROA and the equity multiplier:

Return on equity = Return on assets x Equity multiplier = .0528 x 1.78 = .0940 = 9.40%

Note: This is the same result obtained from the direct calculation of the ROE in Problem 9.

ROE can be further decomposed as follows:

ROE  =  Profit margin x Total asset turnover x  Equity multiplier
$\quad$ = .1056 x .50 x 1.78 = .0940 = 9.40%


## Problem 11

Suppose that Coogan Development Co. has 1,000 shares of common stock outstanding and that the market price per share is $40. Compute earnings per share, the price/earnings ratio and the market-to-book ratio for Coogan Development Co. for the year 2000.

**Solution:**

Earnings per share (EPS) =  ($2,640/1,000) = $2.64
P/E ratio =  $40.00 / $2.64 = 15.2
Market-to-book =  $40.00 / $28.08 = 1.42 times
Book value per share  =  $28,084 / 1,000  =  $28.08


## Problem 12

Suppose that Coogan Development Co. decides to reduce its total debt ratio to 0.20 from 0.44 by selling new common stock and using the proceeds to repay principal on some of its outstanding long-term debt. Compute the resulting value for each of the following: debt/equity ratio, equity multiplier, and return on equity.  How much equity financing will the firm need in order to accomplish this reduction in the total debt ratio?

**Solution:**   The debt/equity ratio can be computed from the total debt ratio. The new total debt ratio indicates that Coogan would have $0.20 of debt for each dollar of assets, or $0.20 of debt and ($1.00 - $0.20) = $0.80 of equity financing for each dollar of assets. Therefore, the debt/equity ratio is ($0.20 / $0.80) = 0.25. The equity multiplier can be computed from the debt/equity ratio in two ways.  First, using the fact that Coogan has $0.80 of equity for each $1.00 of assets, then the equity multiplier is  = $1.00 / $0.80 = 1.25.  Alternatively, the equity multiplier is equal to (1 + debt/equity ratio) = 1 + 0.25 = 1.25. The new return on equity can now be computed using the Du Pont identity:

ROE = Profit margin x Total asset turnover x  Equity multiplier  = .1056 x .50 x 1.25 =  6.60%

To determine the amount of new equity financing required, we use the new total debt ratio to determine total equity for Coogan Development after the new financing.

Total debt ratio = ($50,000 -  Total equity) / $50,000 = .20

Solving, total equity is $40,000.  Therefore, the additional equity financing is ($40,000 - $28,084) = $11,916. Notice that this also represents a reduction of $11,916 in outstanding long-term debt, to ($13,000 - $11,916) = $1,084.

## Problem 13

Suppose that Coogan decides to increase its total debt ratio to 0.80 by borrowing additional long-term funds, and uses the proceeds to buy some of its own outstanding common stock. Compute the resulting value for each of the following: debt/equity ratio, equity multiplier, and return on equity. How much long-term debt financing will Coogan have to obtain in order to accomplish this increase in the total debt ratio?

**Solution:** The debt/equity ratio can be computed from the new total debt ratio. Coogan Development would have $0.80 of debt for each dollar of assets, or $0.80 of debt and ($1.00 - $0.80) = $0.20 of equity financing for each dollar of assets. Therefore, the debt/equity ratio is ($0.80/$0.20) = 4.00. The equity multiplier = (1 + 4.00) = 5.00. The new return on equity is: ROE = .1056 x .50 x 5.00 = .2640 = 26.40%. The total equity after the new financing is obtained by solving:

Total debt ratio = ($50,000 - Total equity) / $50,000 = .80

The firm's equity is $10,000. The additional long-term debt financing is ($18,084 - $10,000) = $8.084.

## Problem 14

Suppose that Coogan decides to reduce its average collection period (ACP) to 120 days from 161 days. How much of its current outstanding accounts receivable would the firm have to collect in order to accomplish this reduction? If the collected funds were held as cash, how would this change affect the firm's current ratio and quick ratio? If the collected funds were used to repay notes payable, how would this change affect the firm's current ratio and quick ratio?

**Solution:** Also called the days' sales in receivables, we can determine the required reduction in accounts receivable, by first solving the equation below for the receivables turnover required to accomplish the reduction in ACP:

Days' sales in receivables = 365 days / Receivables turnover = 120 days

Solving, the receivables turnover is 3.04 times. Then, solving for the required level of accounts receivable:

Receivables turnover = $25,000 / Accounts receivable = 3.04 times

The required level of accounts receivable is $8,223.68. Therefore, the firm would have to collect ($11,000 - $8,223.68) = $2,776.32 of its accounts receivable.

If the collected funds were held as cash, it would not have any effect on either the current ratio or the quick ratio, because total current assets and total current liabilities would not be affected. However, if the collected funds were used to pay outstanding notes payable, both current assets and current liabilities would be reduced by $2,776.32. Then, both the numerator and denominator of these ratios would be reduced by this amount. The current ratio would increase from 2.07 to 2.56 and the quick ratio would increase from 1.57 to 1.82.

## Problem 15

The following information was taken from the financial statements of Bombitdear Corporation: Cash = $25,000; Accounts Receivable = $211,000; Inventory = $72,223.35; Sales = $2,081,486.50; Total Assets = $828,595; Shareholders' Equity = $291,308.25; and the firm has no current assets other than those given. What is the firm's fixed asset turnover?

**Solution:** Fixed asset turnover = $2,081,486.50 / ($828,595 - $25,000 - $211,000 - $72,223.35) = 4.0

## Problem 16

Your firm's financial statements indicate cash of $75,000; accounts receivable of $672,000; inventory of $96,750; total assets of $1,663,000; and shareholder's equity of $490,000. Assuming a fixed asset turnover of 3.5, what is the level of sales?

**Solution:** 3.5 = Sales/($1,663,000 - $75,000 - $672,000 - 96,750)
              Sales = $2,867,375

## Problem 17

Concord Ltd. is a 100% equity financed firm with net fixed assets of $500,000. It has a net profit margin of 8%, a fixed asset turnover of 8 times, a total asset turnover of 5 times, and earnings per share of $2. How many Concord common shares are outstanding?

**Solution:**   Sales = $500,000 x 8 = $4,000,000
               Net income = .08 x $4,000,000 = $320,000
               Number of common shares = $320,000 / $2 =160,000

## Problem 18

Forgetit Ltd. has a gross profit margin (net income/sales) of 25% on sales of $500,000 (90% credit). Cash and marketable securities are $10,000, accounts receivable are $40,000, inventory is $50,000, and the current ratio is 2.0. What are Forgetit's average collection period and inventory turnover? (use a 365-day year). How much inventory should there be if management wants the inventory turnover to be 10 times a year? What would the accounts receivable be if management wants the average collection period to be 22 days?

**Solution:**   Receivables turnover  =  ($500,000 x .90) / $40,000   =   11.25
               Average collection period  =  365 / 11.25   =   32.44 days
               Inventory turnover = ($500,000 x .75) / $50,000   =   7.5 times

               Solve for inventory in the Inventory turnover ratio: ($500,000 x .75) / inventory   =   10. The solution
               is inventory   =   $37,500.

               Solve for accounts receivable in the days' sales in receivables ratio: 365 / Receivables turnover   = 22
               days.   Receivables turnover must be 16.59.  Now solve for accounts receivable in the Receivables
               turnover ratio:  ($500,000 x .90) / receivables   =  16.59.  The level of receivables should be $27,125.

**Problem 19**

Go Broke, Ltd. has a profit margin of 30% on sales of $6 million. All sales are for cash. The firm's cash and marketable securities are $130,000; accounts receivable are $240,000; inventory is valued at $700,000. What is Go Broke's average collection period (days' sales in receivables)? If the inventory turnover is 4 times per year, what is the firm's cost of goods sold?

**Solution:**   Receivables turnover  =  $6,000,000 / $240,000  = 25
                  Days' sales in receivables  =  365 / 25  =  14.6 days (15 days)

Solve for COGS in the inventory turnover ratio: COGS / $700,000  =  4
COGS is $2,800,000.

**Problem 20**

Sam's Supply Company Limited, a small manufacturer of surgical supplies and equipment, has been plagued with low profitability in recent years. As a result, the board of directors replaced the president of the firm. The new president has asked you to conduct an analysis of the firm's financial condition. The most recent financial statements and selected industry average ratios are reproduced below:

Balance Sheet
November 30, 2000 *(thousands of dollars)*

| | | | |
|---|---|---|---|
| Cash | $ 450 | Accounts payable | $ 610 |
| Marketable securities | 330 | Notes payable | 200 |
| Accounts receivable | 660 | Other current liabilities | 150 |
| Inventory | 1,590 | Total current liabilities | $ 960 |
| Total current assets | $3,030 | | |
| | | | |
| Gross fixed assets | $2,250 | Long-term debt | $1,000 |
| Less: Depreciation | (780) | Common shares | 2,100 |
| Net fixed assets | $1,470 | Retained earnings | 440 |
| | | | |
| Total assets | $4,500 | Total liabilities & owners' equity | $4,500 |

## INCOME STATEMENT
### Year Ended November 30, 2000
*(thousands of dollars)*

| | | |
|---|---|---:|
| Net sales | | $ 7,950 |
| Cost of goods sold | | 6,600 |
| Gross profit | | 1,350 |
| Operating expenses | | 735 |
| Depreciation | | 120 |
| Interest | | 45 |
| Taxable income | $  450 | |
| Taxes (47.1%) | | 212 |
| Net income | | $   238 |

### *Selected Industry Average Ratios*

| | | | |
|---|---|---|---|
| Debt to total assets | 40% | Fixed asset turnover | 5 times |
| Times interest earned | 7 times | Total asset turnover | 3 times |
| Inventory turnover | 9 times | Net profit on sales | 3% |
| Avg. collection period | 21 days | Return on total assets | 9% |
| Return on equity | 15% | | |

NOTE: Use year-end balance sheet figures in the computation of all ratios embodying balance sheet items.

Use the Du Pont equation to identify whether balance sheet accounts or income statement figures seem to be primarily responsible for Sam's low return on common equity relative to the industry average of 15%. Which specific **accounts** are most out of line in relation to other firms in the industry? What additional information would be most useful in analyzing Sam's financial condition?

**Solution:**

ROE  = (Net income / Sales) x (Sales / Total assets) x (Total assets / Common equity)
       = ($238 / $7,950) x ($7,950 / $4,500) x ($4,500 / $2,100)
       = 3%   x   1.77 x 2.14  =  11.4%

   Industry ROE  =  3% x 3 x 1.67  =  15%

Note: Indusry asset/equity ratio is found by recognizing that equity is 60% of assets, so assets/equity
=      1.0 / .60  =  1.67.

Balance Sheet accounts seem to be responsible for Sam's low return on common equity because there is a high investment in assets for the level of sales being generated. Also, note the lower use of debt financing (30%) versus the industry average of 40%.

Previous years' information which would allow one to do a hard analysis; industry averages relating to liquidity ratios; and, number of shares outstanding, market price data, etc., in order to calculate market value ratios.

# 4       <u>Long-Term Financial Planning and Corporate Growth</u>

## CHAPTER HIGHLIGHTS

This chapter is primarily concerned with long-term financial planning and financial planning models. The guidelines established as part of the financial planning process should identify the firm's financial goals, analyze the difference between the firm's current status and the established goals, and identify the actions required to achieve those goals. Large corporations tend to use an overall growth rate in sales as a major planning component. As this chapter describes, there are explicit links between potential growth, investment decisions, and financing decisions.

The basic policy elements which must be established by management in order to develop a financial plan are:

1. The firm's needed investment in new assets.
2. The degree of financial leverage.
3. The dividend payment to shareholders.
4. The firm's liquidity and working capital requirements.

These four areas represent, respectively, the firm's capital budgeting decisions, capital structure policy, dividend policy, and net working capital decisions. These decisions affect the firm's future profitability, its need for external financing, and its growth opportunities.

## WHAT IS FINANCIAL PLANNING?

The financial plan identifies the method for achieving the firm's financial goals. Since the implementation of a financial decision may require substantial lead time, financial planning is required in order to successfully meet the firm's goals.

**Growth as a Financial Management Goal:** We have learned that the appropriate goal for the financial manager is to maximize share (equity) value. Growth, by itself, is *not* an appropriate goal. However, growth rates are commonly used in the financial planning process. Therefore, we emphasize growth in this chapter as a way to summarize the various elements of a firm's financial and investment policies.

**Dimensions of Financial Planning:** A financial plan has two dimensions: the *planning horizon* and the process of *aggregation*. A long-term plan usually covers two to five years; the short-term is generally considered to be the next 12 months. In this chapter, we are primarily concerned with a long-term planning horizon.

The creation of a financial plan typically involves a process of combining smaller investment proposals into larger units, so that we treat the sum of these smaller proposals as if they were one larger investment. This process is called aggregation.

Financial plans often require alternative sets of assumptions. For example, a firm might require that each of its divisions prepare alternative plans under different assumptions regarding the state of the economy and the firm's prospects. These might include a worst case, most likely (or normal) case, and best case set of assumptions.

**What Can Planning Accomplish?**   First, the plan makes clear the link between investment proposals and the firm's financing alternatives.  Second, the plan allows the firm to evaluate different investment and financing options and their long-run impact on firm value.  Third, a financial plan helps identify what may happen if today's assumptions about the future are incorrect.  This enables the firm to develop contingency plans that may avoid unpleasant surprises.  Finally, a plan helps establish whether individual objectives and goals are feasible and consistent with overall corporate objectives.

## FINANCIAL PLANNING MODELS: A FIRST LOOK

The exact form and level of detail in a financial plan varies from firm to firm. In this section, we describe some of the common elements of a financial plan and develop a simple financial planning model.

**A Financial Planning Model - The Ingredients**: Most financial planning models include the following components:

1. *Sales forecast*. An externally supplied sales forecast is the foundation of most planning models. All other values in the planning model are derived from this forecast.

2. *Pro forma statements*. These are projected, or forecasted, accounting statements, including balance sheet, income statement, and statement of cash flows.

3. *Asset requirements*. The financial plan describes projected capital expenditures (i.e., investments in fixed assets) and working capital needs.

4. *Financial requirements*. This part of the plan details the necessary financial arrangements. The firm's debt policy and dividend policy are also relevant here because of their impact on the required financing.

5. *The 'plug.'* The projected growth rates in sales, assets, and financial requirements are generally not compatible without some adjustment; in other words, the balance sheet will not balance. Often, the 'plug' variable is the amount of external financing (i.e., new debt and/or equity) required in order to finance the projected increase in assets.

6. *Economic assumptions*. Assumptions about the future state of the economy, including such variables as interest rates, tax rates, and the general state of the economy, must be explicitly stated.

**A Simple Financial Planning Model - An Example:**  The purpose of the financial planning model described in this section is to illustrate the relationships mentioned earlier.  The approach to financial planning in the following example is highly simplified, and therefore is not necessarily practical.

The most recent income statement and balance sheet for the Tinker Corporation are presented here:

TINKER CORPORATION
Financial Statements

Income Statement

| | |
|---|---|
| Sales | $ 2,000 |
| Costs | 1,500 |
| Net income | $   500 |

### Balance Sheet

| | | | |
|---|---|---|---|
| Current assets | $ 800 | Current liabilities | $ 600 |
| Fixed assets | 3,600 | Long-term debt | 1,500 |
| | | Equity | 2,300 |
| Total | $4,400 | Total | $ 4,400 |

Suppose that Tinker forecasts a 10% increase in sales, and that all income statement and balance sheet variables will grow at the same rate as sales. These assumptions result in the following pro forma statements:

### Pro Forma Income Statement

| | |
|---|---|
| Sales | $ 2,200 |
| Costs | 1,650 |
| Net income | $ 550 |

### Pro Forma Balance Sheet

| | | | |
|---|---|---|---|
| Current assets | $ 880 (+$ 80) | Current liabilities | $ 660 (+$ 60) |
| Fixed assets | 3,960 (+$360) | Long-term debt | 1,650 (+$150) |
| | | Equity | 2,530 (+$230) |
| Total | $4,840 (+$440) | Total | $ 4,840 (+$440) |

The assumption that all variables grow at the same rate as sales implies that all variables maintain the same proportionate relationship after the increase in sales. In the example, costs are 75% of sales and current assets are 40% of sales. This is true for both the current and pro forma income statements. All other balance sheet items maintain the same proportionate relationships. For example, the debt/equity ratio remains constant at 34%.

The link between the pro forma income statement and balance sheet is retained earnings. However, Tinker's pro forma statements are inconsistent because our model has not yet accounted for this interaction. The pro forma income statement shows net income equal to $550. Without any dividend payments, retained earnings should increase by $550. The pro forma balance sheet, though, shows increased equity of only $230. This inconsistency can be resolved in several ways. For example, if dividends are used as the 'plug' figure, the data imply dividend payments to common shareholders of ($550 − $230) = $320.

Alternatively, long-term debt could be the 'plug' figure. If no dividends are paid, then equity increases to ($2,300 + $550) = $2,850. Since current liabilities increase to $660, the right side of the balance sheet, exclusive of long-term debt, totals ($2,850 + $660) = $3,510. Total assets are $4,840, so long-term debt must be ($4,840 − $3,510) = $1,330. This represents a decrease in long-term debt equal to ($1,500 − $1,330) = $170, which means that the firm repays existing long-term debt. The resulting pro forma balance sheet is:

### Pro Forma Balance Sheet

| | | | |
|---|---|---|---|
| Current assets | $ 880 (+$ 80) | Current liabilities | $ 660 (+$ 60) |
| Fixed assets | 3,960 (+$360) | Long-term debt | 1,330 (− $170) |
| | | Equity | 2,530 (+$550) |
| Total | $4,840 (+$440) | Total | $ 4,840 (+$440) |

Although this example is highly simplified, it demonstrates the interdependencies among the relevant variables and policies in financial planning models: growth in sales, growth in assets, dividend policy, and financing (capital structure) policy.


## THE PERCENTAGE OF SALES APPROACH

The simple financial planning model of the preceding section is based on the assumption that all income statement and balance sheet items increase proportionately with sales.  We can modify this approach somewhat by acknowledging that not all accounts are likely to increase with sales. This model is the percentage of sales approach.

**An Example:**   The most recent income statement and balance sheet for the Evers Corporation are presented here:

**EVERS CORPORATION**
Income Statement

| | |
|---|---|
| Sales | $ 5,000 |
| Costs | 4,000 |
| Taxable income | $ 1,000 |
| Taxes (34%) | 340 |
| Net income | $   660 |
| | |
| Retained earnings | $   495 |
| Dividends | $   165 |

**EVERS CORPORATION**
Balance Sheet

| Current assets | | | Current liabilities | | |
|---|---|---|---|---|---|
| Cash | $   500 | (10%) | Accounts payable | $ 1,000 (20%) | |
| Accounts receivable | 1,000 | (20%) | Notes payable | 500 ( n/a ) | |
| Inventory | 2,000 | (40%) | Total | $ 1,500 ( n/a ) | |
| Total | $ 3,500 | (70%) | | | |
| | | | Long-term debt | $ 2,500 ( n/a ) | |
| Fixed assets | | | Owners' equity | | |
| Net plant | $ 6,500 | (130%) | Common stock | $ 4,000 ( n/a ) | |
| | | | Retained earnings | 2,000 ( n/a ) | |
| | | | Total | $ 6,000 ( n/a ) | |
| Total assets | $10,000 | (200%) | Total | $10,000 ( n/a ) | |

For each balance sheet item, the percentage in parentheses represents the given item as a percentage of annual sales.  Those items which are not expected to increase proportionately with sales are identified by 'n/a,' indicating that the percentage calculation is not applicable.

The Evers Corporation has projected a 20% increase in sales.  The pro forma income statement is based on the assumption that costs, as a percentage of sales, remain constant.  That is, (costs/sales) = ($4,000/$5,000) = 80%. The consequence of this assumption is that the profit margin also remains constant at ($660/$5,000) = 13.2%.

The ratio of total assets to sales is sometimes called the *capital intensity ratio*. It indicates the level of assets needed to generate $1 in sales. The higher the ratio, the more capital intensive is the firm. Notice also that this ratio is just the reciprocal of the total asset turnover we defined in Chapter 3.

For Evers, this ratio is $10,000 / $5,000 = 2. That means (assuming this ratio is constant) it takes $2 in total assets to generate $1 in sales.

The *dividend payout ratio* is the percentage of net income paid as dividends: cash dividends/net income. For Evers Corporation, the dividend payout ratio is ($165/$660) = 25%. The *retention ratio* or *plowback ratio* is the percentage of net income which is retained: retained earnings/net income. It is equal to 1 minus the dividend payout ratio because everything not paid out is retained. Evers Corporation's retention ratio is ($495/$660) = 75%. In preparing the pro forma income statement, we assume that the dividend payout ratio is constant. This is equivalent to assuming that the retention ratio is constant.

### EVERS CORPORATION
#### Pro Forma Income Statement

| | | |
|---|---:|---:|
| Sales | | $ 6,000 |
| Costs | | 4,800 |
| Taxable income | $ 1,200 | |
| Taxes (34%) | | 408 |
| Net income | | $  792 |
| | | |
| Retained earnings | | $  594 |
| Dividends | | $  198 |

The pro forma balance sheet is derived by applying the respective percentages of sales to the projected sales levels for those items which are expected to increase proportionately with sales. Retained earnings on the pro forma balance sheet is computed by adding the retained earnings figure from the pro forma income statement to the current balance sheet retained earnings figure. All other balance sheet accounts remain constant, and the 'plug' figure is *external financing needed* (EFN). The figures in parentheses on the following partial pro forma balance sheet represent the respective increases from the current balance sheet.

### EVERS CORPORATION
#### Partial Pro Forma Balance Sheet

| Current assets | | | | Current liabilities | | |
|---|---:|---|---:|---|---:|---|
| Cash | $   600 | ($ 100) | | Accounts payable | $ 1,200 | ($ 200) |
| Accounts receivable | 1,200 | ( 200) | | Notes payable | 500 | ( 0) |
| Inventory | 2,400 | ( 400) | | Total | $ 1,700 | ($ 200) |
| Total | $ 4,200 | ( 700) | | | | |
| | | | | Long-term debt | $ 2,500 | ($  0) |
| Fixed assets | | | | Owners' equity | | |
| Net plant | $ 7,800 | ($ 1,300) | | Common stock | $ 4,000 | ( 0) |
| | | | | Retained earnings | 2,594 | ( 594) |
| | | | | Total | $ 6,594 | ( 594) |
| Total assets | $12,000 | ($2,000) | | Total | $10,794 | ($ 794) |
| | | | | | | |
| | | | | EFN | | $ 1,206 |

This statement is considered a partial pro forma balance sheet because the firm must next determine how the $1,206 of external financing will be obtained.  That is, we need to raise $1,206 in new financing in order to generate the expected 20% increase in sales.  The pro forma balance sheet is then complete when the source, or sources, of the external financing are determined and indicated appropriately on the balance sheet. The possible sources of external financing are: short-term debt, long-term debt, and new equity financing.  If, for example, all of the external financing is obtained in the form of additional long-term debt, then the pro forma balance sheet would indicate long-term debt equal to ($2,500 +$1,206) = $3,706.

**An Alternative Scenario:**  The assumption that assets are a fixed percentage of sales may not always be suitable. For example, suppose that Evers is using its fixed assets at only 60% of full capacity.  The need for external financing will be quite different.  This means that the current sales level is 60% of the full capacity sales level: Current sales = $5,000;  Full capacity sales = $5,000/.60 = $8,333.  This means that sales could increase by 67% [($8,333 –$5,000) / $5,000] before the firm needs to invest in new fixed assets.

In our previous scenario, we assumed that it would be necessary to add $1,300 in net fixed assets.  In the current scenario, no spending on net fixed assets is needed, because sales are projected to rise to $6,000, which is substantially less than the $8,333 full capacity level.  As a result, our original estimate of $1,206 in external funds needed is too high because we do not have to spend $1,300 in net fixed assets.  In fact, $94 ($1,300 –$1,206) will be injected into the firm with excess capacity, making a considerable difference in our projections.

## EXTERNAL FINANCING AND GROWTH

Growth and external financing needed (EFN) are positively related.  That is, the higher the rate of growth in sales (and assets), the greater the need for external financing.  In this section, we investigate the relationship between these two aspects of financial planning by first assuming a given financial policy for the firm, and then assessing the impact of that policy on the firm's financing requirements and ability to grow.

**EFN and Growth:**  We will use the following simplified example for Chance Corporation to establish the relationship between EFN and growth. The most recent income statement and balance sheet for the Chance Corporation are below:

CHANCE CORPORATION
Income Statement

| | |
|---|---:|
| Sales | $ 2,000 |
| Costs | 1,400 |
| Taxable income | $   600 |
| Taxes (34%) | 204 |
| Net Income | $   396 |
| | |
| Retained earnings | $    99 |
| Dividends | $   297 |

## CHANCE CORPORATION
### Balance Sheet

| | | | |
|---|---|---|---|
| Current assets | $ 2,000 | Total debt | $ 1,000 |
| Fixed assets | 3,000 | Owners' equity | 4,000 |
| | | | |
| Total assets | $ 5,000 | Total liabilities | $ 5,000 |

Chance is forecasting a 25% increase in sales for the coming year.  They predict that  assets increase directly with sales, while liabilities and equity do not increase spontaneously with sales.

The following notation and data will be used in this example:

| | | | | | |
|---|---|---|---|---|---|
| S | = | Previous year's sales | = | $2,000 | |
| A | = | Total assets | = | $5,000 | |
| D | = | Total debt | = | $1,000 | |
| E | = | Total equity | = | $4,000 | |
| g | = | Growth rate | = | 25% | |

The following ratios can be computed for Chance Corporation:

| | | | | | |
|---|---|---|---|---|---|
| p | = | Profit margin | = | $396 / $2,000 | = 19.80% |
| R | = | Retention ratio = | $99 / $396 | = 25.00% | |
| ROA | = | Return on assets | = | $396 / $5,000 | = 7.92% |
| ROE | = | Return on equity | = | $396 / $4,000 | = 9.90% |
| D/E | = | Debt/equity ratio | = | $1,000 / $4,000 | = 25.00% |

Assuming a constant capital intensity ratio, the increase in total assets is equal to:

$$A \times g = \$5{,}000 \times .25 = \$1{,}250$$

where g is the growth rate.  The pro forma income statement generated by the forecasted 25% sales increase is below.

## CHANCE CORPORATION
### Pro Forma Income Statement

| | |
|---|---|
| Sales | $ 2,500 |
| Costs | 1,750 |
| Taxable income | $   750 |
| Taxes (34%) | 255 |
| Net Income | $   495 |
| | |
| Retained earnings | $   123.75 |
| Dividends | $   371.25 |

The projected sales level is:

$$S \times (1 + g) = \$2{,}000 \times 1.25 = \$2{,}500$$

Projected net income is then equal to the profit margin times projected sales:

$$p\,S \times (1 + g) \;=\; .198 \times \$2,\!500 \;=\; \$495$$

And, the projected addition to retained earnings is the retention ratio times projected net income:

$$R\,p\,S \times (1 + g) \;=\; .25 \times \$495 \;=\; \$123.75$$

Therefore, the external financing needed is:

$$EFN \;=\; (A \times g) - [R \times p \times S \times (1 + g)] \;=\; \$1,\!250 - \$123.75 = \$1,\!126.25$$

The amount of external financing needed is the difference between the increase in assets and the projected addition to retained earnings.

The pro forma balance sheet for Chance Corporation is:

**CHANCE CORPORATION**
Pro Forma Balance Sheet

| Current assets | $ 2,500.00 | Total debt | $ 1,000.00 |
|---|---|---|---|
| Fixed assets | 3,750.00 | Owners' equity | 4,123.75 |
| Total assets | $ 6,250.00 | Total liabilities | $ 5,123.75 |
|  |  | External funds needed | $ 1,126.25 |

The relationship between EFN and g can be clarified by algebraically rearranging the above equation for EFN:

$$EFN \;=\; (A \times g) - [R \times p \times S \times (1 + g)]$$

$$EFN \;=\; -(R \times p \times S) + [A - (R \times p \times S)] \times g$$

Substituting the data for the Chance Corporation:

$$EFN \;=\; -(.25 \times .198 \times \$2,\!000) + [\$5,\!000 - (.25 \times .198 \times \$2,\!000)] \times g$$

$$EFN \;=\; -\$99 + (\$4,\!901 \times g)$$

This is the equation for a straight line with independent variable g and dependent variable EFN. The y-intercept is −$99 and the slope is $4,901. The y-intercept signifies that, when g = 0, EFN = −$99. In other words, if the growth rate is zero, the addition to retained earnings is the same as it was for the previous year. Furthermore, since there is no growth in sales or assets, EFN is negative, indicating that surplus financing is available.

The slope of $4,901 signifies that, for each 1% increase in the growth rate, ($4,901 × .01) = $49.01 of external financing is required. For our example, g is 25%, so that external financing needed is:

$$EFN \;=\; -\$99 + (\$4,\!901 \times .25) \;=\; \$1,\!126.25$$

**Internal Growth Rate:** The above equation lets us determine the firm's internal growth rate; the growth rate which can be achieved without any external financing. To find this growth rate, set EFN equal to zero and solve for g:

$$EFN = -\$99 + (\$4{,}901 \times g) = 0$$

$$\$99 = \$4{,}901 \times g$$

$$g = \$99/\$4{,}901 = .02020 = 2.02\%$$

**Financial Policy and Growth:** The 2.02% growth rate computed above would allow Chance Corporation to grow indefinitely without obtaining external financing. Because all internal financing is derived from retained earnings, and the firm obtains no new external debt financing, the firm's debt/equity ratio will decrease over time. The *sustainable growth rate* (SGR) is the growth rate which the firm could maintain without issuing any new equity, while maintaining the current debt/equity ratio. That is, all external financing is debt financing, which is obtained in a sufficient amount to maintain the existing debt/equity ratio. Algebraically, the sustainable growth rate (g*) is:

$$g^* = \frac{ROE \times R}{1 - (ROE \times R)}$$

For Chance Corporation, the sustainable growth rate is:

$$g^* = \frac{.099 \times .25}{1 - (.099 \times .25)} = .02538 = 2.54\%$$

In order to verify this result, prepare the pro forma income statement and balance sheet for Chance using the 2.538% sustainable growth rate, as follows:

CHANCE CORPORATION
Pro Forma Income Statement

| | |
|---|---|
| Sales | $ 2,050.76 |
| Costs | 1,435.53 |
| Taxable income | $   615.23 |
| Taxes (34%) | 209.18 |
| Net income | $   406.05 |
| | |
| Retained earnings | $   101.51 |
| Dividends | $   304.54 |

Pro Forma Balance Sheet

| | | | |
|---|---|---|---|
| Current assets | $ 2,050.76 | Total debt | $ 1,000.00 |
| Fixed assets | 3,076.14 | Owners' equity | 4,101.51 |
| Total assets | $ 5,126.90 | Total liabilities | $ 5,101.51 |
| | | External funds needed | $      25.39 |

Since the external financing is all debt, the debt/equity ratio is constant: ($1,025.39/$4,101.51) = 25%.

**Determinants of Growth:**  The Du Pont identity developed in the previous chapter specifies that return on equity (ROE) can be written as:  ROE = Profit margin × Total asset turnover × Equity multiplier.  Using the notation introduced in this chapter, the Du Pont identity can be rewritten as:

$$ROE = p \times (S/A) \times [1 + (D/E)]$$

Since ROE is a determinant of the sustainable growth rate, the three determinants of ROE are determinants of the SGR. This relationship is made explicit by substituting the above expression for ROE into the formula for the SGR:

$$g^* \ = \ \frac{ROE \times R}{1 - (ROE \times R)} \ = \ \frac{p \times (S/A) \times [1 + (D/E)] \times R}{1 - \{p \times (S/A) \times [1 + (D/E)] \times R\}}$$

In this form, it is now clear that the sustainable growth rate depends on four factors:

1. *Profit margin.*  An increase in the profit margin (p) increases the firm's ability to generate internal financing, and, consequently, increases the firm's SGR.

2. *Dividend policy.*  An increase in the retention ratio (R) increases both retained earnings and the SGR.

3. *Financial policy.*  An increase in the debt/equity ratio (D/E) increases financial leverage, thereby making additional debt financing available and increasing the SGR.

4. *Total asset turnover.*  An increase in total asset turnover (S/A) decreases the need for financing of new assets and consequently increases the SGR.

This view of the sustainable growth rate clarifies the relationship among the four aspects of financial decision making and their respective effects on the firm's ability to grow.  If management desires a growth rate higher than the sustainable growth rate, then one of the stated assumptions must be modified.  In this way, firms may use the financial planning model to reconcile potentially conflicting goals and objectives.

## SOME CAVEATS TO FINANCIAL PLANNING MODELS

Financial planning models do not necessarily identify optimal financial policies.  Furthermore, the assumptions of the financial planning models we have discussed are too simple to accurately represent reality. Financial planning models are useful for pointing out inconsistencies, but offer limited guidance concerning the resolution of these inconsistencies. The main reason for these deficiencies is that financial planning models are typically based on accounting relationships. They focus attention on matters such as the association between the debt/equity ratio and firm growth.  But, they do not focus on the three basic determinants of firm value: size, risk, and timing of cash flows.

## CONCEPT TEST

1.      The basic policy elements which must be established by management to develop a financial plan are:
            1. The firm's needed investment in new assets.
            2. The degree of financial leverage the firm elects to employ.
            3. The dividend payment to shareholders.
            4. The firm's liquidity and working capital requirements.

These four areas represent, respectively, the firm's _____ decisions, _____ policy, _____ policy, and _____ decision.

2.  A financial plan which covers a period of 2 to 5 years is generally considered a _____ plan. A plan which covers only a 12-month period is considered a _____ plan.

3.  Creation of a financial plan typically involves a process of combining smaller investment proposals into larger units. This process is called _____ .

4.  A universal requirement for financial planning is the _____ forecast. Projected, or forecasted, accounting statements are referred to as _____ statements.

5.  The financial plan describes projected capital expenditures and working capital needs. These are _____ requirements. The firm's financial requirements detail the manner in which required financing will be obtained. The firm's _____ policy and _____ policy are also relevant here because of their impact on the required financing.

6.  The projected growth rates in sales, assets, and financial requirements are generally not compatible without some adjustment. The amount of external financing required in order to finance the projected increase in assets is referred to as the _____ variable.

7.  Assumptions about variables such as interest rates, tax rates, and the general state of the economy, must be explicitly stated; these are called _____ assumptions.

8.  The financial planning model based on the assumption that some, but not all, accounting statement data increase proportionately with sales is called the _____ approach. Using this approach, we assume that costs, as a percentage of sales, __(do/do not)__ remain constant. A consequence of this assumption is that the profit margin __(does/does not)__ remain constant.

9.  The dividend payout ratio is the percentage of _____ paid as dividends. That is, the dividend payout ratio is equal to (_____ /_____ ).

10. The retention ratio is the percentage of _____ which is _____ . That is, the retention ratio is equal to (_____ /_____ ).

11. If, in preparing the pro forma income statement, we assume that the dividend payout ratio is constant, this (is/is not) equivalent to assuming that the retention ratio is constant.

12. For the financial planning model described in the preceding question, it is generally assumed that assets __(do/do not)__ increase proportionately with sales. It is also assumed that liabilities (other than accounts payable) and owners' equity __(do/do not)__ increase proportionately with sales.

13. Retained earnings on the pro forma balance sheet is computed by adding the retained earnings figure from the _____ statement to the current balance sheet retained earnings figure. All other balance sheet accounts remain constant, and external financing needed is the _____ figure. The pro forma balance sheet is then complete when the source, or sources, of the external financing are determined and indicated appropriately on the balance sheet. The possible sources of financing are: _____ debt, _____ debt, and _____ .

14.  Since assets are assumed to increase directly with sales, the increase in total assets is equal to: _____ . Projected sales level is equal to: _____ . Projected net income is equal to _____ times projected _____ ; that is: _____ . The projected addition to retained earnings is _____ times _____ ; that is: _____ .

15.  External financing needed is: EFN = _____ . The relationship between EFN and g can be clarified by algebraically rearranging the above equation for EFN:
     EFN = –_____ + _____ × g. This is the formula for a linear equation with g as the _____ variable and EFN as the _____ variable. The y-intercept is _____ and the slope is _____ .

16.  The y-intercept in the EFN equation signifies that, when g = 0, EFN = _____ . In other words, if the growth rate is zero, the addition to retained earnings is _____ . Also, since there is no growth in sales or assets, EFN is negative, indicating that _____ .

17.  The EFN equation allows us to determine the growth rate which the firm can achieve without any external financing. This growth rate is ascertained by setting EFN equal to _____ and solving for g. This growth rate allows the firm to grow indefinitely without obtaining external financing. Since all internal financing is derived from _____ , and the firm obtains no new external debt financing, the firm's debt/equity ratio will (increase/decrease) over time.

18.  The growth rate which the firm could maintain without issuing any new equity, while maintaining the current debt/equity ratio, is called the _____ . It is computed: g* = _____ .

19.  The Du Pont identity specifies that return on equity can be written: ROE = _____ .

20.  The Du Pont identity can also be written as: ROE = _____ .

21.  By substituting the above expression for ROE into the formula for the sustainable growth rate, this latter formula is written as follows: g* = (_____ )/(_____ ). In this form it is clear that the sustainable growth rate depends on four factors: (1) An increase in the profit margin (increases/decreases) the firm's ability to generate internal financing, and, consequently, (increases/decreases) the firm's SGR. (2) An increase in the retention ratio (increases/decreases) retained earnings and, thus, (increases/decreases) the SGR. (3) An increase in the debt/equity ratio (increases/decreases) financial leverage, and thereby makes additional debt financing available and (increases/decreases) the SGR. (4) An increase in total asset turnover (increases/decreases) the need for financing of new assets and consequently (increases/decreases) the SGR.

## ANSWERS TO CONCEPT TEST

1.  capital budgeting; capital structure; dividend; net working capital

2.  long-term; short-term

3.  aggregation

4.  sales; pro forma

5.      asset; debt; dividend

6.      plug

7.      economic

8.      percentage of sales; do; does

9.      net income; cash dividends; net income

10.     net income; retained; retained earnings; net income

11.     is

12.     do; do not

13.     pro forma income; plug; short-term; long-term; new equity financing

14.     $(A \times g)$; $[S \times (1 + g)]$; the profit margin; sales; $p \times S \times (1 + g)$; the retention ratio; projected net income; $R \times p \times S \times (1 + g)$

15.     $(A \times g) - [R \times p \times S \times (1 + g)]$; $(R \times p \times S)$; $A - (R \times p \times S)$; independent; dependent; $-(R \times p \times S)$; $A - (R \times p \times S)$

16.     $-(R \times p \times S)$; $-(R \times p \times S)$; surplus financing is available

17.     zero; retained earnings; decrease

18.     sustainable growth rate; $(ROE \times R)/[1 - (ROE \times R)]$

19.     Profit margin $\times$ Total asset turnover $\times$ Equity multiplier

20.     $p \times (S/A) \times [1 + (D/E)]$

21.     $p \times (S/A) \times [1 + (D/E)] \times R$; $1 - \{p \times (S/A) \times [1 + (D/E)] \times R\}$; increases; increases; increases; increases; increases; increases; decreases; increases

## PROBLEMS AND SOLUTIONS

### Problem 1

The most recent income statement and balance sheet for the G. T. Seaver Corporation are presented below:

**G. T. SEAVER CORPORATION**
Financial Statements

**Income Statement**

| | |
|---|---|
| Sales | $ 80,000 |
| Costs | 56,000 |
| Net income | $ 24,000 |

**Balance Sheet**

| | | | |
|---|---|---|---|
| Current assets | $ 15,000 | Current liabilities | $ 10,000 |
| Fixed assets | 85,000 | Long-term debt | 25,000 |
| | | Owners' equity | 65,000 |
| Total | $100,000 | Total | $100,000 |

Seaver expects sales to increase by 15% in the coming year. Suppose that all income statement and balance sheet variables will grow at the same rate as sales. Prepare the pro forma income statement and balance sheet. Reconcile these statements using dividends as the 'plug' figure.

**Solution:** Increasing all income statement and balance sheet items by 15% results in the following pro forma statements:

**G. T. SEAVER CORPORATION**
Pro Forma Income Statement

| | |
|---|---|
| Sales | $ 92,000 |
| Costs | 64,400 |
| Net income | $ 27,600 |

**Pro Forma Balance Sheet**

| | | | |
|---|---|---|---|
| Current assets | $ 17,250 (+ $ 2,250) | Current liabilities | $ 11,500 (+ $ 1,500) |
| Fixed assets | 97,750 (+ $12,750) | Long-term debt | 28,750 (+ $ 3,750) |
| | | Owners' equity | 74,750 (+ $ 9,750) |
| Total | $115,000 (+ $15,000) | Total | $115,000 (+ $15,000) |

The figures in parentheses indicate the increase in the respective balance sheet items. The increase of $9,750 in equity is inconsistent with the net income figure of $27,600 from the pro forma income statement. If these figures are reconciled using dividends as the 'plug' figure, then the total cash dividends for the year must be ($27,600 – $9,750) = $17,850.

## Problem 2

Reconcile the pro forma statements in the solution to Problem 1, using long-term debt as the 'plug' figure, under the assumption that Seaver Corporation pays no dividends.

**Solution:**  If dividends are zero, then retained earnings are $27,600 and equity on the pro forma balance sheet is equal to ($65,000 + $27,600) = $92,600. Equity plus current liabilities are equal to ($92,600 + $11,500) = $104,100, so that long-term debt is ($115,000 – $104,100) = $10,900. Seaver must pay off ($25,000 – $10,900) = $14,100 of long-term debt.

The pro forma balance sheet appears as follows:

**G. T. SEAVER CORPORATION**
Pro Forma Balance Sheet

| Current assets | $ 17,250 (+ $  2,250) | Current liabilities | $ 11,500  (+ $  1,500) |
|---|---|---|---|
| Fixed assets | 97,750 (+ $12,750) | Long-term debt | 10,900  (- $ 14,100) |
| | | Owners' equity | 92,600  (+ $27,600) |
| Total | $115,000 (+ $15,000) | Total | $115,000  (+ $15,000) |

## Problem 3

Reconcile the pro forma statements in the solution to Problem 1, using long-term debt as the 'plug' figure, under the assumption that Seaver Corporation has a dividend payout ratio of 80%.

**Solution:**  Dividends are ($27,600 × .80) = $22,080, and retained earnings are ($27,600 – $22,080) = $5,520. Equity on the pro forma balance sheet is equal to ($65,000 + $5,520) = $70,520.  Equity plus current liabilities are equal to ($70,520 + $11,500) = $82,020.  Long-term debt must be ($115,000 – $82,020) = $32,980, so that Seaver must borrow ($32,980 – $25,000) = $7,980. The pro forma balance sheet appears below:

**G. T. SEAVER CORPORATION**
Pro Forma Balance Sheet

| Current assets | $ 17,250 (+ $  2,250) | Current liabilities | $ 11,500  (+ $  1,500) |
|---|---|---|---|
| Fixed assets | 97,750 (+ $12,750) | Long-term debt | 32,980  (+ $  7,980) |
| | | Owners' equity | 70,520  (+ $  5,520) |
| Total | $115,000 (+ $15,000) | Total | $115,000  (+ $15,000) |

## Problem 4

The most recent income statement and balance sheet for DMB, Inc. are presented below:

DMB, Inc.
Income statement for the year ending December 31, 2000

| Sales | $108,000 |
|---|---|
| Total costs | 72,000 |
| Net income | $ 36,000 |
| | |
| Retained earnings | $  9,000 |
| Dividends | $ 27,000 |

DMB, Inc.
Balance Sheet as of December 31, 2000

| Current assets | $ 60,000 | Current liabilities | $ 15,000 |
|---|---|---|---|
| Fixed assets | 120,000 | Long-term debt | 70,000 |
| | | Owners' equity | 95,000 |
| Total | $180,000 | Total | $180,000 |

DMB expects sales to increase by 25% in the year 2001. Prepare a pro forma income statement and balance sheet, assuming all income statement variables will grow at the same rate as sales, and that long-term debt remains constant while all other balance sheet variables increase at the same rate (25%). Assuming that DMB maintains the same retention ration, determine the amount of external financing needed.

## Solution:

DMB, Inc.
Pro Forma Income Statement for 2001

| Sales | $135,000 |
|---|---|
| COGS | 90,000 |
| Net income | $ 45,000 |
| | |
| Retained earnings | $ 11,250 |
| Dividends | $ 33,750 |

DMB, Inc.
Pro Forma Balance Sheet for 2001

| Current assets | $ 75,000 (+15,000) | Current liabilities | $ 18,750 (+3,750) |
|---|---|---|---|
| Fixed assets | 150,000 (+30,000) | Long-term debt | 70,000 |
| | | Owners' equity | 106,250 (+11,250) |
| Total | $225,000 (+45,000) | Total | $195,000 (+15,000) |

External financing needed: EFN  =  $225,000 - $195,000  =  $30,000
Note: Change in owners' equity is the increase in retained earnings: $95,000 x 1.25  =  $11,250

**Problem 5:** The most recent balance sheet and income statement for Grote & Co., Inc., are presented here:

### GROTE & CO., INC.
### Financial Statements

Income Statement

| | | | |
|---|---|---|---|
| Sales | | | $ 20,000 |
| Costs | | | 17,000 |
| Taxable income | | $ 3,000 | |
| Taxes (34%) | | | 1,020 |
| Net income | | | $ 1,980 |
| Retained earnings | | | $ 1,188 |
| Dividends | | | $    792 |

Balance Sheet

| Current assets | | | Current liabilities | | |
|---|---|---|---|---|---|
| Cash | $ 3,000 (15%) | | Accounts payable | $ 6,000 (30%) | |
| Accounts receivable | 5,000 (25%) | | Notes payable | 3,000 ( n/a ) | |
| Inventory | 7,000 (35%) | | Total | $ 9,000 ( n/a ) | |
| Total | $15,000 (75%) | | | | |
| | | | Long-term debt | $ 15,000 ( n/a ) | |
| Fixed assets | | | Owners' equity | | |
| Net plant | $30,000 (150%) | | Common stock | $ 13,000 ( n/a ) | |
| | | | Retained earnings | 8,000 ( n/a ) | |
| | | | Total | $ 21,000 ( n/a ) | |
| Total assets | $45,000 (225%) | | Total liabilities | $ 45,000 ( n/a ) | |

For each balance sheet item, the percentage in parentheses represents the given item as a percentage of annual sales. Those items which are not expected to increase proportionately with sales are identified by 'n/a,' indicating that the percentage calculation is not applicable. Grote & Co. has projected a 25% increase in sales. The dividend payout ratio is expected to remain constant. Use the percentage of sales approach to prepare the pro forma statements and to compute the external financing needed.

**Solution:** The pro forma income statement is based on the assumption that costs, as a percentage of sales, remain constant. That is, (costs/sales) = ($17,000/$20,000) = 85%. Consequently, the profit margin also remains constant at ($1,980/$20,000) = 9.9%. The dividend payout ratio is ($990/$2,475) = 40%.

### GROTE & CO., INC.

Pro Forma Income Statement

| | | |
|---|---|---|
| Sales | | $ 25,000 |
| Costs | | 21,250 |
| Taxable income | $ 3,750 | |
| Taxes (34%) | | 1,275 |
| Net income | | $ 2,475 |
| | | |
| Retained earnings | | $ 1,485 |
| Dividends | | $    990 |

The pro forma balance sheet is derived by applying the respective percentages of sales to the projected sales levels for those items which are expected to increase proportionately with sales. Retained earnings on the pro forma balance sheet is computed by adding the retained earnings figure from the pro forma income statement to the current balance sheet retained earnings figure. All other balance sheet accounts remain constant, and the 'plug' figure is external financing needed (EFN). The figures in parentheses on the partial pro forma balance sheet represent the respective increases from the current balance sheet.

GROTE & CO., INC.

Partial Pro Forma Balance Sheet

| Current assets | | | Current liabilities | | |
|---|---|---|---|---|---|
| Cash | $ 3,750 ($ | 750) | Accounts payable | $ 7,500 ($ 1,500) | |
| Accounts receivable | 6,250 ( | 1,250) | Notes payable | 3,000 ( | 0) |
| Inventory | 8,750 ( | 1,750) | Total | $10,500 ($ 1,500) | |
| Total | $18,750 ($ 3,750) | | | | |
| | | | Long-term debt | $15,000 ( $ | 0) |
| Fixed assets | | | Owners' equity | | |
| Net plant | $37,500 ($ 7,500) | | Common stock | $13,000 ($ | 0) |
| | | | Retained earnings | 9,485 ( | 1,485) |
| | | | Total | $22,485 ($ 1,485) | |
| Total assets | $56,250 ($ 11,250) | | Total liabilities | $47,985 ($ 2,985) | |
| | | | EFN | $ 8,265 | |

The balance sheet is considered a partial pro forma balance sheet because the firm must determine how the external financing of $8,265 is to be obtained. The pro forma balance sheet is completed when the source, or sources, of the external financing are determined and indicated appropriately on the balance sheet. If, for example, all of the external financing is obtained in the form of additional long-term debt, then the pro forma balance sheet would indicate long-term debt equal to ($15,000 + $8,265) = $23,265.

## Problem 6

The most recent income statement and balance sheet for the T. McGraw Corporation are as follows:

T. McGRAW CORPORATION
Income Statement

| | | |
|---|---|---|
| Sales | | $ 10,000 |
| Costs | | 7,500 |
| Taxable income | $ 2,500 | |
| Taxes (34%) | | 850 |
| Net income | | $ 1,650 |
| | | |
| Retained earnings | $ | 660 |
| Dividends | $ | 990 |

## Balance Sheet

| | | | | |
|---|---|---|---|---|
| Current assets | $  5,000 | | Total debt | $  6,000 |
| Fixed assets | 10,000 | | Owners' equity | 9,000 |
| | | | | |
| Total | $ 15,000 | | Total | $ 15,000 |

McGraw is forecasting a 20% increase in sales for the coming year. Assets increase directly with sales, while liabilities and equity do not increase spontaneously with sales. Compute the following for McGraw: profit margin (p), retention ratio (R), return on assets (ROA), return on equity (ROE), and debt/equity ratio (D/E).

**Solution:** These ratios are computed as follows:

| | | | | |
|---|---|---|---|---|
| p | = | $1,650 / $10,000 | = | 16.5% |
| R | = | $660 / $1,650 | = | 40% |
| ROA | = | $1,650 / $15,000 | = | 11% |
| ROE | = | $1,650 / $9,000 = | 18.33% | |
| D/E | = | $6,000 / $9,000 = | 66.67% | |

## Problem 7

Use the ratios computed in the solution to Problem 6 to calculate the external financing required by T. McGraw.

**Solution:** The increase in assets to be financed is: $A \times g = \$15,000 \times .20 = \$3,000$. In order to compute the financing available in the form of retained earnings, we first compute the projected sales level: $S \times (1 + g) = \$10,000 \times 1.20 = \$12,000$. Projected net income is equal to the profit margin times projected sales: $p \times S \times (1 + g) = .165 \times \$12,000 = \$1,980$. The projected addition to retained earnings is the retention ratio times projected net income: $R \times p \times S \times (1 + g) = .40 \times \$1,980 = \$792$. Therefore, the external financing needed is:

$$EFN = (A \times g) - [R \times p \times S \times (1 + g)]$$
$$= \$3,000 - \$792 = \$2,208$$

## Problem 8

Use pro forma statements to verify the results in the solution to Problem 7.

**Solution:**

### T. McGraw CORPORATION
### Pro Forma Income Statement

| | |
|---|---|
| Sales | $ 12,000 |
| Costs | 9,000 |
| Taxable income | $ 3,000 |
| Taxes (34%) | 1,020 |
| Net income | $ 1,980 |
| Retained earnings | $   792 |
| Dividends | $ 1,188 |

Pro Forma Balance Sheet

| Current assets | $ 6,000 | Total debt | $ 6,000 |
| Fixed assets | 12,000 | Owners' equity | 9,792 |
| Total | $ 18,000 | Total | $ 15,792 |
| | | EFN | $ 2,208 |

## Problem 9

Use the solution to Problem 7 to determine the growth rate McGraw can maintain if no external financing is used.

**Solution:**   From the solution to Problem 7, EFN can be written as:

$$EFN = (A \times g) - [R \times p \times S \times (1 + g)]$$

This can be rearranged algebraically as:

$$EFN = -(R \times p \times S) + [A - (R \times p \times S)] \times g$$

Substituting the data for McGraw:

$$EFN = -(.40 \times .165 \times \$10,000) + [\$15,000 - (.40 \times .165 \times \$10,000)] \times g$$
$$EFN = -\$660 + (\$14,340 \times g)$$

This equation allows us to determine the growth rate which the firm can achieve without any external financing, by setting EFN equal to zero and solving for g:

$$EFN = -\$660 + (\$14,340 \times g)$$
$$g = \$660/\$14,340 = .04603 = 4.603\%$$

## Problem 10

Use the linear equation developed in the solution to Problem 9 to determine the external financing needed for a growth rate equal to zero. Also, determine EFN for a growth rate of 1% and a growth rate of 10%.

**Solution:**   If the growth rate is zero, then:  $EFN = -\$660 + (\$14,340 \times g) = -\$660 + (\$14,340 \times 0) = -\$660$

This indicates that when growth is zero (i.e., when sales are constant), the firm has surplus financing of $660 available.  When g increases by .01, then EFN increases by ($14,340 × .01) = $143.40. Therefore, when g is 1%, EFN is equal to (−$660 + $143.40) = −$516.60.  Again, the negative sign indicates surplus financing. When g = 10%, EFN is equal to: $EFN = -\$660 + (\$14,340 \times g) = -\$660 + (\$14,340 \times .10) = \$774$.

## Problem 11

Use the data from the solution to Problem 6 to determine the sustainable growth rate for McGraw.

**Solution:**  The sustainable growth rate is computed as follows:

$$g^* = [ROE \times R] / [\, 1 - (ROE \times R)\, ]$$

For the T. McGraw Corporation, the sustainable growth rate is:

$$g^* = (.18333 \times .40) / [\, 1 - (.18333 \times .40)] = .07914 = 7.914\%$$

Therefore, T. McGraw Corporation can grow at a rate of 7.914% without issuing new equity, while maintaining the current debt/equity ratio.

## Problem 12

Use the Du Pont identity to verify the calculations in the solution to Problem 11.

**Solution:**   According to the Du Pont identity, return on equity (ROE) for McGraw can be written:

$$ROE = .165 \times (\$10,000/\$15,000) \times [1 + (\$6,000/\$9,000)] = .18333$$

Therefore, return on equity is 18.333%, as previously computed in the solution to Problem 6. Using the Du Pont identity, the sustainable growth rate is computed as follows:

$$g^* = p \times (S/A) \times [1 + (D/E)] \times R / [1 - \{p \times (S/A) \times [1 + (D/E)] \times R\}\,]$$

$$= .165 \times (\$10,000/\$15,000) \times [1 + (\$6,000/\$9,000)] \times .40 / [1 - \{.165 \times (\$10,000/\$15,000) \times [1 + (\$6,000/\$9,000)] \times .40\}] = 7.914\%$$

## Problem 13

Verify the results in the solutions to Problems 11 and 12 by preparing the pro forma income statement and balance sheet for McGraw, using the 7.914% sustainable growth rate.

**Solution:** McGraw's pro forma income statement and balance sheet, assuming a growth rate of 7.914%, are:

### T. McGRAW CORPORATION
### Pro Forma Income Statement

| | |
|---|---|
| Sales | $ 10,791.40 |
| Costs | 8,093.55 |
| Taxable income | $  2,697.85 |
| Taxes (34%) | 917.27 |
| Net income | $  1,780.58 |
| | |
| Retained earnings | $     712.23 |
| Dividends | $  1,068.35 |

### Pro Forma Balance Sheet

| Current assets | $ 5,395.70 | Total debt | $ 6,000.00 |
|---|---|---|---|
| Fixed assets | 10,791.40 | Owners' equity | 9,712.23 |
| Total | $ 16,187.10 | Total | $ 15,712.23 |
| | | EFN | $ 474.87 |

Since the external financing is all debt, the debt/equity ratio is ($6,474.87/$9,712.23) = 66.667%; the debt/equity ratio is unchanged from the calculation in the solution to Problem 6.

## Use the following information to solve Problems 14 to 17:

The most recent financial statements for Ryan & Co., Inc. are shown below:

### RYAN & CO., INC.
### Financial Statements

#### Income Statement

| Sales | $ 2,000 |
|---|---|
| Costs | 1,800 |
| Taxable income | $ 200 |
| Taxes (34%) | 68 |
| Net income | $ 132 |

| Retained earnings | $ 88 |
|---|---|
| Dividends | $ 44 |

#### Balance Sheet

| Current assets | $ 500 | Current liabilities | $ 165 |
|---|---|---|---|
| Fixed assets | 1,150 | Long-term debt | 535 |
| | | Owners' equity | 950 |
| Total | $ 1,650 | Total | $ 1,650 |

## Problem 14

Ryan & Co. forecasts next year's sales as $2,200. Costs, assets, and current liabilities increase proportionately with sales, and the retention ratio remains constant. Compute external financing needed for Ryan.

**Solution:**  The retention ratio is ($88/$132) = 2/3, and the growth rate for sales is ($200/$2,000) = 10%. Applying this growth rate to the income statement and balance sheet items, the pro forma income statement and partial pro forma balance sheet are as follows:

RYAN & CO., INC.
Pro Forma Income Statement

| | | |
|---|---|---|
| Sales | | $ 2,200.00 |
| Costs | | 1,980.00 |
| Taxable income | $ 220.00 | |
| Taxes (34%) | | 74.80 |
| Net income | | $ 145.20 |
| | | |
| Retained earnings | $ 96.80 | |
| Dividends | $ 48.40 | |

Partial Pro Forma Balance Sheet

| Current assets | $ 550.00 | Current liabilities | $ 181.50 |
|---|---|---|---|
| Fixed assets | 1,265.00 | Long-term debt | 535.00 |
| | | Owners' equity | 1,046.80 |
| Total | $ 1,650.00 | Total | $ 1,763.30 |

## Problem 15

Assume that Ryan currently has sufficient excess capacity to support a sales level of $2,100 without any additional fixed assets.  Calculate external financing needed for projected sales of $2,200.

**Solution:**  At the full capacity sales level of $2,100, the ratio of fixed assets to sales is:

(Fixed assets/Full capacity sales) = $1,150/$2,100 = .548

If this ratio is maintained at a sales level of $2,200, then Ryan requires (.548 × $2,200) = $1,205.60 of fixed assets. The solution to Problem 14 indicates a fixed asset level of $1,265. Therefore, total assets required are now ($1,265 − $1,205.60) = $59.40 less than previously calculated, so that external financing needed is also $59.40 less than previously calculated. External financing needed is now ($51.70 − $59.40) = −$7.70. The negative figure signifies the fact that Ryan now has excess financing of $7.70.

## Problem 16

Assume that Ryan is currently operating at 80% of its capacity.  Calculate external financing needed for projected sales of $2,200.

**Solution:**  It is first necessary to determine Ryan's full capacity sales level given its current level of fixed assets. The statement that Ryan is currently operating at 80% of its capacity implies that 80% of Ryan's capacity is equal to a sales level of $2,000. That is,  .80 × X = $2,000.  Here,  X is Ryan's full capacity sales level. Solving for X, we find that full capacity is ($2,000/.80) = $2,500. Therefore, no additional fixed assets are required in order to increase sales to $2,200. The solution to Problem 14 indicates additional fixed assets of $115 and external financing needed of $51.70. Since Ryan does not require the additional fixed assets, then external financing needed is equal to ($51.70 − $115) = −$63.30, or excess financing of $63.30.


## Problem 17

Assume that Ryan is currently operating at 95% of its capacity.  Calculate external financing needed for projected sales of $2,200.

**Solution:**  Ryan's full capacity sales level is the value of X in the following equation: $.95 \times X = \$2,000$.  Therefore, the full capacity sales level is ($2,000/.95) = $2,105.26. At this full capacity sales level, the ratio of fixed assets to sales is:

(Fixed assets/Full capacity sales) = $1,150/$2,105.26 = 0.546

For sales of $2,200, Ryan requires (.546 × $2,200) = $1,201.20 of fixed assets. The solution to Problem 14 indicates a fixed asset level of $1,265, so that total assets required are now ($1,265 − $1,201.20) = $63.80 less than previously calculated. External financing needed is also $63.80 less than previously calculated; that is, external financing needed is now ($51.70 − $63.80) = −$12.10, representing excess financing of $12.10.

# 5     <u>Introduction to Valuation: The Time Value of Money</u>

## CHAPTER HIGHLIGHTS

This chapter deals with one of the most important concepts of finance: the time value of money. The material presented provides the foundations used by corporate managers for financial decision making, and it has important applications for financial decisions made by individual consumers. For example, anyone who makes a bank deposit, takes out a loan, or buys a share of stock should understand the importance of the time value of money.

A thorough knowledge of this chapter is essential to an understanding of the material which follows. Furthermore, since the topics in the chapter are developed sequentially, it is crucial that each subject in the chapter be understood before moving to the next topic.

While the mathematical concepts presented in this chapter are not especially complicated, the mechanics of the calculations often require the use of financial tables or a calculator. The tables provided in Appendix A of your text are sufficient for most problems in the chapter, but a financial calculator can be a valuable time-saving aid.

## THE TIME VALUE OF MONEY

Financial managers must be able to determine the value today of cash flows that are expected in the future. This value depends on the time value of money. Put simply, the *time value of money* means that a dollar today is worth more than a dollar promised in the future. This is because today's dollar could have earned interest while you waited. So, it would grow to more than a dollar in the future. The tradeoff between money today and money later depends on several factors. One of them is the interest rate.

The difference between the *nominal rate of interest* (the stated rate you earn or pay) and the inflation rate is called the *real interest rate*. Whether your money will grow in real purchasing power depends upon whether the nominal interest rate exceeds inflation. This issue will be further discussed in later chapters.

## FUTURE VALUE AND COMPOUNDING

*Future value* is the amount to which an initial dollar will grow over some length of time at some interest rate. We first consider investing for a single time period.

**Investing for a Single Period - An Example:** Consider a deposit of $500 in a savings account paying 10% interest per year. The $500 deposit is the original *principal*. The future value is the account balance at some later date. If the $500 is invested for one year, it will earn $50 interest, so you will have a balance of $550 in the account. The calculation of this future value can be thought of as principal plus interest.

$$\$500 + (.10 \times \$500) = \$500 + \$50 = \$550$$

Alternatively, the future value can be determined as follows:

$$\$500 \times (1.10) = \$550, \text{ where } 1.10 \text{ is one plus the interest rate.}$$

Note that these two alternative approaches are mathematically equivalent. However, when performing future value calculations over time periods greater than one year, the second approach is significantly more efficient. In general, the future value (FV) for an investment over a one-year period can be determined from the following equation:

$$FV = P \times (1 + r)$$

where P is the original principal and r is the annual interest rate.

**Investing for More than One Period:**  Suppose the $500 principal above is left for two years. What is the future value (balance in the account at the end of the two-year period)? We will assume the bank continues to pay 10% interest.

First, assume the $50 interest earned the first year is withdrawn and put into a non-interest bearing account. During the second year, the $500 principal amount will earn another $50 in interest.  The interest paid in the first year, however, will earn nothing.  At the end of the second year, the total value (from both accounts) will be:

|  |  |
|---|---|
| $500 | principal |
| 50 | interest on principal, year 1 |
| 50 | interest on principal, year 2 |
| $600 | Total value in year 2 |

Note that, because the first year's interest was placed in a non-interest bearing account, the investor earns exactly $50 interest in each year. That is, the first year's interest payment is not reinvested at the 10% rate, so interest is earned only on the original principal amount invested. This is referred to as *simple interest*.

Now, assume the depositor reinvests the interest from year 1 by leaving it in the account paying 10%. The account balance at the end of year 1 is $550, and the investor will earn 10% interest on this entire amount over the second year.  Since the depositor earns interest on the previous year's interest (as well as the principal), this is referred to as *compound interest*, or the process of *compounding* interest. The value at the end of year 2 will have four components:

|  |  |
|---|---|
| $500 | principal |
| 50 | interest on principal, year 1 |
| 50 | interest on principal, year 2 |
| 5 | interest on year 1 interest, invested for year 2 |
| $605 | Total value in year 2 |

It is important to compare the two calculations above: future value with simple interest, and future value with compound interest.  Note that the future value using compound interest is $605, not $600 as in the simple interest case.  The additional $5 future value represents the "interest earned on interest" in the second year. Although the difference may seem small in this example, over longer periods of time, the difference between compound and simple interest can become extremely large.

Remember, we wrote the future value at the end of the year 1 as:

$$FV = P \times (1 + r) = \$500 \times (1.10) = \$550$$

If we consider the future value in year 1 as the beginning principal in year 2, we can write the future value at the end of year 2 as:

$$FV_2 = P \times (1 + r) = \$550 \times (1.10) = \$605$$

Alternatively, we can think of this calculation as:

$$FV_2 = FV_1 \times (1 + r) = \$550 \times (1.10) = \$605$$

The notation $FV_2$ is used here to indicate the future value at the end of the second year, in order to distinguish it from the future value at the end of the first year, $FV_1$, which is $550. Therefore, the principal at the beginning of the second year (i.e., $FV_1$ = $550) is the future value of the $500 deposited at the beginning of the first year.

$$FV_1 = P \times (1 + r) = \$500 \times (1.10) = \$550$$

Combining these last two equations, we have:

$$
\begin{aligned}
FV_2 &= FV_1 \times (1 + r) \\
&= [P \times (1 + r)] \times (1 + r) \\
&= [\$500 \times (1.10)] \times (1.10) = \$500 \times (1.10)^2 = \$605
\end{aligned}
$$

In general, the future value at the end of year 2 is equal to the original principal times $[(1 + r) \times (1 + r)]$, or:

$$FV_2 = P \times (1 + r)^2$$

To find the future value at the end of year 3 ($FV_3$), we compound the future value at the end of year 2 for one more year by multiplying by the factor $(1 + r)$, as follows:

$$FV_3 = P \times (1 + r)^3$$

For the $500 deposit, receiving 10% interest, for a three-year period:

$$FV_3 = \$500 \times (1.10)^3 = \$500 \times (1.331) = \$665.50$$

In general, the future value of an original principal P, invested for any given number of years t, at an interest rate r, is given by:

$$FV_t = P \times (1 + r)^t$$

The expression $(1 + r)^t$ is often referred to as *the future value interest factor,* or simply future value factor, and is sometimes abbreviated as FVIF(r,t).

Consider the future value of a deposit of $1,000, invested at a 5% interest rate for 7 years:

$$FV_7 = \$1,000 \times (1.05)^7 = \$1,000 \times (1.40710) = \$1,407.10$$

The future value interest factor is: $(1 + r)^t = (1.05)^7 = 1.40710$.  There are several alternative approaches to determining this value.  Using  pencil and paper or a basic four-function calculator, we could multiply seven factors of 1.05.  More efficient alternatives include the use of a calculator with a $[y^x]$ function key, or tables of future value interest factors, such as Table A.1 in Appendix A of your text.

If you are using a calculator with a [y$^x$] function key, first realize that we must enter $(1 + r)$ as the base (that is, y on the calculator), and t as the exponent (that is, x on the calculator). For the above example, this is generally calculated using the following sequence:   1.05 [y$^x$] 7 =   1.40710042. This value is then multiplied by the original principal to determine the future value.  But, if you are using a calculator, be sure you are familiar with it, because not all calculators use exactly the same sequence just discussed.

If you are using Table A.1, the appropriate future value interest factor is in the seventh row under the 5% column.  This indicates that (1.05) is equal to 1.4071.  Note that the use of the table provides a less accurate result than does the calculator.  Furthermore, the use of the table is limited to problems for which the interest rate and time period are provided in the tables.  Therefore, the use of a calculator with a [y$^x$] function key is usually preferable to the use of Table A.1 because the calculator provides a more accurate answer and can also be used for any combination of interest rate and time period.

**An Example:**  You make a $2,000 deposit in a Registered Retirement Savings Plan (RRSP) at a bank which will pay 8% interest per year for the next forty years, at which time you plan to retire.  The future value of your RRSP account at the end of forty years is given by:

$$FV_t = P \times (1 + r)^t$$

$$FV_{40} \quad = \quad \$2{,}000 \times (1.08)^{40} \quad = \quad \$2{,}000 \times (21.72452150) \quad = \quad \$43{,}449.04$$

Table A.1 indicates that $(1.08)^{40} = 21.725$, so that:

$$FV_{40} \quad = \quad \$2{,}000 \times (21.725) \quad = \quad \$43{,}450.00$$

Clearly, the difference of $.96 in these results has little practical significance.  However, it should be kept in mind that this discrepancy arises from the fact that the future value interest factor in Table A.1 is rounded to three decimal places, and therefore is somewhat less accurate than the result obtained using a [y$^x$] function key on a calculator.

The interest earned over the forty-year period is:

$$\$43{,}449.04 - \$2{,}000 = \$41{,}449.04$$

If the deposit earned simple interest, the interest would be $(.08 \times \$2{,}000) = \$160$ per year, or $(\$160 \times 40) = \$6{,}400$ for the forty-year period.  Therefore, the compounding of interest, or interest paid on interest previously received, accounts for $(\$41{,}449.04 - \$6{,}400) = \$35{,}049.04$ of the total interest received.

**A Note on Compound Growth:**  The interest rate earned on a savings account deposit can be thought of as a compound growth rate.  That is, the annual interest rate is actually the rate at which the balance in the account grows each year.  Since an interest rate is one specific example of a compound growth rate, the mathematics of future value calculations can be applied to any quantity which grows at a given compound rate over a period of time.  For example, the population of a given geographic area may grow at a specified annual rate.  Similarly, compound growth rates can be used to describe the growth of economic variables, such as Gross National Product (GNP), or financial values such as a company's sales or profits.

**An Example:** The dividends of the TTK Corporation are expected to grow at a compound rate of 6% each year for the next five years. The most recent annual dividend was $3.50 per share. What is TTK's dividend per share expected to be five years from now?

Think of the current year's dividend as the original 'principal' and the compound growth rate as r: P = $3.50 and r

$= 6\%$. We determine the dividend five years from now as follows:

$$FV_5 \quad = \quad \$3.50 \times (1.06)^5 \quad = \quad \$4.68$$

Therefore, we conclude that TTK will pay an annual dividend of $4.68 five years from now.

## PRESENT VALUE AND DISCOUNTING

In the previous section, we used the future value concept to answer the following question: If you deposit $2,000 today in a savings account paying 8% interest per year, what is the balance in the account forty years from now? (Recall that the answer is $43,449.04.)  In this section we ask a different, but closely related question: What deposit is required today, in an account paying 8% interest, in order to have $250,000 forty years from now? The answer to this question is $11,507.73.  We refer to $11,507.73 as the present value of $250,000 to be received forty years from now, when the appropriate interest rate is 8%. We first examine the single-period case.

**The Single Period Case:**  Consider the situation faced by Kris, an investor who can earn 8% interest in her savings account during the next year.  Kris would like to be able to withdraw $1,200 from her account one year from now. That is, she wants the future value of the account to be $1,200. How much should she deposit today to have a future value of $1,200? To find out, we work with the future value equation, putting in the known values for FV and r. Then we solve for P, which we do not know.

$$
\begin{aligned}
FV \quad &= \quad P \times (1 + r) \\
\$1,200 \quad &= \quad P \times (1 + .08)
\end{aligned}
$$

Solving for P:

$$P \quad = \quad \$1,200 \,/\, 1.08 \quad = \quad \$1,111.11$$

At an 8% rate of interest, Kris would have to deposit $1,111.11 today in order to receive a return of $1,200 one year from now.  In the above calculation, $1,111.11 is referred to as the present value of $1,200, to be received one year from today, when the relevant interest rate is 8%.

It is important to note that the present value depends on three factors: the amount of the future payment (i.e., the future value), the time period, and the market rate of interest. The process of computing a present value is often referred to as *discounting*. The interest rate used in a present value calculation is often referred to as the *discount rate*.

We can derive the above result in another manner. First, we repeat the future value formula of the previous section: $FV = P \times (1 + r)$.  Next, we note that, for our present value calculations, it might be more convenient to replace the notation P, which we used earlier to denote the original principal, with the notation PV, to represent present value:

$$FV \quad = \quad PV \times (1 + r)$$

Now, solve for PV, by dividing both sides of the equation by $(1 + r)$:

$$PV \quad = \quad FV \,/\, (1 + r)$$

If we now substitute the known values of FV and r ($FV = \$1,200$; $r = .08$), we have the same result as before:

$$PV \quad = \quad \$1,200 \,/\, (1.08) \quad = \quad \$1,111.11$$

Clearly, the results obtained with the two solution techniques are identical.  In the first approach, we substituted the known values of FV and r, and then solved for the unknown PV.  In the second approach, we simply reversed the order of these two steps, first solving the equation for the unknown PV and then substituting the known values of FV and r.  This gives us a general formula for present value in the single-period case:

$$PV = FV / (1 + r)$$

Since dividing by the term $(1 + r)$ is equivalent to multiplying by the reciprocal $1/(1 + r)$, the above present value formula can also be rewritten as:

$$PV = FV \times [1 / (1 + r)]$$

**Present Values for Multiple Periods:**  Suppose that Kris has two years, rather than one year, to accumulate $1,200, and that her bank will pay 8% interest per year for the next two years.  What deposit would Kris have to make today in order to obtain a future value of $1,200 two years from today?  We can use the future value formula developed earlier to solve this problem.

First, we repeat the future value formula for multiple periods:

$$FV_t = PV \times (1 + r)^t$$

(Note that we have changed the notation P to PV in this multiple-period problem, as we did earlier for the single-period case.)  Next, we substitute the known values ($FV_2 = \$1,200$; $r = .08$; $t = 2$):

$$\$1,200 = PV \times (1.08)^2$$

Finally, we solve for PV:

$$PV = \$1,200 / (1.08)^2 = \$1,200 / 1.1664 = \$1,028.81$$

Kris would have to deposit $1,028.81 today, in an account paying 8% interest per year, in order to be able to withdraw $1,200 two years from today.  Therefore, $1,028.81 is the present value of $1,200, to be received two years from today, when the appropriate interest rate (or discount rate) is 8%.

Note that we can check the answer by using the future value formula. That is, if Kris invests $1,028.81 today at 8%, how much will she have at the end of two years?

$$FV = PV \times (1 + r)^t = \$1,028.81 \times (1.08)^2 = \$1,200$$

As in the single-period case, it is helpful to consider an alternative approach to this problem.  We first solve for PV and then substitute the known values of $FV_2$, r and t:

$$PV = FV_t / (1 + r)^t$$

$$PV = \$1,200 / (1.08)^2 = \$1,200 / 1.1664 = \$1,028.81$$

The advantage of this latter approach is that we have now developed a general formula for present value in the multiple-period case:

$$PV = FV_t / (1 + r)^t$$

Also, as we observed in the single-period case, we can write the above formula in a somewhat different form. Note that dividing by the term $(1 + r)^t$ is equivalent to multiplying by its reciprocal $1/(1 + r)^t$:

$$PV = FV_t \times [1 / (1 + r)^{t]}$$

The term $[1/(1 + r)^t]$ in the above formula is sometimes referred to as the *present value interest factor*, and can be abbreviated PVIF (r,t). Since the process of calculating a present value is sometimes called discounting, we also refer to the term $[1/(1 + r)^t]$ as the *discount factor*. The process of computing a present value is also referred to as *discounted cash flow* (DCF) valuation.

Note here that the present value interest factor PVIF (8%,2) is equal to $1/(1.08)^2 = 1/1.1664 = .857339$. Using Table A.2 in Appendix A, the above problem can be solved as follows:

$$PV = FV_t \times PVIF\ (r, t) = \$1,200 \times PVIF\ (8\%, 2) = \$1,200 \times .8573 = \$1,028.76$$

(Note that the answer here is slightly inaccurate because the factors in Table A.2 are rounded to four decimal places.) You should be comfortable with using both the tables and a handheld calculator in order to understand and apply present value concepts and calculations.

## MORE ON PRESENT AND FUTURE VALUES

In this section, we discuss further the relationship between present values and future values. We also analyze some additional aspects of these concepts.

**Present versus Future Value:** In the previous sections of this chapter, we developed the future value and present value concepts which are fundamental to corporate financial decision-making. It is important to emphasize that the basic equations we have developed with regard to each of these concepts are, in fact, two algebraically equivalent versions of the same equation. We repeat here the future value and present value equations, respectively:

$$FV_t = PV \times (1 + r)^t$$

$$PV = FV_t / (1 + r)^t$$

Remember that the present value equation is derived simply and directly from the future value equation. By writing the present value equation in its alternative form, we can demonstrate the fact that the present value interest factor is simply the reciprocal of the future value interest factor. That is, as we indicated earlier, the present value equation can be written:

$$PV = FV_t / (1 + r)^t = FV_t \times [1 / (1 + r)^t]$$

where $1/(1 + r)^t$ is the present value interest factor. The future value interest factor is the denominator of the expression for the present value interest factor. Therefore, the present value interest factor is the reciprocal of the future value interest factor.

One of our major concerns in the study of corporate finance is the evaluation of investment opportunities. The desirability of an investment can be determined in several ways. Two alternative, but equivalent, approaches to evaluating investment opportunities are based on the future value and present value concepts, respectively. To illustrate these techniques, we consider the following example.

**An Example:** Suppose that an investor is contemplating the purchase of an antique automobile. The automobile can be purchased for $60,000 today. The investor expects that it can be sold for $70,000 one year from today.

The investor believes this is a very safe investment. But, the investor can invest the $60,000 elsewhere at 12%, also for very little risk. Which investment is better? We can use future-value analysis to calculate the value of $60,000 invested at 12% to determine the amount at the end of one year.

$$FV = PV \times (1 + r) = \$60,000 \times (1.12) = \$67,200$$

At the end of one year, the investor will have $67,200. But, he will have $70,000 if he buys the antique car. Since both opportunities require a $60,000 outlay today, the investor will choose the automobile because it provides a larger future return.

Present-value analysis of this problem requires that the investor determine the amount he would have to invest today, at the 12% rate of interest, in order to obtain a return of $70,000 one year from today. That is, he would calculate the present value of $70,000 to be received one year from today, discounted at the 12% interest rate. The present value is computed as follows:

$$PV = FV_t / (1 + r)^t$$

$$PV = \$70,000 / (1.12) = \$62,500$$

In order to obtain a return of $70,000 one year from now, the required investment today is $62,500. Consequently, the investor can obtain a $70,000 payoff with a smaller initial investment by purchasing the automobile for $60,000.

Both the future value analysis and the present-value analysis indicate that the investment in the antique automobile is preferable to the alternative investment opportunity with a 12% interest rate. Since the two approaches are mathematically equivalent, we would expect the conclusions to be the same in the two cases.

**Determining the Discount Rate:** A third approach to evaluating the investment opportunity is based on calculating the rate of return implicit in the automobile investment. This rate of return is then compared to the 12% interest rate available for the other investment. Since this approach is also based on the fundamental future value concept, it too is mathematically equivalent to the future-value and present-value analyses described above.

In order to determine the rate of return for the investment in the antique automobile, we begin with the basic future value equation and substitute for the known values ($FV = \$70,000$; $PV = \$60,000$; $t = 1$):

$$FV_t = PV \times (1 + r)^1$$

$$\$70,000 = \$60,000 \times (1 + r)^1$$

Dividing both sides of the above equation by $60,000, we find that:

$$(1 + r) = 1.16667$$

so that $r = .166667 = 16.667\%$. This result indicates that an investment which grows in value from $60,000 to $70,000 in one year provides a rate of return equal to 16.667%. Since the alternative investment opportunity available pays a rate of only 12% return, clearly the investment in the antique automobile is the preferable investment opportunity.

In this example, we have indicated the procedure for determining the rate of return, or interest rate, for an investment over a one-year time period. The calculation is somewhat more complicated when the relevant time period is more than one year. Consider the following example, which demonstrates the procedure for computing the interest rate for a particular investment or loan.

**An Example:**  If you were to borrow $5,000 today in exchange for a promise to repay $7,500 six years from today, what is the annual interest rate you are paying for this loan?  The answer can be determined by using the basic future value formula along with either Table A.1 or a financial calculator.

Substitute $FV_6 = \$7,500$, $PV = \$5,000$, $t = 6$ in the future value formula:

$$FV_t \quad = \quad PV \times (1 + r)^t$$

$$\$7,500 = \$5,000 \times (1 + r)^6 ; \quad 1.500 = (1 + r)^6$$

An approximate value for r can now be determined from Table A.1.  The value for r is found by locating, in Table A.1, the future value interest factor for a six-year period which is closest to 1.500. The future value factor 1.5007 in the sixth row, under the 7% column, indicates that $(1.07)^6 = 1.5007$, so that r is approximately 7%.

The alternative approach to solving for r is to take the sixth root of both sides of the above equation.  The right hand side of the equation becomes $(1 + r)$. In order to find the sixth root of 1.500 (i.e., to raise 1.5 to the one-sixth power), use the following sequence with a financial calculator:

$$1.5 \ [y^x] \ 6 \ [1/x] \ [=]$$

Note that this calculation enters 1.5 as the base, y, and the reciprocal of 6, or 1/6, as the exponent, x: $y^x = 1.5^{1/6}$
The sixth root is 1.069913, so that:

$$1.069913 = (1 + r)$$

and, subtracting 1.0 from both sides of the equation, r = 0.069913 or 6.9913%.  This is a more precise value than the one obtained from the tables.

**Finding the Number of Periods:**  We can also use the present value or future value approach to determine  how long it takes to have a certain amount of money.  Suppose an investor has $15,000 to invest in a savings account that pays 7% interest per year.  How long will it take the investor to have $25,000?  To find out, we start with the same future value equation:  $FV_t \quad = \quad PV \ x \ (1 + r)^t$

We can substitute the known values for FV, PV, and r.  Then solve the equation for t.

$$\$25,000 \quad = \quad \$15,000 \ x \ (1.07)^t$$

The future value factor is $25,000 / $15,000  =  1.6667.  Looking in Table A.1 under the 7% column, the factor for 7 years at 7% is 1.6058; the factor for 8 years at 7% is 1.7182.  So, it will take between 7 and 8 years to have $25,000.

## CONCEPT TEST

1.      When a deposit or investment earns interest on interest previously received, it is said to be earning
        _____ .  This process is referred to as _____ .

2.      A _____ is the  amount to which an initial dollar deposit, called the _____ , will grow when
        interest is compounded at a specified interest rate for a specified number of years. The future value ($FV_t$)
        of an initial deposit (PV) which earns interest at the rate r for t years is given by the following formula: $FV_t$
        = _____ .   The expression _____ is referred to as the future value interest factor, and is
        abbreviated as _____ .

3.      A present value is the amount which must be invested today, at a specified _____ , in order to grow
        to a specified _____ , at a specified _____ .   Therefore, a present value is dependent on three
        things: the _____ , the amount of the _____ , and the _____ .

4.      The process of computing a present value is referred to as _____ . The interest rate used in a present
        value calculation is referred to as the _____ .

5.      A present value can be calculated by substituting the known values of the _____ , the _____ , and
        the _____ into the basic present value equation, as follows:  PV = _____

6.      An alternative approach is to rearrange the basic present value equation so that the present value is
        determined by multiplying the future value times the _____ of the future value interest factor, as
        follows:  PV = _____ .

7.      The term _____ is referred to as the present value interest factor, and can be abbreviated _____ .
        The present value interest factor can be determined from tables. The present value interest factor is also
        called the _____ and the process of computing a present value is also referred to as _____
        valuation.

## ANSWERS TO CONCEPT TEST

1.      compound interest; compounding

2.      future value; principal; $PV \times (1 + r)^t$; $(1 + r)^t$; FVIF(r,t)

3.      interest rate; dollar amount; future date; interest rate; future payment; time period

4.      discounting; discount rate

5.      interest rate; future payment; time period; $FV_t / (1 + r)^t$

6.      reciprocal; $FV \times [1/(1 + r)^t]$
7.      $1/(1 + r)^t$; PVIF(r,t); discount factor; discounted cash flow (DCF)

## PROBLEMS AND SOLUTIONS

### Problem 1

If you deposit $10,000 today in a bank account paying 10.38%, how much will you have in one year? (That is, what
is the future value of your investment?) If you need $12,000 in one year, how much do you have to deposit today?
(That is, what is the present value of your investment?)

**Solution:**  If you deposit $10,000 today, the balance in the account at the end of the year will be:

$$FV_1 = \$10,000 \times 1.1038 = \$11,038$$

If you need $12,000 one year from now, the amount you will have to deposit today is:

$$PV = \$12,000 / 1.1038 = \$10,871.53$$

## Problem 2

Calculate the future value for each of the following cash flows to be received one year from now:

| Today's cash flow | Interest rate |
|---|---|
| $ 60,000 | 12.0 % |
| 273,000 | 10.0 |
| 1,500 | 9.0 |
| 27,634 | 6.7 |
| 135,000 | 3.0 |

**Solution:**

| Today's cash flow | Interest rate | Future value |
|---|---|---|
| $ 60,000 | 12.0 % | $ 67,200.00 |
| 273,000 | 10.0 | 300,300.00 |
| 1,500 | 9.0 | 1,635.00 |
| 27,634 | 6.7 | 29,485.48 |
| 135,000 | 3.0 | 139,050.00 |

## Problem 3

If you deposit $2,500 in a savings account at Tightfist Bank, how long will it take before your balance is $5,000? The bank uses simple interest at a rate of 10%. How long will it take to have a $5,000 balance if the interest rate is double to 20%? If instead, the bank compounds interest annually, how long will it take to have a $5,000 balance, using the 10% rate?

**Solution:** The bank pays interest on your $2,500 deposit only at the end of each year. Your interest each year is equal to $2,500 x 0.1 = $250. To reach a $5,000 balance, you need to leave your money in the bank for $2,500 / $250 = 10 years.

If the interest rate is doubled, you would receive $500 per year, rather than $250. This cuts the time required in half to five years.

If interest is compounded annually,

$$\begin{aligned} FV &= \$2,500 \times (1.10)^t \\ \$5,000 &= \$2,500 \times (1.10)^t \\ 2 &= (1.10)^t \end{aligned}$$

Using Table A.3 in Appendix A, at 10%, a future value factor of 2 relates to approximately 7 years. This means that, at an interest rate of 10%, your money will be doubled in 7 years.

## Problem 4

Eddie is wondering if he should invest $2,000 in a rare coin that he expects will be worth $2,500 two years from today. Alternatively, he can invest his $2,000 in a savings account and earn 10%. Using both present value and future value analysis, determine whether or not Eddie should invest in the coin.

**Solution:**   Using future value analysis to calculate the value of investing $2,000 in the savings account:

$$FV_t \; = \; PV \times (1 + r)^t$$

$$FV_2 \; = \; \$2,000 \times (1.10)^2 \; = \; \$2,420.00$$

According to future value analysis, Eddie should invest in the rare coin.

Using present value analysis:

$$PV \; = \; FV / (1 + r)^t$$

$$PV \; = \; \$2,500 / (1.10)^2 \; = \; \$2,066.12$$

According to present value analysis, Eddie should also invest in the rare coin.

Note: The decision is the same, regardless of whether you use future or present value analysis. This is *always* the case.

## Problem 5

After talking to your friend who is completing a business degree, you have learned about compound interest. You decide to take your money out of your account at Tightfist Bank (see Problem 3) and transfer it to JPH Direct, which pays 10% compound interest. If you leave your $2,500 in this account, how much money will you be able to withdraw in five years? What if the interest rate doubled to 20%?
**Solution:**   To calculate how much money you will have in five years, use the FV formula.

$$FV_5 \; = \; \$2,500 \times (1.10)^5 \; = \; \$4,026.28$$

If the interest rate is 20%:

$$FV_5 \; = \; \$2,500 \times (1.20)^5 \; = \; \$6,220.80$$

Note: Although the interest rate doubled, the amount of interest you received over five years *more* than doubled: ($6,220.80 - $2,500) / ($4,026.28 - $2,500)  = 2.44 times. This is the magic of compound interest!

## Problem 6

An art collector has the opportunity to invest in paintings. The investment requires an initial outlay of $2 million today. The collector is certain that he will be able to sell the paintings for $2.18 million one year from now. He also has the opportunity to invest in bank certificates of deposit which pay 10% per year.  What is the future value of the $2 million in one year if the collector elects to purchase a bank certificate of deposit?  Is the investment in the paintings a good investment?

**Solution:**  If the collector invests $2 million in the bank certificates of deposit, the value of the certificates one year from now will be:

$$FV_1 \ = \ \$2,000,000 \times 1.10 \ = \ \$2.2 \text{ million}$$

Consequently, the investment in the paintings is not a good investment.  The collector will have a greater cash flow one year from now if he purchases the bank certificates of deposit.

**Problem 7**

In Problem 6, what is the rate of return for the investment in paintings?

**Solution:**

$$FV_1 = PV \times (1 + r)^1$$
$$\$2.18 \text{ million} \ = \ \$2.00 \text{ million} \times (1 + r)^1$$
$$1.09 \ = \ 1 + r$$
$$r \ = \ .09 \ = \ 9\%$$

Since the rate of return for the investment in paintings is less than that available on the bank certificates of deposit, it is clear that the paintings are an unacceptable investment. Notice that this is the same conclusion reached in the previous problem, where we used future value analysis to evaluate the desirability of the investment.  Since these two procedures for evaluating the desirability of the investment are mathematically equivalent, it must be true that the conclusions reached are the same.

**Problem 8**

For the paintings described in Problem 6, what is the present value of the future cash flow the collector would receive if he sold the paintings one year from now?  What is the value of the paintings to the collector?

**Solution:**  The present value is:

$$PV \;=\; \$2.18 \text{ million} \,/\, 1.10 \;=\; \$1.982 \text{ million}$$

The present value is the amount the collector would have to invest today in the alternative investment (i.e., the bank certificates) in order to duplicate the cash flow he would receive by selling the paintings one year from today. Therefore, since the collector can duplicate the $2.18 million cash flow for only $1.982 million, he would not be willing to pay more than $1.982 million for the paintings today.

**Problem 9**

You plan to live very well when you retire in 35 years and have calculated that you will require $3,000,000 when you retire.  If the rate of interest available is 9%, how much do you need to invest today in order to live comfortably during your retirement?

**Solution:**

$$PV \;=\; FV_t \,/\, (1 + r)^t$$

$$PV \;=\; \$3,000,000 \,/\, (1.09)^{35} \;=\; \$3,000,000 \,/\, 20.413968 \;=\; \$146,958.20$$

You need to invest $146,958.20 at 9% in order to have $3,000,000 when you retire in 35 years.

**Problem 10**

Calculate the present value for each of the following cash flows to be received one year from now:

| Future cash flow | Interest rate |
|---|---|
| $  10,000 | 10% |
| 153,000 | 12 |
| 153,200 | 10 |
| 2,567,450 | 5 |
| 120,600 | 9 |

**Solution:**

| Future cash flow | Interest rate | Present value |
|---|---|---|
| $ 10,000 | 10% $ | 9,090.91 |
| 153,000 | 12 | 136,607.14 |
| 153,200 | 10 | 139,272.73 |
| 2,567,450 | 5 | 2,445,190.48 |
| 120,600 | 9 | 110,642.20 |

In the second and third cases, notice that the future cash flow is the same, but the present value is greater when the market interest rate is 10% than for a market interest rate of 12%. This result illustrates the fact that present value and interest rates are inversely related.


## Problem 11

As a recently graduated finance major embarking on a career in investment banking, you naturally must own a BMW 325 IS immediately. The car costs $28,320. You also have to spend $3,248 on blue pin-stripe suits. Your salary this year is $42,000, and next year it will be $46,000. Your routine living expenses this year will be $34,000. You plan to make up the difference between current income and current consumption by borrowing; the interest rate for the loan is 14% and you intend to repay the loan, plus interest, in one year. How much will you have left to spend next year?

**Solution:** This year you need a total of ($28,320 + $3,248 + $34,000) = $65,568. So, you must borrow ($65,568 – $42,000) = $23,568 this year. The amount you will have to repay next year is:

$$FV_1 = \$23,568 \times 1.14 = \$26,867.52$$

Therefore, you will have ($46,000 – $26,867.52) = $19,132.48 of next year's income left to spend.


## Problem 12

An individual has the opportunity to invest $1,000 today to acquire an asset which will generate $300 in income one year from today and which can be sold for $900 at that time. Determine the minimum level of the market interest rate for which this investment would be attractive.

**Solution:** Substitute the relevant values (PV = $1,000; FV = $1,200) into either the future value formula or the present value formula, and then solve for the interest rate r. Using the future value formula:

$$
\begin{aligned}
FV &= PV \times (1 + r) \\
\$1,200 &= \$1,000 \times (1 + r) \\
1 + r &= 1.20 \\
r &= .20 = 20\%
\end{aligned}
$$

Therefore, the rate of return for the investment is 20%. If the rate of return available on alternative investments is less than 20%, then the investment opportunity described above is acceptable. On the other hand, if the rate of return available elsewhere is greater than 20%, then the investment described above is unacceptable.

**Problem 13**

An entrepreneur has purchased an asset for $200,000 which will produce a cash inflow of $300,000 one year from today. He plans to issue himself 100 shares of common stock and sell 900 shares to the general public. His business, which consists entirely of this one asset, will cease to exist after one year. The market rate of interest is 20%, and the future cash inflow to the firm is guaranteed. At what price per share should the entrepreneur sell the common stock?

**Solution:** The present value of the future cash inflow is:

$$PV = \$300,000/1.20 = \$250,000$$

Therefore, each of the 1,000 shares is worth $250. This can be demonstrated several different ways. An individual who owns one of the shares is entitled to 1/1,000 of the future cash inflow or, $(1/1,000) \times \$300,000 = \$300$. The present value of the $300 is:

$$PV = \$300/1.20 = \$250$$

Alternatively, an individual who owns one share is the owner of 1/1,000 of the present value of the asset, or $(1/1,000) \times \$250,000 = \$250$. Furthermore, an individual who buys a share for $250 today and receives $300 one year from today earns a rate of return equal to 20%. Since this is the same as the rate of return available on alternative investments, an investor would be willing to pay $250 for a share.

**Problem 14**

What is the present value of $145 to be received in five years if the market interest rate is 8%?

**Solution:**    PV  =   $145/(1.08)^5$  =   $98.69

This means that an investor would have to deposit $98.69 today, at an 8% interest rate, in order to be able to withdraw $145 five years from today.

**Problem 15**

What is the future value of $235 dollars invested at 12% for four years?

**Solution:**   $FV_4$  =   $\$235 \times (1.12)^4$  =   $369.78

This means that an investor who deposits $235 today in an account paying 12% interest per year will have a balance of $369.78 in his account four years from today.

## Problem 16

For each of the following, compute the present value:

| Future value | Years | Interest rate |
|---|---|---|
| $   498 | 7 | 13.0% |
| 1,033 | 13 | 6.0 |
| 14,784 | 23 | 4.0 |
| 898,156 | 4 | 31.0 |
| 75,000 | 3 | 10.5 |
| 169,700 | 9 | 4.6 |

**Solution:**

| Future value | Years | Interest rate | Present value |
|---|---|---|---|
| $   498 | 7 | 13.0% | $      211.68 |
| 1,033 | 13 | 6.0 | 484.31 |
| 14,784 | 23 | 4.0 | 5,998.26 |
| 898,156 | 4 | 31.0 | 304,976.65 |
| 75,000 | 3 | 10.5 | 55,587.15 |
| 169,700 | 9 | 4.6 | 113,213.10 |

## Problem 17

For each of the following, compute the future value:

| Present value | Years | Interest rate | Future value |
|---|---|---|---|
| $    123 | 13 | 13.0% | |
| 4,555 | 8 | 8.0 | |
| 74,484 | 5 | 10.0 | |
| 167,332 | 9 | 1.0 | |
| 108,350 | 24 | 3.8 | |
| 57,300 | 16 | 12.4 | |

**Solution:**

| Present value | Years | Interest rate | Future value |
|---|---|---|---|
| $    123 | 13 | 13.0% | $     602.46 |
| 4,555 | 8 | 8.0 | 8,430.99 |
| 74,484 | 5 | 10.0 | 119,957.23 |
| 167,332 | 9 | 1.0 | 183,008.54 |
| 108,350 | 24 | 3.8 | 265,195.04 |
| 57,300 | 16 | 12.4 | 371,890.94 |

## Problem 18

Solve for the unknown time period in each of the following:

| Present value | Future value | Interest rate | Time (years) |
|---|---|---|---|
| $  100 | $   350 | 12% | |
| 123 | 351 | 10 | |
| 4,100 | 8,524 | 5 | |
| 10,543 | 26,783 | 6 | |

**Solution:**

| Present value | Future value | Interest rate | Time (years) |
|---|---|---|---|
| $  100 | $   350 | 12% | 11.05 |
| 123 | 351 | 10 | 11.00 |
| 4,100 | 8,524 | 5 | 15.00 |
| 10,543 | 26,783 | 6 | 16.00 |

## Problem 19

Solve for the unknown interest rate in each of the following:

| Present value | Future value | Interest rate | Time (years) |
|---|---|---|---|
| $  100 | $   305 | | 5 |
| 123 | 218 | | 6 |
| 4,100 | 8,524 | | 7 |
| 10,543 | 21,215 | | 12 |

**Solution:**

| Present value | Future value | Interest rate | Time (years) |
|---|---|---|---|
| $  100 | $   305 | 25% | 5 |
| 123 | 218 | 10 | 6 |
| 4,100 | 8,524 | 11 | 7 |
| 10,543 | 21,215 | 6 | 12 |

## Problem 20

Your Aunt Nell has promised you a two week trip to Europe when you graduate from university in two years, providing your grades are good. She estimates that the trip will cost $5,000. How much money should Aunt Nell put aside today to pay for your trip? She earns 8% on her money.

**Solution:** Your aunt needs to save:  $5,000  =  PV x $(1.08)^2$. Solving for PV leaves $4,286.69.

**Problem 21**

Unfortunately, Aunt Nell just discovered that you and your friends hit several hockey pucks into her front windows. Repair costs are $2,500.  Aunt Nell now has only $2,500 toward your trip. You must come up with the remaining $2,500.  If you earn 6% interest, how much must you save this summer in order to take the trip?

**Solution:**   You need to save: $2,500 $= $ PV x $(1.06)^2$. Solving, you need $2,224.99.

# 6     <u>Discounted Cash Flow Valuation</u>

## CHAPTER HIGHLIGHTS

In Chapter 5, we discussed the basic concept of the time value of money. These concepts form the foundation for *discounted cash flow* analysis, which we will discuss in more detail in this chapter. So far, we have only found present and future values for single cash flows. In this chapter, we extend the analysis to situations which have multiple cash flows. The tools you will learn in this chapter will be very valuable to you because they have many practical applications in everyday life.

## FUTURE AND PRESENT VALUES OF MULTIPLE CASH FLOWS

To this point, our future value and present value calculations have been restricted to problems involving only a single future cash flow. We now analyse future value and present value problems with multiple cash flows.

**Future Value with Multiple Cash Flows:** In an earlier example, we computed the future value of a $2,000 deposit in an RRSP account which pays 8% interest per year for the next 40 years. Recall that the balance in the account at the end of 40 years is:

$$FV_{40} \quad = \quad \$2,000 \times (1.08)^{40} \quad = \quad \$43,449.04$$

The issue we raise in this section is how to compute the balance in an account when several deposits are made over a period of years. For example, the depositor described above might make a $2,000 deposit each year for the next 40 years, or he might make deposits of different amounts each year. We would like to be able to determine the future value regardless of the number, size, and timing of the deposits.

For simplicity, we begin our discussion with an example involving only three deposits: $2,000 deposited today, $1,000 deposited one year from today, and $3,000 deposited two years from today in an account paying 8% interest per year. If these deposits are made into an RRSP account, we might be interested in computing the balance in the account 30 or 40 years from today. Again, for the sake of simplicity, we first discuss the procedure for calculating the balance in the account three years from today.

A very useful tool to help visualize the problem is a *timeline*, which illustrates the pattern of cash flows over the investment horizon. The timeline for this example is:

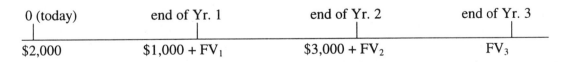

A future value with multiple cash flows can be computed in at least two different ways. First, we can compute the balance in the account year-by-year, adding both the subsequent deposits and compound interest to the account each year. Alternatively, we can separately compute the future value of each deposit and then sum the separate future values. We discuss these alternative, but equivalent, procedures below.

Since the account pays 8% interest, the future value of the first deposit, after one year, is:

$$FV_1 = \$2,000 \times (1.08) = \$2,160$$

Since the second deposit is also made one year from now, the balance in the account after one year is ($2,160 + $1,000) = $3,160.

The depositor now earns interest on the $3,160 balance for one year, and also deposits $3,000 in the account, so that the balance at the end of two years is:

$$[\$3,160 \times (1.08)] + \$3,000 = \$3,412.80 + \$3,000 = \$6,412.80$$

This balance remains on deposit for one more year, earning 8% interest, and no additional deposit is made, so that the balance in the account at the end of three years is:

$$\$6,412.80 \times (1.08) = \$6,925.82$$

The time line showing the calculations is:

| 0 (today) | end of Yr. 1 | end of Yr. 2 | end of Yr. 3 |
|---|---|---|---|
| $2,000 | $1,000 | $3,000.00 | $6,925.82 |
|  | 2,160 | 3,412.80 |  |
|  | $3,160 | $6,412.80 |  |

If no additional deposits are made to the account, and if the depositor continues to receive 8% interest per year, we can compute the future value for any given time period by compounding this balance for the appropriate number of years. For example, suppose the depositor plans to retire 40 years after the initial deposit is made. Then, in order to determine the balance in the account at retirement, the balance at the end of the third year is compounded for 37 more years:

$$\$6,925.82 \times (1.08)^{37} = \$119,440.10$$

As noted earlier, the future value of multiple cash flows can also be determined by compounding each deposit for the appropriate number of years. In order to compute the future value three years from now, we compound the three deposits as follows: the $2,000 deposit is compounded for three years, the $1,000 deposit is compounded for two years, and the $3,000 deposit is compounded for one year.

$$\$2,000 \times (1.08)^3 = \$2,519.42$$
$$\$1,000 \times (1.08)^2 = \$1,166.40$$
$$\$3,000 \times (1.08)^1 = \$3,240.00$$

The time line for this method of calculation is:

| 0 (today) | end of Yr. 1 | end of Yr. 2 | end of Yr. 3 |
|---|---|---|---|
| $2,000 | $1,000 | $ 3,000.00 | $2,519.42 |
|  |  |  | 1,166.40 |
|  |  |  | 3,240.00 |
|  |  |  | $6,925.82 |

The total of these three values is the future value of all three deposits three years from now: ($2,519.42 + $1,166.40 + $3,240.00) = $6,925.82.  Note that this is the same result derived earlier by computing the balance in the account year-by-year.

In order to determine the balance in the account at the end of 40 years, this balance at the end of three years can be compounded for 37 more years, as indicated above. The same result can also be obtained by compounding the three deposits for 40, 39, and 38 years, respectively:

$$\$2,000 \times (1.08)^{40} \;=\; \$43,449.04$$
$$\$1,000 \times (1.08)^{39} \;=\; \$20,115.30$$
$$\$3,000 \times (1.08)^{38} \;=\; \$55,875.83$$

The total future value of the three deposits is $119,440.17. (This result differs by $.07 from that obtained earlier because of rounding error in the previous calculation.)

**Present Value with Multiple Cash Flows:**  As in the case for future value problems involving multiple cash flows, there are two techniques which can be used to determine the present value of multiple cash flows. First, we can discount future payments year-by-year. Second, we can separately compute the present value of each future cash flow and then sum the separate present values to determine the total present value for all the cash flows. Although the two approaches are mathematically equivalent, we discuss only the second technique in this section.

Recall the earlier example of Kris, the investor who has two years to accumulate $1,200 in a bank account that will pay 8% interest per year for the next two years. We computed the present value as follows:

$$PV \;=\; FV_t / (1 + r)^t \;=\; \$1,200 / (1.08)^2 \;=\; \$1,200 / 1.1664 \;=\; \$1,028.81$$

Kris would have to deposit $1,028.81 today, in an account paying 8% interest per year, in order to be able to withdraw $1,200 two years from today.  Therefore, $1,028.81 is the present value of $1,200, to be received two years from today, when the appropriate interest rate (or discount rate) is 8%.

Now we will consider the following example which requires the calculation of the present value for multiple cash flows.

**An Example:**  Kris intends to make the following withdrawals from her account: $1,200 one year from now, $1,200 two years from now, and $2,000 three years from now. She would like to determine the size of the deposit she needs to make today, into an account paying 8% interest, which will enable her to make these withdrawals.

Kris can solve the problem by first thinking of this as three separate problems. First, what deposit today will allow her to withdraw $1,200 one year from today? Second, what deposit today will allow her to withdraw $1,200 two years from today? And, third, what deposit today will allow her to withdraw $2,000 three years from today? The answer to each of these questions is derived from a basic present value calculation as follows:

$$PV \;=\; \$1,200 / (1.08) \;=\; \$1,111.11$$
$$PV \;=\; \$1,200 / (1.08)^2 \;=\; \$1,200 / 1.16644 \;=\; \$1,028.81$$
$$PV \;=\; \$2,000 / (1.08)^3 \;=\; \$2,000 / 1.259712 \;=\; \$1,587.66$$

The time line for this problem is:

| 0 (today) | end of Yr. 1 | end of Yr. 2 | end of Yr. 3 |
|---|---|---|---|
| $1,111.11 | $1,200 | $ 1,200 | $2,000 |
| 1,028.81 | | | |
| 1,587.66 | | | |
| $3,727.58 | | | |

These calculations indicate three things. First, a deposit of $1,111.11 today, in an account paying 8% interest, will allow Kris to withdraw $1,200 one year from today. Second, a deposit of $1,028.81 today will allow Kris to withdraw $1,200 two years from today. Third, a deposit of $1,587.66 today will allow Kris to withdraw $2,000 three years from today. Clearly, then, a deposit equal to

$$\$1,111.11 + \$1,028.81 + \$1,587.66 \quad = \quad \$3,727.58$$

will enable Kris to make the three desired withdrawals.

The conclusion we derive from this example is simply that the present value of a series of cash flows is equal to the sum of the present values of the individual cash flows in the series. To further explore the significance of this result, we consider the following example.

**An Example:** Kris' broker has offered her the opportunity to make the following investment today: if she invests $4,000 today, she will receive $1,200 one year from today, $1,200 two years from today, and $2,000 three years from today. Should she make the investment?

The answer to this question is based on the interpretation of the present value calculation in the previous example. That calculation indicated that a deposit of $3,727.58 today, in an account paying 8 percent interest, would allow Kris to withdraw $1,200 one year from today, $1,200 two years from today, and $2,000 three years from today. This alternative is superior to the investment offered to Kris by her broker, because she can deposit fewer dollars in her account (i.e., $3,727.58 compared to $4,000) and still receive the same payments that she would receive if she made the investment offered by her broker. How much would Kris be willing to pay for the investment offered by the broker? The answer is that she would pay no more than $3,727.58, the present value of the future cash flows, discounted at the appropriate interest rate.

## VALUING LEVEL CASH FLOWS: ANNUITIES AND PERPETUITIES

An *annuity* is a series of constant cash flows that occur at regular intervals for a fixed number of time periods. For example, the payments on a five-year car loan are in the form of a 60-month annuity. Typically, the payments for a car loan begin one month after the car is purchased. When the payments for an annuity occur at the end of the relevant time period, the annuity is referred to as an ordinary annuity.

If payments are at the beginning of the time period, we call the annuity a deferred annuity (or *annuity due*). Deferred annuities are common for leases, which generally require that the first payment be made immediately upon taking possession of the leased asset. Financial calculations frequently involve annuities over long periods of time.

A perpetuity is a perpetual ordinary annuity. They are not as common as annuities for a fixed number of time periods. Although it might seem that the mathematics of an infinite series of payments would be difficult, this is not the case, as we will demonstrate below. We discuss financial calculations involving both annuities and perpetuities in this section.

**Present Value for Annuity Cash Flows:** We introduce the present value of an annuity with an example similar to that of the previous section.

**An Example:** Suppose that Kris, the investor from the previous example, is evaluating another investment proposed by her broker. The cost of the investment is $3,000 and it pays a guaranteed $1,200 per year at the end of each of the next three years. Notice that this example differs from the previous one in that the three payments here are identical, so that we are analyzing a $1,200 ordinary annuity which continues for three years.

In order to evaluate the investment opportunity, Kris first establishes the fact that the three $1,200 payments are guaranteed. Next, she determines that her opportunity cost for a similarly risky investment is 8%. Kris can now proceed to calculate the present value of the three payments, as was done in the previous example.

$$PV = \$1,200 \text{ x PVIF}(8\%,1) = \$1,200 \text{ x } (1/1.08) = \$1,200 \times .925926 = \$1,111.11$$

$$PV = \$1,200 \text{ x PVIF}(8\%,2) = \$1,200 \text{ x } (1/1.08^2) = \$1,200 \times .857339 = \$1,028.81$$

$$PV = \$1,200 \text{ x PVIF}(8\%,3) = \$1,200 \times (1/1.08^3) = \$1,200 \text{ x } .79382 = \$ 952.60$$

The present value of the investment is equal to:

$$\$1,111.11 + \$1,028.81 + \$952.60 = \$3,092.52$$

Kris would have to deposit $3,092.52 in her bank account today in order to be able to withdraw $1,200 per year at the end of each of the next three years. Since she can receive $1,200 per year at the end of each of the next three years for only $3,000 if she purchases the investment suggested by her broker, it would be preferable for her to purchase the investment from her broker.

Note: the present value factors could have been found using the tables in Appendix A.

This calculation can be simplified in the following way. First computing the total of the three present value interest factors. Then, we multiply this total by $1,200 (the size of the payment):

$$0.925926 + 0.857339 + 0.793832 = 2.577097$$
$$2.577097 \times \$1,200 = \$3,092.52$$

The total of the present value interest factors is often referred to as a *present value interest factor for an annuity*, PVIFA(r,t). Although the use of the present value interest factor for an annuity does not seem particularly easier in this example, two important facts must be considered. First, this alternative procedure is noticeably more efficient for annuities over long periods of time. Second, regardless of the time period, a table can be used to find the value of PVIFA(r,t). Table A.3 indicates that PVIFA(8%,3) = 2.5771. Consequently, we can compute the present value of the annuity in this example as follows:

$$PV = C \times PVIFA(r,t) = \$1,200 \times PVIFA(8\%,3) = \$1,200 \times 2.5771 = \$3,092.52$$

where C represents the constant annuity payment and PV is the present value of the annuity. Clearly, this approach is more efficient than calculating and then totalling the three individual present values.

Another alternative for computing the present value of an annuity uses a formula to determine the value of PVIFA(r,t). The sum of the present value interest factors is regarded by mathematicians as the sum of a geometric progression and, using algebraic techniques, it can be shown that the value of PVIFA(r,t) is given by the following formula:

$$\text{PVIFA(r,t)} \;=\; \frac{1 - [1 / (1+r)^t]}{r}$$

Since the term in brackets in the numerator of this expression is the present value interest factor, we can write this formula as:

$$\text{PVIFA(r,t)} \;=\; \frac{1 - [\text{PVIF(r,t)}]}{r}$$

To calculate the value of PVIFA(8%,3), first compute PVIF(8%,3) $= 1/(1.08)^3 = 1/1.259712 = 0.793832$. So,

$$\text{PVIFA(8\%,3)} \;=\; (1 - .79382) / r \;=\; 0,20618 / .08 \;=\; 2.5771$$

This is the same value we determined earlier from Table A.3. The present value of the annuity is:

$$\$1,200 \times 2.5771 \;=\; \$3,092.52$$

Thus far, we have solved for the present value of the annuity using three different procedures: computing and totalling the present values of the individual payments; using Table A.3 to determine the value of PVIFA(8%,3) and then multiplying this factor times the constant payment; and using the formula to determine the value of PVIFA(8%,3) and then multiplying by the constant payment.

The fourth alternative is to use a financial calculator with annuity functions. If you do, be sure you read the manual so that you know exactly how to enter the variables to get the correct answer. That means **be sure to read the instruction manual for *your* calculator. And, practice solving problems with your calculator before you take an exam!**

**Finding the Payment - An Example:**  If we know the interest rate, the present value of the annuity, and the number of times payments will be made, we can use the annuity equation to find out the size of each payment.

Suppose you intend to purchase a $15,000 automobile. You must put down 10% of the purchase price of the car and you can borrow 90% of the price from a bank. The bank will give you a five-year loan, to be repaid in equal monthly instalments, at an interest rate of 12% per year, or 1% per month. What are the monthly payments?

The loan will be for $(.90 \times \$15,000) = 13,500$, so that PV = $13,500. The monthly interest rate is 1%, so that r = .01. The loan will be repaid in 60 equal monthly instalments, so that t = 60 months. We substitute these known values in the formula developed earlier in this section for the present value of an annuity:

$$\text{PV} \;=\; \text{C} \times \text{PVIFA(r,t)}$$

$$\$13,500 \;=\; \text{C} \times \text{PVIFA(1\%,60)}$$

$$\text{PVIFA(1\%,60)} \;=\; \frac{1 - [1/(1.01)^{60}]}{0.01} \;=\; (1 - .550450) / .01 \;=\; 44.9550$$

Substitute PVIFA(1%,60) into the above equation and solve for C:

$13,500  =  C × 44.9550
C  =  $13,500 / 44.9550  =  $300.30

The loan requires 60 monthly payments of $300.30, beginning one month after the loan is made.

You can also solve the problem using the financial tables or a financial calculator. You will get the same answer (except for small rounding errors).

**Finding the Interest Rate - An Example:** Life insurance companies sell annuities to investors who wish to receive constant periodic payments at retirement . For example, a 64 year-old investor might purchase an annuity, to begin one year later, at age 65.  Such annuities are generally paid on a monthly basis; however, in this example, we assume that the annuity payments are made annually.  Suppose that, for the 64 year-old investor, a guaranteed ten-year annuity, paying $15,000 per year, beginning one year from now, costs $120,000. What is the interest rate implicit in this annuity?

As in the previous example, we begin by identifying the known values and substituting into the formula for the present value of an annuity (PV = $120,000; C = $15,000; t = 10):

$$PV  =  C \times PVIFA(r,t)$$

$$\$120,000  =  \$15,000 \times PVIFA(r,10)$$

$$PVIFA(r,10) = \$120,000 / \$15,000  =  8 \quad or \quad \frac{1 - [1/(1 + r)^{10}]}{r}  =  8$$

Unfortunately, it is impossible to directly compute the solution to this equation.  An approximate answer can be determined from Table A.3, table of present value interest factors for an annuity.  A more precise solution can be computed using trial-and-error, while a financial calculator will quickly and easily compute the precise value of r.

First, we consider the approximate solution for r which can be obtained from Table A.3. Values of PVIFA(r,10) are in the tenth row of the table.  Note that PVIFA(4%,10) = 8.1109 and PVIFA(5%,10) = 7.7217.  Since our calculation above indicates that PVIFA(r,10) = 8.0, clearly r must be between 4% and 5%. Since our tables do not provide values of PVIFA(r,10) for r between 4% and 5%, we could proceed to find a more precise value using trial-and-error and the formula for PVIFA indicated earlier in this section.  For example, we might guess that the value of r is closer to 4% than to 5%, since PVIFA(4%, 10) is closer to 8.0 than is PVIFA(5%,10).  If we guess that r = 4.1%, we then calculate the value of PVIFA(4.1%,10) as follows:

$$PVIFA(4.1\%,10)  = \frac{1 - [1/(1.041)^{10}]}{.041}  =  8.070669$$

Since the value of PVIFA(4.1%,10) is greater than 8.0, we now guess that r is greater than 4.1%.  The values of PVIFA(r,10), for r = 4.2% and 4.3%, are 8.030740 and 7.991107, respectively.  Consequently, r is between 4.2% and 4.3%, and closer to 4.3%.  Further trial-and-error indicates that the values of PVIFA(r,10), for r = 4.27% and 4.28%, are 8.002966 and 7.999010, respectively. This procedure can be continued to any desired degree of accuracy, although the process is clearly time-consuming and tedious. The precise value of r can be easily determined with a financial calculator.

**Finding the Number of Payments - An Example**: If we know the interest rate, the present value, and the amount of the annuity payments, we can also determine how many payments will be made.

Let's say you are buying a new living room set for $8,200.39. Annual payments, based on an interest rate of 7%, will be $2000. How many payments must you make? Using the same formula:

$8,200.39   =   $2,000 x PVIFA(7%,t)
$8,200.39/ $2,000   =   4.100195   =   PVIFA(7%,t)

Using the tables, you'll see that you must make five annual payments.

We can use the annuity formula to check:   $\{1 - [(1/1.07)^5]\} / .07$   =   4.100197

**Future Value for Annuities:**  The future value of an annuity can be calculated using procedures analogous to those described in the preceding section for computing the present value of an annuity. First, the future value of an annuity can be determined by computing and then summing the future values of the individual cash flows. Second, Table A.4 can be used to determine the future value interest factor for an annuity, FVIFA(r,t). This factor, which is the sum of the individual future value interest factors for each payment in an annuity, is then multiplied by the constant payment to determine the future value. Third, FVIFA(r,t) can be computed from a formula, indicated below, and is then multiplied by the constant payment to calculate the future value of the annuity. Fourth, a financial calculator can be used to determine the future value of an annuity. Since all but one of these procedures is directly analogous to the comparable present value calculation, in this section we discuss only the use of the formula to determine FVIFA(r,t). The formula is provided here:

$$FVIFA(r,t)   =   \frac{(1 + r)^t - 1}{r}$$

Since $(1 + r)^t$ is the future value interest factor, this formula can be written:

$$FVIFA(r,t)   =   [FVIF(r,t) - 1] / r   =   (Future\ value\ factor - 1) / r$$

In order to determine the future value of an annuity, multiply FVIFA(r,t) times the constant annuity payment, as indicated in the following formula:

$$FV   =   C \times FVIFA(r,t)$$

**A Note on Annuities Due - An Example:**  As mentioned earlier, annuity contracts sometimes specify payments or receipts at the beginning of each period.  Suppose you want to set aside $10,000 at the beginning of each of the next three years, given an interest rate of 10% per annum. What is the future value of this annuity due? What is this annuity due worth today (i.e., the present value of the annuity due)?

The first question can be solved in two ways, by using either of the following equations:

Annuity due FV factor   =   Annuity FV factor x (1 + r)
                        =   FVIFA (10%,3) × (1.10)
                        =   3.310 × 1.1   =   3.6410

The future value of this annuity due is:   $10,000 × 3.6410 = $36,410

Note that, because payments are made at the *beginning* of the year, each payment earns interest for one additional period. That means the future value of an annuity due is greater than the future value of an ordinary annuity.

Alternately, we can use the following equation:

$$\text{Annuity due FV factor} = [\text{FVIFA} (r\%, n + 1)] - 1$$
$$= 4.6410 - 1 = 3.6410$$

The future value of the annuity due is the same $36,410.

To answer the second question, again we have two alternative solutions:

$$\text{. Annuity due PV factor} = \text{Annuity PV factor} \times (1 + r)$$
$$= \text{PVIFA} (10\%, 3) \times (1.10)$$
$$= 2.486852 \times 1.10 = 2.735537$$

The present value of the annuity due is:

$$\$10,000 \times 2.735537 = \$27,355.37$$

In this case, because payments are made at the beginning of the year, each payment is *discounted* for one period *less*. Thus, the present value of an annuity due is greater than the present value of an ordinary annuity.

Note: If using Table A.3, the present value factor for an ordinary annuity is 2.4869, so the factor for an annuity due is 1.1 x 2.4869  = 2.73559.

Alternately,

$$\text{Annuity due PV factor} = [\text{PVIFA} (r\%, n - 1)] + 1$$
$$= 1.735537 + 1 = 2.735537$$

Again, the present value of the annuity due is $27,355.37.

**Perpetuities:**  A *perpetuity* (or perpetual annuity) is a constant series of cash flows, occurring at regular intervals, which continues forever.  The series of dividend payments for a share of preferred stock is often thought of as a perpetuity.  Applying the techniques described earlier, the present value of a perpetuity would be:

$$\text{PV} = C/(1+r)^1 + C/(1+2)^2 + C/(1+r)^3 + \dots \quad C/(1+r)^n$$

where C is the constant payment or cash flow.  This looks complicated.  Mathematically, though, this is the easiest type of cash flow to value.  The above formula reduces to a very simple equation:

$$\text{PV} = C \times (1/r) = C/r$$

**An Example:**  Suppose that a share of preferred stock pays an annual dividend of $8 and that the return you require is 5%. Under these circumstances, what is the present value of the $8 perpetuity?  In other words, what would an investor be willing to pay to purchase the share of preferred stock?

The answer is that the investor would pay whatever price would equate the $8 payments to a 5% interest rate or, algebraically:

PV × .05 = $8
PV  =  $8 / .05  =  $160

The formula can also be written as:  PV × r = C.  It might be helpful to think of this latter form of the equation in terms of a deposit in a bank account which pays the constant rate r for the indefinite future. If r = 5%, as in the above example, an investor could deposit $160 in a bank account today.  The account would earn ($160 × .05) = $8 at the end of the first year. If the investor withdraws the $8 interest immediately after it is paid, his account will still have a balance of $160 beginning the second year.  This balance would again earn ($160 × .05) = $8 interest at the end of the second year, which the investor could then immediately withdraw.  Since this procedure can be repeated every year, and assuming the account continues to pay 5% interest, the investor has created a perpetuity of $8 per year.  The interest at the end of each year is given by the above formula.  Consequently, the mathematics of perpetuities is based on this simple algebraic relationship.

It might be helpful to note that this formula can also be presented in a third form by solving for r:

r  =  C / PV

This form of the equation emphasizes the fact that the rate of return for a perpetuity is simply the size of the constant payment divided by the price of the perpetuity.

## GROWING PERPETUITIES

Today, it is common to find perpetuities for which the payment *grows* over time.  This is referred to as a *growing perpetuity*  - an endless,  constant stream that is expected to increase indefinitely.  The algebraic formula for a growing perpetuity is complicated, but it reduces to a very simple formula:

$$PV = \frac{C}{r - g}$$

Here, C is the cash flow at the end of the first period, r is the interest rate, and g is the growth rate for future cash flows.

Using this simplified formula requires an important assumption about the timing of cash flows.  It assumes that cash inflows and outflows occur at regular, discrete  intervals.

**An example:** You are interested in buying a growing perpetuity issued by a major corporation.  The stated cash flow is 12% of face value, or $120 per year.  These cash flows are expected to grow at an annual rate of 3% forever.  If the return on similar securities is 8%, what is the value of the growing perpetuity today?

The value is computed very easily as:

PV  =  C / (r - g)   =   $120 / (.08 - .03)   =   $2,400

This is the amount you should expect to pay for the security.

## GROWING ANNUITY

A *growing annuity* is different from a growing perpetuity in that it is a *finite* series of cash flows that grows over time.   The formula for a growing annuity is somewhat similar to that for an ordinary annuity, but there are differences:

$$PV \;=\; C/(r-g) \;\times\; \{\,1 - [(1+g)/(1+r)]^{t}\,\}$$

As before, C is the cash flow at the end of the first period, r is the interest rate, and g is the growth rate in cash flows.  T is the number of periods for the annuity.  Note that the first term, C / ( r - g ) is the same as the equation for finding the value of a growing perpetuity.  The second term adjusts for the fact that this is a finite stream of cash flows.

**An example:**  Let's use the same values as we did for the growing perpetuity example, but assume that the payments will be made for 20 years.  The value of the growing annuity is:

$$PV \;=\; [\$120 / (.08 - .03)\,] \;\times\; \{\,1 - [\,(1+.03)/(1+.08)\,]^{\,20}\,\}$$

$$=\; \$2,400 \;\times\; [\,1 - (1.03/1.08)^{20}\,] \;=\; \$2,400 \;\times\; (1 - 0.32874979)$$

$$=\; \$2,400 \times 0.612502 \;=\; \$1,470.00$$

As you can see, the fact that the growing annuity is a finite stream of cash flows reduces its value relative to that of a growing perpetuity.

## COMPARING RATES: THE EFFECT OF COMPOUNDING PERIODS

The preceding discussion of future-value and present-value analysis was based on the assumption of annually compounded interest rates.  However, banks and other financial institutions often compound interest on deposits more frequently.  Below, we discuss how different compounding periods affect financial calculations.

**Effective Annual Rates and Compounding:**  Consider a bank which advertises that it pays 12% interest per year, compounded quarterly.  This rate is equivalent to 3% interest each quarter. The 12% interest rate in this example is sometimes referred to as the *stated interest rate*, the *quoted interest rate* or the *nominal interest rate*. Financial institutions often refer to the 'annual rate' or simply the 'rate.'  However, when interest is compounded more frequently than once a year, the actual interest rate the depositor receives is greater than the quoted interest rate. The actual interest rate is often called the *effective annual interest rate* or the *effective annual yield*.

Note: When comparing the returns offered on two different investments, we must *always* convert to effective rates.

**Calculating and Comparing Effective Annual Rates:**  With quarterly compounding, the depositor begins to receive interest on interest during the second quarter, rather than after the first year, as in the case of annual compounding.   In order to calculate the future value for a deposit in the account described above, it is only necessary to determine the quarterly interest rate (i.e., 3% in this example) and to treat the quarter, rather than the year, as the relevant time period.  Therefore, the future value, after one year, of a $1,000 deposit is:

$$FV \;=\; \$1,000 \times (1.03)^{4} \;=\; \$1,000 \times 1.12551 \;=\; \$1,125.51$$

If the account paid 12% interest per year, compounded annually, the future value would be $1,120, so that the additional ($1,125.51 − $1,120) = $5.51 is the interest on interest earned during the second, third, and fourth quarters of the year. If the bank paid 12.551% interest per year, compounded annually, the future value for a $1,000 deposit over a one-year period would also be $1,125.51:

$$FV = \$1,000 \times (1.12551)^1 = \$1,000 \times 1.12551 = \$1,125.51$$

Therefore, a quoted annual interest rate of 12%, compounded quarterly, is equivalent to an effective annual interest rate of 12.551%. This can be seen directly in the example by noting that: $(1.03)^4 = (1.12551)^1$, so that the effective annual interest rate is simply

$$(1.03)^4 - 1 = (1.12551)^1 - 1.0 = .12551 = 12.551\%$$

In general, this result is presented algebraically as follows:

$$\text{effective annual rate} = \text{EAR} = [1 + (\text{quoted rate}/m)]^m - 1$$

where m is the number of times per year interest is compounded.

**An Example:** Suppose that, for the $1,000 deposit in the account described earlier, the investor would like to compare the future value at the end of 30 years for two accounts, one paying 12% interest per year, compounded annually, and the other paying 12% interest per year, compounded quarterly.

The future value for the first account is:  $FV = \$1,000 \times (1.12)^{30} = \$29,959.92$

For the second account, we use an interest rate of $(.12/4) = .03 = 3\%$ per quarter and a time period of $(30 \times 4$ quarters$) = 120$ quarters, so that the future value is:  $FV = \$1,000 \times (1.03)^{120} = \$34,710.99$.

Notice that the substantial difference of $(\$34,710.99 - \$29,959.92) = \$4,751.07$ in these future values results from the difference between annual and quarterly compounding.

The calculation procedure for compounding m times per year over a period of t years can be summarized as:

$$FV = PV \times [1 + (r/m)]^{mt}$$

**Quoting a Rate - An Example:** Suppose as a banker you have determined that you must earn 12% EAR on a loan with interest compounded monthly. What rate do you quote?  Since $\text{EAR} = [1 + \text{quoted rate}/m)]^m - 1$, we can solve for q as follows:

$$.12 = [1 + \text{quoted rate}/12]^{12} - 1$$

$$1.12 = [1 + \text{quoted rate}/12]^{12}$$

$$(1.12)^{1/12} = 1 + \text{quoted rate}/12$$

$$1.0095 = 1 + \text{quoted rate}/12$$

$$.0095 = \text{quoted rate}/12$$

$$\text{quoted rate} = .1139 \quad \text{or} \quad 11.39\%$$

**Mortgages:** Although mortgages are examples of an annuity with monthly payments, regulations for Canadian financial institutions require that mortgage rates be quoted with semiannual compounding. Furthermore, payments are usually calculated to maturity (25 years).

**An Example:** Loyal Bank is offering a $100,000, 25-year mortgage at a quoted rate of 9%. What are the monthly payments?

First we need to find the quoted monthly rate. We do this by converting the quoted semiannual rate to an EAR:

$$\text{EAR} = [1 + \text{quoted rate}/m]^m - 1$$
$$= [1 + .09/2]^2 - 1 = 9.2025\%$$

Then we find the quoted monthly rate to calculate the payments:

$$\text{quoted rate}/m = (\text{EAR} + 1)^{1/m} - 1$$
$$\text{quoted rate}/12 = (1.092025)^{1/12} - 1 = .007363\%$$

To find the payments, we use the annuity present value formula:

$$\text{Annuity present value} = \$100,000 = C \times (1 - \text{PV factor})/r$$
$$\$100,000 = C \times (1 - 1/1.007363^{300})/.007363$$
$$\$100,000 = C \times 120.7777$$
$$C = \$827.97$$

Note that the number of payments is $12 \times 25 = 300$.

**An Example:** Suppose that the rate of 9% in the above example is fixed for five years and you are wondering whether to lock in this rate or take a lower rate of 8% fixed for one year. If you choose the lower one-year rate, how much lower will your payments be for the first year?

Following the steps outlined in the previous solution, your payments are $763.21, a reduction of $64.76 per month. By taking the option, you are betting that rates will not increase over the next year. This trade off between lower payments and the added uncertainty of interest rate fluctuations reflects the fundamental nature of most financial decisions and is discussed in more detail under risk and return in later chapters.

**Annual Percentage Rate (APR):** The Bank Act in Canada requires that lenders must disclose an APR on virtually all consumer loans. The question is whether an APR is an effective annual rate (EAR). The answer is not all that clear, because lenders are required by law to compute the APR in a particular way. The law states that the APR is simply equal to the interest rate per period multiplied by the number of periods in a year. For example, if a Trust Company charges 3% every quarter then the APR reported must be 12% (3% × 4). However, as demonstrated earlier, the EAR is 12.55% $[(1.03)^4 - 1]$.

**An Example:** Your credit card company quotes an interest rate of 18% APR where monthly payments are required. Your uncle is willing to lend you money at 19% with annual repayments. Who is offering the better rate? Your uncle, since the EAR on the credit card is: $[1 + .18/12]^{12} - 1 = 19.56\%$

**Taking It to the Limit - A Note on Continuous Compounding:** Quarterly, monthly and daily compounding are commonly used by financial institutions, and it is even possible to compound interest hourly, or each minute or second. While these latter compounding periods are not common, continuous compounding, which is equivalent to compounding over the smallest possible period of time, is frequently used in financial calculations. Suppose that an insurance company pays 12% interest per year, compounded continuously. It can be shown that the following formula applies:

$$FV = PV \times e^{qt}$$

where e is a constant whose value is approximately 2.71828 and q is the quoted interest rate.

Therefore, if a $1,000 deposit is compounded continuously for three years, the future value is:

$$FV_3 \;=\; PV \times e^{qt} \;=\; \$1,000 \times e^{(.12 \times 3)} \;=\; \$1,000 \times e^{.36}$$

The value of $e^{.36}$ is 1.43333, which can be determined using a calculator. The future value is $1,433.33.

In the previous section, we first computed the effective annual interest rate by comparing the future value, after one year, for an account which compounds quarterly with an account which compounds annually. We can use the same kind of comparison here to establish the effective annual interest rate for an account which pays interest compounded continuously. The future value, at the end of one year, for a $1,000 deposit in an account which pays 12% interest per year, compounded continuously, is:

$$FV_1 \;=\; PV \times e^{qt} \;=\; \$1,000 \times e^{(.12 \times 1)} \;=\; \$1,000 \times e^{.12} = \$1,000 \times 1.12750 = \$1,127.50$$

An account which paid interest compounded annually would have to pay 12.75% to provide the depositor with a future value of $1,127.50, as demonstrated by the following:

$$FV_1 \;=\; \$1,000 \times (1.1275)^1 \;=\; \$1,127.50$$

Therefore, the effective annual interest rate is 12.75%. This result is obtained directly as follows:

$$effective \; annual \; interest \; rate \;=\; EAR \;=\; e^q - 1$$

where q is the quoted interest rate.

## LOAN TYPES AND LOAN AMORTIZATION

The three basic forms of loans are: pure-discount loans, interest-only loans, and amortized loans. We now discuss the application of present value principles to these three kinds of loans.

**Pure Discount Loans:** A *pure-discount loan* is a loan which is repaid in a single payment. The single payment therefore represents principal plus interest for the period of the loan. The mathematics of pure-discount loans is simply the mathematics of single cash flows.

**An Example:** Melissa borrows $2,500 today, at an interest rate of 11% per year, and agrees to repay the loan three years from today. Since the loan is a pure-discount loan, Melissa will pay principal plus interest three years from today. What is the required payment?

The payment is simply the future value of $2,500, compounded for three years at 11% per year:

$$FV_3 = \$2,500 \times (1.11)^3 = \$3,419.08$$

Suppose that Melissa determines that she must borrow substantially more than $2,500. However, she can only afford to repay $4,500 three years from today. If the interest rate is 11% per year, what is the maximum amount she can borrow today?

The maximum amount Melissa can borrow is the present value of $4,500, discounted at 11%, for three years:

$$PV = \$4,500 / (1.11)^3 = \$3,290.36$$

Suppose that Melissa finds another lender who is willing to lend her $7,500. This is also a pure-discount loan; Melissa must repay $12,500 three years from today. What is the interest rate this new lender is charging?

The interest rate for the loan is determined by substituting the known values of FV, PV, and t, into the basic future value equation and then solving for r:

$$FV_t = PV \times (1 + r)^t$$

$$\$12,500 = \$7,500 \times (1 + r)^3$$

$$1.66666 = (1 + r)^3$$

$$(1.66666)^{(1/3)} = (1 + r)$$

$$1.1856311 = (1 + r)$$

$$r = .1856311 \qquad \text{The interest rate is 18.563\%.}$$

Pure-discount loans are very common when the loan is less than one year.

**An Example - Treasury Bills:** Treasury Bills issued by the Government of Canada are pure discount loans with maturities typically between 3 to 12 months. If a T-bill promises to pay $1,000 in 12 months and the market interest rate is 7%, how much should the bill sell for in the market?

The T-bill should sell for the present value of $1,000, to be paid in one year at 7% or: $1,000/1.07 = $934.58.

**Interest-Only Loans:** *Interest-only loans* require the payment of interest each year, and then repayment of the entire principal at a later date. The mathematics of such loans is generally fairly uncomplicated, because there is no compounding of interest for such loans.

**An Example:** Suppose that Melissa is able to obtain an interest-only loan which requires her to pay 11% interest per year and repay the principal in three years. What are the payments Melissa is required to make on a $2,500 loan?

The annual payment is (.11 × $2,500) = $275. Melissa pays $275 per year at the end of each of the next three years. Then, at the end of the third year, she also repays the $2,500 principal, for a total payment of [($275 x 3) + $2,500] = $3,325. Most bonds issued by the Government of Canada and the provinces have the general form of an interest-only loan.

**Amortized Loans:**  An *amortized loan* requires that the lender make periodic payments which include interest plus repayment of a portion of the principal.  Amortized loans can take several forms.  Two of the most common are: first, a loan payment schedule which requires periodic repayment of a fixed portion of the principal, plus interest; and second, a loan payment which remains constant throughout the life of the loan, so that successive payments repay progressively increasing portions of the principal and correspondingly decreasing interest payments.  The latter form of amortized loan is the typical mortgage or consumer loan.

**An Example:**  Melissa has the opportunity to borrow $7,500 in the form of an amortized loan which requires repayment of one-third of the principal each year, and annual interest payments equal to 15% of the remaining principal.  What are the annual payments for this loan?

At the end of each year, Melissa repays (1/3 × $7,500) = $2,500 principal.  At the end of the first year, she also pays (.15 × $7,500) = $1,125 in interest, so that her first-year payment is ($2,500 + $1,125) = $3,625.  Since Melissa repays $2,500 of the principal at the end of the first year, the remaining balance on the loan beginning the second year is $5,000.  Therefore, the interest payment at the end of the second year is (.15 × $5,000) = $750 and the total payment, including principal repayment, is ($2,500 + $750) = $3,250.  Beginning the third year, the remaining balance is $2,500, so that the interest payment due at the end of the third year is (.15 × $2,500) = $375; the total payment is ($2,500 + $375) = $2,875.

Suppose that the loan described in the preceding example is to be amortized with constant annual payments.  What are the annual payments?  How much of each payment is applied to repayment of principal? How much of each payment represents interest?  This type of computation is referred to as an *amortization schedule*.

**Amortization Schedules - An Example:**  Earlier in this chapter, we discussed the procedure for determining the size of the constant payment, C, for a loan which is to be repaid in the form of an annuity.  This example is solved using the same procedure.  First, substitute the known values (PV = $7,500; r = 11% = .11; t = 3) into the formula for the present value of an annuity:

$$PV \ = \ C \times PVIFA(r,t)$$

$$\$7,500 \ = \ C \times PVIFA(11\%,3)$$

Next, compute the value of PVIFA(11%,3):

$$PVIFA(11\%,3) \ = \ \{1 - [1/(1.11)^3]\} \ / \ .11 = (1 - .731191) \ / \ .11 = 2.443715$$

Now, substitute the value of PVIFA(11%,3) into the above equation and solve for C:

$$\$7,500 \ = \ C \times PVIFA(11\%,3)$$
$$\$7,500 \ = \ C \times 2.443715$$
$$C \ = \ \$7,500/2.443715 \ = \ \$3,069.10$$

The loan requires three annual payments of $3,069.10.  The total of the payments is (3 × $3,069.10) = $9,207.30.  Since $7,500 is applied to repayment of principal, the total interest paid is ($9,207.30 – $7,500) = $1,707.30.

In order to determine what portion of each payment is applied to payment of principal and what portion is interest, we prepare an *amortization schedule*, which also indicates the principal balance remaining on the loan at the end of each of the three years.  Since the principal is $7,500, the interest for the first year is (.11 × $7.500) = $825. For the first payment, the principal repayment is the difference between the size of the payment and the first year's interest, or ($3,069.10 – $825) = $2,244.10.  After the first payment is made, the principal balance is reduced to ($7,500 – $2,244.10) = $5,255.90.  Since this is the principal balance during the second year, the interest paid at the end of the second year is (.11 × $5,255.90) = $578.15.  Notice that the interest paid at the end of the second year is less than that paid at the end of the first year, because the principal balance is less during the second year than during the first.  The remainder of the second payment is applied to repayment of principal: ($3,069.10 – $578.15) = $2,490.95.  This payment leaves a principal balance of ($5,255.90 – $2,490.95) = $2,764.95. The figures for the third year are indicated in the amortization schedule below.  Note that the ending balance is –$.01, indicating that the principal is overpaid by $.01; this results from a rounding error in the calculations.

| Year | Beginning Balance | Total Payment | Interest Paid | Principal Paid | Ending Balance |
|------|-------------------|---------------|---------------|----------------|----------------|
| 1 | $7,500.00 | $3,069.10 | $825.00 | $2,244.10 | $5,255.90 |
| 2 | 5,255.90 | 3,069.10 | 578.15 | 2,490.95 | 2,764.95 |
| 3 | 2,764.95 | 3,069.10 | 304.14 | 2,764.96 | - .01 |

## CONCEPT TEST

1.  A future value with multiple cash flows can be computed by separately computing the _____ of each deposit and then summing the separate _____ .

2.  A present value with multiple cash flows can be calculated by separately computing the _____ of each cash flow and then summing the separate _____ .

3.  An annuity is a series of _____ cash flows that occur at _____ intervals for a _____ number of time periods.

4.  When annuity payments occur at the end of the relevant time period, the annuity is referred to as an _____ annuity or a _____ annuity. If payments are at the beginning of the time period, we call the annuity a _____ annuity or an _____ .

5.  The present value of an annuity can be determined according to the equation: PV = _____ . In the equation, PV is the present value of the annuity, C represents the _____ , and PVIFA(r,t) is the _____ .

6.  PVIFA(r,t) can be determined from a table or from the  formula:  PVIFA(r,t) = _____ .

7.  The future value of an annuity can be determined by the equation:  FV = _____ .  In this equation, FV is the future value of the annuity, C represents the _____ , and FVIFA(r,t) is the _____

8.  FVIFA(r,t) can be determined either from a table or from the formula: FVIFA(r,t) = _____ .

9.  A perpetuity is a series of _____ cash flows, occurring at _____ intervals, which continues perpetually.  The formula for the present value of a perpetuity is:  PV = _____ .

10.  The formula can also be solved for C, and can be written as:  C = _____ .  This formula can also be presented in a third form, solving for r:  r = _____ .

11.    A quoted interest rate is also referred to as a _____ interest rate or a _____ interest rate. When interest is compounded more frequently than once a year, the actual interest rate is _____ than the quoted interest rate.  The actual interest rate is often called the effective annual interest rate or the _____ .

12.    The effective annual interest rate (EAR) is computed as follows:  EAR = _____ , where m is the number of times per year interest is compounded .

13.    When interest is compounded m times per year, the future value is computed as follows:
       FV = _____

14.    In the case of continuous compounding the future value is determined according to the following formula:
       FV = _____ .

15.    A pure-discount loan is a loan which is repaid in a _____ which represents _____ plus _____ for the period of the loan. The mathematics of pure-discount loans is simply the mathematics of single cash flows.

16.    Interest-only loans require the payment of _____ each year, and then repayment of the _____ at a later date.  The mathematics of such loans is relatively uncomplicated, because there is no compounding of interest.

17.    An amortized loan requires that the borrower make periodic payments which include _____ plus repayment of a portion of the _____ .

18.    Two common forms of amortized loans are: a loan payment schedule which requires periodic repayment of a fixed portion of the _____ plus _____ ; and, a loan payment which remains constant throughout the life of the loan, so that successive payments repay progressively _____ portions of the principal and correspondingly _____ interest payments. The latter form of amortized loan is the typical mortgage or consumer loan.

## ANSWERS TO CONCEPT TEST

1.    future value; future values

2.    present value; present values

3.    constant; regular; fixed

4.    ordinary; regular; deferred; annuity due

5.    $C \times PVIFA\ (r,t)$; constant annuity payment; present value interest factor for an annuity

6.    $1 - [1/(1 + r)^t]/r$

7.    $C \times FVIFA(r,t)$; constant annuity payment; future value interest factor for an annuity

8.    $[(1 + r)^t - 1]/r$

9.      constant; regular; C/r

10.     PV × r; C/PV

11.     stated; nominal; greater; effective annual yield

12.     $[1 + (\text{quoted rate}/m)^m] - 1$

13.     $PV \times [1 + (r/m)]^{mt}$

14.     $PV \times e^{qt}$

15.     single payment; interest; principal

16.     interest; principal

17.     interest; principal

18.     principal; interest; larger; smaller

## PROBLEMS AND SOLUTIONS

### Problem 1

An investment requires an initial outlay of $195. The cash inflow from this investment will be $114 one year from today (year 1) and $144 two years from today (year 2). The market rate of interest is 20%. Find the present value for this investment. Is the investment acceptable?

**Solution:** This solution calculates the present value by finding the present value of each cash flow separately, then finding the total. You should confirm this result by also calculating the present value year-by-year.

| Year | Cash Flow | PV (at 20%) |
|------|-----------|-------------|
| 1    | $114      | $ 95        |
| 2    | 144       | 100         |
|      |           | $ 195       |

The present value for the investment is therefore $195. Since $195 is precisely the cost of the investment, the investor is indifferent between the investment opportunity described here and an investment at the market rate of interest. Consequently, this calculation also demonstrates that the rate of return for the investment is the same as the market rate of interest, 20%.

**Problem 2**

Mike is going to deposit $3,000 into his bank account today, $4,000 two years from now, and $1,000 five years from now.  Given that Mike's bank account earns 7% (compounded annually), how much will his deposits be worth at the end of Year 2? Year 5? Year 10?

**Solution:** The time line for this problem is:

```
0 (today)          end of Yr. 2              end of Yr. 5                              end of Yr. 10
   |                    |                         |                                         |
$3,000      $4,000 + FV (from Yr. 0)   $1,000 + FV (from Yr. 2)                    FV (from Yr. 5)
```

The future value of the first deposit, after two years is:

$$FV_2 \ = \ \$3,000 \times (1.07)^2 \ = \ \$3,000 \times 1.1449 \ = \ \$3,434.70$$

The account balance includes the $4,000 deposited in Year 2:  FV $= \$3,434.70 + \$4,000 = \$7,434.70$.

This balance will earn interest for three years until the $1,000 deposit in Year 5.  At the end of Year 5, the total account balance will be:

$$FV_5 \ = \ \$7,434.70 \times (1.07)^3 \ + \ \$1,000 \ = \ \$7,434.70 \times 1.2250 \ + \ \$1,000 \ = \ \$10,107.83.$$

This amount will earn interest for another five years.  The balance in Year 10 will be:

$$FV_{10} \ = \ \$10,107.83 \times 1.4123 \ = \ \$14,176.75.$$

**Problem 3**

An investment which requires a cash outlay of $1,243 today will provide cash inflows of $400, $889, and $432 at the end of one year, two years, and three years, respectively.  The market interest rate is 12%. Is this a good investment?

**Solution:**  Compute the present value for the investment as follows:

$$PV \ = \ (\$400/1.12) \ + \ (\$889/1.12^2) \ + \ (\$432/1.12^3) \ = \ \$1,373.34$$

This indicates that an investor could invest $1,373.34 today in an investment which pays 12% interest per year and then withdraw $400 one year from today, $889 two years from today, and $432 three years from today. The investment described above requires an outlay of only $1,243 and still provides cash flows of $400, $889 and $432 at the end of one year, two years, and three years, respectively.  Therefore, the investment described here is preferable to the alternative opportunity at the market interest rate of 12%.

## Problem 4

Below are four different investment opportunities, with the cost of each investment. Project 1 costs $2,000; Project 2 costs $5,000, and Project 3 costs $4,000. Using an 8% discount rate, determine which of the projects are good investments.

| Project | End of Yr. 1 | End of Yr. 2 | End of Yr. 3 |
|---------|--------------|--------------|--------------|
| 1 | $1,000 | $ 800 | $ 600 |
| 2 | 1,900 | 1,900 | 1,900 |
| 3 | 1,400 | 1,600 | 1,800 |

**Solution:** We need to find the present value of each investment opportunity. If the present value is greater than the cost, the opportunity is good.

$$\text{Project 1:} \quad PV = \$1,000/1.08 + \$800/(1.08)^2 + \$600/(1.08)^3$$
$$= \$2,088.10$$

The project costs $2,000, so it is a good investment.

$$\text{Project 2:} \quad PV = \$1,900/(1.08) + \$1,900/(1.08)^2 + \$1,900/(1.08)^3$$
$$= \$4,896.48$$

The project costs $5,000, though, so it is not a good investment.

$$\text{Project 3:} \quad PV = \$1,400/(1.08) + \$1,600/(1.08)^2 + \$1,800/(1.08)^3$$
$$= \$4,096.94$$

Since the project only costs $4,000, it is a good investment.

## Problem 5

Your banker is trying to interest you in a small-scale investment project for the next three years. The banker says you will receive payments of $800, $1,500, and $1,600 in years 1, 2, and 3, respectively. The cost to get in on the investment is $3,000. Currently, your savings are in an account earning an annual rate of 8%. Should you take your funds out of the account to participate in this investment?

**Solution:** We need to find the present values of the cash flows from the investment:

$$PV = \$800/(1.08) + \$1,500/(1.08)^2 + \$1,600/(1.08)^3$$
$$= \$3,296.88$$

Your banker is giving you good advice. You would earn less from the funds in your savings account.

## Problem 6

A widget machine can be purchased for $1,200 and will create cash flows of $300 per year for the first two years, $500 in Year 3, and $100 in Year 4. At the end of Year 4 the machine can be sold for $200. The market rate of interest is 8.5%. Should you buy the machine?

**Solution:** Note that the net cash flow in Year 4 is the $100 from use of the machine plus the $200 from selling the machine.

$$PV \; = \; \$300 / (1.085) \; + \; \$300 / (1.085)^2 \; + \; \$500 / (1.085)^3 \; + \; \$300 / (1.085)^4$$

$$= \; \$276.50 \; + \; \$254.84 \; + \; \$391.45 \; + \; \$216.47 \; = \; \$1,139.26$$

Since the present value of the cash inflows is less than the $1,200 needed to purchases the machine, this is not a good investment.

Alternatively, you could have solved the problem another way by recognizing that all four years have a cash flow of $300 (an annuity), with an extra $200 cash flow in year 3. The present value equation becomes:

$$PV \; = \; \$300 \text{ x PVIFA } (8.5\%, 4) \; + \; \$200 / (1.085)^3$$

$$= \; \$982.68 \; + \; \$156.58 \; = \; \$1,139.26$$

The present value of the cash flows, and the investment decision are the same either way.

## Problem 7

Now suppose that, instead of getting the cash flows from Project 2 in Problem 4, you get them at the beginning of each year. Does this change your decision?

**Solution:** Effectively, you are receiving each cash flow one year earlier, so the discount period is one year less for each cash flow. The present value is:

$$PV \; = \; \$1,900 / (1.08)^0 \; + \; \$1,900 / (1.08) \; + \; \$1,900 / (1.08)^2$$
$$= \; \$5,288.20$$

The project is now a good investment.

Note: $1.08^0 = 1$. Also, you might recognize this series of cash flows as an annuity, discussed later in the chapter.

## Problem 8

You are entering graduate school tomorrow. You have $35,000 saved to fund your education over the next three years. If you can deposit your savings in an account paying 9% annually, how much can you withdraw each year (assuming withdrawals at the end of the year)?

**Solution:**

First, compute the value factor for an annuity:

$$\text{PVIFA}(9\%,3) = \{1 - [1/(1.09)^3]\} / .09 = (1 - .7721830) / .09 = 2.531295$$

Then use the formula for the present value of an annuity to solve for C, the amount to withdraw:

$$\text{PV} = \$35,000 = C \times 2.531295$$

$$C = \$35,000 / 2.531295 = 13,826.91$$

So, you can withdraw $13,826.91 each year while you are in school.

## Problem 9

Unfortunately, after computing the amount you can withdraw above, you realize that you need the funds at the *beginning* of each year. How much can you withdraw each year now?

**Solution:** Because withdrawals are made at the beginning of the year, this is an annuity due. We can solve the problem two ways. First, we can compute the annuity due PV factor as:

$$\text{Annuity due PV factor} = \text{PVIFA}(r\%, n-1) + 1 = \{1 - [1/(1.09)^2]\} / .09 + 1$$

$$= 1.75911 + 1 = 2.75911$$

So, the withdrawal amount can be found as:

$$\$35,000 = C \times 2.75911 = \$35,000 / 2.75911 = \$12,685.25$$

Alternatively, we can find the annuity due PV factor as:

$$\text{Annuity due PV factor} = \text{PVIFA}(9\%,3)(1+r)$$

$$= 2.531295(1.09) = 2.759112$$

Then, solving as before:  $C = \$35,000 / 2.759112 = \$12,685.24$

Notice that the amount of the withdrawal is smaller when it occurs at the beginning of the year.

## Problem 10

You have just joined the investment banking firm of Knot, Wirthem, *et al.* They have offered you two different salary arrangements. You can have $50,000 per year for the next three years or $25,000 per year for the next three years, along with a $50,000 signing bonus today. If the market interest rate is 16%, which salary arrangement do you prefer?

**Solution:** We will compare the two alternatives by computing the present value of each series of payments. (Note that these alternatives can also be compared on the basis of the future values; the conclusion is the same for either approach.)  The payment of $50,000 per year for the next three years is an ordinary annuity. We first compute the present value interest factor for an annuity:

$$PVIFA(16\%,3) \ = \ \{1 - [1/(1.16)^3]\} \ / \ .16 = (1 - .640658) \ / \ .16 \ = \ 2.245888$$

The present value of the annuity of $50,000 per year for three years is:

$$PV \ = \ \$50,000 \times 2.245888 \ = \ \$112,294.40$$

The present value of the annuity of $25,000 per year for three years is half as much, or $56,147.20.  The total value of the second option is $106,147.20. You should select the $50,000 per year option.

## Problem 11

You expect to receive an annuity of $1,000 per year for the next five years. The market rate of interest is 12%. Assuming that you do not spend any of the income at any other time, what is the maximum you can spend from these payments at the end of five years? What is the maximum amount you can spend today?

**Solution:** The first question requires that you find the future value of the annuity. This can be done as follows:

$$\begin{aligned} FV \ &= \ \$1,000 \times (1.12^4 + 1.12^3 + 1.12^2 + 1.12^1 + 1.12^0) \\ &= \ \$1,000 \times (6.35285) \ = \ \$6,352.85 \end{aligned}$$

Note that the term in parentheses is a future value annuity factor, which can be found in Table A.4 of Appendix A. This calculation indicates that you could invest your first $1,000 payment, to be received at the end of one year, for a period of four years, at a 12% rate; the second payment could be invested for three years, and so on; the proceeds of these investments could then be spent five years from now.

The second question requires that you find the present value of the annuity. This can be done as follows:

$$\begin{aligned} PV \ &= \ \$1,000 \times [1/(1.12)^1 + 1/(1.12)^2 \ + \ 1/(1.12)^3 + 1/(1.12)^4 + 1/(1.12)^5] \\ &= \ \$1,000 \times (3.60478) \ = \ \$3,604.78 \end{aligned}$$

The term in parentheses is a present value annuity factor, which can be found in Table A.3. This calculation indicates that you could borrow $3,604.78 today, at a 12% interest rate, and repay the loan in five annual instalments of $1,000 each.

Note that both the future value and the present value problems can be solved using the appropriate formulas to determine the values of FVIFA(12%,5) and PVIFA(12%,5), respectively.

## Problem 12

Find the present value of the following series of cash flows, using a discount rate of 10%.

| Year | Cash Flow |
|------|-----------|
| 1 | $100 |
| 2 | 200 |
| 3 | 300 |
| 4 | 300 |
| 5 | 300 |

**Solution:** You can find the answer by computing the present value of each cash flow, then finding the total. However, a more efficient way is to recognize that the cash flows in years 3, 4, 5 constitute a 3-year annuity. We can find the value of the annuity at the beginning of year 3 (end of year 2). Then, that value is discounted for two more years in order to find the value today. Find the present values of the cash flows for the first two years, then compute the total.

| Year | Calculation | Present Value |
|------|-------------|---------------|
| 1 | $100 \times PVIF(10\%,1) = 100 \times .909091$ | $ 90.91 |
| 2 | $200 \times PVIF(10\%,2) = 200 \times .826446$ | 165.29 |
| 3-5 | $300 \times PVIFA(10\%,3) \times PVIF(10\%,2)$ | |
|     | $= 300 \times 2.486852 \times .826446$ | 616.57 |
|     | | $ 872.77 |

## Problem 13

Consider a perpetuity which pays $100 per year; the market rate of interest is 10%. What is the present value of the perpetuity? What is the present value of the perpetuity three years from now? What is the present value of the perpetuity n years from now? Under what circumstances does the value of a perpetuity change?

**Solution:** The present value of the perpetuity is given by the following formula:

$$PV = C/r = \$100/.10 = \$1,000$$

Three years from now (or n years from now) the value of the perpetuity is still $1,000; the above calculation applies in either case, as long as the market rate of interest is 10%. The value of the perpetuity changes only if the market rate of interest changes.

## Problem 14

A firm invests $3 million in a project which will yield a perpetuity of $1 million per year. What is the discount rate, r, for which this project's present value is $4.5 million?

**Solution:** Solve the following equation for r: $\$1,000,000/r = \$4,500,000$. The solution is $r = .2222 = 22.22\%$. For values of r less than 22.22%, the present value of the project is greater than $4,500,000.

**Problem 15**

What is the present value of a perpetuity which pays $1,000 per year if the market rate of interest is 8%?  What about a 50-year annuity with the same annual payments?  What is it for a 100-year annuity?

**Solution:** The present value of the perpetuity is:

$$PV = C/r = \$1,000/.08 = \$12,500$$

The value of the 50-year annuity is:

$$PV = \$1,000 \times PVIFA (8\%, 50) = \$1,000 \times 12.23348 = \$12,233.48$$

The value of the 100-year annuity is:

$$PV = \$1,000 \times PVIFA (8\%, 100) = \$1,000 \times 12.49432 = \$12,494.32$$

Note: The longer the life of an annuity, the close its value approaches that of a perpetuity.  This is because the present value interest factor, PVIF, gets smaller as t increases.  For example:

$$PVIF (8\%, 250) = 1/(1.08)^{250} = 0.000000004$$

That makes the present value factor 4 billionths.  So, the present value of the 250th payment $1,000 x 0.000000004 = 4 millionths of a cent!

**Problem 16**

WeGrow.com is going to the market, offering a perpetuity.  However, because they anticipate that the recent slow-down in dot.com securities will be short-lived, they believe it will be less expensive to issue the security as a growing annuity.  They plan to offer 150% of $100 face value and will use an interest rate of 9% in the analysis.  If they issue the security as a 25-year growing annuity, they will use a constant growth rate of 4% per year.  Are they right that issuing a growing perpetuity will be less expensive?  What will happen if they issue the security as a growing *perpetuity*?

**Solution:** The cost of issuing a perpetuity is the present value of the cash flows:

$$PV = C/r = \$150/.09 = \$1,666.67$$

If they issue a growing annuity instead, the cost is:

$$PV = [C/(r-g)] \times \{1 - [(1+g)/(1+r)]^t\} = [\$150/(.09-.04)] \times [1 - (1.04/1.09)^{25}]$$

$$= (\$150/.05) \times (1 - 0.30915) = \$3,000 \times .69085 = \$2,072.55$$

If they issue a growing perpetuity, the cost is:

$$PV = C/(r-g) = \$150/(.09-.04) = \$150/.05 = \$3,000$$

WeGrow.com has it backwards.  Their best alternative is to issue an ordinary perpetuity.  The worst alternative is to issue a growing perpetuity.  This makes sense, because as the value to investors increases, the cost to the company must increase.  Looks like WeGrow.com needs to take a finance course!

**Problem 17**

A local bank is offering 9% interest, compounded monthly, on savings accounts. If you deposit $700 today, how much will you have in two years? How much will you have in two and one-half years?

**Solution:** The interest rate is actually $(.09/12) = .0075 = .75\%$ per month.  Since there are 24 months in two years, the future value factor is:

$$(1.0075)^{24} = 1.1964$$

Multiply the future value factor times the $700 deposit; you will have $837.49 after two years.

This problem can also be solved by first calculating the effective annual rate:

$$[1 + (.09/12)]^{12} - 1 = 9.38069\%$$

After two years, you will have:

$$\$700 \times (1.0938069)^{2} = \$837.49$$

After two and one-half years (or 30 months), you will have:

$$\$700 \times (1.0075)^{30} = \$700 \times (1.0938069)^{2.5} = \$875.89$$

**Problem 18**

For each of the following, calculate the effective annual rate:

| Stated Rate | Number of Times Compounded |
|---|---|
| 5% | semiannually |
| 11 | quarterly |
| 16 | daily |
| 20 | continuously |

**Solution:**

| Stated Rate | Number of times Compounded | Effective Rate |
|---|---|---|
| 5% | semiannually | 5.063% |
| 11 | quarterly | 11.462 |
| 16 | daily | 17.347 |
| 20 | continuously | 22.140 |

## Problem 19

A bank pays interest compounded monthly; the effective annual interest rate is 8%.  What is the quoted rate?

**Solution:**  Solve the following equation for the quoted rate:

$$[1 + (\text{quoted rate}/12)]^{12} - 1 \ = \ .08$$

$$[1 + (\text{quoted rate}/12)]^{12} \ = \ 1.08$$

$$1 + (\text{quoted rate}/12) \ = \ (1.08)^{1/12}$$

Find the twelfth root of 1.08:   $(1.08)^{1/12} \ = \ 1.006434$

$$\text{quoted rate}/12 \ = \ 1.006434 - 1 \ = \ .006434$$

$$\text{quoted rate} \ = \ 12 \times .006434 \ = \ 0.077208 \ = \ 7.7208\%$$

## Problem 20

Mike, from Problem 2, just learned that his bank is offering to change his account so that interest is compounded semi-annually, rather than annually.  Redo Problem 2 to find the value of Mike's account after 2, 5, and 10 years.

**Solution:** The period interest rate is now $.07 / 2 \ = \ 0.35 \ = \ 3.5\%$

After 2 years (4 periods), the balance will be: $FV_4 \ = \ \$3,000 \times (1.035)^4 \ + \ \$4,000 \ = \ \$7,442.57.$

After 5 years (6 additional periods), the balance will be: $FV_5 \ = \ \$7,442.75 \times (1.035)^6 + \$1,000 \ = \ \$10,148.82.$

After 10 years (10 additional periods), $FV_{10} \ = \ \$10,148.82 \times (1.035)^{10} \ = \ \$14,315.91$

Note: The subscripts on the term FV refer to the value in the *actual* year.  However, when computing that value, the *compounding interval* (the exponent) is multiplied by 2 to reflect semiannual compounding.

## Problem 21

A local loan shark offers 'four for five on payday.'   This means you borrow $4 today and you must repay $5, six days from now, when you get your next paycheque.  What is the effective annual interest rate for this loan?

**Solution:**  The interest rate is $[(5/4) - 1] \ = \ 25\%$ for 6 days.  There are about $(365/6) = 60.8333$ such periods in a year.   The effective rate is thus 1.25 raised to the power 60.8333, minus 1.  This works out to be a nice round 78.59 million %.  This is high, but it beats having your legs broken (or worse yet, "feedin' the fishies" or "going for a swim with cement boots").

## Problem 22

A local bank is offering an account that has an effective annual interest rate of 12.75%. If the bank is using continuous compounding, what is the quoted rate?

**Solution:** Solve for q in the following equation:

$$e^q - 1 = .1275$$
$$e^q = 1.1275$$

where e is the constant 2.7183. The solution requires finding the natural logarithm of both sides of the above equation. The natural logarithm of $e^r$ is r. The natural logarithm of 1.1275 is determined by using the following sequence on a financial calculator: 1.1275 [1n]. Thus, r = .12 = 12%.

If logarithms make you nervous, then it may help to know that compounding 5,000 times per year is nearly the same as continuous compounding. With this in mind, you can solve this problem the same way that Problem 15 was solved. The five thousandth root of 1.1275 is 1.000024, and (5,000 × .000024) is approximately .12.

## Problem 23

Suppose you are offered an investment that pays 13.98% continuously compounded. How long will it take your money to double?

**Solution:** There are two ways to solve this problem. First, calculate the effective annual rate and then find out how long it would take to double your money at that rate. The effective annual rate is 15%, so it will take just under five years (4.96 years) to double your money.

Alternatively, solve the following equation for t:  $\$1 \times (e^{.1398\,t}) = \$2$

Solve for t by taking the natural log of 2 and dividing by .1398. The solution is 4.96 years.

## Problem 24

An investment will increase in value by 270% over the next 17 years. What is the annual interest rate which, when compounded quarterly, provides this return?

**Solution:** Set $1 as the beginning amount. In 17 years, it will be worth $270. There are 68 quarterly compounding periods in 17 years. Then solve for the value of r:

$$\$1 \times (1 + r/4)^{68} = \$270 \qquad \text{OR} \qquad (1 + r/4)^{68} = \$270$$

$$(1 + r/4) = (270)^{1/68}$$

$$1 + r/4 = 1.085814$$

Therefore,  r = .343255 = 34.3255%. This is very easily done on a financial calculator.

## Problem 25

Attempt the following two parts independently from each other:

a) The Bank of Notreal offers a two-year Investment Certificate (IC) that pays 10% compounded annually. The Bank of Goners offers a two-year Investment Certificate that is compounded semiannually. The IC's have identical risk. What is the stated, or nominal, rate that the Bank of Goners would have to offer to make you indifferent between the two investments?

b) For a 10-year deposit, what annual rate payable semiannually will produce the same effective rate as 4% compounded continuously?

### Solution:

a) In order for you to be indifferent between the two alternatives, the returns must be equal. Therefore, you set the effective annual rate for Goners equal to the known 10% rate for Notreal. Then solve for q:

$$(1 + q/2)^2 - 1 = .10$$

Solving, we get q = 9.76%.

b)   $e^{.04 \times 10} = (1 + q/2)^{20}$

$1.491825 = (1 + q/2)^{20};\quad 1.020201 = 1 + q/2;\quad q = .040403 = 4.04\%$

## Problem 26

Suppose your firm is planning to invest in a project that will generate the following income stream: a negative flow of $250,000 per year for five years, a positive flow of $450,000 in the sixth year, and a positive flow of $650,000 per year in years 7 through 9. What is the present value of this income stream if the appropriate discount rate is 10% for the first three years and 12% thereafter?

**Solution:** With DCF valuation, we can evaluate investment opportunities when discount rates change over time.

$$
\begin{aligned}
PV &= -\$250,000 \ (\text{PVIFA } 10\%, 5) + \$450,000 \ (\text{PVIF } 12\%, 1)(\text{PVIF } 10\%,5) + \\
&\quad \ \$650,000 \ (\text{PVIFA } 12\%,3)(\text{PVIF } 12\%,1)(\text{PVIF } 10\%, 5)
\end{aligned}
$$

$= -\$250,000 \ (3.7908) + \$450,000 \ (.8929)(.6209) + \$650,000 \ (2.4018)(.8929)(.6209)$

$= -\$947,700 + \$249,480.72 + \$865,515.16$

Note: PVIF interest factors are from Table A.2.

$= \ \$167,295.88$

## Problem 27

Calculate the sum one would need to deposit today at 12% interest in order to pay the following amounts in the periods indicated:

| Period | Amount Paid (at the end of the period) |
|--------|-----------------------------------------|
| 6 | $1,000,000 |
| 7 | 2,000,000 |
| 8 | 2,500,000 |

**Solution:**  $1,000,000 (.5066) + $2,000,000 (.4523) + $2,500,000 (.4039) = $2,420,950

## Problem 28

A lease financing company has determined that it must charge 14% on amortized loans in order to be profitable. What semiannual payment would be required from a borrower who would pay off a four-year loan of $25,000 assuming beginning-of-period payments?

**Solution:**  Semiannual payment = $25,000 / [(PVIFA 7%,7) + 1] = $25,000 / 6.3893 = $3,912.79

## Problem 29

You intend to open a business three years from today, after you have finished your bachelor's in business administration.  You currently have $30,000 in your savings account and estimate that capital expenditures of $27,500 per year-end for six years after the business opens, will be necessary. The only other source available to you (other than your own funds) will be a loan from your generous Aunt Looney. How much will Aunt Looney have to lend you the day the business opens? Assume the appropriate interest rate is 12% throughout the period.

**Solution:** Funds Required: $27,500 (PVIFA 12%, 6) = $27,500 (4.1114) = $113,063.50

Savings in FV:  = $30,000 (FVIF 12%, 3) = $30,000 (1.4049) = $42,147

Borrow (113,063.50 – 42,147) = $70,916.50

## Problem 30

Expansion of your business has resulted in moving to a new building. This entails obtaining a new 25 year mortgage of $100,000 at an annual rate of 12% fixed for a five year term. What is the effective monthly interest rate and the monthly payments?

**Solution:** First, we convert the quoted semiannual rate to an EAR:

$$EAR = [1 + .12/2]^2 - 1 = 12.36\%$$

Then we find the effective monthly rate:

$$= \ (1.1236)^{1/12} - 1 \ = \ .009759$$

To find the payments, we use the annuity present value formula:

$$\$100,000 \ = \ C \times (1 - 1/1.009759^{300}) / .009759$$

$$\$100,000 \ = \ C \times 96.906953$$

$$C = \$1,031.92$$

## Problem 31

Given the information in Problem 30, attempt the following two parts independently from each other.

a) What portion of the first payment will be for interest and what portion represents the payment of principal?

b) Suppose the mortgage was variable-rate where interest is compounded monthly.  However, assuming that interest rates do not fluctuate during the first year, what are the monthly payments? Are you better or worse off with the variable rate mortgage?

**Solution:**

a)      $\$100,000 \times .009759 = \$975.90$  will be interest and only $\$56.02$ ($\$1,031.92 - \$975.90$) for payment of principal.

b)      Using monthly compounding the payments would be:

$$\$100,000 \ = \ C \times \{1 - [1/(1.01)^{300}]\} / \ 0.01$$

$$C \ = \ \$1,053.22$$

You are worse off by $\$21.30$ if the variable rate mortgage is chosen ($\$1,053.22 - \$1,031.92$)
Note: The effective monthly rate is $[1 + (0.12 / 12)]^{12} - 1 \ = \ 0.01$.

## Problem 32

Suppose your firm needs $\$100,000$ in working capital and your bank manager has responded with the following three alternatives:

1)      A lump sum repayment of $\$133,100$ payable at the end of three years.

2)      An interest-only loan where your firm must pay $\$10,500$ for each of the next two years plus $\$110,500$ at the end of the third year.

3)      Annual end-of-period payments of $\$40,921.31$ for each of the next three years.

What alternative should your firm choose?

**Solution:**  Alternative 1 represents a pure discount loan, where the interest rate is 10% [$133,100/(1 + r)^3$]. Since alternative 2 is an interest-only loan, the interest rate is 10.5%  = ($10,500/$100,000). Alternative 3 is an amortized loan where the interest rate works out to 11% [$40,921.31 = $100,000/PVIFA r%, 3$].

Note: The PVIF ($100,000 / $40,921.31  =  2.4427) was found by looking in the row for three periods.  The PFIV factor is approximately between the factors for 10% and 12%.

Your firm should select alternative 1.

# 7     <u>Interest Rates and Bond Valuation</u>

## CHAPTER HIGHLIGHTS

This chapter extends the present value concepts introduced in Chapters 5 and 6 to the valuation of bonds. It then discusses the basic features of bonds and how they are traded in financial markets. Finally, it explains the way in which bond values depend on interest rates. We will also discuss the function of interest rates in our economy and factors which cause them to change.

It is important while studying this chapter to remember that the value of a bond, or any other security, is simply the present value of the future cash payments to the holder of the security.

## BONDS AND BOND VALUATION

Bonds are long-term debt securities issued by corporations as well as governmental units, including the Bank of Canada, and provincial and municipal governments. Although bonds can take many different forms, the basic form discussed in this section is the level-coupon bond. The valuation of these securities is based on the present value concepts developed in the preceding chapter.

**Bond Features and Prices:** Bond owners are typically paid only the interest on the loan every period; the principal is not repaid until the end of the loan. A *level-coupon bond* promises regular interest payments (either annually or semi-annually), as well as a specified principal payment, or face value, at the *maturity date*. The annual interest payment is called the bond's *coupon interest payment*, or simply *coupon* for short. The face value is also referred to as the *par value* or *maturity value* of the bond.

**An Example:** Consider a corporate bond issued by MAM industries. The bond promises a 9% coupon rate and has a face value of $1,000, payable on January 1, 2015. The annual interest payment to the bondholder is the coupon rate times the face value: .09 × $1,000 = $90 per year. The *maturity date* is January 1, 2015. This is the date of the last interest payment and the date of the principal repayment to the bondholder. If today is January 1, 1995, there are still 20 years of coupon payments left. Therefore, the *maturity* of the bond is 20 years. So, bondholders will receive $90 interest per year for 20 years, and they will also receive the $1,000 face value at the end of 20 years.

For most bonds, the coupon payment is made in the form of two semiannual payments. In this case the semi-annual coupon payment would be $90/2 = $45. Most of the examples and problems in this study guide will be based on semiannual payments.

Note:    When working problems based on semiannual coupon payments, remember to make three adjustments:

      1.     coupon payment is ½ the annual payment ($45)
      2.     number of periods = 2 × years to maturity (20 × 2 = 40)
      3.     discount rate = ½ annual rate (.12/2 = .06)

Note: The discount rate of 12% is the same rate investors would earn on other bonds of similar risk and maturity. This is the annual discount rate; 6% represents the rate for one 6-month period.

**Bond Values and Yields:**   The value of the MAM Industries bond is the present value of the future coupon payments and principal payment discounted at the appropriate opportunity cost for bonds of similar characteristics. The opportunity cost is the rate of return, or yield, available on other corporate bonds with approximately 20 years to maturity and risk level comparable to that of the MAM bond.  If the market interest rate for such bonds is 12%, then the value of the MAM bond is given by:

$$PV = \$45 / (1.06)^1 + \$45 / (1.06)^2 + ... + \$45 / (1.06)^{40} + \$1,000 / (1.06)^{40} = \$774.31$$

In general, the above calculation can be represented as follows:

$$P = C / (1 + r)^1 + C / (1 + r)^2 + ... + C / (1 + r)^t + \$1,000 / (1 + r)^t$$

Where C is the semiannual coupon payment, t is the number of semiannual time periods to the maturity date, r is the appropriate semiannual opportunity cost, and $1,000 is the principal payment at maturity.  Since the coupon payments are in the form of an annuity, the above equation can be rewritten as:

$$PV = C \times PVIFA(r,t) + \$1,000 / (1 + r)^t$$

where:  $PVIFA(r,t) = \{1 - [1/(1 + r)^t]\} / r$

Recall that PVIFA(r,t) can be determined by using either the above formula or Table A.3. Using the formula, the value of PVIFA(r,t) for the MAM Industries bond is:

$$PVIFA(6\%,40) = \{1 - [1/(1.06)^{40}]\} / .06 = \{1 - .0972222\} / .06 = 15.046297$$

Therefore, the present value of the bond is calculated as follows:

$$PV = [\$45 \times PVIFA(6\%,40)] + \$1,000 / (1.06)^{40}$$

$$= (\$45 \times 15.046297) + (\$1,000 \times .0972222) = \$774.31$$

Notice that the bond value is simply the present value of the stream of coupon payments plus the present value of the face value paid when the bond matures.

The interest rate required in the market (12% in the example above) is also known as the bond's *yield to maturity,* or YTM.  Bond yields are quoted like APRs; the quoted rate is equal to the actual rate per period multiplied by the number of periods per year.  In our case, the yield is 6% every six months, or .06 x 2 = .12 = 12% per year.  To calculate the effective yield on this bond, note that 6% every six months is equivalent to: Effective annual rate = (1 + .06)$^2$ − 1 = 12.36%. The effective yield, therefore, is 12.36%.

Further discussion of the level-coupon bond described above can provide insight regarding two additional aspects of bond valuation: the relationship between interest rates and bond prices, and the concept of a bond's yield to maturity, which is the rate of return for a bond.

A change in the market interest rate changes the value of the bond.  Suppose an investor purchased the bond for $744.31 and, immediately after, market interest rates increased from 12% to 14%.  If the investor wants to sell the bond, he will no longer be able to sell it for the same price.  The bond, if bought at $744.31 is providing a 12% return.  Other investors will find this unacceptable because other bonds return 14%. Therefore, they will no longer pay $744.31 for the bond. The new price of the bond will be:

$$PV = [\$45 \times PVIFA(7\%,40)] + \$1,000 / (1.07)^{40}$$

$$= (\$45 \times 13.331709) + (\$1,000 \times .066780) = \$666.71$$

Mathematically, it is clear that the value of the bond decreases when the market rate of interest increases, because the interest rate is in the denominator of the basic present value formula. An increase in the denominator reduces the present value.

A decrease in the market rate of interest increases the value of the bond. For example, if YTM = 8%, then the value of the bond is:

$$PV = [\$45 \times PVIFA(4\%,40)] + \$1,000 / (1.04)^{40}$$

$$= (\$45 \times 19.792774) + (\$1,000 \times .208289) = \$1,098.96$$

The fact that the bond's value increases with the decrease in interest rates is consistent with both a mathematical and an intuitive understanding of the relationship between interest rates and bond values. From a mathematical perspective, the decrease in the appropriate discount rate from 12% to 8% results in an increase in the value of the bond because the discount rate is in the denominator of the basic present value calculation; a decrease in the size of the denominator increases the present value.

To understand this result intuitively, we again suppose that an investor bought the bond at a price of $774.31, when the market rate of interest was 12%. If the market rate of interest then declines to 8%, the holder of the bond is not willing to sell the bond for $774.31. At that price, a subsequent buyer would be earning a 12% rate of interest at a time when the rate available on comparable bonds is only 8%. Therefore, the holder of the bond would be able to sell the bond at a higher price (i.e., $1,098.96). The price is determined such that a subsequent buyer would earn the new 8% market rate of interest. A subsequent buyer would not be willing to pay a price higher than $1,098.96, because the buyer would then earn less than the 8% market interest rate. On the other hand, the current owner of the bond has no incentive to sell it for less than $1,098.96, since a subsequent buyer would be satisfied with a price at which he earns the current 8% market rate.

When the bond value is greater than its $1,000 face value, the bond is said to be selling at a *premium* and is referred to as a *premium bond*. A bond which sells for less than face value is selling at a *discount* and is called a *discount bond*. When the market rate of interest is equal to the bond's coupon rate (i.e., 9% in this case), the bond value is $1,000. An investor who pays $1,000 for a bond and receives annual coupon payments of $90 earns a 9% rate of return on the investment.

**Interest Rate Risk:**   An investor buying a bond is faced with the possibility that the value of the bond will change if market interest rates change. The risk that arises for bond owners from fluctuating interest rates is called *interest rate risk*. The amount of interest rate risk depends on how sensitive the bond's price is to changes in interest rates. This sensitivity depends on two things:

1.   time left until maturity: interest rate risk increases as time to maturity increases
2.   coupon rate: interest rate risk increases as coupon rates are lowered

The reason that longer-term bonds have greater interest rate sensitivity is that a large portion of the bond's value comes from the $1,000 face amount. The present value of the amount isn't greatly affected by a change in interest rate if it is to be received in one year, as opposed to 20 years. Similarly, if two bonds with different coupon rates have the same maturity, the value of the lower-coupon bond is proportionately more dependent on the face amount to be received at maturity. As a result, its value will fluctuate more as interest rates change. In other words, the higher-coupon bond has a larger cash flow early in its life, so its value is less sensitive to changes in the discount rate.

**Finding the Yield to Maturity:**    An understanding of the relationship between interest rates and bond values is essential in determining the rate of return, or yield to maturity, for a given bond. For example, suppose that the MAM bond described earlier is known to be selling for $915. What yield to maturity will an investor who purchases the bond for this price earn? To simplify, we will assume that coupon payments are made *annually*. Therefore, the values calculated in the above example will change slightly. Specifically, when r = 8%, PV = $1,098.18; when r = 12%, PV = $775.92. The answer to this question is the value of r which solves the equation:

$$PV \ = \ [C \times PVIFA(r,t)] \ + \ \$1,000 \,/\,(1+r)^t$$

$$\$915 \ = \ [\$90 \times PVIFA(r,20)] \ + \ \$1,000 \,/\,(1+r)^{20}$$

This equation can also be written as:

$$\$915 \ = \ \$90 \times \{\,1 - [\,1/(1+r)^{20}\,]\,\}\,/\,r \ + \ \$1,000 \,/\,(1+r)^{20}$$

Even though there is only one unknown in this equation, it is not mathematically possible to solve for r directly. The solution can, however, be obtained in three alternative ways: using a trial-and-error approach (taking successive 'guesses' at the value of r which solves the equation); using a financial calculator; or, using a shortcut formula.

Also notice that when r is equal to the coupon rate (i.e., 9% for this bond):

$$PV \ = \ (C/r) \ = \ (\$90/.09) \ = \ \$1,000$$

Given the inverse relationship between interest rates and bond prices, it is clear that the yield to maturity for the bond selling at a price of $915 is between 9% and 12%. A good starting 'guess' is that r is approximately 10% or 11%; if r = 11%, PV = $840.73. Since a decrease in r increases PV, the next 'trial' or 'guess' should be 10%, resulting in PV = $914.86. (Note: these last two PV calculations are obtained with a financial calculator; they can also be computed using the PVIF and PVIFA tables in Appendix A.) Therefore, for a purchase price of $915, the yield to maturity is approximately 10%.

The precise yield to maturity can be found using a financial calculator. But again, if you're using a calculator **be sure you know to how solve the problems using your calculator before taking a test!**

There is also a shortcut to guessing the yield on a bond; it uses the following approximate yield formula:

$$Yield \ = \ \frac{[Coupon + (Face\ Value - Price)/Maturity]}{(Price + Face\ Value)/2}$$

In the example above, the approximate yield is:

$$Yield \ = \ \frac{[\$90 + (\$1,000 - \$915)/20]}{(\$915 + \$1,000)/2} \ = \ 9.84\%$$

Although the shortcut approximation is a good starting point, it ignores the time value of money and can be significantly different from the true yield when the bond is selling at a large premium or discount.

## MORE ON BOND FEATURES

A debt is a promise to repay principal (i.e., the original amount of the loan) plus interest at a specified time to the *lender,* or *creditor.* The corporation is the *debtor* or *borrower,* and the amount owed to the creditor is a liability of the corporation.

Three features distinguish debt from equity:

1.   Debt does not represent an ownership interest; creditors have no voting power.
2.   Interest paid on debt is tax-deductible; dividends paid to shareholders are not.
3.   Failure to pay creditors can result in bankruptcy; thus there is a cost to issuing debt which is not present if the firm issues equity.

**Is it Debt or Equity?**   With the many types of securities available to corporations and investors today, it is not always clear whether a particular security is debt or equity.  In general though, equity represents an ownership interest in the firm.  Shareholders have a residual claim, meaning that they are paid after debt holders.  This affects both the risks and benefits of holding one security or the other.

**Long-term Debt - The Basics:**   Debt securities are often classified according to the maturity of the debt, which is the length of time that an unpaid balance remains outstanding.  Debt that matures within one year is considered short-term debt; debt with a maturity greater than one year is considered long-term debt.

Typically, corporate debt securities are notes, debentures, or bonds.  Strictly speaking, a *bond* is secured debt; however, the word 'bond' is often used generically.  A note is a debt security with a maturity less than 10 years.

A long-term debt security can also be classified by whether it is a public issue or a private placement.  This chapter discusses primarily publicly issued debt, which means it is sold to the general public.  The terms of privately placed debt are negotiated directly between the borrower and the lender, and the security is issued directly to the lender, rather than to the general public. The remainder of this section discusses many of the provisions of publicly issued long-term debt securities.

There are many other dimensions to long-term debt, including such things as security, call features, sinking funds, ratings, and protective covenants.   The table on page 203 of your text lists and gives a brief explanation of many of these features.  They are discussed in more detail below.

**The Indenture:**   The *indenture* is the written agreement between the corporation and its bondholders. The indenture sets forth the terms of the loan (the interest rate, the maturity date, the property which serves as security for the loan, and other features) and identifies all *protective covenants* which restrict certain actions on the part of the corporation. The indenture also identifies the *trustee* appointed by the corporation to represent the bondholders.  The trustee's job is to make sure that the terms of the indenture are obeyed.

**Terms of a Bond:** Long-term corporate debt is usually issued as a bond with a principal (face) value of $1,000. Annual interest is generally specified as a coupon rate equal to a percentage of face value.  Interest payments are made semiannually.  A bond with interest payments equal to 8.4% of face value might pay $42 on March 1 and September 1 of each year. Principal, plus the last interest payment, is repaid to the bondholder on the maturity date.

Bonds can be either *registered bonds* or *bearer bonds*. For registered bonds, the company mails the interest payment directly to the owner of record.  Bearer bonds have dated coupons attached. The bondholder must detach a coupon and mail it to the company; the company mails the interest payment to the coupon holder.  Ownership of a bearer bond is not registered with the company.  Therefore, recovery is more difficult if the bonds are lost or stolen.  However, since bearer bonds are not easily traceable, they may have advantages to some investors.

**Security:** Debt securities differ with regard to the collateral pledged as security for the repayment of debt. *Mortgage securities* are secured by a mortgage on real property, usually real estate.  The mortgage is described in a legal document called the mortgage-trust indenture or trust deed.  An open-end mortgage permits the company to issue additional mortgage bonds on the specified property, while a closed-end mortgage restricts the company's ability to do so.  A mortgage may be on a specific piece of property (a building, for example) or it may be a *blanket mortgage* which pledges all of the company's real property.

A *debenture* is not secured by specific property.  Holders of debentures are paid only when all claims to secured debt have been satisfied.  Most of the corporate bonds issued today are debentures, although public utilities and railroads issue primarily mortgage bonds.

**Seniority:** *Seniority* governs priority of payment to creditors in the event of bankruptcy.  Some debt is *subordinated,* which means that other creditors must be repaid first in the event of bankruptcy.

**Repayment:** The face value of most corporate bonds is repaid prior to maturity.  For public issues, repayment takes place through the use of a sinking fund or a call provision (described in the next section). A *sinking fund* requires the corporation to make annual payments to the bond trustee, who then repurchases bonds.  Bonds may be either repurchased in the open market or selected by lottery and redeemed at a specified price.

Sinking fund arrangements vary.  Most start between five and ten years after the original issue date.  Some call for equal annual payments throughout the life of the bond.  The amount paid into the sinking fund may be insufficient to redeem the entire issue so that the corporation must make a large 'balloon' payment at maturity. Sinking funds provide additional security to bondholders by providing for the orderly retirement of debt and by serving as an early warning system regarding potential problems.

**The Call Provision:**  A *call provision* allows the company to repurchase, or call, the entire debt issue prior to maturity at a specified price.  Most debentures are callable.  The call price is usually the face value of the bond plus a *call premium*.  The call premium might be one year's interest initially and decrease every year as maturity approaches.  Often, bonds cannot be called for some number of years following issue (a *deferred call*) and are said to be *call protected* during this period.

**Protective Covenants:** A *protective covenant* restricts certain actions of the company.  A *negative covenant* (such as a dividend restriction) disallows certain actions.  A *positive covenant* (such as a requirement that working capital be maintained at a specified minimum level) requires that certain actions be taken by the corporation.

## BOND RATINGS

Firms typically pay to have a credit rating assigned to their bonds by either one or both of the two leading bond rating firms in Canada: Canadian Bond Rating Service (CBRS) and Dominion Bond Rating Service (DBRS). The largest U.S. rating agencies are Moody's Investor Services and Standard & Poor's Corporation (S&P).  Bonds are rated according to the likelihood of default and the protection afforded the bondholders in the event of default.  The two highest ratings are AAA and AA (DBRS) or A++ and A+ (CBRS).  These ratings indicate a very low probability of default.  Bonds rated at least BBB (DBRS) or B++ (CBRS) are considered investment grade, while lower-rate bonds are referred to as low-grade or high-yield bonds, commonly called 'junk' bonds.  A bond  in default is given a C rating. Because of their higher risk, bonds with lower ratings pay higher interest rates.

## SOME DIFFERENT TYPES OF BONDS

In this section, we discuss the basic features of some bonds with unusual characteristics.

**Financial Engineering:** The design of new securities is referred to as *financial engineering*. The goal of financial engineering is to minimize taxes and to reduce and control risk. In addition, financial engineering may help reduce costs associated with issuing and servicing debt and complying with various regulations. Some debt instruments created through the process of financial engineering are described below.

**Stripped Bonds:** Bonds that pay no coupons are called stripped bonds or zero-coupon bonds. These bonds sell at a price much lower than the par value. Consider a 10-year stripped bond issued when the market rate of interest is 10%. The bond price is $1,000, discounted at 10% for 10 years:

$$PV = [\$1,000/(1.10)^{10}] = \$385.54$$

Over the life of the bond, the issuer pays ($1,000 - $385.54) = $614.46 in interest. The issuer deducts interest every year for tax purposes, even though no interest is paid. And, the owner pays taxes on accrued interest every year, even though no interest is received until maturity. Stripped bonds are popular with tax-exempt investors.

**Floating-Rate Bonds:** The coupon interest payments on a *floating-rate* bond are adjusted as interest rates change. This adjustment is based on an interest rate index such as the Treasury bill interest rate. The value of a floating-rate bond depends on the nature of the adjustment mechanism and the frequency of the adjustments. Most 'floaters' have a 'put' provision giving the holder the option to redeem the bond at face value. Usually, a put provision takes effect following a specified time period after the bond is issued. Another feature of most floaters is a floor-and-ceiling provision, specifying the minimum and maximum coupon rates payable throughout the life of the bond.

**Other Types of Bonds:** The coupon payment for an *income bond* depends on corporate income. The firm is obligated to make interest payments only if income is sufficient. Income bonds offer the advantage of the tax deduction for interest expense without the risk of financial distress; an income bond is not in default when a coupon payment is omitted due to insufficient income. Despite these advantages, corporations rarely issue income bonds.

Other kinds of bonds include *convertible bonds* and *retractable bonds* (put bonds), which are discussed in more detail in Chapter 25.

## BOND MARKETS

There is a huge trading volume in bonds every day, much larger than the trading volume in stocks. In fact, the largest securities market in the world, in terms of volume, is the U.S. Treasury market, which oversees the trading of U.S. government securities.

**How Bonds Are Bought and Sold:** Most bonds are traded *over the counter* (OTC). Dealers all around the world are connected electronically. While most firms have only one stock issue outstanding, they typically have many bond issues outstanding. This means that the number of bond issues is far greater than the number of stock issues. We say that the bond market has very little *transparency*, mostly because it is an OTC market. This means it is difficult for investors to observe trading prices and volume. Transactions are often privately negotiated, and there is little centralized reporting of transactions. Although the trading volume of bonds exceeds that of stocks, only a small portion of total bond issues trade on a given day. This adds to the difficulty in getting current and accurate bond prices.

## INFLATION AND INTEREST RATES

This section discusses the importance of inflation on interest rates, bond yields, and returns.

**Real versus Nominal Rates:** *Nominal rates* are interest rates that have not been adjusted for the effect of inflation. *Real rates*, on the other hand, have been adjusted for inflation. If prices are increasing by 3% a year, then we say the inflation rate is 3%. The real rate is concerned with whether or not $1 will purchase the same amount of goods after adjusting for inflation. When inflation is increasing, the nominal rate is adjusted downward to reflect that prices are higher in real dollar terms. As an example, suppose you invest $50 in an account that pays a nominal rate of 10%. That means you will have $55 at the end of the year. The return on your investment is clearly 10%, but we have not considered the impact of inflation. Suppose that inexpensive winter scarves sell for $10 each at the beginning of the year. With $50, you could buy five scarves. By the end of the year, the price of the scarves has increased by 3% to $10.30 each. Your $55 will now buy you  $55 / $10.30  =  5.34 scarves. The rate of return on the scarves is (5.34/5) - 1  =  6.8%. So, even though the nominal return on the investment was 10%, buying power went up only 6.8%. So, your real rate of return is 6.8%. (The remaining 3.2% is due to inflation.)

**The Fisher Effect:** The Fisher effect describes mathematically the relationship between the real and nominal rates of interest and the rate of inflation. This relationship is expressed by the equation:

$$1 + R  =  (1 + r) \times (1 + h)$$

where R is the nominal rate of interest, r is the real rate, and h is the inflation rate. Rearranging:

$$R  =  r + h + (r \times h)$$

This equation tells us that the three components of the nominal rate are: the real rate, the inflation rate (which compensates for the decrease in the purchasing value of money), and (r x h), which compensates for the loss in value on your investment earnings due to inflation. The third term is very small and is usually dropped from the equation. So, the Fisher effect is usually stated simply as:

$$R  \approx r + h$$

**An Example:** Investors require a 12% rate of return, and the inflation rate is 4%. What is the exact nominal rate? The approximate nominal rate?

      Exact rate:  $1 + R  =  (1.12  \times  1.04)  =  1.1648$   Or   $R  =  16.48\%$

      Approximate rate   $R  =  .12  +  .04  =  .16  =  16\%$

## DETERMINANTS OF BOND YIELDS

Bond yields depend on many factors. These are discussed below.

**The Term Structure of Interest Rates:** The *term structure of interest rates* establishes the relationship between short-term and long-term interest rates. Specifically, it tells us the nominal interest rates on default-free, pure discount bonds with different maturities. It represents the 'pure' time value of money for different lengths of time.

The graphical representation of the term structure is referred to as the *yield curve*. Usually, the yield curve is upward-sloping because long-term rates are higher than short-term rates. It can also be downward-sloping if short-term rates are higher. A 'humped' term structure occurs when rates rise at first, then fall with increasing maturity. Three basic factors influence the shape of the term structure:

    1.  The real rate of interest

    2.  The rate of inflation

    3.  The interest rate risk premium

The real rate of interest compensates investors for the pure time value of money. It influences the *level* of interest rates, rather than the actual shape of the term structure. Term structure *shape* is strongly influenced by investors' expectations about future inflation rates. If they expect inflation to increase, they will demand a higher nominal rate as compensation for the loss of future purchasing power. This addition to the real rate is referred to as the *inflation premium*. Finally, longer-term bonds are more subject to price changes due to changes in interest rates. The compensation required by investors for bearing this additional risk is referred to as the *interest rate risk premium*.

So far, the discussion has involved essentially default-free bonds. What we know as the yield curve typically uses the default-free bonds of the Government of Canada. In determining an appropriate yield for a corporate or municipal bond, investors consider the probability of default. The additional compensation for bearing this default risk is referred to as the *default risk premium*. An additional consideration is that Canadian bonds are taxable; corporate bonds are not. Taxability, therefore, is another concern for investors.

Finally, investors prefer liquid, rather than illiquid, securities. Therefore, they also demand additional compensation if they buy a relatively less liquid bond. This compensation is referred to as the *liquidity risk premium*.

## ON DURATION (APPENDIX 7A)

*Duration* is a measure of a bond's *effective maturity*. We learned earlier that fluctuations in bond value due to interest rate changes depend on the bond's coupon and its maturity. Duration incorporates both these factors to allow us to measure how sensitive a bond's price is to changes in interest rates.

First, note that for pure discount bonds, only the time to maturity affects interest rate sensitivity (because there are no coupon payments). So, time to maturity would be an appropriate measure of volatility. Duration enables us to compute an effective maturity that allows us to measure this volatility for bonds that pay coupons. Essentially, we are determining the *average maturity* of the various payments received by the bondholders.

Duration is computed as follows:

    1.     Compute the present value of each payment
    2.     Calculate the relative value of each payment as the ratio of the
            payment's present value to the value of the bond
    3.     Weight the maturity of each payment by its relative value

The bond's duration is the sum of these weighted payments. In general, bonds with a higher duration have more sensitivity to interest rate changes than those with lower durations.

**An Example:** Calculate the duration of a three-year bond, with a coupon rate of 9%.

First, we calculate the present value of each payment:

$$PV \text{ (Pymt 1)} = \$90 / 1.09 = \$82.57$$

$$PV(\text{Pymt 2}) = \$90 / (1.09)^2 = \$75.75$$

$$PV(\text{Pymt 3}) = \$1,090 / (1.09)^3 = \$841.68$$

Note that the payment in period 3 includes both a coupon payment and repayment of the principal.  Note also that the sum of these present values is the same as the value of the bond we computed above.

Now find the relative weight of each payment:

$$\text{Pymt 1} = \$82.57 / \$1,000 = .082570$$

$$\text{Pymt 2} = \$75.75 / \$1,000 = .075750$$

$$\text{Pymt 3} = \$841.68 / \$1,000 = .841680$$

To find the duration, we multiply the maturity of each payment by its relative weight

$$\text{Duration} = 1 \times .082570 + 2 \times .075750 + 3 \times .841680 = 2.759 \text{ years}$$

## CALLABLE BONDS AND BOND REFUNDING (APPENDIX 7C)

**The Call Provision:** *Bond refunding* is the process of replacing all or part of a bond issue. Call provisions have value to the issuing firm.  If interest rates decline subsequent to the original issue of the bond, the firm has the option to replace the bond issue with bonds paying a lower interest rate. On the other hand, a call provision is disadvantageous for bondholders.  Bonds are called when interest rates decline, so that bondholders are forced to sell their bonds back to the issuing company and are then unable to earn a return on their investment equal to that earned on the called bond.  Consequently, bondholders require compensation for the possibility that their bonds may be called away.  As a result, a firm must pay a higher interest rate on a callable bond than on a comparable non-callable bond.

**Cost of the Call Provision:** Suppose a firm plans to issue a perpetual bond which pays 9% interest.  There is an equal chance that the market interest rate will be either 11.25% or 7.5% one year from now.  What is the price of the bond today if it is not callable?  The price is the present value of next year's coupon interest payment plus the present value of next year's expected price. Since the bond is a perpetuity, its value at the end of the year will be either ($90/.1125) = $800 or ($90/.075) = $1,200.  The expected value of the future price is [.5($800) + .5($1,200)] = $1,000.  Therefore, the price of the bond today is:

$$P_{NC} = \frac{\$90 + \$1,000}{1.09} = \$1,000$$

where $P_{NC}$ is the price of the bond if it is not callable.

Now suppose the bond described above is callable next year at $1,090, and that it will be called if the interest rate drops to 7.5%. What must the coupon interest payment (C) be in order for the firm to be able to issue the bond at the par value of $1,000? At the end of the year, the bondholder will have an interest payment of C dollars plus either $1,090 (the call price) or a bond worth (C/.1125). The expected value of the future price is therefore:

$$.50(\$1,090) + .50(C/.1125)$$

In order for the bond to sell for $1,000 today, the present value of the coupon interest payment (C) plus the present value of the expected future price must equal $1,000:

$$P_C \quad = \quad \$1,000 \quad = \quad \frac{C + [(.50)(\$1,090) + (.50)(C/.1125)]}{1.09}$$

where $P_C$ is the price of the callable bond. Solving for C, we find that the coupon payment must be $100.10. This is the coupon interest payment the firm must pay to sell the callable bond for $1,000. (Recall that the coupon interest payment for the noncallable bond is $90.)

The cost of the call provision to the issuing firm can be determined by computing the price at which the firm could sell a bond with C = $100.10 if the bond is *not* callable. This price ($P_{NC}$) is equal to the present value of next year's coupon interest payment plus the present value of next year's expected price. Since the bond is a perpetuity, its value at the end of the year will be either ($100.10/.075) = $1,334.67 or ($100.10/.1125) = $889.78. The expected value of next year's price is [.5($1,334.67) + .5($889.78)] = $1,112.225.

$$P_{NC} \quad = \quad \frac{\$100.10 + \$1,112.225}{1.09} \quad = \quad \$1,112.23$$

The difference $P_{NC} - P_C$ = $1,112.23 - $1,000) = $112.23, so the firm is paying $112.23 for the call option.

**Value of the Call Provision:** The value of the call provision is the present value of the firm's interest savings minus the present value of the call premium. If the bond above is called one year from now, the coupon interest payment would decline from $100.10 to (.075 x $1,000) = $75, for interest savings of ($100.10 - $75) = $25.10. This is a perpetuity of $25.10, which has a present value, as of next year, of ($25.10/.075) = $334.67. However, the call premium next year will be $90, so the net savings equals ($334.67- $90) = $244.67. Since there is only a 50% probability that the interest rate will decline, there is only a 50% probability that the savings will be realized. Therefore, the expected value of the savings is (.50 x $224.67) = $112.34 and the present value is ($122.34 / 1.09) = $112.24. Except for a rounding error, this is identical to the cost of the call provision computed earlier. This result indicates that the net present value of the call provision, to either the issuer or the bondholders, is zero, because the bondholders require compensation for the call provision which exactly offsets their expected loss.

## THE REFUNDING ISSUE

**When Should Firms Refund Callable Bonds?** A firm should refund callable bonds when the net present value of the refunding is positive. In other words, the firm will refund the callable bonds next year if the net present value of the transaction, at that time, is positive. If the market rate of interest declines to 7.5% one year from now, then the present value of the savings on interest payments is the present value of the $25.10 perpetuity, or ($25.10/.075) = $334.67. Since the call premium is $90, the net present value is ($334.67 - $90) = $224.67, as we computed earlier. The bond should be refunded next year if the market interest rate declines to 7.5%, because the net present value of the refunding, at that time, would be positive.

Continue to assume that:

1. Bonds are perpetuities
2. There are no taxes
3. There are no refunding costs other than the call premium and the refunding is instantaneous (no overlap period)
4. The refunding takes place today

The following notation is used

$C_O$ = Coupon rate on outstanding bonds
$C_N$ = Coupon rate on new issue, equal to the current market rate
$CP$ = Call of premium per bond
$[(C_O - C_N) (\$1,000)] / C_N$ = PV of interest savings
$NPV = [(C_O - C_N) \times (\$1,000)] / C_N - CP$

**An Example:**   Assume that Minerva, Inc., has outstanding bonds originally issued with a 16.3% coupon. The market interest rate is 7% and the call premium is 18%. What is the NPV of refunding?

$$NPV = [(.163 - .07) (\$1,000)] / .07 - [(\$1,000) (.18)]$$

$$= \$1,328.57 - \$180 = \$1,148.57 \text{ per bond}$$

**Relaxing the Assumptions:**   Realistically, the refunding procedure must incorporate finite maturities, taxes, flotation costs, and an overlap period that incorporates the timing problem of issuing new bonds while the outstanding issue comes in. These can be best understood by following the procedure outlined in the solution to the example below.

**An Example:**   WeCall Inc. has a $25 million outstanding bond issue bearing a 15% coupon sold to the public in 1987. The bonds mature in 2002 but are callable today for a 6% call premium. Investment bankers have assured WeCall that a new $30 million, nine-year issue, also maturing in 2002, can be sold with a 10% coupon. The new bonds will be sold two months before the old bonds are to be called, in order to eliminate timing problems with the two issues. Although WeCall has to pay the coupons on both issues during these two months, the issue can be invested at 8% interest in the bank. The flotation costs for the $25 million issue would be $1,406,250 and the firm's tax rate is 30%. Should the bonds be refunded?

The analysis can be broken down into three steps: the cost of refunding, interest savings, and the NPV.

**Cost of Refunding:**   This step consists of: the call premium, the flotation costs and related tax savings, and any extra interest that must be paid or can be earned. Call premium = 0.06 x ($25,000,000) = $1,500,000. Note, the call premium is not tax-deductible. Flotation costs are amortized over the life of the issue or five years, whichever is less. For WeCall: $1,406,250/5 = $281,250 which produces an annual tax shield of $84,375 ($281,250 x .30). The present value of this tax shield is discounted at the after-tax cost of new debt [.10(1 - .30) = 7%] which amounts to: $84,375 (PVIFA 7%,5) = $84,375 (4.100197) = $345,954.12. Therefore, the after-tax flotation costs are:

| | |
|---|---|
| Flotation costs | $1,406,250.00 |
| PV of tax savings | (345,954.12) |
| After-tax cost | $1,060,295.88 |

The incremental interest paid (after taxes) is calculated as the difference between the interest earned by investing the new issue at the short-term rate and the interest paid on the old issue during the overlap period.

Extra interest paid on the old issue after tax is: $25,000,000 (.15 ) (2/12) (1 - .30) = $437,500. This is offset by the interest earned on the new issue after taxes: $25,000,000 (.08) (2/12) (1 - .30) = $233,333.33.

Total additional interest is:

| | |
|---|---|
| Extra interest paid | $ 437,500.00 |
| Extra interest earned | ( 233,333.33) |
| Total additional interest | $ 204,166.67 |

These three items give us the total cost of refunding:

| | |
|---|---|
| Call premium | $1,500,000.00 |
| Flotation costs | 1,060,295.88 |
| Additional interest | 204,166.67 |
| Total after-tax investment | $2,764,462.55 |

**Interest Savings:**  The annual incremental interest savings after taxes is: $25,000,000 (.15 - .10)(1 - .30) = $875,000. The PV of annual savings over nine years is $875,000 x PVIFA (7%,9) = $875,000 x (6.515232) = $5,700,828.00.

**NPV for Refunding:**  The NPV consists of interest savings less the cost of refunding:

| | |
|---|---|
| Interest savings | $5,700,828.00 |
| Cost of refunding | 2,764,462.55 |
| NPV | $2,936,365.45 |

WeCall Inc. can save almost $3 million by proceeding to call in the old bond issue and refunding them with the new issue.  This example illustrates the importance of a call provision when interest rates are relatively high.

## CONCEPT TEST

1.   A long-term debt instrument issued by a corporation is called a _____.

2.   A long-term debt instrument promising regular interest payments and a specified principal payment at a specified date is called a _____.  The regular interest payment is called the _____ payment and the principal payment is called either the _____ value, the _____ value or the _____ value.

3.   The principal payment for most corporate bonds is $_____.  The regular interest payment is indicated by the _____, which is multiplied by the principal to determine the dollar amount of the payment. The date of the principal payment (and of the last regular interest payment) is called the _____ date.

4.    The value of a bond (or of any asset) is equal to the _____ of the future _____ to the holder of the bond.  The valuation of a bond requires that we determine the relevant future _____ and the appropriate market rate of interest, or _____ for the bond.  Then the _____ of the future _____ is calculated, using the appropriate opportunity cost, or _____ rate.

5.    The _____ is the amount an individual would have to invest at the relevant _____ today in order to duplicate the future cash payments promised to the holder of the security.

6.    Bond prices and interest rates are said to have an inverse relationship.  That is, when the relevant market interest rate for a particular bond increases, the price of the bond _____, and when the market interest rate decreases, the bond price _____.

7.    This relationship can be understood mathematically by noting that the interest rate is in the _____ of the basic present value equation, so that when the interest rate increases (or decreases) the size of the denominator _____ (or _____), resulting in a(n) _____ (or _____) in the present value of the bond. This result means that investors will pay less (more) for bonds with fixed annual payment when the level of interest rates available on comparable investments _____ (or _____).

8.    When the market rate of interest is equal to the _____ for a particular bond, the present value of the bond is equal to its _____.  When the market rate of interest is greater than the coupon interest rate, the present value of the bond is _____ than its face value, and the bond is called a _____ bond.  When the market rate of interest is less than the coupon interest rate, the present value of the bond is _____ than its face value, and the bond is called a _____ bond.

9.    A bond with a market value equal to its face value is equivalent to an _____ loan. The mathematics of such a bond are summarized by the equation: C = _____. Alternatively, this equation can be expressed as PV = _____ or r = _____.

10.   The yield to maturity for a bond is the bond's _____.  Unless the market value of the bond is equal to its _____, the yield to maturity is determined by using a _____ approach. The process requires taking successive 'guesses' at the _____ which equates the _____ of the bond's future _____ with its current market value.

11.   A corporate debt is a promise by a corporation to repay the original amount of a loan, called the _____, plus interest, at a specified time.  The lender is also called the _____, and the corporation is the borrower or _____.

12.   Three features distinguish debt from equity. First, debt (does/does not) represent an ownership interest. Second, interest paid on a debt (is/is not) tax-deductible while dividends paid on common stock (are/are not) tax-deductible. Third, failure to pay creditors can result in _____.

13.   Debt securities are often classified according to the length of time that an unpaid balance remains outstanding; this time period is called the _____ of the security. A debt security is considered _____ if its _____ is less than one year; a debt security is considered _____ if its _____ is greater than one year.

14.   A _____ is secured by a mortgage on specific property, whereas a _____ is unsecured.

15.   The written agreement between the corporation and its bondholders is called the _____.

16. Bonds can be either registered bonds or bearer bonds. If a bond is _____, the company's appointed registrar mails the interest payment directly to the owner of record. _____ bonds have dated coupons attached; every six months, the bondholder detaches a coupon and mails it to the company, which then makes the interest payment to the bondholder. The ownership of a _____ bond is not recorded with the company.

17. _____ governs priority of payment to creditors in the event of bankruptcy. Some debt is _____ which means that other creditors must be repaid first in the event of bankruptcy.

18. Most corporate bonds (are/are not) repaid prior to maturity. Repayment takes place through the use of a _____, which is an arrangement requiring the corporation to make annual payments to the bond trustee, who then repurchases bonds.

19. A _____ provision allows the company to repurchase the entire debt issue prior to maturity. The call price is equal to the _____ of the bond plus a _____. Often, bonds cannot be called for some number of years following issue; this is a _____ call, and the bonds are _____ during this period.

20. A _____ restricts certain actions of the company. A _____ disallows certain actions. A _____ requires that certain actions be taken by the corporation.

21. Firms typically pay to have a credit rating assigned to their bonds. Bonds are rated according to the likelihood of _____ and the protection afforded the bondholders in the event of _____. The highest ratings indicate a _____ probability of default.

22. A stripped bond does not pay annual _____; _____ and _____ are paid at maturity. The price of a stripped bond is the present value of its _____, discounted at the appropriate market rate of interest. The difference between the price at which the bond is issued and the _____ of the bond is the interest paid by the issuing corporation. For tax purposes, the implicit interest expense for any given year is the difference between the _____ and the _____. This amount (is/is not) taxable income for the holder of the bond.

23. The coupon interest payments on a _____ bond are adjusted as interest rates change. This adjustment is based on an _____ index. The coupon payment for an _____ bond is dependent on corporate income; that is, the company is obligated to make interest payments only if _____.

24. A call provision has value to the issuing firm because it gives the firm the option to replace a bond issue with bonds paying a _____ interest rate if interest rates _____ subsequent to the original issue of the bond. A call provision is disadvantageous for bondholders because bonds are called when interest rates _____.

25. The cost of a call provision, to the issuing firm, is equal to the price at which the firm could sell a comparable _____ bond minus the price at which the firm could sell the _____ bond. The value of the call provision, to the issuing firm, is equal to the present value of the firm's _____ minus the present value of the _____. The _____ of the call provision is equal to the _____ of the call provision, so that the net present value of the call provision, to either the issuer or the bondholders, is _____. Consequently, a firm should generally be indifferent as to whether it issues callable bonds.

26. A firm should refund callable bonds if the NPV of refunding is _____. The NPV of the refunding is equal to the present value, as of the date of the refunding, of _____ minus the _____.

27.   The effective maturity of a bond is measured by its _____ . This provides information about how
      sensitive bond value is to changes in the _____ .

28.   In general, bonds with _____ are more sensitive to changes in interest rates than bonds with
      _____ .

29.   The graphical representation of the term structure is know as a _____ .


## ANSWERS TO CONCEPT TEST

1.    bond

2.    level-coupon bond; coupon interest; face; par; maturity

3.    $1,000; coupon interest rate; maturity

4.    present value; cash payments; cash payments; opportunity cost; present value; cash payments; discount

5.    present value; market rate of interest

6.    decreases; increases

7.    denominator; increases; decreases; decrease; increase; increases; decreases

8.    coupon interest rate; face value; less; discount; greater; premium

9.    interest-only; $PV \times r$;  $C/r$ ;   $C/PV$

10.   rate of return; face value; trial-and-error; discount rate; present value; cash payments

11.   principal; creditor; debtor

12.   does not; is; are not; bankruptcy

13.   maturity; short-term; maturity; long-term; maturity

14.   bond; debenture

15.   indenture

16.   registered; bearer; bearer

17.   seniority; subordinated

18.   are; sinking fund

19.   call; face value; call premium; deferred; call-protected

20.    protective covenant; negative covenant; positive covenant

21.    default; default; low

22.    interest; interest; principal; face value; face value; value of the bond at the end of the year; value of the bond
       at the beginning of the year; is

23.    floating-rate; interest-rate; income; income is sufficient

24.    lower; decline; decline

25.    non-callable; callable; expected future interest savings; call premium; cost; value; zero

26.    positive; future interest savings; call premium

27.    duration; interest rates

28.    higher duration; lower duration

29.    yield curve

## PROBLEMS AND SOLUTIONS

### Problem 1

Verbrugge Company has a level-coupon bond outstanding that pays coupon interest of $120 per year and has 10
years to maturity. The face value of the bond is $1,000. If the yield for similar bonds is currently 14%, what is the
bond's value? Assume that interest is paid annually.

**Solution:** The bond's value is the present value of the coupon payment plus the present value of the $1,000 face
amount:

$$PV = \frac{\$120}{(1.14)^1} + \frac{\$120}{(1.14)^2} + ... + \frac{\$120}{(1.14)^{10}} + \frac{\$1,000}{(1.14)^{10}}$$

$$= \$120 \times PVIFA(14\%,10) + \$1,000 / (1.14)^{10}$$

$$= \$120 \times 5.216116 + \$1,000 \times .2697438$$

$$= \$895.68$$

The bond is selling for less than its face value because the yield is greater than the coupon interest rate. This bond
is a discount bond.

**Problem 2**

For the Verbrugge Company bond described in Problem 1, find the bond's value if the yield for similar bonds decreases to 12%.

**Solution:**  The value of the bond is now given by:

$$PV \; = \; \$120 \times PVIFA(12\%,10) \; + \; \$1,000 \, / \, (1.12)^{10}$$

$$= \; \$120 \times 5.650223 \; + \; \$1,000 \times .3219732 \; = \; \$1,000$$

Notice that the bond is selling for its face value. Once you recognize that the coupon and market interest rates are equal, you realize this is a par bond. Therefore, no calculations are necessary; the bond will sell at face value.

**Problem 3**

For the Verbrugge Company bond described in Problem 1, find the bond's value if the yield for similar bonds decreases to 9%.

**Solution:** The value of the bond is now given by:

$$PV \; = \; \$120 \times PVIFA(9\%,10) \; + \; \$1,000 \, / \, (1.09)^{10}$$

$$= \; \$120 \times 6.417658 \; + \; \$1,000 \times .4224108 \; = \; \$1,192.53$$

Now the bond is a premium bond, because the bond's yield is less than its coupon rate. Also, notice that as the yield decreases, the value of the bond increases.

**Problem 4**

Suppose the Verbrugge Company bond pays semiannual coupon interest payments. What would its value be if the yield is 14%?

**Solution:**  The coupon interest payments are now $60 per period for 20 time periods; the relevant discount rate is 7%.  The present value is:

$$PV \; = \; \frac{\$60}{(1.07)} \; + \; \frac{\$60}{(1.07)^2} \; + ....+ \; \frac{\$60}{(1.07)^{20}} \; + \; \frac{\$1,000}{(1.07)^{20}}$$

$$PV \; = \; \$60 \times PVIFA(7\%,20) \; + \; \$1,000 \, / \, (1.07)^{20}$$

$$= \; \$60 \times 10.594014 \; + \; \$1,000 \times .2584190 \; = \; \$894.06$$

Notice that this value differs somewhat from the result obtained in Problem 1; this difference results from the assumption of annual interest payments in the earlier problem.

## Problem 5

Now find the value of the Verbrugge Company bond if rates drop to 9%, assuming semiannual coupon interest payments.

**Solution:**  $\begin{aligned} PV &= \$60 \times \text{PVIFA}(4.5\%, 20) + \$1,000/(1.045)^{20} \\ &= \$60 \times 13.007936 + \$1,000 \times .414643 = \$1,195.12 \end{aligned}$

## Problem 6

For your birthday, your great uncle has given you a choice between a bond with a face value of $1,000 and an 8% coupon paid annually, and a vintage chardonnay which will sell for $2,500 in 10 years. You can sell the wine the same year the bond matures. The market rate of interest is 12%. Which gift should you pick?

**Solution:** The present value of the wine bottle is an easy one:

$$PV = \$2,500 \times (1.12)^{10} = \$804.93$$

The value of the bond is:

$$PV = \$80 \times \text{PVIFA}(12\%, 10) + \$1,000 / (1.12)^{10} = \$773.99$$

The wine is the better gift (unless you plan to drink it rather than sell it).

## Problem 7

Sasha Company has a level-coupon bond outstanding with a 9% coupon interest rate; interest is payable annually. The bond has 20 years to maturity and a face value of $1,000; similar bonds currently yield 7%. By prior agreement the company will skip the coupon interest payments in years 8, 9, and 10. These payments will be repaid, without interest, at maturity. What is the bond's value?

**Solution:** This problem can be solved by calculating the present value of each coupon interest payment, plus the present value of the face value. An easier approach is to first calculate the present value of the bond under the assumption that all the coupon interest is paid. Then deduct the present value of the payments that are skipped and add the present value of the payments made at maturity. The value of the bond, ignoring the skipped and repaid coupons, is $1,211.88 (check this for practice). The present value of the skipped coupons is:

$$PV = \frac{\$90}{(1.07)^8} + \frac{\$90}{(1.07)^9} + \frac{\$90}{(1.07)^{10}} = \$147.09$$

At maturity, an extra $(3 \times \$90) = \$270$ will be paid. The present value of this $270 is $69.77. Thus, the value of the bond is $(\$1,211.88 - \$147.09 + \$69.77) = \$1,134.56$.

**Problem 8**

A corporation issues a bond today with a $1,000 face value, maturity in 25 years, and an 8% coupon interest rate; interest is paid annually.  An investor purchases the bond for $1,000. What is the yield to maturity?

**Solution:**   The yield to maturity is the value of r which solves the equation:

$$\$1{,}000 \;=\; [\$80 \times PVIFA(r,25)] \;+\; \$1{,}000 / (1+r)^t$$

This equation can also be written as:

$$\$1{,}000 \;=\; \$80 \times \frac{1 - [1/(1+r)^{25}]}{r} \;+\; \frac{\$1{,}000}{(1+r)^{25}}$$

Trial-and-error indicates that the solution is r = .08 = 8%; that is, when r = .08, the present value of the future payments is exactly $1,000.

You should recognize that this is a par bond; that is, it sells for face value. Therefore, the coupon interest rate must be the same as the market interest rate. Therefore, with no calculations, you can determine that the market rate, or the yield, must be 8%.


**Problem 9**

Suppose that the investor bought the bond described in the previous problem for $900. What is the yield to maturity?

**Solution:**   The yield to maturity is the value of r in the following equation:

$$PV \;=\; C \times [PVIFA(r,t)] \;+\; \$1{,}000 / (1+r)^t$$

$$\$900 \;=\; [\$80 \times PVIFA(r,25)] \;+\; \$1{,}000 / (1+r)^t$$

This equation can also be written as:

$$\$900 \;=\; \$80 \times \frac{1 - [1/(1+r)^{25}]}{r} \;+\; \frac{\$1{,}000}{(1+r)^{25}}$$

We determined in the previous problem that the yield to maturity is 8% when the price of the bond is $1,000. Now, the purchase price is less than $1,000, so that the yield to maturity must be greater than 8%. Therefore, using trial-and-error, we 'guess' that the yield to maturity is 10% and then calculate the present value:

$$PV \;=\; \$80 \times PVIFA(10\%,25) \;+\; \$1{,}000 / (1.10)^{25} \quad \$818.46$$

Since a price of $818.46 implies a yield to maturity of 10%, the yield to maturity for the $900 price is less than 10%. 'Guessing' that the yield is 9%, we find that the present value is $901.78. Therefore, the yield to maturity is slightly greater than 9%. The precise value of the yield to maturity is 9.01969%, as determined using a financial calculator.

## Problem 10

Suppose that the bond described in the previous two problems has a price of $1,100 five years after it is issued. What is the yield to maturity at that time?

**Solution:** The yield to maturity is the value of r in the following equation:

$$PV = C \times [PVIFA(r,t)] + \$1,000 / (1 + r)^t$$

$$\$1,100 = [\$80 \times PVIFA(r,20)] + \$1,000 / (1 + r)^t$$

We know that the yield to maturity is less than the coupon rate because the bond is selling at a premium. Therefore, we will 'guess' that r = 6%, and calculate PV = $1,229.40. Our second 'guess' is that r = 7% and PV = $1,105.94. Therefore, the yield to maturity is slightly greater than 7%. The exact value is 7.05224%.

## Problem 11

A level coupon bond paying 8% interest semiannually has a face value of $1,000 and 10 years left to maturity. If the present market rate of interest is 6%, what is the present value of this bond?

**Solution:** First, the semiannual interest payment is $1,000 x (.08 / 2) = $40. The discount rate is 0.06 / 2 = 0.03, and the number of periods is 10 x 2 = 20.

$$PV = \$40 \times PVIFA (3\%, 20) + \$1,000 / 1.03^{20} = \$40 \times 14.877475 + \$1,000 \times 0.553676$$

$$= \$1,148.78$$

Note: This is a *premium bond* because the coupon payment is higher than the current discount rate.

## Problem 12

Calculate the value of the bond in the previous problem assuming the market interest increases to 10%.

**Solution:** The value of this bond should be less than that of the bond in the previous problem because interest rates have increased. Since the discount rate is now higher than the coupon rate, the bond should sell at a discount.

$$PV = \$40 \times PVIFA (5\%, 20) + \$1,000 / 1.05^{20} = \$40 \times 12.462210 + \$1,000 \times 0.376890$$

$$= \$875.38$$

## Problem 13

Calculate the approximate yield to maturity, on an annual basis, of an 8% coupon, 10-year bond that pays interest semiannually if its price now is $770.60 (use the approximation formula). Based on your results, calculate the effective yield on the bond.

**Solution:**  The semi-annual yield is:

$$\frac{40 + [(1,000 - 770.6) / 20]}{(1,000 + 770.6)/2} \quad = \quad 5.8138\%$$

The annual yield is $5.8138\% \times 2 = 11.63\%$ and the effective yield is $(1 + .1163/2)^2 - 1 = 11.97\%$

**Problem 14**

A bond pays annual interest of 8% and has a face value of $1,000. The life of the bond is 20 years. If you purchase the bond for $700, what is its YTM? Find the YTM using the approximation formula also.

**Solution:**

$$\$700 \quad = \quad \$80 \text{ x PFIVA } (r\%, 20) + \$1,000 / (1 + r)^{20}$$

Because the bond is selling at a discount, the YTM must be greater than the 8% coupon rate. At 10%, bond value would be $829.73. At 11%, the value would be $761.10. At 12%, the value is $1,001.22. So, the YTM is slightly above 12%. Using a financial calculator, the actual YTM is 12.02211%.

Using the approximate formula:

$$YTM \quad = \quad \frac{\$80 \; + \; (\$1,000 - \$700) / 20}{(\$700 + \$1,000) / 2} \quad = \quad 0.111765 \; = \; 11.18\%$$

**Problem 15**

In December 1995, Campough Inc. issued 10-year maturity, $400,000,000 worth of long-term debt that matures in December 2005. The annual interest rate was 14% with semiannual interest paid on June 1 and December 1. In December 1999, interest rates on similar debt of equivalent risk had fallen to 10%. What was the total value of the Campough Inc. 14% debt on December 1999? (Note: the appropriate discount rate for semiannual periods is 5%.)

**Solution:**  First we calculate the market value of one bond:

$$
\begin{array}{lllll}
\$70 \times \text{PVIFA}(5\%,12) & = & \$70 \text{ x } (8.8633) & = & \$\ 620.431 \\
+\ \$1,000 \times \text{PVIF}(5\%,12) & = & \$70 \text{ x } (.5568) & = & \underline{\$\ 556.800} \\
\text{Price of 1 Bond} & & & & \$1,177.231
\end{array}
$$

Since the bond issue is worth $400,000,000 and the face value of each bond is $1,000, there are 400,000 bonds outstanding. The total value is:

$$\text{Price of 400,000 bonds} \;=\; \$1,177.231 \times 400,000 \;=\; \$470,892,400$$

Note: If you rounded the $1,177.231 to $1,177.23, the price for 400,000 bonds will be $470,892,000.

**Problem 16**

Find the duration of a four-year, 10% coupon bond .

**Solution:** First, find the present value of each payment:

$$
\begin{aligned}
\text{PV (Pymt 1)} &= \$100 \,/\, 1.10 &&= \$\ 90.9091 \\
\text{PV (Pymt 2)} &= \$100 \,/\, (1.10)^2 &&=\ \ \ \ 82.6446 \\
\text{PV (Pymt 3)} &= \$100 \,/\, (1.10)^3 &&=\ \ \ \ 75.1315 \\
\text{PV (Pymt 4)} &= \$1{,}100 \,/\, (1.10)^4 &&=\ \ 751.3148
\end{aligned}
$$

Next, find the relative weights:

$$
\begin{aligned}
\text{Pymt 1} &= \$90.9091 \,/\, \$1{,}000 &&=\ \ .090909 \\
\text{Pymt 2} &= \$82.6446 \,/\, \$1{,}000 &&=\ \ .082645 \\
\text{Pymt 3} &= \$75.1315 \,/\, \$1{,}000 &&=\ \ .075132 \\
\text{Pymt 4} &= \$751.3148 \,/\, \$1{,}000 &&=\ \ .751315
\end{aligned}
$$

Duration is the maturity of each payment times the relative weight:

$$
\text{Duration} = 1 \times .090909 + 2 \times .082645 + 3 \times .075132 + 4 \times .751315 = 3.486855 \text{ years}
$$

**Problem 17**

A corporate bond with a face value of $1,000, is currently quoted at 90. The coupon interest rate is 8%. What is the price of the bond? What coupon interest payment does the holder of the bond receive?

**Solution:** Assuming that this is a typical level-coupon bond, the price is (.90 x $1,000) = $900 per bond. The annual coupon interest payment is (.08 x $1,000) = $80 per year; payments are typically in the form of two $40 semi-annual amounts.

**Problem 18**

A corporation issued a five-year stripped bond, with a $1,000 face value, at a time when the market rate of interest was 12%. At what price did the bond originally sell?

**Solution:** The market value of a stripped bond is the present value of the face value, discounted at the market rate of interest. Therefore, the price of the five-year zero-coupon bond is: $1,000 / (1.12)^5 = $567.43.

**Problem 19**

Gilliam Industries has decided to float a perpetual bond issue. The coupon interest payment will be 12%, which is the current market interest rate. There is an equal chance that, in one year, the market rate of interest for the Gilliam Industries bond will be either 8% or 24%. What will the market value of the bonds be one year from now if they are noncallable? At what price can the bonds be sold today if they are noncallable?

**Solution:**  The bond is a perpetuity; therefore, if it is not callable, its value at the end of the year will be either ($120/.08) = $1,500 or ($120/.24) = $500.  The price today is the present value of next year's coupon interest payment plus the present value of next year's expected price. The expected value of the future price is [.5($1,500) + .5($500)] = $1,000.  Therefore, the bond price today is:

$$P_{NC} \;=\; (\$120 + \$1,000) \,/\, 1.12 \;=\; \$1,000$$

where $P_{NC}$ is the price of the bond if it is not callable.

## Problem 20

Suppose that the Gilliam Industries bonds described in Problem 19 are callable at par value plus $120.  At what price can the bonds be sold today?

**Solution:**  If the bond is callable, then, one year from now, it will either be called at $1,120 (if rates fall to 8%) or it will have a market value of ($120/.24) = $500.  The price today is the present value of next year's coupon interest payment plus the present value of next year's expected price.  The expected value of the future price is [.5($1,120) + .5($500)] = $810. Therefore, the price of the bond today is: ($810 + $120) / 1.12 = $830.36.

## Problem 21

If the Gilliam Industries bond in Problem 19 is callable and sells at par, what is the coupon interest payment (C)?

**Solution:**  At the end of the year, the bondholder will have an interest payment of C dollars plus either $1,120 (the call price) or a bond worth (C/.24).  The expected value of the future price is therefore:

$$.50(\$1,120) \;+\; .50(C/.24)$$

In order for the bond to sell for $1,000 today, the present value of the coupon interest payment (C) plus the present value of the expected future price must equal $1,000. Algebraically:

$$P_C \;=\; \$1,000 \;=\; \frac{C + [(.50)\,(\$1,120) + (.50)\,(C/.24)]}{1.12}$$

$$\$1,120 \;=\; C + (\$560) + (.50)(C/.24)$$

$$\$560 \;=\; C + (.50)(C/.24)$$

$$\$134.40 \;=\; .24C + .50C \;=\; .74C$$

$$C \;=\; \$134.40/.74 \;=\; \$181.62$$

Therefore, if the coupon interest payment is $181.62, then the bond will sell for $1,000.

## Problem 22

What is the cost of the call provision to Gilliam?

**Solution:** The cost of the call provision is determined by first computing the price at which the firm could sell a bond with C = $181.62 if the bond is not callable. This price $P_{NC}$ is equal to the present value of next year's coupon interest payment plus the present value of next year's price. Since the bond is a perpetuity, its value at the end of the year will be either ($181.62/.08) = $2,270.25 or ($181.62/.24) = $756.75.

The expected value of next year's price is [.5($2,270.25) + .5($756.75)] = $1,513.50. Therefore, the price of the bond if it were not callable is: $P_{NC}$ = ($181.62 + $1,513.50) / 1.12 = $1,513.50. The difference between $P_{NC}$ and $P_C$ is ($1,513.50 - $1,000) = $513.50, so the firm is paying $513.50 for the call option.

## Problem 23

What is the value of the call provision to Gilliam Industries?

**Solution:** The value of the call provision is the present value of the firm's interest savings minus the present value of the call premium. If the bond is called one year from now, the coupon interest payment would decline from $181.62 to (.08 x $1,000) = $80, for interest savings of ($181.62 - $80) = $101.62. This is a perpetuity of $101.62, which has a present value, as of next year, of ($101.62 / .08) = $1,270.25. However, the call premium next year will be $120, so the net savings equals ($1,270.25 - $120) = $1,150.25. The expected value of the savings is (.50 x $1,150.25) = $575.125 and the present value is ($575.125/1.12) = $513.50. This is identical to the cost of the call provision computed in the solution to Problem 22. This result indicates that the net present value of the call provision, to either the issuer or the bondholders, is zero.

Note: Because the value of a call provision, to either the issuer or the bondholders, is zero, you can actually answer this question without calculations.

## Problem 24

Suppose that Gilliam Industries issues the callable bonds described in Problem 21, and that, one year later, the market rate of interest declines to 8%. Should Gilliam refund the bonds at that time?

**Solution:** Gilliam will refund the callable bonds if the net present value of the transaction is positive. If the market rate of interest declines to 8%, then the present value of the savings on interest payments is the present value of the $101.62 perpetuity, or ($101.62/.08) = $1,270.25. Since the call premium is $120, the net present value is ($1,270.25 - $120) = $1,150.25. If the market interest rate declines to 8% at the end of the year, the bond should be refunded because the net present value of the refunding, at that time, would be positive.

## Problem 25

Fundit Inc. is considering whether to refund a $40 million, 14% coupon, 30-year bond issue that was sold five years ago. Fundit's investment dealers have indicated that although current yields on 25-year bonds of similar risk are 11%, the new (potential) bondholders would require a liquidity premium of 0.5% which will ensure refinancing. A call premium of 7.5% would be required to retire the old bonds, and flotation costs on the new issue would amount to $3.5 million.  Fundit's marginal tax rate is 40%. The new bonds would be issued 1.5 months before the old bonds were called, with the proceeds being invested in short-term government securities returning 9% annually. Fundit estimates the appropriate discount rate to be 7%.  What is the bond refunding's NPV?

**Solution:**  The cost of refunding includes:

Call premium:   $40,000,000 (.075)   =   $3,000,000

Flotation costs:   Annual tax shield after tax: ($3,500,000/5)(.40)   =   $280,000

The PV of this tax shield discounted at 7% is: $280,000 (PVIFA 7%, 5) = $280,000 (4.100197) = $1,148,055.28

The total after tax flotation costs are: $3,500,000 -  $1,148,055.28   =   $2,351,944.72

Additional interest: The extra interest paid on the old issue after taxes is: $40,000,000 (.14)(1.5/12)(1 -  .40) = $420,000.

The extra interest earned from short-term securities after taxes is: $40,000,000 (.09)(1.5/12)(1 -  .40) = $270,000

The total additional interest is: $420,000 - $270,000 = $150,000.

The total cost of refunding is therefore, $3,000,000 + $2,351,944.72 + $150,000 = $5,501,944.72.

The annual interest savings on the issue after taxes is: $40,000,000 (.14 -  .115) (1  - .40) = $600,000.

The PV of annual savings over 25 years is: $600,000 [PVIFA(7%,25)] = $600,000 (11.653583) = $6,992,149.91.

The NPV = $6,992,149.91  -  $5,501,944.72 = $1,490,205.19.

Since the NPV is positive, Fundit Inc. should proceed with the refunding.


**Problem 26**

Your firm is considering refunding $16,000,000 face-value, 12% preferred shares outstanding with a similar issue but a lower dividend rate. Current dividend yields on 20-year term preferred shares of similar risk are 9%, but you estimate that potential preferred shareholders investing in a perpetuity would require a premium of 1% above the term preferred shares. The outstanding preferred shares were issued 44 months ago costing the firm a total of $235,000 in before-tax issue costs and have a call premium equal to a rate that is 4% higher than the prevailing yield on perpetual preferred shares. The new preferreds would be issued three months before the old preferreds are called, with before-tax issue costs amounting to $300,000 where the proceeds of the issue would be invested in a bank deposit that yields 6%. Issue costs could be amortized over five years. The applicable discount rate is 8%. The firm's tax rate is 40%. Should the refunding take place?

**Solution:**  The cost of refunding includes:

Call premium: $16,000,000 (.09 + .01 + .04) = $2,240,000

Flotation costs: Annual tax shield after tax: ($300,000/5)(.40) = $24,000

The PV of this tax shield discounted at 8% is: $24,000 [PVIFA(8%,5)] = $24,000 (3.992710) = $95,825.04

The total after tax flotation costs are: $300,000 -  $95,825.04 = $204,174.96

The extra dividend paid on the old issue is: $16,000,000 (.12)(3/12) = $480,000

Note: Dividends are not tax deductible. The extra interest earned from the bank deposit after taxes is: $16,000,000 (.06)(3/12)(1 - .40) = $144,000.

The additional dividend net of additional interest earned is: $480,000 - $144,000 = $336,000.

The total cost of refunding includes: $2,240,000 + $204,174.96 + $336,000 = $2,780,174.96.

The annual dividend savings are: $16,000,000 (.12 - .10) = $320,000. The PV of these perpetual dividend savings at 8% is  $320,000 / .08 = $4,000,000.

The NPV is = $4,000,000 - $2,780,174.96 = $1,219,825.04.  Since the NPV is positive, your firm should proceed with refunding the preferred share issue.

# 8          <u>Stock Valuation</u>

## CHAPTER HIGHLIGHTS

It is more difficult to value shares of common stock than it is to value bonds.  First, unlike bonds, the promised cash flows are not known in advance.  Secondly, while bonds have a fixed maturity date, the life of a share of stock is essentially forever.  Finally, there is no easy way to observe the return investors require on their shares (as bondholders can do by observing the yield to maturity).  In this chapter we will discuss ways to estimate the value of future cash flows and use them to determine the value of shares of stock.

**Common Share Cash Flows:** Although investors purchase common shares expecting returns in the form of dividends and/or future price appreciation, it is not immediately apparent which of these cash flows are relevant for the purpose of valuation. For example, an investor who plans to hold a share of stock for one year might compute the value of a share as follows:

$$P_0 = PV = \frac{D_1}{(1+r)} + \frac{P_1}{(1+r)}$$

Where $P_0$ and $P_1$ are the price of the share today and one year from today, respectively, and $D_1$ is the next year's dividend.  In order to determine the price at which the share can be sold next year ($P_1$), the investor must determine the present value, as of next year, of dividends and the future selling price to be realized subsequent to next year.  However, any future selling price is the present value of all subsequent dividend payments, so that regardless of any particular investor's time horizon, *the present value of a share of common stock is the present value of all future dividends.*  We represent this conclusion algebraically as follows:

$$P_0 = PV = D_1/(1+r)^1 + D_2/(1+r)^2 + D_3/(1+r)^3 + D_4/(1+r)^4 + \ldots$$

Our conclusion in this section is that the value of a share of stock is equal to the present value of all future dividend payments.  It is virtually impossible to accurately forecast dividend payments far into the future. Consequently, in applying the present value approach to stock valuation, a simplifying assumption is generally made regarding the pattern of dividend payments.  Alternative approaches to stock valuation are discussed in the next section.

**Common Stock Valuation - Some Special Cases:** Three alternative, simplifying assumptions regarding the pattern of future dividend payments are considered in this section.  They are: (1) zero growth in dividends, or constant dividends;  (2) constant growth in dividends; and,  (3) nonconstant growth in dividends.

**Zero growth:**  A stock with constant dividends is a perpetuity.   In Chapter 6, we developed the following equation for the value of a perpetuity:      $PV = C/r$

If we relate this to a constant dividend, then the dividend payment is equivalent to the variable C in the perpetuity equation.  So, we can write the value of a share of stock as:

$P_0 = PV = D/r$

where D is the constant annual dividend and r is the required rate of return.

**An Example:**   Consider a $12 preferred stock with an annual dividend payment of $12. What is the price of a share of $12 preferred stock, if the relevant opportunity cost is 15%?
We use the formula for the present value of a perpetuity, as follows:

$$P_0 \;=\; D/r \;=\; \$12/.15 \;=\; \$80$$

Therefore, the price of the $12 preferred stock is $80.

**Constant Growth:**   A *growing perpetuity* is a series of cash flows, occurring at regular intervals, which grows perpetually at a constant rate.  In certain circumstances, the series of dividend payments for a share of common stock can be considered a growing perpetuity, as long as the size of the dividend payment increases at the same rate each year.  Consider, for example, an investor who intends to purchase a share of Furillo Farms common stock, which has recently paid an annual dividend of $2 per share.  The investor expects dividends to increase at the rate of 5% per year indefinitely.  Next year's dividend is expected to be:

$$D_1 \;=\; D_0 \times (1+g) \;=\; \$2 \times (1.05) \;=\; \$2.10$$

where $D_0$ and $D_1$ are the current year's dividend and next year's dividend, respectively, and $g$ is the annual growth rate in dividends.  Similarly, the dividend expected two years from now ($D_2$) is:

$$D_2 \;=\; D_0 \times (1+g)^2 \;=\; \$2 \times (1.05)^2 \;=\; \$2.21$$

and the dividend at any future date ($D_t$) is:

$$D_t \;=\; D_0 \times (1+g)^t$$

If the appropriate opportunity cost is 12%, the present value calculation for Furillo Farms stock is:

$$P_0 \;=\; \frac{\$2\,(1.05)^1}{(1.12)^1} + \frac{\$2\,(1.05)^2}{(1.12)^2} + \frac{\$2\,(1.05)^3}{(1.12)^3} + \ldots\ldots + \frac{\$2\,(1.05)^t}{(1.12)^t}$$

In general, this formula is:

$$P_0 \;=\; \frac{D_0\,(1+g)^1}{(1+r)^1} + \frac{D_0\,(1+g)^2}{(1+r)^2} + \frac{D_0\,(1+g)^3}{(1+r)^3} + \ldots\ldots + \frac{D_0\,(1+g)^t}{(1+r)^t}$$

It can be shown that, as long as $r$ is greater than $g$, the above formula is equivalent to:

$$P_0 \;=\; \frac{D_0\,(1+g)}{r-g} \;=\; \frac{D_1}{r-g}$$

Applying this result to the Furillo Farms example above, the present value is:

$$P_0 \;=\; \frac{\$2\,(1.05)}{.12-.05} \;=\; \$30$$

It is important to note here that this result is the exact present value of the growing perpetuity; that is, this simplifying formula is not an approximation of the present value.

**Nonconstant Growth:** The assumption of nonconstant (supernormal) growth is best illustrated with an example.

Suppose that Husky Corporation's dividend this year is $1.20 per share and that dividends will grow at 10% per year for the next three years, followed by 6% annual growth. The appropriate discount rate for Husky common stock is 12%. What is the value of a share of Husky Corporation common stock?

To value this stock, first compute the present value of the first three dividend payments as follows:

| Year | Growth rate (g) | Expected dividend | Present value |
|------|------|------|------|
| 1 | 10% | $1.3200 | $1.1786 |
| 2 | 10 | 1.4520 | 1.1575 |
| 3 | 10 | 1.5972 | 1.1369 |

The present value of the first three dividend payments is $3.4730. Next, compute the dividend for year 4:

$$D_4 = \$1.20 \times (1.10)^3 \times (1.06) = \$1.6930$$

The price as of year 3 can be determined by using the formula for the present value of a stock whose dividends grow at a constant rate:

$$P_3 = \frac{D_4}{(r - g)} = \frac{\$1.6930}{(.12 - .06)} = \$28.2167$$

Note that the above formula values the stock as of year 3, using the year 4 dividend in the numerator. To find the present value, as of year 0, of this year 3 price:

$$PV = \$28.2167 / (1.12)^3 = \$20.0841$$

Therefore, $P_0 = (\$3.4730 + \$20.0841) = \$23.5571$ or $23.56.

In other words, the stock price is the present value of the dividends for three years plus the present value of the expected stock price in year 3.

**Components of the Required Return:** In this section, we demonstrate the fact that the rate of return for an investment in a stock whose dividends grow at a constant rate can be thought of as having two components, a dividend component and a capital gains component. To establish this result, we first repeat here the formula developed above for the present value of a constant growth stock:

$$P_0 = \frac{D_1}{r - g}$$

Next, we solve this equation for r:

$$r = D_1 / P_0 + g$$

Here we see that r, the rate of return for a constant growth stock, is composed of two components. The first is referred to as the dividend yield. The second is called the *capital gains yield*. The dividend yield can be thought of as the rate of return for a stock whose dividend is constant. An investor who purchased a share of common stock for a price $P_0$, and who received a constant dividend of $D_1$, would be receiving a perpetuity whose yield is equal to

$D_1/P_0$. To demonstrate the reason that g is identified as the capital gains yield, we refer to the earlier example of Furillo Farms common stock. In that example, we assumed that the company recently paid an annual dividend of $2 per share, that dividends will increase at the rate of 5% per year, and that the relevant opportunity cost is 12%. Given a 5% growth rate in dividends, what is the growth rate in the value of the common stock? For example, what is the price of the common stock four years from now, and what is the growth rate for the price of the stock?

In order to determine the value of $P_4$, we first compute the dividend to be paid in year 5 ($D_5$):

$$D_5 = D_0 \times (1 + g)^5 = \$2 \times (1.05)^5 = \$2.5526$$

Next, using the constant growth formula, we compute $P_4$ as follows:

$$P_4 = D_5 / (r - g) = \$2.5526 / (.12 - .05) = \$36.47$$

What is the growth rate for Furillo Farms common stock? Earlier, we determined that $P_0 = \$30$. An increase in value from $30 to $36.47 over a four-year period is an annual growth rate of 5%, as demonstrated by the following calculation:

$$\$30 \times (1.05)^4 = \$36.47$$

It is not coincidental that the price of the stock grows at the same rate as the dividend. The reason for this can be seen by examining the numerator of the formula for the value of a constant growth stock. When computing $P_0$, we first determine the value of $D_1$ as follows:

$$D_1 = D_0 \times (1 + g)^1$$

Similarly, computing the value of $P_4$ requires that we first determine the value of $D_5$:

$$D_5 = D_0 \times (1 + g)^5$$

Therefore, it can readily be seen that the relationship between $D_5$ and $D_1$ is given by:

$$D_5 = D_1 \times (1 + g)^4$$

This equation indicates that the value of $D_5$ can be derived from the value of $D_1$ by compounding $D_1$ at the rate g for four years. Note also that the denominator in the calculation of $P_4$ is (r–g), which is identical to the denominator in the calculation of $P_0$. Therefore, the difference between $P_0$ and $P_4$ is determined by the difference, in the numerator, between $D_1$ and $D_5$. Since $D_5$ is simply the value of $D_1$ compounded at the rate g for four years, then $P_4$ must be the value of $P_0$ compounded at the rate g for four years. This is the result demonstrated above.

The significance of this result in describing the components of the rate of return is that the growth rate g can be regarded as the growth rate in the price of a share of stock, which is the same as the capital gain to the investor. It is important to note that the conclusions of this section apply regardless of the time period during which the investor holds the stock. For any time period, the capital gains yield, or the rate of growth in the price of the stock, is equal to the rate of growth of the dividends.

# COMMON STOCK FEATURES

In general, *common stock* refers to a share that has no preference in either dividend payments or bankruptcy. They are paid dividends only after all other payments have been met (and dividends are not obligatory). In the case of bankruptcy, shareholders are only entitled to 'the remains' after all other claimants have been satisfied.

**Shareholders' Rights:** As the owners of the firm, shareholders essentially control the corporation through their right to elect the directors. This usually occurs at the annual shareholders meeting. Directors are elected by shareholder vote. Election requires winning the vote of a majority of shareholders represented and entitled to vote. The mechanics of electing directors may vary from firm to firm.

**Other Rights:** In addition to the right to elect the directors, shareholders have three other primary rights:

1. The right to a proportionate share of dividends paid
2. The right to a proportionate share of assets remaining in a liquidation
3. The right to vote on important matters, usually at the annual meeting or a special meeting.

Sometimes shareholders have a *preemptive right*, the right to share proportionately in any new shares sold. If a firm wishes to issue new stock, they must first offer shares to the existing shareholders. This allows shareholders to protect their proportionate ownership position in the firm.

**Dividends:** Dividends provide shareholders with a return on the capital they have contributed to the corporation. Dividends are paid at the discretion of the board of directors. Important characteristics of dividends include:

1. Dividends are not a corporate liability until declared by the board of directors.
2. Dividends are *not* tax-deductible because they are not considered a business expense.
3. Individuals receive a dividend tax credit which partially shelters income received. This avoids the problem of double taxation discussed in Chapter 2.

**Classes of Stock:** Many firms have more than one class of common shares, typically with different voting rights. Some firms also issue *restricted stock*, which is non-voting. The main reason for dual classes of stock has to do with retaining control of the firm. Issuing shares with limited voting rights allows managers to raise equity capital without losing control of the firm.

# PREFERRED STOCK FEATURES

Preferred stock differs from common stock in that preferred shareholders must be paid a stated dividend before dividends can be paid to common shareholders. If the firm liquidates, the claim of preferred shareholders has priority over that of common shareholders. Preferred shares usually do not have voting rights.

**Stated Value:** A preferred share normally has a stated liquidating value. For example, a share of preferred stock might be identified as an '8% preferred,' indicating a dividend yield equal to 8% of the stated value.

**Cumulative and Noncumulative Dividends:** A corporation is not legally obligated to pay dividends on preferred stock. If dividends are *cumulative,* then any dividends not paid are accumulated, and the entire amount must be paid before any dividends on common stock can be paid. Usually, preferred shareholders are granted voting rights if some specified number of dividends have not been paid.

**Is Preferred Stock Really Debt?**  In many ways, preferred stock resembles a perpetual bond. The dividend is fixed, and preferred shareholders receive a stated value in the event of liquidation. In recent years, many preferred issues have also had sinking funds. This provision effectively creates a maturity date for the preferred stock since some portion of the original issue is retired each year.

**Preferred Stock and Taxes:**  On the other hand, the preferred dividend is not tax-deductible for the issuing corporation, as it would be if it were interest on a debt security. Corporations find preferred stocks an attractive investment because 100% of the dividends received by the investing corporation are exempt from corporate income tax. Since individual investors do not receive this exclusion, most preferred stock is held by corporations.

**Beyond Taxes:**  The fact that the dividend is not deductible creates a tax disadvantage, relative to debt, for the issuer. To some extent, this disadvantage is offset by the fact that corporate investors are willing to accept a lower return on preferred stock because of the 100% dividend exclusion. However, the result of these two tax effects is a net disadvantage to issuers of preferred stock. The question arises, then, as to why a corporation would ever choose to issue preferred stock rather than debt securities. Three reasons are commonly cited.

1. Most preferred stock is issued by regulated public utilities; these firms are allowed to pass the additional cost of preferred stock on to consumers.
2. Preferred stock, unlike debt, does not increase the firm's risk of bankruptcy.
3. Preferred shareholders do not have voting rights; firms can issue preferred shares without affecting control of the corporation.

## STOCK MARKET REPORTING

If you look in a financial newspaper, you would see information on many stocks in different markets. Suppose you encounter the following in *The Globe and Mail:*

*52 Week*

| High | Low | Stock | Div | High | Low | Close | Change | Vol |
|------|-----|-------|-----|------|-----|-------|--------|-----|
| 32 1/8 | 19 3/8 | Cdn Pacific | .93 | $23 5/8 23 ½ | 23 7/8 | –3/8 | | 258,641 |

The first two columns indicate the highest and lowest share prices during the last 52 weeks. The third column indicates the company (Canadian Pacific in our example). The Dividend Column indicates the annual cash dividend. The next three columns indicate the high, low, and closing (last) price for the day. Change indicates the difference between the quoted closing price and the closing price on the preceding day. In our case, closing price was down three-eighths (or $0.375) from the closing price of the previous trading day. Notice that shares are quoted in dollars and fractions down to 1/8 whereas bonds are quoted in dollars, percents, and basis points. The volume column indicates the number of shares traded on the trading day reported.

Prices for over-the-counter (OTC) stocks are quoted under the columns 'Bid' and 'Ask.' This is because unlisted quotations reflect transactions between security dealers, who *bid* (what they would pay to buy the stock) and *ask* (what they would sell if for) and not actual sales or purchases by investors.

**Growth Opportunities:**  Suppose a company has a level stream of earnings in perpetuity and it pays all earnings out as dividends. Therefore, EPS = DPS (dividend per share). From the perpetuity formula in Chapter 5, the value of a share is:       $PV = EPS / r = DPS / r$

where r is the required return (or discount rate) on the firm's stock.

Now consider that many firms have growth opportunities, that is, opportunities to invest in profitable projects. Since these investment projects can represent a significant fraction of the firm's value, it would be unwise to forego them in order to pay out all earnings as dividends.

Assume that the set of growth opportunities means investment in a single project and that the firm will retain the entire dividend at date 1 in order to invest in a particular project. If the net present value *per share* of the project as of date 0 is *NPVGO* (net present value per share of the growth opportunity), what is the price of a share at date 0 if the firm decides to take on the project at date 1? Because the per share value of the project is added to the original share price, the new share price (after the firm commits to the new project) must be:

$$P_0 = (EPS/r) + NPVGO$$

Therefore, the price of a share is equal to the value of the firm if it distributed all earnings to the shareholders (EPS/r) plus the *additional* value if the firm retains earnings in order to finance new projects.

**Application - The Price Earnings Ratio:**   A common application of this equation is to the price earnings ratio. Suppose we divide the above equation by EPS. Then:

$$\frac{\text{Price per Share}}{\text{EPS}} = \frac{1}{r} + \frac{\text{NPVGO}}{\text{EPS}}$$

The left hand side is the P/E ratio which is obviously related to NPVGO.  For example, assume two firms have EPS of $2 but only one of them has valuable growth opportunities. Consequently, the one with growth opportunities will sell at a higher price because an investor is buying both $2 income and growth opportunities. If this price is $24 and assuming a price of $16 for the firm with no growth opportunities, and since $2 appears in the denominator of the P/E ratio for both, the P/E is 12 for the firm with growth ($24/$2),  but only 8 for the firm without any opportunities ($16/$2).

Thus, investors who expect a higher growth in one firm over another explains why the higher growth firm will have a higher P/E ratio.  Other factors causing a high P/E are low risk, a low discount rate, r, and conservative accounting.

Note however, that P/E ratios by themselves are not a shortcut for stock analysis, but should be followed up with cash flow analysis using the dividend valuation model.

## CONCEPT TEST

1.      Theoretically, the value of a share of common stock is equal to the _____ of the future _____ to the holder of the stock.  The relevant cash flows for a share of common stock are future _____ and future _____ value of a share.

2.      Application of the present value concept to common stock valuation is more difficult than for bond valuation because each of the following is unknown for a share of common stock: (1) future _____ payments (2) future _____ value; and (3) appropriate _____.

3.      Three alternative simplifying assumptions sometimes made for the purpose of common stock valuation are: (1) zero growth in dividends, or _____ dividends; (2) constant _____ in dividends; and,      (3) _____ in dividends.

4.    The mathematics of a zero-growth stock are summarized by the equation: $P_0 = PV =$ _____.
      Alternatively, this equation can be expressed as D = _____ or r = _____.

5.    The mathematics of a constant-growth stock are summarized by the equation: $P_0 = PV =$ _____.

6.    The case of nonconstant growth requires the calculation of the _____ of several initial dividend
      payments and then the application of the formula for _____ to subsequent dividend payments.

7.    The rate of return for a _____ stock can be thought of as having two components: the dividend yield
      and the capital gains yield. The former is equal to _____ and the latter is equal to the _____.

8.    The capital gains yield is equal to the _____ because the rate at which the _____ of a constant
      growth stock increases is equal to the rate of growth in dividends.

9.    If a firm pays out all of its level, perpetual earnings as dividends, then the value of the stock is equal to
      _____ or _____. The firm with growth opportunities will have a stock price comprised of two
      components; _____ + _____. The firm with higher growth opportunities will also tend to have
      a higher _____ ratio.

10.   Because they are the owners of the firm, the shareholders have the right to _____ the _____ of
      the firm.

11.   Three other rights important to shareholders are: the right to share _____ in _____ paid;
      the right to share _____ in remaining assets after a _____ ; and the right to _____
      ___ on matters of _____ at either the annual or a special meeting.

12.   The right stating that firms must first offer any new equity issue to existing shareholders is called the
      _____ .   This allows shareholders to protect their _____ in the firm.

13.   Dividends do not become a _____ of the corporation until they have been _____ by the
      board of directors.

14.   Unlike interest payments, dividends paid are not _____ . This is because they are not considered
      to be a _____ .

15.   Dividend payments to individuals are partially sheltered by a _____ . This is to avoid the problem
      of _____ associated with dividend payments.

16.   The primary reason firms issue dual classes of stock is so that they can _____ without
      _____ of the firm.

17.   Preferred shareholders must be paid a _____ dividend before _____ can be paid to
      _____ shareholders, and preferred shareholders have preference over _____
      shareholders to the _____ value of assets following _____ of the company.

18.   A corporation (is/is not) legally obligated to pay dividends on preferred stock.  If dividends are
      _____ , then any dividends not paid are accumulated.  The entire amount must be paid before any
      dividends on common stock can be paid.

19.     In many ways, preferred stock resembles a _____ bond.  For example, the dividend is _____and
        preferred shareholders receive a _____ value in the event of _____ .

20.     On the other hand, the preferred dividend (is/is not) tax-deductible for the issuing corporation.


## ANSWERS TO CONCEPT TEST

1.      present value; cash payments; dividends; market

2.      dividend; market; opportunity cost

3.      constant;  growth; nonconstant growth

4.      D/r;  PV×r ;  D/PV

5.       $D_1 / (r-g)$

6.      present value; constant growth

7.      constant growth; $D_1/P_0$; dividend growth rate

8.      dividend growth rate; price

9.      EPS/r;  DPS/r;  EPS/r;  NPVGO;  P/E

10.     elect; directors

11.     proportionately; dividends; proportionately; liquidation; vote; importance

12.     preemptive right; proportionate ownership

13.     liability; declared

14.     tax-deductible; business expense

15.     dividend tax credit; double taxation

16.     raise equity capital; losing control

17.     stated; dividends; common; common; residual; liquidation

18.     is not; cumulative

19.     perpetual; fixed; stated; liquidation

20.     is not

## PROBLEMS AND SOLUTIONS

### Problem 1

Security analysts have forecasted the dividends of Hodges Enterprises for the next three years as:   $D_1 = \$1.50$; $D_2 = \$1.75$; $D_3 = \$2.20$.  The forecasted selling price in three years is $48.50. The rate of return for common stock with a risk level comparable to that of Hodges Enterprises is 14%.  What is the value of Hodges common stock?

**Solution:**  The value of Hodges common stock is the present value of the future dividend payments plus the present value of the future selling price, as follows:

$$P_0 = \frac{D_1}{(1+r)^1} + \frac{D_2}{(1+r)^2} + \frac{D_3}{(1+r)^3} + \frac{P_3}{(1+r)^3}$$

$$= \frac{\$1.50}{(1.14)^1} + \frac{\$1.75}{(1.14)^2} + \frac{\$2.20}{(1.14)^3} + \frac{\$48.50}{(1.14)^3} = \$36.88$$

Therefore, the price of the Hodges common stock is $36.88.

### Problem 2

A share of TTK Corporation preferred stock pays a $10 annual dividend. What is the price of a share of TTK preferred stock if preferred stock with comparable risk has a yield of 8%? What is the price if comparable preferred stock has a yield of 11%?

**Solution:**  The TTK Corporation preferred stock can be referred to as a $10 preferred stock. The 8% yield for preferred stock with comparable risk is the relevant opportunity cost for the TTK stock. To find the value of the preferred share, we use the formula for the present value of a perpetuity, as follows:

$$P_0 = D/r = \$10/.08 = \$125$$

Therefore, the price of the $10 preferred share is $125. If the relevant opportunity cost is 11%, then the price of the TTK preferred shared is ($10/.11) = $90.91.

### Problem 3

A share of preferred stock with a $12 annual dividend is selling for $75. What is the rate of return?

**Solution:**   Substitute $D = \$12$ and $P_0 = \$75$ into the following equation and solve for r:

$$P_0 = D/r, \quad \text{so} \quad \$75 = \$12/r$$

Therefore, $r = .16 = 16\%$. The solution can be obtained directly from the following algebraic rearrangement of the above equation:

$$r = D/P_0 = \$12/\$75 = .16 = 16\%$$

## Problem 4

If a share pays a constant annual dividend of $10 and is selling for $50, what is the rate of the return for the share? What if the share price changes to $65?

**Solution:**

$P_0 = D / r$ can be rearranged as: $r = D / P_0$

$r = \$10 / \$50 = 0.20 = 20\%$

If $P_0 = \$65$, then $r = \$10 / \$65 = 0.1538 = 15.38\%$

## Problem 5

Hilliard, Inc. has just paid a $2 annual dividend on its common stock. The dividend is expected to increase at a constant rate of 8% per year indefinitely.  If the required rate of return on Hilliard's stock is 16%, what is its current value?

**Solution:**  Hilliard is a constant growth stock with $D_0 = \$2.00$ and:

$D_1 = \$2.00 \times 1.08 = \$2.16$

Therefore, the current value of Hilliard stock is:

$$P_0 = \frac{D_0 \times (1 + g)}{r - g} = \frac{D_1}{r - g}$$

$$= \frac{\$2 \times (1.08)}{.16 - .08} = \frac{\$2.16}{.08} = \$27.00$$

## Problem 6

The dividend paid this year on a share of common stock is $10. Assuming dividends grow at a 5% rate for the foreseeable future, and that the required rate of return is 10%, what is the value of the share today? Last year (date −1)? Next year (date 1)?

**Solution:**  The value today ($P_0$) is:

$$P_0 = \frac{D_1}{r - g} = \frac{\$10 \times (1.05)}{.10 - .05} = \$210$$

The value last year ($P_{-1}$) was:

$$P_{-1} = \frac{D_0}{r - g} = \frac{\$10}{.10 - .05} = \$200$$

The value next year ($P_1$) will be:

$$P_1 \ = \ \frac{D_2}{r - g} \ = \ \frac{\$10\,(1.05)^2}{.10 - .05} \ = \ \$220.50$$

Notice that the price increases at the same growth rate that the dividends increase; that is:

$$P_{-1} \times (1 + g) \ = \ \$200 \times 1.05 \ = \ \$210 \ = \ P_0$$
$$P_0 \times (1 + g) \ = \ \$210 \times 1.05 \ = \ \$220.50 \ = \ P_1$$

## Problem 7

The current price of a share is $20 and last year's price was $18.87. The current year's dividend is $2. Assume a constant growth rate in dividends and share price. What is the stock's rate of return for the coming year?

**Solution:**  This problem can be solved by finding the solution for r in the following equation:

$$P_0 \ = \ \frac{D_1}{r - g}, \qquad \text{so} \qquad r \ = \ \frac{D_1}{P_0} + g$$

We know that $P_0 = \$20$. We can determine the values of both g and $D_1$ from the information given. The growth rate for dividends is the same as the growth rate for share price. Solve for g in the following equation:

$$P_0 \ = \ P_{-1} \times (1 + g)$$
$$\$20 \ = \ \$18.87 \times (1 + g)$$
$$(1 + g) \ = \ \$20 \,/\, \$18.87 \ = \ 1.05988$$
$$g \ = \ 0.059883 \ = 6\%$$

Therefore, g is approximately 6%. Applying the growth rate to dividends, we see that:

$$D_1 \ = \ \$2 \times 1.06 \ = \ \$2.12$$

Substituting these values into the above equation for r, we find that $r = .166 = 16.6\%$.

## Problem 8

The current year's dividend for a share of common stock is $2 and the current share price is $30. Dividends are expected to grow at a 5% rate for the foreseeable future. What is the current rate of return for this stock? What is the capital gain (or loss) on the stock over the past year if the required rate of return was 10% last year?

**Solution:**  Substitute $P_0 = \$30$, $D_0 = \$2$, $g = .05$ into the following equation and solve for r:

$$P_0 \ = \ \frac{D_1}{r - g} \ = \ \frac{\$2\,(1.05)}{r - .05} \ = \ \$30$$

The rate of return is r = .12 = 12%. In order to determine the capital gain (or loss) find the value of the stock last year (P.₁):

$$P_{-1} = \frac{D_0}{r-g} = \frac{\$2}{.10-.05} = \$40$$

Therefore, the capital loss is ($40 - $30) = $10.

## Problem 9

Jeff is considering buying shares in PMG Corporation. PMG has just paid dividends of $2.25 per share. Dividends are expected to grow at a constant annual rate of 5%. What would Jeff be willing to pay for a share of PMG? The market rate of interest is 10%.

**Solution:** Using the constant growth model, the price per share is:

$$P_0 = D_0(1+g)/(r-g) = (\$2.25 \times 1.05)/(0.10 - 0.05) = \$2.3625/0.05 = \$47.25$$

## Problem 10

Pettway Corporation's next annual dividend is expected to be $4. The growth rate in dividends over the following three years is forecasted at 15%. After that, Pettway's growth rate is anticipated to be equal to the industry average of 5%. If the required rate of return is 18%, what is the current value of the stock?

**Solution:** The current value of the stock is equal to the present value of the dividends from the high growth phase plus the present value of the share price when the high growth phase ends. Notice that the next dividend is forecasted at $4. Calculate the present value of the first four dividend payments as follows:

| Year | Growth rate (g) | Expected dividend | Present value |
|------|-----------------|-------------------|---------------|
| 1    | 15%             | $4.000            | $3.3898       |
| 2    | 15              | 4.600             | 3.3036        |
| 3    | 15              | 5.290             | 3.2197        |
| 4    | 15              | 6.084             | 3.1381        |

The total present value for the first four dividend payments is $13.0512.

Now, calculate the dividend payment for year 5 and use that amount to calculate the value of the share in year 4.

$$D_5 = \$4 \times (1.15)^3 \times (1.05) = \$6.39$$

The price at year 4 (P₄) is thus:

$$P_4 = \frac{D_5}{r-g} = \frac{\$6.39}{.18-.05} = \$49.15$$

The present value is $49.15/(1.18^4) = $25.35. The share value is ($25.34 + $13.05) = $38.39.

**Problem 11**

A company pays a current dividend of $1.20 per share on its common stock. The annual dividend will increase by 3%, 4%, and 5%, respectively, over the next three years, and then by 6% per year thereafter. The appropriate discount rate is 12%. What is the current price of the stock? What is the capital gain (or loss) on the stock over the past year?

**Solution:**   Dividends for the next three years are determined as follows:

$$D_1 \; = \; \$1.20 \times (1.03) \; = \; \$1.24$$
$$D_2 \; = \; \$1.20 \times (1.03) \times (1.04) \; = \; \$1.29$$
$$D_3 \; = \; \$1.20 \times (1.03) \times (1.04) \times (1.05) \; = \; \$1.35$$

The year 3 price is:

$$P_3 \; = \; \frac{D_4}{r-g} \; = \; \frac{\$1.35\,(1.06)}{.12-.06} \; = \; \$23.85$$

The current price is the present value of the next three year's dividends plus the present value of $P_3$, discounted at 12%; $P_0$ is $20.06. In order to find the capital gain, we first determine last year's price ($P_{-1}$), by finding the present value of the dividends $D_0$ to $D_3$, discounted to last year, plus the present value of $P_3$, also discounted to last year. $P_{-1}$ is equal to $18.98, so that the capital gain is ($20.06 – $18.98) = $1.08.

**Problem 12**

JPH Corporation has just signed a large deal with one of its customers. Dividends are expected to grow at rates of 10%, 15%, and 20% over the next three years. For the fourth year and all following years, growth is expected to be 10%. If Pat is interested in purchasing 20 shares of JPH, how much would he be willing to pay if the market rate of interest is 12% and JPH has just paid dividends of $2 per share?

**Solution:** Dividends for the next four years are:

| | | | | |
|---|---|---|---|---|
| $D_1$ | = | $2.00 x 1.10 | = | $2.20 |
| $D_2$ | = | $2.00 x 1.10 x 1.15 | = | $2.53 |
| $D_3$ | = | $2.00 x 1.10 x 1.15 x 1.20 | = | $3.036 |
| $D_4$ | = | $2.00 x 1.10 x 1.15 x 1.20 x 1.10 = | | $3.3396 |

The present value for the first three years of dividends is $6.14.

The Year 3 price can be found using the constant growth model:

$$P_3 \quad = \quad D_4 / (r-g) \; = \; \$3.34 / (.12 - .10) \; = \; \$167.$$

Today's share price is $167 / (1.12)^3 + $6.14 = $125.01. Pat will pay 20 x $125.01 = $2,500.20 for 20 shares.

## Problem 13

A company's dividend this year is $2.25 per share, and dividends are expected to grow at 12% for the next four years and at 5% indefinitely after that.  If the firm's discount rate is 8%, what is the value of one share today?

**Solution:** To value this share, calculate the present value of the first four dividend payments and then the present value of the share once it grows at a constant rate.

Year 1: expected dividend  $=$  $2,5200;  PV  $=$  $2.3333
Year 2: expected dividend  $=$  $2.8224;  PV  $=$  $2.4198
Year 3: expected dividend  $=$  $3.1611;  PV  $=$  $2.5094
Year 4: expected dividend  $=$  $3.5404;  PV  $=$  $2.6023

The present value of the first four dividend payments is $9.8648.  The present value of the share when it reaches constant growth is:

$$P_4 \ = \ D_5 / (r - g) \ = \ \$3.7174 / (.08 - .05) \ = \ \$123.91$$

$$PV \ = \ \$123.91 / (1.08)^4 \ = \ \$91.08$$

So, $P_0$  $=$  $9.8648  +  $91.08  $=$  $100.95.

## Problem 14

The No Can Do Company has been hit hard due to increased competition.  The company's analysts predict that earnings (and dividends) will decline at a rate of 5% annually for an indefinite period of time.  Assume that the required return consists of a 3% dividend yield and 8% capital gain components, and that the most recent dividend per share was $2. What will be the price of the company's stock in three years?

**Solution:**       $D_1$  $=$  $1.90 ($2 × .95)
                      $D_2$  $=$  $1.805 ($1.9 × .95)
                      $D_3$  $=$  $1.7147 ($1.805 × .95)
                      $D_4$  $=$  $1.63 (1.7147 x .95)

The price in year 3:  $P_3 = $1.63/ [.11 - (-.05)] = $10.19

# 9        Net Present Value and Other Investment Criteria

## CHAPTER HIGHLIGHTS

Many of the criteria used for capital budgeting decision-making are discussed in this chapter. The criteria analyzed include: net present value, the payback period, the discounted payback period, the average accounting return, the internal rate of return, and the profitability index.  Our major conclusion is that net present value (NPV) is unequivocally the appropriate criterion for capital budgeting decisions. Consequently, we begin with a discussion of net present value.  Then we compare each of the alternative approaches to the present value. Each of the alternative criteria is deficient in some important ways.  However, we must consider these alternatives and understand their deficiencies because they are used in practice.

## NET PRESENT VALUE

We will demonstrate that the use of the net present value criterion in making capital budgeting decisions is consistent with the goal of financial managers examined in Chapter 1.  That is, the manager who uses the net present value criterion when making capital budgeting decisions is maximizing the current price of the firm's common shares.

**The Basic Idea:**  Consider an investment in an asset (e.g., a piece of real estate) for a price of $2,000.  Assume that the asset can be sold for $2,500 one year from today.  Alternatively, the investor has the opportunity to earn an 8% rate of return on an investment of similar risk.  To decide whether to acquire the real estate, we compare the acquisition of the asset with the investment at 8%. We can make the comparison based on: (1) future value; (2) present value; or (3) rate of return.  First we will compare the investments based on future value, then based on present value.  A comparison based on rates of return will be discussed later in the chapter.

The two alternatives which the investor must consider are: first, he can invest $2,000 at 8% for one year or, second, he can invest $2,000 to acquire the real estate today.  If he selects the first alternative, then one year from today he will receive:

$$FV_1 \; = \; PV \times (1 + r) \; = \; \$2,000 \times (1 + .08) \; = \; \$2,160$$

Clearly, the second alternative is preferable since the investor will have $2,500, rather than $2,160, one year from today.  Therefore, the investor should acquire the real estate today for $2,000.

The investor can also use present value analysis to evaluate the investment opportunity.  This analysis requires that the investor answer the following question:  At the 8% opportunity cost, what deposit would the investor have to make today in order to receive a return (i.e., future value) of $2,500 one year from today?  This question can be answered by using the present value formula developed in Chapter 5:

$$PV \; = \; \frac{FV}{(1 + r)} \quad \frac{\$2,500}{(1.08)} \; = \; \$2,314.81$$

At the 8% opportunity cost, the investor would have to invest $2,314.81 today in a one-year certificate of deposit in order to receive a return of $2,500 one year from now.  Consequently, the investor would select the investment providing the opportunity to purchase real estate for only $2,000, returning $2,500 one year from today.

The present value approach to investment decision-making can also be described in terms of the difference between the present value of the investment (i.e., $2,314.81 in the above example) and the cost of the investment ($2,000). This difference ($314.81 in this example) is called the *net present value*. The NPV for this example is:

$$\text{NPV} \quad = \quad \text{PV} - \text{Cost} \quad = \quad \$2,314.81 - \$2,000 \quad = \quad \$314.81$$

Net present value not only provides a criterion for determining whether an investment is acceptable, but it is also an unambiguous measure of the value of the investment. Note that the investor could sell the real estate for $2,314.81 immediately after purchasing it. The $2,314.81 represents the market value of the asset. Thus, the net present value (NPV) is the difference between an investment's market value and its cost. An investment with a positive net present value provides a net benefit to the investor equal to the net present value; an investment with a negative net present value is unacceptable.

The above interpretation of the net present value applies to corporate investment decision-making as well. We demonstrate this conclusion by considering the following simplified example.

**An Example:**   Suppose you want to form a corporation with a one-year life. The corporation is being formed in order to acquire an asset which costs $200,000 and which can be sold one year from now for $250,000. You would like to convince each of 100 investors (including yourself) to purchase a share in this corporation for $2,000. Since each investor is a 1% owner, each investor would then receive 1% of $250,000, or $2,500, one year from now. Assume that the market rate of interest is 8%. Is this investment opportunity attractive to potential investors?

Suppose that an investor is not willing to wait one year for his $2,500 share of the selling price of the asset. If the corporation purchases the asset today, the present value of the $250,000 to be received next year is:

$$\text{PV} \quad = \quad \$250,000 \, / \, (1.08) \quad = \quad \$231,481.48$$

Since the entire corporation consists of this one asset, this present value is the value of the corporation once the asset is purchased. An investor who purchases one share for $2,000 and then immediately sells the share in the financial market will be able to sell his share for $2,314.81. This figure can be viewed as 1% of the value of the firm (.01 × $231,481.48), or as the present value of 1% of the $250,000 future value of the asset:

$$\text{PV} \quad = \quad \$2,500 \, / \, (1.08) = \$2,314.81$$

The net present value of an investor's share is the difference between $2,314.81 and the cost of one share.

$$\text{NPV} \quad = \quad \$2,314.81 - \$2,000 \quad = \quad \$314.81$$

The above example demonstrates that a corporate investment with a positive net present value provides a net benefit to the shareholder equal to his proportionate share of the net present value of the corporate investment. Management must accept investments with positive net present value, since such investments provide value to the shareholders. Consequently, the net present value criterion indicates that corporate financial managers should seek to maximize the current value of the shares of the firm by adopting investments with positive net present value.

**Estimating Net Present Value - An Example:**  We now consider an example which further develops some aspects of the net present value concept introduced in the previous section.

Campanella Construction, Inc. is considering the acquisition of new construction equipment. Management estimates that it will cost $10,000 to acquire the equipment and that the availability of the equipment will increase the company's cash revenues by $9,000 per year for each of the next two years. However, cash expenses will increase by $4,000 per year; these expenses include, among other expenses, labour costs and additional income taxes. (Note that the above expenses do not include depreciation, which is not a cash expense; the relevance of depreciation expenses in capital budgeting decisions is discussed in detail in Chapter 10.) The equipment is expected to have a useful life of two years. At the end of two years, the equipment is expected to have a salvage value of $3,000. We assume an opportunity cost of 12% for this investment. Should Campanella invest in the new equipment?

Note: when calculating NPV, it is critical to remember that we always deal with *incremental* cash flows. That is, the difference between any cash flow increases and any cash flow decreases (or revenue increases – cost increases). The net cash inflow to Campanella is expected to be ($9,000 – $4,000) = $5,000 per year for each of the next two years. In addition, Campanella expects to be able to sell the equipment for $3,000 at the end of the two-year life of the asset. Therefore, the relevant cash inflows are $5,000 at the end of the first year and $8,000 at the end of the second year. Next, compute the present value of the cash inflows, using the 12% discount rate specified above:

$$PV = \frac{\$5,000}{(1.12)^1} = \frac{\$5,000}{(1.12)} = \$4,464.29$$

$$PV = \frac{\$5,000 + \$3,000}{(1.12)^2} = \frac{\$8,000}{(1.12)^2} = \$6,377.55$$

The sum of these present values is $10,841.84. This calculation indicates that Campanella would have to invest $10,841.84, at the 12% market interest rate, in order for the firm to receive payments of $5,000 after one year and $8,000 after two years. Since Campanella Construction has the opportunity to invest only $10,000 in the new equipment in order to receive cash inflows of $5,000 at the end of one year and $8,000 at the end of two years, this latter alternative is clearly preferable to the market alternative.

The difference between the present value calculated above (i.e., $10,841.84) and the $10,000 cost of the asset is the net present value of the asset (i.e., $841.84). In our example of the previous section, we interpreted the net present value as the net benefit to the owners of the firm. For each shareholder, the net benefit is equal to his proportionate share of the net present value of the corporate investment. In that earlier example, we hypothesized that the asset acquired represented the total assets of the firm. However, the interpretation of the net present value of a given investment is still appropriate even though the new equipment to be acquired by Campanella is only a portion of the firm's assets. This result is a consequence of the fact that the acquisition of the new equipment by Campanella increases the amount that prospective investors would be willing to pay to acquire ownership of the firm. The net benefit of this increased value accrues to the existing shareholders of the firm.

Algebraically, the net present value calculation for this example can be summarized as follows:

$$NPV = -C_0 + \frac{C_1}{(1+r)^1} + \frac{C_2}{(1+r)^2}$$

where $C_0$ is the initial $10,000 outlay, $C_1$ is the $5,000 payment one year from now, $C_2$ is the $8,000 payment two years from now and r is the 12% market interest rate. The more general formula for net present value is:

$$NPV = -C_0 + \frac{C_1}{(1+r)^1} + \frac{C_2}{(1+r)^2} + \ldots + \frac{C_t}{(1+r)^t}$$

where t represents the last period during which a payment is received.

To summarize the NPV rule, *an investment should be accepted if the NPV is positive and rejected if it is negative.*

## THE PAYBACK RULE

The *payback period* is the amount of time required to recover the initial investment for a capital budgeting project from the subsequent cash inflows produced by the project. The payback period is easy to calculate and the payback period rule is equally simple to apply. However, the payback period rule has several major deficiencies which generally make it an inappropriate criterion for capital budgeting decisions.

**Defining the Rule:** The *payback period rule* specifies that an investment is acceptable if the sum of its undiscounted cash flows equals the initial investment before some specified cutoff time period.

**An Example:** Consider an investment with the following cash flows: an initial investment of $10,000, and cash inflows of $2,000, $5,000, $3,000, and $6,000 at the end of years 1, 2, 3 and 4, respectively. What is the payback period? According to the payback period rule, should the investment be accepted?

The initial investment is $10,000. After three years, the sum of the cash inflows equals $10,000, so the payback period for this investment is three years. Consequently, this investment would be rejected if the cutoff time period were, for example, two years. Managers would accept the project if their cutoff date was greater than three years.

In the above example, if the initial investment were $13,000 instead of $10,000, what is the payback? Clearly, another $3,000 must be recovered in the fourth year during which the cash inflow is $6,000. To figure out the fractional year, we simply divide $3,000 by $6,000 (=.50). So, the payback is 3.50 years. Note, the payback rule assumes that the cash inflows and outflows occur at a *constant rate throughout the year.*

**Analyzing the Payback Period Rule:** The deficiencies of the payback rule are:

1.      The timing of cash flows within the payback period is ignored, thereby treating all cash flows as equally valuable. In contrast, the net present value properly discounts these cash flows.
2.      All cash flows after the cutoff time period are ignored, while NPV considers all cash flows.
3.      There is no objective criterion for choosing the cutoff time period, while the net present value criterion is based on market interest rates and the creation of wealth.

The primary advantage of the payback rule is its simplicity; it is both easy to compute and easy to understand. It is often used in practice for making low-level, relatively small investment decisions.

**The Discounted Payback Rule:** The *discounted payback period rule* specifies that a project is acceptable if the sum of the discounted cash flows equals the initial investment before a specified cutoff time period. This rule is identical to the payback period rule except that the time value of money is considered since the cash flows are discounted.

**An Example:** We will use the cash flow data from the preceding problem and a 10% discount rate. Would the investment be acceptable for a company that requires a discounted payback period of three years?

The sum of the discounted cash flows is the present value of the future cash inflows. For the first three years, the sum of the discounted cash flows is $8,204.36. For the first four years, the sum is $12,302.44. Therefore, this project has a discounted payback period between three and four years, and it would be rejected according to the discounted payback period rule. The exact discounted payback is (3 + $1795.44 / $4098.08) = 3.44 years where the fractional year is computed by taking the amount to be recovered in the fourth year, $1,795.64 ($10,000 – $8,204.36) and dividing by the present value equivalent of the fourth year cash inflow: [$6,000/(1.1)$^4$] = $4098.08. Notice that the net present value for this investment is ($12,302.44 – $10,000) = $2,302.44, indicating that the investment should be accepted.

The discounted payback period rule may appear preferable to the payback period rule because cash flows are discounted.  However, two of the three deficiencies of the payback period criterion also apply to the discounted payback period.  That is, cash flows after the cutoff time period are ignored and there is no objective criterion for choosing the cutoff time period.  Consequently, the discounted payback period lacks the simplicity of the payback period and is still less meaningful than the net present value.

## THE AVERAGE ACCOUNTING RETURN

The *average accounting return* (AAR) is defined as average net income attributed to an investment divided by the average book value of the asset.  The *average accounting return rule* specifies that an investment is acceptable if its average accounting return exceeds a specified target level.

**An Example:**  Suppose that the cash inflow data of the preceding problems represent accounting net income rather than cash flows. What is the average accounting return? According to the average accounting return criterion, is the capital budgeting project acceptable?

The average net income is:

($2,000 + $5,000 + $3,000 + $6,000) / 4  =  $4,000

If the $10,000 investment is depreciated to a value of zero, on a straight-line basis, over a four-year period, then the book value decreases by ($10,000/4) = $2,500 per year.  The average book value is:

($10,000 + $7,500 + $5,000 + $2,500 + $0) / 5  =  $5,000

Note that even though the asset is depreciated over a four-year period, the average book value is the average of five observations, beginning with the year 0 book value, and ending with the year 4 book value. So, if an asset will be fully depreciated over the project's life, the average book value is simply the investment divided by 2.

$$\text{AAR} = \frac{\text{Avg. Net Income}}{\text{Avg. Book Value}} = \frac{\$4,000}{\$5,000} = 80\%$$

The project is acceptable if the firm's target AAR is less than 80%.

The AAR rule has several serious deficiencies.  First, the AAR method uses accounting income and book value data which generally are not closely related to cash flows, the relevant data for financial decision-making. Second, the AAR ignores the time value of money.  Income received in three years, for example, is treated as equivalent to income received in one year. Third, the target AAR must be arbitrarily specified because it is not a rate of return in the financial market sense.

The only redeeming features for the AAR rule are that it is easy to calculate and that the information needed for the calculation is almost always available. Nevertheless, these features do not compensate for the disadvantages of this method.

## THE INTERNAL RATE OF RETURN

The *internal rate of return* (IRR) criterion is the most significant alternative to the net present value criterion. For any investment, the IRR is the rate of return (or discount rate) which equates the present value of the cash inflows with the cash outlay, or cost, of the investment. In other words, the IRR is the unique discount rate that makes the NPV of an investment zero. Alternatively, the IRR is defined as the rate of return for an investment. Algebraically, the IRR is the solution for the discount rate in the following equation:

$$NPV = 0 = -C_0 + \frac{C_1}{(1 + IRR)^1} + \frac{C_2}{(1 + IRR)^2} + \ldots + \frac{C_t}{(1 + IRR)^t}$$

Here, IRR = r at which NPV = 0.

**An Example:**   Consider the investment described earlier in this chapter; the cash outlay ($C_0$) is $10,000, and the cash inflows are $C_1 = \$2,000$, $C_2 = \$5,000$, $C_3 = \$3,000$, $C_4 = \$6,000$.   What is the internal rate of return for this investment?

To calculate the internal rate of return, substitute the known $C_i$ values into the above equation:

$$NPV = 0 = -\$10,000 + \frac{\$2,000}{(1 + IRR)^1} + \frac{\$5,000}{(1 + IRR)^2} + \frac{\$3,000}{(1 + IRR)^3} + \frac{\$6,000}{(1 + IRR)^4}$$

Alternatively, we can rewrite the equation as:

$$\$10,000 = \frac{\$2,000}{(1 + IRR)^1} + \frac{\$5,000}{(1 + IRR)^2} + \frac{\$3,000}{(1 + IRR)^3} + \frac{\$6,000}{(1 + IRR)^4}$$

Solving this equation for r is equivalent to solving for the yield to maturity of a level coupon bond, as discussed in Chapter 7. Therefore, the value of r can be determined by using either trial-and-error or a financial calculator. For either approach, the solution technique is analogous to the corresponding solution of the yield to maturity problem presented in the preceding chapter.

Using trial-and-error, one might 'guess' that IRR is 5%. Since this is purely a guess, two different individuals solving the same problem could very well make different first 'guesses.' To determine whether the guess is correct, find the present value of the cash inflows, discounted at 5%:

$$\frac{\$2,000}{(1.05)^1} + \frac{\$5,000}{(1.05)^2} + \frac{\$3,000}{(1.05)^3} + \frac{\$6,000}{(1.05)^4} = \$13,967.64$$

The present value is greater than $C_0$, which is $10,000.   Consequently, IRR = 5% is not the solution to the above equation. The next 'guess' at a solution must be a value of IRR greater than 5% because a larger denominator in the above equation reduces the present value. Therefore, a reasonable second guess might be 10%. (A student might wonder why 10% would be a more reasonable guess than, say, 6% or 60%. The answer is that none of these guesses is more or less reasonable than another; at this point it is not yet possible to determine which of these rates is closest to the correct value for r.)   Substituting a discount rate of 10% in the above equation:

$$\frac{\$2,000}{(1.10)^1} + \frac{\$5,000}{(1.10)^2} + \frac{\$3,000}{(1.10)^3} + \frac{\$6,000}{(1.10)^4} = \$12,302.44$$

Again, the discount rate must be increased, because the present value of the cash inflows exceeds the cash outlay ($C_0$). Extrapolating the above results indicates that the IRR must be substantially greater than 10%, so that a reasonable guess would be that IRR is approximately 20%:

$$\frac{\$2,000}{(1.20)^1} + \frac{\$5,000}{(1.20)^2} + \frac{\$3,000}{(1.20)^3} + \frac{\$6,000}{(1.20)^4} = \$9,768.52$$

Now it is clear that the internal rate of return is between 10% and 20% and substantially closer to 20%. Subsequent trials reveal that for discount rates of 18% and 19%, the present values are $10,206.46 and $9,983.76, respectively, so that the IRR is between 18% and 19%. A reasonable next guess would be r = 18.5%, which results in a present value of $10,094.16. Therefore, the IRR is between 18.5% and 19%. The above procedure can be continued until the desired degree of accuracy is reached, but it is apparent that the trial-and-error process is both tedious and time consuming. An accurate solution can be reached quickly with a financial calculator, which works out the IRR to be 18.9259%. Students using financial calculators should become familiar with using it to solve these types of problems. The exact procedure depends on the model of financial calculator. Read the instruction manual for examples of how to work these problems on your particular calculator. **Again, be sure you know how to use the calculator before an exam.**

The trial-and-error procedure requires finding the value of r which equates the present value of the future cash flows with the cash outlay. When the present value and the cash outlay are equal, the net present value is zero. Therefore, the above solution technique can also be described as the process of finding the value of r which equates the net present value to zero. This interpretation of the trial-and-error process can be seen in the following table, which summarizes the calculations above:

| Discount Rate | Present Value | Net Present Value |
|---|---|---|
| 5.0% | $13,967.64 | +$3,967.64 |
| 10.0 | 12,302.44 | + 2,302.44 |
| 20.0 | 9,768.52 | − 231.48 |
| 18.0 | 10,206.46 | + 206.46 |
| 19.0 | 9,983.76 | − 16.24 |
| 18.5 | 10,094.16 | + 94.16 |

The first two columns in this table represent the trial-and-error process used in the previous example in order to determine the discount rate for which the present value of the investment is equal to the cost of the investment (i.e., $10,000). In the third column, we view these calculations as a process of identifying the discount rate for which the net present value is zero. Since these procedures are equivalent, our conclusion, in either case, is that the internal rate of return is between 18.5% and 19.0%.

In part, the appeal of IRR is the simplicity in applying and understanding the criterion. An investment project is acceptable if the IRR is greater than the rate of return the firm could earn on investments of equal risk. An investment project is unacceptable if the IRR is less than the rate of return required by the firm.

If the investment under consideration is free of risk, then the relevant comparison in applying the above criterion is between the IRR and the rate of return in the financial markets for investments which are riskless. On the other hand, since most capital budgeting projects are risky to some extent, then the comparison must be between the IRR and the rate available in the financial markets for investments with risk level equal to that of the investment under consideration. As noted in the preceding chapters, this rate is often referred to as the 'discount rate,' although alternative terminology is also used, including 'opportunity cost,' 'required rate of return,' or 'the cost of capital.'

A useful tool in understanding the relationship between NPV and IRR is the *net present value profile* for a given investment opportunity. The NPV profile summarizes the relationship between the discount rate (r) and the NPV of the investment.   The NPV profile for the above investment opportunity is below.

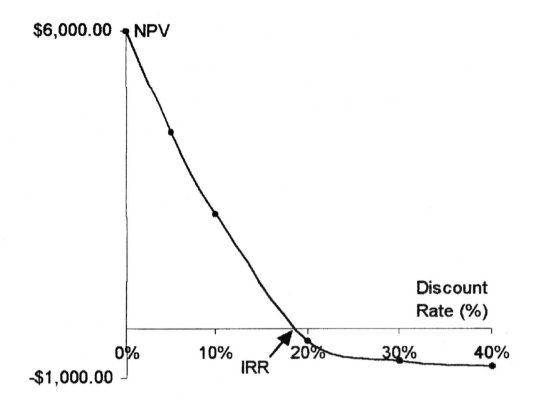

Clearly, as the discount rate increases, the NPV decreases.  The IRR is indicated as the value of r for which the NPV is zero.

The NPV profile illustrates the reason why, under certain circumstances, the IRR and the NPV criteria lead to identical decisions regarding the acceptability of an investment. If the IRR for a particular investment is greater than the required rate of return, then the following conclusions apply: first, according to the IRR criterion, the investment is acceptable; second, the NPV discounted at the required rate of return is positive (that is, on the NPV profile, the NPV is positive for any discount rate less than the IRR); and, third, since the NPV is positive, the investment is also acceptable according to the NPV criterion. Consequently, both criteria lead to the same decision. (The same conclusion applies when the IRR is less than the required rate of return.  That is, both criteria indicate that the investment is unacceptable.)

**Problems with the IRR:**  The above discussion seems to imply that the IRR criterion is equivalent to the NPV criterion in its ability to identify acceptable investments. However, under certain circumstances, the IRR criterion does not correctly indicate whether an investment is acceptable.  Problems with applying the IRR criterion are associated with the following situations: nonconventional cash flows and mutually exclusive investments.  These situations are analyzed below.

**Nonconventional Cash Flows:**  In order to understand the problem associated with nonconventional cash flows, we first define a cash inflow as having a positive sign and a cash outflow as having a negative sign. Therefore, a conventional cash flow for a capital budgeting project has a negative cash flow (i.e., an outlay) followed by positive cash flows (i.e., inflows).  A nonconventional series of cash flows changes sign (from negative to positive, or positive to negative) more than once.

Consider the following cash flows for an investment: (–$80, $500, –$500). This sequence indicates an outlay of $80 followed by an inflow of $500 at the end of year 1 and then an outlay of $500 at the end of year 2. Thus, the equation for calculating the NPV is:

$$NPV = -\$80 + \frac{\$500}{(1 + IRR)^1} - \frac{\$500}{(1 + IRR)^2}$$

To find the IRR, the equation must be solved for the value of r at which the NPV equals zero. The NPV for this series of cash flows is zero when the discount rate is 25%, and is also zero when the discount rate is 400%. There are two internal rates of return. This situation is an example of the *multiple rates of return* problem. Since there is no basis for choosing either one of these rates as the relevant IRR for such an investment, it is impossible to apply the IRR criterion when cash flows change sign more than once. In these cases, the NPV must be used as the decision rule.

**Mutually Exclusive Investments**:  An *independent investment project* is an investment whose acceptance or rejection does not affect, and is not affected by, the acceptance or rejection of any other projects. A set of *mutually exclusive investment projects* is a set of projects for which the acceptance of any one project in the set implies the rejection of all other projects in the set. For example, a company which is considering the purchase of a delivery truck may have under consideration numerous models produced by several manufacturers. Since only one truck will be purchased, the alternatives under consideration comprise a set of mutually exclusive investments.

The difficulties encountered in applying the IRR criterion to mutually exclusive projects arise when the projects being compared differ with respect to either scale or timing. In the former case, there are differences in the size of the initial outlay for the projects under consideration.  In the latter case, the differences are generally between one project whose cash flows are concentrated in the early years of the project's life and another project whose cash flows are concentrated in the later years. The scale problem is discussed in detail here.

Suppose we have two mutually exclusive investments, X and Y, with the following respective cash flows:

    X:        –$200, $100, $300, $400
    Y:        –$5,000, $4,000, $1,000, $2,000

Project X requires an outlay of $200 today in exchange for returns of $100, $300, and $400 in Years 1, 2, and 3, respectively. These investments are said to differ in scale because the cash flows for Y are substantially larger than those for X.  Further, suppose that the relevant opportunity cost is 10%. Since these investments are mutually exclusive, we must determine, first, whether each investment is acceptable and, second, in the event that both are acceptable, which is preferable.  At the 10% discount rate, the net present values are $439.37 and $965.44 for X and Y, respectively, indicating that both investments are acceptable. The internal rates of return are 87.20% and 22.81%, respectively, for X and Y.  Note that X has the higher IRR while Y has the higher NPV, so that it is not immediately apparent which is the preferable alternative.

It is important to remember here the discussion earlier in this chapter, establishing the validity of the NPV criterion for investment decision-making.  Given those conclusions, it is clear that Y is the preferable alternative. Although this decision is correct, it often seems inappropriate to those encountering this result for the first time. In order to understand why the IRR criterion can, under certain circumstances, mislead a decision-maker, it is helpful to think of the choice between X and Y in terms of the cross-over rate.

In order to understand the significance of the cross-over rate, we first define a hypothetical investment (Y–X); this is an investment which, when implemented along with investment X, will have the same cost and will generate the same cash flows as investment Y. Therefore, (Y–X) can be thought of as the incremental cash flows which would result if Y were accepted in place of X. (Y–X) requires that an additional ($5,000 – $200) = $4,800 be invested in order to receive incremental cash flows of $3,900, $700, and $1,600.

$$NPV(Y-X) = -\$4,800 + \frac{\$3,900}{(1.10)^1} + \frac{\$700}{(1.10)^2} + \frac{\$1,600}{(1.10)^3}$$

Next, we ascertain whether investment X (the investment with the smaller outlay and cash inflows), would be acceptable if it were treated as an independent investment, both the NPV and IRR criteria indicate that X is acceptable. Finally, we determine whether the investment (Y–X) is acceptable. (Y–X) has an IRR of 17.70% and an NPV (discounted at the 10% opportunity cost) of $526.07, so it is an acceptable investment. We have determined that X is acceptable and that (Y–X) is acceptable. Viewed in this way, accepting project Y amounts to accepting project X plus another acceptable investment (Y–X). Therefore, Y is the preferable alternative.

The internal rate of return for (Y–X) is referred to as the *cross-over rate*. In this example and as shown in the figure below, it indicates that we are indifferent between investments X and Y if the opportunity cost is equal to the 17.70% cross-over rate. If the opportunity cost is less than the cross-over rate, then investment Y is preferable; if the opportunity cost is greater than the cross-over rate, then investment X is preferable.

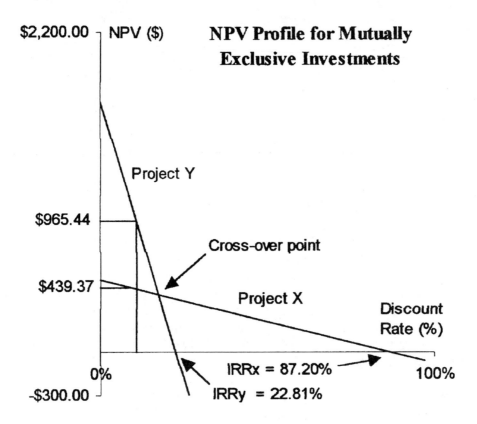

The timing problem mentioned at the beginning of this section occurs when two investments requiring the same initial outlay differ substantially in terms of the timing of the cash inflows. That is, the larger cash inflows for one investment occur early in the life of the asset, while the larger inflows for the other occur later; or in the case when two projects have different lives. As is the case for the scale problem, it is possible that the IRR criterion will mislead the decision-maker into selecting the less desirable alternative. As described above for the scale problem, this can be avoided by: (1) applying the NPV criterion; or, (2) comparing the incremental IRR with the required rate of return.

**Redeeming Qualities of the IRR:** Although NPV is the superior tool for analysing investment opportunities, IRR is actually more widely used. This is largely because investors and financial analysts prefer to discuss rates of return; this is a concept most people are familiar with. In addition, IRR is an easily understood way to communicate information about the profitability of a project.

IRR actually has one advantage over NPV. Using NPV requires being able to estimate an appropriate discount rate. We can compute the IRR without this information.

## THE PROFITABILITY INDEX

The *profitability index* (PI), also known as the *benefit/cost ratio,* is defined as the present value of the future cash flows divided by the initial investment. In one sense, the profitability index is comparable to the NPV criterion, because it provides an indication of whether the present value of the future cash flows exceeds the initial investment. If this ratio is greater than one, then the investment is desirable, because the present value of the future cash flows is greater than the initial outlay. Any independent investment shown to be acceptable according to the PI criterion is also acceptable according to the NPV criterion. However, as in the case of the IRR, problems may arise in applying the PI to mutually exclusive investment projects. For example, a smaller project may have a higher PI, but a lower NPV than a larger project. Incorrect decisions are avoided by: (1) applying the NPV criterion; or, (2) applying the PI criterion to the incremental cash flows.

In our earlier example where the NPV was $2,302.44 for an initial investment of $10,000, the PI is simply 1.23 ($12,302.44/$10,000). This tells us that for every dollar invested, $.23 in NPV is created ($.23 is the value created per dollar invested).

## THE PRACTICE OF CAPITAL BUDGETING

In surveys of large corporations, discounted cash flow approaches (i.e., NPV, IRR, PI) are the most commonly used capital budgeting techniques. It appears that 80% or more use discounted cash flow (NPV and/or IRR), but not necessarily to the exclusion of other procedures.

## CONCEPT TEST

1.  Present value analysis of an investment opportunity specifies that the investment is _____ if the present value of the future cash inflows is _____ the cash outlay. The investment is_____ if the present value of the future cash inflows is _____ the cash outlay.

2.  The net present value of an asset is equal to the difference between the present value of the future_____ produced by the asset and the _____ of the asset.

3.  An investment is acceptable if its net present value is _____. This is consistent with present value analysis because an asset with a _____ net present value has a present value greater than its cost, which makes the investment _____.

4.      An investment is unacceptable if its net present value is _____.  This is consistent with present value analysis because an investment with a_____ net present value has a present value less than its cost, which makes the investment _____.

5.      The net present value of an asset measures the _____ which accrues to the _____ of the firm if the asset is acquired.  Therefore, the use of the net present value criterion is consistent with the financial manager's goal of maximizing the _____ of the firm's common shares.

6.      The payback period is the amount of time required to recover the _____ for a capital budgeting project from the future _____ produced by the project. The payback period rule specifies that an investment is _____ if the payback period is less than a specified _____.

7.      The deficiencies of the payback rule are: the _____ of cash flows within the payback period is ignored, thereby treating these cash flows as _____; all cash flows after the _____ are ignored; there is no objective criterion for choosing the _____.

8.      The primary advantage of the payback rule is its _____.

9.      The discounted payback period for an asset is the time period required for the sum of the discounted future _____ to equal the _____ for the asset.  The discounted payback period rule specifies that a project is _____ if the discounted payback period is less than a specified _____.

10.     The deficiencies of the discounted payback period rule are: cash flows after the_____ are ignored; and there is no objective criterion for choosing the _____.

11.     The average accounting return (AAR) for an investment project is defined as _____ attributed to the asset divided by _____ of the asset. The average accounting return rule specifies that an investment is _____ if its average accounting return exceeds a _____.

12.     The deficiencies of the AAR are: the AAR method uses _____ income and _____ value data, rather than _____; the AAR ignores the _____; and, the_____ must be arbitrarily specified.

13.     The internal rate of return is the rate of return (or discount rate) which equates the _____ of the future _____ for an investment with the _____ of the investment. The IRR can also be defined as the rate of return which equates the net present value of an investment to _____.

14.     An investment project is _____ if the IRR is greater than the rate of return which could be earned in the financial markets on investments of equal risk. An investment project is _____ if the IRR is less than the relevant rate of return in the financial markets.

15.     The IRR criterion may not correctly indicate whether an investment is acceptable. The problems which arise in applying the internal rate of return criterion are associated with the following situations: _____ cash flows and _____ investments.

16.     A conventional cash flow for a capital budgeting project has a _____ cash flow (i.e., an outlay) followed by _____ cash flows (i.e., inflows). A _____ series of cash flows changes sign more than once, and may have more than one IRR. It is impossible to apply the IRR criterion in the case of a _____ series of cash flows.

17.  An _____ investment project is an investment whose acceptance or rejection does not affect, and is not affected by, the acceptance or rejection of any other projects. A set of mutually exclusive investment projects is a set of projects for which the acceptance of any one project in the set implies the _____ of all other projects in the set.

18.  The difficulties encountered in applying the IRR criterion to mutually exclusive projects arise when the projects being compared differ with respect to either _____ or _____. Incorrect decisions are avoided by: (1) applying the_____ criterion; or, (2) applying the IRR criterion to the _____ cash flows.

19.  The profitability index is defined as the _____ of the future _____ divided by the _____. If the PI is greater than _____, then the investment is_____, because the present value of the future cash inflows is greater than the _____. Any _____ investment shown to be acceptable according to the PI criterion is also acceptable according to the NPV criterion.

20.  Problems may arise in applying the PI to_____ investment projects. Incorrect decisions are avoided by: (1) applying the_____ criterion; or, (2) applying the PI criterion to the _____ cash flows.

## ANSWERS TO CONCEPT TEST

1.  acceptable; greater than; unacceptable; less than

2.  cash flows; cost

3.  positive; positive; acceptable

4.  negative; negative; unacceptable

5.  value; shareholders; current price

6.  initial investment; cash inflows; acceptable; cutoff time period

7.  timing; equally valuable; cutoff time period; cutoff time period

8.  simplicity

9.  cash inflows; initial investment; acceptable; cutoff time period

10.  cutoff time period; cutoff time period

11.  average net income; average book value; acceptable; specified target level

12.  accounting; book; cash flows; time value of money; target AAR

13.  present value; cash inflows; cost; zero

14.  acceptable; unacceptable

15.     nonconventional; mutually exclusive

16.     negative; positive; nonconventional; nonconventional

17.     independent; rejection

18.     scale; timing; net present value; incremental

19.     present value; cash inflows; initial investment; one; acceptable; initial investment; independent

20.     mutually exclusive; net present value; incremental


## PROBLEMS AND SOLUTIONS


### Problem 1

Christine is considering purchasing a new piece of equipment for her factory.  The equipment costs $10,000 and will increase revenues by $4,000 per year for the next three years, and $2,000 per year for two years after that.  It will cost Christine $1,000 per year to run the equipment, and at the end of the five years the equipment is expected to have a salvage value of $2,500.  Use the net present value criterion to determine whether Christine should invest in this equipment, assuming an opportunity cost of 10%.

**Solution:** Remember that net present value is concerned with *incremental* cash flows.  During the first three years, the equipment will generate cash flows of (4,000 - $1,000) = $3,000 per year, and during the fourth and fifth years it will generate cash flows of ($2,000 - $1,000) = $1,000 per year.  The NPV can then be calculated as:

$$\text{NPV} = -\$10,000 + \$3,000 \times \text{PVIFA}\,(10\%, 3) \ + \ \$1,000 / (1.10)^4 \ + \ \$3,500 / (1.10)^5$$

$$= \ -\$10,000 \ + \ \$7,460.56 \ + \ \$683.01 \ + \ \$2,173.22 \ = \ \$316.79$$

Christine should accept the investment and purchase the equipment, because the NPV was positive.


**For Problems 2 to7, use the following cash flows for projects A and B:**

> A:      −$2,000, $500, $600, $700, $800
> B:      −$2,000, $950, $850, $400, $300


### Problem 2

Calculate the payback period for projects A and B.  If the target payback period is three years for each project, will the projects be accepted?

**Solution:** The sum of the first three cash flows for project A is $1,800, and the sum of the first four cash flows is $2,600, so the payback period for A is between three and four years. After three years, A is within $200 of paying back the initial cost. The cash flow in the fourth year is $800. The fractional year is thus ($200/$800) = .25, so the payback period is 3.25 years. The payback period for project B is 2.5 years.

Project A's payback period is greater than the target cutoff, so it will be rejected. Project B will be accepted.

## Problem 3

If the discount rate is 12%, what is the discounted payback period for project A? For project B?

**Solution:** The sum of the four discounted cash flows for project A is $1,931.41, so A does not pay back its initial cost. For B, the sum of the four discounted cash flows is $2,001.20, so the payback period is almost exactly four years.

## Problem 4

Calculate by trial-and-error the internal rate of return for projects A and B.

**Solution:** The solution to Problem 2 provides some useful information for solving this problem. For project B, the discounted payback period is almost exactly equal to the life of the project, so the internal rate of return must be slightly greater than the 12% discount rate. The exact value of the IRR is 12.0351%. For project A, the NPV is –$68.59 at a 12% discount rate, so the IRR is somewhat less than 12%. At discount rates of 10% and 11%, the NPV is $22.74 and –$23.76, respectively. Therefore, the IRR must be between 10% and 11%. The exact value is 10.4845%.

## Problem 5

If A and B are mutually exclusive and the required rate of return is 5%, which project should be accepted?

**Solution:** Using a discount rate of 5%, the NPV for A is $283.26 and the NPV for B is $268.08. Therefore, A is preferred even though it has the lower IRR.

## Problem 6

If the discount rate is 12%, and A and B are mutually exclusive, which project should be accepted?

**Solution:**   In Problem 3, A is shown to have a negative NPV at a 12% discount rate (–$68.59), making it unacceptable. B has an NPV of $1.20, so it is acceptable and preferred.

## Problem 7

At what discount rate will we be indifferent between A and B?

**Solution:** To solve for the rate at which we are indifferent between A and B, we compute the discount rate such that A and B have the same net present value. That is:

$$NPV_A = NPV_B$$

This is equivalent to finding the discount rate such that:

$$NPV_A - NPV_B = 0$$

This is solved by finding the internal rate of return for the incremental cash flows for an investment (A –B): ($0, –$450, –$250, $300, $500). This is the cross-over rate. This rate is found by trial and error or with the use of a financial calculator. The latter approach indicates that the rate is 6.0654%. At this discount rate, both A and B have an NPV of $223.51.


## Problem 8

Compute the internal rate of return for investments with the following cash flows in years 0, 1 and 2, respectively:

A:     –$60, $155, –$100
B:     $60, –$155, $100

How do you interpret the results in terms of the IRR criterion?

**Solution:** Since the cash flows for each of these investments change sign more than once, each investment has more than one internal rate of return. These can be determined by trial and error, but since these cash flows extend over only three time periods, it is possible to solve algebraically for the two IRR values. Consider, for example, the first of the two investments. The IRR is the rate r which is the solution to the following equation:

$$\$60 = \frac{\$155}{(1 + IRR)} - \frac{\$100}{(1 + IRR)^2}$$

Algebraically, this is a quadratic equation. In general, a quadratic equation has two solutions, which can be determined directly by using the quadratic formula. The two solutions here are $IRR_1 = .25 = 25\%$ and $IRR_2 = .3333 = 33.33\%$. These same values are also the two solutions for the second investment above.

To interpret these results, we can compute the net present value at a rate between the two IRRs. At a discount rate of 30%, for example, the NPV is +$.06 for the first investment and –$.06 for the second. The first investment is acceptable only if the required rate of return is between 25% and 33.33%. The second investment is acceptable only if the required return is outside the range 25% to 33.33%. This conclusion derives from the fact that a quadratic equation, when graphed, has the shape of a parabola, so that the net present value must be either exclusively negative or exclusively positive between the two solutions identified here, and has the opposite sign outside the range of the two solutions.

## Problem 9

You have been asked to analyze an investment with the following cash flows in years 0, 1, and 2, respectively: –$51, $100, –$50. Compute the internal rate of return for this investment. Is the investment acceptable? The required return is unknown.

**Solution:** This is a problem designed to keep students out of trouble by keeping them busy. There is no IRR! All this means is that there is no real number for which the NPV is zero. For example, consider the lowest possible discount rate, r = 0%. The NPV becomes:

$$NPV = -\$51 + \frac{\$100}{(1.0)} - \frac{\$50}{(1.0)^2} = -\$1$$

At any positive discount rate, the NPV becomes more negative. At any discount rate, the NPV is negative, so the required return is irrelevant. This result can also be demonstrated algebraically because the IRR is the solution to a quadratic equation, as discussed in the solution to Problem 8. For this problem, however, the quadratic equation does not have an x-intercept and, therefore, no solution.

## Problem 10

Pete is considering two investment opportunities. Investment P requires an initial cash outflow of $900 and is expected to return $225 for each of the following six years. Investment J requires an initial investment of $1,200 and will provide cash inflows of $300 for the next five years. Use the profitability index criterion to determine which investment Pete should choose, given that his required rate of return is 8%.

**Solution:** To solve for the profitability index, we need to calculate the present value of the future cash flows for each investment option, using a discount rate of 8%. We then divide the present value of the future cash flows by the initial investment to determine the profitability index. The present value of the future cash flows for Investment P is:

$$PV = \$225 \times PVIFA\ (8\%,\ 6) = \$225 \times 4.6229 = \$1,040.15$$

The profitability index for Investment P is ($1,040.15 / $900) = 1.1557. With a profitability index above 1, the investment is acceptable, and its NPV is $140.15.

The present value of the future cash flows for Investment J is:

$$PV = \$300 \times PVIFA\ (8\%,\ 5) = \$300 \times 3.9927 = \$1,197.81$$

The profitability index for Investment J is ($1,197.81 / $1,200) = 0.99818, making it unacceptable. The NPV of Investment J is -$2.19. Clearly, Pete should select Investment P.

## Problem 11

Use the following abbreviated financial statements to calculate the average accounting return for a proposed investment:

|                             | Year   |        |        |        |        |
|-----------------------------|--------|--------|--------|--------|--------|
|                             | 0      | 1      | 2      | 3      | 4      |
| Gross book value            | $160   | $160   | $160   | $160   | $160   |
| Less: Accumulated depreciation |     | 40     | 80     | 120    | 160    |
| Net book value              | $160   | $120   | $ 80   | $ 40   | $ 0    |
|                             |        |        |        |        |        |
| Sales                       |        | $ 95   | $ 90   | $ 97   | $ 80   |
| Costs                       |        | 33     | 30     | 25     | 10     |
| Depreciation                |        | 40     | 40     | 40     | 40     |
| Taxes (50%)                 |        | 11     | 10     | 16     | 15     |
| Net income                  |        | $ 11   | $ 10   | $ 16   | $ 15   |

**Solution:** The average net income is ($11 + $10 + $16 + $15) / 4 = $13. The average book value is ($160 + $120 + $80 + $40 + $0) / 5 = $80, so the AAR is ($13/$80) = .1625 = 16.25%.

## Problem 12

What is the internal rate of return for the investment described in Problem 11?

**Solution:** To compute the internal rate of return, the cash flows must first be tabulated. Remember, operating cash flow can be derived by adding depreciation to net income. So, cash flows are $51, $50, $56, and $55, respectively over the four-year period. The initial investment is $160. Using trial-and-error, it can be shown that the IRR is approximately 12%. For a 12% discount rate, the present value of the cash flows is $160.21 and the net present value is ($160.21 − $160) = $.21. The exact value of the IRR is 12.0608%.

## Problem 13

What is the IRR of a project with a cash outflow of $600 in year 0, followed by yearly cash inflows of $200, $200, and $400?

**Solution:**

$$\text{NPV} = -\$600 + \$200 / (1 + \text{IRR}) + \$200 / (1 + \text{IRR})^2 + \$400 / (1 + \text{IRR})^3$$

Using a trial-and-error approach, the following IRRs can be found:

| Discount rate | NPV     |
|---------------|---------|
| 12%           | $22.72  |
| 13            | 10.84   |
| 14            | - 0.68  |

Using a financial calculator, the exact answer is 13.0402%.

## Problem 14

You have the opportunity to borrow $8,000, to be repaid in yearly instalments of $2,200 at the end of each of the next five years.  Use the IRR criterion to determine whether this loan is preferable to borrowing at the market rate of 11.5%.

**Solution:**  The IRR is the solution for r in the following equation:

$$PV = C \times PVIFA(r,t)$$
$$\$8,000 = \$2,200 \times PVIFA(r,5)$$
$$PVIFA(r,5) = 3.63636$$

This last equation can also be written:

$$\frac{1 - [1 / (1 + r)^5]}{r} = 3.63636$$

Although it is impossible to directly compute the solution to this equation, an approximate answer can be determined from Table A.3.  A more precise solution can be computed using trial-and-error, while a financial calculator will quickly and easily compute the precise value of r.

First, we consider the approximate solution for r which can be derived from Table A.3.  Values of PVIFA(r,5) are in the fifth row of the table. PVIFA(11%,5) = 3.6959 and PVIFA(12%,5) = 3.6048.  Note that, in order to find the PVIFA for 11%, it is necessary to interpolate because the table only gives the PVIFA for 10% and 12%. The PVIFA for 11% is exactly halfway between the two. Since our calculation indicates that PVIFA(r,5) = 3.63636, r is between 11% and 12%.  We could proceed to derive a more precise value using trial-and-error and the formula for PVIFA.  For example, it would be reasonable to 'guess' that the value of r is closer to 12% than to 11%, since PVIFA(12%,5) is closer to 3.63636 than is PVIFA(11%,5).  If we guess that r = 11.7%, we then calculate the value of PVIFA(11.7%,5) as follows:

$$PVIFA(11.7\%,5) = \frac{1 - [1/(1.117)^5]}{0.117} = 3.63173$$

Since the value of PVIFA(11.7%,5) is less than 3.63636 we now guess that r is less than 11.7%.  The value of PVIFA(r,5) for r = 11.6% is 3.64078.  Consequently, r is between 11.6% and 11.7%. This procedure can be continued to any desired degree of accuracy.  The precise value of r can be determined with a financial calculator.

The exact interest rate is 11.6488%.  It is clear that borrowing at the market rate of 11.5% is preferable to borrowing at the higher rate indicated in this example.

## Problem 15

A firm is considering the following mutually exclusive investment projects: Project A requires an initial outlay of $500 and will return $120 per year for the next seven years; Project B requires an initial outlay of $5,000 and will return $1,350 per year for the next five years. The required rate of return is 10%. Use the net present value criterion to determine which investment is preferable.

**Solution:** Since the return for each investment is in the form of an annuity, we can use the following formula to determine the net present value for project A:

$$PV = \$120 \times PVIFA(10\%,7)$$

The value of PVIFA(10%,7) is computed as follows:

$$PVIFA(10\%,7) = \frac{1 - [1 / (1.10)^7]}{.10} = 4.86842$$

Therefore, the present value of the annuity is ($120 × 4.86842) = $584.21 and the net present value for project A is $84.20. Similarly, the net present value for project B is $117.56. The net present value criterion indicates that B is the preferred alternative. (Note that there may be an additional problem here arising from the difference in the life of the two assets. If the assets perform a comparable task, the shorter life of project A may imply that a new investment in a replacement is required sooner for A than for B. This possibility is addressed in the next chapter.)

## Problem 16

Calculate the internal rate of return for each of the investment projects described in Problem 15.

**Solution:** Since the returns for each project are in the form of an annuity, we can estimate the IRRs using the solution technique of Problem 15, or we can determine the exact values using the annuity functions of a financial calculator. The latter approach indicates that the internal rates of return are 14.9500% and 10.9162% for projects A and B, respectively. In spite of the fact that project A has the higher IRR, the solution to Problem 15 indicates that project B is preferable. This is an example of the scale problem discussed in the chapter.

## Problem 17

Calculate the profitability index for each of the investment projects described in Problem 15.

**Solution:** The profitability index is defined as the ratio of the present value of the future cash flows divided by the initial investment. For project A, the profitability index is ($584.21/$500) = 1.1684. For project B, the profitability index is ($5,117.58/$5,000) = 1.0235. If these two projects were independent of each other, both would be acceptable according to the profitability index criterion because each of the above values is greater than 1. This conclusion is consistent with that implied by the net present value and internal rate of return criteria for independent projects. However, since the projects are in fact mutually exclusive, the profitability index criterion can not be used to select the preferred alternative.

## Problem 18

Again, refer to the two investments identified in Problem 15. Calculate the internal rate of return, the profitability index, and the net present value for the incremental investment (B–A).

**Solution:** The cash flows for the incremental investment (B–A) are:

(–$4,500, $1,230, $1,230, $1,230, $1,230, $1,230, –$120, –$120)

The internal rate of return for (B–A) is 10.3009%, the present value is $4,533.35, the profitability index is 1.0074, and the net present value is $33.35. (Note that the internal rate of return computed here is also referred to as the cross-over rate.)

All three criteria indicate that the incremental investment (B–A) is acceptable.  It is always true that the three criteria applied to the incremental investment result in the same decision.  Consequently, since project A is acceptable and the incremental investment (B–A) is acceptable, then project B is preferred.  We have demonstrated that the internal rate of return and profitability index criteria, when applied to the incremental investment, result in the same decision derived by applying the NPV criterion in Problem 15.

# 10   Making Capital Investment Decisions

## CHAPTER HIGHLIGHTS

The major emphasis of this chapter is the identification of the relevant cash flows for net present value analysis of a capital budgeting problem. Although financial managers use accounting income data in their decision-making, financial decisions must be based on cash flows rather than income. Consequently, it is important to correctly interpret accounting data in order to identify relevant cash flows.

In the last section of the chapter, we also discuss the application of capital budgeting techniques in two special circumstances: setting a bid price and evaluating equipment with different lives. These problems are illustrative of the numerous variations which arise in capital budgeting problems.

## PROJECT CASH FLOWS: A FIRST LOOK

By undertaking a capital budgeting project, a firm changes current and future cash flows. Capital investment decision-making requires that financial managers determine whether the changes in cash flows which result from undertaking a particular project add value to the firm.

**Relevant Cash Flows:** The relevant cash flows for the analysis of a capital budgeting project are the *incremental cash flows* associated with the project. The incremental cash flows consist of any and all changes in the firm's cash flows *that are a direct consequence of accepting the project.* Even though we use accounting income data, we must be able to interpret the accounting data in such a way as to identify the incremental cash flows.

**The Stand-Alone Principle:** The incremental cash flows for a project can be defined as the difference between the firm's cash flows, now and in the future, if the project is undertaken, and the firm's cash flows if the project is not undertaken. For practical purposes, this is an unwieldy definition because it requires the examination of the firm's total cash flows. Fortunately, a particular project can generally be viewed as having its own cash flows. That is, the stand-alone principle specifies that the financial manager can view the incremental cash flows from the perspective of the project, rather than from the perspective of the entire firm.

## INCREMENTAL CASH FLOWS

The financial manager encounters numerous difficulties in the process of identifying incremental cash flows for a capital budgeting project. Some of the most frequently encountered complications relate to the interpretation of the following concepts: sunk costs, opportunity costs, side effects, net working capital, and financing costs.

**Sunk Costs:** A *sunk cost* is money the firm has already spent, or is committed to spend, regardless of whether it accepts the project under consideration. For instance, the cost of a feasibility study undertaken before the accept/reject decision is made is a sunk cost, because it must be paid regardless of the decision made. This sunk cost is not an incremental cost. Therefore it is not relevant to the capital budgeting decision. Sunk costs are always excluded from the analysis.

**Opportunity Costs:**   Suppose a firm is considering a project that involves building a new factory on land already owned by the firm. The price paid for the land, at some time in the past, is a sunk cost and is therefore not relevant to the current decision.   However, by building a factory on the land, the firm would lose the opportunity to use the land for some alternative project.   One alternative to building the factory would be to sell the property.   By using the property to build the factory, the firm forgoes the proceeds from a sale of the property.   Hence, the market value of the property (net of any capital gains taxes) is an opportunity cost which is an incremental cost to the project.

**Side Effects:**   Capital budgeting projects often have *side effects* which must be taken into consideration. An example of a side effect is *erosion*.   When a consumer products manufacturer introduces a new product, some portion of the new product's sales might come at the expense of reduced sales of the company's other products. The resulting reduction in cash flow to other product lines is a direct consequence of introducing the new consideration.

**Net Working Capital:**   As defined in Chapter 2, net working capital is the difference between current assets and current liabilities.   A capital budgeting project often requires an increase in net working capital during the life of the project.   For example, the development of a new product necessitates increases in cash balances, inventory and accounts receivable.   Some of the financing needed for this expansion of current assets is provided by increases in accounts payable.   However, the increase in accounts payable is typically not sufficient to finance the increase in current assets; hence, additional outlays are normally required to finance the increase in net working capital.   This investment in net working capital is an incremental cash outflow.   At the termination of a project, this outflow is typically recovered, and is therefore an inflow at that time.

**Financing Costs:** Financing costs are *not included* in the computation of incremental cash flows.   Financing costs have an impact on our net present value analysis in that these costs determine the appropriate discount rate in our net present value calculations.   This issue is discussed in detail in later chapters.   In this chapter, we continue to assume that the relevant opportunity cost or discount rate is given and that financing costs are incorporated in the discount rate.

**Inflation:** Typically, because capital budgeting projects span many years, inflation may have an impact on a project's cash flows.   We already know that nominal rates are adjusted for expected inflation.   Similarly any estimates of cash flows must also be adjusted.   Ignoring the impact of inflation could bias against accepting a positive NPV project.

**Government Intervention:**   In Canada, various levels of government offer incentives to promote certain types of capital investment These incentives include grants, investment tax credits and favourable rates for capital cost allowance (CCA) and subsidized loans.   Since these change a project's cash flows, they must be factored into capital budgeting analysis.

**Other Issues:**   Two additional issues associated with the identification of the relevant incremental cash flows are: first, cash flows are measured when they occur, not when they accrue in the accounting sense; and, second, since taxes are clearly cash outflows, *we are concerned with after-tax incremental cash flows*.

## PRO FORMA FINANCIAL STATEMENTS AND PROJECT CASH FLOWS

For a typical capital budgeting project, current cash outflows are followed by future cash inflows. Therefore, it is necessary to forecast, or project, these incremental cash inflows. Projected cash flows for a capital budgeting project are derived from *pro forma financial statements*.   These are projected financial statements for future time periods.

**An Example:** In this section we will determine the NPV for a proposed capital budgeting project for KMS Corporation. However, we must first determine the incremental cash flows. Assume KMS is considering the purchase of new manufacturing equipment, expected to produce a better quality product at a lower cost. Sales revenue is expected to increase by $40,000 the first year, and 10% a year for each of the next four years. Operating costs will decrease by $20,000 per year. The equipment costs $150,000 and is expected to have a useful economic life of five years. The market value at the end of five years will be $60,000. We will assume straight line depreciation and a 40% tax rate for both ordinary income and capital gains. KMS projects an investment of $15,000 in working capital. This investment will be completely recovered at the end of year five.

In Chapter 2, we observed that cash flow from the firm's assets has three components: operating cash flow, capital spending, and additions to net working capital. The capital spending for the new equipment is the amount spent on acquiring the asset, the $150,000 outlay for purchase of the equipment. The addition to net working capital is the $15,000 outlay for the investment in working capital. Therefore, the total outlay at year 0 is $165,000, which consists of $150,000 capital expenditure and a $15,000 addition to net working capital. Operating cash flow is defined in Chapter 2 as:

Earnings before interest and taxes + Depreciation − Taxes

We noted in Chapter 2 that we do not deduct either interest or depreciation in computing operating cash flow. Interest is not deducted because it is not an operating expense. We do not deduct depreciation in computing operating cash flow because depreciation is a non-cash expense. The above definition of operating cash flow specifies that depreciation is added to earnings before interest and taxes (EBIT). The sum of EBIT and depreciation can be thought of as earnings before depreciation, interest, and taxes. The deduction of taxes is because taxes are a cash outflow. In this example, the KMS has no interest expense. For KMS Corporation, we compute operating cash flow as follows:

| | Year 1 | Year 2 | Year 3 | Year 4 | Year 5 |
|---|---|---|---|---|---|
| Sales revenue | $40,000 | $44,000 | $48,400 | $53,240 | $58,564.00 |
| -Operating costs | - 20,000 | - 20,000 | - 20,000 | - 20,000 | - 20,000.00 |
| -Depreciation | 18,000 | 18,000 | 18,000 | 18,000 | 18,000.00 |
| EBIT | $42,000* | $46,000 | $50,400 | $55,240 | $60,564.00 |
| Plus Depreciation | 18,000 | 18,000 | 18,000 | 18,000 | 18,000.00 |
| -Tax on EBIT(at 40%) | 16,800 | 18,400 | 20,160 | 22,096 | 24,225.60 |
| Operating cash flow | $43,200 | $45,600 | $48,240 | $51,144 | $54,338.40 |

*Note that we are subtracting a *decrease* in costs. This actually increases the EBIT. (For Year 1, EBIT = $40,000 − (−20,000) − 18,000 = $42,000.)

For year 5, in addition to operating cash flows, we have cash flows related to the sale of the asset and the recovery of working capital. The sale of the equipment at the end of year 5 results in an inflow to KMS equal to $60,000. In addition, KMS has an inflow in year 5 equal to the $15,000 recovery of the working capital investment.

The total cash flow for year 5 is:

$54,338.40 + $60,000 + $15,000 = $129,338.40

To determine the acceptability of the investment, we compute the NPV of the cash flows. For simplicity, we assume that all cash flows occur at year end. If the opportunity cost for this investment is 16%, then the present value of the cash inflows for years 1 through 5 is $191,861.01. The net present value of the investment is $26,861.

## MORE ON PROJECT CASH FLOW

Two important aspects of the previous example are: first, the relationship between our treatment of net working capital and the issue of the timing of cash flows; and second, various aspects of the tax treatment of depreciation.

**A Closer Look at Net Working Capital:**  When we introduced the cash flow concept in Chapter 2, we observed that Generally Accepted Accounting Principles (GAAP) require that revenue is recorded on the income statement when it is accrued.  Furthermore, for income statement purposes, costs are determined according to the 'matching' principle, which requires that expenses are recognized at the time of the sale.  It is important to adjust this accounting information to reflect the actual timing of cash flows.  It may seem that we have ignored this requirement in our analysis of the KMS Corporation problem of the previous section.  However, the manner in which we have treated additions to net working capital actually makes the necessary adjustment.

**An Example:**  Suppose that, when KMS makes sales of $40,000 during year 1, 20% of the sales are on credit; the credit terms require payment in the month following the sale.  Also assume that sales occur at the rate of $3,333.33 per month.  Therefore, at the end of the first year, $(.20 \times \$3,333.33) = \$666.67$ of sales revenue has not been collected, but the full $3,333.33 has been recorded on the accounting income statement for December sales.  Actual cash inflows, though, are  only $2,666.67.  Consequently, even though year 1 revenue is $40,000, the cash inflow should be $39,333.33. How does our treatment of net working capital correctly account for this fact?

The $666.67 of revenue which appears on the income statement but has not been received by the end of year 1 is recorded as accounts receivable on the firm's balance sheet.  This is an increase in net working capital and, assuming there are no additional changes in current assets or current liabilities during year 1, we would treat the $666.67 increase in net working capital as an outflow for year 1.  So, the net result would be $40,000 in revenue, as an inflow, and a $666.67 addition to net working capital, as an outflow, for a net $39,333.33 inflow.  This is the correct cash flow, as indicated above, so our treatment of additions to net working capital correctly adjusts for the difference between accrued revenue and actual cash inflow.  A comparable conclusion results from an evaluation of other changes in net working capital which arise from changes in other current assets, such as inventory, or current liabilities, such as accounts payable.

**An Example:**   Assume that W.C. Inc. is investing in a new project that will affect certain of the firm's working capital accounts in the next three periods (see table below).  Presently total current assets are $20,000 and total current liabilities are $12,000.  If we assume that the firm's net working capital will revert to its original levels after three years and given a 10% discount rate, what is the impact on cash flow and on NPV?

| Period | Account | $ Increase | $ Decrease |
|--------|---------|-----------|-----------|
| 0 | Accounts Receivable | 9,000 | |
| 1 | Inventory | | 7,000 |
| 2 | Accruals | | 3,000 |
| 3 | Accounts Payable | 8,000 | |
| 3 | Accounts Receivable | 5,000 | |

The table below summarizes the effect on cash flow given changes in working capital.

### Working Capital Effects on Cash Flow

| Funds Required (−) | Funds Released (+) |
|--------------------|---------------------|
| Increase in current assets | Increase in current liabilities |
| Decrease in current liabilities | Decrease in current assets |

Applied to our example, the cash flow would change in present value by [– $9,000 + $7,000 (.9091) – $3,000 (.8264)] + [$8,000 – $5,000 × (.7513)] = –$2,861.60 where the brackets represent present value factors. Therefore, W.C. Inc. will require a net increase in working capital of $2,861.76 over the life of the project. To understand the recovery of working capital, consider the cumulative changes in the working capital accounts:

|  | Current Assets | - | Current Liabilities | = | Net Working Capital | Cumulative Change |
|---|---|---|---|---|---|---|
| Current level | $20,000 |  | $ 12,000 |  | $ 8,000 |  |
| Time  0 | 9,000 |  |  |  | 17,000 | $ 9,000 |
| 1 | –7,000 |  |  |  | –7,000 | 2,000 |
| 2 |  |  | 3,000 |  | 3,000 | 5,000 |
| 3 | 5,000 |  | –8,000 |  | –3,000 | 2,000 |

As shown above, the cumulative change in net working capital is $2,000 at the end of year 3. This $2,000 increase represents the net increase in working capital levels (undiscounted) at the end of the project. Since the problem stated that after the project, working capital levels would revert back to the original levels, the net increase in working capital (–$2,000) becomes an inflow (+$2,000) and in present value is: $2,000 × .7513 = $1,502.60, which should be added to cash flow.

In summary the effect on cash flow, in present value, of changes in working capital are – $2,861.60 + $1,502.60 = –$1,359.00 so that NPV would be reduced by this amount.

## ALTERNATIVE DEFINITIONS OF OPERATING CASH FLOW

In the earlier example of the KMS Corporation, we computed each year's operating cash flow according to the following definition:

Operating Cash Flow = Earnings before interest and taxes + Depreciation – Taxes

For example, the calculation of the year 1 operating cash flow is as follows:

$42,000 + $18,000 – $16,800  =  $43,200

In this section, we develop several alternative, but equivalent, approaches to computing operating cash flow. These alternatives provide insight into various aspects of the cash flow calculation. In order to derive these alternative approaches, we first define the following notation for the various components of the calculation:

| OCF | = | project operating cash flow |
|---|---|---|
| S | = | sales (in dollars) |
| C | = | operating costs |
| D | = | depreciation |
| $T_c$ | = | corporate tax rate |

Therefore, EBIT = (S – C – D) and taxes is equal to:

$$EBIT \times T_c = (S - C - D) \times T_c$$

Substituting these algebraic definitions of EBIT and taxes into the above equation for operating cash flow:

$$
\begin{aligned}
\text{OCF} &= \text{EBIT} + D - \text{Taxes} \\
&= (S - C - D) + D - [(S - C - D) \times T_c]
\end{aligned}
$$

Note that we have simply restated the definition of operating cash flow, as it was computed in the earlier example, in terms of the algebraic notation. We can rearrange this definition in order to derive alternative approaches to the computation of operating cash flow.

**The Bottom-Up Approach:** The *bottom-up approach* to defining operating cash flow accentuates the relationship between net income and operating cash flow. Using the notation introduced earlier, net income is defined as follows:

$$
\begin{aligned}
\text{Net income} &= \text{EBIT} - \text{Taxes} \\
&= (S - C - D) - [(S - C - D) \times T_c] \\
&= (S - C - D) \times (1 - T_c)
\end{aligned}
$$

(Note that this definition of net income ignores financing costs; this is consistent with our earlier discussion regarding these costs.) Our original definition of OCF can be rearranged to emphasize this bottom-up interpretation, as follows:

$$
\begin{aligned}
\text{OCF} &= \text{EBIT} + D - \text{Taxes} \\
&= (\text{EBIT} - \text{Taxes}) + D \\
&= \text{Net income} + \text{Depreciation} \\
&= [(S - C - D) \times (1 - T_c)] + D
\end{aligned}
$$

Using this bottom-up definition for the KMS example for Year 1:

$$
\text{OCF} = \text{Net income} + \text{Depreciation} = \$25{,}200 + \$18{,}000 = \$43{,}200
$$

Again, this value for OCF is identical to that derived earlier, but this calculation focuses on the manner in which net income and depreciation determine operating cash flow.

**The Top-Down Approach:** The *top-down approach* is derived from the basic definition of operating cash flow as follows:

$$
\begin{aligned}
\text{OCF} &= \text{EBIT} + D - \text{Taxes} \\
&= (S - C - D) + D - [(S - C - D) \times T_c] \\
&= (S - C) - D + D - [(S - C - D) \times T_c] \\
&= (S - C) - [(S - C - D) \times T_c] \\
&= \text{Sales} - \text{Costs} - \text{Taxes}
\end{aligned}
$$

This perspective emphasizes the fact that operating cash flow is equal to sales minus expenses (including taxes, but excluding non-cash expenses such as depreciation). For KMS in Year 1, this calculation of operating cash flow is

$$
\text{OCF} = \$40{,}000 - (-\$20{,}000) - \$16{,}800 = \$43{,}200
$$

**The Tax Shield Approach:** The *tax shield approach* to defining operating cash flow emphasizes the manner in which depreciation affects cash flow. Since depreciation is a non-cash expense, its only impact on cash flow is through its effect on taxes; the tax shield approach accentuates this fact. The tax shield approach is derived from the basic definition of operating cash flow as follows:

$$
\begin{aligned}
\text{OCF} \quad &= \quad \text{EBIT} + D - \text{Taxes} \\
&= \quad (S - C - D) + D - [(S - C - D) \times T_c] \\
&= \quad (S - C) - [(S - C) \times T_c] + (D \times T_c) \\
&= \quad [(S - C) \times (1 - T_c)] + (D \times T_c)
\end{aligned}
$$

This definition of operating cash flow has two terms. The first term can be thought of as the project's cash flow in the absence of depreciation. That is, $[(S - C) \times (1 - T_c)]$ would be the project's after-tax income if depreciation were zero. In the absence of depreciation, operating cash flow would equal net income after taxes. Note that we are referring to net operating income. That is, interest costs have been excluded from consideration. The second term in this definition of operating cash flow is referred to as the *depreciation tax shield*. Since depreciation is a non-cash expense, its only impact on operating cash flow calculations is its impact on taxes. The tax savings associated with the tax deductibility of depreciation expense is equal to the depreciation expense (D) multiplied by the tax rate ($T_c$); this tax savings is the depreciation tax shield.

For the KMS example, the calculation of operating cash flow using the tax shield approach is:

$$
\begin{aligned}
\text{OCF} \quad &= \quad [\,(S - C) \times (1 - T_c)\,] + (D \times T_c) \\
&= \quad [\$40,000 - (-\$20,000) \times (1 - .40)] + (\$18,000 \times .40) \\
&= \quad [\$60,000 \times .60] + (\$18,000 \times .40) \\
&= \quad \$36,000 + \$7,200 = \$43,200
\end{aligned}
$$

Notice that this value of OCF is identical to that derived earlier. The tax shield approach emphasizes the fact that the $18,000 depreciation expense produces a $7,200 tax savings for the firm.

## APPLYING THE TAX SHIELD APPROACH: CCA

As we saw in Chapter 2, CCRA forces companies to compute capital cost allowance (CCA) instead of book depreciation. Thirty-seven asset classes have been established along with the maximum CCA rates, and as discussed earlier, the half-year rule is applied. If we go back to our example of KMS Corporation which invested $150,000 in motorcycle equipment manufacturing and assume that the applicable CCA rate is 30% , what are the annual CCA charges that the corporation can claim?

| Year | Beginning UCC | CCA | Ending UCC |
|------|--------------|-----|-----------|
| 1 | $ 75,000.00 | $22,500.00 | $52,500.00 |
| 2 | 127,500.00* | 38,250.00 | 89,250.00 |
| 3 | 89,250.00 | 26,775.00 | 62,475.00 |
| 4 | 62,475.00 | 18,742.50 | 43,732.50 |
| 5 | 43,732.50 | 13,119.75 | 30,612.75 |

*$127,500 = $52,500 + $75,000

The problem with calculating annual CCA is that although the investment project has a finite life, the CCA charges can continue indefinitely since these are calculated by applying a rate on the declining balance. Moreover, not only are we interested in calculating the tax savings that result from claiming CCA, but we also want to convert these future CCA tax savings into their present value equivalent. Fortunately, the following formula does all this for us. That is, it calculates the present value of infinite CCA tax savings incorporating the half-year rule:

$$\frac{CdT_c}{k + d} \quad \times \quad \frac{1 + .5k}{1 + k}$$

where   C  = change in the UCC pool (net of any tax credits)
        d  = CCA rate
        $T_c$ = tax rate
        k  = discount factor
        $\dfrac{1+.5k}{1+k}$  = adjustment for the half-year rule

**An Example:**  Considering the $150,000 investment by KMS Corporation, what is the present value of tax savings they will earn from CCA charges.  Assume a 30% CCA rate, 16% discount rate and a 40% tax rate?

Applying this information in the formula developed, we get:

$$\frac{\$150,000 \times .30 \times .40}{.16 + .30} \quad \times \quad \frac{1.08}{1.16} \quad = \quad \$36,431.78$$

KMS will save $36,431.78 in taxes (today's dollars) by claiming CCA on the investment indefinitely.

**Salvage:**  Since salvage value represents a recoverable amount from the depreciable asset and will reduce the UCC pool, the perpetual CCA tax savings will also be reduced.  These lost tax savings, which reduce net cash flow, are quantifiable in the same way as our declining balance formula, but must then be multiplied by the present value formula to convert the lost CCA tax savings in today's dollars.  In other words, the present value of lost CCA tax savings due to expected salvage can be computed by using the following formula:

$$\frac{- SdT_c}{k + d} \quad \times \quad \frac{1}{(1 + k)^n}$$

where S = incremental salvage value.  Apart from reducing CCA tax savings, the salvage value will also increase future cash inflows as noted earlier in our example for KMS Corporation.

**An Example:**  For KMS, what is the impact of the $60,000 salvage value on the firm's cash flow?

First, using the formula above, we can calculate the lost CCA tax savings:

$$\frac{- \$60,000 \times .30 \times .40}{.16 + .30} \quad \times \quad \frac{1}{(1.16)^5} \quad = \quad - \$15,652.17 \times .476113 \quad = \quad - \$7,452.20$$

Second, we calculate the present value of salvage: $60,000 (.476113) = $28,566.78. Therefore, the impact of salvage value on cash flow is – $7,452.20 + $28,566.78 = $21,114.58.

Also, there are tax implications associated with the sale of an asset whenever the asset is sold for a price which differs from its UCC (undepreciated capital cost) value at the time of the sale. When the asset is sold for more than its UCC value, a tax obligation is created; when the asset is sold for less than its UCC value and there are no assets left in the class, the difference between the two figures is a tax deduction for the firm.  Recall that these situations correspond to our definitions in Chapter 2 of recaptured income and terminal loss.

To complicate matters, the implication of these tax effects is not only that the tax liability will be increased (in the case of a recapture) or reduced (in the case of a terminal loss), but the lost CCA tax savings formula will have to be slightly modified by substituting the value of S by the remaining UCC balance. In other words, since a recapture or terminal loss results in a zero UCC balance, the infinite CCA tax savings must be reduced by the UCC balance at the time the asset sold.

**An Example:**  Carefully reconsider the previous example when KMS sold the equipment for $60,000. Are there any tax implications?

If there were no other assets in the class in which the equipment was placed, the answer is yes. Notice that by investing $150,000 in a class 10 asset where the CCA rate is 30%, KMS was left with $43,732.5 beginning UCC balance in the fifth year. The sale of equipment for $60,000 reduces the UCC pool to a negative amount of ($43,732.50 – $60,000) = $16,267.50 which must be *recaptured* as income. KMS must pay taxes of ($16,267.50 $\times$ .40) = $6,507 on the recapture, which will reduce the cash flow of the project. The NPV would be reduced by ($16,267.5 $\times$ PVIF(16%,5) = $7,745.17. The second impact of a recapture is that the UCC balance reverts to zero for period 6 and onwards, which means that instead of reducing the infinite CCA tax savings by the salvage value, we use the UCC beginning balance in the year in which the recapture occurred. In other words, we calculate the lost CCA tax savings using the same formula introduced earlier, except we substitute UCC for S.

$$\frac{-(\$43,732,50)\,(.30)\,(.40)}{.16 + .30} \quad \times \quad \frac{1}{(1.16)^5} \quad = \quad -\$11,408\,(.476113) \quad = \quad -\$5,431.73$$

To summarize, the tax implications of a recapture are that KMS must pay taxes on the recaptured amount ($7,745.17 in present value) and the present value of lost CCA tax savings are reduced to $5,431.73 (instead of $7,452.20 when salvage was used in the formula).

In general, the entire formula can be written as:

$$\text{PV tax shield on CCA} \quad = \quad \frac{CdT_c}{d+k} \times \frac{1+.5k}{1+k} - \frac{SdT_c}{d+k} \times \frac{1}{(1+k)^n}$$

## SOME SPECIAL CASES OF DISCOUNTED CASH FLOW ANALYSIS

In this section, we analyze three special capital budgeting problems. These examples should be regarded as illustrative of the wide variety of specific circumstances which can arise in the application of discounted cash flow analysis to capital budgeting.

**Replacing an Asset:**  Instead of cutting costs by automation, companies will often attempt to enhance productivity by replacing existing equipment with newer models of advanced technology. The following example demonstrates a replacement decision:

**An Example:**  Firm Publishing Company is considering replacing two of its many printing presses which were purchased five years ago for $40,000 each with an estimated remaining useful life of five years and a salvage value of $1,500 per press. One new press is needed to replace the two old ones which could be sold today for $3,500 each. The new press normally retails for $62,500 but you have found a manufacturer who is willing to sell the same model for a 20% discount. The new press is expected to increase sales by $9,000 per year and economize on annual operating expenses, which were $4,500 per press ($9,000 total), but would be $7,000 per year for the new press. Furthermore, each of the existing presses require one operator who is currently paid $15,000 per year but would not be needed if the new press is purchased. The new press could be sold for $8,000 at the end of the fifth year. The company also foresees a decrease in working capital requirements of $6,000 at the end of the first year of operations, but this decrease will revert to its original level once the project is completed in five years. The applicable discount rate is 16%, the CCA rate is 30% and the tax rate is 40%. Assuming that the sale of the new printing press will not result in any recaptured depreciation or terminal loss, should your company replace the two existing printing presses?

We begin by identifying the initial investment and then discount the relevant cash flows to calculate the NPV: The initial investment consists of the discount price of the new press less the market value of the old presses: ($62,500 × .80) – ($3,500 × 2) = $43,000. The after-tax operating income in present value is: {$9,000 – [$7,000 – ($4,500 × 2) – $15,000]} (1 – .4) [PVIFA(16%,5)], = ($9,000 + $17,000) (.6) (3.274294) = $51,078.99. The incremental salvage value in today's dollars is:   $8,000 – ($1,500 × 2) (PVIF(16%,5))  = $8,000 – ($3,000) (.476113) = $6,571.66.

The present value tax shield for CCA is:

$$\frac{\$43,000\,(.30)\,(.40)}{.16+.30} \quad \times \quad \frac{1.08}{1.16} \quad - \quad \frac{\$5,000\,(.30)\,(.40)}{.16+.30} \quad \times \quad \frac{1}{(1.16)^5}$$

$$= \quad \$10,443.78 \ - \ \$621.02 \ = \ \$9,822.77$$

Finally, the present value of working capital requirements are:

$$\$6,000 \text{ x PVIF}(16\%,1) – \$6,000 \text{ x PVIF }(16\%,5) = \$6,000\,(.862069) – \$6,000\,(.476113) = \$2,315.74$$

Notice that a decrease in working capital requirements means that cash flow increases and, when working capital requirements revert to their original levels, cash flow decreases.

The NPV is:    –$43,000 + $51,078.98 + $6,571.66  + $9,822.76 + $2,315.74 = $26,789.15

The new press should be purchased since the NPV is positive.

**Evaluating Equipment with Different Lives:** A special capital budgeting problem arises when we compare two different machines that provide the same benefits, but have different purchase prices and operating costs. If the benefits are the same, we can simply choose the machine with the lower present value of operating costs. However, the analysis becomes more complicated if the two machines have different operating lives. The problem is resolved by using the *equivalent annual cost* (EAC) method.

**An Example:**   Suppose we are considering the purchase of either Machine X or Machine Y. The two machines provide the same benefit to the company and the machine selected will be replaced at the end of its useful life. The lives and annual costs for each are:

| Year | Machine X | Machine Y |
|------|-----------|-----------|
| 0 | - $100 | - $70 |
| 1 | - 10 | - 15 |
| 2 | - 10 | - 15 |
| 3 | - 10 | |

The firm's opportunity cost is 10%. If we assume no taxes, which machine should be selected?

At a 10% discount rate, the present values of the costs for X and Y are $124.87 and $96.03, respectively. If we ignore the fact that Machine Y would have to be replaced earlier than Machine X, we would select Y because the present value of the costs are less.

The two present values, however, cannot be compared because they cover a different period of years. We must ask the question: what constant dollar amount, paid each year, has exactly the same present value as the machine's purchase price plus operating costs? This amount is the *equivalent annual* cost, EAC. For Machine X, this value is determined by solving for C in the following annuity formula:

$$PV = C \times PVIFA(r,t)$$

$$\$124.87 = C \times PVIFA(10\%,3)$$

The value of PVIFA(10%,3) is computed as follows:

$$PVIFA(10\%,3) = \frac{1 - [1/(1.10)^3]}{.10} = 2.486852$$

Therefore, the value of C is the solution to the following equation:

$$\$124.87 = C \times 2.486852$$

$$C = \$124.87/2.486852 = \$50.21$$

The equivalent annual cost for Machine X is therefore $50.21.

The equivalent annual cost (EAC) for machine Y is:

$$\$96.03 = C \times PVIFA(10\%,2) = C \times 1.73554$$
$$\$96.03/1.73554 = C = \$55.33$$

The EAC for X is less than the EAC for Y, so that X has the lower cost. Therefore, X is the preferable alternative.

**Setting the Bid Price:** Under certain circumstances, a supplier of a product or service submits a bid price to a prospective customer who then purchases the product or service from the supplier who has submitted the lowest bid. This procedure might be used by a governmental unit or agency which is required by law to purchase from the lowest bidder. The problem for the supplier is to set the bid price at the lowest price which still provides the required rate of return. To derive this price, the supplier must solve the capital budgeting problem 'backwards.' That is, rather than using price and cost data to determine cash flows and net present value, the supplier identifies the operating cash flow and then the price which provides the required rate of return.

**An Example:** P. M. Reese Sporting Goods plans to submit a bid to supply baseballs to a high school athletic league. The league will buy 5,000 baseballs per year for the next five years. To supply the baseballs, Reese Sporting Goods must purchase manufacturing equipment which costs $20,000. The equipment has a five-year life and no salvage value at the end of five years. For simplicity, we will assume that the equipment will be depreciated on a straight-line basis. Additional fixed costs will total $3,000 per year and variable costs will be $2 per baseball. An additional investment of $5,000 in net working capital will be required; this investment will be recovered at the end of five years. The firm's tax rate is 40% and the required rate of return is 15%. What is the lowest price Reese can charge for the baseballs?

To solve this problem, we essentially work *backwards,* as follows:

1.  Find the minimum annual operating cash flow (OCF) needed to yield a 15% return.  Note: this means NPV will be zero at that level of OCF
2.  Compute the net income for that level of OCF
3.  Find the required price per unit

1. To find the minimum required OCF, use the basic formula for NPV.  Substitute for r = 15%. The initial outlay, $C_0 = -\$20,000 - \$5,000 = -\$25,000$ (cost of machine plus investment in net working capital). Cash flows for years 1 through 5 are $C_1 = C_2 = C_3 = C_4 = C_5 = OCF$.  Finally, the $5,000 investment in net working capital will be recovered in year 5.

At the required return of 15%, NPV equals zero. So, we can write:

$$0 = -\$25,000 + \frac{OCF}{(1.15)^1} + \frac{OCF}{(1.15)^2} + \frac{OCF}{(1.15)^3} + \frac{OCF}{(1.15)^4} + \frac{OCF}{(1.15)^5} + \frac{\$5,000}{(1.15)^5}$$

The present value of the $5,000 recovery of net working capital is $\$5,000/(1.15)^5 = \$2,485.88$.  Also note that the OCF is actually a five-year annuity. The NPV can be rewritten as:

$$0 = -\$25,000 + OCF \times PVIFA(15\%,5) + \$2,485.88 = -\$22,514.12 + OCF \times 3.352155$$

Now we can solve for OCF:  $\$22,514.12 / 3.352155 = OCF = \$6,716.31$.  So, with an operating cash flow of $6,716.31, NPV equals zero and Reese will earn exactly the required 15% return.

2. Now, we use the bottom-up definition of operating cash flow to determine net income:

$$OCF = \text{Net income} + \text{Depreciation}$$
$$\$6,716.31 = \text{Net income} + \$20,000/5$$
$$\text{Net income} = \$2,716.31$$

3. Now, we use the definition of net income to solve for S, the required sales level.  Note that C is the sum of fixed and variable costs: $C = \$3,000 + \$2 \times 5,000 = \$13,000$.

$$\text{Net income} = (S - C - D) \times (1 - T_c)$$
$$\$2,716.31 = (S - \$13,000 - \$4,000) \times (1 - .40)$$
$$\$2,716.31 = (S - \$17,000) \times (.60)$$
$$\$2,716.31 / .60 = S - \$17,000$$
$$\$4,527.18 + 17,000 = S = \$21,527.18$$

That is, sales of $21,527.18 will generate the required cash flow of $2,716.31.  The bid is for 5,000 baseballs, so the price per unit must be:

$$\text{Sales Revenue} / \text{units} = \text{price per unit}$$
$$\$21,527.18 / 5,000 = \text{price} = \$4.31$$

## CONCEPT TEST

1.  In evaluating a capital budgeting project, the relevant cash flows are the incremental cash flows, which consist of all _____ in the firm's cash flows that are a direct consequence of _____ the project.

2.  The incremental cash flows for a project can be defined as the firm's cash flows if the project is undertaken minus _____. Alternatively, the _____ principle specifies that incremental cash flows can be analyzed from the perspective of the_____, rather than from the perspective of the _____.

3.  A sunk cost for a capital budgeting project is money the firm has already _____, or is_____, regardless of whether it accepts the project under consideration. A sunk cost _(is/is not)_ incremental to a capital budgeting project, and therefore _(is/is not)_ relevant to the capital budgeting decision.

4.  An opportunity cost for a particular capital budgeting project is a benefit which the firm would_____ if it _____ the project.  An opportunity cost_(is/is not)_an incremental cost for a capital budgeting project.

5.  A _____ is the impact which a given capital budgeting project might have on cash flows in another area of the firm. These changes in cash flows _(are/are not)_ incremental cash flows for the project under consideration.

6.  Net working capital is equal to _____ minus _____. A capital budgeting project typically requires an _____ in net working capital during the life of the project.

7.  The investment in net working capital is an incremental cash _____. At the termination of a project, this investment is typically recovered, and is therefore an incremental cash _____ at that time. This treatment of changes in net working capital adjusts accounting data to a cash flow basis. Generally Accepted Accounting Principles require that revenue is recorded on the income statement when it _____, and that costs are determined according to the _____ principle. Consequently, it is essential to adjust accounting information, which is reported on an_____ basis, in such a way that it reflects the actual timing of _____.

8.  Depreciation is a _____ expense; it is relevant to the computation of incremental cash flows only because it affects _____.

9.  Depreciation affects cash flow calculations in two ways: first, depreciation expenses affect operating cash flows, since the deduction of depreciation expense reduces _____; and, second, depreciation affects the _____ value of an asset, and the difference between _____ value and _____ value has tax implications when an asset is sold.

10. There are tax implications associated with the sale of an asset whenever the asset is sold for a price which differs from its _____ value at the time of the sale. When the asset is sold for more than its _____ value, a tax obligation is created; when the asset is sold for less than its _____ value, the difference between the two figures is a _____ for the firm.

11. Projected cash flows for a capital budgeting project are derived from _____ financial statements, which are projected financial statements for future time periods.  Operating cash flow is defined as: _____ + _____ − _____.

12.    We do not deduct either interest or depreciation in computing operating cash flow.  Interest is not deducted because it is not an_____ expense.  Financing costs have an impact on our net present value analysis in that these costs determine the appropriate _____ in our net present value calculations. We do not deduct depreciation in computing operating cash flow because depreciation is a _____ expense.

13.    Algebraically, we define EBIT as _____; taxes as _____; and operating cash flow (OCF) as: _____ + _____ − _____.

14.    The bottom-up approach to defining operating cash flow accentuates the relationship between_____ and operating cash flow. The bottom-up interpretation of operating cash flow can be derived as follows: OCF = _____ + _____ − _____= (EBIT − Taxes) + D = _____ + Depreciation = _____ + D

15.    The top-down approach is derived from the basic definition of operating cash flow as follows: OCF = _____ + _____ − _____ = _____ + D − _____= (S − C) − [(S − C − D) × T$_c$] = Sales − Costs − Taxes.  The top-down approach emphasizes the fact that operating cash flow is equal to _____ minus _____.

16.    The tax shield approach to defining operating cash flow emphasizes the manner in which_____ affects cash flow.  The tax shield approach is derived from the basic definition of operating cash flow as follows:
       OCF = _____ + _____ − _____= (S − C − D) + D − [(S − C − D) × T$_c$] = _____ + _____ . The first term in this definition is the project's _____ in the absence of _____.
       The second term in this definition of operating cash flow is referred to as the _____.

17.    A supplier of a product or service sometimes submits a bid price to a prospective customer who then purchases the product or service from the supplier who has submitted the lowest bid. The problem for the supplier is to set the bid price at the _____ price which still provides the_____. To derive this price, the supplier must solve the capital budgeting problem 'backwards.' The supplier first determines the annual operating cash flow which makes the net present value of the project equal to _____. This value of OCF would provide the supplier with the_____. The supplier then determines the level of _____, and the price per unit, which would provide the required OCF. This price per unit is the supplier's _____.

18.    A special capital budgeting problem arises when a firm compares two different machines that provide the same essential service, but differ with respect to purchase price and operating costs. This is an example of a choice between _____ alternatives.  Such choices can be made on the basis of the _____ criterion.  Since the machines provide the same essential service to the firm, the cash inflows can be ignored because they are not _____ cash flows for either machine.

19.    If the machines have the same operating life, this choice between mutually exclusive alternatives is resolved by choosing the machine with the _____ present value of _____. If the two machines have different operating lives and if the firm will be replacing the selected machine at the end of its useful life, then the problem is resolved by the use of the _____ method.


## ANSWERS TO CONCEPT TEST

1.     changes; accepting

2.     the firm's cash flows if the project is not undertaken; stand-alone; project; entire firm

3.      spent; committed to spend; is not; is not

4.      forego; accepts; is

5.      side effect; are

6.      current assets; current liabilities; increase

7.      outflow; inflow; accrues; matching; accrual; cash flows

8.      non-cash; taxes

9.      taxes; book; book; market

10.     book; book; book; tax deduction

11.     pro forma; earnings before interest and taxes (EBIT); depreciation; taxes

12.     operating; discount rate; non-cash

13.     $(S–C–D)$; $[(S–C–D)\times T_C]$; $(S–C–D)$; D; $[(S–C–D)\times T_C]$

14.     net income; EBIT; D; Taxes; Net income; $[(S–C–D)\times(1–T_c)]$

15.     EBIT; D; Taxes; $(S–C–D)$; $[(S–C–D)\times T_c]$; sales; expenses

16.     depreciation; EBIT; D; Taxes; $[(S–C)\times(1–T_c)]$; $(D\times T_c)$; cash flow; depreciation; depreciation tax shield

17.     lowest; required rate of return; zero; required rate of return; sales; bid price

18.     mutually exclusive; net present value; incremental

19.     lower; operating costs; equivalent annual cost

## PROBLEMS AND SOLUTIONS

### Use the following information to solve Problems 1 and 2:

Frizzle, Inc. manufactures imitation Persian rugs (as opposed to hand-knotted ones). Its owner, Matt Frizzle, has spent $30,000 travelling to Persia to study rugs. On his return he purchased a new weaving machine for $400,000. The machine will be depreciated using a 20% CCA rate. The machine will increase sales by $300,000 in each of the next three years. Annual fixed costs will be $40,000 and variable costs will be 55% of sales. The tax rate is 34%.

## Problem 1

What are the CCA charges and ending UCC for the project?

**Solution:**

| Year | Beginning UCC | CAA | Ending UCC |
|------|---------------|---------|------------|
| 1 | $200,000 | $40,000 | $160,000 |
| 2 | 360,000 | 72,000 | 288,000 |
| 3 | 288,000 | 57,600 | 230,400 |

## Problem 2

Prepare the pro forma income statements for years 1 to 3.

**Solution:**

| | Year 1 | Year 2 | Year 3 |
|------|----------|----------|----------|
| Sales | $300,000 | $300,000 | $300,000 |
| - Variable costs | $165,000 | $165,000 | 165,000 |
| - Fixed costs | 40,000 | 40,000 | 40,000 |
| - Depreciation | 40,000 | 72,000 | 57,600 |
| EBIT | $ 55,000 | $ 23,000 | $ 37,400 |
| - Tax @ 34% | 18,700 | 7,820 | 12,716 |
| Net income | $ 36,300 | $ 15,180 | $ 24,684 |

## Use the following information to solve Problems 3 to 14:

Aunt Sally's Sauces, Inc., is considering expansion into a new line of all-natural, cholesterol-free, sodium-free, fat-free, low-calorie tomato sauces.  Sally paid $50,000 for a marketing study which indicates that sales for the new product line will be $650,000 per year for the next six years.  Manufacturing plant and equipment would cost $500,000.  The appropriate CCA rate is 20% .  Salvage value will be zero.  Annual fixed costs are projected at $80,000 and variable costs are projected at 60% of sales.  Net working capital requirements are $75,000 for the six-year life of the project; the outlay for working capital will be recovered at the end of six years.  Aunt Sally's tax rate is 34%, and the firm requires a 16% return on capital budgeting projects.

## Problem 3

Compute the annual CCA charges and the ending UCC value for the fixed assets.

**Solution:**

| Year | Beginning UCC | CCA | Ending UCC |
|------|---------------|----------|------------|
| 1 | $250,000 | $50,000 | $200,000 |
| 2 | 450,000 | 90,000 | 360,000 |
| 3 | 360,000 | 72,000 | 288,000 |
| 4 | 288,000 | 57,600 | 230,400 |
| 5 | 230,400 | 46,080 | 184,320 |
| 6 | 184,320 | 36,864 | 147,456 |

## Problem 4

Prepare pro forma income statements for years 1 through 6.

**Solution:**   The pro forma income statements are presented in the following table:

|               | Year 1      | Year 2      | Year 3      | Year 4      | Year 5        | Year 6        |
|---------------|-------------|-------------|-------------|-------------|---------------|---------------|
| Sales revenue | $ 650,000   | $ 650,000   | $ 650,000   | $650,000    | $650,000.00   | $ 650,000.00  |
| –Variable Costs | 390,000   | 390,000     | 390,000     | 390,000     | 390,000.00    | 390,000.00    |
| –Fixed Costs  | 80,000      | 80,000      | 80,000      | 80,000      | 80,000.00     | 80,000.00     |
| –Depreciation | 50,000      | 90,000      | 72,000      | 57,600      | 46,080.00     | 36,864.00     |
| EBIT          | $ 130,000   | $ 90,000    | $ 108,000   | $122,400    | $133,920.00   | $ 143,136.00  |
| –Tax (at 34%) | 44,200      | 30,600      | 36,720      | 41,616      | 45,532.80     | 48,666.24     |
| Net Income    | $ 85,800    | $ 59,400    | $ 71,280    | $ 80,784    | $ 88,387.20   | $ 94,469.76   |

## Problem 5

Compute operating cash flow for the project for years 1 through 6.

**Solution:** The operating cash flows are computed in the following table, using data from the pro forma income statements in problem 4:

|               | Year 1      | Year 2      | Year 3      | Year 4      | Year 5        | Year 6        |
|---------------|-------------|-------------|-------------|-------------|---------------|---------------|
| (EBIT)        | $130,000    | $ 90,000    | $108,000    | $122,400    | $133,920.00   | $ 43,136.00   |
| +Depreciation | 50,000      | 90,000      | 72,000      | 57,600      | 46,080.00     | 36,864.00     |
| –Tax (at 34%) | 44,200      | 30,600      | 36,720      | 41,616      | 45,532.80     | 48,666.24     |
| OCF           | $135,800    | $149,400    | $143,280    | $138,384    | $134,467.20   | $131,333.76   |

## Problem 6

Compute total projected cash flows for year 0 through 6 for the project.

**Solution:** Net working capital remains constant from years 1 through 5 and capital expenditures take place only in year zero. Consequently, for years 1 through 5, total cash flow is the same as operating cash flow. For year 0, additions to net working capital are $75,000 and capital expenditures are $500,000. Therefore, year 0 cash outflow is $575,000. For year 6, recovery of net working capital results in a cash inflow of $75,000. The ending UCC value is $147,456 and if there are no assets left in this pool, then the company can realize a terminal loss equal to this amount. The resulting tax savings are equal to $50,135.04 ($147,456 × .34). Note we are assuming that the company will scrap the investment for zero salvage at the end of the sixth year, and claim CCA that year. Total cash inflow for year 6 is equal to the sum of the operating cash flow, the recovery of net working capital, and tax savings from the terminal loss: ($131,333.76 + $75,000 + $50,135.04 = $256,468.80).

**Problem 7**

Compute the net present value and the internal rate of return for the new product line.

**Solution:** The present value of the future cash flows is:

$$\frac{\$135{,}800}{(1.16)} + \frac{\$149{,}400}{(1.16)^2} + \frac{\$143{,}280}{(1.16)^3} + \frac{\$138{,}384}{(1.16)^4} + \frac{\$134.467.20}{(1.16)^5} + \frac{\$256{,}468.80}{(1.16)^6}$$

$$= \$565{,}606.40$$

The net present value is ($565,606.40 – $575,000) = –$9,393.60. Since the net present value is negative, the new product line is not an acceptable investment.

The IRR can be computed using the trial-and-error procedures described in the previous chapter. The calculations require that we determine the discount rate for which the present value of the future cash flows is equal to the current cash outlay. Alternatively, we can think of the internal rate of return as the discount rate which makes the net present value of the project zero. For a discount rate of 16%, the present value is $565,606.40 and the net present value is –$9,393.60. For a discount rate of 15%, the present value and net present value are +$582,117.75 and +$7,117.75, respectively. Therefore, the IRR is between 15% and 16% indicating an unacceptable investment because it is less than the appropriate discount rate. The precise value of the IRR is 15.4255%.

**Problem 8**

Use the tax-shield approach to compute the operating cash flow for years 1 through 6.

**Solution:** The tax-shield approach defines the operating cash flow as follows:

$$OCF = [(S - C) \times (1 - T_c)] + (D \times T_c)$$

This equation is used in the following table to compute operating cash flow for each year of the project's life:

|  | Year 1 | Year 2 | Year 3 | Year 4 | Year 5 | Year 6 |
|---|---|---|---|---|---|---|
| Sales revenue | $650,000 | $650,000 | $650,000 | $650,000 | $650,000 | $650,000 |
| –Total Costs | 470,000 | 470,000 | 470,000 | 470,000 | 470,000 | 470,000 |
| (S - C) | 180,000 | 180,000 | 180,000 | 180,000 | 180,000 | 180,000 |
| $(S - C) \times (1 - T_c)$ | 118,800 | 118,800 | 118,800 | 118,800 | 118,800 | 118,800 |
| | | | | | | |
| Depreciation (D) | 50,000 | 90,000 | 72,000 | 57,600 | 46,080 | 36,864 |
| $(D \times T_c)$ | 17,000 | 30,600 | 24,480 | 19,584 | 15,667.20 | 12,533.76 |
| $OCF = [(S - C) \times (1-T_c)] + (D \times T_c)$ | $135,800 | $149,400 | $143,280 | $138,384 | $134,467.20 | $131,333.76 |

These figures for operating cash flow are identical to those computed in Problem 5.

## Problem 9

Use the 'bottom-up' approach to compute the operating cash flow for years 1 through 6.

**Solution:**  The 'bottom-up' approach defines the operating cash flow as follows:

$$OCF = [(S - C - D) \times (1 - T_c)] + D = \text{Net Income} + \text{Depreciation}$$

In the following table, we use this equation, and data from Problem 4, to compute operating cash flow for each year of the project's life.

|              | Year 1  | Year 2   | Year 3   | Year 4   | Year 5      | Year 6      |
|--------------|---------|----------|----------|----------|-------------|-------------|
| Net income   | 85,800  | 59,400   | 71,280   | 80,784   | 88,387.20   | 94,469.76   |
| +Depreciation| 50,000  | 90,000   | 72,000   | 57,600   | 46,080.00   | 36,864.00   |
| OCF          | 135,800 | $149,400 | $143,280 | $138,384 | $134,467.20 | $131,333.76 |

These figures for operating cash flow are identical to those computed in Problems 5 and 8.

## Problem 10

Use the 'top-down' approach to compute the operating cash flow for years 1 through 6.

**Solution:**

The 'top-down' approach defines the operating cash flow as follows:

$$\begin{aligned} OCF &= (S - C) - [(S - C - D) \times T_c] \\ &= \text{Sales} - \text{Costs} - \text{Taxes} \end{aligned}$$

In the following table, we use this equation and data from Problem 6 to compute operating cash flow for each year of the project's life:

|               | Year 1    | Year 2    | Year 3    | Year 4    | Year 5       | Year 6       |
|---------------|-----------|-----------|-----------|-----------|--------------|--------------|
| Sales revenue | $650,000  | $650,000  | $650,000  | $650,000  | $650,000.00  | $650,000.00  |
| −Total Costs  | 470,000   | 470,000   | 470,000   | 470,000   | 470,000.00   | 470,000.00   |
| −Taxes        | 44,200    | 30,600    | 36,720    | 41,616    | 45,532.80    | 48,666.24    |
| OCF           | $135,800  | $149,400  | $143,280  | $138,384  | $134,467.20  | $131,333.76  |

## Problem 11

Now assume that fixed assets have a salvage value of $100,000 at the end of six years.  What is the total cash flow for year 6?

**Solution:** From Problem 3, we know the beginning UCC value in year 6 is $184,320.  If the fixed assets are sold for $100,000, then the terminal loss is reduced to $84,320.  The resulting tax savings are equal to $28,668.80

($84,320 × .34). For year 6, the total cash flow components consist of salvage value ($100,000), terminal loss tax savings ($28,668.80), recovery of working capital ($75,000) and operating cash flow ($131,333.76) which add up to $335,002.56.

## Problem 12

Using the information in Problem 9 compute the net present value, the benefit-cost ratio, and the internal rate of return for the new product line.

**Solution:**  The present value of the future cash flows is:

$$\frac{\$135,800}{(1.16)} + \frac{\$149,400}{(1.16)^2} + \frac{\$143,280}{(1.16)^3} + \frac{\$138,384}{(1.16)^4} + \frac{\$134,467.2}{(1.16)^5} + \frac{\$335,002.56}{(1.16)^6}$$

The net present value is $22,839.98 ($597,839.98 – $575,000) and the investment project is acceptable mainly because of the large salvage value that is recovered at the end of six years.

The benefit-cost ratio is $597,839.98 / $575,000 = 1.03972, or approximately $0.04 of value created for every $1 invested.

The IRR must be greater than 16%, since the NPV is positive.  The exact IRR is 17.32%.

## Problem 13

Once again, solve Aunt Sally's capital budgeting problem assuming the fixed assets have a salvage value of $100,000 at the end of six years.  This time, use the declining balance formula to calculate the present value of CCA tax savings.

**Solution:**  Calculate the present value of CCA tax savings.  The problem can be solved sequentially by calculating the present value of six different cash flow components:

First, we identify the initial investment: –$500,000.  Second, calculate the present value of after tax operating income excluding CCA:

$$(\$650,000 - \$470,000)\, (1 - .34) \times PVIFA((16\%,6) \;=\; (\$180,000)\, (.66)\, (3.684736) = \$437,746.64$$

Third, calculate the present value of working capital requirements:

$$-\$75,000 + [\$75,000 \times PVIF(16\%,6)] \;=\; -\$75,000 + (\$75,000 \times .410442) \;=\; -\$44,216.85$$

Fourth, calculate the present value of CCA tax savings:

$$\frac{\$500,000\,(.20)\,(.34)}{.16 + .2} \times \frac{1.08}{1.16} \;-\; \frac{\$147,456\,(.20)\,(.34)}{.16 + .2} \times .410442$$

$$= \$87,931.03 - \$11,431.96 = \$76,499.07$$

Note: $147,456 has been used for S (not $100,000) because we want to reduce the infinite CCA tax savings ($87,931.03) by the ending UCC value ($147,456) since there is a terminal loss at the end of the project. If a terminal loss was not anticipated then the infinite CCA tax savings would have been reduced by the salvage amount ($100,000) in the formula.

Fifth, compute the present value of salvage: $100,000 (.410442) = $41,044.2. Finally, calculate the present value of the terminal loss tax savings: $84,320 (.34) (.410442) = $11,766.88.

Note: the terminal loss is equal to the beginning UCC value in year 6 less the salvage value ($184,320 – $100,000). The NPV is therefore: $–500,000 + $437,746.64 – $44,216.85 + $76,499.07 + $41,044.20 + $11,766.88 = $22,839.94 which is the same result as the solution to Problem 12.

## Problem 14

If we go back to Problem 13 and assume that there will be other assets in class 8 so that a terminal loss will not occur in year 6, how would you adjust the NPV of the project?

**Solution:** The fourth component of cash flow in Problem 13, the present value of CCA tax savings, needs to be recomputed:

$$\frac{\$500,000\,(.20)\,(.34)}{.16+.2} \times \frac{1.08}{1.16} \quad - \quad \frac{\$100,000\,(.20)\,(.34)}{.16+.2} \quad \times .410442 \quad = \quad \$80,178.24$$

This amount is greater than the CCA tax savings when a terminal loss was expected ($76,499.07) because the reduction in CCA tax savings was based on the ending UCC balance ($147,456) which is greater than the salvage value ($100,000). The impact on NPV is that it will increase by $3,679.17 ($80,178.24 – $76,499.07), but will be reduced by $11,766.88, which represents the terminal loss tax savings that will not occur. The NPV changes by a reduction of $8,087.71 ($3,679.17 – $11,766.88) so that it decreases to $22,839.95 – $8,087.71  =  $14,752.23.

## Problem 15

To replace an existing non-depreciable asset whose market value is $30,000 requires the purchase of a new asset which costs $60,000 and is expected to generate before-tax cash savings of $11,111.11 per year for each of the next five years. If the discount rate is 10% and the tax rate 46%, what is the NPV of this project? What is the IRR?

**Solution:** The initial investment is $30,000 ($60,000 – $30,000) the total cash flows after taxes are $6,000 [$11,111.11 (1 – .46)] per year. The NPV is: $–30,000 + $6,000 × PVIFA(10%,5) = $–30,000 + $6,000 (3.790787) = –$7,255.28

The IRR of the project is found by solving the following:

$$- \$30,000 \; + \; \$6,000 \times \frac{1 \; - \; 1/(1+IRR)^5}{IRR}$$

The IRR works out to 0.0%. This implies that the present value factor for each of the next five years is 1.0. Therefore, at a 0% discount rate (IRR) the NPV is zero: –30,000 + $6,000 × 5 = 0.

## Problem 16

A company is considering the acquisition of production equipment which will reduce labour and materials costs. The cost of the equipment is $100,000 and it will be depreciated on a straight-line basis over a four-year period. For simplicity, we assume this asset can be depreciated straight-line for tax purposes. However, the useful life of the equipment is five years, and it will have a $20,000 salvage value at the end of five years. Operating costs will be reduced by $30,000 in Year 1, and the savings will increase by $5,000 per year for years 2, 3, and 4. Due to increased maintenance costs, savings in year 5 will be $10,000 less than the year 4 savings. The equipment will also reduce net working capital by $5,000 throughout the life of the project. The firm's tax rate is 34% and the firm requires a 16% return on capital budgeting projects. Compute operating cash flow for the project for years 1 through 5.

**Solution:** The pro forma income statements are presented in the following table:

|                    | Year 1     | Year 2     | Year 3     | Year 4     | Year 5     |
|--------------------|------------|------------|------------|------------|------------|
| Sales revenue      | $    0     | $    0     | $    0     | $    0     | $    0     |
| −Operating costs   | − 30,000   | −35,000    | −40,000    | −45,000    | −35,000    |
| −Depreciation      | 25,000     | 25,000     | 25,000     | 25,000     | 0          |
| (EBIT)             | $ 5,000    | $10,000    | $15,000    | $20,000    | $35,000    |
| −Tax (at 34%)      | 1,700      | 3,400      | 5,100      | 6,800      | 11,900     |
| Net Income         | $ 3,300    | $ 6,600    | $ 9,900    | $13,200    | $23,100    |

Sales revenue does not change. Therefore, since we are concerned with incremental cash flows for the capital budgeting project, we enter zero for sales revenue. The decrease in operating costs results in an increase in EBIT and net income. Operating cash flows using data from the pro forma income statements are below:

|                    | Year 1     | Year 2     | Year 3     | Year 4     | Year 5     |
|--------------------|------------|------------|------------|------------|------------|
| (EBIT)             | $ 5,000    | $10,000    | $15,000    | $20,000    | $35,000    |
| +Depreciation      | 25,000     | 25,000     | 25,000     | 25,000     | 0          |
| −Tax (at 34%)      | 1,700      | 3,400      | 5,100      | 6,800      | 11,900     |
| (OCF)              | $28,300    | $31,600    | $34,900    | $38,200    | $23,100    |

## Problem 17

Compute total projected cash flows for years 0 through 5 for the project.

**Solution:** For years 1 through 4, total cash flow is the same as operating cash flow. For year 0, net working capital is reduced by $5,000 and capital expenditures are $100,000. The reduction in net working capital is a cash inflow, so that the year 0 cash outflow is ($100,000 − $5,000) = $95,000. We assume that the termination of the project terminates the reduction in net working capital, so that, at the end of year 5, we return to the previous level of net working capital. Consequently, the resulting increase in net working capital at the end of year 5 is a cash outflow. Also at the end of year 5, fixed assets have a salvage value of $20,000 and a book value of zero. Therefore, the after-tax cash inflow resulting from the sale of fixed assets is equal to:

$$($20,000 − $0) \times (1 − .34)  =  $13,200$$

Total cash inflow for year 5 is:   $23,100 − $5,000 + $13,200  =  $31,300

## Problem 18

Compute the net present value and the internal rate of return for the production equipment.

**Solution:** The present value of the future cash flows is:

$$\frac{\$28,300}{(1.16)} + \frac{\$31,600}{(1.16)^2} + \frac{\$34,900}{(1.16)^3} + \frac{\$38,200}{(1.16)^4} + \frac{\$31,300}{(1.16)^5} = \$106,239.31$$

The net present value is ($106,239.31 − $95,000) = $11,239.31. Since the net present value is positive, the acquisition of the new production equipment is an acceptable investment.

Using trial-and-error to determine the internal rate of return, we find that the present value is $96,725.37 and the net present value is $1,725.37 for a discount rate of 20%. For a discount rate of 21%, the present value and net present value are: $94,559.88 and −$440.12, respectively. Therefore, the internal rate of return is between 20% and 21%, indicating an acceptable investment. The precise value of the internal rate of return is 20.794%.

## Problem 19

Your company is considering the acquisition of a new machine which must have an IRR of at least 15%. This new machine will have an expected useful life of 10 years and zero salvage value. The firm takes maximum CCA tax savings each year and annual total cash flow (after CCA deductions and taxes), resulting from the addition of the new machine, will begin at the end of the year in which the initial investment has been made and are estimated to be $9,962.60. What is the maximum amount your firm should be willing to pay for the new machine?

**Solution:** The maximum investment ($C_0$) occurs when NPV is equal to zero.

$$\$9,962.60 \times \text{PVIFA}(15\%,10) - C_0 = 0$$
$$C_0 = \$9,962.60 \times 5.018769$$
$$C_0 = \$50,000$$

## Problem 20

Rinki Dink Inc. is considering the purchase of a new ice-making machine that costs $55,500. The firm expects the machine to generate before-tax revenues of $21,500 per year for four years and increase operating costs by $4,500 per year for each of the next four years. At the end of the fourth year, the machine will be sold for its remaining UCC (Undepreciated Capital Cost). A CCA rate of 30% on the declining balance is applicable. In order to support the machine, an additional $7,000 is needed in working capital immediately and another $3,500 is required at the end of the second year of operations. Working capital additions are *not* subsequently recovered. Assume that there will be other assets in the UCC pool so that there will be no recapture or terminal loss.

1... Compute the total after-tax cash flow for each of the next four years, incorporating the half-year rule and given a 40% tax rate.

2. Compute the payback period.

**Solution:**   *All numbers are rounded off to the nearest dollar*

a)      First we calculate a schedule for CCA charges:

| t | UCC Beginning | CCA | UCC ending |
|---|---|---|---|
| 1 | $27,500 | $ 8,250 | $19,250 |
| 2 | 46,750 | 14,025 | 32,725 |
| 3 | 32,725 | 9,818 | 22,907 |
| 4 | 22,907 | 6,872 | 16,035 |

Next, we identify the components for total cash flow:

|  | Year 0 | Year 1 | Year 2 | Year 3 | Year 4 |
|---|---|---|---|---|---|
| Investment | $−55,000 | | | | |
| Revenue | | $21,500 | $21,500 | $21,500 | $21,500 |
| Costs | | 4,500 | 4,500 | 4,500 | 4,500 |
| CCA | | 8,250 | 14,025 | 9,818 | 6,872 |
| EBIT | | 8,750 | 2,975 | 7,182 | 10,128 |
| −Tax (at 40%) | | 3,500 | 1,190 | 2,873 | 4,051 |
| +CCA | | 8,250 | 14,025 | 9,818 | 6,872 |
| Operating cash flow | | 13,500 | 15,810 | 14,127 | 12,949 |
| Working capital | − 7,000 | | − 3,500 | | |
| Salvage value | | | | | 16,035 |
| Total cash flow | $−62,000 | $13,500 | $12,310 | $14,127 | $28,984 |

b)      To calculate the payback period (undiscounted) we add the total cash flows:

|  | Year 0 | Year 1 | Year 2 | Year 3 | Year 4 |
|---|---|---|---|---|---|
| Total cash flows | −$62,000 | $13,500 | $12,310 | $14,127 | $28,984 |
| Cumulative | −$62,000 | − 48,500 | −36,190 | −22,063 | + 6,921 |

From the above table, we can see that Rinki Dink Inc., needs to recover $22,063 from year four cash flows. The fraction of year four in which the payback occurs is ($22,063/$28,984) = .7612. Therefore, the payback period is 3.75 years.

## Problem 21

Referring to Problem 20, determine the NPV of the investment if Rinki Dink's opportunity cost is 10%.  Should the machine be purchased?

**Solution:** The NPV can be computed by discounting the components of total cash flow:

The initial investment is −$62,000

The present value of working capital requirements:

$$-\$7,000 - \$3,500 \ (PVIF \ 10\%, 2) \ = \ -\$7,000 - \$3,500 \ (.8264) \ = \ -\$9,892.40$$

The present value of after-tax operating income is:

$$(\$21,500 - \$4,500)\,(1 - .4)\,(\text{PVIFA }10\%,\,4) = \$17,000\,(.6)\,(3.1699) = \$32,332.63$$

The present value of CCA tax savings is:

$$\frac{\$62,000\,(.30)\,(.40)}{.10 + .3} \times \frac{1.05}{1.10} = \$17,754.55$$

The present value of CCA tax savings lost due to salvage:

$$-\ \frac{\$16,035\,(.30)\,(.40)}{.10 + .3} \times \text{PVIF}\,(10\%,4) = -\ \frac{\$16,035\,(.30)\,(.40)}{.40} \times (.6830) = -\$3,285.57$$

The present value of salvage proceeds received:

$$= \$16,035\,(\text{PVIF }10\%,4) = \$16,035\,(.6830) = \$10,951.91$$

The NPV is:

$$-\$62,000 - \$9,892.40 + \$32,332.63 + \$17,754.55 - \$3,285.57 + \$10,951.91 = -\$14,138.88$$

Decision: Do not purchase the machine.


**Problem 22**

TJR Corporation is going to invest $100,000 in equipment with an applicable CCA rate of 30%. There are no other assets in this pool. The equipment has a useful life of five years. Calculate the annual CCA charges the corporation can claim. Next, assume the equipment has a salvage value of $40,000 and that TJR uses a 14% discount rate. Using a 40% tax rate, apply the tax shield approach to determine the present value of future CCA savings.

**Solution:**

| Year | Beginning UCC | CCA | Ending UCC |
|------|--------------|-----|-----------|
| 1 | $50,000 | $15,000.00 | $35,000.00 |
| 2 | 85,000* | 25,500.00 | 59,500.00 |
| 3 | 59,500 | 17,850.00 | 41,650.00 |
| 4 | 41,650 | 12,495.00 | 29,155.00 |
| 5 | 29,155 | 8,746.50 | 20,408.50 |

\* $85,000 = $35,00 + $50,000

Next, calculate the present value of the tax shield:

$$\text{PV} = \frac{\$100,000\,(.30)\,(.40)}{.30 + .40} \times \frac{1 + (0.50)\,(0.14)}{1 + .14} - \frac{\$29,155\,(.30)\,(.40)}{.30 + .40} \times \frac{1}{(1.14)^5}$$

$$= \$16,090.23 - \$2,595.80 = \$13,494.43$$

Note that the salvage value used to solve this equation is the UCC balance in the beginning of the year the recapture (due to sale and salvage value) occurred. TJR Corporation will have a tax savings of $13,494.43 from the depreciation and subsequent sale of the equipment.


## Problem 23

Wecan Corporation is considering the replacement of existing equipment that is listed on its books for $10,000 but would probably sell for half as much today, with another machine belonging in the same asset class that would cost $65,000. The firm expects this replacement to generate incremental after-tax revenues of $16,800 per year for three years and increase before-tax operating costs by $3,000 per year for each of the next three years. At the end of the third year, the new machine is expected to be scrapped (sold) for $8,750 which is 75% more than the expected salvage value of the old machine, had the old machine been used for another three years. Assume that there will always be another asset in the UCC pool. CCA rate of 20% on the declining balance is applicable. In order to support the machine, an additional $6,000 is needed in working capital immediately. Working capital additions are recovered at the end of the investment project. Compute the total after-tax cash flow for each year of the investment project, using a 40% tax-rate and incorporating the half-year rule.

**Solution:** First, we calculate a schedule for CCA changes:

| t | UCC beginning | CCA | UCC ending |
|---|---|---|---|
| 1 | $30,000 | $ 6,000 | $24,000 |
| 2 | 54,000 | 10,800 | 43,200 |
| 3 | 43,200 | 8,640 | 34,560 |

Note, the UCC beginning balance for the first year is $30,000. This is because the net acquisition is $60,000 [$65,000 – ($10,000 × ½) ] of which only half is added when it is put in use.

Next, we identify the components of total cash flow:

| | Year 0 | Year 1 | Year 2 | Year 3 |
|---|---|---|---|---|
| Net Investment | –$60,000 | | | |
| Revenue | | $28,000 | $28,000 | $28,000 |
| Costs | | 3,000 | 3,000 | 3,000 |
| CCA | | 6,000 | 10,800 | 8,640 |
| EBIT | | 19,000 | 14,200 | 16,360 |
| +CCA | | 6,000 | 10,800 | 8,640 |
| –Tax | | 7,600 | 5,680 | 6,544 |
| Operating cash flow | | 17,400 | 19,320 | 18,456 |
| Working capital | – 6,000 | | | 6,000 |
| Salvage value | | | | 3,750 |
| Total cash flow | –$66,000 | $17,400 | $19,320 | $28,206 |

The change in revenues is calculated by converting the after-tax amount of $16,800 to its before-tax equivalent of $16,800/(1 – .4)  =  $28,000. The salvage value represents the difference between the salvage value of the new equipment of $8,750, and the salvage value of the old equipment if it had been kept, which amounts to $5,000. The difference is ($8,750 – $5,000) = $3,750.

## Problem 24

Referring to Problem 23, if the firm's cost of capital is 8%, determine the NPV of the investment. Should the machine be purchased?

**Solution:** The NPV is calculated by discounting the components of total cash flow:

The initial investment is $60,000.

The present value of working capital requirements is:
   $- \$6,000 + \$6,000 \times PVIF(8\%,3)$  =  $-\$6,000 + \$6,000 \,(.793832)$  =  $-\$1,237$

The present value of after-tax operating income is:

   $(\$28,000 - \$3,000)\,(1 - .4)\,[PVIFA\,(8\%,3)] =$  $(\$25,000)\,(.6)\,(2.577097)$  =  $\$38,656.46$

The present value of the CCA tax savings is:

$$\frac{\$60,000\,(.20)\,(.40)}{.08 + .20} \times \frac{1.04}{1.08} \quad - \quad \frac{\$3,750\,(.20)\,(.40)}{.08 + .20} \times .793832$$

$$= \$16,507.94 - \$850.53 = \$15,657.41$$

The present value of salvage is: $\$3,750\,(.793832)$  =  $\$2,976.87$

The NPV is:  $-\$60,000 + \$38,656.46 - \$1,237 + \$15,657.41 + \$2,976.87$  =  $-\$3,946.26$. Since the NPV is negative, the equipment should not be purchased.

## Problem 25

A firm is considering the purchase of either Machine A or Machine B. The two machines provide the same benefit to the company and the machine selected will be replaced at the end of its useful life. The lives and annual costs for each are:

| Year | Machine A | Machine B |
|------|-----------|-----------|
| 0 | $5,000 | $4,000 |
| 1 | 800 | 1,200 |
| 2 | 800 | 1,200 |
| 3 | 800 | 1,200 |
| 4 | 800 | 1,200 |
| 5 | 800 | |

The firm's opportunity cost is 12%. If we assume no taxes, which machine should be selected? Solve this problem by computing the equivalent annual cost for each machine.

**Solution:**  At a 12% discount rate, the present values of the costs for A and B are $7,883.82 and $7,644.82, respectively.  If we ignore the fact that Machine B would have to be replaced earlier than Machine A, we would select B because the present value of the costs is less.  However, in order to properly evaluate these alternatives, we would compute the equivalent annual cost for each.  For Machine A, the EAC is the solution for C in the following equation:

$$PV \;=\; C \times PVIFA(r,t)$$
$$\$7,883.82 \;=\; C \times PVIFA(12\%,5)$$
$$\$7,883.82 \;=\; C \times 3.604776$$

Therefore,   $C \;=\; \$7,883.82 \,/\, 3.604776 \;=\; \$2,187.05$

The equivalent annual cost for Machine A is therefore $2,187.05.  The EAC for Machine B is $2,516.94.  The EAC for A is less than the EAC for B, so that A has the lower cost, on an annual basis, and is therefore the preferable alternative.

**Problem 26**

Suppose that, in the previous problem, all costs are before-tax costs and the tax rate is 34%; the company will depreciate either machine using straight-line depreciation over the life of the asset, and the salvage value of either asset is zero at the end of the life of the asset.  Compute the EAC for each asset.  Which asset is preferable?

**Solution:**  In order to compute the EAC, we first determine the operating cash flows for each asset. In this problem, operating cash flow is most easily computed using the tax-shield approach, as indicated by the following equation:

$$OCF \;=\; [(S - C) \times (1 - T_c)] \;+\; (D \times T_c)$$

Since incremental sales are zero, the first term in this calculation for Machine A is:

$$[(S - C) \times (1 - T_c)] \;=\; [(\$0 - \$800) \times (1 - .34)] \;=\; -\$528$$

The second term is the depreciation tax shield, which is computed as follows:

$$(D \times T_c) \;=\; (\$5,000 \,/\, 5) \times .34 \;=\; \$340$$

Therefore, operating cash flow is:   $-\$528 + 340 \;=\; -\$188$

Annual operating cash flow is a five-year annuity of $188 in costs per year, so that the present value of the operating cash flow is:

$$-\$188 \times PVIFA(12\%,5) \;=\; -\$188 \times 3.604776 \;=\; -\$677.70$$

The present value of the cash outflows is ($677.70 + $5,000) = $5,677.70. The EAC is the solution for C in the following equation:

$$\$5,677.70 \;=\; C \times 3.604776$$
$$C \;=\; \$5,677.70 \,/\, 3.604776 \;=\; \$1,575.05$$

The equivalent annual cost for Machine A is therefore $1,575.05. For Machine B, the operating cash flow is –$452, the present value of the cash outflows is $5,372.88, and the EAC is $1,786.94. Therefore, Machine A is the preferable alternative.

## Problem 27

A firm is considering the purchase of either Machine X or Machine Y. The two machines provide the same benefit to the company and the machine selected will be replaced at the end of its useful life. The lives and annual costs for each are:

| Year | Machine X | Machine Y |
|------|-----------|-----------|
| 0 | $800 | $600 |
| 1 | 150 | 200 |
| 2 | 150 | 200 |
| 3 | 150 | 200 |
| 4 | 150 | |

The firm's opportunity cost is 15%. If we assume no taxes, which machine should be selected? Solve this problem by computing the equivalent annual cost for each machine.

**Solution:**   At a 15% discount rate, the present values of the costs for X and Y are $1,228.25 and $1,056.65, respectively.  For Machine X, the EAC is the solution for C in the following equation:

$1,228.25   =   C × PVIFA(15%,4)
$1,228.25   = C × 2.854978
  C   =   $1,228.25 / 2.854978   =   $430.21

The equivalent annual cost for Machine X is therefore $430.21; the EAC for Machine Y is $462.79. The EAC for X is less than the EAC for Y, so that X has the lower cost, on an annual basis and is therefore the preferable alternative.

## Problem 28

A manufacturer of hand tools plans to submit a bid to supply hammers to Canada's Department of Defence (DOD). The DOD will buy 1,000 hammers per year for the next three years. To be able to supply the hammers, the manufacturer must acquire manufacturing equipment at a cost of $150,000. The equipment has a five-year life and will be depreciated for tax purposes on a straight-line basis. Since the contract with the DOD is for a three-year period, the manufacturer plans to sell the equipment after three years. At that time, the equipment is expected to have a market value of $50,000. Additional fixed costs will total $38,000 per year and variable costs are expected to be $2 per hammer. An additional investment of $25,000 in net working capital will be required. This investment will be recovered at the end of three years. The firm's tax rate is 34% and the required rate of return is 18%. What is the lowest price the manufacturer can charge for the hammers?

**Solution:** The cash outflow in year 0 is the sum of the additional net working capital and the capital expenditure: ($25,000 + $150,000) = $175,000. The total cash flow in year 3 is the sum of the operating cash flow, the recovery of net working capital, and the inflow from the sale of the equipment. The sale of the equipment has tax implications because the book value of the asset differs from the market value. The book value is the purchase price less the accumulated depreciation. The annual depreciation expense is ($150,000/5) = $30,000, so that the accumulated depreciation is (3 × $30,000) = $90,000 and the book value is ($150,000 − $90,000) = $60,000. The difference between the market value ($50,000) and the book value ($60,000) is a tax deduction because the firm has under-depreciated the asset by $10,000. The tax deduction results in a tax savings of $3,400, so that the inflow resulting from the sale of the equipment at the end of year 3 is ($50,000 + $3,400) = $53,400. The total cash inflow at the end of year 3 is:

$$OCF + \$25,000 + \$53,400 \;=\; OCF + \$78,400$$

where OCF is the operating cash flow.

Now, we solve for the annual operating cash flow (OCF) which will provide the 18% required rate of return. This is the value of OCF which is the solution to the following net present value equation:

$$0 \;=\; -\$175,000 + \frac{OCF}{(1.18)} + \frac{OCF}{(1.18)^2} + \frac{OCF}{(1.18)^3} + \frac{\$78,400}{(1.18)^3}$$

The present value of the $78,400 inflow at the end of year 3 is equal to $[\$78,400/(1.18)^3] = \$47,716.66$. The three terms representing the present value of the annual operating cash flows can be written as an annuity. Therefore the above equation can be rewritten as:

$$0 \;=\; -\$175,000 + [OCF \times PVIFA(18\%,3)] + \$47,716.66$$

$$\$127,283.34 \;=\; [OCF \times 2.174273]$$

Therefore, OCF = ($127,283.34/2.174273) = $58,540.64. This solution indicates that if the firm's operating cash flow for the project is $58,540.64 per year, then the net present value of the project would be zero. Consequently, the rate of return on the firm's investment in equipment and working capital would be 18%, the required rate of return.

The next step is to determine the net income, and then the price per unit, for the project which will provide the necessary operating cash flow. For this purpose, we use the bottom-up definition of operating cash flow:

$$\begin{aligned} OCF \;&=\; \text{Net income} + \text{Depreciation} \\ &=\; [(S - C - D) \times (1 - T_c)] + D \end{aligned}$$

Since OCF = $58,540.64 and D = ($150,000/5) = $30,000, then:

$$\text{Net income} \;=\; OCF - D \;=\; \$58,540.64 - \$30,000 \;=\; \$28,540.64$$

Using the definition of net income in the above equation, we can substitute and solve for S, as follows:

$$\begin{aligned} \text{Net income} \;&=\; [(S - C - D) \times (1 - T_c)] \\ \$28,540.64 \;&=\; (S - \$40,000 - \$30,000) \times (1 - .34) \\ \$28,540.64 \;&=\; (S - \$70,000) \times (.66) \\ (\$28,540.64 \,/\, .66) \;&=\; (S - \$70,000) \\ S \;&=\; \$43,243.39 + \$70,000 \;=\; \$113,243.39 \end{aligned}$$

The value of C in this calculation is the sum of variable and fixed costs for the project.  Fixed costs are $38,000 per year and variable costs are ($2 × 1,000) = $2,000, so that C = ($38,000 + $2,000) = $40,000.  The solution for S represents total sales required to generate the required operating cash flow. Since the bid is for 1,000 hammers, the price per unit is ($113,243.39/1,000) = $113.24.  This price will provide the firm with annual operating cash flow of $58,540.64 and net present value for the project equal to zero, so that the firm would earn the required 18% rate of return.

# 11     <u>Project Analysis and Evaluation</u>

## CHAPTER HIGHLIGHTS

In Chapter 10, our focus was on identifying and computing cash flows for capital budgeting projects. In this chapter, we recognize the fact that these cash flows, as well as the resulting net present value calculations, are estimates which must be evaluated more closely. Therefore, the emphasis is on procedures for assessing these forecasts and estimates.

## EVALUATING NPV ESTIMATES

Remember, a capital budgeting project is acceptable if its market value exceeds its cost, but most of the time, we cannot directly observe market value. Therefore, we estimate it. Market value can be estimated using discounted cash flow analysis. If the present value of the project exceeds its cost, then the project's NPV is positive. Although this is a good sign, we must remember that the numbers used to compute the NPV are estimates. Therefore, the NPV calculations are subject to error. A potential source of error is in the forecast of future cash flows. We must be aware of, and attempt to compensate for, the possibility that actual cash flows will deviate from our forecasts. All NPV calculations, therefore, must be evaluated to determine their reliability.

The first step in evaluation of an NPV estimate is to understand the nature of the cash flow forecasts. In general, these forecasts can be thought of in terms of the expected value concept. For example, consider a forecasted cash flow of $5,000 one year from now. This does not mean that the actual cash flow will be $5,000 or even very close to $5,000. Remember, the expected value refers to a weighted average of all the cash flows which might possibly occur. Therefore, the actual cash flow could be a great deal more or less than $5,000. In interpreting our DCF analysis, we must keep in mind that the actual cash flow can, and most likely will, differ from the expected value.

*Forecasting risk* is the risk that the financial manager makes an incorrect decision because of errors in forecasting future cash flows. If forecasted cash inflows are overly optimistic, a project may appear to have a positive net present value when in fact, the net present value is negative. Many of the techniques described in this chapter are designed to identify sources of potential errors in cash flow forecasts.

## SCENARIO AND OTHER WHAT-IF ANALYSES

Whenever we do capital budgeting, we are dealing with the uncertain future. To the extent that our assumptions about future cash flows are incorrect, our estimates of NPV will be incorrect as well. *Scenario analysis*, *sensitivity analysis*, and *simulation analysis* are commonly used techniques for evaluating the critical assumptions of net present value calculations.

**Getting Started:** Let's assume a firm is considering the production of a new product. The project requires an investment of $1,000,000 in plant and equipment which has a 10-year life and no salvage value. For simplicity, we will assume that, for tax purposes, fixed assets will be depreciated on a straight-line basis. The required rate of return is 16% and the tax rate is 34%. The firm has made the following forecasts:

|                        | Base case | Lower bound | Upper bound |
|------------------------|-----------|-------------|-------------|
| Unit sales             | 10,000    | 9,000       | 11,000      |
| Price per unit         | $200      | $190        | $210        |
| Variable costs per unit| $130      | $125        | $135        |
| Fixed costs per year   | $425,000  | $410,000    | $440,000    |

The 'base case' forecast represents the expected values for each forecasted item.  The 'lower bound' and 'upper bound' forecasts are values such that the firm believes it is unlikely that actual values will be outside these bounds.  What is the net present value of the project using the base case forecast?

First, compute the net income and operating cash flow:

| Sales              | $2,000,000   |
|--------------------|--------------|
| – Variable costs   | 1,300,000    |
| – Fixed costs      | 425,000      |
| – Depreciation     | 100,000      |
| EBIT               | $   175,000  |
| – Taxes (34%)      | 59,500       |
| Net income         | $   115,500  |
|                    |              |
| EBIT               | $   175,000  |
| + Depreciation     | 100,000      |
| – Taxes            | 59,500       |
| Operating Cash Flow| $   215,500  |

Next, compute the present value of an annuity of $215,500 per year for 10 years, discounted at the 16% required rate of return:

$$PV \; = \; \$215,500 \times PVIFA(16\%,10) \; = \; \$215,500 \times 4.833227 \; = \; \$1,041,560$$

The net present value of the project is:

$$\$1,041,560 \; \text{-} \; \$1,000,000 \; = \; \$41,560$$

This net present value can be thought of as the *expected* net present value, the NPV managers deem most likely.

**Scenario Analysis:**  Since the net present value computed in the preceding example is positive, we might conclude that the project is acceptable.  However, in this section, we analyze this result more carefully, in light of the lower and upper bound forecasts mentioned earlier.  *Scenario analysis* examines the effect on all variables, and consequently on NPV, of a hypothetical sequence of events.

**An Example:**  For our scenario analysis, we examine both the worst case scenario and the best case scenario, as indicated in the following table:

|                        | Worst case | Best case |
|------------------------|------------|-----------|
| Unit sales             | 9,000      | 11,000    |
| Price per unit         | $190       | $210      |
| Variable costs per unit| $135       | $125      |
| Fixed costs per year   | $440,000   | $410,000  |

The worst case scenario indicates the least favourable outcome for each of the four forecasted variables while the best case scenario indicates the most favourable outcome for each of the variables. For example, the worst case scenario will use the lower bound for unit sales and price per unit but the upper bound for variable and fixed costs. The best case scenario will use the upper bound for sales and price, and the lower bound for variable and fixed costs. For each scenario, we now compute net income, cash flow, net present value, and internal rate of return for the proposed project. The results are presented in the following table:

| Scenario | Net income | Cash flow | NPV | IRR |
|---|---|---|---|---|
| Base case | $115,500 | $215,500 | $ 41,650 | 17.11% |
| Worst case | – 29,700 | 70,300 | –660,224 | –5.94 |
| Best case | 280,500 | 380,500 | 839,043 | 36.33 |

What conclusions can we draw from these results? The major conclusion seems to be that further analysis is required. While the net present value is positive for the base case scenario, there is some possibility that the net present value will be significantly negative (the NPV for the worst case scenario is –$660,224). In the next section, we use a variant of scenario analysis to evaluate these results further.

**Sensitivity Analysis:** *Sensitivity analysis* is designed to determine the sensitivity of one variable to changes in another variable. For our purposes, we are interested in the sensitivity of NPV to variation in the level of each of the four forecasted variables. For example, we might attempt to determine the change in NPV which results if actual sales are at the lower bound of our forecasted range, while all other variables are held at their base case levels. Sensitivity analysis is a variant of scenario analysis in which each scenario represents a change in only one variable, rather than a number of variables.

**An Example:** Assume that all variables, except unit sales, take on their base case levels. What is the effect on net present value and internal rate of return if unit sales are at their lower bound?

The answer to this question is provided in the following table:

| Scenario | Unit sales | Cash flow | NPV | IRR |
|---|---|---|---|---|
| Base case | 10,000 | $215,500 | $ 41,650 | 17.11% |
| Worst case | 9,000 | 169,300 | –181,735 | 10.93 |
| Best case | 11,000 | 261,700 | 264,856 | 22.82 |

Although the problem posed here concerns the effect on NPV and IRR if unit sales are at their lower bound, we have also included results for the case in which sales are at their upper bound. For both the worst case and best case scenarios here, we assume that price, variable costs, and fixed costs take on their base case values. Before we analyze these results, we perform sensitivity analysis for additional variables.

**An Example:** What is the effect on NPV and IRR if variable costs are at their lower bound and all other variables are at their base value?

Sensitivity analysis of variable costs is performed in the following table:

| Scenario | Variable costs | Cash flow | NPV | IRR |
|---|---|---|---|---|
| Base case | $130 | $215,500 | $ 41,650 | 17.11% |
| Worst case | 135 | 182,500 | –117,936 | 12.76 |
| Best case | 125 | 248,500 | 201,057 | 21.22 |

These results are derived by varying only variable costs. In the worst case scenario, variable costs are $135 per unit and in the best case scenario, variable costs are $125 per unit. For both scenarios, unit sales, price, and fixed costs take on their base case values.

**An Example:**  What is the effect on NPV and IRR if fixed costs are at their lower bound?

Sensitivity analysis of fixed costs is performed in the following table:

| Scenario | Fixed costs | Cash flow | NPV | IRR |
|---|---|---|---|---|
| Base case | $425,000 | $215,500 | $ 41,650 | 17.11% |
| Worst case | 440,000 | 205,600 | – 6,288 | 15.83 |
| Best case | 410,000 | 225,400 | 89,409 | 18.36 |

We have now performed sensitivity analysis for three of our forecasted variables. What conclusions can we derive from this analysis? The first important conclusion is that net present value is more sensitive to changes in the unit sales forecast than to either the variable cost or the fixed cost forecasts. When sales are at the lower bound, net present value is –$181,735; when variable costs and fixed costs are at the lower bound, net present values are – $117,936 and –$6,288, respectively. These are typical results; they reflect the fact that sales are typically more difficult to forecast than costs. In this example, the range of sales levels deviates from the base case sales level by 10 % in either direction. The cost forecasts vary by less than 4% in either direction, thereby contributing to the lower sensitivity of NPV to cost forecasts.

The second important conclusion is that, for each of the three variables subjected to sensitivity analysis, the net present value is negative for the worst case scenario. That is, net present value is negative if any one of the variables takes on its lower bound forecast. This is not a particularly encouraging result. A reasonable conclusion suggested by this outcome might be that further evaluation of the forecasts is appropriate. Especially worthy of attention are the unit sales and variable cost forecasts. The goal of this additional analysis is to obtain more accurate forecasts which might clarify the likelihood that the net present value will be negative.

**Simulation Analysis**: This is another variant of scenario analysis in which we consider a large number of different combinations of the forecasted variables. Unlike scenario analysis, however, the combinations of the variables are selected randomly, rather than with a hypothesized scenario in mind. For each combination of values, net income, cash flow, and net present values are computed. The financial analyst then uses the resulting data to derive estimates of the likelihood that net present value will take on some particular values. For example, the analyst might be interested in estimating the probability that the NPV is negative. Simulation analysis is typically performed with the aid of a computer because it involves a large number of calculations. Furthermore, the manner in which the computer selects combinations of variables must be carefully specified according to reasonable rules of probability if the results are to be meaningful.

## BREAK-EVEN ANALYSIS

In the example analyzed in the previous section, we concluded that unit sales forecast is the crucial variable in ascertaining whether the project is likely to have a positive net present value; this is often the case for a capital budgeting project, especially if the project involves development of a new product. Consequently, the relationship between sales volume and profitability warrants additional attention. In this section, we develop several forms of break-even analysis. In general, the goal of break-even analysis is to identify the level of sales below which a project is unacceptable.

**Fixed and Variable Costs:** Break-even analysis requires that we first distinguish between fixed and variable costs. Variable costs are costs that vary with production. They are frequently assumed to be proportional to the level of production. Direct labour cost is an example of a variable cost. Total variable costs (VC) are equal to variable cost per unit of output (v) multiplied by the number of units of output (Q). This relationship is summarized by:

$$VC = v \times Q$$

Fixed costs do not change over a specified time interval and must be paid regardless of production levels. Rent is an example of a fixed cost. Fixed costs are considered fixed during a given period of time, such as a quarter or a year. However, in the long run, all costs are ultimately variable. Rent, for example, may be fixed over a given time period specified in the lease (for example five years). However, it is variable over a longer period because the contractual obligation may be terminated.

Total costs (TC) for a given level of output in a given period of time are defined as the sum of total variable costs (VC) and fixed costs (FC):

$$TC = VC + FC$$

Since $VC = v \times Q$, the above equation can be rewritten as:

$$TC = (v \times Q) + FC$$

**Accounting Break-Even:** The *accounting break-even point* is the sales level at which net income is zero.

**An Example:**  Heggestad, Inc. has forecasted sales of a new product at 4,400 units per year, with a selling price of $5.95 per unit. Fixed assets will be acquired for $40,000. The fixed assets have a 10-year life and will be depreciated on a straight-line basis; depreciation will be $4,000 annually. Variable costs are $3.45 per unit. Fixed costs will be $2,000 per year. The firm's required rate of return is 18% and the corporate tax rate is 34%. What is the accounting break-even point for Heggestad?

If EBIT is zero, then taxes and net income are also zero. Therefore, we can solve this problem by finding the sales level for which EBIT is zero. First, suppose that sales are zero. Then, EBIT is ($0 – $2,000 – $4,000) = –$6,000. Now suppose that Heggestad increases sales from zero units to one unit, so that EBIT increases by the difference between the selling price and the variable cost per unit: ($5.95 – $3.45) = $2.50. Each additional unit sold will increase EBIT by $2.50, so that, in order to increase EBIT to zero, Heggestad must sell ($6,000/$2.50) = 2,400 units. This example illustrates the fact that, in general, the accounting break-even occurs when the number of units (Q) is equal to:

$$Q = \frac{\text{Total fixed costs} + \text{Depreciation}}{\text{Unit price} - \text{Unit variable cost}}$$

This formula for the accounting break-even point can be derived from the algebraic definition of net income:

$$\text{Net income} = (S - VC - FC - D) \times (1 - t)$$

where S = sales, VC = total variable costs, FC = fixed costs, D = depreciation and t = the tax rate. If we let P = selling price per unit, v = variable cost per unit, and Q = total units sold, then:

$$S = P \times Q \quad \text{and} \quad VC = v \times Q$$

Net income can be rewritten as:

$$\text{Net income} = [(P \times Q) - (v \times Q) - FC - D] \times (1 - t)$$
$$= \{[(P - v) \times Q] - FC - D\} \times (1 - t)$$

Since accounting break-even is the sales level for which net income is zero, then accounting break-even is the value of Q for which:

$$\{[(P - v) \times Q] - FC - D\} \times (1 - t) = 0$$

Dividing both sides of this equation by (1 – t), we have:

$$[(P - v) \times Q] - FC - D = 0$$

The left side of this equation is EBIT, so this statement indicates that the value of Q for which net income is zero is the same value of Q for which EBIT is zero, as we observed earlier.  This equation is solved as follows:

$$[(P - v) \times Q] - FC - D = 0$$
$$(P - v) \times Q = FC + D$$

$$Q = \frac{FC + D}{P - v}$$

This statement is the algebraic equivalent of our earlier definition of the accounting break-even point.

Although the accounting break-even point is widely used for analysis of capital budgeting projects, there is some question as to its usefulness.  The primary reason for this skepticism is the fact that a project whose sales level exceeds the accounting break-even point does not necessarily have a positive net present value.  On the other hand, the accounting break-even point is relatively simple to calculate and understand, and may be useful as a rough guide to the acceptability of a project.  As an example of this latter point, a project which is not expected to break even in the accounting sense is also unacceptable from net present value perspective.


## OPERATING CASH FLOW, SALES, VOLUME, AND BREAK-EVEN

In this section, we consider the accounting break-even point from an alternative perspective, and we develop two additional break-even concepts: cash break-even point and financial break-even point.  In order to simplify our analysis somewhat, we assume that the firm pays no income tax.

**Accounting Break-Even and Cash Flow:**  In the example of the previous section, Heggestad, Inc. had an accounting break-even point of 2,400 units.  Therefore, if Heggestad sells 2,400 units per year, both EBIT and net income are zero.  At this level of sales, what is the firm's operating cash flow?  Recall that the 'bottom-up' approach defines operating cash flow as net income plus depreciation.  For this example:

$$OCF = EBIT + D - T = 0 + \$4,000 - 0 = \$4,000$$

If sales remain at the break-even level, the IRR is zero.  The project will return a cash flow of $4,000 per year for 10 years, on an initial outlay of $40,000.  At any positive discount rate, the NPV is less than zero.  Thus it is easily seen that, even if sales exceed the break-even point, NPV is not necessarily positive.

**Sales Volume and Operating Cash Flow:** Operating cash flow has been defined as:

$$OCF \quad = \quad EBIT + D - Taxes$$

$$= \quad (S - C - D) + D - [(S - C - D) \times T_c]$$

In this section, we have chosen to ignore taxes. Therefore, the above definition becomes:

$$OCF \quad = \quad EBIT + D \quad = \quad (S - C - D) + D$$

In addition, earlier in this chapter, we defined EBIT as follows:

$$EBIT \quad = \quad [(P - v) \times Q] - FC - D$$

Therefore, the above definition of OCF can be rewritten as:

$$
\begin{aligned}
OCF \quad &= \quad EBIT + D \\
&= \quad (S - C - D) + D \\
&= \quad \{[(P - v) \times Q] - FC - D\} + D \\
&= \quad [(P - v) \times Q] - FC
\end{aligned}
$$

**Cash Flow, Accounting, and Financial Break-Even Points:** The above definition of OCF can be rearranged by solving for Q:

$$OCF \quad = \quad [(P - v) \times Q] - FC$$

$$FC + OCF \quad = \quad (P - v) \times Q$$

$$Q \quad = \quad \frac{FC + OCF}{P - v}$$

This relationship specifies the level of Q required in order to achieve any given level of OCF.

For the accounting break-even point, OCF = D. Therefore, the accounting break-even can be defined in terms of the relationship between Q and OCF by simply replacing OCF by D. This verifies that the accounting break-even is:

$$Q \quad = \quad \frac{FC + D}{P - v}$$

The *cash break-even point* is the level of sales for which the operating cash flow is zero. This is easily derived by substituting OCF = 0 in the above relationship between Q and OCF:

$$Q \quad = \quad \frac{FC + 0}{P - v} \quad = \quad \frac{FC}{P - v}$$

**An Example:** Compute the cash break-even point for the Heggestad example.

The cash break-even point is:

$$Q = \frac{FC}{P - v} = \frac{\$2,000}{\$5.95 - \$3.45} = 800$$

Heggestad must sell 800 units to have operating cash flow equal to zero. A project with sales equal to the cash break-even level throughout its life has an internal rate of return of $-100\%$. That is, the $40,000 investment produces no cash inflow, so the investment represents a total loss of the original investment.

The most significant break-even point for the financial manager is the *financial break-even point*, which is the level of sales such that the net present value of the project is zero.

**An Example:** Compute the financial break-even for Heggestad.

We solve the problem by first identifying the level of operating cash flow (OCF) for which net present value is zero. Then, substituting this value of OCF in the earlier equation, we solve for Q. Heggestad's operating cash flow is in the form of a ten-year annuity. The present value of this annuity must equal the initial outlay of $40,000. Solve the following equation for OCF:

$$\$40,000 = OCF \times PVIFA(18\%,10)$$
$$\$40,000 = OCF \times 4.494086$$
$$OCF = \$40,000 / 4.494086 = \$8,900.59$$

Substitute this value of OCF into the earlier equation to determine the financial break-even point:

$$Q = \frac{\$2,000 + \$8,900.59}{\$5.95 - \$3.45} = 4,360.24$$

Therefore, sales must be 4,361 units in order for the project to have a net present value greater than zero.


## OPERATING LEVERAGE

The level of fixed costs for a capital budgeting project, or for a company as a whole, has an important impact on the break-even concepts developed in the previous section. The precise nature of the relationship between fixed costs and break-even points is described in this section.

**The Basic Idea:** *Operating leverage* is the extent to which a capital budgeting project, or a firm as a whole, relies on fixed production costs. A firm or project with a relatively high level of fixed costs has high operating leverage. Generally, a high level of fixed costs is also associated with a relatively large investment in plant and equipment; such a situation is said to be capital-intensive.

**Measuring Operating Leverage:** The *degree of operating leverage* (DOL) is defined as:

$$DOL = \frac{\text{Percentage change in OCF}}{\text{Percentage change in Q}}$$

This is equivalent to:

$$DOL = 1 + FC / OCF$$

**An Example:**  Suppose sales for the project under consideration by Heggestad increase from 2,400 units to 3,000 units.  What is the effect on operating cash flow?  What is the degree of operating leverage?

Remember, OCF is equal to $4,000 at the accounting break-even point of 2,400 units.  To find the DOL, the percentage change in OCF and Q are measured using the break-even point as the base quantity.  Operating cash flow for an output of 3,000 units can be computed as follows:

$$
\begin{aligned}
OCF &= [(P - v) \times Q] - FC \\
&= [(\$5.95 - \$3.45) \times 3,000] - \$2,000 = \$5,500
\end{aligned}
$$

The percentage change in operating cash flow is:

$$\frac{\$5,500 - \$4,000}{\$4,000} = .375 = 37.5\%$$

The percentage change in output is:

$$\frac{3,000 - 2,400}{2,400} = .25 = 25\%$$

Therefore, the degree of operating leverage is $(37.5\%/25\%) = 1.5$.  The alternative calculation of DOL provides the same result:

$$DOL = 1 + FC / OCF = 1 + \$2,000 / \$4,000 = 1.5$$

The following examples illustrate additional aspects of the DOL calculation.

**An Example:**  Suppose that sales for the project under consideration by Heggestad increase from 2,400 units to 3,600 units.  What is the effect on operating cash flow?  What is the degree of operating leverage?

Using OFC = $4,000 when Q = 2,400 units, for Q = 3,600 units:

$$OCF = [(P - v) \times Q] - FC = [(\$5.95 - \$3.45) \times 3,600] - \$2,000 = \$7,000$$

The percentage change in operating cash flow is:

$$\frac{\$7,000 - \$4,000}{\$4,000} = .75 = 75\%$$

The percentage change in output is:

$$\frac{3,600 - 2,400}{2,400} = .50 = 50\%$$

Therefore, the degree of operating leverage is (75%/50%) = 1.5. This example illustrates the fact that, for a given level of output (in this case, Q = 2,400 units), the degree of operating leverage remains constant regardless of the size of the increase in Q. This conclusion can be verified by observing the alternative formula for the calculation of DOL. For a given level of Q, both FC and OCF remain constant regardless of the size of the increase in Q.

**An Example:**   If sales increase from 3,000 units to 3,600 units, what is the degree of operating leverage?

When Q = 3,000 units, OCF = \$5,500; when Q = 3,600 units, OCF = \$7,000. The percentage change in operating cash flow is:

$$\frac{\$7,000 - \$5,500}{\$5,500} \ = \ .272727 \ = \ 27.2727\%$$

The percentage change in output is:

$$\frac{3,600 - 3,000}{3,000} \ = \ .20 \ = \ 20\%$$

The degree of operating leverage is (27.2727%/20%) = 1.3636. The alternative calculation of DOL is:

$$DOL \ = \ 1 + FC \, / \, OCF \ = \ 1 \ + \ \$2,000 \, / \, \$5,500 \ = \ 1.3636$$

This example illustrates the fact that the DOL changes when the level of Q changes. When we consider changes in Q from a base of 2,400 units, DOL = 1.5. For changes in Q from a base of 3,000 units, DOL decreases to 1.3636. This is representative of the general result that DOL decreases when the base level of Q increases.

**An Example:**   Heggestad has determined that an alternative manufacturing process can be used to produce the new product. The alternative process is less capital-intensive, so that fixed costs are reduced but variable costs per unit are increased; annual fixed costs are \$800 and variable costs are \$4.45 per unit. The required investment in fixed assets is \$25,000. Heggestad is using straight-line depreciation to depreciate the asset over its 10-year life. Compute the accounting break-even, the cash break-even and the financial break-even for the alternative process. Also, compute the degree of operating leverage and the net present value for each production process at a forecasted sales level of 4,400 units per year.

Depreciation for the alternative process is D = (\$25,000/10) = \$2,500 and (P – v) = (\$5.95 – \$4.45) = \$1.50. The accounting break-even point is:

$$Q \ = \ \frac{FC + D}{P - v} \ = \ \frac{\$800 \ + \ \$2,500}{\$1.50} \ = \ 2,200$$

The cash break-even point is:

$$Q \ = \ \frac{FC \ + \ OCF}{P - v} \ = \ \frac{\$800 + 0}{\$1.50} \ = \ 533.33 \ = \ 534 \text{ units}$$

To compute the financial break-even, first solve for OCF in the following equation:

$$\$25,000 \ = \ OCF \times PVIFA(18\%,10)$$
$$\$25,000 \ = \ OCF \times 4.494086$$
$$OCF \ = \ \$25,000 \, / \, 4.494086 \ = \ \$5,562.87$$

Substitute this value of OCF into the earlier equation to determine the financial break-even point:

$$Q = \frac{FC + OCF}{P - v} = \frac{\$800 + \$5,562.87}{\$5.95 - \$4.45} = 4,241.91 = 4,242 \text{ units}$$

Notice that each break-even point has decreased relative to the corresponding calculation for the original, capital-intensive process.

At Q = 4,400 units, OCF for the original production process is:

$$OCF = [(P - v) \times Q] - FC = [(\$5.95 - \$3.45) \times 4,400] - \$2,000 = \$9,000$$

The degree of operating leverage is:

$$DOL = 1 + FC / OCF = 1 + \$2,000 / \$9,000 = 1.222$$

The net present value for the original capital-intensive process is:

$$NPV = -\$40,000 + [\$9,000 \times PVIFA(18\%,10)] = -\$40,000 + (\$9,000 \times 4.494086) = +\$446.77$$

For the alternative process:

$$OCF = [(P - v) \times Q] - FC = [(\$5.95 - \$4.45) \times 4,400] - \$800 = \$5,800$$

$$DOL = 1 + \$800 / \$5,800 = 1.138$$

$$NPV = -\$25,000 + (\$5,800 \times 4.494086) = +\$1,065.70$$

The alternative production process has a higher net present value and a lower DOL at the forecasted sales level. Also, as noted earlier, the financial break-even point is lower. Does this mean that the alternative process should be implemented by the firm? There is no simple answer to this question. Clearly, if we were certain that sales would be precisely 4,400 units, this is the preferable alternative. However, as discussed earlier, the forecasting risk can be substantial when a new product is introduced.

Suppose that there is a possibility that sales could be higher than 4,400 units. Does this possibility change our conclusion? The higher degree of operating leverage for the capital-intensive production process indicates that operating cash flow and net present value increase more rapidly with an increase in sales. For example, at a sales level of 5,000 units, the NPV for the original process is +$7,187.90 while NPV for the alternative is +$5,110.38. The original process now has the higher NPV and is therefore preferable. On the other hand, if sales are below the forecasted level, the higher DOL for the capital-intensive process implies a more rapid decline in net present value. There is no clear preference between the two alternatives in this problem.

## ADDITIONAL CONSIDERATIONS IN CAPITAL BUDGETING

The additional considerations discussed in this section are managerial options and capital rationing.

**Managerial Options:**   So far, we have assumed that all basic features of a capital budgeting project will not change throughout the life of the project.   This ignores *managerial options* that might change the course of the project. Management can, for example, change product price, expand production, modify the production process, or even abandon an unsuccessful project.  Ignoring these managerial options may incorrectly estimate the net present value of a project.  A dynamic analysis incorporates the value of managerial options.

Two particularly important managerial options are the option to expand a successful project and the option to reduce the scale of a project, or even abandon a project, if it is unsuccessful.  Since these options have value to the firm, they must be considered in capital budgeting analysis.

In a static analysis, NPV calculations are based on forecasted sales levels throughout the life of the project.  In dynamic capital budgeting, we incorporate the fact that our estimates of projected sales will be revised over the life of the project.  For example, if sales forecasts are revised upward, a firm might expand production and sales. This implies that cash flows and NPV are greater than initially anticipated.  Since static analysis ignores this possibility, it underestimates the net present value of the project.

Similar conclusions apply to the option to abandon an unsuccessful project.  If demand for a new product is significantly below original expectations, it might be less expensive to abandon the project than to proceed with it. Static analysis assumes that an unsuccessful project will continue for a specified number of years.  If abandonment of the project is less expensive than continuing at low sales levels, then the net present value increases if the project is abandoned.  In other words, static analysis again underestimates a project's NPV because it ignores the managerial option to abandon an unsuccessful project.  The analysis of managerial options is difficult because we must predict the probability that a project will be expanded or abandoned.

Suppose a project will be expanded if first-year sales exceed 10,000 units, and it will be abandoned if first-year sales are less than 5,000 units.  Dynamic analysis forecasts the probability that these events will occur.  Then the NPV is determined for each possibility, as well as the possibility that the project is maintained at its expected level.  The net present value of the project is the weighted average (i.e., expected value) of the possible NPVs for each event.  The major difficulty with this analysis is making reasonable forecasts of the probabilities for each possible outcome.  Both forecasting and computation can be quite complicated.

**Capital Rationing:**  Capital rationing exists if a firm, or a unit of a corporation, has identified positive NPV capital budgeting projects but is unable to obtain the financing required for the projects.  One approach to resolving such a problem is to accept the set of projects which maximizes the NPV with the funds available.  This is generally equivalent to accepting those projects with the highest profitability index.  However, the existence of capital rationing raises questions as to whether the firm is employing appropriate discounted cash flow analysis.  For example, if a corporation limits the financing available to a division of the firm, without regard for whether additional positive NPV projects exist, it is questionable whether the corporation is attempting to maximize shareholder value.

## CONCEPT TEST

1.      The risk that a financial manager makes an incorrect decision because of errors in forecasting future cash flows is called _____ .

2.     An analysis of the effect on all forecasted variables, and on NPV, of a hypothetical sequence of events is referred to as _____ .

3.     An assessment of the sensitivity of one variable to changes in another variable is called _____ .

4.     Capital budgeting is concerned about the sensitivity of _____ to variation in the level of a forecasted variable.  For example, the financial managers evaluate the change in _____ which results if actual sales are at the lower bound of a forecasted range, while all other variables are held constant.  The process of analyzing the impact of different forecasted variables on the acceptability of a capital budgeting project is called _____ .  In this process, the combinations of the variables are not selected with any particular scenario in mind, but rather are selected _____ .

5.     Variable costs are costs that vary with the level of _____ and are generally assumed to be proportional to the level of _____ . Total variable costs (VC) are equal to _____ multiplied by _____. This relationship is summarized algebraically as : VC = _____ .

6.     Costs which do not change over a specified time interval and must be paid regardless of production levels are called _____ .

7.     Total costs (TC) for a given level of output in a given period of time are defined as the sum of _____ and _____ .  This relationship can be expressed algebraically as: TC = _____ .

8.     The accounting break-even point is the sales level at which a project's _____ is equal to _____ .   The accounting break-even point is computed as        Q = _____ .   If sales are equal to the accounting break-even point, then both _____ and _____ are equal to zero.

9.     The 'bottom-up' approach defines operating cash flow as _____ plus _____ .  At the break-even sales level, operating cash flow is equal to _____ .  If sales remain at the break-even level throughout the life of a project, then the internal rate of return is equal to _____ . Therefore, at any positive discount rate, the net present value of such a project is _____ .

10.    In the absence of corporate income taxes, the level of output (Q) required to achieve a given level of operating cash flow (OCF) can be written as:  Q = _____ .

11.    The cash break-even point is the level of sales for which the _____ is equal to _____ . The formula for the cash break-even point is derived from the previous equation by substituting _____ = _____ , resulting in the following:  Q = _____ .

12.    A project with sales equal to the cash break-even level throughout the life of the project has an internal rate of return equal to _____ because the initial outlay produces no cash inflow.

13.    The most significant break-even point for the financial manager is the financial break-even point, which is the level of sales such that the _____ of the project is equal to _____ . The financial break-even point is computed by first identifying the level of operating cash flow (OCF) for which _____ is equal to _____ and then substituting this value of OCF in the equation which describes the relationship between Q and OCF.

14.    The extent to which a capital budgeting project, or a firm as a whole, relies on fixed production costs is called _____ . A firm or project with a relatively high level of fixed costs is said to have high _____ . A high level of fixed costs is typically associated with a relatively large investment in plant and equipment; such a situation is said to be _____ .

15.    The degree of operating leverage (DOL) is defined as:  DOL = _____ .    It can be demonstrated algebraically that this definition is equivalent to:  DOL = _____ .

16.    For a given level of output, the degree of operating leverage (increases/decreases/remains constant) as the size of the increase in Q increases.  When the base level of Q increases, the degree of operating leverage (increases/decreases/remains constant) . A capital-intensive production process has a (higher/ lower) DOL than a less capital-intensive process, so that operating cash flow and net present value  increase (more/less) rapidly with an increase in sales; if sales are below the forecasted level, then net present value decreases (more/less) rapidly for the capital-intensive process.

17.    If capital budgeting analysis ignores managerial options, then the net present value of a project is _____ . Such analysis is said to be _____ , because it assumes that changes during the life of a project are not possible.  Capital budgeting analysis which acknowledge the value of managerial options is said to be _____ .

18.    If a firm, or a unit of a corporation, has identified positive NPV capital budgeting projects but is unable to obtain the financing required for the projects, then _____ is said to exist.  One approach to resolving such a problem is to accept the set of projects which maximizes the _____ with the funds available. This is generally equivalent to accepting those projects with the highest _____ . However, the existence of capital rationing raises questions as to whether the firm is employing appropriate discounted cash flow analysis.

## ANSWERS TO CONCEPT TEST

1.    forecasting risk

2.    scenario analysis

3.    sensitivity analysis

4.    net present value; net present value; simulation analysis; randomly

5.    production; production; variable costs per unit of output; number of units of output; $(v \times Q)$

6.    fixed costs

7.    total variable costs; fixed costs; $(v \times Q) + F$]

8.    net income; zero; $(FC + D)/(P - v)$; EBIT; net income

9.    net income; annual depreciation expense; annual depreciation expense; zero; negative

10.     (FC + OCF)/(P − v)

11.     operating cash flow; zero; OCF; zero; FC/(P − v)

12.     −100%

13.     net present value; zero; net present value; zero

14.     operating leverage; operating leverage; capital intensive

15.     (% change in OCF)/(% change in Q); 1 + (FC/OCF)

16.     remains constant; decreases; higher; more; more

17.     underestimated; static; dynamic

18.     capital rationing; net present value; profitability index

## PROBLEMS AND SOLUTIONS

**Use the following information on SDC Corporation to solve Problems 1 to 4:**

|  | Base case | Lower bound | Upper bound |
|---|---|---|---|
| Unit sales | 1,000 | 800 | 1,200 |
| Price per unit | $95 | $90 | $100 |
| Variable costs per unit | $50 | $40 | $ 60 |
| Fixed costs per year | $10,000 | $9,000 | $11,000 |

SDC's required rate of return is 12%, and a $15,000 investment in a new machine is required. The corporate tax rate is 34%. The machine is expected to last five years with no salvage value and will be depreciated on a straight-line basis.

### Problem 1

Compute the annual operating cash flow for the project associated with each of the three cases.

**Solution:** First, compute the net income and operating cash flow for the different scenarios.

|  | Base case | Lower bound | Upper bound |
|---|---|---|---|
| Sales | $95,000 | $72,000 | $120,000 |
| − Variable costs | 50,000 | 32,000 | 72,000 |
| − Fixed costs | 10,000 | 9,000 | 11,000 |
| − Depreciation | 3,000 | 3,000 | 3,000 |
| EBIT | $32,000 | 28,000 | 34,000 |
| − Taxes (34%) | 10,880 | 9,520 | 11,560 |
| Net income | $21,120 | $18,480 | $ 22,440 |

|                       |          |          |          |
|-----------------------|----------|----------|----------|
| EBIT                  | $32,000  | $28,000  | $ 34,000 |
| + Depreciation        | 3,000    | 3,000    | 3,000    |
| – Taxes               | 10,880   | 9,520    | 11,560   |
| Operating Cash Flow   | $24,120  | $21,480  | $ 25,440 |

## Problem 2

Calculate the NPV of the project using each of the scenarios.

**Solution:** The NPV for each scenario is calculated by treating each operating cash flow as the present value of a five-year annuity with a 12% required rate of return.

Base case:    PV    = $24,120 x PVIFA (12%, 5)  =   $24,120 x 3.604776  = $86,947.20

                NPV  = $86,947.20  -  $15,000  =  $71,947.20

Lower bound:  PV    = $21,480 x PVIFA (12%, 5)  =   $21,480 x 3.604776  = $77,430.59

                NPV  = $77,430.59  -  $15,000  =  $62,430.59

Upper bound:  PV    = $25,440 x PVIFA (12%, 5) =   $25,440 x 3.604776   = $91,705.51

                NPV  = $91,705.51  -  $15,000  =  $76,705.51

## Problem 3

What are the operating cash flows and the NPV for the project if all variables are from the base case except fixed costs which take on the lower bound values?

**Solution:**

|                       |          |          |
|-----------------------|----------|----------|
| Sales                 |          | $95,000  |
| – Variable costs      | 50,000   |          |
| – Fixed costs         |          | 9,000    |
| – Depreciation        |          | 3,000    |
| EBIT                  |          | $33,000  |
| – Taxes (34%)         |          | 11,220   |
| Net income            |          | $21,780  |
|                       |          |          |
| EBIT                  |          | $33,000  |
| + Depreciation        |          | 3,000    |
| – Taxes               |          | 11,220   |
| Operating Cash Flow   |          | $24,780  |

NPV    = $24,780 x PVIFA (12%, 5)  -  $15,000  =   $89,326.35 - $15,000  =  $74,326.35

Note: Because the project is not very capital intensive, the majority of costs are variable.  Changes in fixed costs don't cause a large change in the NPV.

## Problem 4

What are the operating cash flows and the NPV for the project if all variables are from the base case except variable costs which take on the upper bound values?

**Solution:**

|                     |                                        |
|---------------------|----------------------------------------|
| Sales               | $95,000                                |
| – Variable costs    | 60,000($60 x 1,000 base case units)    |
| – Fixed costs       | 10,000                                 |
| – Depreciation      | 3,000                                  |
| EBIT                | $22,000                                |
| – Taxes (34%)       | 7,480                                  |
| Net income          | $14,520                                |
|                     |                                        |
| EBIT                | $22,000                                |
| + Depreciation      | 3,000                                  |
| – Taxes             | 7,480                                  |
| Operating Cash Flow | $17,520                                |

NPV   =   $17,520 x PVIFA (12%, 5)  -  $15,000   =   $63,155.68 - $15,000   =   $48,155.68

**Use the following information to solve Problems 5 to 17:**

D. Newcombe & Associates, Inc. is considering the introduction of a new product.  Production of the new product requires an investment of $140,000 in equipment with a five-year life.  The equipment has no salvage value at the end of five years and will be depreciated on a straight-line basis.  Newcombe's required rate of return is 15% and the tax rate is 34%.  The firm has made the following forecasts:

|                         | Base case | Lower bound | Upper bound |
|-------------------------|-----------|-------------|-------------|
| Unit sales              | 2,000     | 1,800       | 2,200       |
| Price per unit          | $55       | $50         | $60         |
| Variable costs per unit | $22       | $21         | $23         |
| Fixed costs per year    | $10,000   | $9,500      | $10,500     |

## Problem 5

Compute the annual operating cash flow for the project, using the base case forecast for each variable.

**Solution:** We first compute the net income and then the operating cash flow, as follows:

| | |
|---|---:|
| Sales | $110,000 |
| – Variable costs | 44,000 |
| – Fixed costs | 10,000 |
| – Depreciation | 28,000 |
| EBIT | $ 28,000 |
| – Taxes (34%) | 9,520 |
| Net income | $ 18,480 |

| | |
|---|---:|
| EBIT | $ 28,000 |
| + Depreciation | 28,000 |
| – Taxes | 9,520 |
| Operating Cash Flow | $ 46,480 |

## Problem 6

Compute the net present value for the project, using the base case forecast for each variable.

**Solution:**   The present value of the project is the present value of an annuity of $46,480 per year for five years, discounted at the 15% required rate of return:

$$PV = \$46,480 \times PVIFA(15\%,5) = \$46,480 \times 3.352155 = \$155,808$$

The net present value of the project is:  $155,808 – $140,000   =   $15,808

## Problem 7

Compute the net present value and the internal rate of return for the Newcombe project under the best case scenario and then under the worst case scenario.

**Solution:**  The worst case scenario is comprised of the least favourable outcome for each of the four forecasted variables, while the best case scenario is comprised of the most favourable outcome for each of the variables. These scenarios are described in the following table:

| | Worst case | Best case |
|---|:---:|:---:|
| Unit sales | 1,800 | 2,200 |
| Price per unit | $50 | $60 |
| Variable costs per unit | $23 | $21 |
| Fixed costs per year | $10,500 | $9,500 |

For each scenario, we compute net income, cash flow, net present value, and internal rate of return for the proposed project.  The results are presented in the following table:

| Scenario | Net income | Cash flow | NPV | IRR |
|----------|-----------|-----------|-----|-----|
| Base case | $18,480 | $46,480 | $15,808 | 19.68% |
| Worst case | 6,666 | 34,666 | –23,794 | 7.57 |
| Best case | 31,878 | 59,878 | 60,720 | 32.16 |

The net present value for the base case scenario is positive, so the project appears to be acceptable. However, the negative net present value for the worst case scenario indicates that further analysis is necessary. Sensitivity analysis might be useful at this point so that Newcombe can identify those forecasted variables which most clearly contribute to the possibility that the net present value will be negative.

## Problem 8

Assume that all variables, except unit sales, take on their base case levels. What is the effect on net present value and internal rate of return if unit sales are at their lower bound? Also, compute net present value and internal rate of return under the assumption that unit sales are at their upper bound.

**Solution:** The solution is provided in the following table:

| Scenario | Unit Sales | Cash flow | NPV | IRR |
|----------|-----------|-----------|-----|-----|
| Base case | 2,000 | $46,480 | $15,808 | 19.68% |
| Worst case | 1,800 | 42,124 | 1,206 | 15.36 |
| Best case | 2,200 | 50,836 | 30,410 | 23.85 |

For both the worst case and best case scenarios here, we assume that price, variable costs and fixed costs take on their base case values. These results indicate that net present value is relatively sensitive to the unit sales forecasts. However, even assuming the lower bound sales level, net present value is still positive. This is an encouraging result, but Newcombe's optimism regarding this result must be tempered by the fact that we assume base case levels for all variables other than sales. If, in fact, any additional variable takes on its 'worst case' value, then it seems likely that net present value would become negative.

## Problem 9

Assume that all variables, except price per unit, take on their base case levels. What is the effect on net present value and internal rate of return if price per unit is at its lower bound? Also, compute net present value and internal rate of return under the assumption that price per unit is at the upper bound.

**Solution:** Sensitivity analysis of unit price is performed in the following table:

| Scenario | Price per unit | Cash flow | NPV | IRR |
|----------|---------------|-----------|-----|-----|
| Base case | $55 | $46,480 | $15,808 | 19.68% |
| Worst case | 50 | 39,880 | – 6,316 | 13.08 |
| Best case | 60 | 53,080 | 37,932 | 25.95 |

Comparison of these results to those in Problem 8 reveals the fact that net present value of the project is more sensitive to changes in unit price than it is to changes in sales level; when unit price is at its lower bound, the net present value of the project is negative. It is essential for Newcombe to further assess the sensitivity of net present value to both sales level and unit price. For example, the likelihood that sales and price both take on their lower bound values may be an important consideration because such a scenario would have a significant impact on the net present value of the project.

## Problem 10

Assume that all variables, except variable costs per unit, take on their base case levels. What is the effect on net present value and internal rate of return if variable costs per unit are at their upper bound? Also, compute net present value and internal rate of return under the assumption that variable costs per unit are at their lower bound.

**Solution:** Sensitivity analysis of variable costs is performed in the following table:

| Scenario | Variable costs | Cash flow | NPV | IRR |
|---|---|---|---|---|
| Base case | $22 | $46,480 | $15,808 | 19.68% |
| Worst case | 23 | 45,160 | 11,383 | 18.39 |
| Best case | 21 | 47,800 | 20,233 | 20.95 |

Net present value is relatively insensitive to changes in variable costs. Therefore, in assessing the acceptability of the project, it may not be particularly important for Newcombe to further evaluate this forecast.

## Problem 11

Assume that all variables, except fixed costs, take on their base case levels. What is the effect on net present value and internal rate of return if fixed costs are at their upper bound? Also, compute net present value and internal rate of return under the assumption that fixed costs are at their lower bound.

**Solution:** Sensitivity analysis of fixed costs is presented in the following table:

| Scenario | Fixed costs | Cash flow | NPV | IRR |
|---|---|---|---|---|
| Base case | $10,000 | $46,480 | $15,808 | 19.68% |
| Worst case | 10,500 | 46,150 | 14,702 | 19.35 |
| Best case | 9,500 | 46,810 | 16,914 | 20.00 |

Net present value is not particularly sensitive to changes in fixed costs. This result follows from the fact that, first, the percentage change in fixed costs from the base case to the upper bound is relatively small, and, second, fixed costs are a relatively small portion of the total costs for the project. It is probably not worthwhile for Newcombe to analyze the fixed costs forecast more closely.

## Problem 12

Assume the base-case forecasts for the Newcombe project. Compute the accounting break-even point for the project.

**Solution:** The accounting break-even point is computed as follows:

$$Q \; = \; \frac{FC + D}{P - v} \; = \; \frac{\$10,000 \; + \; \$28,000}{\$55 \; - \; \$22} \; = \; 1,151.52$$

Net income (and EBIT) will be zero if Newcombe produces and sells 1,151.52 units. In order for the project to produce net income (and EBIT) approximately equal to zero, sales must be 1,152 units.


## Problem 13

Assume the base-case forecasts and no income taxes for the Newcombe project. Compute the cash break-even point for the project.


**Solution:** The cash break-even point is the sales level for which operating cash flow is equal to zero. The relationship between Q and OCF is:

$$Q = \frac{FC + OCF}{P - v} = \frac{FC + 0}{P - v} = \frac{FC}{P - v} = \frac{\$10,000}{\$55 - \$22} = 303.03$$

At sales of 303.03 units, operating cash flow is zero; therefore, Newcombe must sell at least 304 units for cash flow to be positive.


## Problem 14

Assume the base-case forecasts and no income taxes for the Newcombe project. Compute the financial break-even point for the project.

**Solution:** The OCF for the project is a five-year annuity. At the financial break-even point, the net present value of the project is zero, which is equivalent to stating that the present value of the annuity is equal to the $140,000 cash outflow. Therefore, we solve the following equation for OCF:

$$\$140,000 = OCF \times PVIFA(15\%,5) = OCF \times 3.352155$$

$$OCF = \$140,000 / 3.352155 = \$41,764.18$$

Substitute this value of OCF into the following equation to determine the financial break-even point:

$$Q = \frac{FC + OCF}{P - v} = \frac{\$10,000 + \$41,764.18}{\$55 - \$22} = 1,568.61$$

Therefore, sales must be 1,569 units in order for the project to have a net present value greater than zero.


## Problem 15

Suppose that sales for the project under consideration by Newcombe increase from 2,000 units to 2,200 units per year. Compute the degree of operating leverage for the project at sales of 2,000 units. Use both the definition of the degree of operating leverage and its algebraic equivalent for this calculation. Assume Newcombe does not pay income taxes on this project.

**Solution:**  The degree of operating leverage (DOL) is defined as follows:

$$DOL \quad = \quad \frac{\text{Percentage change in OCF}}{\text{Percentage change in Q}}$$

Operating cash flow for output of 2,000 units can be computed as follows:

$$OCF \quad = \quad [(P - v) \times Q] - FC \quad = \quad [(\$55 - \$22) \times 2,000] - \$10,000 \quad = \quad \$56,000$$

OCF for output of 2,200 units is $62,600.  The percentage change in operating cash flow is:

$$\frac{\$62,600 \; - \; \$56,000}{\$56,000} \quad = \quad .11786 \quad = \quad 11.786\%$$

The percentage change in output is:

$$\frac{2,200 \; - \; 2,000}{2,000} \quad = \quad .10 \quad = \quad 10\%$$

Therefore, the degree of operating leverage is (11.786% / 10%) = 1.1786.  The alternative calculation of DOL provides the same result.


**Problem 16**

Suppose that sales for the project under consideration by Newcombe decrease from 2,000 units to 1,600 units per year.  Compute the degree of operating leverage for the project, using the definition of the degree of operating leverage.  Assume Newcombe does not pay income taxes on this project.

**Solution:**  Operating cash flow for output of 2,000 units is $56,000, as computed in the solution to Problem 15.  Operating cash flow for output of 1,600 units is:

$$OCF \quad = \quad [(P - v) \times Q] - FC \quad = \quad [(\$55 - \$22) \times 1,600] - \$10,000 \quad = \quad \$42,800$$

The percentage change in operating cash flow is:

$$\frac{\$42,800 \; - \; \$56,000}{\$56,000} \quad = \quad -.23571 \quad = \quad -23.57\%$$

The percentage change in output is:

$$\frac{1,600 \; - \; 2,000}{2,000} \quad = \quad -.20 \quad = \quad -20\%$$

Therefore, the degree of operating leverage is:

$$DOL \quad = \quad \frac{\text{Percentage change in OCF}}{\text{Percentage change in Q}} \quad = \quad \frac{-23.57\%}{-20\%} \quad = \quad 1.1786$$

This is the same result obtained in the solution to Problem 15.  DOL depends on the current level of Q and OCF, and is constant for any change from that level.


## Problem 17

Assume that sales increase from 1,600 units to 2,000 units for the project.  Compute DOL for the project at sales of 1,600 units.  Use both the definition of the degree of operating leverage and its algebraic equivalent for this calculation.  Assume Newcombe does not pay income taxes on this project.

**Solution:**  The solutions to Problems 15 and 16 indicate the following: when Q = 1,600, OCF = $42,800; when Q = 2,000, OCF = $56,000.  The percentage change in operating cash flow is:

$$\frac{\$56,000 - \$42,800}{\$42,800} \quad = \quad .30841 \quad = \quad 30.84\%$$

The percentage change in output is:

$$\frac{2,000 - 1,600}{1,600} \quad = \quad .25 \quad = \quad 25\%$$

Therefore, the degree of operating leverage is:

$$DOL \quad = \quad \frac{30.84\%}{25\%} \quad = \quad 1.2336$$

The alternative calculation of DOL provides the same result:

$$DOL \quad = \quad 1 \ + \ FC / OCF \quad = \quad 1 \ + \ \$10,000 / \$42,800 \quad = \quad 1.2336$$

The degree of operating leverage is higher for the increase in Q from 1,600 units to 2,000 units than it is for the decrease in Q from 2,000 units to 1,600 units.  Operating leverage decreases as the level of Q increases.


## Problem 18

The following data have been computed for a firm: when output is 20,000 units, operating cash flow is $50,000 and operating leverage is 2.5.  Suppose output increases to 23,000 units.  What is the new level of operating cash flow?

**Solution:**  The definition of the degree of operating leverage is:

$$DOL \quad = \quad \frac{\text{Percentage change in OCF}}{\text{Percentage change in Q}}$$

The percentage change in output is:

$$\frac{23,000 - 20,000}{20,000} \quad = \quad .15 \ = \ 15\%$$

Substituting this percentage change in output, and DOL = 2.5, into the definition of the degree of operating leverage, we can solve for the percentage change in operating cash flow:

$$2.5 \ = \ \frac{\text{Percentage change in OCF}}{.15}$$

Therefore, the percentage change in OCF = $(2.5 \times .15) = .375 = 37.5\%$.  OCF increases by 37.5%, so that the new level of operating cash flow is $(1.375 \times \$50,000) = \$68,750$.

## Problem 19

For the data in Problem 18, compute the firm's fixed costs.

**Solution:**  The alternative formula for computing DOL is:

$$\text{DOL} \ = \ 1 \ + \ \text{FC} / \text{OCF}$$

Substituting DOL = 2.5 and OCF = \$50,000, solve for FC as follows:

$$2.5 \ = \ 1 \ + \ \text{FC} / \$50,000$$

$$1.5 \ = \ \text{FC} / \$50,000$$

Fixed costs therefore equal $(1.5 \times \$50,000) = \$75,000$.

## Problem 20

Suppose an investor is considering a piece of property to use as a parking lot.  The cost of the property is \$10,000. The investor expects that the value of the property will remain constant for the foreseeable future; no depreciation expense will be taken on the property.  The investor expects that, for the foreseeable future, 6,000 cars per year will use the parking lot at a rate of \$3 per car.

Variable costs are zero, but an attendant must be paid \$16,000 per year.  Assume that the required rate of return is 25% and that there are no taxes.  Compute the net present value for the investment.  Is the project acceptable?

**Solution:**   Sales are $(\$3 \times 6,000) = \$18,000$ and net income is $(\$18,000 - \$16,000) = \$2,000$.  Since depreciation and taxes are zero, operating cash flow is also \$2,000.  Treating this cash flow as a perpetuity, the present value is $(\$2,000/.25) = \$8,000$.  The net present value is $(\$8,000 - \$10,000) = -\$2,000$, so the project is unacceptable.

## Problem 21

Suppose that in the previous problem, the investor intends to re-evaluate her forecast at the end of the first year. She believes that usage of the parking lot during the first year will be either 5,500 or 6,500 cars per year, and that the volume of business during the first year will indicate which of these figures will continue beyond the first year. In addition, she believes that each of these figures is equally likely. Compute the net present value of the project. Is the project acceptable?

**Solution:**  If the volume of business is 5,500 cars per year, then sales will be ($3 × 5,500) = $16,500; net income and operating cash flow will be ($16,500 – $16,000) = $500.  At 6,500 cars per year, net income and operating cash flow are $3,500.  Since the two figures are considered equally likely, the expected value of the first year's operating cash flow is [(.5 × $500) + (.5 × $3,500)] = $2,000.

If the volume of business during the first year is 5,500 cars, then the operating cash flow will be $500 for all subsequent years.  The value of this perpetuity, as of the end of the first year, is ($500/.25) = $2,000.   Since the property can be sold for $10,000, the investor would sell the property at the end of the first year.  On the other hand, at 6,500 cars per year, operating cash flow will be $3,500 and the value of the business would be ($3,500/.25) = $14,000.  Under these circumstances, the investor will continue to operate the business.  Therefore, at the end of the first year, the investor will have an expected cash flow of $2,000, plus either $10,000 in cash or a business worth $14,000.  The expected value at the end of the first year is therefore:

$$\$2,000 + [(.5 \times \$10,000) + (.5 \times \$14,000)] \;\; = \;\; \$14,000$$

The present value of this $14,000 is ($14,000/1.25) = $11,200, and the net present value of the investment is ($11,200 – $10,000) = $1,120.  The investment is acceptable.  The option to abandon the investment at the end of the first year has added value to the project, compared to the solution to Problem 20.

# 12     <u>Some Lessons from Capital Market History</u>

## CHAPTER HIGHLIGHTS

The capital budgeting concepts discussed so far have mostly ignored the issue of risk.  However, risk is a critical element in determining the required rate of return used to discount a project's cash flows.  Put simply, the greater the risk, the greater the required return.  This chapter begins the task of understanding the relationship between risk and return.  We begin with a perspective on risk and return as provided by capital market history.  In general, we learn two major lessons: (1) investors earn a reward for taking risk, and (2) the higher the potential reward, the higher the risk.

## RETURNS

In order to understand the relationship between risk and return, we must be able to measure both risk and return for an investment.  In this section, we introduce the measurement of returns, both as dollar returns and as percentage returns.

**Dollar Returns:**  The return on an investment has two components: the income component and the capital gain (or capital loss) component.  It is possible for an investment to have only a capital gain component.  For example, a collectible antique produces no periodic income, but increases in value, providing its owner with a capital gain. Assets purchased for business purposes (machinery, for example) typically produce periodic income but no capital gains.  If you buy common stock, however, your return on the investment usually comes in two forms: dividends (periodic income) and capital gains.

Suppose you buy 100 shares of Ahlers Corporation's common stock for $25 per share.  Over the course of a year, Ahlers pays a cash dividend of $2 per share and the value of the share rises to $30.  At the end of the year, you have received ($2 × 100) = $200 in dividends.  In addition, you own 100 shares of stock worth $30 per share.  The capital gain is [($30 – $25) × 100] = $500.  The total dollar return is therefore:

$$\text{Total dollar return} \; = \; \text{Dividend income} + \text{Capital gain (or loss)} \; = \; \$200 + \$500 \; = \; \$700$$

The total value of your position is $3,200, the total investment is $2,500, and the total return is $700.

**Percentage Returns:**  For financial decision-making, percentage returns are easier to work with because the results apply regardless of the amount invested in a particular asset.  In the case of the investment in Ahlers common stock, you received $700 on a $2,500 investment, so your total percentage return is:

$$[\$200 + (\$3,000 \; - \; \$2,500)] \, / \, \$2,500 \; = \; .28 \; = \; 28\%$$

This calculation can also be expressed on a per share basis.  An investor who purchases one share for $25 receives a $2 dividend during the year and has a share worth $30 at the end of the year.  Therefore, the investor's total percentage return can be computed as:

$$[\$2 + (\$30 \; - \; \$25)] \, / \, \$25 \; = \; .28 \; = \; 28\%$$

This 28% total return is comprised of the dividend yield plus the percentage capital gain (or capital gains yield).

The dividend yield is:

$$D_t / P_t \ = \ \$2 / \$25 \ = \ .08 \ = \ 8\%$$

where $P_t$ is the price of the stock at the beginning of the year, and $D_t$ is the dividend paid during the year.

The capital gains yield is:

$$(P_{t+1} - P_t) / P_t \ = \ (\$30 - \$25) / \$25 \ = \ .20 \ = \ 20\%$$

where $P_t$ is the price of the stock at the beginning of the year and $P_{t+1}$ is the price at the end of the year. The total percentage return is the sum of the dividend yield and the capital gains yield:

$$\text{Total percentage return} \ = \ 8\% + 20\% \ = \ 28\%$$

## AVERAGE RETURNS: THE FIRST LESSON

To use historical stock market returns for financial decisions, we must summarize percentage return data for individual stocks or for the stock market as a whole. To do this, we calculate the average return. The average (mean) return is simply the sum of all returns divided by the number of observations.

Consider an investment which has a guaranteed 100% return the first year and a guaranteed 60% loss the second. The average return is [100% + (–60%)]/2 = 20%. Financial managers are often interested in the answer to the question: "What rate can I expect to earn <u>next</u> year?" In this case, one possible forecast of this expected return may be the average return for some historical period.

A common benchmark used in comparing returns is the return on securities issued by the Canadian government. One form of government security is the Treasury bill or T-bill, which is a security sold by the Bank of Canada maturing in less than one year. We refer to the T-bill rate as the risk-free rate of return.

From 1948 to 1990, the average return on T-bills was 6.1% per year. During the same time period, a portfolio consisting of Canadian common stocks (the TSE 300 Composite Index) had an average return of 12.92%. The difference between the 12.92% return for the common stock portfolio and the 6.1% earned on T-bills is called the excess return for the risky asset. Since the excess return is due to the greater riskiness of stock investments, the excess return is also called the risk premium. The historical risk premium for the Canadian common stock portfolio is (.1292 − .061) = .0682 = 6.82%. The historical existence of risk premiums is the basis for our first lesson: *Risky assets, on average, earn a risk premium.* In other words, there is a reward for bearing risk.

## THE VARIABILITY OF RETURNS

Since riskiness affects returns, we must be able to measure the degree of risk associated with an investment in order to understand the relationship between risk and return. The most common measures are the *variance* and the *standard deviation.*

**The Historical Variance and Standard Deviation:** Suppose that a particular investment returned 8%, 14%, −4%, and 6% over the last four years. The average return is:

$$\text{Avg. Return} \ = \ (.08 + .14 - .04 + .06) / 4 \ = \ .06 \ = \ 6\%$$

Financial economists equate risk with the statistical concept of variability. The most commonly used statistical measures of variability are the variance and the standard deviation. In the financial context, we use the variance to measure the variability of returns from the average return; the greater the deviation from the average, the more variable the rate of return and the higher the level of risk.

To calculate the variance, we first find the squared deviations from the mean (average) return. The sum of these amounts is then divided by the number of returns less 1.

The calculation of the variance is summarized in this table:

| Rate of return | Average return | Deviation from average return | Squared value of deviation |
|---|---|---|---|
| .08 | .06 | .02 | .0004 |
| .14 | .06 | .08 | .0064 |
| - .04 | .06 | - .10 | .0100 |
| .06 | .06 | .00 | .0000 |

The variance is the average squared deviation, or $[.0168/(4 - 1)] = .0056$. The standard deviation is the square root of .0056, which equals .07483. This calculation of the variance is summarized by the following formula:

$$\text{Var(R)} = \sigma^2 = [1/(T-1)] [(R_1 - E(R))^2 + (R_2 - E(R))^2 + ... + (R_T - E(R))^2]$$

where Var(R) and $\sigma^2$ represent alternative notations for variance, $R_1$, $R_2$, and $R_T$ are the returns for each year, and T is the number of observations. The standard deviation is the square root of the variance, and is denoted as either SD(R) or $\sigma$.

**Normal Distribution:** For many random events, the normal distribution (or bell curve) is useful for deriving the probability that the value of a variable falls within a certain range. For example, if stock returns have a normal distribution, the probability that the return in a given year is within one standard deviation of the mean is about 68%, or approximately 2/3. The probability that the return is within two standard deviations of the mean is about 95%. Figure 12.6 on page 393 of your text illustrates a normal return distribution for a portfolio of large common shares.

For the Canadian common stock portfolio, the standard deviation of returns from 1948 to 1999, is approximately 16.62%. The mean return during this period was 13.20%. The probability that the return in a given year is in the range –.0342 to .2982, ( .1392 plus or minus one standard deviation, .1662) is approximately 2/3. Put another way, there is one chance in three that the rate of return would fall outside this range. This result illustrates that the stock market can be quite volatile. However, there is only a 5% chance (approximately) that the mean rate of return would be outside the range –.2004 to .4644 [.1320 plus or minus (2 x .1662)]. Assuming that the return on the Canadian common stock portfolio is normally distributed, these points are illustrated on the graph in your text.

That graph tells us that if you buy stocks in large Canadian corporations, you will be outside the range of –3.42 % to 29.82% one time in three (or one year out of every three years). This is an important observation about the stock market's volatility. However, there is only a 5% chance (approximately) that you would end up outside the range of –20.04% to 46.44%. Thus, this year to year volatility is the basis for our second lesson: *the greater the potential for reward, the greater is the risk.*

Suppose we are interested in evaluating an investment that is about as risky as the Canadian common stock portfolio. What discount rate should we use for our present value analysis?  Recall that the difference between the return on a risky asset and the risk-free return is the risk premium, so that the appropriate discount rate for evaluating a risky investment is the sum of the risk-free rate plus a risk premium.  The historic risk premium for the Canadian common stock portfolio is 6.82%.  If T-bills are currently yielding 7%, then the appropriate rate to use in evaluating this investment would be (6.82% + 7%) = 13.82%.

Clearly, not all risky investments have the same risk level as the Canadian common stock portfolio.  Therefore, we can not use the above procedure for evaluating all risky investments.  So, it is necessary to analyze the relationship between risk and return in the financial markets. We will complete this discussion in the next chapter.

## CAPITAL MARKET EFFICIENCY

The financial markets in Canada have very low trading costs and many buyers and sellers, all of whom have ready access to relevant information. In such a market, all transactions have exactly zero NPV.  That is, assets are worth exactly what they cost.  This premise is the basis for the notion that financial markets are efficient.  We briefly discuss the concept of market efficiency in this section.

**The Efficient Markets Hypothesis:**  An *efficient capital market* is a market in which all transactions have net present value equal to zero.  Alternatively, it can be said that the price of any asset is always equal to its present value, so that the return for an investment is equal to the equilibrium return for a given level of risk.  All that is required for a market to be efficient is that current market prices reflect available information.  If a market is efficient with respect to some piece of information, then that piece of information can not be used to identify a positive NPV investment.

The *efficient markets hypothesis* (EMH) asserts that prices for assets in Canadian capital markets are efficient with respect to available information.  The hypothesis implies that no investment strategy based on current or historical information produces extraordinarily large profits.  With thousands of investment advisory services, mountains of information, and millions of investors (all of whom have the same goals), the adjustment of prices to new information is almost instantaneous.

There are two important implications of market efficiency for investors and firms.  First, investors buying stocks and bonds should expect to earn an equilibrium return commensurate with the level of risk they assume.  Second, firms issuing securities should expect to receive from investors a price equal to the present value of the securities.

**Some Common Misconceptions About the EMH:**  Two objections to the efficient markets hypothesis are frequently raised.  The first is based on the observation that security prices fluctuate every day.  However, this observation is not inconsistent with market efficiency.  On the contrary, since new information arrives every day, the efficient markets hypothesis predicts that prices adjust rapidly to the new information.  The second criticism is that the market cannot be efficient because only a fraction of the outstanding shares are traded every day. Once again, however, this result is actually consistent with the hypothesis.  Investors trade only when they expect to benefit from doing so.  In a market with transaction costs, such as brokerage fees, there is little incentive for trades to take place if securities are correctly valued.

The efficient markets hypothesis does not suggest that the determinants of price changes are unknown.  Prices depend on expected future cash flows.  It is the expectations of these future cash flows that change when new information arrives.  The hypothesis also does not imply that we should select stocks randomly.  The result could be an undiversified portfolio of securities with an undesirable level of risk.  Finally, the EMH does not imply that investors are uninformed.  To the contrary, the hypothesis is based on the assumption that investors are quite rational, and are not easily fooled or manipulated.

**Market Efficiency - Forms and Evidence:**  Financial economists generally identify three forms of market efficiency, based on the kinds of information which might be expected to influence stock prices.  A market is said to be *weak-form efficient* if current security prices completely incorporate the information contained in past prices.  This means that it is pointless to analyze past prices in an attempt to predict future prices.  Such an evaluation procedure is called technical analysis or 'charting,'  Weak-form efficiency implies that technical analysis can not be used successfully to forecast future prices and therefore that technical analysts do not earn extraordinary profits. There is a great deal of evidence indicating that financial markets are weak-form efficient.

A market is said to be *semistrong-form efficient* if current prices incorporate all publicly available information. Semistrong-form efficiency implies that the analysis of published financial statements, for example, does not result in earning excess profits.  Notice that a semistrong efficient market is also weak-form efficient, since past prices are a form of publicly available information.

At the extreme, a market is *strong-form efficient* if current prices reflect *all* information, including inside information; inside information is information about a firm which is available only to 'insiders', including corporate executives and major shareholders.  There seems to be little reason to believe that markets are strong-form efficient; that is, available evidence seems to indicate that valuable inside information does exist.  At the other extreme, there are compelling reasons for believing that markets are weak-form efficient.  There is a great deal of debate, however, over semistrong-form efficiency.  A reasonable compromise view might be summarized as follows: some prices, some of the time, might not reflect all publicly available information, but most assets, most of the time, do reflect this information.

## CONCEPT TEST

1.  The return on an investment comes in either or both of two general forms; these are the _____ component, and the _____ gain or loss.

2.  The return on an investment in common stock usually comes in two forms; _____ and _____ gains. _____ , which are cash payments by a corporation to its shareholders, represent the income component of the return. _____ gains (or losses) for an investment in common stock result from _____ or _____ in the value of the stock.

3.  The total percentage return for an investment is the sum of the _____ yield and the percentage _____ gain (or _____ gains yield). The _____ yield is defined algebraically as _____ . The _____ gains yield is defined algebraically as _____ .

4.  The _____ return or _____ return is simply the ordinary average: the total of the returns divided by the number of observations. The calculation of the average return is summarized algebraically as follows: $E(R) =$ _____ , where T is the number of time periods, and R and E(R) are alternative notations for the average return.

5.  Treasury bills are considered virtually _____ , so that the T-bill rate is often referred to as the _____ . The difference between the rate of return for a particular risky investment and the rate of return earned on T-bills is called the _____ or the _____ for the risky asset.

6.  Financial economists equate risk with the statistical concept of _____ , which is commonly measured by the variance and the standard deviation. The variance is used to measure the variability of return from the average return. The variance is the average of the _____ deviations from the _____ return. This calculation of the variance is summarized by the formula:   $Var(R) = \sigma^2 = $ _____ , where $Var(R)$ and $\sigma^2$ are alternative notation for variance, $R_1$, $R_2$, and $R_T$ are the returns for each year, and T is the number of observations.

7.  The _____ is the square root of the variance, and is denoted as either _____ or _____ .

8.  For many random events, the _____ distribution or the bell curve, is useful for deriving the probability that the value of a variable falls within a certain range. If stock returns have this distribution, then the probability that the rate of return in a given year is within one standard deviation of the mean is _____ . The probability that the return is within two standard deviations of the mean is _____ .

9.  An efficient capital market is a market in which all transactions have net present value equal to _____ . Alternatively, it can be said that in an efficient market, the price of an asset is always equal to its _____ , so that the rate of return for an investment is equal to the equilibrium rate of return for a given level of risk. All that is required for a market to be efficient is that current market prices reflect _____ . If a market is efficient with respect to some piece of information, then that piece of information can not be used to identify an investment with a _____ .

10. The _____ hypothesis asserts that prices for assets in Canadian capital markets are efficient with respect to available information. The hypothesis implies that no investment strategy based on current or historical information produces extraordinarily large profits. The adjustment of prices to new information is _____ .

11. Financial economists identify three forms of market efficiency. A market is said to be _____-form efficient if current security prices completely incorporate the information contained in past prices. A market is said to be _____-form efficient if current prices incorporate all publicly available information. A market is _____-form efficient if current prices reflect all information, including inside information.

12. Available evidence seems to indicate that valuable inside information does exist, so that financial markets (are/are not) strong-form efficient. At the other extreme, there are compelling reasons for believing that markets (are/are not) weak-form efficient. There is a great deal of debate, however, over _____-form efficiency.

## ANSWERS TO CONCEPT TESTS

1.  income; capital

2.  dividends; capital; dividends; capital; increases; decreases

3.  dividend; capital; capital; dividend; $(D_t/P_t)$; capital; $[(P_{t+1} - P_t)/P_t]$

4.  average; mean; $[(R_1 + R_2 + ... + R_T)/T]$

5.  risk-free; risk-free rate of return; excess return; risk premium

6.      variability; squared; average; $[1/(T - 1)] [(R_1 - R)^2 + (R_2 - R)^2 + ... + (R_T - R)^2]$

7.      standard deviation; SD(R); σ

8.      normal; about 68%, or about 2/3; about 95%

9.      zero; present value; available information; positive NPV

10.     efficient markets; almost instantaneous

11.     weak; semistrong; strong

12.     are not; are; semistrong

## PROBLEMS AND SOLUTIONS

### Problem 1

Adam bought 100 shares of TJR Corporation's common stock for $18 per share.  In the following year, he received a cash dividend of $2.50 per share, and the value of the stock increased to $22 per share.  What is Adam's total dollar return? Also calculate his dividend and capital gains yield, and his total percentage return.

**Solution:**  Total dollar return   =   Dividend income + Capital gain (loss)

   =   (100 x $2.50) + [100 x ($22 - $18)   =   $250 + $400   =   $650

   Dividend yield   =   $D_t / P_t$   =   $2.50 / $18   =   0.138889   =   13.89%

   where $P_t$ is the share price at the beginning of the year and $D_t$ is the dividend paid during the year.

   Capital gains yield   =   $(P_{t-1} - P_t) / P_t$   =   ($22 - $18) / $18   =   0.22222   =   22.22 %

   Total percentage return   =   Dividend yield + Capital gains yield   =   13.89% + 22.22%   =   36.11%

OR

   Total percentage return   =   (Dividend + Capital gain) / Original Investment

   =   ($2.50 + $4) / $18   =   0.3611   =   36.11%

### Problem 2

Suppose that, one year ago, you bought 100 shares of Bradley Corporation common stock for $32 per share. During the year, you received dividends of $2.50 per share.  Bradley common stock is currently selling for $33.50 per share. What was your total dividend income during the year?  How much did you earn in capital gains?  What was your total dollar return?  Use these dollar returns to calculate the dividend yield, capital gains yield, and total percentage return for this investment.

**Solution:**  The total dividend income is ($2.50 × 100) = $250.  Capital gains are equal to [($33.50 – $32) × 100] = $150 and total dollar return is ($250 + $150) = $400.  The dividend yield is [$250/($32 × 100)] = .0781 = 7.81%.  The capital gains yield is [$150/($32 × 100)] = .0469 = 4.69%.  The total percentage return is [($150 + $250)/($32 × 100)] = .1250 = 12.50% = (4.69% + 7.81%).

## Problem 3

For the Bradley common stock investment described in Problem 2, compute the dividend yield, the capital gains yield, and the total percentage return on a per share basis.

**Solution:**  The dividend yield is:

$$D_t / P_t \;=\; \$2.50 / \$32 \;=\; .0781 \;=\; 7.81\%$$

where $P_t$ is the price of the stock at the beginning of the year, and $D_t$ is the dividend paid during the year. The capital gains yield is:

$$\frac{P_{t+1} - P_t}{P_t} \;=\; \frac{\$33.50 - \$32}{\$32} \;=\; .0469 \;=\; 4.69\%$$

where $P_t$ is the price of the stock at the beginning of the year and $P_{t+1}$ is the price at the end of the year.  The total percentage return is the sum of the dividend yield and the capital gains yield:

$$\text{Total percentage return} \;=\; 7.81\% + 4.69\% \;=\; 12.50\%$$

## Problem 4

Suppose that, one year from today, you expect the Bradley Corporation common stock described in Problem 2 to be selling for $33 per share, and that during the coming year, you expect to receive dividends of $2 per share. What is the total dividend income expected during the year?  What is the total capital gain expected during the year?  What is the total dollar return expected during the year?  Use these dollar returns to calculate the dividend yield, capital gains yield, and total percentage return expected during the year.

**Solution:**  The total dividend income expected is ($2 × 100) = $200. The expected capital gains are equal to [($33 – $33.50) × 100] = –$50; this is a capital loss of $50.  The total dollar return expected is ($200 – $50) = $150.  The expected dividend yield is [($200/($33.50 × 100)] = .0597 = 5.97%.  The expected capital gains yield is [–$50/($33.50 × 100)] = –.0149 = –1.49%.  The total percentage return is [($200 – $50) / ($33.50 × 100)] = .0448 = 4.48% = (5.97% – 1.49%).

## Problem 5

For the investment described in Problem 4, compute the dividend yield, the capital gains yield, and the total percentage return on a per share basis.

**Solution:** The dividend yield is: $2.00 / $33.50 = .0597 = 5.97%. The capital gains yield is: ($33 - $33.50) / $33.50 = -.0149 = -1.49%. The total percentage return is the sum of the dividend yield and the capital gains yield: 5.97% – 1.49% = 4.48%


## Problem 6

Last year Jacky bought 50 shares of JAG Corporation common stock for $19.73 per share. During the year, she received dividends of $2.70 per share. JAG Corp is now selling for $24.27 per share. What was Jacky's total dividend income during the year? How much did she earn in capital gains? What was her total dollar return? What were the dividend yield and capital gains yield? What was the total percentage return on Jacky's investment?

**Solution:** Total dividend income is ($2.70 x 50) = $135.00, and capital gains were [ ($24.27 - $19.73) x 50 ] = $227.00. Total dollar return is $135 + $227 = $362. Dividend yield was $135 / ($19.73 x 50) = 0.1368 = 13.68%. Capital gains yield was $227 / ($19.73 x 50) = 0.2301 = 23.01%. Total percentage return was 13.68% + 23.01% = 36.69%.


## Problem 7

For JAG Corporation's information in Problem 6, calculate the dividend yield, the capital gains yield, and the total percentage return on a per-share basis.

**Solution:** The dividend yield, capital gains yield, and total percentage return are the same for one share as they are for a group of shares. There are no calculations required to answer this problem. That means the percentage values are the same as those in Problem 6.


## Problem 8

The following table contains information on the rates of return for common shares of the Healy Tire Corporation (HT) and the Smooth Ride Wheel Company (SR) over a five-year period.

| | Returns | |
|---|---|---|
| Year | HT | SR |
| 1 | 7% | 10% |
| 2 | 9 | 12 |
| 3 | -8 | 8 |
| 4 | 4 | -6 |
| 5 | 8 | 6 |

What is the mean return for HT common stock and for SR common stock? Also, calculate the variance and standard deviation for each common stock.

**Solution:** The mean returns are:

For HT:       (.07 + .09 - .08 + .04 + .08) / 5   =   0.04   =   4.0%

For SR:       (.10 + .12 + .08 - .06 + .06) / 5   =   0.06   =   6.0%

The variance calculations are summarized in the following table:

| Year | Rate of Return | | Deviation from Average Return | | Squared value of Deviation | |
|---|---|---|---|---|---|---|
| | HT | SR | HT | SR | HT | SR |
| 1 | .07 | .10 | .03 | .04 | .0009 | .0016 |
| 2 | .09 | .12 | .05 | .06 | .0025 | .0036 |
| 3 | -.08 | .08 | -.12 | .02 | .0144 | .0004 |
| 4 | .04 | -.06 | .00 | -.12 | .0000 | .0144 |
| 5 | .08 | .06 | .04 | .00 | .0016 | .0000 |
| Total | .20 | .30 | .00 | .00 | .0194 | .0200 |

For HT: $\sigma^2$ = 0.0194 / 4 = .00485;   For SR, $\sigma^2$ = .0200 / 4 = .0050

The standard deviation of the return for each stock is the square root of the variance.

For HT: $\sigma$ = $.00485^{1/2}$ = 0.06964 = 6.964%;   For SR, $\sigma$ = $0.0050^{1/2}$ = 0.07071 = 7.071%

**Use the information in the following table to solve Problems 9 to 12:**

Suppose that the following information represents the rate of return for General Motors Canada (GM) common stock and Bell Canada (BC) common stock over a five-year period:

| Year | Returns | |
|---|---|---|
| | GM | BC |
| 1 | .10 | .12 |
| 2 | .04 | .06 |
| 3 | - .09 | - .10 |
| 4 | .20 | .22 |
| 5 | .05 | .05 |

**Problem 9**

What is the mean return for GM common stock?  For BC common stock?

**Solution:** For GM: R  =  (.10 + .04 - .09 + .20 + .05) / 5  =  .06  =  6%
              For BC:  R  =  (.12 + .06 - .10 + .22 + .05) / 5  =  .07  =  7%

**Problem 10**

What is the variance of the return for GM common stock? For BC stock?

**Solution:**  The calculations are summarized in the following table:

| Year | Rate of return | | Deviation from average return | | Squared value of deviation | |
|---|---|---|---|---|---|---|
| | GM | BC | GM | BC | GM | BC |
| 1 | .10 | .12 | .04 | .05 | .0016 | .0025 |
| 2 | .04 | .06 | -.02 | -.01 | .0004 | .0001 |
| 3 | -.09 | -.10 | -.15 | -.17 | .0225 | .0289 |
| 4 | .20 | .22 | .14 | .15 | .0196 | .0225 |
| 5 | .05 | .05 | -.01 | -.02 | .0001 | .0004 |
| Total | .30 | .35 | .00 | .00 | .0442 | .0544 |

For GM: $\sigma^2 = .0442 / 4 = 0.01105$.   For BC: $\sigma^2 = .0544 / 4 = .0136$

## Problem 11

What is the standard deviation of the return for GM common stock? For BC common stock?

**Solution:**  The standard deviation is the square root of the variance.  The standard deviation for GM is: $\sigma = (.01105)^{.5} = .10512 = 10.512\%$.  For BC:  $\sigma = (.0136)^{.5} = .11662 = 11.662\%$.

## Problem 12

Suppose the returns for GM and BC each have a normal distribution with the means and standard deviations calculated in Problem 10 and 11, respectively.  For each stock, determine the range of returns within one standard deviation of the mean and the range of returns within two standard deviations of the mean.  Interpret these results.

**Solution:**  For GM, the range of returns within one standard deviation of the mean is from $[.06 - (1 \times .10512)]$ to $[.06 + (1 \times .10512)]$, or $-4.512\%$ to $16.512\%$.  The range of returns within two standard deviations of the mean is from $[.06 - (2 \times .10512)]$ to $(.06 + (2 \times .10512))$, or $-15.024\%$ to $27.024\%$.  These results indicate that there is approximately a 68% probability that, in any given year, the return for GM common stock will be between $-4.512\%$ and $16.512\%$ and approximately a 95% probability that the return will be between $-15.024\%$ and $27.024\%$.

For BC common stock, the probability is approximately 68% that the return will be between $-4.662\%$ and $18.662\%$, and approximately 95% that the return will be between $-16.324\%$ and $30.324\%$.

## Use the following information to solve Problems 13 to 15:

The returns for the TTK Corporation common stock and the MAX Corporation common stock during the past five years are listed below:

| Year | Returns | |
|---|---|---|
| | TTK | MAX |
| 1 | 12% | 6% |
| 2 | 15 | 14 |
| 3 | 4 | 7 |
| 4 | - 5 | 0 |
| 5 | 9 | 13 |

## Problem 13

Calculate the average return for TTK and for MAX common stock.

**Solution:** The average returns are R = (.35/5) = .07 = 7%   for TTK common stock and  R = (.40/5) = .08 = 8% for MAX common stock.

## Problem 14

Calculate the variance for TTK and for MAX common stock.

**Solution:**   The variances are: $\sigma_{TTK}^2$ = (.0246/4) = .00615 and $\sigma_{MAX}^2$ = (.0130/4) = .00325.

## Problem 15

Calculate the standard deviation for TTK and for MAX common stock.

**Solution:**   The standard deviations are: $\sigma_{TTK}$ = $(.00615)^{.5}$ = .078422 and $\sigma_M$ = $(.00325)^{.5}$ = .05701.

# 13        Return, Risk, and the Security Market Line

## CHAPTER HIGHLIGHTS

We have established that investments with greater risk provide, on average, a higher rate of return. In this chapter, we establish a more precise description of the relationship between risk and return in the securities markets. The relationship between risk and return is called the *security market line* (SML). First, we discuss the appropriate procedures for measuring rates of return and risk.

## EXPECTED RETURNS AND VARIANCES

In the previous chapter, we discussed the calculation of average returns and variances based on historical data. In this chapter, the focus is on rates of return that might occur in the future.

**Expected Return:** The rate of return that might occur in the future is referred to as the *expected return*. Actually, an expected value is an average, or mean, of possible future outcomes.  Here, the term *expected return* refers to the expected value of all possible future rates of return. The *actual* return an investor earns, however, will most likely differ from the expected return.

**An Example:**   The table below summarizes data for GM and Exxon stocks.

| State of economy | Probability of state of economy (Pr) | Rate of return if state occurs (R) | |
|---|---|---|---|
| | | GM | Exxon |
| 1 | .20 | .10 | .03 |
| 2 | .20 | .04 | - .08 |
| 3 | .20 | -.09 | .07 |
| 4 | .20 | .20 | .12 |
| 5 | .20 | .05 | .21 |
| Total | 1.00 | .30 | .35 |

The table represents forecasts of possible returns for each stock during the coming year. The forecasts are based on five equally likely possible states of the economy; a state of the economy might be a severe recession, or a depression, or moderate growth of the economy, for example. For each state of the economy, we have predicted the rate of return which is likely to occur for each common stock. This example is oversimplified. First, we have assumed only five states of the economy. Second, we have assumed that each state is equally likely to occur.  Nevertheless, the concepts presented hold even when the 'real-world' situation becomes more complicated.

Since there are five equally likely possible states of the economy, the probability for any one state is 0.20 or 20%; the total of the probabilities is 1.00, or 100%, indicating that one of the five states must occur during the coming year.

The expected return $E(R_U)$ is computed as the sum of each possible return multiplied by its probability of occurrence.  For GM and Exxon, the expected returns are:

$$E(R_{GM}) \quad = .20 \times .10 \; + \; .20 \times .04 \; + \; .20 \times -.09 \; + \; .20 \times .20 \; + \; .20 \times .05 \; = \; .06$$

$$E(R_{Exxon}) \quad = .20 \times .03 \quad + \quad .20 \times -.08 \quad + \quad .20 \times .07 \quad + \quad .20 \times .12 \quad + \quad .20 \times .21 \quad = \quad .07$$

When the probability of each return is equally likely (as above), the expected return can simply be computed as an average of the possible returns.

$$E(R_{GM}) \quad = \quad (.10 + .04 - .09 + .20 + .05)/5 \quad = \quad .06$$

$$E(R_{Exxon}) \quad = \quad (.03 - .08 + .07 + .12 + .21)/5 \quad = .07$$

In general, though, each state of the economy is not equally likely to occur. Under these circumstances, expected return is calculated as a weighted average of the possible returns. Each possible return is multiplied (weighted) by its probability of occurrence. The expected return is the sum of these weighted returns:

$$E(R) \quad = \quad (Pr_1 \times R_1) + (Pr_2 \times R_2) + (Pr_3 \times R_3) + ..... + (Pr_T \times R_T)$$

where T is the number of possible states of the economy, $Pr_1$, $Pr_2$, $Pr_3$, and $Pr_T$ are the probabilities of the respective states of the economy, and $R_1$, $R_2$, $R_3$, and $R_T$ are the possible rates of return.

We can revise the above table to consider the fact that all states of the economy are not equally likely:

| State of economy | Probability of state of economy (Pr) | Rate of return if state occurs (R) | |
|---|---|---|---|
| | | GM | Exxon |
| 1 | .10 | .10 | .03 |
| 2 | .30 | .04 | -.08 |
| 3 | .30 | -.09 | .07 |
| 4 | .20 | .20 | .12 |
| 5 | .10 | .05 | .21 |
| Total | 1.00 | .30 | .35 |

Computing the new expected returns for GM and Exxon, we have:

$$E(R_{GM}) \quad = .10 \times .10 \quad + \quad .30 \times .04 \quad + \quad .30 \times -.09 \quad + \quad .20 \times .20 \quad + \quad .10 \times .05 \quad = \quad .040$$

$$E(R_{Exxon}) \quad = .10 \times .03 \quad + \quad .30 \times -.08 \quad + \quad .30 \times .07 \quad + \quad .20 \times .12 \quad + \quad .10 \times .21 \quad = \quad .045$$

**Variance:**   Our focus in this section is on the calculation of the variance for data representing future possible rates of return.   To calculate the variance, we determine the squared deviations from the expected return. Each possible squared deviation is multiplied by its probability of occurrence. These are added; the sum is the variance. The standard deviation is simply the square root of the variance.

The generalized equations for the variance and standard deviation are:

$$\sigma^2 \quad = \quad \Sigma_J \, [R_j - E(R)]^2 \times P_j$$

$$\sigma \quad = \quad (\sigma^2)^{1/2}$$

The calculation of the variances for the GM and Exxon example is summarized in the following table.   NOTE: for this example, we are using the scenario where each state of the economy is equally likely to occur. That is, $Pr_1 = Pr_2 = ... = Pr_5 = .20$.

| State of economy | Rate of return if state occurs (R) | | Deviation of return from expected return [R - E(R)] | | Squared deviation of return from expected return [R - E(R)]$^2$ | |
|---|---|---|---|---|---|---|
| | GM | Exxon | GM | Exxon | GM | Exxon |
| 1 | .10 | .03 | .04 | -.04 | .0016 | .0016 |
| 2 | .04 | -.08 | -.02 | -.15 | .0004 | .0225 |
| 3 | -.09 | .07 | -.15 | .00 | .0225 | .0000 |
| 4 | .20 | .12 | .14 | .05 | .0196 | .0025 |
| 5 | .05 | .21 | -.01 | .14 | .0001 | .0196 |
| Total | .30 | .35 | .00 | .00 | .0442 | .0462 |

The variance ($\sigma_{GM}^2$) and standard deviation ($\sigma_{GM}$) for GM are $(.0442 / 45) = 0.01105$ and $[(0.01105)^{.5}] = 0.10512 = 10.512\%$, respectively . The variance ($\sigma_{EX}^2$) and standard deviation ($\sigma_{EX}$) for Exxon are $(.0462 / 4) = 0.01155$ and $[(0.01155)^{.5}] = 0.10747 = 10.747\%$, respectively.

Note that, if the probabilities of each state occurring were not equal, we would have to multiply each squared deviation by its probability. The sum would then be the variance.

## PORTFOLIOS

Most investors own a portfolio of assets, rather than one individual asset. An investor's portfolio is the combination of assets the investor owns. Therefore, investors are more concerned about the characteristics of the portfolio than the characteristics of the individual assets which comprise the portfolio.   In this section we discuss the expected return and variance of a portfolio.

**Portfolio Weights:**  The respective percentages of a portfolio's total value invested in each of the assets in the portfolio are referred to as the portfolio weights.

**An Example:**  An investor has a three-asset portfolio with a total value of $1,000. The values of assets A, B and C are $450, $250, and $300, respectively. What are the portfolio weights for this portfolio?

> Weight invested in Asset A   =   $450 / $1,000   =   45%
> Weight invested in Asset B   =   $250 / $1,000   =   25%
> Weight invested in Asset C   =   $300 / $1,000   =   30%

**Portfolio Expected Returns:**  Consider an individual who invests 60% of his money in GM stock and 40% in Exxon stock (the portfolio weights are 60% and 40%, respectively). For each of the five possible states of the economy indicated in the earlier example, the investor's return on his investment will be equal to a weighted average of the returns in that state for the respective stocks. For example, if state 1 occurs, the portfolio return ($R_p$) would be:

$$R_p = (.60 \times .10) + (.40 \times .03) = .072 = 7.2\%$$

The table below indicates the return for the portfolio in each of the five states of the economy, and the calculations required to compute the expected return for the portfolio, ($E(R_p)$) when each state has an equal probability of occurring:

| State of economy | Probability of state of economy (Pr) | Rate of return if state occurs ($R_{GM}$) | ($R_{exxon}$) | ($R_P$) | (Pr x $R_p$) |
|---|---|---|---|---|---|
| 1 | .20 | .10 | .03 | .072 | .0144 |
| 2 | .20 | .04 | -.08 | -.008 | -.0016 |
| 3 | .20 | -.09 | .07 | -.026 | -.0052 |
| 4 | .20 | .20 | .12 | .168 | .0336 |
| 5 | .20 | .05 | .21 | .114 | .0228 |
| Total | 1.00 | .30 | .35 | .320 | .0640 |

The expected return for the portfolio is 0.0640 = 6.4%. Notice that we have used the weighted-average procedure here to compute $E(R_p)$. Since the five possible values of $R_p$ are equally likely, we could have computed $E(R_p)$ as a simple average of the values of $R_p$. That is, $E(R_p) = (.320/5) = 0.0640 = 6.4\%$.

A more direct approach computes the expected return for a portfolio as a weighted average of the expected returns of the securities in the portfolio. The weights are the portfolio weights. The formula for this calculation is:

$$E(R_p) = [x_1 \times E(R_1)] + [x_2 \times E(R_2)] + [x_3 \times E(R_3)] + \ ... + \ [x_n \times E(R_n)]$$

where n is the number of assets in the portfolio, $x_1$, $x_2$, $x_3$, and $x_n$ are the portfolio weights for the assets, and $E(R_1)$, $E(R_2)$, $E(R_3)$, and $E(R_n)$ are the expected returns for the assets. For the GM-Exxon example:

$$E(R_p) = [x_{GM} \times E(R_{GM})] + [x_{EXXON} \times E(R_{EXXON})] = (.60 \times .06) + (.40 \times .07) = .064 = 6.4\%$$

**Portfolio Variance:** The expected return for a portfolio is a weighted average of the expected returns of the individual securities in the portfolio. However, the variance and standard deviation of a portfolio are *not* weighted averages of the variances and standard deviations of the individual securities. In fact, the way in which assets are combined into a portfolio can significantly change the risks faced by an investor. This is a very important concept.

**Portfolio Standard Deviation and Diversification:** Combining assets into portfolios in order to reduce portfolio risk is know as *diversification*. In general, the process of diversification reduces portfolio risk. This is because of the *correlation* between the returns of the securities in the portfolio. The correlation coefficient tells us the extent to which the returns of two securities move together over time. The correlation coefficient (CORR) can range from +1 (perfectly positive) to –1 (perfectly negative). A coefficient of 0 indicates that there is no relationship.

The graphs in Figure 13.1, on page 417 of your text show three cases for combining two assets, A and B (assume these are returns of securities). The left-hand graphs plot the separate returns for the two securities through time. The right-hand graphs represent the returns for *both* A and B over a particular time interval. The correlation of returns for A and B, CORR($R_A$, $R_B$) ranges from –1.0 to 1.0.

The significance of different degrees of correlation on the standard deviation of a portfolio is intuitively obvious in the extreme case of perfectly negative correlation between the returns of two securities. Whenever security returns are not moving in exactly the same direction over time, then by investing equal amounts in A and B, the portfolio returns are smoothed out and the portfolio standard deviation is reduced. Mathematically, it can be shown that the portfolio variance for a two stock portfolio (Stock A and B) is:

$$\sigma^2_p = x^2_A \sigma^2_A + x^2_B \sigma^2_B + 2x_A x_B \, CORR_{AB} \, \sigma_A \, \sigma_B$$

where   $x$   = proportion of wealth invested in A or B
   $CORR_{AB}$   = Correlation between the returns for A and B
   $CORR_{AB} \, \sigma_A \, \sigma_B$   = Covariance between the returns of A and B

**An Example:**   The standard deviation of the rate of return for CP is 12% and 26% for CAE.  If the correlation between their rates of return is .65, what is the standard deviation of a portfolio consisting of 20% of CAE and the remainder in CP stock?  What is the covariance between the returns of CP and CAE?

The variance of the two stock portfolio is:

$$\sigma^2_p = (.80)^2(.12)^2 + (.20)^2(.26)^2 + 2\,(.80)(.20)(.65)(.12)(.26) = .01841$$

The standard deviation is the square root of the variance: $\sigma_p$   =   $(.01841)^{1/2}$   =   .135682 or 13.57%.

Note, if the correlation coefficient is 1.0, the standard deviation of this portfolio would be 14.8%, which is simply a weighted average of the individual standard deviations :   $(.80)(.12) + (.20)(.26) = 14.8\%$.  Any time the correlation coefficient is *less* than +1, the portfolio standard deviation is less than a weighted average of the individual standard deviations.  This means that, any time the correlation coefficient is less than +1, diversification will reduce portfolio risk.

**An Example:** In the preceding example, what is the standard deviation of the two stock portfolios if the correlation coefficient is zero? What is it if CORR is –1.0?

If $CORR_{A,B}$ = 0:   $\sigma_p^2$   =   $(.80)^2(.12)^2$   +   $(.20)^2(.26)^2$   +   $2(.80)(.20)(0)(.12)(.26)$
   =   .00922   +   .00270 +   0   =   .011920
   $\sigma_p$   =   $(.011920)^{1/2}$   =   .10918   =   10.92%

If $CORR_{A,B}$ = –1:   $\sigma_p^2$   =   $(.80)^2(.12)^2$   +   $(.20)^2(.26)^2$   +   $2(.80)(.20)(-1.0)(.12)(.26)$   = .001936
   $\sigma_p$   =   4.4 %

From the above examples it should be clear that as long as *CORR is less than 1.0, the standard deviation of a portfolio of two securities is* <u>*less*</u> *than the weighted average of the standard deviation of the individual securities.* Notice that the most risk reduction occurred when CORR = –1.0.

Combining securities (or assets) whose CORR is less than +1.0 offers the investor the opportunity to reduce portfolio risk as measured by the portfolio standard deviation. This process is commonly known as *diversification.*

As investors diversify their portfolios by adding securities that have correlation coefficients less than +1.0, and continue to adjust the respective weights in these portfolios, the many possible combinations can be represented in a *feasible set or the efficient set* of portfolio combinations.

## ANNOUNCEMENTS, SURPRISES, AND EXPECTED RETURNS

Our measurement of risk, using variance and standard deviation, is based on the size of the differences between actual returns, R, and expected returns, E(R). In this section, we discuss the reasons why differences between R and E(R) exist.

**Expected and Unexpected Returns:** The actual return (R) on a security consists of two parts: the expected return, which is predicted by participants in the financial markets; and, a 'surprise,' or unexpected, part. The expected return is based on the market's understanding of a large number of factors that may influence a given company's share price.

The second part of the return, the risky part, comes from unexpected information that is revealed during the year.
  For a given stock, we can write:

$$R = E(R) + U$$

where R is the actual total return, E(R) is the expected part of the return and U is the unexpected part of the return. The difference between the actual return, R, and the expected return, E(R), is attributed to surprises reflected in the unexpected return, U.

**Announcements and News:**  Consider the example of Texxon, a large oil company. The expected return on Texxon common stock is partially determined by the expected price of oil.  Suppose the price of oil is currently $12 per barrel and the price is completely controlled by the OPEC cartel.  It is generally expected that the cartel will raise the price to $20 per barrel.  Unexpectedly, however, the cartel announces that the price will be $22. The price changes by $10 per barrel, but $8 of this change was expected and was reflected in Texxon's expected return.  It is the $2 deviation from the expected price that is the 'surprise' portion of the announcement.

In general, an announcement has two components: the expected part and the surprise, or innovation:

Announcement = Expected part + Surprise

In the Texxon example, if a price hike to $20 had actually been announced, there would have been no surprise. In the language of Wall Street, the market has already 'discounted' the news of a price increase to $20, which means that the value of the Texxon shares already reflects this information because it is anticipated by market participants. Therefore, there should be no change in Texxon's stock price if the cartel announces the $20 price. If, however, a $22 price is announced, Texxon's stock price will change.

## RISK: SYSTEMATIC AND UNSYSTEMATIC

The risk of owning an asset, such as common stock, results from unexpected events.  If events always occurred exactly as predicted, there would be no risk. In this section, we identify two types of unexpected events which give rise to two categories of risk; systematic risk and unsystematic risk.

**Systematic and Unsystematic Risk:**  A *systematic* risk tends to affect a large number of assets to a greater or lesser degree; systematic risks are also called *market risks*.  An *unsystematic* risk affects only a single asset or a small group of assets.  Systematic risks arise from uncertainty about economy-wide factors, such as inflation and interest rates, whereas the possibility of a labour strike or lawsuit involving a single company is an unsystematic risk.  These risks are also referred to as unique or asset-specific risk.

**Systematic and Unsystematic Components of Return:**  Remember, the actual return on a security consists of its expected and surprise components:   R = E(R) + U, where U is the surprise component. The surprise component is influenced by two kinds of risk. Therefore, we can rewrite U as follows:

$$U = \text{Systematic portion} + \text{Unsystematic portion} \quad = m + \varepsilon$$

where m represents the systematic, or market, portion of U, and ε represents the unsystematic portion of U. Substituting (m + ε) for U, we can now rewrite R as follows:

$$R = E(R) + U \quad = \quad E(R) + m + \varepsilon$$

The unsystematic risk is particular to an individual asset. As an example, the unsystematic risk for General Motors is unrelated to the unsystematic risk for IBM. This fact has important implications for the risk of a portfolio.

# DIVERSIFICATION AND PORTFOLIO RISK

As we noted earlier, diversification is the process of investing in a portfolio of several assets in order to reduce risk. We will discuss the extent to which risk is reduced by diversification, and the reason why diversification reduces risk.

**The Effect of Diversification - Another Lesson from Market History:**  Studies of common stock listed on the Toronto Stock Exchange (TSE) demonstrate that the standard deviation of a portfolio decreases as the number of securities in the portfolio increases. Significant decreases in standard deviation occur as the number of stocks in the portfolio increases from one to approximately 10. On average, the standard deviation of a 10-stock portfolio is approximately half the standard deviation of a single TSE stock. Further decreases in standard deviation are observed as the number of stocks in the portfolio increases, but decreases in risk become smaller as additional securities are added to the portfolio.  The graph in Figure 13.6 on page 427 of your text shows the way in which adding stocks to a portfolio reduces the standard deviation of the portfolio.

**The Principle of Diversification:**  The principle of diversification indicates that spreading an investment across many assets eliminates some of the risk. The risk which is eliminated by diversification is called *diversifiable* risk.  However, there is a minimum level of risk in a portfolio which cannot be eliminated by diversification. This minimum risk level is called *nondiversifiable* risk.

**Diversification and Unsystematic Risk:**  Why isn't all risk diversifiable? The answer is found in the distinction between *unsystematic* and *systematic* risk.

In a large portfolio of common stocks, the unsystematic risk associated with one stock typically has no impact on the unsystematic risk associated with any other stock. Therefore, in a large portfolio, we would not expect to observe any particular relationship between the unsystematic risks for the individual stocks in the portfolio. In a portfolio of 30 or more stocks, the effects of unsystematic risk of various stocks usually offset each other, thereby eliminating the risk arising from each individual source. The risk which can be eliminated is diversifiable risk; it is the same as unsystematic risk.

**Diversification and Systematic Risk:**  Systematic risk has an impact on all the stocks in a portfolio. For example, a recession will have a negative impact on virtually all the securities in the portfolio, and consequently on the investor's return from the portfolio. Systematic risk cannot be diversified away; hence, the terms systematic risk and nondiversifiable risk are synonymous.

## SYSTEMATIC RISK AND BETA

**The Systematic Risk Principle:** We know that investors will not accept risk without compensation in the form of a higher expected return.  We have established that investors can eliminate unsystematic risk by diversifying. Therefore, it is not necessary for any investor to bear the unsystematic risk of an investment.  The market will not reward investors for taking unnecessary risks.  So, investors are not paid for bearing unsystematic risks.  In other words, the reward for bearing risk depends only on the systematic risk of an investment. This means that *the expected return for an asset depends only on that asset's systematic risk.*

**Measuring Systematic Risk:** The systematic risk of an asset is measured by its beta coefficient, represented by the Greek letter $\beta$.  Beta measures the systematic risk for a particular asset, relative to the systematic risk for the average asset.  For example, the average TSE common stock has a beta value equal to 1.0, so a stock with $\beta = 0.50$ has half the systematic risk of the average TSE stock.  Or, a stock with $\beta = 1.25$ has 25% more systematic risk than the average stock. It is important to remember that, since systematic risk is the relevant risk for an investor, the expected return for an asset is dependent on $\beta$.   A stock with a high value of $\beta$ has a high expected return;  a stock with a lower value of $\beta$  has a lower expected return. This conclusion is true regardless of the standard deviation for a stock.

**Portfolio Betas:** The value of beta for a portfolio ($\beta_p$) is a weighted-average of the betas of the securities which comprise the portfolio, as indicated in the following formula:

$$\beta_p = (x_1 + \beta_1) + (x_2 + \beta_2) + (x_3 + \beta_3) + \dots + (x_n \times \beta_n)$$

where n is the number of assets in the portfolio, $x_1$, $x_2$, $x_3$, and $x_n$ are the portfolio weights, and $\beta_1$, $\beta_2$, $\beta_3$, and $\beta_n$ are the beta values for the assets in the portfolio.

**An Example:**  For the GM-Exxon example presented earlier in the chapter, suppose that $\beta_{GM} = 1.10$ and $\beta_{TEXXON} = 0.70$.  What is the value of $\beta_p$ for a portfolio with portfolio weights of $x_{GM} = 0.40$ and $x_{TEXXON} = 0.60$?

$$\beta_p = (x_{GM} \times \beta_{GM}) + (x_{TEXXON} \times \beta_{TEXXON}) = (.40 \times 1.10) + (.60 \times .70) = .86$$

## THE SECURITY MARKET LINE

We now develop the precise relationship between systematic risk, measured by beta and the expected return. The graphic representation is called the security market line (SML) and the algebraic representation is the *capital asset pricing model* (CAPM).

**Beta and the Risk Premium:** Let's look at an example.  Let asset A be an individual security with $\beta_A = 1.2$ and $E(R_A) = 16\%$.  Assume the risk-free rate ($R_f$) is 5%.  Note that beta for the risk-free asset is zero; since the risk-free asset does not have any risk, it clearly does not have any systematic risk.   If x is the percentage of the portfolio invested in asset A, then $(1 - x)$ is the percentage invested in the risk-free asset, because the total of the portfolio weights must be 1.0 (100%).  The expected return for a portfolio consisting of asset A and the risk-free asset is:

$$E(R_p) = [x \times E(R_A)] + [(1 - x) \times R_f] = (x \times 16\%) + [(1 - x) \times 5\%]$$

Beta for this portfolio is:

$$\beta_p = (x \times \beta_A) + [(1 - x) \times 0] = (x \times 1.2) + (0) = 1.2x$$

By selecting various values of x, and then computing the corresponding values of $E(R_p)$ and $\beta_p$, we can plot expected returns and beta can be plotted on a graph.  Some values of x, $E(R_p)$ and $\beta_p$ are indicated in the following table:

| Percentage of portfolio invested in Asset A (x) | Portfolio expected return $E(R_p)$ | Portfolio Beta $\beta_p$ |
|---|---|---|
| 0 % | 5.0% | 0.00 |
| 20 | 7.2 | 0.24 |
| 50 | 10.5 | 0.60 |
| 90 | 14.9 | 1.08 |
| 100 | 16.0 | 1.20 |
| 150 | 21.5 | 1.80 |
| 200 | 27.0 | 2.40 |

If you plot these points, the important thing to remember is that the relationship between $E(R_p)$ and $\beta_p$ is a *straight line* through the point $R_f$ and the point represented by $\beta_A = 1.2$ and $E(R_A) = 16\%$.

If x is greater than 100%, the portfolio was formed by borrowing at the rate $R_f$ and then investing the borrowed money in Asset A.   For example, if an individual has $1,000 to invest, she might borrow $500 at the rate $R_f = 5\%$, and then invest $1,500 in Asset A.  The total amount invested in Asset A is equal to 150% of her own funds (i.e., x = 1.50) and the value of $(1 - x)$ is $-.50$, indicating that an amount equal to half of the investor's funds is borrowed.

**The Reward-to-Risk Ratio:**  The slope of the line in the graph is called the *reward-to-risk ratio*. The slope of this straight line can be computed between any two points on the line. We will use the following points to compute the slope: the intercept (i.e., $R_f$), and the point representing Asset A [i.e., the point where $\beta = \beta_A = 1.2$, and $E(R) = E(R_A) = 16\%$]. The slope is the change in the 'y' value (expected return) divided by the change in the 'x' value ($\beta$):

$$\text{Slope} \;=\; \frac{E(R_A) - R_f}{\beta_A} \;=\; \frac{.16 - .05}{1.2} \;=\; .09167 \;=\; 9.17\%$$

This reward-to-risk ratio can be interpreted by first assuming that an investor is considering placing her entire investment portfolio in the risk-free asset. Prior to making this decision, the investor might want to know what her compensation would be for taking on risk. The answer is indicated by the reward-to-risk ratio; for each one unit increase in systematic risk (i.e., by increasing the systematic risk in her investment from $\beta = 0$ to $\beta = 1$), she will increase her expected rate of return by 9.167%.  Of course, increases in the value of $\beta$ by more or less than one result in proportionate increases in expected rate of return.

**The Basic Argument:** Assume  we have identified Asset B, with $\beta_B = .6$ and $E(R_B) = 10\%$. Should an investor consider purchasing this asset? In order to answer this question, we compare a portfolio of Asset B and the risk-free asset to the portfolio formed earlier with Asset A and the risk-free asset.  We can prepare a table similar to the one above:

| Percentage of portfolio invested in Asset A (x) | Portfolio expected return $E(R_p)$ | Portfolio Beta $\beta_p$ |
|---|---|---|
| 0 % | 5.0% | 0.00 |
| 20 | 6.0 | 0.12 |
| 50 | 7.5 | 0.30 |
| 90 | 9.5 | 0.54 |
| 100 | 10.0 | 0.60 |
| 150 | 12.5 | 0.90 |
| 200 | 15.0 | 1.20 |

If you graph the portfolios using Asset A and Asset B in combination with the risk-free asset, you will see that, at each point, investors receive a higher return given the risk, if they choose the portfolio with Asset A. This means that the portfolio comprised of Asset A and the riskless asset is superior to the one with Asset B.

We can also demonstrate this result mathematically by computing the reward-to-risk ratio for Asset B:

$$\text{Slope} \;=\; \frac{E(R_B) - R_f}{\beta_B} \;=\; \frac{.10 - .05}{0.6} \;=\; .08333 \;=\; 8.33\%$$

Asset B provides a lower reward-to-risk ratio than does Asset A. Consequently, an investor would not consider purchasing Asset B. The reward-to-risk ratio is the slope of the graph of all possible portfolios formed by combining Asset B with the risk-free asset. Since the slope for Asset B is less steep than the slope for Asset A, while the intercepts are the same (i.e., $R_f$ is the intercept for each line), all portfolios combining Asset A with $R_f$ are preferable to corresponding portfolios combining Asset B with $R_f$.

**Calculating Beta:** A security's beta measures the responsiveness of the security's return to changes in the return on the market as a whole. We can calculate a firm's beta by graphing the relationship between a stock's expected return to different returns on the market. The resulting line, the *characteristic line*, has the same slope as the stock's beta.

**The Security Market Line:**   The line that describes the relationship between systematic risk and expected return is the *security market line* (SML).   This is one of the major concepts in finance. The SML is shown in graphic form on the following page.

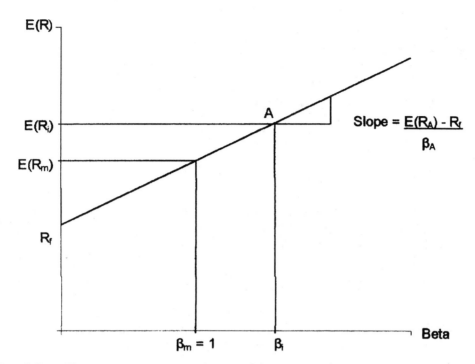

**Market Portfolios:** The most common way of deriving the equation of the SML involves the concept of a *market portfolio*. This is a portfolio made up of all assets in the market. The market portfolio itself is an asset, so its expected return [$E(R_M)$] and beta ($\beta_M$) must be on the security market line. What then is the value of $\beta_M$? We have defined beta as the level of systematic risk for a particular asset relative to the systematic risk of the average asset in the market. The market portfolio is comprised of all assets in the market; furthermore, a portfolio beta is a weighted-average of the betas of the securities in the portfolio. Therefore, the beta for the market portfolio must be equal to beta for the average security; that is, $\beta_m = 1.0$. The beta and expected return for the market portfolio are plotted on the SML graph above. Using the market portfolio, we can write the slope of the SML as:

$$\text{SML Slope} \quad = \quad \frac{E(R_M) - R_f}{\beta_M} \quad = \quad \frac{E(R_M) - R_f}{1} \quad = \quad E(R_M) - R_f$$

Since this slope is the excess return on the market over the risk-free rate, it is often called the *market risk premium*.

**The Capital Asset Pricing Model:** If $E(R_i)$ and $\beta_i$ represent the expected return and beta for any asset on the market, this point must plot on the SML. The reward-to-risk ratio must be the same as that for the market in general. That means,

$$\frac{E(R_i) - R_f}{\beta_i} \quad = \quad E(R_M) - R_f$$

We can rearrange this to write the equation for the SML:

$$E(R_i) \quad = \quad R_f + [E(R_M) - R_f] \times \beta_i$$

where $E(R_i)$ and $\beta_i$ are the expected return and beta for any asset. This equation is referred to as the Capital Asset Pricing Model (CAPM), and it indicates the expected return for any asset for a given level of systematic risk.

This model shows that the expected return for a given asset depends on (1) the pure time value of money, (2) the reward for bearing systematic risk,  and (3) the amount of systematic risk.

## THE SML AND THE COST OF CAPITAL: A PREVIEW

So far, we have discussed risk in terms of investments in securities. However, the same concepts also apply to the capital budgeting process.

**The Basic Idea:**  The security market line describes investors' opportunities in financial markets in terms of systematic risk (i.e., $\beta$) and expected return. A capital budgeting project under consideration by management must provide an expected return to shareholders which exceeds that for other investments with comparable risk. For example, suppose the capital budgeting project has a beta of 0.9, and the expected return in the financial markets for investments with $\beta = 0.9$ is 15%; the capital budgeting project is acceptable only if its expected return exceeds the 15% which investors could earn on their own in the financial markets.

**The Cost of Capital:**  The cost of capital associated with a capital budgeting project is the minimum required return for the investment. Since that return is the expected return available in the financial markets for investments with a specified risk level, it is the shareholders' opportunity cost. Cost of capital is discussed in Part VI.

## ARBITRAGE PRICING THEORY

An alternative model of risk and return is the *arbitrage pricing theory* (APT).  The major advantage of the APT model is that it can handle multiple factors that are not included in CAPM.  Like CAPM, the APT model assumes that stock returns depend on both expected and unexpected returns.  Unlike CAPM, the unexpected return in the APT model is related to several market factors.  Assuming those factors are unanticipated changes in inflation, GNP, and interest rates, the expected return would be written as:

$$E(R) \; = \; R_r \; + \; E[(R_1) - R_f] \times \beta_1 \; + \; E[(R_2) - R_f] \times \beta_2 \; + \; E[(R_3) - R_f] \times \beta_3 \; + \; E[(R_4) - R_f] \times \beta_4$$

Using this concept, the APT model can be expanded to include as many factors as we want.

## CONCEPT TEST

1.      The expected return is the _____ of possible future returns for an investment.

2.      When possible future returns are equally likely to occur, the expected return can be computed in two equivalent ways. The first is the same as the procedure for computing the average of historical data and is given by the formula      $E(R)$  =  _____ , where T is the number of possible future returns, $R_1$, $R_2$, and $R_T$ are the _____ and  $E(R)$ is the _____ . The alternative calculation is a _____ average of the possible future returns:   $E(R) =$  _____ , where T is the number of possible future returns, $Pr_1$, $Pr_2$, and $Pr_T$ are the probabilities of the respective possible returns and $R_1$, $R_2$, and $R_T$ are the _____ . If the returns are not equally likely to occur, then the _____ procedure must be used to compute the expected return.

3.      To calculate the variance of returns, we first compute the _____ of the possible returns from the expected return. Each of these is then multiplied by the _____ . Finally, the variance is the _____ of all these terms.

4.      An investor's portfolio is the _____ which the investor owns. The respective percentages of a portfolio's total value invested in each of the assets in the portfolio are referred to as the _____ .

5.      The expected return for a portfolio is a weighted average of the _____ of the securities which comprise the portfolio, as indicated by the formula   $E(R_p) =$ _____ , where n is the number of assets in the portfolio $x_1$, $x_2$, and $x_n$ are the _____ for the assets, and $E(R_1)$, $E(R_2)$, and $E(R_n)$ are the _____ for the assets.

6.      The _____ represents the statistical relationship between two series of numbers and can range from _____ to _____ .

7.      If the correlation between two securities is +1.0 then the _____ of this portfolio would be equal to a _____ of the individual standard deviations.

8.      The covariance term for securities A and B includes the product of _____ × _____ × _____ .

9.      As long as the correlation coefficient is less than _____ the standard deviation of a two stock portfolio is _____ than the weighted average of the _____ of the individual securities.

10.     Combining securities whose correlation is _____ than _____ in order to reduce portfolio risk is known as the process of _____ .

11.     The actual return (R) on a security consists of two parts: the _____ return, which is the part of the return predicted or expected by participants in the financial markets, and, a 'surprise' or _____ , part.

12.     The risk for a particular asset comes from the _____ part of the return. For a given stock, we can write that   R = E(R) + U,   where R is the actual total return, E(R) is the _____ part of the return and U is the _____ part of the return.

13.     The difference between the actual return and the expected return is attributed to surprises which are reflected in the _____ part of the return. The surprise component is influenced by two kinds of risk, so that we can write U as:   U = _____ portion + _____ portion = _____ , where m represents the _____ , or market, portion of U, and ε represents the _____ portion of U.

14.     Substituting (m + ε) for U, the actual return on a security is:   R = E(R) + U = E(R) + _____.

15.     A _____ risk tends to affect a large number of assets to a greater or lesser degree; this kind of risk is also called a _____ risk, and it arises from uncertainty about economy-wide factors. An _____ risk affects only a single asset or a small group of assets.

16.    As the number of assets in a portfolio increases, the standard deviation of the portfolio _____ .  A significant reduction in portfolio risk occurs by combining as many as ___ assets.  As more assets are added to the portfolio further reductions in risk are _____ .

17.    Increasing the number of assets in a portfolio eliminates a significant portion of the risk to which the investor would be subjected if he held only one stock. The risk which is eliminated by diversification is called _____ risk. However, there is a minimum level of risk in a portfolio of common stocks which can not be eliminated by diversification; this minimum level is referred to as _____ risk.

18.    In a large portfolio of common stocks, the _____ risk associated with one stock typically has no impact on the _____ risk associated with any other stock. In a portfolio of 30 or more stocks, it would be reasonable to expect that the effects of _____ risk on various stocks would offset each other, thereby eliminating the risk to the investor arising from this source. This source of risk is synonymous with _____ risk.

19.    _____ risk has an impact on all the stocks in a portfolio, and cannot be diversified away; hence, the terms _____ risk and _____ risk are synonymous.

20.    Financial markets do not reward investors for taking on risks which can be eliminated by _____ . Investors are not rewarded for taking on _____ risk, because this risk is _____ .

21.    The systematic risk principle states that the reward for bearing risk depends only on the _____ risk of an investment. Consequently, the expected return for an asset depends on that asset's _____ risk.

22.    The systematic risk of an asset is measured by its _____ . This measures the amount of systematic risk for a particular asset, relative to the amount of _____ risk for the average asset. The average common stock has a beta value equal to _____ .

23.    The value of a portfolio beta $(\beta_p)$ is a weighted-average of the _____ of the securities which comprise the portfolio, as indicated by $\beta_p$ = _____ , where n is the number of assets in the portfolio, $x_1$, $x_2$, and $x_n$ are the _____ , and $\beta_1$, $\beta_2$, and $\beta_n$ are the beta values for the assets in the portfolio.


## ANSWERS TO CONCEPT TEST

1.    average

2.    $( R_1 + R_2 + \ldots + R_T )/ T$;  possible future returns;  expected return;  weighted;  $(Pr_1 \times R_1) + (Pr_2 \times R_2) + \ldots + (Pr_T \times R_T)$; possible future returns;  weighted-average

3.    squared standard deviations;  probability of occurrence;  sum

4.    combination of assets;  portfolio weights

5.    expected returns;  $[x_1 \times E(R_1)] + [x_2 \times E(R_2)] + \ldots + [x_n \times E(R_n)]$;  portfolio weights;  expected returns

6.    correlation coefficient; + 1.0; – 1.0

7.      standard deviation;  weighted average

8.      CORR$_{A,B}$;  standard deviation of A; standard deviation of B

9.      +1.0; less; standard deviation

10.     less; +1.0; diversification

11.     expected;  unexpected

12.     unexpected;  expected;  unexpected;

13.      unexpected;  systematic; unsystematic; m + ε; systematic; unsystematic

14.     (m + ε)

15.     systematic; market; unsystematic;

16.     decreases; 10; smaller

17.     diversifiable; nondiversifiable

18.     unsystematic; unsystematic; unsystematic; diversifiable

19.     systematic; nondiversifiable; systematic

20.     diversification; unsystematic; diversifiable

21.     systematic; systematic

22.     beta; systematic; 1.0

23.     betas;  $(x_1 \times \beta_1) + (x_2 \times \beta_2) + \ldots + (x_n \times \beta_n)$;  portfolio weights

## PROBLEMS AND SOLUTIONS

**Use the following information to solve Problems 1 to 3:**

The information below represents possible future returns for Canadian Pacific (CP) common shares next year:

| State of economy | Probability of state of economy (PR) | Rate of return if state occurs (R) |
|---|---|---|
| 1 | .20 | 12% |
| 2 | .20 | 6 |
| 3 | .20 | - 10 |
| 4 | .20 | 22 |
| 5 | .20 | 5 |
| Total | 1.00 | |

## Problem 1

What is the expected rate of return for CP common stock?

**Solution:**

$$E(R) = (.12 + .06 - .10 + .22 + .05)/5 = 0.07 = 7\%$$

OR   $E(R) = (.20 \times .12) + (.20 \times .06) + (.20 \times -.10) + (.20 \times .22) + (.20 \times .05) = .07 = 7\%$

## Problem 2

What is the variance of the return for CP common stock?

**Solution:**

$$\sigma^2 = .2 \times (.12 - .07)^2 + .2 \times (.06 - .07)^2 + .2 \times (-.10 - .07)^2 + .2 \times (.22 - .07)^2 + .2 \times (.05 - .07)^2$$
$$= .2 \times .0025 + .2 \times .0001 + .2 \times .0289 + .2 \times .0225 + .2 \times .0004$$
$$= .01088$$

## Problem 3

What is the standard deviation of the return for CP common stock?

**Solution:**   $\sigma = (.01088)^{1/2} = 0.104307 = 10.4307\%$

**Use the information below to solve Problems 4 and 5.**

The information below provides the possible future returns for common stock for Verine Corporation (VC) and for Xavier Technologies Corporation (XT) during the next year.

| State of economy | Probability of state of economy (PR) | Rate of return if state occurs VC | XT |
|---|---|---|---|
| 1 | .20 | 10% | 5% |
| 2 | .30 | - 8 | 9 |
| 3 | .15 | 14 | 14 |
| 4 | .35 | 11 | -2 |

## Problem 4

What is the expected rate of return for VC and XT common shares, respectively?

**Solution:**

For VC:  E(R)  =  (.20 x .10) + (.30 x -.08) + (.15 x .14) + (.35 x .11)  =  .0555  =  5.55%

For XT:  E(R)  =  (.20 x .05) + (.30 x .09) + (.15 x .14) + (.35 x -.02)  =  .0510  =  5.10%

## Problem 5

What is the variance and standard deviation for VC's shares?  For XT's?

**Solution:**

For VC:  $\sigma^2$  =  .20 (.10 - .0555)$^2$ +  .30 ( -.08 - .0555)$^2$ + .15 (.14 - .0555)$^2$  +  .35 (.11 - .0555)$^2$

   =  .0080

$\sigma$  =  (.0080)$^{1/2}$  =  8.953%

For XT:  $\sigma^2$  =  .20 (.05 - .0510)$^2$ +  .30 (.09 - .0510)$^2$ + .15 (.14 - .0510)$^2$  +  .35 (-.02 - .0510)$^2$

   =  .003409

$\sigma$  =  (.003409)$^{1/2}$  =  5.839%

## Problem 6

You have the following information about returns for two securities, Asset X and Asset Y.  Each return has an equal probability of occurring.

| Asset X | Asset Y |
|---------|---------|
| 11 % | - 3 % |
| 9 % | 15 % |
| 25 % | 2 % |
| 7 % | 20 % |

Calculate the expected return and standard deviation of return for each asset.

**Solution:**     For Asset X:    E(R)  =  (0.11 + 0.09 + 0.25 + 0.07) / 4  =  0.13  =  13 %

$\sigma^2$  =  [(0.11-0.13)$^2$ + (0.09 - 0.13)$^2$ + (0.25 - 0.13)$^2$
         + (0.07 - 0.13)$^2$] /4   =  0.005

$\sigma$  =  0.0707   =  7.07 %

For Asset Y:    E( R)  =  (-0.03 + 0.15 + 0.02 + 0.20) / 4  =  0.085  =            8.5 %

$\sigma^2$   =        0.008725

$\sigma$   =        0.0934  =  9.34 %

Note that in this solution, we used the average way to compute the expected return and standard deviation because the probabilities of each state occurring were the same.

## Problem 7

The probability that the economy will experience a recession next year is .3, while the probabilities of moderate growth or rapid expansion are .5 and .2, respectively. The common stock of Firm A is expected to return 5%, 15% or 20%, depending on whether the economy experiences a recession, moderate growth or rapid expansion, respectively. The returns for Firm B are expected to be 0%, 16%, or 30%, respectively. Calculate the expected rate of return for each firm's common stock.

**Solution:**   The expected rates of return must be computed using a weighted average, because the possible returns are not equally likely.

$E(R_A)$  =  $(.3 \times .05) + (.5 \times .15) + (.2 \times .20)$  =  .13  =  13%

$E(R_B)$  =  $(.3 \times .00) + (.5 \times .16) + (.2 \times .30)$  =  .14  =  14%

## Problem 8

What is the variance of the return for Firm A common stock?   For Firm B common stock?

**Solution:**    For A:    $\sigma^2$  =  $.3 \times (.05 - .13)^2 + .5 \times (.15 - .13)^2 + .2 \times (.20 - .13)^2$  =  0.00310
                 For B:    $\sigma^2$  =  $.3 \times (.00 - .14)^2 + .5 \times (.16 - .14)^2 + .2 \times (.30 - .14)^2$  =  0.01120

## Problem 9

What is the standard deviation of the rate of return for Firm A common stock? For Firm B common stock?

**Solution:**  Firm A:  $\sigma$  =  $(.00310)^{1/2}$  =  .05568  =  5.568%
               Firm B:  $\sigma$  =  $(.01120)^{1/2}$  =  .10583  = 10.583%.

**Use the following information for Stocks K and M to solve Problems 10 to 14.**

| State of economy | Probability of state of economy (Pr) | | Rate of return if state occurs (R) | |
|---|---|---|---|---|
| | | | K | M |
| 1 | .10 | .25 | .18 | |
| 2 | .20 | | .10 | .20 |
| 3 | .50 | | .15 | .04 |
| 4 | .20 | | -.12 | .00 |

## Problem 10

What is the expected return for Stock K? For Stock M?

**Solution:** For K: $E(R)$ = $(.10 \times .25)$ + $(.20 \times .10)$ + $(.50 \times .15)$ + $(.20 \times -.12)$ = .096 = 9.6%

For M: $E(R)$ = $(.10 \times .18)$ + $(.20 \times .20)$ + $(.50 \times .04)$ + $(.20 \times .00)$ = .078 = 7.8%

## Problem 11

What is the variance for Stock K? For Stock M?

**Solution:** For K: $\sigma^2$ = $.1 \times (.25 - .096)^2$ + $.2 \times (.10 - .096)^2$ + $.5 \times (.15 - .096)^2$ + $.2 \times (-.12 - .096)^2$
= 0.013164

For B: $\sigma^2$ = $.1 \times (.18 - .078)^2$ + $.2 \times (.20 - .078)^2$ + $.5 \times (.04 - .078)^2$ + $.2 \times (.00 - .078)^2$
= 0.005956

## Problem 12

What is the standard deviation for Stock K? For Stock M?

**Solution:** For K: $\sigma$ = $(0.013164)^{1/2}$ = 0.11473 = 11.473%
For M: $\sigma$ = $(0.005956)^{1/2}$ = 0.077175 = 7.718%

## Problem 13

An individual plans to invest $5,000; she will invest $3,000 in Stock K and $2,000 in Stock M. What are the portfolio weights for this portfolio?

**Solution:** The portfolio weights are:   $x_K$ = ($3,000/$5,000) = .60 = 60% invested in Stock K
$x_M$ = ($2,000/$5,000) = .40 = 40% invested in Stock M.

## Problem 14

Using the portfolio weights computed in Problem 13, what is the expected return for the portfolio?

**Solution:** The easiest approach is to calculate the weighted average of the expected returns for the individual securities in the portfolio:

$$E(R_p) \ = \ [x_1 \times E(R_K)] + [x_2 \times E(R_M)] \ = (.60 \times .096) + (.40 \times .078) = .0888 = 8.88\%$$

**Use the following information on WAK Corporation and ALH Corporation to answer Problems 15 and 16.**

| State of economy | Probability of state of economy | Rate of return if state occurs | WAK | ALH |
|---|---|---|---|---|
| 1 | .20 | .25 | .18 | |
| 2 | .10 | | .10 | .20 |
| 3 | .50 | | .15 | .04 |
| 4 | .30 | | -.12 | .00 |

## Problem 15

What are the expected returns for WAK and ALH?

**Solution:**

For WAK:   $E(R) \ = \ (.2 \times .1) + (.1 \times .14) + (.5 \times .19) + (.3 \times .51) \ = \ .144 \ = \ 14.4\%$

For ALH:   $(E(R) \ = \ (.2 \times -.05) + (.1 \times .08) + (.5 \times .20) + (.3 \times .18) \ = \ .152 \ = \ 15.2\%$

## Problem 16

What is the variance and standard deviation for WAK?  For ALH?

For WAK:   $\sigma^2 \ = \ .2(.10 - .144)^2 \ + \ .1[(.14 - .144)^2 + .5(.19 - .144)^2 + .5(.05 - .144)^2]$
$= \ .004098$
$\sigma \ = \ (.004098)^{\frac{1}{2}} \ = \ 6.40\%$

For WLH:   $\sigma^2 \ = \ .2(-.05 - .152)^2 \ + [.1(.08 - .152)^2 + .5(.20 - .152)^2 + .5(.18 - .152)^2]$
$= \ .010007$
$\sigma \ = \ (.010007)^{\frac{1}{2}} \ = \ 10.04\%$

## Problem 17

Refer to the information for Assets X and Y in Problem 6.  Assume that $CORR_{X,Y}$ is 0.8.  Find the expected return, the variance, and the standard deviation for a portfolio invested 30% in Asset X, and the rest in Asset Y.  (Note: The actual correlation coefficient must be found by finding the actual covariance of Assets X and Y.  We are assuming CORR = 0.8 to keep the computation simple.)

**Solution:**   $E(R_p)$   =   (.30 x .13)  +  (.70 x .085)   =   .0985   =   9.85%

$$\sigma^2 = x_1^2\sigma_1^2 + x_2^2\sigma_2^2 + 2x_1x_2CORR_{1,2}\sigma_1\sigma_2$$
$$= (.30)^2(0.005) + (.70)^2(0.008725) + 2(.30)(.70)(0.8)(0.0707)(0.0934)$$
$$= 0.006944$$
$$\sigma = (0.006944)^{1/2} = 0.8333 = 8.333\%$$

## Problem 18

Two assets have expected returns of 10% and 4.5%, respectively.  Their standard deviations are 8% and 6.8%.  If you invest 50% in each asset, what is the expected return for the portfolio?  What is the standard deviation of the portfolio's return if the correlation coefficient between the assets is 1.0?  0.50?  0.10?  0.0?  -0.6?  -1.0?

**Solution:**  The expected return is always a weighted average of the expected returns of the assets in the portfolio:

$$E(R_p) = 0.50 \times 10\% + 0.50 \times 4.5\% = 7.25\%$$

For a correlation of 1.0, standard deviation is a weighted of standard deviations of assets in the portfolio::

$$\sigma = 0.50\,(8\%) + 0.50\,(6.8\%) = 7.4\%$$

For a correlation of 0.50, the standard deviation of the portfolio's expected return is:

$$\sigma = [(0.50)^2(0.08)^2 + (0.50)^2(0.068)^2 + 2(0.50)(0.50)(0.50)(0.08)(0.068)]^{.5}$$
$$= 0.064 = 6.4\%$$

For correlations of  0.1, 0.0, -0.6, and -1.0, the standard deviations are 0.055 (5.5%),  0.0525 (5.25%),  0.0335 (3.35%), and  0.006 (0.6%), respectively.

## Problem 19

An individual plans to invest in Stock A and Stock B. The expected returns are 9% and 10% for Stocks A and B, respectively. The beta values are 0.95 and 1.25 for Stocks A and B, respectively. Find the expected return and beta for the portfolio if she invests 75% of her funds in Stock A.

**Solution:**   $E(R_p) = [x_A \times E(R_A)] + [x_B \times E(R_B)] = (.75 \times .09) + (.25 \times .10) = .0925 = 9.25\%$

$$\beta_p = (x_A \times \beta_A) + (x_B \times \beta_B) = (.75 \times .95) + (.25 \times 1.25) = 1.025$$

## Problem 20

Suppose the investor in Problem 19 wants to construct a portfolio with expected return equal to 9.5%. What are the portfolio weights for this portfolio? What is the beta for this portfolio?

**Solution:** In order to form a portfolio with expected return equal to 9.5%, the investor must solve the following equation for $x_A$ (the weight to invest in Asset A):

$$E(R_p) = [x_A \times E(R_A)] + [x_B + E(R_B)]$$
$$.095 = [x_A \times .09] + [(1 - x_A) \times .10]$$

where $x_A$ is the proportion of the portfolio invested in Stock A and $(1 - x_A)$ is the proportion invested in Stock B. The solution for $x_A$ is .50, so that the portfolio weights are $x_A = .50 = 50\%$ and $x_B = (1 - x_A) = .50 = 50\%$. The beta for this portfolio is:     $\beta_p = (x_A \times \beta_A) + (x_B \times \beta_B) = (.50 \times .95) + (.50 \times 1.25) = 1.10$

## Problem 21

Suppose the investor described in Problem 19 decides to form a portfolio consisting of three assets, as follows: 10% invested in Stock A, 30% invested in Stock B, and 60% invested in a risk-free asset with a return of 6%. What is the expected return for this portfolio? What is the standard deviation of return?

**Solution:** The expected return for the portfolio is:

$$E(R_p) = [x_A \times E(R_A)] + [x_B \times E(R_B)] + [x_C \times E(R_C)] = (.10 \times .09) + (.30 \times .10) + (.60 \times .06) = .075 = 7.5\%$$

Beta for the risk-free asset is zero, so the portfolio beta is:

$$\beta_p = (x_A \times \beta_A) + (x_B \times \beta_B) + (x_C \times \beta_C) = (.10 \times .95) + (.30 \times 1.25) + (.60 \times 0) = .470$$

## Problem 22

Market research has shown that the expected returns for Alpha, Inc. and Beta, Inc. are perfectly correlated. The standard deviation of the expected return is 10% for Alpha and 5% for Beta. A portfolio consisting of the stocks of both firms is expected to have a standard deviation of 8%. What percent of the portfolio is invested in each asset?

**Solution:** We know the expected return for the portfolio. If we let $x_1$ be the return for Alpha and $x_2$ be the return for Beta, we can say that:     $x_1 + x_2 = 1$,   so   $x_2 = 1 - x_1$

We also know the formula for the variance of a portfolio of two assets:

$$\sigma^2 = x_1^2 \sigma_1^2 + x_2^2 \sigma_2^2 + 2x_1 x_2 \, CORR_{1,2} \, \sigma_1 \sigma_2$$

Substituting, we have:

$$(0.08)^2 = x_1^2 (0.1)^2 + (1 - x_1)^2 (0.05)^2 + 2x_1(1 - x_1)(1)(0.10)(0.05)$$

$$(0.08)^2 = [\, 0.1 \, x_1 + 0.05 \, (1 - x_1) \,]^2$$

$$0.08 \quad = \quad 0.1\, x_1 \; + \; 0.05\, (1 - x_1)$$

$$0.08 \quad = \quad 0.05 x_1 \; + \; 0.05$$

$$0.03 \quad = \quad 0.05 x_1$$

$$x_1 \quad = \quad .60; \quad 1 - x_1 \; = \; 0.40$$

So, 60% is invested in Alpha, and 40% is invested in Beta.

## Problem 23

Use the following information to compute the reward-to-risk ratio for Stocks A, B, and C:

|                  | Expected return |      | Beta |
| ---------------- | --------------- | ---- | ---- |
| Stock A          | 10.5%           | 0.90 |      |
| Stock B          | 13.0            | 1.15 |      |
| Stock C          | 14.5            | 1.20 |      |
| Risk-free Asset  |                 | 6.0  | 0.00 |

**Solution:** For Stock A:  $\dfrac{E(R_a)\; -\; R_f}{\beta_A} \;=\; \dfrac{.105\; -\; .06}{0.90} \;=\; .050 \;=\; 5.0\%$

For Stocks B and C, the reward-to-risk ratios are 6.087% and 7.083%, respectively.

**For Problems 24 to 28, assume the risk-free rate is 6% and the expected return for the market portfolio is 14%.**

## Problem 24

Write the basic equation for the capital asset pricing model.  Using the information above, what is the intercept of the CAPM? What is the slope of the CAPM?  What is the market risk premium?

**Solution:** The equation for the CAPM is:  $E(R_i) \;=\; R_f \;+\; [E(R_M) - R_f] \times \beta_i$ , where $E(R_i)$ and $\beta_i$ are the expected return and beta, respectively, for any asset.  The intercept of the CAPM is $R_f = 6\%$, and the slope is:

$$[E(R_M) - R_f] = 14\% - 6\% = 8\%$$

Therefore, in this example, the equation for the CAPM is:   $E(R_i) = 6\% + 8\% \times \beta_i$

The market risk premium is the same as the slope of the CAPM:   $[E(R_M) - R_f] = 14\% - 6\% = 8\%$

## Problem 25

Speiss Corporation has a beta of 2. What is its expected return?

**Solution:** $E(R_i) = 6\% + (8\% \times \beta_i) = .06 + (.08 \times 2) = .22 = 22\%$

## Problem 26

Suppose an individual invests $4,000 in a portfolio as follows: $2,800 invested in Speiss common stock and $1,200 invested in the risk-free asset. What are the portfolio weights for this portfolio? What is the expected return for the portfolio? What is the beta for the portfolio?

**Solution:** $x_{risk-free} = (\$1,200 / \$4,000) = .30 = 30\%$   $x_{Speiss} = (\$2,800 / \$4,000) = .70 = 70\%$

The expected return for the portfolio is:  $E(R_p) = (.30 \times .06) + (.70 \times .22) = .172 = 17.2\%$

Beta for the risk-free asset is zero, so the portfolio beta is:  $\beta_p = (.30 \times 0) + (.70 \times 2) = 1.4$

Note: If we substitute this portfolio beta of 1.4 into the CAPM equation, we get the same expected return of 17.2%.

## Problem 27

What are the portfolio weights for a portfolio comprised of Speiss common stock and the risk-free asset which has a portfolio beta equal to 1.5? What is the expected return for this portfolio?

**Solution:** To form a portfolio with beta equal to 1.5, the investor must solve the following equation for $x_1$:

$$\beta_p = (x_1 + \beta_1) + [(1 - x_1) \times \beta_2)] = 1.5 = [x_1 \times 0] + [(1 - x_1) \times 2]$$

where $x_1$ is the proportion of the portfolio invested in the risk-free asset and $(1 - x_1)$ is the proportion invested in Speiss common stock. The solution for $x_1$ is .25, so the portfolio weights are $x_1 = .25 = 25\%$ and $x_2 = (1 - x_1) = .75 = 75\%$. That is, the individual invests 25% of his money in the risk-free asset and 75% in Speiss common stock.

The expected return for the portfolio is:

$$E(R_p) = 6\% + (8\% \times \beta_p) = .06 + (.08 \times 1.5) = .18 = 18\%$$

Alternatively,

$$E(R_p) = 0.25 \times .06 + .75 \times .22 = .18 = 18\%$$

**Problem 28**

Dorigan Corporation has a beta of 1.45 and an expected return of 15%. Given the CAPM equation of Problem 20, is Dorigan common stock correctly priced?

**Solution:** The expected return for a stock with beta equal to 1.45 is:

$$E(R_i) = 6\% + (8\% \times \beta_i) = .06 + (.08 \times 1.45) = .176 = 17.6\%$$

According to the CAPM, a security with $\beta = 1.45$ should have $E(R_i)$ equal to 17.6%. Dorigan Corporation common stock has an expected return of only 15%. Consequently, Dorigan's common stock is over-priced; we would expect that demand for Dorigan will be low, resulting in a lower price and higher expected return.

**Problem 29**

Assume the four stocks below plot on the SML. What is the equation for the SML? Fill in the missing numbers.

| Security | $E(R_j)$ | $Var(R_j)$ | $\beta_j$ |
|---|---|---|---|
| 1 | .07 | .0225 | |
| 2 | .14 | .0400 | 0.8 |
| 3 | .10 | .1225 | |
| 4 | .07 | .0000 | |

**Solution:** Security 4 has a 7% expected return and zero variance. Thus Security 4 is a risk-free asset, and the risk-free rate is 7%. Beta for Security 4 must be zero. Security 1 also has an expected return of 7%. Therefore, Security 1 must also be a risk-free asset and must have beta equal to zero. Security 2 has beta equal to 0.8.

Note: In a strictly theoretical sense, Security 1, being a risk-free asset should have a variance of zero. However, in practical terms, the risk-free asset may have a slight variance (in practice, even T-bills are not completely without risk of any kind). However, the beta of the risk-free asset is always zero.

We can solve for the expected return on the market using the information for Security 2. We know the risk-free rate, the expected return, and the beta. We solve the equation:

$$.14 = .07 + [E(R_M) - .07] \times .8; \quad \text{Solving, } E(R_M) = 15.75\%$$

Security 3 has an expected return [$E(R_3)$] of 10%. We can solve for the beta value of Security 3 ($\beta_3$) by substituting into the CAPM, as follows:

$$.10 = 7\% + (.1575 - .07) \times \beta$$
$$.03 = (.0875 \times \beta_3)$$
$$\beta_3 = (.03/.0875) = .343$$

**Use the following information to solve Problems 30 to 32.**

The possible rates of return for assets X and M for five possible states of the economy are listed in the table below, along with the probability of occurrence:

| State of economy | Probability of state of economy (Pr) | | Rate of return if state occurs (R) | |
|---|---|---|---|---|
| | | | X | M |
| 1 | .20 | .03 | .09 | |
| 2 | .20 | | .17 | .16 |
| 3 | .30 | | .28 | .10 |
| 4 | .20 | | .05 | .02 |
| 5 | .10 | .04 | .16 | |

Work these problems on your own. The answers are given below.

## Problem 30

Calculate the expected return for asset X and asset M.

**Solution:** Asset X:  E(R)  =  13%;   Asset M: E(R)  =  10%

## Problem 31

What is the standard deviation for asset X? For asset M?

**Solution:** Asset X:  11.507%;   Asset M: 4.879%

## Problem 32

Assume that Asset M is the market portfolio, and that Asset X is a capital budgeting project under consideration by a corporation. If Asset X is to be financed with equity, and $\beta_x$ is equal to 1.25, then what is the required rate of return for Asset X, according to the CAPM? (The risk-free rate is 6%.)

**Solution:** The intercept of the CAPM is $R_f = 6\%$ and the slope is:  $[E(R_M) - R_f] = 10\% - 6\% = 4\%$

In this example, the CAPM equation is:  $E(R_i) = 6\% + (4\% \times \beta_i)$

For Asset X:  $E(R_X) = 6\% + (4\% \times \beta_X)$  =  $.06 + (.04 \times 1.25)$  =  $.11 = 11\%$

Therefore, the required return, or cost of capital, is 11%. Since Asset X has an expected return of 13%, it is an acceptable investment.

# 14      <u>Cost of Capital</u>

## CHAPTER HIGHLIGHTS

The appropriate discount rate for evaluating a capital budgeting project depends on the riskiness of the project. In this chapter, we establish the relationship between the risk level of a capital budgeting project and the relevant discount rate for the project. This required rate of return is the weighted average cost of capital.

## THE COST OF CAPITAL: SOME PRELIMINARIES

Remember that firms should undertake investments which have positive NPVs. Another way to state this is that the return provided by the project is greater than the return required by investors for providing the firm with the capital to undertake the project.   When the project is risky, the return required by investors increases to compensate for the additional risk. We refer to the return demanded by investors as the *required return*, the *appropriate discount rate*, and the *cost of capital*. The main concept is that the cost of capital for a given investment depends on the risk of that particular investment. In other words, *the cost of capital depends on the use, not the source, of funds.*

In determining the firm's cost of capital, we will assume that the firm's capital structure is fixed. That is, the firm will maintain a fixed debt/equity ratio that reflects the firm's target capital structure. The firm's overall cost of capital reflects the required return on the firm's total assets. So, we must consider the costs of both debt and equity in determining the overall cost of capital.

## THE COST OF EQUITY

There are two approaches for computing the cost of equity capital: the dividend growth model approach and the security market line approach.

**The Dividend Growth Model Approach:** The constant dividend growth model for a firm's stock price is:

$$P_0 = \frac{D_0 \times (1 + g)}{R_E - g} = \frac{D_1}{R_E - g}$$

where $P_0$ is the current price of the firm's stock, $D_0$ is the most recent dividend paid, $D_1$ is next year's projected dividend, and $R_E$ is the required return on the firm's stock. Solving this equation for $R_E$:

$$R_E = (D_1 / P_0) + g$$

Therefore, if $D_0$, $P_0$, and g are known, the cost of equity capital, $R_E$, can be determined. Note that if $D_0$ and g are known, then $D_1$ can be computed.   The variable g is not directly observable and therefore must be estimated.   If historical data are representative of future growth rates, g can be estimated from historical dividend data. Alternatively, an estimate of g can be based on forecasts of future dividend payments or growth rates.

**An Example:**   A firm has recently declared and paid a dividend of $2.50 per share of common stock. The current price of the common stock is $20 per share, and it is estimated that the dividend will increase at a rate of 4% per year for the foreseeable future. Compute the cost of equity capital.

First, compute $D_1$:       $D_1$   =   $D_0 \times (1 + g)$   =   $\$2.50 \times 1.04$   =   $2.60

Next, using the dividend growth model:

$$R_E   =   (D_1 / P_0)   +   g   =   (\$2.60 / \$20)   +   .04   =   .17   =   17\%$$

**Estimating g:**   There are three ways of estimating the growth rate g.

1)        Using historical growth rates.

**An Example:**   Suppose you observe the following dividends:

| Year | Dividend per share |
|------|--------------------|
| 1993 | $1.87 |
| 1994 | 2.24 |
| 1995 | 2.24 |
| 1996 | 2.48 |
| 1997 | 2.74 |
| 1998 | 3.01 |

What is the compound growth rate in dividends?

The historical compound growth rate (five periods of growth) is approximately 10% (exactly 9.9879%). Then, $1.87 $\times$ FVIF(g%, 5) = $3.01. Solving for g%, we get 10% as an estimate of the growth rate.

2)        Estimate based on retention rate. This can be used when the firm's investment rate is less than its retention rate.  The retention ratio is the percentage of earnings *not* paid out as dividends.  It is defined as retained earnings divided by net revenue (or 1 − payout ratio, payout ratio being dividends divided by net income) and the ROE is net income after interest and taxes divided by common shareholders' equity.  The following equation can be used to solve for the estimated growth rate:

$$1 + g   =   1   +   \text{Retention ratio x Return on retained earnings}$$

3)        Analysts' forecasts of future growth rates (available from the research departments of investment dealers) may also be used to estimate the growth rate.

The deficiencies of the dividend growth model approach are: (1) it is based on an assumption of constant growth in dividends, (2) the value of g must be estimated, and forecasting errors have a direct impact on the estimate of $R_E$, and (3) the dividend growth model does not explicitly consider risk.

**The SML Approach:**   The SML approach is based on the CAPM equation for the expected (required) return on an asset:   $E(R_i) = R_f + \beta_i \times [E(R_M) - R_f]$.   In using the CAPM to compute the cost of equity capital, we assume the required return ($R_E$) is the same as the expected return, $E(R_i)$, so the above equation is now written:

$$R_E = R_f + \beta_E \times (R_M - Rf)$$

**An Example:**  Suppose the market risk premium is 8.5%, the risk-free rate is 5.5%, and the Pettway Company has $\beta$ equal to 0.7. Use the SML to compute the firm's cost of equity capital.

The expected return is:

$$R_E = R_f + \beta_E \times (R_M - R_f) \quad = \quad .055 + (.7 \times .085) = .1145 = 11.45\%$$

Investors expect a return of 11.45% for investing in Pettway common stock.

The advantages of the SML approach are: (1) it explicitly adjusts for risk; and (2) it is applicable to any firm for which the value of $\beta$ can be determined. However, this approach requires that both $\beta$ and the market risk premium $(R_M - R_f)$ be determined. Again, this requires estimation because these values are not known with certainty. And, as with the dividend growth model approach, we are relying on the past to predict future betas and returns.


## THE COSTS OF DEBT AND PREFERRED STOCK

In addition to equity financing, corporations also use debt and preferred stock financing. The costs of these types of financing are discussed below.

**The Cost of Debt:**  The cost of debt financing $(R_D)$ is the market interest rate the firm would pay on new debt. This cost can be observed directly in the financial markets in the following ways:

1)      The rate on new debt will equal the current yield on the firm's existing debt.
2)      The rate on new debt will equal the current yield on debt securities issued by other firms of similar risk.

In each case, the yield to maturity can be determined using the trial-and-error approach described in Chapter 7.

**An Example:** Suppose BC Ltd. will issue bonds with 15-year maturity and a coupon rate of 9.75% for $950.50 each. What is BC's cost of debt?

We can use the approximation formula from Chapter 7 to calculate the yield to maturity on this bond:

$$YTM = \frac{\text{Coupon} + (\text{Face value} - \text{Price}) / \text{Maturity}}{(\text{Price} + \text{Face value}) / 2} = \frac{\$97.50 + (\$1,000 - \$950.50) / 15}{(\$950.50 + \$1,000) / 2} = 10.34\%$$

The exact yield using a financial calculator is 10.42% . This is the cost of new debt issued by the firm.

**The Cost of Preferred Stock:**   The cost of preferred stock financing $(R_p)$ can also be observed in the financial markets.   A firm which expects to issue preferred stock would compute the yield for either its own currently outstanding preferred stock issue or for preferred stock issued by other firms with ratings similar to that which the firm expects to issue.    Since the dividend paid on preferred stock is a perpetuity, the expected return can be computed using the valuation equation from Chapter 8: $R_p \quad = \quad D / P_0$, where D is the constant annual dividend payment and $P_0$ is the current price per share of the preferred stock.

**An Example:**   As of September 21, 1995, the Island Lighting Company (ILCo), a gas and electric utility, had several issues of preferred stock outstanding. One of these issues paid an annual dividend of $4.35 per share and was trading at a price of $42 per share.  Two other issues paid dividends of $8.12 and $8.30  and had market prices of $78.50 and $80.50, respectively.   What is ILCo's cost of preferred stock financing on September 21?

The return for the first issue is:   $4.35 / $42  =  10.357%.  The returns for the other two issues are 10.344% and 10.311%, respectively.  So, the cost of preferred stock financing for ILCo is between 10.3% and 10.4%.

## THE WEIGHTED AVERAGE COST OF CAPITAL

The firm's overall cost of capital is its weighted average cost of capital (WACC). Although the WACC can incorporate many financing sources, our discussion will concentrate on long-term debt and equity as the two major components of the WACC. The discussion will also assume that the firm's optimal mix of debt and equity has already been established.

**The Capital Structure Weights:**  For a firm that uses both debt and equity financing, the average cost of capital is the total amount the firm expects to pay, to both shareholders and bondholders, per dollar of financing obtained.  The total cost of debt, measured in dollars, is $(D \times R_D)$, where D is the market value of the firm's debt. The total cost of equity is $(E \times R_E)$, where E is the market value of the firm's equity. The average cost of capital is the total cost of equity $(E \times R_E)$ plus the total cost of debt $(D \times R_D)$, divided by V, the total value of the firm's capital, where V $= (E + D)$. The firm's *average cost of capital* is:

$$\text{WACC (unadjusted)}  =  (E / V) \times R_E  +  (D / V) \times R_D$$

This expression  indicates that the average cost of capital is a weighted average of the firm's cost of equity $(R_E)$ and the firm's cost of debt $(R_D)$.  The weights are the proportion of the total firm value represented by equity $(E/V)$ and the proportion represented by debt $(D/V)$. This weighted average is the *unadjusted* weighted average cost of capital (WACC).  It is 'unadjusted' in the sense that it ignores the effect of taxes on the firm's cost of debt.

**Taxes and the Weighted Average Cost of Capital:**  Interest is a tax-deductible expense, while dividends paid to shareholders are not tax-deductible.   Consequently, the above calculation of the WACC must be adjusted to reflect this difference in tax treatment.   Consider a firm with $R_D = 10\%$ and a corporate tax rate $(T_c)$ equal to 34%. If the firm pays 10% interest on $1,000 of debt, the before-tax cost of the debt is:   $D \times R_D = \$1,000 \times 10\% = \$100$.  Since the $100 interest expense is tax-deductible, it reduces the firm's taxable income by $100 and consequently reduces the firm's taxes by:   $D \times R_D \times T_C = \$1,000 \times .10 \times .34 = \$34$.  The after-tax cost of debt, measured in dollars, is therefore:   $D \times R_D \times (1 - T_c) = \$1,000 \times .10 \times (1 - .34) = \$66$

The after-tax cost of debt, as an interest rate, is $[R_D \times (1 - T_c)]$, and the unadjusted WACC developed in the preceding section must be adjusted as follows:

$$\text{WACC}  =  (E / V) \times R_E  +  (D / V) \times R_D \times (1 - T_C)$$

The WACC is the rate of return which the firm must earn on its investments in order to be able to exactly compensate the debt holders and equity holders who provide the financing to the firm. The WACC is thus the required return for the firm's investments, and it is the appropriate discount rate to use in analysis of capital budgeting projects.

One important qualification to this interpretation of the WACC must be kept in mind, however. The calculation of both the cost of debt and the cost of equity is based on the implicit assumption that *the risk level of a proposed capital-budgeting project is the same as the existing risk level of the firm*. Therefore, using the WACC as computed above is only appropriate when the project under consideration has the same risk as the overall risk of the firm. If the proposed project has a different risk level, adjustments in the discount rate must be made.

**An Example:**  Assume Pettway's cost of equity is 11.45%. The yield to maturity on Pettway's debt is 8%. The total market value of Pettway's equity is $240 million, and the value of the debt is $160 million. Pettway's corporate tax rate is 34%. Compute the WACC for Pettway.

The WACC is:   WACC   =   ($240 / $400) x .1145  +  ($160 / $400) x .08 x (1 - .34)   =   0.08982   =   8.982%

The WACC can be used as the discount rate for determining the NPV of a proposed capital budgeting project. Consider the following example:

**An Example:** Pettway is considering moving its operations from Quebec to Ontario to obtain a more geographically central location. The cash flows derived from this investment are expected to be $25,000 per year for the next 25 years. The cost of the move is estimated at $175,000. Should Pettway move its operations?

The cash inflows for this investment are in the form of an annuity. The WACC computed in the preceding example is the appropriate discount rate here because this investment can be considered to be in the same risk class as the firm. The present value of the investment is:   PV = C × PVIFA(WACC, t)   =   $25,000 x 9.836922   =   $245,923.05. The NPV is:   $245,923.05   -   $175,000   =   $70,923.05.   Since the net present value is positive, Pettway should relocate.

**Divisional and Project Costs of Capital:** When a proposed investment is in a risk class different from the firm's risk class, we determine the expected return on financial market investments in the same risk class as the proposed investment, and use that rate to discount the cash flows from the new project.   We do *not* use the firm's WACC when the risk of the investment differs from that of the firm.   For a new investment, we require that its return must be at least as great as the return for other investments of similar risk. The project, considered in isolation from the overall firm, can be accepted or rejected on this basis.   Using the WACC to evaluate projects in a different risk class may lead to poor decisions.   The firm will accept risky projects because they have been evaluated at too low a discount rate, and the firm will reject less risky projects because the cost of capital used to evaluate them was too high.

Similarly, projects undertaken by a division cannot be properly evaluated using the firm's WACC.

## FLOTATION COSTS AND THE WEIGHTED AVERAGE COST OF CAPITAL

If the firm must issue new securities to obtain the required financing for a new project, then any flotation costs associated with the new issue are incremental costs. They must be incorporated into the NPV analysis.

**An Example:**   The Brite Lites Production Company, an all-equity firm, is evaluating an investment in a new production studio with a 10-year useful life. The cost of the studio is $460,000, which would be financed by an issue of new common stock. Flotation costs are 8% of the amount of stock issued. The incremental after-tax cash inflow is expected to be $95,000 per year throughout the life of the studio. The corporate tax rate is 34% and the firm's cost of equity capital is 15%.

Brite Lites is an all-equity firm, so the WACC is equal to the cost of equity capital. Because the cash inflows are in the form of an annuity, the present value is computed as follows:

$$PV = C \times PVIFA(WACC, t)   =   \$95,000 \times PVIFA (15\%, 10)   =   \$95,000 \times 5.018769   =   \$476,783.05$$

If we ignore flotation costs for the new stock issue, then the net present value would be:

NPV = $476,783.05 − $460,000 = +$16,783.05

However, the flotation costs represent an additional expense associated with the capital budgeting project, and must be incorporated into the analysis. First, we compute the flotation costs for the new stock issue. Since Brite Lites requires $460,000 of financing, the firm will have to issue more than $460,000 of equity in order to net from the issue the required amount of financing. The dollar value of the stock issue is the value of X in the following equation:
$460,000 = (1 − .08) × X

That is, in order to obtain $460,000 in financing, after paying the 8% flotation costs, the firm must issue $500,000 of common stock to net $460,000 after paying flotation costs.  The flotation costs are ($500,000 − $460,000) = $40,000, and the true cost of the studio is $500,000. The actual net present value is:

NPV = $476,783.05 − $500,000 = −$23,216.95

Therefore, when flotation costs are taken into consideration, the investment in the studio is unacceptable.

In the preceding example, the firm is an all-equity firm. For a firm which uses both debt and equity financing, it is necessary to compute a weighted-average flotation cost.

**An Example:**   Suppose the Brite Lites Production Company has a capital structure of 75% equity and 25% debt. Assume all other relevant data are as presented in the preceding example.  The cost of debt capital is 10%, with flotation costs equal to 4% of the amount of debt issued. Compute the net present value of the investment in the production studio.

First, the WACC is:  WACC  =  0.75 x .15  +  0.25 x 0.10 x (1 - .34)  =  12.90%

The weighted average flotation costs are:

$f_a$  =  (E / V) x $f_E$  +  (D / V) x $f_D$  =  .75 x .08  +  .25 x .04  =  7%

The firm must raise $460,000 / (1 - .07)  =  $494,623.66 in order to net the $460,000 necessary to finance the investment.  So, the project's NPV is:

NPV  =  $95,000 x PVIFA(12.90%, 10 yrs)  -  $494,623.66  =  $517,559.96  -  $494,623.66
        = $22,936.30

The NPV is positive even after taking into consideration the flotation costs, so the firm should proceed with the investment.

## CONCEPT TEST

1.      For a specified level of $\beta$, the CAPM specifies the _____ available in the financial markets.  Since the cost of capital specifies the minimum acceptable return for a capital budgeting project, it is also referred to as the _____ .

2.      Since some financing is obtained through debt and some through equity, the firm's overall cost of capital must reflect both sources.  This overall cost of capital is referred to as the _____ .

3.      Under the assumption that dividends grow at a constant rate (g), the dividend growth model specifies that the price of a share of stock ($P_0$) is given by the equation: $P_0$ = _____ .  Solving this equation for $R_E$, the cost of equity capital is:  $R_E$ = _____ .  Of the required data, only _____ is not directly observable and therefore must be estimated.

4.      The deficiencies of the dividend growth model approach to computing the cost of equity capital are: (1) it is based on an assumption of _____ ; (2) the value of _____ must be estimated, and forecasting errors have a direct impact on the estimate of $R_E$; and, (3) the dividend growth model does not explicitly consider _____ .

5.      The expected or required return for a share of stock can be determined by using CAPM as:  $E(R_i)$ = _____ .

6.      The advantages of the SML approach to computing the cost of equity capital are: (1) it explicitly adjusts for _____ ; and, (2) it is applicable to any firm for which the value of _____ can be determined. However, this approach requires that both _____ and the _____ be determined. Since neither of these quantities can be known with certainty, the value of $R_E$ may be inaccurate.

7.      The cost of debt financing ($R_D$) is the interest rate that the firm will have to pay on new debt. The interest rate investors expect on a new bond issue can be determined by computing the _____ for the company's _____ . Alternatively, it is possible to determine the cost of new debt financing by computing the _____ for bonds with a _____ similar to that of the bonds the firm would issue.

8.      The cost of preferred stock financing ($R_p$) can be observed in the financial markets. A firm which  expects to issue preferred stock would compute the yield for either _____ or for _____ . Since the dividend paid on preferred stock is in the form of a _____ , the dividend yield can be computed directly as:      $R_p$ = _____ .

9.      The overall measure of the cost of capital for the firm is the _____ .  For a firm that uses both debt and equity financing, the average cost of capital is the total amount the firm expects to pay, to both shareholders and bondholders, per dollar of financing obtained.  For a firm with debt level D and cost of debt $R_D$, the before-tax cost of debt, measured in dollars, is _____ . For a firm with equity level E and cost of debt $R_E$, the total cost of equity is _____ . The average cost of capital is the total cost of equity plus the total cost of debt, divided by _____ . The unadjusted weighted average cost of capital (WACC) for the firm is computed as follows: WACC(unadjusted)  = _____ .

10.     Interest (is/is not) a tax-deductible expense, and dividends paid to shareholders (are/are not) tax-deductible. For a firm with debt level D and cost of debt $R_D$, the before-tax cost of the debt is _____ . The payment of this amount of interest reduces the firm's taxes by _____ . The after-tax cost of debt, measured in dollars, is therefore equal to _____ . The after-tax cost of debt, as an interest rate, is _____ .

11.     The (adjusted) weighted average cost of capital (WACC) is:  WACC = _____

12.     The calculation of both the cost of debt and the cost of equity is based on the implicit assumption that  the risk level of a proposed capital-budgeting project is the same as the _____ . Consequently, application of the WACC to a proposed capital-budgeting project is appropriate if the risk level of the

proposed project does not differ significantly from the _____ . The net present value criterion requires that we determine the NPV for an investment, using the appropriate discount rate. The appropriate discount rate to use in computing the NPV depends on the _____ .

13.     When a proposed investment is in a risk class different from the firm's risk class, we determine the expected return on financial market investments in the same _____ as the proposed investment, and use that rate to discount the cash flows from the new project. What we require of a new investment is that its return must be at least as great as the return for other investments of _____ .

14.     Comparable conclusions apply to corporations which have divisions engaged in different businesses with significantly different risk levels; in this case, the relevant cost of capital for each division of the firm depends on the _____ .

15.     If a firm uses its WACC to evaluate projects that do not belong in the same risk class as the firm's other projects, the firm will make incorrect accept/reject decisions. The firm will tend to _____ riskier projects because the discount rate used was too _____ . The firm will tend to _____ less risky projects because the discount rate used was too _____ .

16.     If a capital budgeting project requires the issue of new securities in order to obtain the required financing, then the flotation costs  (are/are not)  incremental costs associated with the project and  (are/are not)  considered in the net present value analysis.  For a firm which uses both debt and equity financing, it is necessary to compute a weighted-average flotation cost: $f_A$  =  _____ .

## ANSWERS TO CONCEPT TEST

1.      expected return;  required return

2.      weighted average cost of capital (WACC)

3.      $D_1/(R_E - g)$;   $(D_1/P_0) + g$;   g, the dividend growth rate

4.      constant growth in dividends; g; risk

5.      $R_f + \beta_E \times [R_M - R_f]$

6.      risk; $\beta$; $\beta$; market risk premium

7.      yield to maturity; outstanding bonds; yield to maturity; risk level

8.      its own currently outstanding preferred stock issue; preferred stock issued by other firms of similar risk; perpetuity;  $(D/P_0)$

9.      weighted average cost of capital; $(D \times R_D)$; $(E \times R_E)$; the total value of the firm's capital; $[(E/V) \times R_E ] + [(D/V) \times R_D]$

10.     is; are not;  $(D \times R_D)$;  $(D \times R_D \times T_c)$;  $D \times R_D \times (1 - T_c)$;  $R_D \times (1 - T_c)$

11.     $[(E/V) \times R_E] + [(D/V) \times R_D \times (1 - T_c)]$

12.     existing risk level of the firm; risk level of the firm; risk level of the investment

13.     risk class;  similar risk

14.     risk level of the division

15.     accept; low; reject; high

16.     are; are; $[(E/V) \times f_E] + [(D/V) \times f_D]$


## PROBLEMS AND SOLUTIONS


### Problem 1

PMR Corporation's current common stock price is $25 per share, and it recently paid a cash dividend of $3 per share. If the estimated dividend growth rate is 5% per year, compute the cost of equity capital.

**Solution:**

$$D_1 = D_0 \times (1 + g) = \$3 \times 1.05 = \$3.15$$

Use the dividend growth model to determine the cost of equity capital ($R_E$)

$$R_E = (D_1 / P_0) + g = (\$3.15 / \$25) + .05 = .176 = 17.6\%$$


### Problem 2

On January 1, 1985 MAM Industries issued a 30-year bond with a 9% coupon and a $1,000 face value, payable on January 1, 2015. The bond is currently selling for $915. Use the outstanding MAM bond to determine the firm's after-tax cost of debt capital if today's date is January 1, 1995. (Assume annual interest payments and a 34% corporate tax rate.)

**Solution:**  The firm's pre-tax cost of debt capital is the yield to maturity for the outstanding bond issue. Although the bond had 30 years to maturity when it was issued, the relevant time period is now the remaining twenty years to maturity. The yield to maturity is the value of r which solves the equation.

$$\$915 = [\$90 \times \text{PVIFA}(r,20 \text{ years})] + \$1,000 / (1 + r)^{20}$$

Trial and error (or financial calculator) gives a before-tax cost of debt equal to 9.998%. The after-tax cost of debt is:  $.09998 \times (1 - .34) = .06599 = 6.599\%$

## Problem 3

Suppose MAM Industries (see Problem 2) also issued a 30-year bond five years ago (in 1990). The bond has a $1,000 face value and a 10% coupon interest rate. If the bond currently sells for $1,000, what is the after-tax cost of debt capital, as indicated by the market value of this outstanding bond?

**Solution:**  Since the 30-year bond was issued five years ago, the current maturity of the bond is 25 years. The pre-tax cost of debt is the yield to maturity for the bond, or the value of r which solves the equation:

$$\$1,000 \;=\; [\$100 \times \text{PVIFA}(r, 25 \text{ years})] \;+\; \$1,000 / (1 + r)^{25}$$

The required before-tax return is 10%. Note: because the bond is selling at par, the yield must be the same as the coupon rate. So, no actual calculations were necessary. The after-tax cost of debt is $.10 \times (1 - .34) \;=\; 6.6\%$

## Problem 4

Suppose that, five years from now, the MAM bond described in Problem 3 has a market price of $1,100. What is the after-tax cost of debt capital at that time?

**Solution:**   Five years from now, the bond will be a 20-year bond. The yield to maturity at that time would be the value of r in the following equation:

$$\$1,100 \;=\; [\$100 \times \text{PVIFA}(r, 20 \text{ years})] \;+\; \$1,000 / (1 + r)^{20} \; ; \; r \;=\; 8.911\%.$$

The after-tax cost of debt is $8.911 \times (1 - .34) \;=\; 5.881\%$

## Problem 5

MAM Industries has recently declared a dividend of $3.50 per share of common stock. The current price of the firm's common stock is $25 per share, and it is estimated that the dividend will increase at a rate of 4% per year for the foreseeable future. Use the dividend growth model approach to compute the cost of equity capital for MAM Industries.

**Solution:**   In order to compute the cost of equity capital ($R_E$), first compute $D_1$ as follows:

$$D_1 = D_0 \times (1 + g) = \$3.50 \times 1.04 = \$3.64$$

Using the dividend growth model to compute $R_E$, we find:

$$R_E \;=\; D_1 / P_0 \;+\; g \;=\; \$3.64 / \$25 \;+\; .04 \;=\; .1856 \;=\; 18.56\%$$

## Problem 6

Suppose that the market risk premium is 8.5%, the risk-free rate is 7.0%, and MAM Industries has β equal to 1.35. Use the SML to compute the firm's cost of equity capital.

**Solution:** The cost of equity capital ($R_E$) is:

$$R_E = R_f + \beta_E \times [R_M - R_f] \quad = \quad .070 + (1.35 \times .085\ ) = \ .18475 \ = \ 18.475\%$$

## Problem 7

MAM industries has paid the following dividends over the last five years:  $2.83, $3.05, $3.27, $3.44, and $3.50. Use the dividend growth model to compute the cost of equity capital.

**Solution:** First, we need to calculate the historical growth rate based on the firm's dividend payouts.  The growth rate is found by solving for g in the following equation:

$$\$3.50 \quad = \quad \$2.83\,(1 + g)^5$$

The growth rate is .0434  =  4.34%.  Then, using the dividend growth model, the required return on equity is:

$$R_E \quad = \quad \$3.50 \,/\, \$25 \ + \ .0434 \ = \ .1834 \ = \ 18.34\%$$

## Problem 8

Suppose that MAM Industries has a debt/equity ratio of 0.50. Use the data in Problems 2, 3, 5, and 6 to compute the unadjusted weighted average cost of capital for MAM Industries.

**Solution:**  Problem 2 indicates the pre-tax cost of debt capital, based on the yield to maturity for a 20-year MAM Industries bond, is 9.998%. In Problem 3, we also determined that the pre-tax cost of debt capital, based on the yield for a 25 year bond, is 10.0%. Therefore, the cost of debt capital ($R_D$) for MAM is essentially equal to 10%. Problems 5 and 6 indicate that the cost of equity capital is 18.56% (using the dividend growth model approach) or 18.475% (using the SML approach).  Consequently, it is appropriate to estimate that the cost of equity capital ($R_E$) is 18.5%.

A debt/equity ratio of 0.50 indicates that the firm has $0.50 of debt financing for each $1 of equity financing. Therefore, (E/V) = [$1/($.50 + $1)] = 2/3, and (D/V) = [$.50/($.50 + $1)] = 1/3. The unadjusted weighted average cost of capital (WACC) is:

$$\text{WACC (unadjusted)} \quad = \quad 2/3 \times .185 \ + \ 1/3 \times .10 \ = \ .15667 \ = \ 15.667\%$$

## Problem 9

Use the data above to compute the adjusted weighted average cost of capital for MAM Industries.

**Solution:** The values of (E/V) and (D/V) are the same as in the solution to Problem 8. The value of $R_E$ is 18.5%, and the value of $R_D$ is 10%.  The WACC, after adjusting for the effect of taxes,  is computed as:

$$\text{WACC}_{(adjusted)} \quad = \quad 2/3 \times .185 \ + \ 1/3 \times .10 \times (1 - .34) \quad = \quad .14533 \ = \ 14.533\%$$

## Problem 10

Filimon Corporation needs to purchase $400,000 worth of new machinery. The machinery will be financed by issuing $150,000 of new equity, the rest in bonds. The firm's required return on equity is 15%, and the return on its bonds is 10%. The corporate tax rate is 34%. What are the unadjusted and adjusted weighted average costs of capital?

**Solution:**

$$WACC_{unadjusted} = (E / V) \times R_E + D (D / V) \times R_D$$
$$= (\$150,000 / \$400,000) \times .15 + (\$250,000 / \$400,000) \times .10 = .11875 = 11.88\%$$

$$WACC_{adjusted} = (E / V) \times R_E + D (D / V) \times R_D \times (1 - T_C)$$
$$= (\$150,000 / \$400,000) \times .15 + (\$250,000 / \$400,000) \times .10 \times (1 - .34) = .0975$$
$$= 9.75\%$$

## Problem 11

Coprez Corporation has issued dividends of $3.15, $3.59, $3.90, and $4.37 over the past four years. Use the dividend growth model to calculate the firm's cost of equity capital if the price per share is currently $27.

**Solution:** The growth rate of Coprez can be found using $4.37 $= \$3.15 \times (1+g)^4$. Solving for g, the growth rate is 8.5%. The cost of equity capital is therefore:

$$R_E = \$4.37 / \$27 + 0.085 = .2469 = 24.69\%$$

## Problem 12

If Coprez Corporation's cost of debt is 8.33% and the firm has a debt/equity ratio of 0.75, what is the firm's WACC if the corporate tax rate is 34%?

**Solution:** A debt/equity ratio of 0.75 means that the firm has $0.75 of debt finance for each $1 of equity of equity financing. E/V is therefore [$1.00 / ($1.00 + $0.75) ] = 4/7, and D/V = [$0.75 / ($1.00 + $0.75)] = 3/7. It follows that:

$$WACC = 4/7 \times 0.2469 + 3/7 \times 0.0833 \times (1 - .34) = .1646 = 16.46\%$$

## Problem 13

Omega Electronics needs to buy $350,000 worth of new equipment. The equipment will be financed by issuing new debt and equity. Omega plans to issue $150,000 in bonds; the remainder will be equity financing. The firm's required return on equity is 17%, and the return on its bonds is 9%. The corporate tax rate is 40%. What are the unadjusted and adjusted weighted average costs of capital?

**Solution:**

$$\text{WACC}_{\text{(unadjusted)}} = (\$200,000 / \$350,000) \times .17 + (\$150,000 / \$350,000) \times .09 = .1357 = 13.57\%$$

$$\text{WACC}_{\text{(adjusted)}} = (\$200,000 / \$350,000) \times .17 + (\$150,000 / \$350,000) \times .09 \times (1 - .4) = 12.03\%$$

## Problem 14

Suppose that MAM Industries is considering an expansion of its facilities. This expansion requires that MAM obtain $690,000 of financing. Flotation costs for debt and equity are 6% and 9%, respectively. If flotation costs are considered, what is the true cost of the expansion?

**Solution:** The weighted average flotation cost for MAM is:

$$f_A = (2/3 \times .09) + (1/3 \times .06) = .08 = 8\%$$

The total financing required is the value of X in the following equation: $\$690,000 = (1 - .08) \times X$. Solving, we find that the firm must obtain total financing of ($690,000/.92) = $750,000. This is the true cost of the expansion.

## Problem 15

Rainy Days real estate development company plans to borrow $900,000 to acquire new properties. The company's cost of debt is 12%, and its corporate tax rate is 30%. If flotation costs are expected to be 2%, how much does Rainy Days need to borrow? What is the after-tax cost of debt financing?

**Solution:** They must borrow $900,000 / .98 = $918,367.35. The after-tax cost of debt financing is .12 x (1 - .30) = 8.4%.

## Problem 16

MAM Industries has an issue of preferred stock outstanding. It pays an annual dividend of $3.25 per share and currently has a market price of $25 per share. Compute the cost of preferred stock capital for MAM.

**Solution:** The yield for the outstanding issue is: $R_P = D / P_0 = \$3.25 / \$25 = .13 = 13\%$

## Problem 17

Suppose that MAM's capital structure is 30% debt, 10% preferred stock, and 60% equity. Use the information from Problems 8 and 16 to compute weighted average cost of capital.

**Solution:** The weighted average cost of capital is computed using the weights for all three sources of capital:

$$\text{WACC} = .60 \times .185 + .10 \times .13 + .30 \times .10 \times (1 - .34) = .1438 = 14.38\%$$

## Problem 18

Refer to the information on MAM in Problems 8 and 14.  If the proposed investment generates after-tax cash flows of $100,000 for the next 10 years, should MAM undertake the project?  Be sure to consider flotation costs..

**Solution:** The weighted average cost of capital, established earlier is 15.667%.  The actual investment, considering flotation costs, is $750,000.  So, the NPV of the proposed project is:

$$NPV = \$100,000 \times PVIFA(15.667\%, 10 \text{ yrs}) - \$750,000 = \$489,375.81 - \$750,000$$
$$= -\$260,624.19$$

The NPV is negative, so they should not take the project.

## Problem 19

As of November 19, 1995, Illinois Power had several outstanding issues of preferred stock listed on the New York Stock Exchange. On November 19, 1995, one issue of Illinois Power preferred stock had a market price of $39 5/8 and paid an annual dividend of $4 per share. As of the same date, two other issues of Illinois Power preferred stock had prices of $21 1/4 and $39 7/8, respectively, and paid annual dividends of $2.13 and $4.12, respectively. What is Illinois Power's cost of preferred stock financing on November 19, 1995?

**Solution:**   The return for the first issue is computed as follows:

$$R_p = \$4.00 / \$39.625 = .100946 = 10.096\%$$

Returns for the other issues are 10.02% and 10.33%, respectively.   So, a good estimate for the required rate of return on preferred stock is between 10.0% and 10.35%.

### Use the following information to solve Problems 20 to 23:

Margo Corporation is a major producer of lawn care products. Margo stock currently sells for $80 per share; there are 10.5 million shares outstanding. Margo also has debt outstanding with an aggregate book value of $400 million. The bonds issued by Margo are currently yielding 10%, and are trading at 90% of face value. The risk-free rate is 8%, the market risk premium is 9%, and Margo has a β equal to 2. The corporate tax rate is 34%.

## Problem 20

Margo is considering expansion of its facilities. Use the SML approach to determine the cost of equity capital for Margo.

**Solution:**   $R_E = .080 + (2.00 \times .090) = .2600 = 26\%$

## Problem 21

Compute the weighted average cost of capital for Margo.

**Solution:**   The market value of Margo's equity is (10.5 million × $80) = $840 million. The market value of Margo's debt is (.90 × $400 million) = $360 million. The total market value of the firm is ($840 million + $360 million) = $1.2 billion.

The weighted average cost of capital is:

$$\text{WACC} = (\$840 / \$1,200) \times .26 + (\$360 / \$1,200) \times .10 \times (1 - .34) = .2018 = 20.18\%$$

## Problem 22

The project under consideration by Margo requires an outlay of $1,000,000. The expansion will produce incremental after-tax cash inflows of $350,000 per year for the next five years. Compute the net present value of the investment, assuming the project has the same risk as Margo's other projects.

**Solution:**   The weighted average cost of capital is the appropriate discount rate for this investment since the expansion is in the same risk class as the firm itself. The net present value of the investment is:

$$\text{NPV} = \$350,000 \times \text{PVIFA}(20.18\%, 5 \text{ yrs}) - \$1,000,000 = \$1,042,582 - \$1,000,000 = \$42,582$$

They should accept the project.

## Problem 23

Flotation costs are 5% of the amount of common stock issued and 2% of the amount of debt issued. Using the data from the previous problems, compute the weighted average flotation cost for Margo. Also, compute the net present value of the investment when flotation costs are taken into account.  Should they undertake the project?

**Solution:** The weighted average flotation cost is: $f_A = (\$840 / \$1,200) \times .05 + (\$360 / 1,200) \times .02 = .041 = 4.1\%$. So, the actual cost of the investment is $\$1,000,000 / (1 - .041) = \$1,042,752.87$. And, the NPV is $\$1,042,582 - \$1,042,752.87 = -\$170.87$. They should not accept the project.

## Problem 24

Now assume that the project under consideration is riskier than Margo's existing projects.  The beta for the new project is 2.4.  How should this affect their decision?  (Ignore flotation costs.)

**Solution:** The appropriate cost of equity is $R_E = .08 + .09 \times 2.4 = 29.6\%$. The appropriate discount rate is: $(\$840 / \$1,200) \times .296 + (\$360 / \$1,200) \times .10 \times (1 - .34) = 22.7\%$.

The NPV is: $\$350,000 \times \text{PVIFA}(22.7\%, 5 \text{ yrs}) - \$1,000,000 = \$987,455.13 - \$1,000,000 = -\$12,544.87$.

They should not take the project.  Evaluating the project at the firm's weighted average cost of capital (20.18%) would cause them to accept an unprofitable project.

**Problem 25**

Now assume that the proposed project only has a beta of 1.8.  How does the firm's decision change?

**Solution:**  The appropriate cost of equity is $R_E$  =  .08  + .09 x 1.8  =  24.2%. The appropriate discount rate is:  ($840 / $1,200) x .242  +  ($360 / $1,200) x .10 x (1 - .34)  =  18.92.

The NPV is:  $350,000 x PVIFA(18.92%, 5 yrs)  -  $1,000,000  =  $1,072,086.29 - $1,000,000  = $72,086.29.  They should take the project.  Evaluating the project at the firm's weighted average cost of capital (20.18%) would cause them to reject a profitable project.

# 15     <u>Raising Capital</u>

## CHAPTER HIGHLIGHTS

The sale of securities to the investing public is an essential source of long-term financing for a corporation. To a great extent, the procedures described in this chapter apply to new issues of both debt and equity, but the emphasis is on equity.

Corporations typically use an investment dealer to assist them in a new security issue. The assistance from the investment dealer may include a variety of services including advice on which securities to issue, how to structure and price a deal, complying with disclosure requirements, and guaranteeing the amount of funds the issuer will receive from the new issue.

Securities may be public issues, offered to investors on the primary market. Alternatively, they may be private placements, sold directly to a small number of buyers. Public issues account for the majority of new financing, comprising almost 79% of new Canadian issues in 1998.

## THE FINANCING LIFE CYCLE OF A FIRM: EARLY-STAGE FINANCING AND VENTURE CAPITAL

Start-up companies typically have no assets except for their idea about what their new firm will deliver. That is, they have no track record. Entrepreneurs very often find funding in the *venture capital* market.

**Venture capital:** In general, *venture capital* refers to financing for new, typically high-risk ventures. Venture capital firms pool funds from different sources and invest them in start-up companies. Most often, the source of funds is 'private equity.'

The risk associated with funding a start-up project is quite high. Most will fail. However, when a start-up company succeeds, the profits are huge. To limit their risk, venture capitalists usually supply their funding in stages. That allows the venture capitalist (VC) to get out of the deal if, at any given stage, the venture does not look promising.

**Some Venture Capital Realities:** There is quite a large market for venture capital. However, access to this market is very limited. Much of the access to these markets requires 'networking'; personal contacts are extremely important in gaining access to funds for starting up a business.

**Choosing a Venture Capitalist:** The following should be considered:

    1. Financial strength - Can the venture capitalist support the project through successive phases needed to bring the product to market?

    2. Style - Will the VC be involved in day-to-day operations or be involved on a monthly or yearly basis?

    3. References for the VC - What is their success record?

    4. Contacts - Who does the VC firm know? Specialization may be important here.

5. Exit strategy - Given that VCs are typically short-term investors, how do you negotiate the terms under which they can 'cash out' of the project?

## THE PUBLIC ISSUE

In 1983, the Ontario Securities Commission (OSC) introduced the *Prompt Offering Prospectus* (POP), a streamlined reporting and registration system for large companies that frequently issue securities. Since POP was introduced, *bought deals* have become the most common way to raise new equity. In these offerings, the underwriter takes all the pricing risk.

The Canadian securities market is regulated by provincial commissions and provincial securities acts. Only five provinces have such commissions. In contrast, the U.S. securities market is regulated by a federal body, the Securities and Exchange Commission (SEC). The goal of regulation is an efficient flow of information about securities and the smooth function of securities markets.

The Toronto Stock Exchange (TSE) is Canada's largest securities market, and the major regulatory body in Canada is the Ontario Securities Commission (OSC). The OSC's goal is to ensure that investors receive any relevant information about new issues, through the registration statement and the prospectus.

The OSC also regulates the trading of securities to ensure adequate disclosure of information, establishes disclosure rules for asset transitions between related parties, publishes *insider reports* filed by major shareholders, officers and directors of TSE listed firms, and oversees training and supervision of investment dealers and monitors their capital positions.

**The Basic Procedure for a New Issue:** The first step in issuing new securities is to obtain approval from the board of directors to increase the number of authorized shares. The firm then distributes a *preliminary prospectus* to the OSC and potential investors. This contains much of the financial information that will be included in the final prospectus, but it does not give the offer price. The preliminary prospectus is sometimes called a *red herring*, in part because bold red letters are printed on the cover warning that the OSC has neither approved nor disapproved of the offering. Once the revised, final prospectus meets with the OSC's approval, an offer price is determined and the selling effort gets under way.

*Tombstone advertisements* are used by underwriters during and after the waiting period. They contain information about the issue and list the investment dealers involved in selling the issue. The investment dealers are divided into groups called *brackets* on the tombstone; the higher the bracket, the greater the underwriter's prestige.

An *initial public offering* (IPO), as opposed to a *seasoned new issue* for companies already trading on the TSE, represents a company's first equity issue made available to the public (also known as an unseasoned new issue). Researchers have found that IPOs with prestigious underwriters perform better.

The *Prompt Offering Prospectus* (POP) system has reduced repetitive filing requirements for large companies by allowing them to file interim and annual financial statements regardless of whether they plan an issue during a given year. To use the POP system, issuers must have complied with the continuous disclosure requirements for a period of 36 months. This gives the firms prompt access to capital markets without the need to file detailed financial statements before the issue. A *Multi-Jurisdictional Disclosure System* (MJDS) allows issuers easier and frequent access to both the U.S. and Canadian markets.

## THE CASH OFFER

For a cash offer, *underwriters* help to formulate the method used to issue the securities, price the securities, and sell the securities to the public. The underwriter normally buys the securities from the firm and offers them to the public at a higher price. The difference between the underwriter's buying price and the price at which the underwriter offers the security to the public is called the *spread* or the discount. For large issues, the risk associated with selling the securities to the public is shared by forming a group of investment dealers, called a *syndicate* or *banking group*, headed by a lead underwriter.

**Types of Underwriting:** If the underwriter purchases the entire issue, the issuing firm receives a fixed price for the securities, and all the risk associated with the sale of the securities is transferred to the underwriter. This procedure is called *firm-commitment underwriting*. The underwriter accepts the risk of not being able to sell the securities, in exchange for compensation received in the form of the spread. A related procedure, *regular underwriting*, differs from firm-commitment underwriting in that the banking group has the option to drop the issue if the price drops significantly.

In a *best-efforts offering*, the underwriter does not purchase the securities, but rather acts as an agent and receives a commission for each share sold. The issuing firm bears the risk that the securities cannot be sold at the offer price. This type of underwriting is mostly used for IPOs.

In a *bought deal*, the issuer sells the entire issue to one investment dealer or to a group who then attempts to resell it. Although bought deals are the most popular form of underwriting in Canada today, some investment dealers criticize bought deals for excluding retail investors from access to many new issues and from due diligence investigation. With a bought deal, all the risk of selling the issue is transferred to the underwriter.

**The Selling Period:** The time period immediately after the sale is called the *aftermarket*. The principal underwriter is allowed to buy shares in the aftermarket in order to 'support' or stabilize the price.

**The Overallotment Option:** Underwriting contracts frequently contain an overallotment option (*Green Shoe Provision*), allowing the investment dealer to buy additional shares at the offer price to cover any excess demand. This option is beneficial to the underwriter if the stock price quickly rises above the initial offer price.

**Investment Dealers:** The services of underwriters include providing advice to the issuing firm, underwriting the issue, and marketing the securities. The leading underwriters in Canada are RBC Dominion Securities and BMO Nesbitt Burns. The setting of an appropriate issue price is essential to the investment banker's business. Mispricing affects the issuing firm and the investor, as well as the investment banker's ability to attract underwriting business in the future.

**The Offering Price and Underpricing:** One of the most difficult tasks for an investment banker is the pricing of an IPO. If the price is too low, the firm's existing shareholders incur an opportunity loss; if it is too high, the issue fails to sell. New issues are typically underpriced, which is beneficial to new shareholders, but detrimental to existing shareholders. Existing shareholders are, in effect, selling a portion of the firm they own at a price below its market value. The degree of underpricing varies considerably, but underpricing is usually greater for smaller issues.

**The Decision to Go Public:** The major advantages of going public are: greater access to new capital, more information available to new investors because of disclosure requirements, and the possibility for owners to diversify their personal portfolios by selling some shares yet retaining control of the firm. The disadvantages are: stricter (and costly) disclosure and regulatory requirements, and the time spent by management in complying with these requirements and providing information to investment analysts.

**Pricing IPOs:** In general, firms providing lots of high-quality information get higher prices for their IPOs. This implies that larger firms have an advantage in going public. The reputation of the underwriter has an impact on the IPO price. Higher offering prices are associated with prestigious underwriters. Investors also assume that, if owners retain a substantial portion of the firm's stock after the offering, they must expect the firm to do well in the future. So, the IPO price is higher when managers keep a larger portion of the firm's shares.

**Why does underpricing exist?** Consider the following analogy. Suppose 1,000 used Chevrolets are for sale at $600 each. On average, used Chevys are worth $600. So if you buy all of them, your profit will be zero. However, some are worth more than $600, and some are worth less. Suppose you are unable to make this distinction, but car dealers can. They bid on the good ones. If you try to buy all of the cars, the good ones will be rationed because demand will exceed supply, and you will be able to purchase only a percentage of them. On the other hand, you will get all the bad ones, and, on average, you will lose money. As a result of this 'winner's curse,' you will not bid at all unless the price is less than $600. This reasoning is thought to be at least part of the explanation for the fact that new issues are, on average, underpriced. If they were not underpriced, ordinary investors would not buy them.

## NEW EQUITY SALES AND THE VALUE OF THE FIRM

The announcement of a new equity issue is often regarded as a negative signal to the securities market. Managers with special inside information about the future of their firm may issue new equity when they know the firm's stock is overvalued. Additionally, firms that choose an equity issue may be those that have excess debt. In both cases, an equity issue signals this negative information to investors. There are also substantial costs associated with issuing new shares. Therefore, the response to the announcement of an equity issue is a drop in the firm's stock price.

## THE COSTS OF ISSUING SECURITIES

Flotation costs are the costs incurred in bringing a new issue to market. These costs include the underwriter's spread, other direct expenses (such as legal fees), indirect costs (managers' time), abnormal returns (the drop in stock price), and costs to existing shareholders resulting from underwriting and the overallotment option. Direct costs typically average 13% of the issue value. Indirect costs, although difficult to precisely quantify, are also substantial. Total costs of going public, including underpricing, have been estimated at 14% from 1984 through 1997.

Based on issuer experience, three observations have been made: (1) raising equity is less expensive for larger firms; (2) costs associated with underpricing can be substantial; and (3) issue costs are higher for IPOs than for seasoned offerings.

## RIGHTS

A firm's articles of incorporation may contain a preemptive right, specifying that any new issue of common stock must first be offered to existing shareholders. The preemptive right gives shareholders the opportunity to maintain their percentage ownership of the firm when new securities are sold.

In a rights offering, a shareholder receives one right for each share owned. For a specified number of rights, the shareholder has the option to purchase a new share of stock at a fixed price (the subscription price) for a given period of time. Shareholders can exercise their rights by purchasing the stock, or they can sell the rights to someone else.

**The Mechanics of a Rights Offering:** The financial manager must determine the following for a rights offering: (1) the subscription price; (2) the number of shares to be sold; (3) the number of rights required to purchase a new share; and (4) the impact of the rights offering on the value of the existing common stock.

**An Example:** The MRR Corporation intends to raise $20 million in new equity financing through a rights offering. The firm's outstanding common stock currently sells for $40 per share; 10 million shares are outstanding. What is the subscription price for the rights offering? How many new shares must be sold? How many rights are required to purchase a new share? What is the value of a right? How does the rights offering affect the value of the existing shares?

**Number of Rights Needed to Purchase a Share:** The subscription price must be set below the market price in order for the rights offering to succeed. If the subscription price for the new issues is set at $20 per share, one million new shares will be sold in order to raise the $20 million. The number of new shares to be issued is computed by dividing the total funds to be raised by the subscription price. For the MRR Corporation:

$$\text{Number of new shares} \ = \ \frac{\text{Funds to be raised}}{\text{Subscription price}} \ = \ \frac{\$20,000,000}{\$20} \ = \ 1,000,000 \text{ shares}$$

Each shareholder receives one right for each share owned. Since there are 10 million shares outstanding, the firm will issue 10 million rights. These rights will be used to purchase the one million new shares issued. For MRR, the number of rights needed to buy one share is:

$$\text{Number of rights} \ = \ \frac{\text{Old shares}}{\text{New shares}} \ = \ \frac{10,000,000}{1,000,000} \ = \ 10 \text{ rights}$$

That is, it will take 10 rights to buy one new share at the subscription price of $20.

**The Value of a Right:** The holder of 10 shares of MRR Corporation stock has the right to purchase, for $20 a share, stock which is currently selling for $40 per share. Clearly, this offer has value to the existing shareholders. Consider an investor who buys 10 shares of MRR common stock for $400, receives 10 rights, and then exercises the rights to obtain another share for $20. In this way, the investor will have obtained 11 shares for a total cost of $420. Since any investor can acquire 11 shares for $420, the price per share must fall to ($420/11) = $38.18 following the exercise of the rights.

The original 10 shares each carried a right, whereas the new share does not. Also, after the 10 rights are exercised, none of the 11 shares include a right. Therefore, the difference between the value of one of the original shares and the value of the shares after the rights are exercised is ($40 − $38.18) = $1.82. Since the only difference between the shares is that each of the original 10 shares entitles its holder to one right, then the difference between the prices is the value of a right. This means the value of each right is $1.82.

**Theoretical Value of a Right:** Mathematically, the equation for the theoretical value of a right during the rights-on period is:

$$R_0 = (M_0 - S) / (N + 1)$$

where

$M_0$ = Common share price during the right-on period

$S$ = Subscriptions price

$N$ = Number of rights required to buy one new share

For MRR the value of one right is:

$$R_o = (\$40 - \$20) / (10 + 1) = \$1.82, \text{ which is the same answer we got earlier.}$$

**Ex-Rights:**  For rights offerings, the firm establishes the holder-of-record date.  An investor who is a 'holder-of-record' on that date receives one right for each share owned.  According to stock exchange rules, the *ex-rights date* is four trading days prior to the holder-of-record date.  An investor must purchase the stock prior to the ex-rights date in order to be considered the owner of the stock on the holder-of-record date.  If a share is sold before the ex-rights date, it is said to be trading 'rights-on' or 'cum rights,' and the purchaser receives the right.  At the close of trading on the fifth day prior to the holder-of-record date, the stock goes ex-rights, so that any subsequent purchaser does not receive the right (the right goes to the original owner).  At the start of trading on the next day, which is the ex-rights date, the price of the stock decreases by the value of the right.  In the MRR example above, the price of the stock will decline from \$40 to \$38.18 on the ex-rights date.

**Value of Rights after Ex-Rights Date:**  When the stock goes ex-rights, we saw that its price drops by the value of one right.  However, even when the stock sells 'ex-rights,' investors can exercise their rights, and buy new shares, until the rights offering expires.  The value of a right during the ex-rights period is:

$$R_e = (M_e - S) / N$$

where $M_e$ = common share price during the ex-rights period.  In the case of MRR, $M_e$ = \$40 − \$1.82 = \$38.18.
$R_e$ = (\$38.18 − \$20) / 10 = \$1.82

**The Underwriting Arrangements:**   A rights offering often involves *standby underwriting*. The underwriter is paid a *standby fee* and agrees to purchase any unsubscribed shares.  Only a small portion of a rights offering would normally not be subscribed.  Furthermore, shareholders are usually given an *oversubscription privilege*, which gives them the option to buy additional shares at the subscription price, should any be available.  Thus it is generally unlikely that the standby underwriter will need to 'take up' any unsold shares.

**Effects on Shareholders:**  As long as shareholders either exercise or sell their rights, they are not harmed by the rights offering and the subsequent decline in stock price.  Suppose that, in the MRR Corporation example, an owner of 10 shares exercises the 10 rights and purchases a share for \$20.  Prior to the announcement of the rights offering, the 10 shares were worth a total of \$400.  After exercising the rights and paying an additional \$20, the investor owns 11 shares worth \$420.  Therefore, at a cost of \$20 the total value of the  holdings has increased by \$20.  So, there is no gain or loss as a result of the transaction.

On the other hand, the investor may choose to sell the rights for (10 × \$1.82)  =  \$18.20.  The ten shares will be worth (10 × \$38.18) = \$381.80, which, when added to the \$18.20 value of the rights, leaves total wealth unchanged at \$400.  Consequently, exercising or selling the rights does not affect the investor's total wealth. If, however,  the investor allows the rights to expire, there is a loss equal to the decline in the value of the stock, or (\$40 − \$38.18)  = \$1.82 per share.  As computed earlier, this is the same as the value of a right.  In this case, the investor loses 10 x \$1.82  =  \$18.20, and total wealth drops from \$400 to \$381.80.


## DILUTION

Dilution is a decrease in the value of the common shareholders' position resulting from the issue of new common stock.   There are three aspects of dilution: (1) dilution of proportionate ownership; (2) dilution of book value and earnings per share; and (3) dilution of market value. Each of these concepts are illustrated in the following example.

**An Example:**  The Polo Company currently has 100 shares outstanding.  Of these, R. Branca owns 40 shares and B. Thompson owns 30 shares. The market value of the firm's stock is $40 per share. The book value of the firm is $5,000, so that book value per share is $50.  The firm's return on equity, ROE, is 20%.  The firm intends to issue 50 new shares.  How does this new issue affect the current shareholders?

First, we can solve for net income in the following equation for ROE:

$$ROE = \text{Net income / Common equity;} \quad .20 = \text{Net income / \$5,000, and Net income} = \$1,000.$$

This means that EPS is $1,000 / 100 = $10.

**Dilution of Proportionate Ownership:**  The impact of the issue of 50 new shares on the voting rights of the current shareholders depends on the nature of the new issue.   If the new issue is a rights offering, then each existing shareholder will be able to purchase one new share for each two shares currently owned.  For example, Thompson will be able to purchase 15 new shares and, after the rights offering, will own 45 of 150 shares outstanding, or 30% of the outstanding shares, the same percentage currently owned.  In this case, there is no dilution of ownership.  If the new issue is a general cash offer, however,  Thompson does not purchase any of the new shares.  The ownership stake decreases to (30/150) = 20%, reducing Thompson's influence on corporate decisions.

**Dilution of Value - Book versus Market Values:**   The impact of the new stock issue on book value and earnings per share depends on the price at which the new shares are sold and the firm's ROE before and after the new issue. If ROE remains constant at 20% , and the new shares are sold for a price equal to the current book value per share ($50 in the Polo example), then there is no dilution of book value and earnings per share. Book value for the firm will increase by  (50 × $50)  =  $2,500 to ($5,000 + $2,500) = $7,500 and net income will be (.20 × $7,500) = $1,500.  Book value per share will be ($7,500/150) = $50 and EPS will be ($1,500/150) = $10.  The fact that book value per share remains constant results from the fact that the book value per share for both the old shares and the newly issued shares is $50.  That is, since the new shares are sold at a price equal to the book value of the old shares, and the price of the new shares becomes their book value once they are sold, the book value per share does not change.   Furthermore, the ROE for both the old shares and the new shares is 20%, so that EPS can be thought of as (.20 × $50) = $10 for both the old and new shares.

On the other hand, if the new shares are sold for a price below the book value of the old shares, then the book value per share and EPS are diluted.  This reduction in both book value per share and EPS is referred to as accounting dilution.  Suppose the new shares are sold for $40 per share and ROE remains at 20%. Clearly, book value per share is reduced, since 50 shares with a book value of $40 per share are now added to the existing equity of 100 shares with a book value of $50 per share. Book value of the firm is increased by (50 × $40) = $2,000, to a total of ($5,000 + $2,000) = $7,000, and the book value per share is ($7,000/150) = $46.67.  EPS is also reduced because the new shares contribute only (.20 × $40) = $8 per share to the firm's total earnings, which is less than the $10 EPS of the firm's existing shares.  After the new issue, total earnings are (.20 × $7,000) = $1,400 and EPS equals ($1,400/150) = $9.33.  Thus, accounting dilution occurs if the firm issues new shares at a price below the current book value per share while ROE remains constant.

Market value dilution is a decrease in the market value per share of the firm's stock following the issue of new shares of common stock.  Whether market value dilution occurs depends on the purpose of the additional financing obtained by Polo.

Suppose the $2,000 obtained from this issue will be used to finance a capital budgeting project whose net present value is zero.  How will this affect the market value of the firm's stock?  The market value of the existing stock is $40 per share, so that the market value of the firm is ($40 × 100) = $4,000. The assets for the new capital budgeting project will increase the firm's market value to ($4,000 + $2,000) = $6,000 and the market price per share will be ($6,000/150) = $40.  If, however, the net present value of the capital budgeting project is +$2,450, then the market value of the firm will increase to ($4,000 + $2,450) = $6,450 and the price per share will be ($6,450/150) = $43. Market value increases because the project being financed has a positive net present value.  If, however, the project had a negative NPV, we would see dilution of market value.

For our purposes, we are concerned with market value dilution, not with accounting dilution.

## ISSUING LONG-TERM DEBT

A public issue of bonds requires the issuing firm to register the issue with the OSC and other relevant provincial securities commissions.  The registration process is similar to that required for a common stock issue.  However, for bonds, the registration statement must indicate an indenture.

More than 50% of all debt is directly placed, either as *term loans* or *private placements*.  A term loan is a direct business loan that is normally amortized over a period of one to five years.  The major lenders are commercial banks and insurance companies.  A private placement is similar to a term loan except for the fact that the maturity is generally longer and comes under OSC regulation.  A private placement does not require a full prospectus. Instead, the firm and its investment dealer draw up an *offering memorandum* briefly describing the issuer and the issue. Most privately placed debt is sold to *exempt purchasers* who are large insurance companies, pension funds, and other institutions who do not require protection provided by studying a full prospectus.

Private placements tend to have higher interest rates than public issues and are also more likely to have restrictive covenants.  The benefits of private placements are that they are easier to renegotiate and incur lower distribution costs.  The interest rates on term loans and private placements are usually higher than those on equivalent public issues.  This reflects the trade-off between a higher interest rate and more flexible arrangements in the event of financial distress, as well as lower costs associated with private placements.

## CONCEPT TEST

1.      When a firm sells a new issue of securities in Ontario, the firm must file a _____ statement  with the _____.  This statement is a detailed financial disclosure. The OSC studies the registration statement during the _____.  The buyer of the securities must receive a _____, which contains much of the information in the registration statement.

2.      A public offering of a new issue may be either a _____ offer or a _____ offer.  Some equity securities, and almost all debt securities, are sold through a _____ offer,  which is an offer to sell securities to the general public.

3.      A _____ offering is an offer to sell common stock to the firm's existing shareholders.

4.      A company's first public offering of equity securities is called an _____ offering or an _____.  A _____ new issue is a new issue by a company that has previously issued securities.

5. For a cash offer, the underwriter, or _____, normally buys the securities from the firm and offers them to the public at a higher price. The difference between the underwriter's buying price and the price at which the underwriter offers the security to the public is called the _____ or the _____.

6. If the underwriter purchases the entire issue, then the issuing firm receives a fixed price for the securities, and all the risk associated with the sale of the securities is transferred to the _____. This procedure is called _____ underwriting.

7. For a _____ offering, the underwriter does not purchase the securities, but rather acts as an agent and receives a commission for each share. The _____ bears the risk that the securities cannot be sold at the specified price.

8. One of the most difficult tasks for an investment banker is the pricing of an initial public offering. If the price is set too low, the firm's existing shareholders incur an _____ loss; if it is set too high, the issue _____. New issues are typically _____, which is beneficial to new shareholders, but detrimental to existing shareholders.

9. The announcement of a new issue is often regarded as a _____ signal to the securities markets. If the firm has a superior opportunity, it _(is/is not)_ beneficial to existing shareholders to share this information by selling new shares of stock.

10. A firm's _____ may contain a preemptive right, which specifies that any new issue of common stock must be first offered to existing shareholders. A common stock issue offered to existing shareholders is called a _____ offering. A specified number of rights gives the shareholder the option to buy a new share at a fixed price, called the _____ price, during a specified time period, after which the rights _____.

11. In order for a rights offering to succeed, the subscription price must be set below the _____. The number of new shares to be issued is: Number of new shares = _____. The price per share after the rights are exercised can be computed as [(N × _____) + (_____)] / (_____) where N is the number of rights required to purchase one new share. The value of a right is equal to the _____ minus the _____.

12. For a rights offering, an investor who is a 'holder-of-record' on the holder-of-record date receives _____ right(s) for each share owned. The _____ date is four business days prior to the holder-of-record date. An investor must purchase the stock prior to the _____ date to be considered the owner of the stock on the holder-of-record date. At the close of trading on the fifth day prior to the holder-of-record date, the stock goes _____, so that any subsequent purchaser does not receive the right.

13. As long as shareholders either _____ or _____ their rights, they are not harmed by the rights offering and the subsequent decline in stock price. That is, if the investor either _____ or _____ the rights, total wealth is unchanged. If the investor allows a right to expire, the loss is equal to _____.

14. Dilution is a decrease in the value of the common shareholders' position which results from the issue of new common stock. Dilution of voting rights _(does/does not)_ occur if the new issue is a rights offering. If the new issue is a public offering, and if an existing shareholder does not purchase any of the new shares, dilution of voting rights _(does/does not)_ occur.

15.     Accounting dilution is a reduction in both _____ per share and _____.   Whether a new stock issue results in accounting dilution depends on the _____ and the firm's _____ . If ROE remains constant after the new issue is sold, and the new shares are sold for a price equal to the current book value per share then accounting dilution  (does/does not) occur.  If the new shares are sold for a price below the book value of the old shares, then dilution of book value per share and EPS  (does/does not) occur.

16.     Market value dilution is a decrease in the _____ of the firm's stock following the issue of new shares of common stock.  Market value dilution  (does/does not) occur if the funds obtained are used to finance a capital budgeting project whose net present value is zero or positive.  It does occur when the net present value of a capital budgeting project is _____.

17.     A public issue of bonds requires that the issuing firm file a _____ statement with the SEC.  More than 50% of all debt is directly placed, either as _____ loans or _____ placements.

18.     A _____ loan is a direct business loan that is normally amortized over a period of one to five years.   A _____ placement is similar to a term loan except for the fact that the _____.

19.     A corporation may register with the OSC an offering it expects to sell in the near future. This _____ procedure permits large corporations to reduce repetitive filing requirements.

20.     To use the POP system, issuers must have been reporting for _____ months and have complied with continuous _____.

21.     In 1991, securities regulators in Canada and in the U.S. introduced a _____ where large issuers are allowed to issue securities in both countries under disclosure documents satisfactory to regulators in the _____ country.

22.     Underwriting contracts often contain an _____ which allows the _____ to purchase additional shares in order to cover excess demand.

23.     In a _____ the issuer sells the entire issue to one investment dealer who takes all the risk of _____.

24.     For debt, a _____ does not require a full prospectus. Instead an _____ briefly describes the issuer and the issue.


## ANSWERS TO CONCEPT TEST

1.      registration; Ontario Securities Commission; waiting period; prospectus

2.      cash; rights; cash

3.      rights

4.      initial public; unseasoned new issue; seasoned

5.      investment dealer; spread; discount

6.      underwriter; firm-commitment

7. best-efforts; issuing firm

8. opportunity; fails to sell; underpriced

9. negative; is not

10. articles of incorporation; rights; subscription; expire

11. market price; (Funds to be raised/Subscription price); price per share before the rights offering; subscription price; N + 1; price per share before the rights offering; price per share after the rights are exercised

12. one; ex-rights; ex-rights; ex-rights

13. exercise; sell; exercises; sells; the value of a right

14. does not; does

15. book value; earnings per share; price at which the new shares are sold; return on equity; does not; does

16. market value; does not; negative

17. registration; term; private

18. term; private; maturity is longer

19. prompt offering prospectus (POP)

20. 36; disclosure requirements

21. Multi-Jurisdictional Disclosure System (MJDS); home

22. overallotment option (or green shoe provision); investment dealers

23. bought deal; selling the issue

24. private placement; offering memorandum

## PROBLEMS AND SOLUTIONS

### Problem 1

Yul Company has just floated an IPO. Under a firm-commitment underwriting agreement, Yul received $10 for each of the one million shares sold. The initial offering price was $11 per share, and the stock price rose to $14 per share in the first few minutes of trading. Yul paid $60,000 in direct legal and other costs; indirect costs were $40,000. What was the flotation cost as a percentage of funds raised?

**Solution:** Yul obtained financing of ($10 × 1,000,000) = $10 million. Flotation costs included:

| | |
|---|---:|
| Underwriter's spread ($11 – $10) × 1,000,000 | $ 1,000,000 |
| Direct costs | 60,000 |
| Indirect costs | 40,000 |
| Underpricing ($14 - 11) x 1,000,000 | 3,000,000 |
| Total | $ 4,100,000 |

Flotation costs were $4,100,000 / $10,000,000 = 41% of the financing obtained.

## Problem 2

The Canuck Corporation plans to raise $10 million in new equity financing through a rights offering. The firm's stock is valued at $30 per share, and 20 million shares are outstanding. If the firm sets the subscription price at $20 per share, how many new shares must be sold? How many rights are required to purchase a new share? What is the value of a right? How does the rights offering affect the value of Canuck Corporation's existing shares?

**Solution:** The number of new shares to be issued in order to raise the required funds is:

$$\text{Number of new shares} = \text{Funds to be raised / Subscription price}$$
$$= \$10,000,000 / \$20 = 500,000 \text{ shares}$$

The number of rights required to purchase a new share is:

$$\text{Number of rights} = \text{Olds shares / New shares} = 20,000,000 / 500,000 = 40$$

It will take 40 rights to buy one new share at a subscription price of $20 per share.

To determine the value of a right, use the following equation:

$$R_0 = (M_0 - S) / (N + 1) = (\$30 - \$20) / (40 + 1) = \$0.24$$

Therefore, the price per share will fall to ($30 - $.24) = $29.76 on the ex-rights day.

## Problem 3

Suppose a shareholder with 120 shares of Canuck Corporation decides to sell the rights to the new offering. Does doing this harm the shareholder? What if the shareholder decides to exercise the rights?

**Solution:** Prior to the rights offering, the shareholder owns stock with a value of (120 x $30) = $3,600. Selling the rights will yield (120 x $.24) = $28.80, plus the value of the shares (120 x $29.76) = $3,571.20. The total value of the investment is $28.80 + $3,571.20 = $3,600. Therefore, the shareholder is not harmed, as the total wealth is unchanged. If the shareholder exercises the rights, he/she can purchase new shares of (120 / 40) = 3 for (3 x $20) = $60. The holdings would be worth (123 x $29.76) = $3,660.48. Subtracting $60 paid for the new shares, the position is worth $3,600.48. (The difference is due to rounding errors.)

**Problem 4**

A company requires $15 million in equity financing.  Direct costs of a cash offering (including the spread, but excluding underpricing) are equal to 12% of the financing obtained. How large does the issue have to be in order to provide the company with the $15 million of required financing? What is the dollar amount of the flotation costs for this offering?

**Solution:**  We need to solve for issue size in the equation:  $(1 - .12) \times$ issue size   =  $15 million.  That is, $(1 - .12)$ = .88 = 88% of the size of the issue is financing available to the firm.  The firm must issue ($15 million / .88)   = $17,045,455 in equity.   The flotation costs are $17,045,455 – $15,000,000 = $2,045,455.

**Problem 5**

Dumas Corporation needs $19 million in equity financing.  Direct costs of the cash offering (including the spread, excluding underpricing) are equal to 11% of the financing obtained.  How large does the issue need to be in order to raise the required $19 million?  What is the dollar amount of flotation costs?

**Solution:** The size of the issue is equal to $(1 - .11)$ x issue size = $19 million.  Issue size is equal to $21,348,314.61.  The flotation costs are therefore ($21,348,314.61  - $19,000,000)   =  $2,348,314.61.

**Problem 6**

Firms A and B have announced IPOs.  Each firm's stock will be sold for $10 per share.  One of these issues is undervalued by $1, while the other is overvalued by $.50.  You are not able to determine which is undervalued and which is overvalued.  You plan to buy 100 shares of each firm's stock.  If an issue is rationed, you will be able to purchase only half of your order.  If you are able to buy 100 shares of each firm's stock, what is your profit? What profit do you actually expect?

**Solution:**  If you are able to purchase all the shares for which you bid, you would earn a profit of $100 on the undervalued stock, while you would lose $50 on the overvalued stock, for a total profit of ($100 – $50) = $50. However, the undervalued issue will be rationed while the overvalued issue will not be rationed. You should therefore expect to get 50 shares of the undervalued issue, for a profit of $50, and 100 shares of the overvalued issue, for a loss of $50.  Therefore, you expect to earn no profit.  Notice that, on average, these new issues are underpriced by ($.25 / $10) = 2.5%.   The fact that you expect to earn a zero profit, even though the two issues are, on average, underpriced, illustrates the winner's curse.

**Problem 7**

Emery Enterprises has announced a rights offering to obtain $10 million of equity financing for a new publishing project. The stock currently sells for $80 per share, and there are two million shares outstanding.  If Emery sets the subscription price at $20 per share, how many shares must be sold? How many rights are required in order to buy one share?

**Solution:**  At a subscription price of $20 per share, ($10,000,000/$20) = 500,000 shares must be sold.  There are two million shares outstanding, so that (2,000,000/500,000) = four rights are required in order to buy one new share.

## Problem 8

For the rights offering described in Problem 7, what is the ex-rights price? What is the value of a right?

**Solution:**   An investor could buy four shares of Emery common stock for ($80 × 4) = $320, and then exercise the rights to acquire a fifth share for $20. Thus, five shares can be purchased for $340, or ($340/5) = $68 per share. Therefore, the ex-rights price is $68 per share, and the value of one right is ($80 – $68) = $12.

Using the equation for the value of a right:  $M_o$  =   ($80 - $20) / (4 + 1)   =   $12.   The ex-rights price is $80 - $12  =  $68.

## Problem 9

Suppose that an investor who owns 100 shares of Emery common stock intends to sell the rights, rather than purchase additional shares of stock. Demonstrate the fact that the shareholder is not harmed by the rights offering described in Problem 7.

**Solution:**  Before the rights offering, the 100 shares were worth ($80 × 100) = $8,000.   The solution to Problem 8 indicates that the ex-rights price of the Emery stock is $68.   Therefore, after the offering, the shares are worth ($68 × 100) = $6,800. The solution to Problem 8 indicates that the value of a right is $12, so that the 100 rights can be sold for ($12 × 100) = $1,200. Therefore, after the rights offering, the investor has stock whose value is $6,800, plus $1,200 in cash, for a total of $8,000.  The total wealth is unchanged.

## Problem 10

Suppose that the investor described in Problem 9 decides to exercise, rather than sell, the rights. How does this course of action affect the investor's  total wealth?

**Solution:**  The solution to Problem 7 indicates that the investor will be able to purchase one additional share for every four shares currently owned.   Thus, the holder of 100 shares will be able to purchase 25 new shares for ($20 × 25) = $500.  From Problem 8,  the ex-rights price of the stock is $68.   Therefore, after exercising the rights, the value of the investor's stock is ($68 × 125) = $8,500.  The investor originally owned $8,000 of Emery stock. After purchasing $500 of additional stock,  the total value of the stock is now $8,500.  The investor's wealth is $8,500 less the $500 spent on new shares, or $8,000.  The rights offering has not affected the shareholder's wealth.

## Problem 11

Suppose that the rights described in Problems 7 and 8 are trading for less than the $12 value computed in the solution to Problem 8.  For example, assume that the market value of a right is $10.  How will this affect the investor who owns 100 shares of Emery common stock?  What action would you recommend to an investor who does not own Emery common stock?

**Solution:**  An investor who owns 100 shares of Emery common stock would lose ($2 × 100) = $200 by selling the rights.  That is, as described in the solution to Problem 9, the stock would be worth ($68 × 100) = $6,800, but the value of the rights would be only ($10 × 100) = $1,000, for a total value of only ($6,800 + $1,000) = $7,800. Therefore, it would be preferable for this investor to exercise the rights, as described in the solution to Problem 10.

An investor who does not own Emery common stock could purchase four rights for ($10 × 4) = $40, and then exercise the rights to acquire a share for $20. The total cost to the investor would be ($40 + $20) = $60 per share. Since the ex-rights price of the stock is $68, the investor could then sell the share for an $8 gain. This transaction could be repeated many times, by any investor, whether or not they currently own Emery common stock. The demand for the rights at a price of $10 would result in an increase in the price of the rights. Furthermore, as described in the first part of this problem, those who own stock would not be willing to sell their rights at the $10 price. The conclusion here is that the rights could not have a price of less than $12, because there would be an extremely large demand for, and essentially no supply of, rights at the $10 price. The equilibrium price for the rights would be the $12 established in the above problems.

## Problem 12

Suppose that the rights described in Problems 7 and 8 are trading for more than the $12 value computed in the solution to Problem 8. For example, assume that the market value of a right is $13. How will this affect the investor who owns 100 shares of Emery common stock? What action would you recommend to an investor who does not own Emery common stock?

**Solution:** An investor who owns 100 shares of Emery common stock should sell the rights for $13. This would result in a $100 gain, compared to the result described in the solution to Problem 9. That is, the investor would have 100 shares worth ($68 × 100) = $6,800, plus ($13 × 100) = $1,300, for a total of ($6,800 + $1,300) = $8,100. An investor who does not own Emery stock would not be willing to purchase a right for $13. Four rights would cost ($13 × 4) = $52. In order to exercise the rights, the investor would pay the subscription price of $20, for a total cost of ($52 + $20) = $72 per share. Since the ex-rights price is $68, this would not be a reasonable investment. Consequently, Emery shareholders would be willing to sell a right for $13, but a rational investor would not be willing to buy a right for this price. Thus, the price of the rights cannot be greater than the $12 value computed in the solution to Problem 8.

## Problem 13

Try this one on your own, referring to the information in Problem 7. Suppose that Emery Enterprises had set the subscription price at $50. How many shares of stock must Emery sell? How many rights are required in order to buy one new share?

**Solution:** Number of shares to sell = 200,000.   Number of rights to buy one share  =  10.

## Problem 14

Based on your answer to Problem 13, what is the ex-rights price? What is the value of one right?

**Solution 11:** $R_o$  =  $2.73;  Ex-rights price  =  $77.27.

## Problem 15

An investor owns 100 shares of Emery common stock. Demonstrate the fact that the investor's wealth is unchanged by the rights offering described in Problem 13, regardless of whether the investor sells or exercises the rights.

**Solution:**   Prior to the rights offering, the investor owns stock whose value is ($80 × 100) = $8,000. The investor can sell the rights and receive ($2.73 × 100) = $273.00 cash.  In addition, the shares are worth ($77.27 × 100) = $7,727.00. Therefore, total wealth is unchanged: ($7,727.00 + $273.00) = $8,000.

The investor can exercise the rights and purchase 10 new shares for ($50 × 10) = $500. Then, the investor owns 110 shares worth ($77.27 × 110) = $8,499.70. This value differs slightly from $8,500 due to a rounding error in computing the ex-rights price in Problem 14.   Total wealth is ($8,499.70  - $500) = $7,999.70.   That is, it is unchanged.

## Problem 16

Assume that an investor owns 100 shares of Emery common stock, and will sell the rights regardless of the subscription price. Demonstrate that the investor's wealth is unaffected by a rights offering, regardless of the subscription price.

**Solution:**  Assume that an investor owns one share of Emery common stock. The value of the share is $M_o$, the rights-on price.   On the ex-rights date, the value of the share decreases to the ex-rights price, $M_e$, so that the loss to the investor is $(M_o - M_e)$.   However, the value of the right is the difference between the rights-on price and the ex-rights price, that is, $(M_o - M_e)$.   Therefore, the value of the right exactly compensates the investor for the loss in the value of the stock, so that the investor's wealth is left unchanged by selling the right. Since this conclusion applies to the holder of one share, it applies to the holder of any number of shares, and it is unaffected by the subscription price of the rights offering.

## Problem 17

What is the maximum possible subscription price for the Emery Enterprises rights offering? What is the minimum price?

**Solution:**    The solution to Problem 16 demonstrates that the subscription price does not affect the existing shareholders of Emery.  That is, regardless of whether the existing shareholders exercise or sell their rights, their wealth is unchanged by the rights offering, regardless of the subscription price.  Theoretically, then, the minimum subscription price could be arbitrarily small, as long as it is not zero.  This illustrates the fact that a rights offering cannot be underpriced, although, as a practical matter, extremely low values are unreasonable. The maximum subscription price is $80, because the issue would not sell at a price higher than the current market value.  In practice, a subscription price close to $80 would be too high because the market price could decline during the offer, so that the issue would not sell.

## Problem 18

Delefes Enterprises has announced a rights offering to raise $15 million in equity financing for a new theatre in the downtown core.  Shares currently cost $34 and there are 1.2 million shares outstanding.  How many shares must be sold if the subscription price is $25?  How many rights are required to buy one share?  What is the ex-rights price and the value of a right?

**Solution:** The number of shares to be sold is ($15,000,000 / $25)  =  600,000 and (1,200,000 / 600,000)  = two rights are required to buy one share.

Value of one right  =  ($34 - $25) / (2+1)  =  $3

Ex-rights price  =  $34 - $3 = $31

## Problem 19

Aardvark Industries needs to raise $270 million in capital. They plan a rights offering with a subscription price of $75 per share. The firm's stock is currently trading at $90 per share and there are nine million shares outstanding. Find the value of a right and the ex-rights share price.

**Solution:** Aardvark must sell ($270,000,000 / $90)  =  three million shares. Investors need 9 million / 3 million  = 3 rights to buy one share. The value of one right is $R_o$  =  ($90 - $75) / (3 + 1)  =  $3.75. The ex-rights stock price is $90  - $3.75  =  $86.25.

## Problem 20

Demonstrate that an investor with 180 shares of Aardvark is equally well off by exercising or selling the rights.

**Solution:** Before the rights offering, the value of the investor's position is 180 x $90  =  $16,200. If the investor exercises the rights, the investor's total wealth will be:

| | |
|---|---|
| Value of old shares (180 x $86.25) | $15,525 |
| Value of new shares (180 / 3) x $86.25 | 5,175 |
| Less cash to buy shares (60 x $75) | ( 4,500) |
| Total wealth | $16,200 |

If the investor sells the rights, the total wealth will be:

| | |
|---|---|
| Old shares (180 x $86.25) | $15,525 |
| Cash from selling rights (180 x $3.75) | 675 |
| Total wealth | $16,200 |

In either case, the investor's wealth remains unchanged at $16,200.

## Problem 21

Now suppose the investor in Problem 20 decides to sell half the rights and exercise the rest. How does this affect the investor's financial position?

**Solution:** The investor's wealth will be:

| | |
|---|---:|
| Old shares (180 x $86.25) | $15,525.00 |
| New shares (90 / 3) x $86.25 | 2,587.50 |
| Cash from selling rights (90 x $3.75) | 337.50 |
| Less cash for new shares (30 x $75) | ( 2,250.00) |
| Total wealth | $16,200.00 |

## Problem 22

Finally, assume that the investor lets the Aardvark rights expire.  How does this affect the financial position?

**Solution:** The investor's wealth will be:  180 x $86.25  =  $15,525.  This is a loss of $16,200 - $15,525  =  $675, which is equal to the value of the rights, (180 x $3.75)  =  $675.

## Use the following information to solve Problems 23 to 26:

Ebbets Manufacturing Company has been experiencing financial difficulties ever since its major customer moved to Chavez Ravine. However, Ebbets is considering expansion into a new line of business. The expansion requires $4,500,000 of financing, which will be obtained through a cash offering of common stock. Ebbets currently has 5,000,000 shares of common stock outstanding and no debt. The firm's book value is $60,000,000 and net income is currently $7,500,000. Ebbets common stock currently sells for $9 per share.

## Problem 23

Calculate each of the following for Ebbets, without the expansion: book value per share, earnings per share (EPS), price earnings (P/E) ratio, return on equity (ROE), and market-to-book value ratio.

**Solution:**  Book value per share  =   ($60,000,000/$5,000,000) = $12.  EPS  =  ($7,500,000/5,000,000) = $1.50.  The P/E ratio equals market value per share divided by EPS: ($9/$1.50) = 6.   ROE equals EPS divided by book value per share: ($1.50/$12.00) = .125 = 12.5%. The market-to-book ratio is market value per share divided by book value per share: ($9/$12) = .75.

## Problem 24

Assume that the firm's P/E ratio and ROE remain constant. Calculate each of the following for Ebbets, after the expansion: book value per share, EPS, market price per share, market-to-book ratio.

**Solution:**   Total book value is ($60,000,000 + $4,500,000) = $64,500,000.   The number of shares issued equals ($4,500,000/$9) = 500,000.   Total shares outstanding equal (5,000,000 + 500,000) = 5,500,000.  Book value per share is ($64,500,000/5,500,000) = $11.73.  If ROE remains constant at 12.5% (as computed in Problem 23), then net income is (.125 × $64,500,000) = $8,062,500.  EPS equals ($8,062,500/5,500,000) = $1.47.  If the P/E ratio remains constant at 6 (as computed in Problem 23), then the market price per share is ($1.47 × 6) = $8.82.  The market-to-book ratio equals ($8.82/$11.73) = .75.  Notice that both accounting dilution and market value dilution have taken place here.  Accounting dilution is the reduction in book value per share and earnings per share which results from the sale of a new issue of common stock at a price below the book value per share of the firm's outstanding common stock.   Book value per share decreases because the book value of the new shares is $9, which is less than the book value of the existing shares.  Given a constant ROE, then EPS for the new shares can be thought of as $(.125 \times \$9) = \$1.125$; since this is less than the EPS computed in Problem 23, EPS must decrease.  Accounting dilution is not relevant to the shareholder, but market value dilution is relevant. The dilution of market value is not caused by the accounting dilution; the cause of the market value dilution is the fact that the expansion under consideration by Ebbets has a negative net present value. This result is developed in the next problem.

## Problem 25

What is the net present value of the expansion under consideration by Ebbets?

**Solution:** The market value of the firm prior to the expansion is $(\$9 \times 5,000,000) = \$45,000,00$. After the expansion, the market value is $(\$8.80 \times 5,500,000) = \$48,400,000$.  This represents an increase in market value of $3,400,000.
  Ebbets proposes spending $4,500,000 on a capital budgeting project which increases the firm's market value by only $3,400,000.  This project has a net present value of $(\$3,400,000 - \$4,500,000) = -\$1,100,000$. It is this negative net present value which causes the dilution in the market value of the firm's common stock.  The loss per share of stock is $-\$1,100,000 / 5,500,000 = -\$.20$.  This is reflected in the drop in share price from $9 to $8.80 per share.

## Problem 26

Suppose that the net present value of the expansion is $1,000,000. What is the market value of the firm's common stock after the expansion?

**Solution:** The market value of the firm will be $(\$45,000,000 + \$1,000,000 + \$4,500,000) = \$50,500,000$. Market value per share will be $(\$50,500,000/5,500,000) = \$9.18$.   Note that the accounting dilution and the market value dilution are independent of each other.   The accounting dilution occurs because the new shares are sold for a price which is below the book value of the firm's existing shares.   Market value dilution occurs only if the project being financed has a negative net present value.   In this problem, we hypothesize that the project has a positive net present value; the negative net present value computed in Problem 25 results from the assumptions that the firm's P/E ratio and ROE remain constant after the expansion. There is no reason to believe that these ratios will necessarily remain constant simply because the firm sells shares for a price below their book value.   Therefore, there is no reason to believe that market value dilution occurs whenever accounting dilution occurs.

Note that the gain per share is NPV / number of shares   =   $1,000,000 / 5,500,000   =   $.18. This is reflected in the increase in share price from $9 to $9.18.

# 16     <u>Financial Leverage and Capital Structure Policy</u>

## CHAPTER HIGHLIGHTS

Firms have considerable flexibility in choosing their capital structure–that is, the way they finance their assets. To simplify the choice of capital structure, our discussion is limited to the choice between debt and equity. The objective of the capital structure decision, like any corporate objective, should be to maximize the wealth of the firm's owners, the shareholders. In this chapter, we will assume the firm's investment decision is already made. That is, the firm is choosing the appropriate capital structure to finance a given set of assets.

## THE CAPITAL STRUCTURE QUESTION

There are two major issues related to the capital structure decision. First, should shareholders be concerned about maximizing the value of the entire firm, rather than maximizing the value of the firm's equity? And, second, what is the ratio of debt to equity that maximizes shareholders'interests?

**Firm Value and Stock Value:**  First, we can demonstrate that maximizing the value of the firm's equity is equivalent to maximizing the value of the firm.

Consider an all-equity firm with a market value of $100,000. That is, both the firm's existing assets and its common stock are valued at $100,000. Managers are considering the possibility $40,000 and using the proceeds of the loan to pay dividends to the shareholders.

If this financial restructuring does not affect the value of the firm's assets, then the wealth of the shareholders is unaffected. Before the restructuring, they owned 100% of a firm worth $100,000. After the restructuring, they own 60% of a firm worth $100,000 = $60,000 + $40,000 in dividends = $100,000. Their total wealth is the same.

If restructuring increases the value of the firm, then shareholders benefit. If, for example, restructuring increases the value of the firm to $110,000, the shareholders now own equity in the firm worth ($110,000 − $40,000) = $70,000 plus dividends of $40,000, for a total of $110,000.  In other words, the increase in firm value accrues to the shareholders. Likewise, any loss in value also accrues to the firm's shareholders. Consequently, maximizing the value of the firm is equivalent to maximizing the value of the shareholders' position.

Therefore, from the shareholders' point of view, if there is a capital structure which maximizes the value of the firm, the same capital structure also maximizes the value of the shareholders' position.

**Capital Structure and the Cost of Capital:** Remember that the value of a firm is the present value of the firm's cash flows, discounted at the WACC.  If capital structure decisions have an impact on the WACC, then these decisions affect the value of the firm. The capital structure which minimizes the WACC is also the capital structure which maximizes the value of the firm.

## THE EFFECT OF FINANCIAL LEVERAGE

Financial leverage is the extent to which a firm uses debt, rather than equity, financing.  In this section, we investigate the relationship between financial leverage and the returns to the firm's shareholders.

**The Basics of Financial Leverage:**  We discuss the impact of leverage on shareholders in terms of the effect on earnings per share (EPS) and return on equity (ROE).   For now, we will ignore the impact of taxes.

**An Example:**  W. Reed & Company is an all-equity firm with 20,000 shares of common stock outstanding. The market value per share is $25, so the firm's market value  ($25 × 20,000) = $500,000. The CFO has proposed to issue $300,000 of debt in order to repurchase ($300,000/$25) = 12,000 shares of the firm's outstanding stock.  The interest rate on the debt is 10%. The restructuring would leave (20,000 − 12,000) = 8,000 shares outstanding. The current and proposed capital structures are summarized in the following table:

|                     | Current   | Proposed  |
|---------------------|-----------|-----------|
| Assets              | $500,000  | $500,000  |
| Debt                | 0         | 300,000   |
| Equity              | 500,000   | 200,000   |
|                     |           |           |
| Debt/equity ratio   | 0.0       | 1.5       |
| Share price         | $25       | $25       |
| Shares outstanding  | 20,000    | 8,000     |
| Interest rate       |           | 10%       |

The following table illustrates the impact of the restructuring on ROE and EPS under each of three alternative scenarios (i.e., recession, expected, and expansion):

| Current capital structure: No debt | | | |
|------------|-----------|-----------|-----------|
|            | Recession | Expected  | Expansion |
| EBIT       | $40,000   | $60,000   | $100,000  |
| Interest   | 0         | 0         | 0         |
| Net income | $40,000   | $60,000   | $100,000  |
|            |           |           |           |
| ROE        | 8.00%     | 12.00%    | 20.00%    |
| EPS        | $2.00     | $3.00     | $5.00     |

| Proposed capital structure: Debt = $300,000 | | | |
|------------|-----------|-----------|-----------|
|            | Recession | Expected  | Expansion |
| EBIT       | $40,000   | $60,000   | $100,000  |
| Interest   | 30,000    | 30,000    | 30,000    |
| Net income | $10,000   | $ 30,000  | $ 70,000  |
|            |           |           |           |
| ROE        | 5.00%     | 15.00%    | 35.00%    |
| EPS        | $1.25     | $3.75     | $8.75     |

Since the current capital structure of Reed & Company is 100% equity, the net income is the same as earnings before interest and taxes (EBIT) for each of the three possible scenarios.   ROE is equal to net income divided by total equity.  For example, ROE in a recession would be ($40,000/$500,000)  = .08 = 8%. EPS is equal to net income divided by the number of shares outstanding. In a recession, EPS would be ($40,000/20,000) = $2.00.

For the proposed capital structure, interest is (.10 × $300,000) = $30,000, so net income is $30,000 less for each scenario than it would be with the current capital structure. In a recession:   ROE = $10,000/$200,000 = .05 = 5%. EPS = $10,000/8,000 = $1.25

Notice that, for each capital structure, both ROE and EPS change as EBIT changes. For the expected EBIT, both ROE and EPS are higher under the proposed plan. However, in the event of a recession, ROE and EPS are lower under the proposed structure. The reverse is true for an economic expansion.

In general, leverage has a beneficial impact on shareholders when EBIT is high and a detrimental impact when EBIT is low. This is due to the fixed interest cost associated with debt financing. When EBIT is low, the fixed obligation to creditors consumes a substantial portion of the firm's earnings, so the return to shareholders is relatively low. However, at higher levels of EBIT, the return to creditors remains constant, while the shareholders derive a proportionately larger benefit from the increased earnings. Financial leverage magnifies both the benefits and the losses to shareholders. In other words, the variability in returns to shareholders increases with increases in financial leverage.

**Degree of Financial Leverage:**   Financial leverage measures how much earnings per share respond to changes in EBIT.   Financial leverage is an extension of our discussion of operating leverage in Chapter 2. The *degree of financial leverage* (DFL) can be computed with the following formula:

$$DFL = \frac{\text{Percentage change in EPS}}{\text{Percentage change in EBIT}}$$

If there is debt in the capital structure, the DFL varies for different ranges of EPS and EBIT. For example, given the current capital structure, the DFL for Reed & Company for each possible EBIT will be:

$$\text{EBIT} = \$40,000: \quad DFL = \frac{(\$3 - \$2) / \$2}{(\$60,000 - \$40,000) / \$40,000} = \frac{0.50}{0.50} = 1.0$$

$$\text{EBIT} = \$60,000: \quad DFL = \frac{(\$5 - \$3) / \$3}{(\$100,000 - \$60,000) / \$60,000} = \frac{0.67}{0.67} = 1.0$$

Because there is no debt in the capital structure, the DFL is the same regardless of the level of EBIT. However, for the *proposed* capital structure, the DFL changes as EBIT increases from $40,000 to $60,000:

$$\text{EBIT} = \$40,000: \quad DFL = \frac{(\$3.75 - \$1.25) / \$1.25}{(\$60,000 - \$40,000) / \$40,000} = \frac{2.0}{0.5} = 4.0$$

$$\text{EBIT} = \$60,000: \quad DFL = \frac{(\$8.75 - \$3.75) / \$3.75}{(\$100,000 - \$60,000) / \$60,000} = \frac{1.33}{0.67} = 2.0$$

The following formula may also be used to calculate DFL:

$$DFL = \frac{\text{EBIT}}{\text{EBIT - Interest}}$$

Recalculating the DFL for the proposed capital structure and EBIT of $40,000 and $60,000, you see that the results are the same using either equation.

$$DFL_{\$40,000} = \frac{\$40,000}{\$40,000 - \$30,000} = 4.0 \qquad DFL_{\$60,000} = \frac{\$60,000}{\$60,000 - \$30,000} = 2.0$$

The importance of calculating DFL is apparent when this result is used in the context of changes in EBIT and net income.   For example, under the proposed capital structure, the EBIT increased by 67% (from $60,000 to $100,000).   Since the DFL at EBIT of $60,000 is 2.0 we can conclude that net income will increase by 134% (67% × 2).   This means that ROE and EPS will also increase by 134%.   In other words, given a DFL, the analyst can predict the impact on net income (magnification or demagnification), given his forecast of changes in EBIT.   If EBIT were to decrease by a given percentage, net income would decrease by that given percentage times the DFL factor.

**Indifference EBIT:**   The results for Reed & Company imply that, at some level of EBIT between $40,000 and $60,000, EPS will be the same for either capital structure.   We can determine the indifference EBIT (the level of EBIT at which EPS is the same).   For the current capital structure, EPS is equal to (EBIT - $0) / 20,000.   For the proposed capital structure, EPS is equal to (EBIT – $30,000) / 8,000.   The indifference EBIT is found by equating these two expressions and solving for EBIT:

$$\frac{(EBIT - \$0)}{20,000} = \frac{(EBIT - \$30,000)}{8,000}$$

$$8,000 \times EBIT = 20,000 \times EBIT - \$600,000,000$$

$$-12,000 \times EBIT = -\$600,000,000$$

$$EBIT = \$50,000$$

When EBIT is $50,000,   EPS is equal to $2.50 for either capital structure.   If the analyst is forecasting higher levels of EBIT (above $50,000), this favours debt financing since EPS will be increased.

**Corporate Borrowing and Homemade Leverage:**   The discussion above seems to suggest that the firm's capital structure is important to the shareholders.   However, in a world of perfect capital markets, this conclusion is incorrect.   Shareholders can adjust the amount of leverage in their position by borrowing or lending on their own, thereby creating *homemade leverage*. In these situations, investors are indifferent to the firm's choice of capital structure because their total wealth is unchanged.

**An Example:**   Using Reed & Company again, assume that an investor owns 100 shares of stock.  The table below shows the investor's financial position if the firm adopts the proposed capital structure. The next table shows that the investor can create homemade leverage by borrowing and purchasing additional shares, thus achieving the same level of wealth even if the firm does not adopt the proposed plan.

| Proposed capital structure | | | |
|---|---|---|---|
| | Recession | Expected | Expansion |
| EPS | $    1.25 | $   3.75 | $    8.75 |
| Total earnings (100 shares) | 125.00 | 375.00 | 875.00 |
| Net cost   =   (100 x $25)   =   $2,500.00 | | | |

| Original capital structure and homemade leverage | | | |
|---|---|---|---|
| | Recession | Expected | Expansion |
| EPS | $     2.00 | $   3.00 | $     5.00 |
| Earnings for 250 shares | 500.00 | 750.00 | 1,250.00 |
| Less interest ($3,750 @ 10%) | 375.00 | 375.00 | 375.00 |
| Net earnings | $   125.00 | $375.00 | $  875.00 |

Net cost   =   (250 x $25)  - Amount borrowed   =   $6,250  -  $3,750  =  $2,500

The homemade leverage in the second section exactly duplicates the leverage of the Reed & Company roposed capital structure.  The proposed capital structure has a debt/equity ratio of ($3,750 / $2,500) = 1.50. The shareholder can create the same financial leverage by *borrowing* an amount equal to 1.50 times the equity in the 100 share position, and investing this amount in additional shares.  That is, borrow (1.50 × $2,500) = $3,750 and then purchase ($3,750/$25) = 150 additional shares of stock.  The total number of shares owned is then (100 + 150) = 250 shares.  In the event of a recession, for example, the shareholder's total earnings on this position would be ($2.00 × 250) = $500, and the total interest paid would be (.10 × $3,750) = $375.  The net earnings would then be ($500 – $375) = $125, the same as the total earnings under the proposed capital structure.

If the firm adopts the proposed capital structure, a shareholder who prefers less leverage can *unlever* the position by *lending* an amount sufficient to duplicate the earnings the shareholder would receive under the original capital structure. The table below demonstrates that these earnings could be duplicated if the shareholder were to sell 60 shares, for a total of ($25 × 60) = $1,500, and then lend this $1,500 at a 10% interest rate.

|  | Original capital structure | | | |
|---|---|---|---|---|
|  | Recession | Expected | Expansion | EPS |
| EPS | $ 2.00 | $ 3.00 | $ 5.00 | |
| Total earnings(100 shares) | $ 200.00 | $300.00 | $500.00 | |

Net cost  =  (100 x $25)  = $2,500.00

|  | Proposed capital structure and homemade leverage | | |
|---|---|---|---|
|  | Recession | Expected | Expansion |
| EPS | $ 1.25 | $ 3.75 | $ 8.75 |
| Earnings for 40 shares | 50.00 | 150.00 | 350.00 |
| Plus interest ($1,500 @ 10%) | 150.00 | 150.00 | 150.00 |
| Net earnings | $ 200.00 | $300.00 | $ 500.00 |

Net cost  =  (40 x $25) + Amount loaned  =  $1,000  +  $1,500  =  $2,500

Thus, an investor is indifferent to the capital structure decisions of the firm since the shareholder can duplicate the preferred capital structure, regardless of the firm's actual capital structure, by borrowing or lending.

## CAPITAL STRUCTURE AND THE COST OF EQUITY CAPITAL

The discussion above indicates that, under certain circumstances, the price of a firm's common stock is not dependent on the firm's capital structure.   This conclusion was initially derived by Modigliani and Miller (M&M) in 1958.  We refer to this result as **M&M Proposition I.**   Their derivation of this result is based on the following two assumptions: first, there are no taxes; and second, investors can borrow on their own account at the same rate that the firm pays on its debt.

**M&M Proposition I - The Pie Model:**  Recall that the market value of a firm (V) is equal to the sum of the equity value (E) and the debt value (D).  The value of the firm can be viewed as a pie, and the firm's capital structure is represented by the way in which the pie is sliced; this is referred to as the pie model.  The slices of the pie are the equity and debt portions.  M&M Proposition 1 states that the size of the pie is not affected by the manner in which the pie is sliced.  That is, the total value of the firm's assets is not affected by the manner in which the financing is obtained.  It is the assets of a firm that generate cash flow and determine the firm's value.  The firm's capital structure is simply a way of packaging those cash flows and selling them in financial markets.

Proposition I is expressed in the following formula:

$$V_u = EBIT / R_e^u = V_L = E_L + D_L$$

where: 
$V_u$ = Value of the unlevered firm
$V_L$ = Value of the levered firm
EBIT = Perpetual operating income
$R_e^u$ = Equity required return for the unlevered firm
$E_L$ = Market value of equity for a levered firm
$D_L$ = Market value of debt for a levered firm

**An Example:** AA International is an all-equity firm that generates EBIT of $3 million per year. The required rate of return, $R_E^u$, is 15%. If Proposition I holds, how would the market value of AA International change if it issued $4 million in debt, using the proceeds to retire equity?

Currently the market value of the firm is equal to the market value of equity, since there is no debt: $V_u$ = $3,000,000 / .15 = $20,000,000. According to Proposition I, the value of AA would remain the same since $V_u = V_L$. In other words, $V_L$ would be the sum of $E_L$ and $D_L$ ($16,000,000 + $4,000,000 = $20,000,000). Note that, because the market value of the firm doesn't change, the equity value drops by $4,000,000 to $16,000,000.

**The Cost of Equity and Financial Leverage - M&M Proposition II:** M&M Proposition II addresses the relationship between the firm's debt/equity ratio (i.e., the capital structure) and the firm's cost of equity capital. Specifically, M&M Proposition II establishes a positive relationship between leverage and the expected return on equity. That is, the risk (and the cost) of a firm's equity increases as the degree of leverage increases.

The equation for the weighted average cost of capital (WACC) is below. Also, because the WACC represents the firm's required return on its overall assets, we can replace the WACC in the equation with $R_A$, the return on assets.

$$WACC = R_A = (E/V) \times R_E + (D/V) \times R_D$$

Solving for the return on equity ($R_E$), we have:

$$R_E = R_A + (R_A - R_D) \times (D/E)$$

This relationship indicates that the required return on equity is a linear function of the firm's debt/equity ratio. We know from Proposition I that the value of the firm is not affected by changes in the debt/equity ratio, so that it must also be true that the firm's overall cost of capital $R_A$ does not change with changes in the firm's financial structure. Also, if $R_A$ is greater than $R_D$, the $R_E$ increases with the debt/equity ratio. Intuitively, this last conclusion results from the fact that additional debt increases the risk of the firm's equity, and consequently increases the required return on equity.

M&M Proposition II states that the cost of equity is given by a straight line with a slope of $(R_A - R_D)$ and a y-intercept of $R_A$. The y-intercept indicates that $R_E = R_A$ for a firm with no debt (i.e., for a firm with D/E = 0). As the debt/equity ratio (D/E) increases, the cost of equity ($R_E$) rises in a linear fashion, but the increased cost of equity is exactly offset by the increased use of cheaper debt. The overall cost of capital ($R_A$) is the same regardless of the value of the debt/equity ratio. Since $R_A$ never changes, and the firm's cash flows are constant, the value of the firm is unaffected by changes in the capital structure.

**An Example:**   Reconsider AA International by assuming that the new issue of debt could cost the firm 8%. What is the required equity return for the levered firm and its overall weighted average cost of capital?

The debt to equity ratio is 25%  ($4,000,000 / $16,000,000).  Using Proposition II, the equity required return for the levered firm is $R_E$  =  15% + [(15% – 8%) x (.25)]  =  16.75%. The weighted average cost of capital will remain unchanged at 15%:

$$\text{WACC} = R_A = .1675 \times (.80) + .08 \times (.20) = 0.15 = 15\%$$

WACC does not change because the use of cheaper debt is exactly offset by the increase in the cost of equity.

**Business and Financial Risk:**  Combining the results of Proposition II and the SML (used earlier to estimate the cost of equity), we can rewrite the required return on the firm's assets as:  $R_A = R_f + (R_M - R_f) \times \beta_A$.

The beta coefficient here, $\beta_A$ is called the *asset* beta as it measures the systematic risk of the firm's assets.   If we combine the above equation with the cost of equity from the SML, $R_E = R_f + (R_M - R_f) \beta_E$, we can write the relationship between the equity beta, $\beta_E$, and the asset beta,  $\beta_A$: $\beta_E = \beta_A \times (1 + D/E)$.

The term $(1 + D/E)$ is the same as the equity multiplier in chapter 3.  Here, though, it is measured in market, instead of book values.  The result is that the risk premium for the firm's equity is equal to the risk premium on the firm's assets times the equity multiplier.  The real insight of this equation appears when it is rewritten in the following manner: $\beta_E = \beta_A + \beta_A \times (D/E)$.

The first component, $\beta_A$, is a measure of the riskiness of the firm's assets. In other words, it measures the *business risk* of the firm.  The second component, $\beta_A \times (D/E)$ depends upon the firm's financial policy or the *financial risk* of the equity.

Therefore, the total systematic risk of the firm's equity has two parts; business risk and financial risk. As we saw earlier, the cost of equity rises when the firm increases its use of financial leverage (debt) because the financial risk of the stock increases.


## M&M PROPOSITIONS I & II WITH CORPORATE TAXES

The conclusions of the previous section are derived under a set of fairly unrealistic assumptions.  In addition, the conclusion that the debt/equity ratio does not affect value cannot explain the fact that debt/equity ratios seem to vary with industry characteristics.  These observations make it necessary to assess the validity of the M&M conclusions under a more realistic set of assumptions.  Specifically, we consider how the introduction of corporate taxes affects the M&M propositions.

Remember that interest payments on debt are tax deductible. Therefore, if corporate income is taxed, the *tax subsidy* for debt increases the attractiveness of debt in the firm's capital structure.

**An Example:** Two firms, Firm U and Firm L, both have earnings before interest and taxes (EBIT) of $1,000 in perpetuity.  Firm L has issued perpetual bonds in the amount of $500 on which it pays 12% interest, and the corporate tax rate is 30%. Firm U has 100% equity.  We can summarize this information as follows:

|                    |      | Firm U   |       | Firm L  |
| ------------------ | ---- | -------- | ----- | ------- |
| EBIT               |      | $1,000   |       | $1,000  |
| Interest           |      | 0        |       | 60      |
| Taxable income     | $1,000 |        | $ 940 |         |
| Taxes (30%)        |      | 300      |       | 282     |
| Net income         |      | $ 700    |       | $ 658   |

**The Interest Tax Shield:** Since depreciation, capital spending and changes in net working capital are all zero, the cash flow from each firm's assets is equal to (EBIT – Taxes), as indicated in the following table:

| Cash flow from assets |       | Firm U |       | Firm L |
| --------------------- | ----- | ------ | ----- | ------ |
| EBIT                  |       | $1,000 |       | $1,000 |
| - Taxes               | 300   |        | 282   |        |
| Total                 |       | $ 700  |       | $ 718  |

We can now compute the total cash flow to both shareholders and bondholders:

| Cash flow       |        | Firm U |        | Firm L |
| --------------- | ------ | ------ | ------ | ------ |
| To shareholders | $ 700  |        | $ 658  |        |
| To bondholders  |        | 0      |        | 60     |
| Total           | $ 700  |        | $ 718  |        |

The total cash flow for Firm L is $18 greater than the cash flow for Firm U. This occurs because Firm L's tax bill, which is a cash outflow, is $18 less. The interest expense has generated a tax saving equal to the interest payment ($60) multiplied by the corporate tax rate (30%). This tax saving is called the *interest tax shield.*

**Taxes and M&M Proposition I:** Since the debt is perpetual, this same interest tax shield will be generated every year forever. The after-tax cash flow to Firm L will be the same $700 that accrues to Firm U, plus the $18 tax shield. Because the tax shield is generated by paying interest, it has the same risk as the firm's debt, so that 12% is the appropriate discount rate for valuing the tax shield. The value of the tax shield is thus:

$$\text{PV(tax shield)} \;=\; \$18 \,/\, .12 \;=\; (.30 \times .12 \times \$500) \,/\, .12 \;=\; \$150$$

In general, the value of the interest tax shield is computed as: Tax shield $= T_C \times D$.

The after-tax cash flow to the shareholders of the unlevered firm is $[EBIT \times (1 - T_C)]$. If we assume that all cash flows are perpetual and constant, then the value of the unlevered firm is:

$$V_U \;=\; \frac{EBIT\,(1 - T_C)}{\rho}$$

where $\rho$ is the unlevered cost of capital. This means that $\rho$ is the cost of capital the firm would have if it had no debt.

Suppose that the cost of capital for Firm U is 20% (i.e., $\rho = 20\%$). The value of Firm U is:

$$V_U \;=\; \frac{\$1,000\,(1 - .30)}{.20} \;=\; \$3,500$$

M&M Proposition I (with corporate taxes) states that the value of a levered firm, $V_L$, is equal to the value of the unlevered firm plus the value of the interest tax shield:

$$V_L = V_U + (T_C \times D)$$

For Firm L:   $V_L = \$3,500 + \$150 = \$3,650$

These results demonstrate that, in a world with corporate taxes, the firm has an incentive to increase its debt/equity ratio. A higher debt/equity ratio lowers taxes and increases the total value of the firm. In fact, the above results indicate that a firm should move as close as possible to an all-debt capital structure. Clearly, this conclusion is inconsistent with reality, since firms do not choose capital structures which are virtually all debt. It is important to keep in mind here that this conclusion is derived under the assumption that there are no bankruptcy costs. These are discussed later in the chapter.

**Taxes, the WACC, and Proposition II:** M&M demonstrates that, in a world with corporate taxes, the following equation describes the relationship between the debt/equity ratio and the cost of equity capital:

$$R_E = \rho + (\rho - R_D) \times (D / E) \times (1 - T_C)$$

This result is known as M&M Proposition II (with corporate taxes). It indicates a positive relationship between expected return on equity and the debt/equity ratio. It also implies that the firm's overall cost of capital decreases as the amount of debt increases, which leads to the conclusion that a capital structure of 100% debt is optimal. This is the same conclusion implied by M&M Proposition I (with corporate taxes). Note that, again, the cost of equity is a linear function of the firm's debt/equity ratio.

**An Example:** We can use this equation to compute the WACC for Firm L in the above example.

Since $V_L = \$3,650$, and the firm's debt has a value of $D = \$500$, the equity for Firm L has a value of $E = (\$3,650 - \$500) = \$3,150$. The cost of equity for Firm L is:

$$R_E = .20 + (.20 - .12) \times (\$500 / \$3,150) \times (1 - .30) = .20889 = 20.889\%$$

The weighted average cost of capital is:

$$WACC = (\$3,150 / \$3,650) \times .20889 + (\$500 / \$3,650) \times .12 \times (1 - .30) = .1918 = 19.18\%$$

The weighted average cost of capital for an unlevered firm is 20% (i.e., WACC = $\rho$ = 20%), while the WACC for Firm L is 19.18%. Since the cash flows are the same for the two firms, the firm with the lower WACC (Firm L) has the greater value.

## BANKRUPTCY COSTS

The M&M Propositions (with taxes) state that a firm can increase its value by increasing leverage. This implies that firms should be financed largely by debt. Most firms, though, are not highly leveraged. In part, the explanation for this discrepancy lies in the fact that we have ignored the cost of bankruptcy, which increases with the firm's level of debt. The impact of bankruptcy costs is discussed below.

The obligation to pay principal and interest on debt puts pressure on the firm since failure to meet the obligation results in *financial distress*. The ultimate financial distress is bankruptcy, in which case ownership of the firm's assets is transferred to the bondholders. Costs of financial distress offset the advantages of debt under certain circumstances.

**Direct Bankruptcy Costs:** Economically, bankruptcy occurs when the value of a firm's assets is equal to or less than the value of its debt. Legally, though, bankruptcy occurs when the firm's assets are turned over to the firm's bondholders. This process involves significant expenses, referred to as *direct bankruptcy costs*, which include attorneys' fees, administrative and accounting fees, and, in the event of a trial, fees to expert witnesses. These costs represent a disadvantage to debt financing, which, to some extent, offsets the advantage of tax deductibility of interest.

**Indirect Bankruptcy Costs:** Bankruptcy often results in an impaired ability to conduct business. Customers may question the ability of the firm to provide service subsequent to a purchase, and are consequently less likely to buy from a firm in bankruptcy. Although these costs are difficult to estimate, they are generally thought to be much greater than the direct costs cited above.

**Agency Costs of Equity:** Bankruptcy costs are agency costs of debt that increase as financial leverage increases. Agency costs of equity can result from shirking by owner-managers and can work in the opposite manner. The implication here is that, when the firm issues equity, the owner-entrepreneur's stake is diluted, with the effect that the entrepreneur works shorter hours and consumes more perquisites (a big office, company car, larger expense account, etc.) than if the firm issues debt.

## OPTIMAL CAPITAL STRUCTURE

Financial distress costs are insignificant for a firm with little or no debt. If the firm adds a small amount of debt to its capital structure, it derives the benefit of the tax shield on debt without incurring significant costs of financial distress. As a firm uses more and more debt, however, the tax savings are eventually offset by the increased likelihood that financial distress costs will be incurred. Conceivably, there exists a point where these two factors exactly offset each other, and the value of the firm is maximized.

The *static theory of capital structure* states that a firm uses additional debt financing in its capital structure up to the point where the tax benefit derived from an additional dollar of debt exactly offsets the cost associated with an increased likelihood of financial distress. An optimum (or target) capital structure exists when the benefit of another dollar in debt is exactly balanced by the increased likelihood of financial distress.

The graph below demonstrates this discussion in terms of the value of the firm. If we begin with no debt, the value of the firm increases as debt is added. The incremental gains from additional debt begin diminishing, however, because of the increased likelihood of financial distress. An optimal capital structure occurs when the present value of the tax saving from an additional dollar of debt (the marginal benefit of leverage) equals the increase in the present value of expected bankruptcy costs (the marginal cost of leverage). At this point, the value of the firm is maximized.

Two qualitative conclusions are derived from this analysis: firms with higher tax rates should borrow more, and firms with higher risks of financial distress (perhaps those with higher operating risks) should borrow less.

## THE PIE AGAIN

We initially viewed the value of the firm as being equal to the value of the stock plus the value of the debt. A way of reconciling much of the discussion in this chapter is to recognize that the pie representing the firm is actually comprised of much more than just the debt and equity portions. For example, the government takes a substantial slice in the form of taxes. In the event of bankruptcy, many other parties will take a slice. Therefore, many different types of claims on the firm's cash flow may exist at any time.

All the claims to the firm's cash flow can nonetheless be divided into two groups. The debt and equity are the *marketed claims* and the rest are *nonmarketed claims*. When we speak of the capital structure issue, we are really investigating whether the total value of the marketed claims can be increased by decreasing the size of the nonmarketed claims. For example, the interest tax shield increases the size of the marketed claims by decreasing the size of the nonmarketed government claim. It is important to keep in mind that the size of the pie is constant when we include all the claims. The issue under consideration is how the cash flow from operations is paid out. The optimum capital structure minimizes the 'nibbling' by those who hold nonmarketed claims.

## OBSERVED CAPITAL STRUCTURES

The results of this chapter do not provide an exact formula for evaluating the relationship between leverage and firm value. So, it is important to also consider evidence from the real world in establishing capital structure policy.

There are certain observed regularities in corporate capital structures which indicate that the firm's choice of capital structure does matter. First, most firms do not use a great deal of debt, and many of these firms pay substantial taxes. There appears to be a limit on the ability of firms to exploit the interest tax shield. Second, firms in similar industries tend to have similar capital structures, but capital structures appear to vary widely across industries. This fact suggests that capital structure is influenced by the nature of a firm's assets.

## LONG-TERM FINANCING UNDER FINANCIAL DISTRESS AND BANKRUPTCY

One of the disadvantages of the use of debt is the possibility of financial distress. Financial distress includes:

1.  *Business failure* is the termination of a business, resulting in a loss to the firm's creditors.
2.  *Legal bankruptcy* is a legal proceeding resulting in the liquidation or reorganization of the firm.
3.  *Technical insolvency* results from a firm's default on a legal obligation to pay a debt.
4.  *Accounting insolvency* occurs when the firm's liabilities exceed the firm's assets, so the firm's net worth is negative.

**Liquidation and Reorganization:** Liquidation and reorganization are the two possible outcomes of a legal bankruptcy. *Liquidation* is the termination of a firm, following a bankruptcy proceeding. The firm's assets are sold and the proceeds of the sale are distributed to those who have claims against the firm, including employees, consumers, governments, creditors, and shareholders. *Reorganization* is a plan that allows the firm to continue to operate, but generally requires a restructuring of the firm's debts. The restructuring includes some payments to creditors and shareholders, and often includes the issuing of new securities to replace existing securities.

## APPENDIX 16A: CAPITAL STRUCTURE AND PERSONAL TAXES

Earlier we saw that the value of a levered firm equals the value of an identical unlevered firm, $V_u$, plus the present value of the interest tax shield, $T_C \times D$. The following equation represents the value of a levered firm taking into account personal as well as corporate taxes.

$$V_L \ = \ V_U \ + \ 1 \ - \frac{(1 - T_C)(1 - T_S)}{(1 - T_b)} \ \times \ D$$

where   $T_b$ = personal tax rate on ordinary income, such as interest

$T_S$ = personal tax rate on equity distributions – dividends and capital gains

Note that, if $T_b$ and $T_s$ are equal, the above equation simplifies to the case when there are no personal taxes:

$$V_L = V_u + T_C \times D$$

This means that personal taxes do not affect our valuation formula as long as equity distributions are taxed identically to interest at the personal level.  However, the gain from leverage is reduced when equity distributions are taxed more lightly than interest (i.e., when $T_s$ is less than $T_b$).  In other words, more taxes are paid at the personal level for a levered firm than for an unlevered firm. The reason why there is no gain from leverage is that the lower corporate taxes for a levered firm are *exactly* offset by higher personal taxes.

**An Example:**  Black, Inc. expects a perpetual pre-tax earning stream of $500,000 and faces a 46 % corporate tax rate.  Investors discount the earnings stream after corporate taxes at 14%.  The personal tax rate on equity distributions is 25% and the personal tax rate on interest is 48%.  Black has an all equity capital structure but is considering borrowing $250,000 at 8%.  What is the advantage of leveraging if personal taxes are considered and if personal taxes are ignored?

The value of the all-equity firm is:

$$V_U \ = \ \frac{\$500,000 \times (1 - .46)}{.14} \ = \ \$1,928,571.43$$

The value of the levered firm, after considering personal taxes, is:

$$V_L \ = \ \$1,928,571.43 \ + \ 1 \ - \ \frac{(1 - .46)(1 - .25)}{(1 - .48)} \ \times \$250,000 \ = \ \$1,983,859.89$$

If there are no personal taxes, the value of the levered firm is:

$$V_L \ = \ \$1,928,571.43 \ + \ .46 \times \$250,000 \ = \ \$2,043,571.43$$

Therefore, the advantage of leverage with personal taxes ($55,288.46) is less than with no personal taxes ($115,000).

## CONCEPT TEST

1.  In making capital structure decisions, the firm considers whether or not the way it _____ its assets makes any economic difference.  That is, we are focusing only on the issue of how a firm _____ a given collection of _____.

2.  Shareholders benefit from a financial restructuring only if _____.  This occurs because any increase in the value of the firm as a result of restructuring accrues to the _____.  Consequently, maximizing the value of the shareholders' position is equivalent to maximizing the _____.

3.  The value of a firm is the _____ of the firm's cash flows discounted at the _____.  The capital structure which maximizes the value of the firm is the capital structure which minimizes the _____.

4.  Financial leverage is the extent to which a firm uses _____ financing. Leverage has a beneficial impact on stockholders when EBIT is (high/low) and a detrimental impact when EBIT is (high/low). It is said that financial leverage _____ both the benefits and the losses to shareholders. The variability in the return to shareholders is (greater/less) for a firm that uses debt financing than for an all-equity firm. The variability in returns to shareholders (increases/decreases) with increases in financial leverage.

5.  In a world of perfect capital markets, the firm's capital structure (is/is not) important to the shareholders. Shareholders can adjust the amount of leverage in their position by _____ or _____ on their own, thereby creating _____.  A shareholder who prefers a capital structure with more leverage than that which the firm has adopted can duplicate the preferred capital structure by _____ an amount sufficient to create a personal debt/equity ratio equal to that of the preferred capital structure.  A shareholder who prefers a capital structure with less leverage than that which the firm has adopted can duplicate the preferred capital structure by _____ an amount sufficient to create a personal debt/equity ratio equal to that of the preferred capital structure.

6.  Under the above circumstances, the price of a firm's common stock (is/is not) dependent on the firm's capital structure. This conclusion is referred to as _____.  This result is based on the following two assumptions: first, _____; and, second, investors can borrow on their own account at the _____.

7.  According to the pie model, the value of the firm can be viewed as a pie, and the firm's capital structure is represented by _____.  M&M Proposition I states that the size of the pie is not affected by the manner in which the pie is sliced; that is, the total value of the firm's assets is not affected by the manner in which _____.  The firm's cash flow is generated by its _____; the firm's capital structure is a way of packaging those cash flows and selling them in financial markets.

8.  Proposition I is expressed in the following formula, where $V_u = $ _____ and $V_L = $ _____.

9.  M&M Proposition II addresses the relationship between the firm's debt/equity ratio and the firm's _____.  M&M Proposition II establishes a positive relationship between leverage and the _____.

10. M&M Proposition II (no taxes) is stated algebraically as:  $R_E = $ _____ . This relationship indicates that the required return on equity is a linear function of the _____.  M&M Proposition II states that the cost of equity is given by a straight line with a slope of _____ and a y-intercept of _____. The y-intercept indicates that, for a firm with no debt, $R_E = $ _____.

11.   As the debt/equity ratio increases, the cost of equity rises in a _____ fashion, but the increased cost of equity is exactly offset by the _____. As a result, the overall cost of capital (does/does not) change as the debt/equity ratio changes. Therefore, the value of the firm (is/is not) affected by changes in the capital structure.

12.   A primary difference between debt and equity is that interest (is/is not) tax-deductible, whereas dividends (are/are not) tax deductible. The tax subsidy on interest (increases/decreases) the attractiveness of debt. The capital structure (does/does not) have an impact on the firm's cash flows. The interest expense on debt generates a tax saving equal to the _____ multiplied by the _____. This tax saving is called the _____, and its value is computed in either of the following alternative ways: _____ = _____ .

13.   The after-tax cash flow to the shareholders of an unlevered firm is equal to _____ × _____. If we assume that all cash flows are perpetual and constant, then the value of an unlevered firm is: $V_U$ = _____ .

14.   M&M Proposition I (with corporate taxes) states that the value of a levered firm, $V_L$, is equal to the value of the _____ plus the value of the _____: $V_L$ = _____ . These results demonstrate that, in a world with corporate taxes, the firm has an incentive to (increase/decrease) its debt/equity ratio. A higher debt/equity ratio (increases/decreases) taxes and (increases/decreases) the total value of the firm. In fact, the above results indicate that a firm should move as close as possible to _____. This conclusion is derived under the assumption that there are no _____.

15.   M&M Proposition II (with corporate taxes) describes the relationship between the debt/equity ratio and the cost of equity capital as: $R_E$ = _____ . It indicates a positive relationship between expected return on equity and the _____ . It also implies that the firm's overall cost of capital (increases/decreases) as the amount of debt increases.

16.   The M&M Propositions (with taxes) state that a firm can increase its value by (increasing/decreasing) leverage. However, these propositions ignore the cost of _____, which (increases/decreases)with increases in the firm's level of debt.

17.   When we combine the SML and Proposition II, the relationship between the equity beta, $\beta_E$, and the asset beta, $\beta_A$ is: _____ . This can be rewritten as: _____ .

18.   $\beta_A$ is a measure of the riskiness of the firm's assets, as it measures the _____ of the firm. $\beta_A \times (D/E)$ measures the _____ of the firm's equity.

19.   The ultimate financial distress is _____, in which case ownership of the firm's assets is transferred to the _____. The legal interpretation of bankruptcy is the process whereby the firm's assets are turned over to the firm's _____. This process involves significant expenses, referred to as _____, which include attorneys' fees, administrative and accounting fees, and, in the event of a trial, fees to expert witnesses. Bankruptcy often results in an impaired ability to conduct business; costs associated with this impaired ability are referred to as _____ .

20.   The _____ theory of capital structure states that a firm uses additional debt financing up to the point where the _____ benefit derived from an additional dollar of debt exactly offsets the cost associated with an increased likelihood of _____. The _____ capital structure occurs when the present value of the tax savings from an additional dollar of debt equals the increase in the present value of expected bankruptcy costs; at this point, the value of the firm is _____ .

21. A large number of different types of claims to the firm's cash flow may exist at any time. All the claims to the firm's cash flow can nonetheless be divided into two groups; the debt and equity are the _____ claims and the rest are _____ claims. The capital structure issue is really the question of whether the total value of the _____ claims can be increased by decreasing the size of the _____ claims.

22. The value of the levered firm taking into account personal taxes is: _____ . However, if $T_b$ and $T_s$ are equal, then the value of the levered firm is: _____ .

23. The reason why there may be no gain from leverage is that the lower corporate taxes for a levered firm are exactly offset by higher _____ .

24. It is important to consider evidence from the real world in establishing capital structure policy.  Most firms (do/do not) use a great deal of debt; there would appear to be limits on the ability of firms to exploit the _____ . Firms in similar industries (do/do not) tend to have similar capital structures, while capital structures (do/do not) vary widely across industries. This fact suggests that capital structure is influenced by the nature of a firm's _____ .

25. _____ is the termination of a business which results in a loss to the firm's creditors. _____is a legal proceeding which results in the liquidation or reorganization of the firm.

26. _____ results from a firm's default on a legal obligation to pay a debt. _____ is a condition in which the firm's liabilities exceed the firm's assets, so that the firm's net worth is negative.

27. _____ is the termination of a firm, following a bankruptcy proceeding.  The firm's assets are sold and the proceeds of the sale are distributed to those with claims against the firm. _____ is a plan that allows the firm to continue to operate, but generally requires a restructuring of the firm's debts.

## ANSWERS TO CONCEPT TEST

1. finances; finances; assets

2. the value of the firm increases; shareholders; value of the firm

3. present value; weighted average cost of capital; weighted average cost of capital

4. debt; high; low; magnifies; greater; increases

5. is not; borrowing; lending; homemade leverage; borrowing; lending

6. is not; M&M Proposition I (no taxes); there are no taxes; same rate that the firm pays on its debt

7. the way in which the pie is sliced; financing is obtained; assets

8. $EBIT / R_E^U$ ;   $E_L + D_L$

9. cost of equity capital; expected return on equity

10. $R_A + (R_A - R_D) \times (D/E)$;  debt/equity ratio;  $(R_A - R_D)$;  $R_A$;  $R_A$

11.    linear;  increased use of cheaper debt; does not; is not

12.    is; are not; increases; does; interest payment; corporate tax rate; interest tax shield; $[(T_C \times R_D \times D)/R_D]$; $(T_C \times D)$

13.    EBIT;  $(1 - T_C)$;  $[EBIT \times (1 - T_C)]/\rho$

14.    unlevered firm; interest tax shield;  $V_U + (T_C \times D)$; increase; decreases; increases; an all-debt capital structure; bankruptcy costs

15.    $\rho + [(\rho - R_D) \times (D/E) \times (1 - T_C)]$;  debt/equity ratio; decreases

16.    increasing; bankruptcy; increases

17.    $\beta_E = \beta_A \times (1 + D/E)$; $\beta_E = \beta_A + \beta_A (D/E)$

18.    business risk; financial risk

19.    bankruptcy; bondholders; bondholders; direct bankruptcy costs; indirect bankruptcy costs

20.    static; tax; financial distress; optimal; maximized

21.    marketed; nonmarketed; marketed; nonmarketed

22.    $V_L = V_U + 1 - \dfrac{(1 - T_C)(1 - T_S)}{(1 - T_b)} \times D$;  $V_L = V_u + (T_c \times D)$

23     personal taxes

24.    do not; interest tax shield; do; do; assets

25.    business failure; legal bankruptcy

26.    technical insolvency; accounting insolvency

27.    liquidation; reorganization


## PROBLEMS AND SOLUTIONS

### Problem 1

Vancom Corporation is an all-equity firm with 10,000 shares of stock outstanding.  The market value per share is $20, making the market value of the company 10,000 x $20  =  $200,000.  The CFO is recommending issuing $80,000 of debt in order to repurchase ($80,000 / $20) = 4,000 shares of the firm's outstanding stock.  The interest rate on debt is 15%. Given the different EBIT scenarios for Vancom Company below, calculate net income, ROE, and EPS with its current capital structure and under the CFO's proposal.

| | Scenario | | |
| | Recession | Expected | Unexpected |
| --- | --- | --- | --- |
| EBIT | $25,000 | $50,000 | $75,000 |

**Solution:**

| | Current structure: no debt | | |
| | Recession | Expected | Unexpected |
| --- | --- | --- | --- |
| EBIT | $25,000 | $50,000 | $75,000 |
| Interest | 0 | 0 | 0 |
| Net income | $25,000 | $50,000 | $75,000 |
| | | | |
| ROE | 12.5% | 25.0% | 37.5% |
| EPS | $ 2.50 | $ 5.00 | $ 7.50 |

| | Proposed structure: Debt = $80,000 | | |
| | Recession | Expected | Unexpected |
| --- | --- | --- | --- |
| EBIT | $25,000 | $50,000 | $75,000 |
| Interest | 12,000 | 12,000 | 12,000 |
| Net income | $13,000 | $38,000 | $63,000 |
| | | | |
| ROE | 10.8% | 31.7% | 52.5% |
| EPS | $ 2.17 | $6.33 | $10.50 |

## Problem 2

Given the above findings, use the DFL to determine the indifference EBIT for Vancom Company.

**Solution:** The indifference EBIT is determined by equating the two expressions for EPS with all-equity, and with debt, and then solving for EBIT:

$$\frac{EBIT - \$0}{10,000} = \frac{EBIT - \$12,000}{6,000}$$

$$6,000 \times EBIT = 10,000 \times EBIT - \$120,000,000$$

$$-4,000 \times EBIT = -\$120,000,000$$

$$EBIT = \$30,000$$

At an EBIT of $30,000, EPS is $3 for either capital structure. For an EBIT below $30,000, Vancom will prefer an all-equity structure, while for any EBIT above $30,000, debt financing will be preferred, because EPS is higher.

## Use the information below to solve Problems 3 to 11:

Maxlever and Nolever are identical firms in all ways except that Maxlever employs debt in its capital structure and Nolever does not. Earnings before interest and taxes (EBIT) for each firm are expected to be $10,000. The total value of equity is $40,000 for Maxlever and $80,000 for Nolever. Maxlever has 1,000 shares outstanding; Nolever has 2,000 shares outstanding. Maxlever's bonds have a market value and a face value of $40,000. The interest rate is 10% and there are no taxes.

## Problem 3

Compute earnings per share (EPS), return on equity (ROE), and price per share for Nolever and for Maxlever.

**Solution:** For a firm with no debt, net income equals EBIT. Nolever's EPS is ($10,000/2,000) = $5.00. ROE is ($10,000/$80,000) = .125 = 12.5%. The price per share is ($80,000/2,000) = $40.

For Maxlever, net income is EBIT less interest. The firm's interest payment is (.10 × $40,000) = $4,000, and net income is ($10,000 – $4,000) = $6,000. EPS is ($6,000 / 1,000) = $6.00. ROE is ($6,000 / $40,000) = 15%. Price per share is ($40,000 / 1,000) = $40.

## Problem 4

In the event of a recession, both Maxlever and Nolever will have EBIT equal to $5,000. EBIT will be $20,000 in the event of an economic expansion. Compute EPS and ROE for each firm under each of these scenarios.

**Solution:** The calculations for this problem and the results from Problem 3 are summarized below:

### Nolever: No debt

|            | Recession | Expected | Expansion |
|------------|-----------|----------|-----------|
| EBIT       | $ 5,000   | $ 10,000 | $ 20,000  |
| Interest   | 0         | 0        | 0         |
| Net income | $ 5,000   | $ 10,000 | $ 20,000  |
|            |           |          |           |
| ROE        | 6.25%     | 12.50%   | 25.00%    |
| EPS        | $2.50     | $5.00    | $10.00    |

### Maxlever: Debt = $40,000

|            | Recession | Expected | Expansion |
|------------|-----------|----------|-----------|
| EBIT       | $ 5,000   | $10,000  | $ 20,000  |
| Interest   | 4,000     | 4,000    | 4,000     |
| Net income | $ 1,000   | $ 6,000  | $ 16,000  |
|            |           |          |           |
| ROE        | 2.50%     | 15.00%   | 40.00%    |
| EPS        | $1.00     | $6.00    | $16.00    |

## Problem 5

Compute the level of EBIT such that Maxlever and Nolever have the same earnings per share.

**Solution:**  The level of EBIT such that the two firms have the same earnings per share is the indifference EBIT discussed in the chapter.  For Nolever, EPS is (EBIT - $0)/2,000)); for Maxlever, EPS is (EBIT – $4,000)/1,000.  Equating these two expressions and solving for EBIT, we find the indifference level of EBIT as follows:

$$\frac{\text{EBIT} - \$0}{2,000} = \frac{\text{EBIT} - \$4,000}{1,000}$$

$$1,000 \times \text{EBIT} = 2,000 \times \text{EBIT} - \$8,000,000$$

$$\text{EBIT} = \$8,000$$

When EBIT is $8,000, EPS is equal to $4 for both Maxlever and Nolever.

## Problem 6

Suppose that an investor purchased 200 shares of Maxlever.  Compute the cost of this investment and the earnings for this position under each of the three scenarios described in Problems 1 and 2.

**Solution:**  The net cost of this investment is ($40 × 200) = $8,000. In the event of a recession, the total earnings for this investment will be ($1 × 200) = $200. Earnings for the expected scenario and the recession scenario are $1,200 and $3,200, respectively.

## Problem 7

Explain how the investor described in Problem 6 can duplicate the earnings from the investment in Maxlever by borrowing and investing in the shares of Nolever.

**Solution:**   The debt/equity ratio of Maxlever is 1.00.   Therefore, the investor must purchase $8,000 of the equity of Nolever, and borrow an amount equal to the equity investment.   That is, the investor borrows $8,000 and purchases an additional $8,000 of Nolever common stock.   The returns for this position, and for the investment described in Problem 6 are summarized in the following table:

|                              | Maxlever | | | | |
|------------------------------|----------|-----------|--------|---------|-----------|
|                              | Recession | | Expected | | Expansion |
| EPS                          | $  1.00  |           | $  6.00 |         | $  16.00  |
| Total earnings (200 shares)  | 200.00   |           | 1,200.00 |        | 3,200.00  |

Net cost   =   (200 x $40)   =   $8,000.00

|                              | Nolever | | |
|------------------------------|---------|----------|-----------|
|                              | Recession | Expected | Expansion |
| EPS                          | $   2.50 | $   5.00 | $   10.00 |
| Earnings for 400 shares      | 1,000.00 | 2,000.00 | 4,000.00  |
| Less interest ($8,000 @ 10%) | 800.00  | 800.00   | 800.00    |
| Net earnings                 | $   200.00 | $1,200.00 | $3,200.00 |

Net cost   =   (400 x $40) - Amount borrowed   =   $16,000 - $8,000   =   $8,000

## Problem 8

Suppose that increased leverage increased the value of the firm, so that the market value of Maxlever is $90,000, while the market value of Nolever remains at $80,000. How would the investor above react to this information?

**Solution:**   The investor's return is the same for the two strategies in Problems 4 and 5.   However, if the market value of Maxlever is $90,000, rather than $80,000, the cost of buying 200 shares of Maxlever is now higher.   The market value of equity is now ($90,000 – $40,000) = $50,000;   the value of a share is ($50,000/1,000) = $50.   The cost of 200 shares of Maxlever is ($50 × 200) = $10,000. The strategy of Problem 5 duplicates the cash flows from 200 shares of Maxlever, but the cost is only $8,000.   As a result, a rational investor would pursue the strategy of Problem 7.   This would increase the value of Nolever and decrease the value of Maxlever.  Prices will adjust until the market values of the two firms are equal. The interpretation of this result is that corporate leverage does not have value to the shareholder, since the same effect can be created with homemade leverage.

## Problem 9

Suppose that an investor purchased 200 shares of Nolever. Compute the cost of this investment and the earnings for this position under each of the three scenarios described in Problems 3 and 4.

**Solution:**  The net cost of this investment is ($40 × 200) = $8,000. In the event of a recession, the total earnings for this investment will be ($2.50 × 200) = $500.   Earnings for the expected scenario and the recession scenario are $1,000 and $2,000, respectively.

## Problem 10

Explain how the investor described in Problem 9 can duplicate the earnings from the investment in Nolever by lending and investing in the shares of Maxlever.

**Solution:** The investor would purchase 100 shares of Maxlever, and lend $4,000 at 10% interest. The returns for this position, and for the investment described in Problem 9, are summarized in the following table:

| | Nolever | | |
|---|---|---|---|
| | Recession | Expected | Expansion |
| EPS | $ 2.50 | $ 5.00 | $ 10.00 |
| Total earnings (200 shares) | $ 500.00 | $1,000.00 | $ 2,000.00 |

Net cost = (200 x $40) = $8,000.00

| | Nolever | | |
|---|---|---|---|
| | Recession | Expected | Expansion |
| EPS | $ 1.00 | $ 6.00 | $ 16.00 |
| Earnings for 100 shares | 100.00 | 600.00 | 1,600.00 |
| Plus interest ($4,000 @ 10%) | 400.00 | 400.00 | 400.00 |
| Net earnings | $ 520.00 | $ 1,000.00 | $ 2,000.00 |

Net cost = (100 x $40) + Amount loaned = $4,000 +$4,000 = $8,000

## Problem 11

Suppose that increased leverage decreased the value of the firm, so that the market value of Maxlever is $70,000, while the market value of Nolever remains at $80,000. How would the investor described in Problems 7 and 8 react to this information?

**Solution:** The solutions to Problems 7 and 8 indicate that the investor can earn the same returns from either strategy. The net cost of purchasing 200 shares of Nolever is $8,000. If the market value of Maxlever is $70,000, then the market value of the firm's equity is ($70,000 − $40,000) = $30,000, and the market value of a share is ($30,000/1,000) = $30. Consequently, the cost of the strategy of Problem 8 is $7,000. Since the same returns can be earned for a lower cost, any rational investor would purchase the stock of Maxlever, rather than the stock of Nolever. This would result in an adjustment of the values of the two firms, until the values are equal. As in Problem 6, this example demonstrates the fact that leverage does not affect the value of the firm.

## Problem 12

Ice King Industries makes artificial snow for use on movie sets. It is an all-equity firm with cash flow of $275,000 per year forever. Its discount rate is 10%. In a perfect market setting, what is the value of the firm? What would be the value of an identical, but levered firm?

**Solution:**  $V_U$ = $275,000 / .10 = $2,750,000. The value of the levered firm is the same $2,750,000 because, in a perfect market setting, capital structure has no effect on the value of the firm.

## Problem 13

Now assume Ice King borrows $500,000 to repurchase equity. The cost of debt is 7%. The firm's asset beta equals one, and the market portfolio returns 10%. What is the new value of the equity when adjusted for the increased financial risk?

**Solution:**   New  cash flow = $275,000 - ($500,000 x 0.07) = $240,000. The new equity value is the value of the levered firm less the value of the debt: Equity value  =  $2,750,000  -  $500,000  =  $2,250,000. The firm's new equity beta is: Equity beta  =  1 x [1 + ($500,000 / 2,250,000)]  =  1.2222. The new required return on equity  = .070 + (0.10 - 0 .07) x 1.2222 = .10667.   The new value of the equity  = $240, 000 / 0.10667  = $2,250,000.

## Problem 14

Island  Cruises expects pre-tax cash flows of $2 million in perpetuity. The company has no debt. The asset beta of cruise lines is 1.5. Assuming perfect markets with a riskless interest rate of 5% and a 12% return on the market index, what is the required return on assets and on equity? If the company has one million shares outstanding, what is the value of a single share?

**Solution:**   $R_A$   =   0.05  +  (0.12  -  0.05) x 1.5  =  0.155  =  15.5%
$R_E$   =   $R_D$   =   15.5%   because the firm has no debt
$V_u$   =   $2,000,000 / 0.155  =  $12,903,225.81
Value of each share  =  $12.90

## Problem 15

If Ice King (from problems 12 and  13 above) shares traded for $10 each before the capital restructuring, what is the price per share after the firm issues $500,000 in debt?

**Solution:**  When Ice King was an all-equity firm, there were $2,750,000 / 10 = 275,000 shares outstanding. The firm repurchased $500,000 / $10  = 50,000 shares,  so there are now 225,000 shares outstanding. The new share price is $2,250,000 / 225,000 = $10. As expected, the price per share was not affected by the change in capital structure.

## Problem 16

Assume that you own 2,250 shares or 1% of Ice King stock after the capital restructuring. Demonstrate that, even if Ice King decides not to restructure, you could use personal leverage to receive the same net cash flows as you now receive.

**Solution:**  After the restructuring, your share of Ice King's cash flow is $240,000 x .01  =  $2,400. Before the restructuring, the value of your equity position was  $10 x 2,250 shares = $22,500.  In order to have the same D/E ratio as the leveraged firm, you should  borrow 0.01 x $500,000 = $5,000, which you will use to buy new shares. You now own [2,250 + ($5,000 / $10)] = 2,750 shares.

Your ownership percentage is 2,750 / 275,000  =  0.01 of the firm.  Therefore, your net cash flow (after subtracting interest on your debt) will be ($275,000 x .01)  -  ($5,000 x .07)  =  $2,400.  This is the same cash flow whether the firm decides to issues debt or to remain as an all-equity firm.

## Problem 17

Show that, for Ice King, both the unlevered company and the new leveraged company have the same weighted average cost of capital.

**Solution:**  The WACC for the unlevered firm is  ( 0 / $2,750,000) x 0.07  +  ($2,750,000 / $2,750,000) x 0.10   =  0.10  =  10%.  The WACC for the levered firm is ($500,000 / $2,750,000) x 0.07   +  ($2,250,000 / $2,750,000) x 0.10667  =  0.10  =  10%.

## Use the information below to solve Problems 18 to 21.

The North Company, a major manufacturer of document shredders, has a perpetual expected EBIT of $200. The interest rate for North's debt is 12%.

## Problem 18

Assuming that there are no taxes or bankruptcy costs, what is the value of North Company if its debt/equity ratio is .25 and its weighted average cost of capital is 16%?  What is the value of North's equity?  What is the value of North's debt?

**Solution:**   If there are no taxes, then M&M Proposition I (no taxes) applies and North's capital structure is irrelevant.  The value of the firm is: $EBIT / R_A$   =   $200 / .16   =   $1,250.   A debt/equity ratio of .25 indicates that the firm has $0.25 of debt for each dollar of equity.  Therefore, North's capital structure is 80% equity, and the value of the equity is (.80 × $1,250) = $1,000.  The value of the debt is ($1,250 – $1,000) = $250.

## Problem 19

What is the cost of equity capital for North Company?

**Solution:** The cost of equity capital can be computed using M&M Proposition II as:  $R_E$  =  .16 + [(.16 – .12) × .25] = .17 = 17%.   Alternatively, we can compute the cash flow to shareholders as: $200 – (.12 × $250) = $170.  Since the value of the equity is $1,000, the cost of capital is ($170 / $1,000) = .17 = 17%.

## Problem 20

Suppose the corporate tax rate is 30%, there are no personal taxes or bankruptcy costs, and North has $400 in debt outstanding. If the unlevered cost of equity is 20%, what is the value of North Company?  What is the value of the firm's equity?

**Solution:**  The value of North as an unlevered firm is:  $V_U$  =  $[EBIT \times (1 - T_C)] / \rho$  =  [$200 x .70] / .20  =  $700.   Proposition I (with corporate taxes) states that the value of a levered firm, $V_L$, is equal to the value of the unlevered firm plus the value of the interest tax shield: $V_L$  =  $V_U$  +  $(T_C \times D)$  =  $700  +  (.30 x $400)  =  $820.  The value of the firm's equity is ($820 – $400) = $420.

## Problem 21

What is the weighted average cost of capital for North Company?

**Solution:**   Following M&M Proposition II (with corporate taxes), the cost of equity for North is: $R_E$ = $\rho$ + ($\rho$ - $R_D$) x (D / E) x (1 - $T_C$)  =  .20  +  (.20 - .12) x ($400 / $420) x (1 - .30) =  .25333  =  25.33%. Alternatively, the cost of equity capital can be computed by first calculating the cash flow to shareholders as: [$200 – (.12 × $400)] × (1 – .30) = $106.40.  Using this method, the return on equity is ($106.40/$420) = 25.333%, as previously calculated.

The weighted average cost of capital is: WACC  =  ($420 / $820) x .25333  +  ($400 / $820) x .12 x .70  = .17073  =  17.07%.   Therefore, the weighted average cost of capital for an unlevered firm is 20% (i.e., WACC = $\rho$ = 20%), while the WACC for North Company is 17.073%.

## Problem 22

Coprez Corporation has an EBIT of $400 per year.  The interest rate on debt is 10% and Coprez does not pay taxes. If there are no bankruptcy costs and the debt/equity ratio is 0.5, what is the value of Coprez's debt and equity if the WACC is 12%?

**Solution:** The value of the firm is EBIT / $R_A$  =  $400 / 0.12  =  $3,333.  With a 0.5 debt/equity ratio, Coprez's capital structure is 1/3 debt and 2/3 equity.  The value of the debt is therefore $3,333 x 1/3  =  $1,111.  The value of the equity is $3,333 - $1,111 =  $2,222.

## Problem 23

What is the cost of equity capital for Coprez Corporation?

**Solution:** $R_E$  =  0.12 + [(0.12 - 0.10) x 0.5 ] =  0.13  =  13%

The cost of equity can also be computed as $400  - (0.10 x $1,111) / $2,222  = $289 / $2,222 = 0.13 = 13%

## Use the following information to solve Problems 24 to 28:

Merrick Motors is an all-equity firm with earnings expected to be $450,000 in perpetuity.  The firm has 100,000 shares outstanding.  The cost of capital is 15%. MM is considering a major expansion of its facilities which will require an initial outlay of $400,000 and is expected to produce additional annual earnings of $150,000 per year in perpetuity.  Management considers the expansion to have the same risk as the firm's existing assets.  Assume throughout that there are no taxes and no costs of bankruptcy.

## Problem 24

What is the value of the firm's assets prior to undertaking the proposed expansion?  What is the value of the firm's equity?  What is the price per share of the firm's stock?

**Solution:** The value of the firm is ($450,000/.15) = $3,000,000. Since MM is an all-equity firm, the value of the firm's equity is also $3,000,000. Price per share is ($3,000,000/100,000) = $30.

## Problem 25

Suppose MM plans to finance the expansion by issuing common stock. How many shares of stock must be issued? What is the value of the firm's equity after the new stock issue? What is the price per share of the firm's stock?

**Solution:** The NPV of the expansion is: –$400,000 + ($150,000/.15) = $600,000. Therefore, when the firm announces the expansion, the value of the firm increases to ($3,000,000 + $600,000) = $3,600,000. That is, the value of the firm's assets and the value of the equity each increase to $3,600,000. Price per share increases to ($3,600,000/100,000) = $36. Note that this increase in value occurs immediately following the announcement of the expansion, but before financing is obtained. To obtain $400,000 in equity financing, the firm sells ($400,000/$36) = 11,111 shares of stock. The proceeds of the stock issue are used to acquire the new assets, so that the value of the firm becomes ($3,000,000 + $600,000 + $400,000) = $4,000,000, which is the value of the firm's equity. The price per share is still $36 after the financing; that is, ($4,000,000/111,111) = $36. Note that the $6 gain in share price is the project's NPV divided by the original number of shares outstanding: $600,000 / 100,000 = $6.

## Problem 26

Suppose MM plans to finance the expansion by issuing bonds with an interest rate of 10%. What is the value of the firm after the new bond issue? What is the value of the firm's equity? What is the price per share of the firm's stock?

**Solution:** As in Problem 25, the value of the firm increases to $3,600,000 after the announcement of the expansion. When the firm issues $400,000 of new debt, the value of the firm's assets increases to $4,000,000, but the value of the firm's equity remains at $3,600,000. The value of the firm is the same as under the equity financing arrangement, as indicated by M&M Proposition I (no taxes). The price per share of the firm's stock is $36 after the announcement and before the financing is obtained, and remains at $36 after the financing is obtained. Again, the gain in share price is equal to the project's NPV divided by the original number of shares outstanding, $6.

## Problem 27

Calculate the expected yearly income after interest for the equityholders. Use the expected yearly income to calculate the expected return for the equityholders.

**Solution:** Expected yearly income is  $450,000 + $150,000 – (.10 × $400,000) = $560,000. The expected return for the equityholders is ($560,000/$3,600,000) = 15.556%.

## Problem 28

Use M&M Proposition II (no taxes) to determine the expected return for the equityholders.

**Solution:** M&M Proposition II (no taxes) indicates that the return to equityholders is: $560,000 / $3,600,000 = .15556 = 15.556%.

## Problem 29

Maestro Frozen Foods expects to earn $365,000 in perpetuity before interest and taxes from its line of gourmet TV dinners. The company has a debt to assets ratio of 40%. The cost of debt is 10%. If the company had no debt, its cost of capital would have been 15%. The firm's tax rate is 30%. What is the value of the firm? The value of its equity? The required rate of return on equity? The weighted average cost of capital?

**Solution:**  $V_u$  =  $365,000 \times (1 - 0.30) / 0.15$   =   $1,703,333. To find the value of the levered firm, you should recognize that debt is 40% of total asset value. So, for the present value of the interest tax shield ($T_c \times D$), we can substitute ($V_L \times 0.40$) for D.  $V_L =$   $V_u + T_c \times D$  =   $1,703,333 + 0.30 \times V_L (0.4)$. Solving, $0.88 V_L =$ $1,703,333 and  $V_L$  =  $1,935,606.

We know that the value of the debt is 40% of total firm value, so  D  =  $1,935,606 x (0.4)  =  $774,242.40.  This means the equity value is:  E  =  $1,935,606  -  $774,242.40  =  $1,161,364.

The return on equity and WACC are:

$$R_E \quad = \quad 0.15 + (0.15 - 0.10) \times [(0.40 / 0.60) \times (1 - 0.30)] \quad = \quad 0.173 \quad = \quad 17.3\%$$
$$\text{WACC} = \quad 0.15 \times [1 - (0.30 \times 0.40)] \quad = \quad 0.132 \quad = \quad 13.2\%$$

## Problem 30

Now suppose that Maestro decides to issue equity and retire its debt. What will happen to the value of the firm? Assume that, under the current capital structure, there are 100,000 shares outstanding.

**Solution:** With debt, the share price is $1,161,363 / 100,000  =  $11.61 per share. The firm's current debt level is $774,242.40, so they need to issue $774,242.49 / $11.61 = 66,687.55 shares. The entire after-tax cash flow goes to the shareholders: $365,000 x (1 - 0.30)  =  $255,500. Each share receives $255,500 / 166,687.55  =  $1.5328. The present value is $1.5328 / 0.15  =  $10.2187. The value of the equity (and the unlevered firm) is $10.2187 x 166,687.55  =  $1,703,333. This is the same answer we would have obtained using the equation for the value of the levered firm. (Note: You may have slightly different answers, due to rounding.)

## Problem 31

Now, using the information for Maestro above, assume that the personal tax rate on equity income is 20 % and the tax rate on interest income is 35%. How will this affect the value of the company?

**Solution:**  $V_L$   =   $1,703,333 + $774,242.40 x [1 - (1 - .30) x (1 - .20) / (1 - .35)]  =  $1,810,536

# 17        <u>Dividends and Dividend Policy</u>

## CHAPTER HIGHLIGHTS

Simple intuition suggests that dividend policy should not matter a great deal. Investors wishing a cash payout from their stock portfolios can simply sell some stock and pay themselves a cash 'dividend.' Investors who do not want a cash dividend can simply reinvest dividends received. However, the argument is slightly more complicated. Certain factors favour high dividend payouts; others favour low payouts. Then, some argue that dividend policy is irrelevant. These points of view are addressed below.

## CASH DIVIDENDS AND DIVIDEND PAYMENT

A *dividend* is a cash payment, made to shareholders, from the firm's earnings. If the payment is from sources other than current earnings, it is called a *distribution from capital* or a *liquidating dividend*. The basic types of cash dividends are:

1.    Regular cash dividends
2.    Extra dividends
3.    Liquidating dividends

**Cash Dividends:** Typically, a corporation pays a *regular cash dividend* four times a year. An *extra cash dividend* may also be paid periodically, but not on a regular basis. A *liquidating dividend* results from the liquidation of all or part of the corporation.

**Standard Method of Cash Dividend Payment:** A cash dividend can be expressed as either dollars per share (*dividends per share*), a percentage of market price (*dividend yield*), or as a percentage of earnings per share (*dividend payout*). A dividend becomes a liability of the firm once it is declared by the board of directors.

**Dividend Payment - A Chronology:** The chronology of a dividend payment involves the following four dates: the *declaration date*, the *ex-dividend date*, the *date of record*, and the *date of payment*. On the declaration date, the board of directors announces the amount of the dividend and the date of record. The dividend is paid to shareholders who are holders of record as of the date of record. The dividend cheques are mailed to these owners on the date of payment.

If you buy a share the day before the date of record, this fact would not be reflected in the corporation's records on the date of record because of processing delays; the previous owner would be the shareholder of record. To avoid inconsistencies created by such delays, brokerage firms set the ex-dividend date four business days prior to the record date. Anyone purchasing a share on or after the ex-dividend date does not receive the dividend. Prior to the ex-dividend date, the stock is said to be trading *cum dividend* (with dividend). Subsequently, it trades *ex-dividend*.

**More on the Ex-Dividend Date:** Suppose a stock pays a $1 dividend and goes ex-dividend on Wednesday. If you buy the stock on Tuesday, just before the market closes, you will receive the dividend. If you buy on Wednesday, just as the market opens, you will not. The price of the stock declines overnight by approximately the amount of the dividend. Since dividends are taxed as ordinary income, the price decline is actually closer to the after-tax value of the dividend, rather than the full amount of the dividend.

## DOES DIVIDEND POLICY MATTER?

A firm's dividend policy determines the pattern of dividend payment over time.  A firm can choose to pay a large percentage of earnings to shareholders in the form of dividends, or to pay a small percentage of earnings as dividends and to reinvest a large portion of earnings with the expectation that larger dividend payments will be made in the future.  The issue of dividend policy concerns the question of whether one or the other of these approaches is more advantageous to the shareholders.

**An Illustration of the Irrelevance of Dividend Policy:**  The basic argument for dividend irrelevance can be illustrated with a simple numerical example.  Consider a corporation with 100 shares outstanding and which will have a certain cash flow of $110 at date 1, and will liquidate for a certain $242 at date 2.  If 10% is the required rate of return, then the total value of the firm is:

$$\frac{\$110}{1.10} + \frac{\$242}{(1.10)^2} = \$300$$

Each share is worth ($300/100) = $3.

One possible dividend policy is to pay $110 at date 1 and $242 at date 2.  Suppose that, instead, the shareholders prefer a $200 dividend at date 1.  To pay this amount, the firm could sell $90 worth of new stock at year's end and pay out a total of $200.  What dividend would be paid to the old shareholders at date 2?  There is $242 available at date 2.  The new shareholders require a 10% return, so they would have to be paid ($90 × 1.10) = $99, leaving ($242 – $99) = $143 for the old shareholders. The present value of the dividends the old shareholders receive is:

$$\frac{\$200}{1.10} + \frac{\$143}{(1.10)^2} = \$300$$

The present value of this dividend policy is therefore identical to the present value of the previous policy.  In fact, no matter how the available cash is paid out as dividends, the present value is always $300.

**Homemade Dividends:**  Suppose you own 10 shares of stock in the company described above, and the firm has decided to pay out $110 and $242 at date 1 and date 2, respectively.  You will receive $11 and $24.20, respectively.  Also, suppose that you would rather receive $20 and $14.30, at dates 1 and 2. Given the firm's dividend policy, you can create the cash flows you prefer by selling enough shares at the end of the first year to receive the extra $9.  In doing so, you forfeit ($9 × 1.10) = $9.90 at date 2. Thus, you will receive ($24.20 – $9.90) = $14.30, effectively creating a new dividend policy or *homemade dividend.*

Some corporations assist their shareholders by offering *automatic dividend reinvestment plans* (ADPs or DRIPs), which give the shareholder the option to automatically reinvest some or all of their cash dividend in shares acquired at a small discount.  Investment dealers have also created homemade dividends (or homemade capital gains) called *stripped common shares* which entitle holders to receive either all the dividends of one or a group of well-known companies which packages any capital gain in the form of a call option.  The investor has the right to buy the underlying shares at a fixed price.  The option value increases as share price increases.

It is important to keep in mind that we are not saying that dividends themselves are irrelevant; rather, the decision to pay dividends now or later is irrelevant.  It is also important to note that it is assumed here that the firm's dividend policy does not affect its investment policy.  That is, we assume that the firm accepts all positive NPV investment opportunities prior to making the dividend decision.

## REAL-WORLD FACTORS FAVOURING A LOW PAYOUT

The irrelevance of dividend policy established in the previous section is based on the assumption that there are no taxes or flotation costs. Clearly, these assumptions are inconsistent with reality. The current section is devoted to a discussion of how existing tax laws affect the earlier conclusions.

**Taxes:** Under current tax laws in Canada, both dividend income and capital gains are taxed at effective rates *less than* the marginal tax rates on ordinary income. Investors receiving dividend income face a lower tax rate due to the dividend tax credit. Capital gains are taxed at 75% of the marginal rate. Since taxation takes place only when capital gains are realized, capital gains are very lightly taxed in Canada and generally taxed lower than dividends.

A policy of low dividend payout means that earnings are reinvested in the firm. The value of the firm increases, resulting in capital gains for the shareholders. Consequently, the taxation of capital gains has implications for the firm's dividend policy. The lower effective tax rate for capital gains is a factor encouraging a low dividend payout.

Suppose a firm has adopted all available capital-budgeting projects with a positive net present value, and still has $1,000 in cash. This excess cash is sometimes referred to as *free cash flow*. Should such a firm pay the $1,000 in dividends to its shareholders, in spite of the tax implications and transactions costs noted above? Consider some alternatives to a dividend payment: (1) select additional capital-budgeting projects; (2) repurchase shares; (3) acquire other companies; (4) purchase financial assets.

Since the firm has already taken all positive NPV projects, any additional capital budgeting projects have negative NPVs. Therefore, alternative (1) is unacceptable. Alternative (2), repurchasing shares, may be viewed as dividends for tax purposes, so this alternative may not be very attractive. Alternative (3), acquisition of another company is generally not profitable for the acquiring firm. If the only motive for the acquisition is to avoid dividends, the acquisition will probably not succeed.

Alternative (4), the purchase of financial assets, may be advantageous to shareholders under certain circumstances. When the corporate tax rate exceeds the individual tax rate, investors would prefer to receive dividend income. Consider the following example:

Assume a firm has $10 extra cash, the corporate tax rate is 30%, and the individual tax rate is 20%. If the firm pays a $10 dividend, shareholders receive [$10 × (1 − .20)] = $8 after tax. If this is invested for five years at a 10% rate, investors will earn 8% on an after-tax basis. The investment will be worth [$8 × (1.08)$^5$] = $11.75 in five years. If the firm invested the $10 at a 10% rate instead of paying a dividend, the after-tax return would be 7%. After five years, the investment would be worth [$10 × (1.07)$^5$] = $14.03. If this amount is paid to shareholders, they will be able to keep the after-tax amount of [$14.03 × (1 − .20)] = $11.22. Clearly, the investors in this case would prefer the firm to pay the dividend today, so that they could invest for themselves.

On the other hand, if individual taxes are higher, the firm has an incentive to reduce dividend payouts.

**Flotation Costs:** In an earlier example, we noted that a firm could issue common stock in order to pay dividends. However, we ignored the fact that this would require the firm to pay flotation costs. These flotation costs can be substantial. So, this is an additional incentive in favour of a low dividend payout policy.

**Dividend Restrictions:** Bond indentures often limit a corporation's dividend payout. This protects bondholders in the event shareholders want to pay themselves a large dividend, possibly limiting their ability to meet interest payment to bondholders. Dividend restriction helps to resolve the agency conflict between bondholders and shareholders.

## REAL-WORLD FACTORS FAVOURING A HIGH PAYOUT

Some have argued that shareholders prefer a high dividend payout policy because of the desire for current income and the resolution of uncertainty.

**Desire for Current Income:**  Some investors, including many on fixed incomes, undoubtedly desire current income.  These investors might conceivably pay a premium for stocks with high dividends.  Selling a portion of the stock each period in order to produce current income may be undesirable because of brokerage fees, among other reasons.  However, a mutual fund could very easily provide this service by regularly selling its holdings of low-dividend stocks to pay dividends to its shareholders.  Therefore, high dividend payout is not necessarily preferable, even for shareholders who desire current income.

**Uncertainty Resolution:**  A dollar received in the form of a dividend has a known value, while a dollar reinvested by the corporation has an uncertain future value.  The 'bird-in-hand' story argues that the cash dividend reduces the risk of owning the stock.  However, this conclusion is erroneous because a shareholder can accomplish the same result by selling shares of a low-dividend stock in order to create homemade dividends.

**Tax and Legal Benefits from High Dividends:**  Tax considerations which reduce the effective tax rate for capital gains generally lead individual investors to prefer common stocks with low dividend payouts.  However, other investors are not subjected to higher tax rates on dividends.  For corporations which own the securities of other corporations, 100% of dividend income received is excluded from the firm's taxable income.  Consequently, these investors often prefer to own common stocks, or preferred stocks, with high dividend payouts, rather than either common stocks with low dividend payouts or corporate bonds.  In addition, pension funds, endowment funds, and trust funds favour stocks with high dividend payouts because these institutions are tax-exempt.

## A RESOLUTION OF REAL-WORLD FACTORS?

The general consensus is that several factors are important in establishing dividend policy.  Tax effects and flotation costs lead some investors to favour a low payout, whereas the desire for current income influences others to favour a high payout.  Although the issue has been studied extensively, it is not possible to determine which of these factors dominates, so the policy question is unresolved.  As explained below, the evidence is not easy to interpret.

**Information Content of Dividends:**  The *information content effect* is the market's reaction to a change in corporate dividend payout.  It is generally established that stock prices increase following an announcement of a dividend increase.  This fact seems to support the contention that investors prefer a high dividend payout. However, financial actions by the firm are sometimes regarded as a way of signalling future prospects to the financial markets.  Firms resist cutting dividends, so an announcement of an increase in dividends indicates that the firm expects future cash flow to be sufficient to support a higher level of dividends.  This is a positive signal, and consequently the stock price increases.  It is difficult to separate the information content of the announcement from the dividend itself.

**The Clientele Effect:**  Some investors prefer high dividend payouts while others prefer low payouts.  Different firms may cater to one group (or clientele) or the other.  As long as both groups are satisfied, the corporation does not benefit from a change in its dividend policy; doing so simply attracts a different clientele.  This scenario is called the *clientele effect*.  A natural type of clientele is based on tax brackets.  Evidence suggests that investors in low tax brackets tend to hold high payout stocks, and investors in high brackets hold low payout stocks.

# ESTABLISHING A DIVIDEND POLICY

In this section, we discuss alternative approaches to establishing a dividend policy.

**Residual Dividend Approach:**  Firms with low dividend payout ratios require less external financing than firms with high payout ratios.  Since external financing requires that the firm pay flotation costs, it is less expensive to obtain financing by retaining earnings; that is, by adopting a low dividend payout ratio.  In this section, we assume that the firm seeks to minimize the need to issue new common stock.  We also assume that the firm will maintain its existing capital structure.

A firm that adopts the *residual dividend approach* relies primarily on internally generated funds to finance positive NPV projects while maintaining a desired debt/equity ratio.  After allocating internally generated equity funds to all positive NPV projects, the firm pays dividends from any residual funds which remain after financing these projects.

**An Example:**  A firm with a residual dividend approach has $5,000 in earnings and a debt/equity ratio of 0.25.  What is the maximum amount of capital spending possible if the firm does not obtain any new equity financing and maintains the current debt/equity ratio?  If the firm has positive NPV projects available which require the investment of $4,000, how much will the firm pay in dividends?

A debt/equity ratio of 0.25 indicates the firm has $0.25 of debt for each dollar of equity.  The $5,000 in earnings represents available equity financing so that the firm must raise (.25 × $5,000) = $1,250 of debt financing.  Therefore, the total financing available, if the firm does not obtain any new equity financing, is ($5,000 + $1,250) = $6,250.

The debt/equity ratio of 0.25 means that the firm's capital structure is comprised of $0.25 of debt and $1.00 of equity for each $1.25 of total financing.  The capital structure is therefore ($0.25/$1.25) = 20% debt and ($1.00/$1.25) = 80% equity.  In order to finance capital expenditures of $4,000, while maintaining the existing capital structure, the firm will use debt financing of (.20 × $4,000) = $800, and equity financing of (.80 × $4,000) = $3,200.  Since the firm has $5,000 of internal equity financing available, dividends are ($5,000 – $3,200) = $1,800.

Since the total financing available is $6,250, the firm will obtain additional equity financing only if positive NPV projects require financing greater than this total.  Twenty percent of any additional financing, in excess of the available $6,250, is debt financing and 80% is equity financing.

Now assume the firm requires $10,000 of financing for positive NPV projects and $5,000 of equity financing is derived from retained earnings.  This $5,000 of equity financing implies debt financing of $1,250 in order to maintain the firm's debt/equity ratio, as described earlier.  Additional financing equal to ($10,000 – $6,250) = $3,750 is then obtained as follows: (.20 × $3,750) = $750 of additional debt financing and (.80 × $3,750) = $3,000 of additional equity financing.  Therefore, total equity financing consists of $5,000 of internally generated funds and $3,000 of new equity.  Total debt financing is equal to ($1,250 + $750) = $2,000.

**Dividend Stability:**  Under the residual dividend approach, the dividend paid depends on both the firm's earnings for the quarter and the firm's investment opportunities.  Because these quantities can vary significantly over time, the actual dividend paid can be very unstable. Since investors seem to value stability in dividends, alternative dividend policies might be preferable.  Dividend stability complements investor objectives of information content, income, and reduction in uncertainty.  Institutional investors often follow 'prudence' tests which restrict investment in firms that do not pay regular dividends.  One such policy is a cyclical dividend policy which sets each quarter's dividend equal to a fixed fraction of the quarter's earnings; this policy is cyclical because earnings, and consequently dividends, may vary throughout the year, but total annual dividends might remain relatively stable.

A second alternative policy sets quarterly dividends equal to a specified fraction of annual earnings, rather than quarterly earnings. This is a stable dividend policy if earnings are relatively stable from one year to the next.

**A Compromise Dividend Policy:** Many firms follow a compromise dividend policy based on the following goals:

1.  Avoid the rejection of positive NPV projects in order to pay a dividend.
2.  Avoid reducing dividends.
3.  Avoid issuing new equity.
4.  Maintain a target debt/equity ratio.
5.  Maintain a target dividend payout ratio.

For this kind of compromise dividend policy, both the target debt/equity ratio and the target dividend payout ratio are regarded as long-term goals, rather than strict requirements. The long-run *target payout ratio* is the fraction of earnings the firm normally expects to pay as dividends. If earnings are unusually low in a given quarter, the firm might choose to temporarily increase the payout ratio in order to avoid reducing dividends.

## STOCK REPURCHASE: AN ALTERNATIVE TO CASH DIVIDENDS

As an alternative to paying cash dividends, a firm can pay cash to its shareholders by a *repurchase* of its own stock from the shareholders. This alternative to cash dividends is discussed below.

**Cash Dividend versus Repurchase:** In the absence of taxes and transactions costs, a share repurchase has the same effect on shareholders as a dividend payment of the same dollar amount. Consider an all-equity firm with the following market value balance sheet:

| Market value balance sheet | | | |
|---|---|---|---|
| Excess cash | $ 60,000 | Debt | $ 0 |
| Other assets | 240,000 | Equity | 300,000 |
| Total | $ 300,000 | Total | $ 300,000 |

The firm has 6,000 shares outstanding, so the market value per share is ($300,000/6,000) = $50.

The firm is considering the following alternative uses of the excess cash: (1) pay a dividend of ($60,000/6,000) = $10 per share; or, (2) repurchase ($60,000/$50) = 1,200 shares of its common stock. The firm's balance sheet and the impact on an individual shareholder are the same for these two alternatives.

For the first alternative, the firm's balance sheet appears as follows after paying the dividend:

| Market value balance sheet : Pay cash dividend | | | |
|---|---|---|---|
| Excess cash | $ 0 | Debt | $ 0 |
| Other assets | 240,000 | Equity | 240,000 |
| Total | $ 240,000 | Total | $ 240,000 |

For a shareholder who owns 200 shares of stock, the market value prior to the dividend payment is ($50 × 200) = $10,000. After the dividend is paid, each share of stock has a value of ($240,000/6,000) = $40. Consequently, the shareholder who owns 200 shares now owns stock whose value is ($40 × 200) = $8,000. In addition, the investor receives dividends of ($10 × 200) = $2,000. The total value is unaffected by the dividend payment.

If instead, the firm repurchases 1,200 shares, its market value balance sheet is identical to its appearance after the dividend payment.  There would be (6,000 – 1,200) = 4,800 shares outstanding, each with a market value of ($240,000/4,800) = $50.  Assuming shareholders keep their shares, the market value of their position is unchanged after the share repurchase.  The investor has 200 shares with a total value of ($50 × 200) = $10,000. Selling all 200 shares would also leave the investor with $10,000 cash.  Alternatively, the investor could sell a portion of the shares, creating homemade dividends.  If, for example, 40 shares were sold, the homemade dividends would be ($50 × 40) = $2,000.  The remaining stock would be worth ($50 × 160) = $8,000.  In other words, the value of the position is still $10,000.

**Real-World Considerations in a Repurchase:**  As demonstrated above, in the absence of taxes and transactions costs, shareholders are indifferent between a dividend payment and a stock repurchase.  However, existing tax laws may lead shareholders to favour a stock repurchase.

Consider the previous case.  If the firm elected to pay dividends, the investor would receive $2,000 in dividends.  Assuming a tax rate of 28%, the taxes on dividends would be $560.  However, if the firm repurchases stock, the investor might pay no taxes.  For example, if the investor chooses not to sell any shares, then there is no taxable income.  If the investor creates homemade dividends by selling 40 shares, the tax liability will still be less than if the investor received $2,000 in dividends because the tax is paid only on capital gains resulting from the sale. If the shares were bought for $30, the capital gain would be ($50 – $30) = $20 per share.  Taxable income would be ($20 × 40) = $800.  Taxes would be only ($800 × .28) = $224.

## STOCK DIVIDENDS AND STOCK SPLITS

A *stock dividend* is paid in the form of additional shares of stock.  A 10% stock dividend, for example, increases by 10% the number of shares held by each shareholder.  Suppose an individual owns 200 shares of the common stock of a firm that has 1,000 shares outstanding.  If a 10% stock dividend is declared, this shareholder receives an additional (.10 × 200) = 20 shares.  Since all shareholders receive the same 10% stock dividend, the number of shares outstanding increases to (1.10 × 1,000) = 1,100.  Shareholders who owned 200 shares prior to the 10% stock dividend owned (200/1,000) = 20% of the outstanding shares.  After the stock dividend, they still own (220/1,100) = 20% of the outstanding shares.  The total value of the firm does not change when a stock dividend is declared. Since there are no cash flows associated with a stock dividend, the total value of the firm is not affected. Consequently, the investor who owned 20% of the firm prior to the stock dividend still owns 20% of the firm after the stock dividend.  Since the value of the firm is unchanged, the value of the individual's holdings is also unchanged by the stock dividend.  Because the number of shares outstanding is increased by 10%, without any change in the total value of the firm, each share is worth correspondingly less.

A *stock split* is essentially equivalent to a stock dividend, except that a split is expressed as a ratio rather than as a percentage.  Under the TSE rules, the maximum stock dividend is 25%; anything larger is considered a stock split.  For example, a five-for-four stock split gives a shareholder five shares for every four owned prior to the split.  Since a five-for-four stock split results in the distribution of one additional share for every four the shareholder owns, it is equivalent to a (1/4) = 25% stock dividend.  Stock splits and stock dividends are, for the most part, just paper transactions which do not change either the total value of the firm or the value of the shareholder's position.

**Some Details on Stock Splits and Stock Dividends:**  For accounting purposes, stock splits and stock dividends are classified as: (1) small stock dividends; (2) large stock dividends; and, (3) stock splits.  Stock dividends of less than approximately 20% to 25% are classified as small stock dividends.  For each of these categories, accountants adjust the firm's balance sheet somewhat differently.  However, in all three cases, the total owners' equity is unaffected by the distribution.  Furthermore, the total market value of the firm or individual's holdings does not change.

**Value of Stock Splits and Stock Dividends:** Consider the earlier example of a 10% stock dividend declared by a firm with 1,000 shares outstanding. If the market value of a share prior to the stock dividend is $22, then the total market value of the firm's equity is ($22 × 1,000) = $22,000. After the 10% stock dividend, the 1,100 outstanding shares must have the same market value because the value of the firm cannot change by simply sending pieces of paper (i.e., additional stock certificates) to the shareholders. Therefore, each of the 1,100 shares must now have a market value of $20, so the total value of the firm is still ($20 × 1,100) = $22,000. Also consider the shareholder with 200 shares prior to the stock dividend; the value is ($22 × 200) = $4,400. After the stock dividend, the investor has 220 shares with a total market value of ($20 × 220) = $4,400. Clearly, the value of the holdings has not changed.

The individual shareholder's position can also be viewed from the perspective of proportionate ownership of the firm before and after the stock dividend. Prior to the stock dividend, the investor owns (200/1,000) = 20% of the equity in the company. Since the total market value of the firm's equity is $22,000, the value is (.20 × $22,000) = $4,400. After the stock dividend, the investor still owns (220/1,100) = 20% of the equity, so that the value is still $4,400.

**Popular Trading Range:** Those who contend that stock splits and stock dividends have value to shareholders often argue that the value of a stock is enhanced if its price is within a certain trading range. Investors may be more likely to buy round lots (i.e., multiples of 100 shares) of a stock whose price is within the appropriate trading range. The reasoning is that broker's commissions are lower for stocks traded in round lots, and investors are more likely to be able to afford 100 shares of a stock priced in a moderate range (say, less than $100 per share) than for shares priced above this trading range. There is, however, little empirical evidence to support this contention.

**Reverse Splits:** A less frequently encountered manoeuvre is the reverse split, in which a firm's number of shares outstanding is *reduced*. In a one-for-three reverse split, each investor exchanges three old shares for one new share.

## CONCEPT TEST

1.      A dividend is a cash payment, made to shareholders, from earnings. If the payment is from sources other than current earnings, it is called a(n) _____ or a(n) _____ dividend.

2.      A dividend which is typically paid four times a year is a(n) _____ cash dividend. A dividend which is paid periodically, but which may not continue in the future, is a(n) _____ dividend. A dividend paid subsequent to the liquidation of part or all of the corporation is a(n) _____ dividend.

3.      When the size of a cash dividend is expressed as dollars per share, it is identified in terms of _____ . When the size of the dividend is stated as a percentage of market price, it is called the _____ . When the size of the dividend is expressed as a percentage of earnings per share, it is referred to as the _____ .

4.      The date on which the board of directors announces the amount of the dividend is called the _____ . The dividend is paid to shareholders who are holders of record as of the _____ . The dividend cheques are mailed to these owners on the _____ .

5.      The _____ date is four business days before the record date. Anyone purchasing a share before the ex-dividend date <u>does/does not</u> receive the dividend. Prior to the ex-dividend date, the stock is said to be trading _____ . Subsequently, it trades _____ . Prior to the ex-dividend date, the price of the stock declines overnight by approximately _____ .

6.      A stock dividend is paid in the form of _____ . Therefore, a stock dividend <u>(is/is not)</u> a true dividend.

The total value of the firm (does/does not) change when a stock dividend is declared, and the total value of an individual's holdings (does/does not) change.

7. A stock split (is/is not) essentially equivalent to a stock dividend. A split is expressed as a _____ , while a stock dividend is expressed as a _____ .

8. When a 20% stock dividend is declared, an investor who owns 100 shares of stock receives _____ new shares, so the total number of shares he owns after the stock dividend is _____ .

9. When a three-for-two stock split is declared, an investor who owns 100 shares of stock receives _____ new shares, so the total number of shares he owns after the stock split is _____ . A three-for-two stock split is equivalent to a _____ % stock dividend. A 20% stock dividend is equivalent to a _____-for-_____ stock split.

10. Those who contend that stock splits and stock dividends have value to shareholders often argue that the value of a stock is enhanced if its price is within a certain _____ .

11. The argument for the irrelevance of dividend policy is based on the conclusion that an investor can create a new dividend policy, or _____ dividends, if the firm's pattern of dividend payments does not match the investor's preferences.

12. The irrelevance of dividend policy is based on the assumptions that there are no _____ or _____ . Under current tax laws in Canada, dividend income and capital gains (are/are not) both taxed as ordinary income and (are/are not) subject to the same tax rates. They are taxed at _____ than the ordinary income tax rate. Capital gains taxes are deferred until the stock is sold, so that effective tax rates are (lower/higher) for capital gains.

13. A policy of (low/high) dividend payout means that earnings are reinvested in the firm, so that the value of the firm (increases/ decreases) , resulting in capital gains for shareholders. Consequently, the taxation of capital gains has implications for the firm's dividend policy. The lower effective tax rate for capital gains is a factor encouraging a (low/high) dividend payout.

14. The existence of flotation costs provides an incentive for firms to adopt a policy of (low/high) dividend payout.

15. Some have argued that a (low/high) dividend payout policy is preferable because of the desire for current income and the resolution of uncertainty. It has been argued that the payment of a cash dividend (increases/decreases) the risk of owning a stock. However, a shareholder can accomplish the same result by _____ in order to create _____ dividends.

16. Some investors are not subjected to higher tax rates on dividends than on capital gains. One such group of investors consists of corporations which own the securities of other corporations. For such investors, _____ % of dividend income received is excluded from the firm's taxable income. Consequently, these investors often prefer to own common stocks with (low/high) dividend payouts. In addition, pension funds, endowment funds, and trust funds favour stocks with (low/high) dividend payouts because these institutions are _____ .

17. Some investors prefer high dividend payouts while others prefer low payouts. Different firms may end up catering to one group or the other; this is called the _____ . Evidence suggests that investors in low tax brackets tend to hold (low/high) payout stocks, and investors in high brackets hold (low/high) payout

stocks.

18.     Firms with low dividend payout ratios require (less/more) external financing than firms with high dividend payout ratios.  Since external financing requires that the firm pay flotation costs, it is less expensive to obtain financing by retaining earnings and consequently adopting a (low/high) dividend payout ratio.

19.     A firm which adopts the _____ approach relies primarily on internally generated funds to finance positive NPV projects.  After allocating internally generated equity funds to all positive NPV projects, the firm pays dividends only from any _____ funds which remain after financing these projects.

20.     Under the residual dividend approach, the dividend paid to shareholders each quarter depends on both the firm's _____ and the firm's _____ .  Therefore, the actual dividend paid can be very unstable.  Since investors seem to value stability in dividends, alternative dividend policies which lead to more stability in dividends might be preferable. One such policy, which sets each quarter's dividend equal to a fixed fraction of the quarter's earnings, is referred to as a _____ dividend policy. A second alternative policy sets quarterly dividends equal to a specified fraction of annual earnings; this is a _____ dividend policy if earnings are relatively stable from one year to the next.

21.     Many firms seem to follow a compromise dividend policy based on the following goals:

        1.      Avoid the rejection of _____ projects in order to pay a dividend.
        2.      Avoid reducing _____ .
        3.      Avoid issuing _____ .
        4.      Maintain a target _____ .
        5.      Maintain a target _____ .

        For this kind of compromise policy, both the target _____ and the target _____ are regarded as long-term goals, rather than strict requirements.

22.     As an alternative to paying cash dividends, a firm can pay cash to its shareholders by a repurchase of its own stock from the shareholders.  In the absence of _____ and _____ , shareholders are indifferent between a dividend payment and a stock repurchase.  However, existing tax laws lead shareholders to favour a _____ .

## ANSWERS TO CONCEPT TEST

1.      distribution from capital; liquidating

2.      regular; extra; liquidating

3.      dividends per share; dividend yield; dividend payout

4.      declaration date; date of record; date of payment

5.      ex-dividend; does; cum dividend; ex-dividend; the after-tax value of the dividend

6.      additional shares of stock; is not; does not; does not

7.      is; ratio; percentage

8.      20; 120

9.      50; 150; 50; six; five

10.     trading range

11.     homemade

12.     taxes; flotation costs; are not; are not; less; lower

13.     low; increases; low

14.     low

15.     high; decreases; selling shares of stock; homemade

16.     100; high; high; tax-exempt

17.     clientele effect; high; low

18.     less; low

19.     residual dividend; residual

20.     earnings for the quarter; investment opportunities; cyclical; stable

21.     positive NPV; dividends; new equity; debt/equity ratio; dividend payout ratio; debt/equity ratio; dividend payout ratio

22.     taxes; transaction costs; stock repurchase

## PROBLEMS AND SOLUTIONS

### Problem 1

The market value balance sheet for Agee Jones Associates, Inc., is shown below:

| Market value balance sheet | | | |
|---|---|---|---|
| Cash | $ 20,000 | Debt | $ 10,000 |
| Fixed assets | 30,000 | Equity | 40,000 |
| Total | $ 50,000 | Total | $ 50,000 |

The firm has 1,000 shares outstanding and has declared a 25% stock dividend. T. Agee owns 400 shares of the firm's common stock. What is the effect of the stock dividend on the firm's market value? How does the stock dividend affect the value of a share of stock? How does the stock dividend affect the value of T. Agee's holdings?

**Solution:** Prior to the stock dividend, the market value of the firm's equity is $40,000 and the market value per share is ($40,000/1,000) = $40. The stock dividend does not affect the total market value of the firm's equity, so that the market value balance sheet does not change. However, since there are now an additional (.25 x 1,000) = 250 shares outstanding, the value per share declines. After the stock dividend, the market value per share is:

Price per share  x  1,250  =  $40,000

The market value per share is ($40,000/1,250)  =  $32 after the stock dividend.

Prior to the stock dividend, the market value of T. Agee's holdings is ($40 x 400) = $16,000. Alternatively, since T. Agee owns (400/1,000) = 40% of the firm, the market value of his position is (.40 x $40,000) = $16,000. After the stock dividend, T. Agee owns (1.25 x 400) = 500 shares, which still represents (500/1,250) = 40% of the firm. The market value of his position is:  $32 x 500  =  .40 x $40,000  =  $16,000.

### Problem 2

An all-equity firm has the following market-value balance sheet:

| Market value balance sheet | | | |
|---|---|---|---|
| Excess cash | $ 80,000 | Debt | $ 0 |
| Other assets | 360,000 | Equity | 440,000 |
| Total | $ 440,000 | Total | $440,000 |

The firm currently has 13,750 common shares outstanding. Market value per share os $440,000 / 13,750 = $32. The firm is considering using the excess cash to either repurchase ($80,000 / $32)  =  2,500 shares or pay a dividend of ($80,000 / 13,750)  =  $5.82 per share.

Maureen owns 300 shares of stock in the firm. Assuming no transaction costs, show that either action by the firm has no impact on Maureen's wealth.

**Solution:** The market value of Maureen's shares before the dividend payment is (300 x $32) = $9,600. After the dividend is paid Maureen has shares worth ($32 - $5.82) x 300   +   $5.82 x 300 in cash.  The total is $7,854 + $1,746   =   $9,600, the same as before.

If the firm repurchases 2,500 shares, there would be 13,750 - 2,500   =   11,250 shares outstanding with a market value of $360,000 / 11,250 = $32 per share.  If Maureen keeps her shares, they are worth 300 x $32   =   $9,600. Regardless of which alternative the firm chooses, the value of Maureen's position stays the same.

## Problem 3

In the scenario from Problem 2, suppose that Maureen sold 80 of her shares, creating homemade dividends.  Does her total wealth change?

**Solution:** By selling 80 shares, Maureen receives homemade dividends (cash) of ($32 x 80)   =   $2,560.  Her remaining shares are worth (220 x $32)   =   $7,040.  Her total wealth is still $9,600 = ($2,560 + $7,040).

## Problem 4

Suppose that, for the data of Problem 1, Agee Jones declares a two-for-one stock split.  What is the effect of the stock split on the firm's market value?  How does the stock split affect the value of a share of stock?  How does the stock split affect the value of T. Agee's holdings?

**Solution:**  As in the case of the stock dividend, the stock split does not affect the total market value of the firm's equity. The stock split results in the distribution of one new share for each existing share.  Therefore, it is equivalent to a 100% stock dividend and results in the distribution of 1,000 new shares.  The total number of shares is then (1,000 + 1,000) = 2,000.   The market value per share, after the stock split, is:

Market value per share x 2,000   =   $40,000

The market value per share is ($40,000/2,000)   =   $20 after the stock dividend.

After the stock split, T. Agee owns (2.00 x  400)   =   800 shares.  The market value of his position is:

$20 x   800   =   .40 x $40,000   =   $16,000

## Problem 5

Glennie's VCR Company has 2,500 shares outstanding and is debt-free.  Glennie expects to pay dividends of $3,000 one year from now and will pay liquidating dividends of $123,000 three years from now.  If Glennie's required rate of return is 16.5%, what is the value of the firm and the value of one share of Glennie?

**Solution:** The value of Glennie is:

$3,000 / 1.165  +  $123,000 / 1.165^3   =   $80,365.75
The value of one share is $80,365.85 / 2,500   =   $32.15

## Problem 6

The Krane Pools Company is an all-equity firm with 1,000 shares outstanding. The firm expects to pay total dividends of $6,000 one year from now and total liquidating dividends of $72,000 two years from now. The required rate of return for Krane Pools is 20%. What is the total value of the firm? What is the value of a share of common stock?

**Solution:** The total value of Krane Pools is:

$$\frac{\$6,000}{1.20} + \frac{\$72,000}{(1.20)^2} = \$55,000$$

The market value of a share is ($55,000/1,000) = $55. Alternatively, the market value of one share can be computed as the present value of the dividends per share to be paid at the end of each of the next two years:

$$\frac{\$6.00}{1.20} + \frac{\$72.00}{(1.20)^2} = \$55$$

## Problem 7

Suppose that the shareholders of Krane Pools prefer total dividend payments of $30,000 at the end of one year, rather than dividend payments described in Problem 6. What dividend payment will the firm make at the end of the second year? What is the value of the firm if it adopts the new dividend payment schedule? What is the value of a share of stock?

**Solution:** In order to pay $30,000 in dividends at the end of one year, Krane Pools could sell ($30,000 - $6,000) = $24,000 of common stock at the end of the year. The holders of this new common stock require a 20% rate of return, so that they will require ($24,000 x 1.20) = $28,800 in dividends. The dividend payment to the existing shareholders at the end of the second year will therefore be ($72,000 - $28,800) = $43,200. The value of the firm today is the present value of the future dividends to be paid to the existing shareholders:

$$\frac{\$30,000}{1.20} + \frac{\$43,200}{(1.20)^2} = \$55,000$$

The value of the firm does not change with the change in dividend payments. Furthermore, the value per share remains $55 under the new dividend policy.

## Problem 8

E. Charles owns 100 shares of Krane Pools common stock. The firm plans to pay dividends as described in Problem 6, but E. Charles would like to receive the dividend payments he would receive if the firm paid dividends as described in Problem 7. How can E. Charles use homemade dividends to duplicate his desired dividend payments?

**Solution:** The dividend payments in Problem 7 imply dividends per share of ($30,000/1,000) = $30 and ($43,200/1,000) = $43.20 at the end of one and two years, respectively. Therefore, Charles prefers to receive the following dividend payments at the end of one and two years: ($30 x 100) = $3,000 and ($43.20 x 100) =

$4,320. According to the dividend payments in Problem 6, dividends paid to Charles at the end of one year will be ($6 x 100) = $600. Therefore, Charles will sell ($3,000 - $600) = $2,400 of common stock at the end of the first year. By doing so, he forfeits ($2,400 x 1.20) = $2,880 at the end of the second year. Therefore, his total payment at the end of the second year is ($7,200 - $2,880) = $4,320. This is the same payment he would have received at the end of year two if Krane Pools followed the dividend policy described in Problem 7.

## Problem 9

Lankester Corporation has a debt/equity ratio of 1/5 and earnings of $55,000. What is the maximum amount of capital spending for Lankester if the current debt/equity ratio must be maintained and the firm doesn't want to obtain additional equity financing?

**Solution:** To maintain the current capital structure, Lankester must borrow $1 for every $5 of equity financing (from earnings) used. So, they must borrow 1/5 x $55,000 = $11,000. Total capital spending possible is $66,000.

## Problem 10

A firm that has adopted a residual dividend approach has $30,000 in earnings and a debt/equity ratio of 1/3. What is the maximum amount of capital spending possible if the firm does not obtain any new equity financing and maintains the current debt/equity ratio?

**Solution:** The debt/equity ratio of 1/3 signifies that the firm has $1 of debt for every $3 of equity. If the firm retains all of the available $30,000 as the equity financing portion, to maintain the existing debt/equity ratio, the firm must raise (1/3 x $30,000) = $10,000 of debt financing. Therefore, the total financing available, if the firm does not obtain any new equity financing, is ($30,000 + $10,000) = $40,000.

## Problem 11

Suppose that the firm described in Problem 10 has positive NPV projects available which require the investment of $24,000. How will these projects be financed? How much will the firm pay in dividends?

**Solution:** The debt/equity ratio of 1/3 signifies that the firm's capital structure consists of $1 of debt and $3 of equity for each $4 of total financing. The capital structure is ($1 / $4) = 25% debt and ($3 / $4) = 75% equity. In order to finance expenditures of $24,000, while maintaining the existing capital structure, the firm will use debt financing of (.25 x $24,000) = $6,000, and equity financing of (.75 x $24,000) = $18,000. The firm has $30,000 of internal equity financing available, so that dividends are ($30,000 - $18,000) = $12,000.

## Problem 12

Suppose that the firm described in Problem 10 has $60,000 of positive NPV projects available. How will these projects be financed? How much will the firm pay in dividends?

**Solution:** From Problem 10, if no external equity financing is obtained, the total financing available is $40,000. To maintain the debt/equity ratio of 1/3, any additional financing is obtained as follows: 25% is debt financing and 75% is equity financing. The firm requires additional financing of ($60,000 - $40,000) = $20,000, which is obtained as follows: (.25 x $20,000) = $5,000 of additional debt financing and (.75 x  $20,000) = $15,000 of additional equity financing. Total equity financing consists of $30,000 of internally generated funds and $15,000 of new equity. Total debt financing is equal to ($10,000 + $5,000) = $15,000. In this situation, the firm pays no dividends.

## Problem 13

An all-equity firm has the following market value balance sheet:

| Market value balance sheet | | | |
|---|---|---|---|
| Excess cash | $  10,000 | Debt | $          0 |
| Other assets | 90,000 | Equity | 100,000 |
| Total | $ 100,000 | Total | $ 100,000 |

The firm has 2,000 shares outstanding and is considering paying dividends with the excess cash. What is the impact on the firm's market value balance sheet? How does the dividend payment affect a stockholder who owns 500 shares of stock?

**Solution:** Prior to the payment of the dividend, the market value per share is ($100,000/2,000) = $50. The owner of 500 shares owns stock with a total market value of ($50 x  500) = $25,000. After the payment of the dividends, the market value balance sheet appears as follows:

| Market value balance sheet | | | |
|---|---|---|---|
| Excess cash | $       0 | Debt | $       0 |
| Other assets | 90,000 | Equity | 90,000 |
| Total | $  90,000 | Total | $  90,000 |

Dividends are ($10,000 / 2,000) = $5 per share. The market value per share is now ($90,000 / 2,000) = $45. The owner of 500 shares owns stock with a market value of ($45 x  500) = $22,500, and he has received dividends of ($5 x  500) = $2,500. Therefore, the market value of his position is ($22,500 + $2,500) = $25,000, which is the same as it was prior to the dividend payment.

## Problem 14

Suppose that the firm described in Problem 13 is considering a stock repurchase rather than the dividend payment. What is the impact on the firm's market value balance sheet? How does the stock repurchase affect a shareholder who owns 500 shares of stock?

**Solution:** The firm's market value balance sheet is identical to the balance sheet in the solution to Problem 13. At a market value of $50 per share, the firm can repurchase ($10,000 / $50) = 200 shares. Since there are now (2,000 - 200) = 1,800 shares outstanding, the value of a share of stock is ($90,000/1,800) = $50. The shareholder who owns 500 shares has a position with a total market value of ($50 x  500) = $25,000. Since this market value is the same as that computed in Problem 13, the shareholder is unaffected by either the dividend payment or the stock repurchase. However, the advantage of the stock repurchase is that the shareholder's tax payments are less than they would be with a dividend payment. In Problem 13, the shareholder pays income taxes on the total dividend payment of $2,500.

With the stock repurchase, the shareholder does not pay any income taxes, unless he chooses to create homemade dividends by selling a portion of his holdings. If, for example, he chooses to sell stock in an amount sufficient to duplicate the $2,500 dividend payment he would have received with the dividend payment described in Problem 13, he would sell ($2,500/$50) = 50 shares.

However, even in this case, his tax payment is less than it would be in the event of the dividend payment. Here, he would pay taxes only on the capital gain resulting from the sale of stock, rather than on the full $2,500.

**Use the following information to solve Problems 15 to 19:**

The balance sheet for Reebop Corporation is shown. Reebop has 1,000 shares outstanding.

| Market value balance sheet | | | |
|---|---|---|---|
| Cash | $ 10,000 | Debt | $        0 |
| Fixed assets | 50,000 | Equity | 60,000 |
| Total | $ 60,000 | Total | $ 60,000 |

## Problem 15

Reebop has declared a dividend of $3 per share. The stock goes ex-dividend tomorrow. What is the price of the stock today? What will its price be tomorrow? Assume no taxes.

**Solution:** Since the balance sheet shows market values, the stock is worth ($60,000/1,000) = $60 per share today (cum dividend). The ex-dividend price will be ($60 - $3) = $57. Notice that once the dividend is paid, Reebop has $3,000 less cash, so the total equity is worth $57,000, or ($57,000/1,000) = $57 per share.

## Problem 16

Reebop has declared a 20% stock dividend, rather than the cash dividend described in Problem 15. The stock goes ex-dividend tomorrow. What is the ex-dividend price?

**Solution:** After the stock dividend is distributed, (1,000 x 1.20) = 1,200 shares will be outstanding. The total value of the shares is still $60,000. That is, the total market value of the equity is unchanged. Therefore, the per share value is ($60,000/1,200) = $50. Notice that this is not 20% less than the old price. Rather the old price is 120% of the new price: ($50 x 1.20) = $60.

## Problem 17

Instead of paying a cash dividend, Reebop has announced that it is going to repurchase $3,000 of stock. What is the effect of this repurchase? Ignoring taxes, show how this repurchase is effectively the same as a $3 dividend per share.

**Solution:** Reebop will purchase ($3,000/$60) = 50 shares, leaving 950 outstanding. The total equity value will be $57,000, so that the market price is still ($57,000/950) = $60 per share.

Consider an investor who owns 100 shares. With the cash dividend, this investor receives ($3.00 x 100) = $300 in cash and has 100 shares with a total value of ($57 x 100) = $5,700. Using the $300, the investor could purchase ($300/$57) = 5.263 more shares and have 105.263 shares worth $57 each, for a total value of $6,000. With the repurchase, the investor has 100 shares worth $60 each, if she does not sell any shares. Alternatively, she could sell ($300/$60) = 5 shares. As a result, she would have 95 shares, with a total value of ($60 x 95) = $5,700, and $300 in cash, for a total of $6,000 again.

## Problem 18

Suppose that capital gains are not taxed, but dividends are taxed at a 40% rate, and that taxes are withheld at the time the dividend is paid. If Reebop is going to pay a $4 dividend per share, what is the ex-dividend price?

**Solution:** The price will decrease by the after-tax amount of the dividend, or [$4 x (1 - .40)] = $2.40. The ex-dividend price will be ($60.00 - $2.40) = $57.60.

## Problem 19

Suppose that, in Problem 18, capital gains are taxed at a 20% rate. What is the ex-dividend price?

**Solution:** This problem is somewhat more difficult. Consider the following scenario: suppose you buy a share just before the stock goes ex-dividend, and then sell immediately thereafter. You will have an after-tax dividend of $2.40 and a capital loss of D, the decline in the stock price. Since this loss is tax deductible, your after-tax loss is [D x (1 - .20)]. You will be indifferent with regard to buying the share with the dividend only if:

$$\$2.40 = D \times (1 - .20)$$

In this scenario, the price decrease will be D = ($2.40/.80) = $3. In reality, capital gains are only taxed when the gain (loss) is realized. In the case of a realized capital loss, the loss is only applied against realized capital gains, so the size of the price decline is more difficult to determine. However, it would probably be less than the amount of the dividend but more than the after-tax value of the dividend.

## Problem 20

Dadadas Company is in the same risk class as Old Balance Company. Dadadas has an expected dividend yield over the next year of 10%, while Old Balance pays no dividends. The required return on Old Balance is 20%. Capital gains are not taxed, but dividends are effectively taxed at 40%. What is the required pre-tax return on Dadadas?

**Solution:** The 10% dividend yield is equivalent to a 6% after-tax return. Since the total expected after-tax return is 20%, the expected capital gain is (20% - 6%) = 14%. The after-tax return is thus 'grossed up' to a pre-tax return of (10% + 14%) = 24%.

## Problem 21

You own 20 shares of stock in King Aircraft. You are certain you will receive a $.50 per share dividend at date 1. At date 2, King will pay a liquidating dividend of $13.80 per share. The required return is 20%. Assuming no taxes, what is the price per share of the common stock? Suppose that you would rather have equal dividends in each of the next two years. How can you accomplish this by using homemade dividends?

**Solution:**  The value of your position is the present value of the dividends, ($.50 / 1.20) + (13.80 / 1.20$^2$) = $10 per share. Therefore, the total value of your position is $200.  An annuity of $130.91 per year for two years has the same present value.  At date 1, your stock will be worth the present value of the liquidating dividend, or $11.50 per share.  You will receive $10 in total dividends at date 1.  You will have to sell $120.91 worth of stock, or ($120.91/11.5) = 10.514 shares, leaving you with 9.486 shares.  At the end of the second year, you will receive (9.486 x $13.80) in dividends, for a total of $130.91, thereby accomplishing your goal.

**Problem 22**

Try this one on your own. Suppose that, in Problem 21, you wanted only $5 at date 1.  What is your homemade dividend at date 2?

**Solution:**  Your liquidating dividend will be $282, which is $6 greater than it would have been.

# 18         Short-Term Finance and Planning

## CHAPTER HIGHLIGHTS

This chapter introduces the fundamentals of short-term financial management: the analysis of decisions involving cash flows which occur within a year or less. Because they affect the firm's current assets and current liabilities, these decisions are referred to as working capital management. Some examples of short-term financial decisions are questions such as: How much inventory should be kept on hand? How much cash should be kept on hand? Should goods be sold on credit? How should the firm borrow short-term?

## TRACING CASH AND NET WORKING CAPITAL

*Current assets* include cash and other assets expected to be converted to cash within one year. The four major categories of current assets are: cash, marketable securities, accounts receivable, and inventory. Current assets appear on the balance sheet in order of the ease and time involved in converting the assets to cash.

Current liabilities are short-term obligations which require payment within one year. The three major categories are: accounts payable, expenses payable, and notes payable.

**Defining Cash in Terms of Other Elements:** The balance sheet identity can be written as:

Current assets + Fixed assets  =  Current liabilities + Long-term debt + Equity

Alternatively, by rearranging terms, this identity can be written:

(Cash + Other current assets) – Current liabilities + Fixed assets  =  Long-term debt + Equity

Solving this equation for cash:

Cash  =  Long-term debt + Equity + Current liabilities – Current assets (excluding cash) – Fixed assets

This equation clearly indicates those actions which increase cash and those which decrease cash:

Activities which increase cash:

> Increase long-term debt (borrowing long-term);
> Increase equity (sell common stock);
> Increase current liabilities (borrow short-term);
> Decrease current assets other than cash (sell inventory for cash);
> Decrease fixed assets (sell fixed assets).

Activities which decrease cash:

> Decrease long-term debt (repay long-term debt);
> Decrease equity (repurchase common stock);
> Decrease current liabilities (repay short-term debt);
> Increase current assets other than cash (buy inventory for cash);
> Increase fixed assets (buy fixed assets).

Activities that increase cash are called sources of cash; those that decrease cash are called uses of cash.  Sources of cash always involve increasing a liability or equity account and/or decreasing an asset account.  Uses of cash involve increasing an asset account or decreasing a liability (equity) account.


## THE OPERATING CYCLE AND THE CASH CYCLE

A typical manufacturing firm's short-run operating and financing activities might consist of the following events and decisions:

| Events | Decisions |
|---|---|
| 1. Buying raw materials | 1. How much inventory to order? |
| 2. Paying cash for purchases | 2. To borrow, or draw down cash balance? |
| 3. Manufacturing the product | 3. What choice of production technology? |
| 4. Selling the product | 4. To offer cash terms or credit terms to customers? |
| 5. Collecting cash | 5. How to collect cash? |

These activities create cash inflows and outflows that are both unsynchronized and uncertain.  Cash flows are unsynchronized because inflows from the sale of a product do not occur at the same time as outflows to acquire raw materials.  The uncertainty of cash flows arises from the fact that future sales and costs cannot be predicted with certainty.

**Defining the Operating and Cash Cycles:**  Short-term operating activities and cash flows can be represented by a *cash flow time line* (see the example in your text).  This time line consists of an operating cycle and a cash cycle.  The length of the *operating cycle* is equal to the sum of the inventory period and the accounts receivable period.  The *inventory period* is the time required from receipt of inventory to sale of the finished goods.  The *accounts receivable period* is the time required to collect cash from a credit sale.  The *accounts payable period* is the length of time the firm can delay payment on its purchases.

The *cash cycle* is the difference between the operating cycle and the accounts payable period.  A cash cycle of 30 days means that inflows occur 30 days after outflows. This mismatch suggests the need for short-term financing, which can be provided either by borrowing or by maintaining a liquid reserve of marketable securities. Alternatively, the cash cycle can be shortened by changing the inventory, accounts receivable, or accounts payable periods.

**Calculating the Operating and Cash Cycles:**  The operating and cash cycles can be calculated from balance sheet and income statement information.

**An Example:**  The following information for D. Drysdale & Co., Inc. represents balance sheet data for the beginning and end of 2000, and income statement data for the year 2000:

| Balance sheet item | Beginning | Ending | Average |
|---|---|---|---|
| Inventory | $4,500 | $5,000 | $4,750 |
| Accounts receivable | 3,500 | 4,500 | 4,000 |
| Accounts payable | 2,250 | 2,500 | 2,375 |

| Income statement item | Annual |
|---|---|
| Net sales (all credit) | $18,000 |
| Cost of goods sold | 13,300 |

Calculate the operating cycle and the cash cycle for Drysdale & Co.

The operating cycle is equal to the inventory period plus the accounts receivable period. We compute these from the inventory turnover ratio and the receivables turnover ratio, respectively.

$$\text{Inventory turnover} = \frac{\text{Cost of goods sold}}{\text{Average inventory}} = \frac{\$13,300}{\$4,750} = 2.80 \text{ times}$$

Inventory is 'turned over' 2.80 times per year. Therefore, the inventory period is determined as follows:

$$\text{Inventory period} = \frac{365}{\text{Inventory turnover}} = \frac{365}{2.8} = 130.36 \text{ days}$$

Assuming that all sales are credit sales, then:

$$\text{Receivables turnover} = \frac{\text{Credit sales}}{\text{Average receivables}} = \frac{\$18,000}{\$4,000} = 4.50 \text{ times}$$

$$\text{Receivables period} = \frac{365}{\text{Receivables turnover}} = \frac{365}{4.50} = 81.11 \text{ days}$$

The operating cycle is:

$$\begin{aligned}
\text{Operating cycle} &= \text{Inventory period} + \text{Accounts receivable period} \\
&= 130.36 \text{ days} + 81.11 \text{ days} = 211.47 \text{ days} = 211 \text{ days}
\end{aligned}$$

In order to determine the cash cycle, we first compute the accounts payable turnover and then the accounts payable period:

$$\text{Payables turnover} = \frac{\text{Cost of goods sold}}{\text{Average payables}} = \frac{\$13,300}{\$2,375} = 5.60 \text{ times}$$

$$\text{Payables period} = \frac{365}{\text{Payables turnover}} = \frac{365}{5.60} = 65.18 \text{ days}$$

Therefore, the cash cycle is:

$$\begin{aligned}
\text{Cash cycle} &= \text{Operating cycle} - \text{Accounts payable period} \\
&= 211.47 \text{ days} - 65.18 \text{ days} = 146.29 \text{ days} = 146 \text{ days}
\end{aligned}$$

These calculations indicate that, on average, the time between Drysdale's acquisition of inventory and collection of payment on sales is approximately 211 days, and the time between Drysdale's payment for acquisitions and collection of payment on sales is approximately 146 days.

## SOME ASPECTS OF SHORT-TERM FINANCIAL POLICY

A firm's short-term financial policy has two dimensions: the size of the investment in current assets, and the financing of current assets. A *flexible* current-asset policy requires maintaining a relatively high ratio of current assets to sales, while a *restrictive* policy implies a relatively low ratio. A flexible financing policy employs relatively less short-term debt and more long-term debt; a restrictive financing policy requires that current assets are financed primarily by short-term debt.

**The Size of the Firm's Investment in Current Assets:**  A flexible current asset policy implies that the firm maintains relatively high levels of cash, marketable securities, and inventories, and grants liberal credit terms resulting in relatively high levels of accounts receivable. Firms with restrictive policies maintain relatively low levels of current assets.   In order to determine the optimal levels of current assets, the costs and benefits associated with each policy must be identified.

A flexible policy requires greater initial cash outflows in order to purchase inventory, finance credit sales, and maintain high levels of cash and marketable securities. Future cash inflows, however, should be higher for a flexible policy.  Similarly, liberal credit policies also stimulate sales.  In addition, the larger cash balances associated with a flexible policy ensure that bills can be paid promptly, thereby increasing discounts taken on accounts payable and reducing borrowing costs required in order to meet expenditures.

The costs associated with managing current assets can be classified as: *carrying costs*, which increase with increases in current assets; and, *shortage costs* which decrease with increases in current assets.  Carrying costs are the opportunity costs of investment in current assets because,  if the firm holds idle cash, it forgoes the opportunity to earn interest on the investment of that cash.  Similarly, investment in inventory also implies an opportunity cost.  The two kinds of shortage costs are *trading costs (order costs),* and costs related to safety reserves.  Trading (order) costs arise when the firm runs out of cash or inventory and must consequently incur the cost of restocking.   Costs related to safety reserves include loss of sales, customer goodwill, or production time when a *stock out (cash out)* occurs.

The figure below illustrates the firm's carrying and shortage costs associated with the investment in current assets.  The optimal investment in current assets (CA*) is the level that minimizes *total costs* (that is, the sum of carrying and shortage costs).

Optimal Amount of Current Assets.
This point minimizes costs

A flexible policy is most appropriate when carrying costs are low relative to shortage costs.   This results in a higher optimal level of current assets.  This is shown in the graph below.

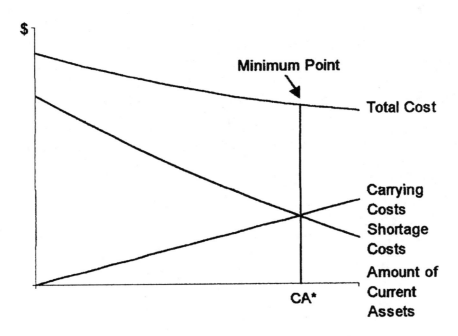

Alternatively, a restrictive policy is most appropriate when carrying costs are high relative to shortage costs.  This results in a lower optimal level of current assets as shown in the following graph.

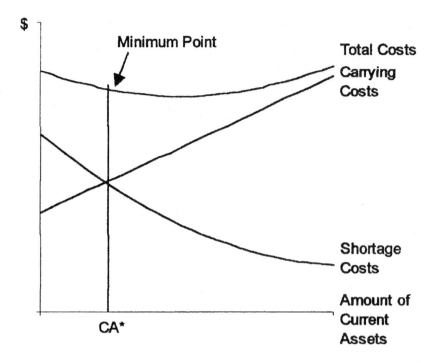

**Alternative Financing Policies for Current Assets:**  For a given level of current assets, different financing policies are feasible.  Under ideal circumstances, short-term assets are financed by short-term debts with maturity equal to the life of the assets; net working capital would always be zero.

In the real world, firms almost always require a *permanent investment* in current assets because current assets never decline to zero.  This permanent investment is generally a result of growth in sales, seasonal variation, and unpredictable fluctuations.  To finance the permanent component of working capital, a firm could use long-term debt.  Then the firm will have excess cash available for investment in marketable securities.  The alternative to this flexible strategy is a restrictive strategy that involves the use of permanent short-term borrowing to finance any deficit between long-term financing and total assets.

**Which Financing Policy is Best?**  There is no definitive answer to the question: "How much short-term borrowing is optimal?"  Several factors must be considered.  First, firms with flexible policies and *cash reserves* are generally less likely to experience financial distress since these policies imply less difficulty in meeting short-term obligations.  Second, most firms hedge interest-rate risk by matching debt maturities with asset maturities known as *maturity hedging*.  A policy of financing long-term assets with short-term debt is inherently risky since frequent refinancing is needed, and short-term interest rates are more volatile than long-term rates.  Finally, short-term interest rates tend to be lower than long-term rates.  This implies that, on average, borrowing long-term is costlier.

*Flexible policies* (F) and *restrictive policies* (R) are extreme cases, since, with F, the firm never does any short-term borrowing, and, with R, the firm never has a cash reserve (an investment in marketable securities).  Figure 18.6 on page 615 of your text illustrates these two policies along with a compromise, Policy C.

With a compromise policy, the firm borrows short-term to cover peak financing needs, but maintains a cash reserve in the form of marketable securities during slow periods.  As current assets build up, the firm draws down this reserve before engaging in any short-term borrowing.

## THE CASH BUDGET

The *cash budget* is a forecast of estimated cash inflows and outflows over a period of time.  It is the primary tool of short-run financial planning.  The following example illustrates the preparation of a cash budget.

**An Example:**  C. Erskine & Company has estimated sales for the next four quarters as follows:

|  | Qtr 1 | Qtr 2 | Qtr 3 | Qtr 4 |
|---|---|---|---|---|
| Sales | $150 | $200 | $300 | $250 |

Accounts receivable at the beginning of the year are $100.  Erskine has a 54-day collection period.  Cash outflows consist of: (1) payments to suppliers; (2) wages, taxes, and other expenses; (3) capital expenditures; and, (4) long-term financing payments.  Purchases from suppliers during a quarter are equal to 50% of next quarter's forecast sales. Payments to suppliers are equal to the previous period's purchases.  In the most recent quarter, Erskine's purchases are $(.50 \times \$150) = \$75$, which will be paid during the first quarter.  Wages, taxes, and other expenses are 30% of sales.  Interest and dividends are $20 per quarter.  A capital expenditure of $100 is planned in the second quarter. Erskine maintains a $10 minimum cash balance to guard against unforseen contingencies and forecasting errors. Prepare a cash budget for C. Erskine & Co.

**Sales and Cash Collections:** First, compute the cash collections for each quarter.  The 54-day collection period implies that $[(90 - 54)/90] = 40\%$ of the sales in a given quarter will be collected during the current quarter and $(54/90) = 60\%$ during the following quarter.  That is, sales made during the first $(90 - 54) = 36$ days of the quarter will be collected before the end of the quarter, while sales during the remaining 54 days will be collected during the following quarter.  Therefore, ending receivables for a given quarter are 60% of sales during that quarter.  In the first quarter, cash collections are the beginning receivables of $100 plus 40% of sales, or:

$$\text{Cash collections} = \text{Beginning accounts receivable} + (40\% \times \text{Sales})$$
$$= \$100 + (.40 \times \$150) = \$100 + \$60 = \$160$$

Cash collections for each quarter are:

|  | Qtr 1 | Qtr 2 | Qtr 3 | Qtr 4 |
|---|---|---|---|---|
| Beginning Receivables | $100 | $ 90 | $120 | $180 |
| Sales | 150 | 200 | 300 | 250 |
| Cash Collections | 160 | 170 | 240 | 280 |
| Ending Receivables | 90 | 120 | 180 | 150 |

The cash outflows for Erskine are:

|  | Qtr 1 | Qtr 2 | Qtr 3 | Qtr 4 |
|---|---|---|---|---|
| Payment of Accounts | $ 75 | $100 | $150 | $125 |
| Wages, taxes, other expenses | 45 | 60 | 90 | 75 |
| Capital Expenditures | 0 | 100 | 0 | 0 |
| Long-term financing expenses (interest and dividends) | 20 | 20 | 20 | 20 |
| Total | $140 | $280 | $260 | $220 |

**The Cash Balance:** The forecasted *net cash inflow* is the difference between cash collections and cash outflows. The net cash inflow is determined as follows:

|                         | Qtr 1 | Qtr 2  | Qtr 3  | Qtr 4 |
|-------------------------|-------|--------|--------|-------|
| Total cash collections  | $160  | $170   | $240   | $280  |
| Total cash disbursements| 140   | 280    | 260    | 220   |
| Net cash inflow         | $ 20  | -$110  | -$ 20  | $ 60  |

Erskine maintains a $10 minimum cash balance.  Assuming that $10 balance existed at the beginning of the first quarter, we can compute the cumulative surplus, or deficit, at the end of each quarter:

|                              | Qtr 1 | Qtr 2  | Qtr 3  | Qtr 4  |
|------------------------------|-------|--------|--------|--------|
| Beginning cash balance       | $ 10  | $ 30   | -$ 80  | -$100  |
| Net cash inflow              | 20    | - 110  | - 20   | 60     |
| Ending cash balance          | $ 30  | -$ 80  | -$100  | -$ 40  |
| Minimum cash balance         | 10    | 10     | 10     | 10     |
| Cumulative surplus (deficit) | $ 20  | -$ 90  | -$110  | -$ 50  |

Beginning in the second quarter, Erskine has a cash shortfall.  It occurs because of the seasonal pattern of sales, the delay in collections, and the planned capital expenditure.

## A SHORT-TERM FINANCIAL PLAN

In this section, we use the C. Erskine & Co. example to illustrate a completed short-term financial plan, which includes short-term borrowing of needed funds.

**An Example:**  Erskine will borrow needed funds at a rate of 12% APR, or (.12/4) = .03 = 3% per quarter. Assume that they begin the year with no short-term debt, and repay short-term debt as soon as possible.  Ignore taxes, and assume that the cash surplus during the first quarter does not earn interest.  Prepare a complete short-term financial plan for the year.

The complete short-term financial plan is below.  With no borrowing, the cumulative deficit at the end of quarter 2 is $90.  Consequently, short-term borrowing of $90 is required in quarter 2.  Interest of (.03 × $90) = $2.70 must be paid during quarter 3, which increases the cumulative deficit for the quarter from $90 to $92.70. Therefore, additional short-term borrowing of $22.70 is required during the quarter.  Ending short-term debt is ($90 + $22.70) = $112.70, which covers the cumulative deficit of $112.70.  Interest paid during quarter 4 is (.03 × $112.70) = $3.38, so that ($60 − $3.38) = $56.62 of the $60 cash inflow is available to repay short-term debt.

|                                    | Qtr 1 | Qtr 2 | Qtr 3    | Qtr 4    |
|------------------------------------|-------|-------|----------|----------|
| Beginning cash balance             | $10   | $ 30  | $ 10.00  | $ 10.00  |
| + Net cash inflow                  | 20    | - 110 | - 20.00  | 60.00    |
| + New short-term borrowing         |       | 90    | 22.70    |          |
| - Interest on short-term borrowing |       |       | 2.70     | 3.38     |
| - Short-term borrowing repaid      |       |       |          | 56.62    |
| Ending cash balance                | $30   | $ 10  | $ 10.00  | $ 10.00  |
| - Minimum cash balance             | 10    | 10    | 10.00    | 10.00    |
| Cumulative surplus (deficit)       | $20   | $ 0   | $ 0.00   | $ 0.00   |
| Beginning short-term borrowing     | 0     | 0     | 90.00    | 112.70   |
| + Change in short-term debt        | 0     | 90    | 22.70    | - 56.62  |
| Ending short-term debt             | $ 0   | $ 90  | $112.70  | $ 56.08  |

## SHORT-TERM BORROWING

Erskine must finance the cash shortfall beginning in the second quarter. Two options are unsecured and secured short-term financing.

**Operating Loans:** An *operating loan* is a form of short-term financing which allows the firm to borrow up to a given amount over a specified time period (usually one year). These loans may be either secured or unsecured. These short-term lines of credit are referred to as either *committed* or *noncommitted*. Committed line of credit agreements are more formal than uncommitted agreements. Under a committed agreement, the bank guarantees that funds will be available when needed. For this guarantee, the firm pays a fee, which is usually a percentage of the total committed funds.

**Compensating the Bank:** The interest rate on an operating loan is usually stated as a specified number of percentage points above the prime rate. In addition, banks often require that a firm maintain a *compensating balance* on deposit in either a low- or zero-interest account. This compensating balance serves to increase the effective rate on the loan because interest on the loan is paid on the full amount borrowed, even though some portion of the loan is not available to the borrower.

**An Example:**   A bank offers a line of credit with a 15% annual interest rate and a 5% compensating balance. How much interest is paid on a $20,000, one-year loan? What is the compensating balance requirement? What is the effective interest rate?

Assuming a single payment at the end of the year, with no compounding of interest, we have the following calculations:

$$\text{Interest paid} \;\; = \;\; .15 \times \$20,000 \;\; = \;\; \$3,000$$
$$\text{Compensating balance} \;\; = \;\; .05 \times \$20,000 \;\; = \;\; \$1,000$$

$$\text{Effective interest rate} \;\; = \;\; \frac{\text{Interest paid}}{\text{Amount available}} \;\; = \;\; \frac{\$3,000}{\$19,000} \;\; = \;\; .15789 \;\; = \;\; 15.789\%$$

The last calculation indicates that the borrower has only ($20,000 – $1,000)  =  $19,000 available because $1,000 must be left on deposit at the bank earning no interest. The effective rate is therefore 15.789%, rather than the stated 15%, because the interest paid is computed on the basis of a $20,000 loan, whereas the actual proceeds of the loan to the borrower are only $19,000.

**An Example:**  For the loan terms described above, what size loan is necessary if the borrower requires net proceeds of $25,000? What is the compensating balance requirement? How much interest is paid on the loan for one year? What is the effective interest rate?

The borrower must apply for a loan which is large enough so that 95% of the proceeds of the loan will provide the required $25,000. The size of the loan is the solution to the following equation:

$$(1 - .05) \times \text{Loan size} \;\; = \;\; \$25,000$$
$$\text{Loan size} \;\; = \;\; \$25,000 \,/\, .95 \;\; = \;\; \$26,315.79$$

Therefore, the size of the loan is $26,315.79 and the compensating balance requirement is ($26,315.79 – $25,000) = (.05 × $26,315.79) = $1,315.79.

Interest paid  =  .15 × $26,315.79  =  $3,947.37

$$\text{Effective interest rate} \;=\; \frac{\$3,947.37}{\$25,000} \;=\; .15789 \;=\; 15.789\%$$

The effective interest rate is 15.789%, as in the previous example, because the interest rate and the compensating balance percentage are constant regardless of the size of the loan. The borrower pays $.15 interest for each $.95 borrowed, or an effective rate of ($.15/$.95) = 15.789%.

**Letters of Credit:** A letter of credit (LC) is a common arrangement in international finance, where the bank issuing the letter promises to make a loan if certain conditions are met, including that the goods arrive as promised. An LC can be revocable (subject to cancellation) or irrevocable.

**Secured Loans:** Secured short-term loans usually require either accounts receivable or inventories as security for the loan. In addition, banks routinely limit risk through *covenants* that impose constraints that protect the interest of the debt holder. With accounts receivable financing, accounts are either *assigned* or *factored*.

Under assignment, the lender has a lien on receivables, and the borrower is responsible for bad accounts. The lending agreement establishes a margin (usually 75%) of current (less than 90 days) receivables. As the firm makes sales, it submits its invoices to the bank and can borrow up to 75% of their value.

**Factoring:** A factor is an independent company that acts as an 'outside credit department' for the client. In *maturity factoring*, as the accounts are collected, the factor pays the client the face amount of the invoice less a discount (usually below 2%). If any accounts are late, the factor still pays the firm on an average maturity date determined in advance. Legally, the factor purchases the accounts receivable from the firm, thus providing insurance against bad debts because default or bad debts are the factor's problem. It may also reduce costs associated with granting credit since factors do business with many firms, achieving scale economies and risk reduction through diversification.

Firms that finance their receivables through a chartered bank may also use the services of a factor to improve the receivables' collateral value. Here the factor buys the receivables and assigns them to the bank. This is called maturity factoring with assignment of equity. In the case of *advance factoring*, the factor will provide an advance on the receivables and charge interest at prime plus 2 to3%.

**An Example:** Pat's Pet Products, Inc. factors receivables by selling them for 98 cents on the dollar; it can also be said that Pat's sells receivables at a 2% discount. Pat's average collection period is 30 days. What is the effective annual interest rate?

Pat receives $.98 for each dollar of receivables, but does not have to wait 30 days to collect payment. At the end of 30 days, Pat's customers pay the full amount of the receivables to the factor. This is equivalent to paying $.02 to obtain financing of $.98 for 30 days, which is an interest rate of ($.02/$.98) = .020408 = 2.0408% for 30 days. Assuming, for simplicity, twelve 30-day periods in a year, the effective annual rate is:

$$\text{EAR} \;=\; (1.020408)^{12} - 1 \;=\; 27.43\%$$

**Securitized Receivables - A Financial Innovation:** A new approach to receivables financing is *securitized receivables*. Under this arrangement, large corporations may sell securitized receivables to a wholly-owned financial subsidiary. The subsidiary issues debentures and commercial paper backed by a diversified portfolio of receivables.

Since receivables are liquid, the subsidiary debt is less risky than lending to the parent company which can benefit from the interest savings.

**Inventory loans** involve either a *blanket inventory lien* (a lien on the borrower's entire inventory), a *trust receipt* (the borrower holds specific items of inventory 'in trust' for the lender), or *warehouse financing* (a public warehouse company controls the inventory for the lender).  The legal form of the security arrangement can be tailored to the type of inventory.

**Trade Credit:**  Another alternative source of financing is trade credit, which is equivalent to borrowing from suppliers.

Suppose a supplier offers terms of 2/10 net 30.  If your firm makes a $10,000 purchase, you can pay on the tenth day taking a cash discount or pay the full $10,000 on the thirtieth day.  Or, you may be able to 'stretch' your payables by paying the $10,000 after 60 days.  The longer you wait, the longer the supplier is providing you with trade credit financing.

**An Example:**  For the $10,000 purchase mentioned above, what should your company do?

The buyer is effectively borrowing $9,800 for 20 days, so that the buyer pays $200 in interest on the 'loan' from the supplier.  The interest rate for the 20-day period (net 30 less the discount period of 10 days) is 2.0408% = ($200/$9,800).  Since there are 18.25 such periods in a year (365/20), the buyer is paying an effective annual rate (EAR) of:

$$EAR \; = \; (1.020408)^{18.25} - 1 \; = \; 44.6\%.$$

If the buyer can stretch and pay in 60 days, the EAR is based on 6.0833 periods a year (365/60):

$$EAR \; = \; (1.020408)^{6.0833} - 1 \; = \; 13.08\%.$$

This is a significant improvement for the buyer.  However, companies that continually make late payments to their suppliers risk supplier illwill and possibly a loss in their reputation and credit rating.

**Money Market Financing:** There are two important money market instruments for firms with excellent credit ratings.  *Commercial paper* is offered in denominations of $100,000 and up with maturities ranging from 30 to 90 days (with some up to 365 days).  These short-term notes are issued directly by the corporation and backed by a special line of credit.  So, the interest rate the firm obtains is below the rate a bank would charge for a direct loan.  Also, commercial paper offers the issuer flexibility in tailoring the maturity and size of borrowing.

*Bankers acceptances* (BAs) are notes backed by the bank which guarantee the paper's principal and interest.  When the bank 'accepts' paper, it charges a stamping fee ranging from 0.20% to 0.75%.  The most common buyers of BAs are mutual funds, insurance companies, and banks.

## CONCEPT TEST

1.      Current assets are defined as cash and other assets expected to be converted to _____ within _____ .

2.      The four major categories of current assets are: _____, _____, _____, and _
        _____ . Current assets appear on the balance sheet in order of _____ , which is the ease and time
        involved in converting the assets to _____ .

3.      Short-term obligations which require payment within one year are called _____ . Three major
        categories are: _____ , _____ , and _____ .

4.      The balance sheet identity can be written as: Current assets + Fixed assets   =   _____   +
        _____  +  _____ . Rearranging terms and solving for cash, cash  =
        _____  +  _____  +  _____  -  _____  -  _____ .

5.      The equation in (4) indicates those actions which increase cash and those which decrease cash. Activities
        which increase cash are: (increase/decrease) long-term debt; (increase/decrease) equity; (increase/decrease)
        current liabilities; (increase/decrease) current assets other than cash; and (increase/decrease) fixed assets.
        Activities which decrease cash are: (increase/decrease) long-term debt; (increase/decrease) equity;
        (increase/decrease) current liabilities; (increase/decrease) current assets other than cash; and
        (increase/decrease) fixed assets.

6.      The length of the operating cycle is equal to the sum of the _____ period and the _____
        period.

7.      The cash cycle is the difference between the _____ and the _____ period. A cash cycle of
        30 days means that _____ occur 30 days after _____ .

8.      A firm's short-term financial policy has two dimensions: the size of the investment in current assets, and the
        financing of current assets. A flexible current asset policy implies that the firm maintains relatively
        (high/low) levels of cash, marketable securities, and inventories, and grants (liberal/restrictive) credit terms
        which result in relatively (high/low) levels of accounts receivable. Restrictive policies mean that the firm
        maintains relatively (high/low) levels of current assets.

9.      A flexible policy requires (larger/ smaller) initial cash outflows, and future cash inflows should be
        (larger/smaller) . The (higher/lower) level of inventory associated with a flexible policy (reduces/increases)
        the likelihood of inventory stockouts, so that sales are (increased/decreased). Similarly, the
        (liberal/restrictive) credit policies associated with a flexible policy result in (increased/decreased) sales.
        Also, the (larger/smaller) cash balances associated with a flexible policy result in (increased/decreased)
        discounts taken on accounts payable and (reduced/increased) borrowing costs.

10.     A flexible financing policy employs relatively (less/more) short-term debt and (less/more) long-term debt.
        A restrictive financing policy employs relatively (less/more) short-term debt and (less/more) long-term debt.

11.     The costs associated with managing current assets can be classified as follows: carrying costs, which are costs
        that (increase/decrease) with increases in the level of investment in current assets; and, shortage costs, which
        are those that (increase/decrease) with increases in the level of investment in current assets.

12.     Carrying costs are the _____ costs of investment in current assets. The two kinds of shortage costs are:
        (1) _____ or _____ costs; and, (2) costs related to _____ . The optimal investment
        in current assets is the level that _____ the sum of the carrying costs and the shortage costs.

13.     Firms almost always require a permanent investment in current assets because _____ . To finance
        the permanent component of working capital, a firm could use a (flexible/restrictive) strategy for which the
        amount of long-term debt always exceeds the firm's total asset requirement. The alternative to this strategy

is a (flexible/restrictive) strategy which involves the use of permanent short-term borrowing to finance any deficit between long-term financing and total assets.  Firms with (flexible/ restrictive) policies are generally less likely to experience financial distress.

14.     Most firms hedge interest-rate risk by matching _____ with _____ .

15.     A policy of financing long-term assets with short-term debt is inherently risky since frequent refinancing is needed, and short-term interest rates are (more/less) volatile than long-term rates.  Short-term interest rates tend to be (higher/lower) than long-term rates so that, on average, borrowing long-term is (more/less) costly.

16.     A common arrangement in international finance is known as a _____ where the bank issuing the letter promises to make a loan under certain conditions.  This LC can be _____ or _____ .

17.     The _____ is a forecasted estimate of cash inflows and outflows over a period of time.  The forecasted net cash inflow is the difference between cash _____ and cash _____ .

18.     Short-term borrowing used to cover a temporary cash deficit most often takes the form of _____ loan.  A _____ is an informal agreement allowing the firm to borrow without submitting the usual paperwork.  A _____ is a formal legal agreement specifying that the bank will lend up to a specified amount to the firm.  The interest rate is usually stated as a specified number of percentage points above the _____ .

19.     A line of credit arrangement often requires that the firm keep some amount of money on deposit in a low-interest (or zero-interest) account; this arrangement is called a _____ and serves to (increase/decrease) the effective rate on the loan because interest on the loan is paid on the full amount borrowed, even though some portion of the loan is not available to the borrower.

20.     Loans that usually require either accounts receivable or inventories as security for the loan are _____ loans.  When accounts receivable are sold to the lender, they are said to be _____ .  In this case, the (lender/borrower) assumes the risk of default on the part of the borrower's customer.  Under the arrangement referred to as _____ of accounts receivable, the lender has a lien on receivables, and the (lender/borrower) assumes the risk of default on the part of the borrower's customer.

21.     If the factoring company pays the client the face amount of the invoice less a fee as the accounts are collected, this is referred to as _____ .  In the case of _____, the factor will provide an advance on the receivables and charge interest at _____ plus 2-3 %.  If the factor buys the receivables and assigns them to the bank, this is called maturity factoring with _____ .

22.     Large corporations may sell _____ to a wholly-owned financial subsidiary.  The subsidiary issues debentures and commercial paper which are backed by a diversified portfolio of _____ .

23.     When an inventory loan involves a lien on all of the borrower's inventory, the arrangement is referred to as _____ .  Inventory loans for which the borrower holds specific items of inventory 'in trust' for the lender involve the use of a _____ .  When a public warehouse company controls the inventory for the lender, this arrangement is referred to as _____ .

24.     It is (cheaper/more expensive) to purchase supplies from a source with credit terms of 2/15 net 45, whose annual percentage cost is _____ as opposed to another source with credit terms of 2/10 net 30.  But you can 'stretch' by paying on the sixtieth day, reducing the annual  cost to _____ .

25.    _____ are short-term notes issued in denominations of _____ and up, issued by large corporations, with yields that are approximately one percentage (higher/lower) than the bank prime rate.

26.    By '_____' the paper, which means the bank guarantees the paper's principal and interest, a _____ is charged which ranges from 0.20% to 0.75%.


## ANSWERS TO CONCEPT TEST

1.    cash; one year

2.    cash; marketable securities; accounts receivable; inventory; accounting liquidity; cash

3.    current liabilities; accounts payable; expenses payable; notes payable

4.    current liabilities; long-term debt; equity; long-term debt; equity; current liabilities; current assets (excluding cash); fixed assets

5.    increase; increase; increase; decrease; decrease; decrease; decrease; decrease; increase; increase

6.    inventory; accounts receivable

7.    operating cycle; accounts payable; inflows; outflows

8.    high; liberal; high; low

9.    larger; larger; higher; reduces; increased; liberal; increased; larger; increased; reduced

10.   less; more; more; less

11.   increase; decrease

12.   opportunity; trading; order; safety reserves; minimizes

13.   current assets never decline to zero; flexible; restrictive; flexible

14.   debt maturities; asset maturities

15.   more; lower; more

16.   letter of credit; revocable; irrevocable

17.   cash budget; collections; outflows

18.   an unsecured short-term bank; noncommitted line of credit; committed line of credit; prime rate

19.   compensating balance; increase

20.   secured short-term; factored; lender; assignment; borrower

21. maturity factoring; advance factoring; prime; assignment of equity

22. securitized receivables; receivables

23. a blanket inventory lien; trust receipt; warehouse financing

24. more expensive; 17.81%; 13.08%

25. commercial paper; $100,000; lower

26. accepting; stamping fee

## PROBLEMS AND SOLUTIONS

### Problem 1

The following data for the Bleys Company applies to the year just ended:

1. Accounts payable increased by $20
2. A $10 dividend was paid
3. Inventories were increased by $120
4. Short-term bank borrowing increased by $80
5. Accounts receivable increased by $30

Identify each of the above as either a source or a use of cash.

**Solution:**   1.   source of cash
2.   use of cash
3.   use of cash
4.   source of cash
5.   use of cash

**Some selected items from Oberon Corporation's balance sheets for the beginning and ending of 2000, respectively, and income statement for 2000 are shown below. Use this information to solve Problems 2 - 6:**

| Balance sheet item | Beginning | Ending | Average |
|---|---|---|---|
| Inventory | $1,000 | $1,400 | $1,200 |
| Accounts receivable | 1,800 | 2,100 | 1,950 |
| Accounts payable | 900 | 1,100 | 1,000 |

| Income statement item | Annual |
|---|---|
| Net sales (all credit) | $30,000 |
| Cost of goods sold | 16,000 |

## Problem 2

Calculate the inventory period.

**Solution:** First compute the inventory turnover ratio:

$$\text{Inventory turnover} = \frac{\text{Costs of goods sold}}{\text{Average inventory}} = \frac{\$16,000}{\$1,200} = 13.33 \text{ times}$$

$$\text{Inventory period} = \frac{365}{\text{Inventory turnover}} = \frac{365}{13.33} = 27.38 \text{ days}$$

The inventory turnover period is the average length of time required to order, produce, and sell a product. Inventory turned over every 27.38 days, on average.

## Problem 3

Calculate the accounts receivable period.

**Solution:** First, compute the accounts receivable turnover ratio:

$$\text{Receivables turnover} = \frac{\text{Credit sales}}{\text{Average receivables}} = \frac{\$30,000}{\$1,950} = 15.38 \text{ times}$$

$$\text{Receivables period} = \frac{365}{\text{Receivables turnover}} = \frac{365}{15.38} = 23.73 \text{ days}$$

Receivables turned over 15.38 times during the year, or every 23.73 days, on average.

## Problem 4

Calculate the accounts payable period.

**Solution:**  First, compute the accounts payable turnover ratio:

$$\text{Payables turnover} = \frac{\text{Cost of goods sold}}{\text{Average payables}} = \frac{\$16,000}{\$1,000} = 16.0 \text{ times}$$

$$\text{Payables period} = \frac{365}{\text{Payables turnover}} = \frac{365}{16.0} = 22.81 \text{ days}$$

Payables turned over 16 times during the year, or every 22.81 days, on average.

**Problem 5**

Calculate the operating cycle.

**Solution:** Using the results from Problems 2 and 3, the operating cycle is:

Operating cycle   =   Inventory period + Accounts Receivable period
                  =   27.38 days + 23.73 days   =   51.11 days   =   51 days

**Problem 6**

Calculate the cash cycle.

**Solution:** Using the results from Problems 4 and 5, the cash cycle is:

Cash cycle   =   Operating cycle – Accounts payable period
             =   51.11 days – 22.81 days   =   28.30 days   =   28 days

**Problem 7**

The balance sheet and income statement data for the Martin Corporation (year 2000) are below.

| Balance sheet item | Beginning | Ending | Average |
|---|---|---|---|
| Inventory | $10,500 | $8,000 | $9,250 |
| Accounts receivable | 5,000 | 6,500 | 5,750 |
| Accounts payable | 2,500 | 3,250 | 2,875 |

| Income statement item | | | |
|---|---|---|---|
| Net sales (all credit) | $17,000 | | |
| Cost of goods sold | 12,250 | | |

Calculate the inventory period, the accounts receivable period, and the accounts payable period.

**Solution:**

Inventory turnover   =   $12,250 / $9,250   =   1.32 times
Inventory period     =   365 / 1.32   =   275.52 days

Receivables turnover   =   $17,000 / $5,750   =   2.96 times
Accounts receivable period   =   365 / 2.96   =   123.31 days

Payables turnover   =   $12,250 / $2,875   =   4.26 times
Accounts payable period   =   365 / 4.26   =   85.68 days

## Problem 8

What are the operating and cash cycles for Martin Corporation?

**Solution:**

Operating cycle  =  Inventory period + Accounts receivable period  =  276.52 + 123.31  =  399.83 days
Cash cycle  =  Operating cycle - Accounts payable period  =  399.83 - 85.68  =  314.15 days

## Problem 9

The balance sheet and income statement for Iago Corporation for the year 2000 are presented below. Calculate the inventory period, the accounts receivable period, and the accounts payable period.

| Balance sheet item | Beginning | Ending | Average |
|---|---|---|---|
| Inventory | $27,400 | $24,600 | $26,000 |
| Accounts receivable | 7,800 | 8,400 | 8,100 |
| Accounts payable | 3,200 | 4,150 | 3,675 |

| Income statement item | | | |
|---|---|---|---|
| Net sales (all credit) | $42,300 | | |
| Cost of goods sold | $28,000 | | |

**Solution:**

Inventory turnover  =  $28,000 / $26,000  =  1.08 times
Inventory period    =  365 / 1.08  =  337.96 days

Receivables turnover  =  $42,300 / $8,100  =  5.22 times
Accounts receivable period  =  365 / 5.22  =  69.92 days

Payables turnover  =  $28,000 / $3,675  =  7.62 times
Accounts payable period  =  365 / 7.62  =  47.90 days

## Problem 10

What are the operating and cash cycles for Iago Corporation?

**Solution:**

Operating cycle  =  337.96 + 69.92  =  407.88 days
Cash cycle  =  407.88 - 47.90  =  359.98 days

**Use the following information on Osiris Company to solve Problems 11 to 18:**

Osiris has estimated sales for the next four quarters as:

|       | Qtr 1 | Qtr 2 | Qtr 3 | Qtr 4 |
|-------|-------|-------|-------|-------|
| Sales | $510  | $870  | $450  | $600  |

Accounts receivable at the beginning of the year were $210. Osiris has a 60-day accounts receivable collection period. Osiris' purchases from suppliers during a quarter are equal to 50% of the next quarter's forecast sales. Projected sales for each quarter of the year following the current one are uniformly 10% higher than the corresponding quarter's forecast sales during the current year. The accounts payable period is 45 days. Wages, taxes, and other expenses are one-third of sales, and interest and dividends are $10 per quarter. No capital expenditures are planned. Osiris is required to maintain a $10 minimum compensating balance, but currently has a cash balance of $0.

## Problem 11

Calculate Osiris's projected cash collections.

**Solution:** With a 60-day collection period, Osiris collects $(30/90) = 1/3$ of sales in the quarter in which they occur; 2/3 of sales are collected the following quarter. Cash collections for the first quarter are:

$$
\begin{aligned}
\text{Cash collections} &= \text{Beginning accounts receivable} + (1/3 \times \text{Sales}) \\
&= \$210 + (1/3 \times \$510) \quad = \quad \$210 + \$170 \quad = \quad \$380
\end{aligned}
$$

Cash collections for each quarter are indicated in the following table:

|                       |     | Qtr 1 |     | Qtr 2 |     | Qtr 3 |     | Qtr 4 |
|-----------------------|-----|-------|-----|-------|-----|-------|-----|-------|
| Beginning receivables |     | $210  |     | $340  |     | $580  |     | $300  |
| Sales                 |     | 510   |     | 870   |     | 450   |     | 600   |
| Cash collections      | 380 |       | 630 |       | 730 |       | 500 |       |
| Ending receivables    |     | 340   |     | 580   |     | 300   |     | 400   |

## Problem 12

Calculate Osiris's projected cash outflows.

**Solution:** With a 45-day accounts payable period, half of purchases from suppliers are paid in the quarter in which they are ordered and half are deferred one quarter. Projected sales in the first quarter of the next year are $(\$510 \times 1.10) = \$561$. The projected cash outflows are:

|                                                        | Qtr 1 | Qtr 2 | Qtr 3 | Qtr 4 |
|--------------------------------------------------------|-------|-------|-------|-------|
| Payment of accounts                                    | $345  | $330  | $263  | $290  |
| Wages, taxes, other expenses                           | 170   | 290   | 150   | 200   |
| Long-term financing expenses (interest and dividends)  | 10    | 10    | 10    | 10    |
| Total                                                  | $525  | $630  | $423  | $500  |

## Problem 13

Calculate the net cash inflow and cumulative financing surplus (or deficit) for Osiris.  What do you observe?

**Solution:**

|                           | Qtr 1   | Qtr 2  | Qtr 3  | Qtr 4  |
|---------------------------|---------|--------|--------|--------|
| Total cash collections    | $380    | $630   | $730   | $500   |
| - Total cash disbursements| 525     | 630    | 423    | 500    |
| Net cash inflow           | -$145   | $  0   | $307   | $  0   |

The cumulative surplus (or deficit) is computed as follows:

|                              | Qtr 1   | Qtr 2   | Qtr 3   | Qtr 4  |
|------------------------------|---------|---------|---------|--------|
| Beginning cash balance       | $  0    | -$145   | -$145   | $162   |
| + Net cash inflow            | - 145   | 0       | 307     | 0      |
| Ending cash balance          | - 145   | - 145   | 162     | 162    |
| Minimum cash balance         | 10      | 10      | 10      | 10     |
| Cumulative surplus (deficit) | -$155   | -$155   | $152    | $152   |

Osiris has a highly seasonal sales pattern.  Because purchases are made in advance and collections are deferred, Osiris will have an ongoing pattern of short-term deficits followed by surpluses.

## Problem 14

Osiris will borrow needed funds at an interest rate of 16% APR, or (.16/4) = .04 = 4% per quarter.  Assume that Osiris begins the year with no short-term debt, and repays short-term debt as soon as possible.  Ignore taxes, and assume that any cash surplus does not earn interest.  Prepare a short-term financial plan for Osiris for the year.

**Solution:**   The complete short-term financial plan is presented in the following table:

|                                | Qtr 1       | Qtr 2       | Qtr 3     | Qtr 4     |
|--------------------------------|-------------|-------------|-----------|-----------|
| Beginning cash balance         | $    0      | $   10.00   | $  10.00  | $149.35   |
| + Net cash inflow              | −   145     | 0.00        | 307.00    | 00.00     |
| + New short-term borrowing     | 155         | 6.20        |           |           |
| – Interest on short-term borrowing |         | 6.20        | 6.45      |           |
| –Short-term borrowing repaid   |             |             | 161.20    |           |
| +Ending cash balance           | $    10     | $   10.00   | $ 149.35  | $ 149.35  |
| –Minimum cash balance          | 10          | 10.00       | 10.00     | 10.00     |
| Cumulative surplus (deficit)   | $    0      | $    0.00   | $139.35   | $ 139.35  |
| Beginning short-term borrowing | $    0      | $155.00     | $161.20   | $   0.00  |
| +Change in short-term debt     | 155         | 6.20        | - 161.20  | 0.00      |
| Ending short-term debt         | $  155      | $161.20     | $  0.00   | $  0.00   |

With no borrowing, the cumulative deficit at the end of quarter 1 is $155.  Consequently, short-term borrowing of $155 is required in quarter 1.  Interest of (.04 × $155) = $6.20 must be paid during quarter 2, and additional short-term borrowing of $6.20 is required during the quarter because the net cash inflow is zero.  Ending short-term debt is ($155 + $6.20) = $161.20.  Interest paid during quarter 3 is (.04 × $161.20) = $6.45, and the net cash inflow of $307 is more than sufficient to pay the total short-term debt of $161.20.

## Problem 15

Suppose that the following changes occur: the accounts receivable collection period decreases from 60 days to 30 days, and the accounts payable period increases from 45 days to 72 days. Calculate Osiris's projected cash collections.

**Solution:** With a 30-day collection period, Osiris collects (60/90) = 2/3 of sales in the quarter in which they occur; 1/3 of sales are collected the following quarter. Cash collections for the first quarter are:

$$\text{Cash collections} = \text{Beginning accounts receivable} + (2/3 \times \text{Sales})$$
$$= \$210 + (2/3 \times \$510) = \$210 + \$340 = \$550$$

Cash collections for each quarter are indicated in the following table:

|  | | Qtr 1 | | Qtr 2 | | Qtr 3 | | Qtr 4 |
|---|---|---|---|---|---|---|---|---|
| Beginning receivables | | $210 | | $170 | | $290 | | $150 |
| Sales | | 510 | | 870 | | 450 | | 600 |
| Cash collections | 550 | | 750 | | 590 | | 550 | |
| Ending receivables | | 170 | | 290 | | 150 | | 200 |

## Problem 16

Calculate Osiris's projected cash outflows, based on the changes described in Problem 15.

**Solution:** With a 72-day accounts payable period, 20% of purchases from suppliers are paid in the quarter in which they are ordered and 80% are deferred one quarter. Only payment of accounts, and, consequently, total cash outflows are affected by the change in the accounts payable period. The projected cash outflows are:

|  | Qtr 1 | Qtr 2 | Qtr 3 | Qtr 4 |
|---|---|---|---|---|
| Payment of accounts | $291 | $393 | $240 | $296 |
| Wages, taxes, other expenses | 170 | 290 | 150 | 200 |
| Long-term financing expenses (interest and dividends) | 10 | 10 | 10 | 10 |
| Total | $471 | $693 | $400 | $506 |

## Problem 17

Calculate the net cash inflow and cumulative financing surplus (or deficit) for Osiris.

**Solution:** The net cash inflows are:

|  | Qtr 1 | Qtr 2 | Qtr 3 | Qtr 4 |
|---|---|---|---|---|
| Total cash collections | $550 | $750 | $590 | $550 |
| - Total cash disbursements | 471 | 693 | 400 | 506 |
| Net cash inflow | $ 79 | $ 57 | $190 | $ 44 |

The cumulative surplus (or deficit) is computed as follows:

|                              | Qtr 1 | Qtr 2 | Qtr 3 | Qtr 4 |
|------------------------------|-------|-------|-------|-------|
| Beginning cash balance       | $   0 | $  79 | $136  | $326  |
| + Net cash inflow            |   79  |   57  |  190  |   44  |
| Ending cash balance          |   79  |  136  |  326  |  370  |
| Minimum cash balance         |   10  |   10  |   10  |   10  |
| Cumulative surplus (deficit) | $  69 | $126  | $316  | $360  |

In comparing the results of this problem with those of Problem 13, we note that Osiris now expects a positive cash inflow for all four quarters, and that the firm has a cumulative surplus throughout the year.  In the earlier problem, a deficit occurs during the first two quarters due to delays in collections.  The differences in this problem result primarily from the earlier collections, although the delayed payments also contribute.  It is important to note that total collections and outflows for the year do not change substantially.  Rather, it is the timing of cash flows which produce the results observed here.


**Problem 18**

Prepare a complete short-term financial plan for Osiris for the year.

**Solution:**   The complete short-term financial plan is presented in the following table:

|                                     | Qtr 1 |    | Qtr 2 | Qtr 3 |    | Qtr 4 |    |
|-------------------------------------|-------|----|-------|-------|----|-------|----|
| Beginning cash balance              | $   0 | $ 79 |     | $ 136 |    | $ 326 |    |
| + Net cash inflow                   |   79  | 57 |       |  190  | 44 |       |    |
| + New short-term borrowing          |       |    |       |       |    |       |    |
| – Interest on short-term borrowing  |       |    |       |       |    |       |    |
| –Short-term borrowing repaid        |       |    |       |       |    |       |    |
| +Ending cash balance                | $  79 |    | $  136 | $ 326 |    | $ 370 |    |
| –Minimum cash balance               |   10  |    |   10  |   10  |    |   10  |    |
| Cumulative surplus (deficit)        | $  69 |    | $  126 | $ 316 |    | $  360 |    |
| –Beginning short-term borrowing     | $   0 |    | $   0 | $  0  |    | $   0 |    |
| +Change in short-term debt          |    0  |    |    0  |   0   |    |    0  |    |
| Ending short-term debt              | $   0 |    | $   0 | $  0  |    | $   0 |    |

There are no deficits, and we have assumed that a surplus does not earn interest.  The complete financial plan does not add any information not already apparent from the solution to Problem 17.


**Some selected items from Isis Company's balance sheets for the beginning and ending of 2000, respectively, and income statement for 2000 are shown below. Use this information to solve Problems 19 to 24.**

|                     | Beginning | Ending | Average |
|---------------------|-----------|--------|---------|
| Inventory           | $600      | $ 700  | $650    |
| Accounts receivable | 800       | 900    | 850     |
| Accounts payable    | 200       | 250    | 225     |

| Income statement item | Annual |
|---|---|
| Net sales (all credit) | $10,000 |
| Cost of goods sold | 6,000 |

## Problem 19

Calculate the inventory turnover period, the accounts receivable turnover period, and the operating cycle.

**Solution:**  The inventory period is 39.54 days, the accounts receivable period is 31.04 days, and the operating cycle is 70.58 days.

## Problem 20

Calculate the accounts payable period and the cash cycle for Isis.

**Solution:**  The accounts payable period is 13.69 days, and the cash cycle is 56.89 days.

## Problem 21

Suppose that Isis is able to reduce its inventory period from 39.54 days to 30 days.  How will this affect the firm's short-term financing requirements?

**Solution:**  An inventory period of 30 days is equivalent to inventory turnover of (365/30) = 12.17 times per year.  With cost of goods sold equal to $6,000 per year, the average inventory level which would be required is: $6,000 / Average inventory   =   12.17

The solution to the above equation is $493.02, which is a reduction of ($650 – $493.02) = $156.98 in the level of inventory.  Consequently, the firm will require, on average, $156.98 less short-term financing with this reduction in the inventory turnover period.

## Problem 22

Suppose that Isis is able to reduce its accounts receivable turnover period from 31.04 days to 25 days.  How will this affect its short-term financing requirements?

**Solution:**  An accounts receivable turnover period of 25 days is equivalent to accounts receivable turnover of 14.60 times per year.  The average level of accounts receivable is determined by :   $10,000 / average receivables  = 14.60.

Therefore, the new level of accounts receivable is $684.93, which represents a reduction of ($850 – $684.93) = $165.07 in the average level of accounts receivable and, consequently, in the average amount of short-term financing required by the firm.

## Problem 23

Suppose that Isis is able to extend its accounts payable period to 18 days, from the current 13.69 days. How will this affect the firm's short-term financing requirements?

**Solution:** An accounts payable period of 18 days is equivalent to accounts payable turnover of (365/18) = 20.28 times per year. The average level of accounts payable which results from this increase is indicated by: $6,000 / Average payables = 20.28.

The new level of accounts payable increases to $295.86, which is an increase of ($295.86 – $225) = $70.86 in the level of accounts payable and consequently a decrease in the amount of short-term financing required from other sources.

## Problem 24

Given the changes presented in Problems 21 to 23, what is the new operating cycle? What is the new cash cycle?

**Solution:** The operating cycle is 55 days and the cash cycle is 37 days. We have indicated a reduction in the cash cycle here and a resulting reduction in short-term financing requirements as calculated in Problems 21 to 23. However, it is important to realize that changes such as those suggested above cannot be achieved without incurring related costs. Therefore, the benefit associated with reductions in financing requirements must be weighed against costs such as potential loss of sales due to reduction in credit period.

## Problem 25

A bank offers a line of credit with a 13% annual interest rate and a 6% compensating balance. How much interest is paid on a $400,000, one-year loan? What is the compensating balance requirement? What is the effective interest rate?

**Solution:** Assuming a single payment at the end of the year, with no compounding of interest, we have the following calculations:

$$\text{Interest paid} = .13 \times \$400,000 = \$52,000$$
$$\text{Compensating balance} = .06 \times \$400,000 = \$24,000$$

$$\text{Effective interest rate} = \frac{\text{Interest paid}}{\text{Amount available}} = \frac{\$52,000}{\$376,000} = .13830$$

The effective rate is 13.830%, rather than the stated 13%, because the interest paid is computed on the basis of a $400,000 loan, whereas the actual proceeds of the loan to the borrower are only $376,000. The effective interest rate can also be computed on a per dollar basis. The interest paid per dollar borrowed is $.13, and the actual amount available per dollar borrowed is $.94, so that the effective interest rate is ($.13/$.94) = 13.830%.

**Problem 26**

Refer to the loan terms described in Problem 25.   What size loan is necessary if the borrower requires net proceeds of $500,000? What is the compensating balance requirement?  How much interest is paid on the loan for one year?  What is the effective interest rate?

**Solution:**  The size of the loan is the solution for the following equation:

$$(1 - .06) \times \text{loan size} = \$500,000$$
$$\text{loan size} = \$500,000 / .94 = \$531,914.89$$

The size of the loan is $531,914.89 and the compensating balance requirement is ($531,914.89 – $500,000) = (.06 × $531,914.89) = $31,914.89

$$\text{Interest paid} = .13 \times \$531,914.89 = \$69,148.94$$

$$\text{Effective interest rate} = \frac{\$69,148.94}{\$500,000} = .13830$$

The effective interest rate is 13.830%, as computed in Problem 25.

**Problem 27**

Kristy Konstruction Supplies, Inc. factors its receivables at a 2.5% discount.  The firm's average collection period is 40 days.  What is the effective annual interest rate?  Assume 360 days in a year.

**Solution:**  Kristy receives 97.5 cents for each dollar of receivables, but does not have to wait 40 days to collect payment.  At the end of 40 days, Kristy's customers pay the full amount of the receivables to the factor. This is equivalent to paying 2.5 cents to obtain financing of 97.5 cents for 40 days, which is an interest rate of ($.025 / $.975) = .025641 = 2.5641% for 40 days.  Assuming 360 days in a year, and therefore nine 40-day periods in a year, the effective annual rate is:

$$\text{EAR} = (1.025641)^9 - 1 = 25.59\%$$

# 19       Cash and Liquidity Management

## CHAPTER HIGHLIGHTS

Corporations hold cash to provide the liquidity necessary for efficient operations. Holding cash, however, means foregoing the return that could be earned by investing in marketable securities. Cash management involves evaluating the tradeoff between the benefits of liquidity and the opportunity cost of foregone interest. Effective cash management requires that financial managers address three basic concerns. First, how much cash should the firm keep on hand? Second, how should the firm manage cash collection and disbursement? Third, how should 'excess' cash be invested?

## REASONS FOR HOLDING CASH

There are three reasons for holding cash: the precautionary motive, the speculative motive, and the transaction motive.

**Speculative and Precautionary Motives:** The speculative motive is the need for cash to take advantage of investment opportunities which might arise in the future. The precautionary motive is the need to hold cash as a financial reserve in the event of unanticipated decreases in cash inflows. Both of these motives can be satisfied by access to reserve borrowing ability and holding of marketable securities, rather than holding cash. Consequently, it would be more appropriate to refer to these as motives for liquidity, rather than motives for holding cash.

**The Transaction Motive:** Firms require cash to meet their regular disbursements. This reason for holding cash is referred to as the transaction motive. The need arises because the timing of cash inflows and outflows do not exactly match.

**Compensating Balances:** Additionally, firms may hold cash in the form of compensating balances. A compensating balance is a minimum deposit required by a commercial bank as compensation for bank services. Compensating balance requirements together with the minimum necessary transactions balance establish the minimum total cash requirement.

**Costs of Holding Cash:** Firms with cash balances in excess of the minimum total cash requirement incur opportunity costs. The opportunity cost is the interest income foregone by holding cash rather than investing in marketable securities, for example. However, firms with low cash balances run the risk of not meeting required disbursements.

## DETERMINING THE TARGET CASH BALANCE

The opportunity costs of holding cash are carrying costs, which are costs which increase with an increase in the cash balance. The costs of holding too little cash are shortage costs, or adjustment costs. The target cash balance is the firm's desired level of cash, which is the cash balance that minimizes the sum of carrying costs and shortage costs.

Firms with a flexible working capital policy hold marketable securities to satisfy the transaction and precautionary motives. The adjustment costs incurred are the trading costs associated with buying and selling marketable securities. Firms with restrictive policies face adjustment costs in the form of interest expense and other expenses associated with short-term debt.

A firm which holds an extremely low cash balance incurs high trading costs, but little or no opportunity costs. These firms sell marketable securities to meet a cash shortage, and then buy marketable securities with excess cash balances. As the cash balance increases, the firm's opportunity costs increase, while trading costs decrease; sales and purchases of marketable securities are less frequent because cash shortages occur less frequently. With extremely high cash balances, opportunity costs are very high, but trading costs are very low, cash shortages are infrequent, so that sales and purchases of securities are infrequent. The optimal cash balance, or target cash balance, is the cash balance which minimizes the sum of the opportunity costs and the trading costs.

**Other Factors Influencing the Target Cash Balance:**  Firms can raise cash by borrowing, rather than by selling securities. However, the interest rate on short-term debt is usually higher than the rate the firm would have earned on marketable securities. And, firms with greater cash flow variability and low investment in marketable securities typically have to borrow more; thus, interest costs are higher.

For large firms, the transaction cost of buying and selling Treasury bills is almost certainly less than the interest that can be earned on T-bills, even for an overnight investment. As a result, the primary reasons for such firms to hold cash relate to compensating balance requirements. A large firm may have thousands of accounts so that it may not be worthwhile to manage them all on a daily basis.

## UNDERSTANDING FLOAT

The amount of cash on a firm's financial statements (the 'book' or 'ledger' balance) is not the same as the firm's bank balance (the firm's 'available' or 'collected' balance). The difference between the firm's available balance and its book balance is called float.

**Disbursement Float:**  Cheques written by the firm reduce the book balance immediately, but do not affect the available balance until the cheque is actually presented to the firm's bank for payment. The difference in the balances is called *disbursement float.* For example, suppose you have $100 on deposit in a chequing account, and you write a cheque for $100 to pay for supplies. Once you write the cheque, you show a balance of zero on your books (i.e., in your cheque book), but the bank shows an available balance of $100 during the time that the cheque is clearing. You have a positive disbursement float of $100 during that time. The firm can obtain the benefits of this cash while the cheque is clearing by temporarily investing the balance in marketable securities.

Prior to writing the cheque, you have zero disbursement float:

$$\text{Float} = \text{Available balance} - \text{Book balance} = \$100 - \$100 = \$0$$

Once you write the cheque, but before the cheque is presented to your bank:

$$\text{Float} = \text{Available balance} - \text{Book balance} = \$100 - \$0 = \$100$$

When the cheque is presented to your bank:

$$\text{Float} = \text{Available balance} - \text{Book balance} = \$0 - \$0 = \$0$$

**Collection Float and Net Float:**  Cheques received increase your book balance but not your available balance until payment is actually received by the bank. The difference is called *collection float.* If you deposit a $200 pay cheque, then you show an increase in your book balance of $200, but your bank balance does not increase by $200 until the cheque clears. This difference is a negative collection float equal to –$200. That is, when the cheque is deposited:

$$\text{Float} = \text{Available balance} - \text{Book balance} = \$0 - \$200 = -\$200$$

When the cheque has cleared, so that the $200 is available to you:

Float  =  Available balance – Book balance  =  $200 – $200  =  $0

Net float is the sum of collection and disbursement floats.  Suppose you deposit the $200 pay cheque at the same time that you write the $100 cheque to pay for supplies.  At that time, the book balance is $200 (i.e., the $200 pay cheque which has been deposited), but the available balance is $100 (i.e., the original $100 balance in the account).  Therefore the net discrepancy, or the net float is negative.

Float  =  Available balance – Book balance  =  $100 – $200  =  –$100

This negative net float is a disadvantage since, if you were to write another cheque for $150, the bank balance would not be sufficient to cover the cheque even though your book balance is sufficient.  Financial managers are more concerned with the available balance than with the book balance.

**Float Management:**  Float management involves speeding up collections and delaying disbursements.  Float can be broken down into three parts: *mail float* (the time the cheque is in the mail), *processing float* (the time between the receipt and deposit of a cheque), and *availability float* (the time required to clear the cheque through the banking system).  Study Figure 19.2 on page 648 of your text to see the relationship between the three different types of float.

**Measuring Float:**  The size of the float depends on both the dollar amount and the time delay involved.  Suppose a customer places an order through a mail-order catalogue; the customer mails a $300 cheque to the firm from another province.  It takes four days for the cheque to reach the firm, and one day for the firm to deposit the cheque in the bank.  The bank holds out-of-province cheques for two days before crediting the firm's account.  The total float is [$300 \times (4 + 1 + 2)] = $2,100.  Assume, for simplicity, that this is the only cheque received by the firm during the month.  The average daily float is computed as follows:

$$\text{Average daily float}  =  \frac{\text{Total float}}{\text{Total days}}  =  \frac{\$2,100}{30}  =  \$70$$

During the month, the firm's book balance is, on average, $70 greater than the available balance.

**An Example:**  Suppose that the firm receives two cheques every month: one cheque is for $2,000 and is delayed a total of 15 days; the other is for $3,000 and is delayed five days.  Compute the total float and the average daily float.

The total float is:  ($2,000 \times 15) + ($3,000 \times 5)  =  $45,000

The average daily float, assuming a 30-day month, is: Average daily float  =  $45,000 / 30  =  $1,500

Alternatively, the average daily float can be computed by first calculating the weighted average delay.  For the above example, total receipts for the month are ($2,000 + $3,000) = $5,000.  The weighted average delay is:

[($2,000/$5,000) \times 15]  +  [($3,000/$5,000) \times 5]  =  9 days

The calculation indicates that ($2,000/$5,000) = 40% of the firm's receipts are delayed 15 days, and ($3,000/$5,000) = 60% of the receipts are delayed five days, so that the weighted average delay is nine days. Average daily receipts are ($5,000/30) = $166.67.  Since this amount is delayed nine days, on average, then the average daily float is:

Average daily float = Average daily receipts × Weighted average delay  =  $166.67 \times 9 = $1,500

**Cost of the Float:** The cost of the float is the opportunity cost resulting from not being able to use the money. The calculation of this cost is based on the average daily float. Suppose a firm received a $100 payment each day from its customers, and the cheques require three days to clear through the banking system. Therefore, a cheque received Day 1 is available to the firm on Day 4, and float, as of Day 4, is $300. Float remains constant at $300, and the firm receives payment of $100 each day while a cheque deposited three days earlier becomes available each day. Now, suppose that, as of Day t, the three-day delay could be completely eliminated, so that all payments were available immediately; what would such a change be worth to the firm? The answer is $300. On Day 5, $400 would become available, representing the $100 payment received from customers on Day t plus payments received from customers on each of the three preceding days. This results in an incremental cash inflow of $300, and float would be reduced from $300 to $0 on Day t. On Day (t + 1), and on every subsequent day, the firm would continue to receive $100 per day. Therefore, the only change in cash flows is the additional $300 received on Day t.

Suppose that, instead of a reduction from a three-day delay to no delay, the reduction is from a three-day delay to a one-day delay. What is the value of this reduction to the firm? Float will decrease from $300 to $100, a $200 decrease, and the incremental cash flow will be $200, the same as the reduction in float. That is, on Day t, $300 becomes available, rather than $100, because cheques which were deposited on Days (t–3), (t–2), and (t–1) all become available on Day t. With the previous arrangement, only the cheque deposited on Day (t–3) would become available on Day t.

A reduction in float has value to the firm, but there is generally a cost associated with accomplishing such a reduction. Some procedures for reducing float are described in the remainder of this section. Adopting these techniques is appropriate only if they have positive net present value; that is, the benefit derived from the reduction in float must exceed the cost of implementing a change.

**Accelerating Collections:** Techniques to accelerate collections include systems to expedite mail and cheque processing, lockboxes, concentration banking, and wire transfers.

The key tasks of the firm's cash flow information system are tracking payments through the system and providing up-to-date cash balances and investment rates. Linking the manager's terminal with the bank's on-line, real time system, gives the financial manager access to account balances and transactions and information on money market rates. Electronic banking systems also allow the manager to transfer funds and make money market investments. Today *smart cards* are much like an Automated Teller Machine Card and are used within corporations to control access to information by its employees.

**Over-the-Counter Collections:** Most large retailers and other firms receive collections over the counter at field offices or at stores. Firms also may instruct customers to mail cheques to a given collection point address. By distributing these collection points locally, the firm can reduce mail float (instead of collecting at head office).

**Lockboxes:** A *lockbox* is the most common approach used to accelerate collections. A firm arranges for customers to mail payments to a post office box maintained by a local bank. The bank collects the cheques from the post office box several times a day, and deposits them in the firm's account. Lockboxes reduce mailing time, because customers mail payment to a local post office rather than to company headquarters. Use of lockboxes also eliminates the time the corporation would spend processing cheques prior to making the deposit.

**Electronic Collection Systems:** Many firms today use some type of electronic funds transfer system. Examples in Canada include *pre-authorized payments,* which are paperless transfers of instalment payments from the customer's account directly to the firm's (mortgage payments, rent, insurance, cable TV, etc.); *point-of-sales transfers* which use *debit cards* to transfer funds directly from a customer's bank account to a retailer's, and *electronic trade payables* (discussed later under disbursements).

**Cash Concentration:**  With a *concentration banking system*, a firm's sales offices are used to receive and process cheques.  Since customer payments are then deposited in local banks, this process speeds up cheque-clearing because customer's cheques also tend to be drawn on local banks.  In addition, mailing time is reduced because cheques are mailed to local sales offices.  Surplus funds are subsequently transferred to the firm's main bank (or to a small number of banks), called the concentration bank (or concentration banks). Concentration banking is often combined with lockboxes.

**Controlling Disbursements:**  There are three common approaches to controlling delaying disbursements by delaying receipt of payment.  The first is to make payments from as far away as possible.  For example, pay Vancouver suppliers with cheques drawn on a Montreal bank, thus increasing the disbursement float by increasing the time required for the cheque to clear.  The second is to postmark a payment, but delay mailing it. The third is to mail cheques from remote post offices.

A cheque is drawn on a bank while a draft is drawn on the issuer (the firm) and cannot be paid until it is presented to, and accepted by, the issuer. The issuer then deposits the required amount in order to cover payment of the draft. The use of drafts slows up payments and allows the firm to keep a lower cash balance than would otherwise be required.

Electronic payments made from disbursement accounts (for example, payroll, vendor disbursements, customer refunds etc.) are kept separate from the concentration account to ease accounting and control. Firms use *zero balance accounts* to avoid carrying extra balances in each disbursement account. A zero balance is maintained by transfers of funds from a master account in an amount only large enough to cover cheques presented.

It is often possible for firms to draw on and invest uncollected funds. A systematic policy of exploiting the float is potentially quite profitable, though it presents ethical and legal questions.

## INVESTING IDLE CASH

Canadian chartered banks offer arrangements in which the bank takes all excess available funds at the close of each business day and invests them for the firm.

Idle cash can be invested in short-term securities. The market for these securities is called the money market. Most large firms do their own investing in money-market securities. Smaller firms often rely on money-market mutual funds, some of which specialize in corporate cash management. These funds buy money market instruments and manage them for a fee.

**Temporary Cash Surpluses:**  Temporary cash surpluses help finance seasonal or cyclical activities, as well as planned or possible expenditures.  Some firms, such as retailers, have a predictable seasonal cash flow pattern. These firms regularly invest in marketable securities during periods of surplus cash flows and sell securities, or obtain bank loans, during deficit periods.  Firms frequently accumulate cash in anticipation of a large expenditure on a new plant, for example.  Stocks and bonds might be sold to finance the expenditure; the proceeds are then temporarily invested and drawn down as construction progresses.

**Characteristics of Short-Term Securities:**  The most important characteristics of short-term marketable securities are the maturity, default risk, marketability, and tax status of the securities.

Most firms limit their investments in money-market securities to those with maturity of 90 days or less.  This strategy virtually eliminates interest-rate risk, which is the change in the value of an asset resulting from changes in interest rates.  Firms also restrict their short-term investments to highly-rated securities with little or no default risk.  Firms usually prefer to invest in securities which are highly marketable, or liquid, meaning that they can be quickly sold without loss of value.  Finally, interest earned on money-market securities is subject to federal and provincial tax.

**Some Different Types of Money-Market Securities:**   *Treasury bills* are direct obligations of the federal government.  At weekly auctions, they are issued with maturities of 90 and 180 days.  At monthly auctions, the maturities are 270 and 360 days.  These securities are actively traded by banks and investment dealers over the counter.

*Commercial paper* is short-term, unsecured debt, issued by businesses with maturities ranging from a few weeks to 270 days.  Since there is no active secondary market for commercial paper, marketability is low. DBRS and CBRS publish quality ratings and default risk varies with the issuer's strength.

*Repurchase agreements* are transactions involving the purchase of an instrument (usually Treasury securities) and a simultaneous agreement to sell it back at a higher price in the future. *Dollar swaps* are foreign currency deposits that will be converted or swapped back into Canadian dollars at a predetermined rate. They allow the manager to place funds in major money markets outside Canada without measuring foreign exchange risk.

## CASH MANAGEMENT MODELS (APPENDIX 19A)

**The BAT Model:**  The Baumol-Allais-Tobin (BAT) model is the simplest formal approach to establishing a target cash balance.  Consider the following example:

$$T = \$240 = \text{the total cash needed for transactions over a period (e.g., a year);}$$
$$F = \$1 \quad = \text{the fixed cost of making a securities trade to replenish cash balances;}$$
$$R = 10\% = \text{the interest rate on marketable securities (i.e., the opportunity cost);}$$
$$C = \$10 \quad = \text{the beginning cash balance.}$$

We assume the cash balance is initially at C and declines to zero.  When the balance reaches zero, it is replenished to the level C by the sale of marketable securities.  Therefore, the average cash balance over the period is $[(C + 0)/2]$ = ($10/2) = $5.  The total opportunity cost is the average cash balance times the interest rate on marketable securities:

$$\text{Opportunity costs} = (C/2) \times R = \$5 \times .10 = \$.50.$$

The number of times that the cash balance is replenished during the year is:   $(T/C) = (\$240/\$10) = 24$ times.

The total trading cost for the year is:

$$\text{Trading costs} = (T/C) \times F = 24 \times \$1 = \$24$$

The following figure illustrates the characteristic 'sawtooth' pattern of the BAT model.

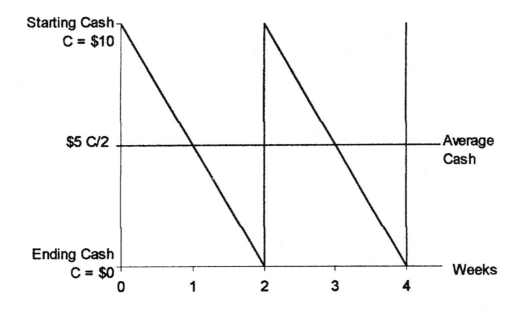

The BAT model identifies the cash balance (C*) which minimizes the sum of the two costs. The total cost is:

Total cost   =   Opportunity costs + Trading costs

=   $[(C/2) \times R] + [(T/C) \times F]$

It can be shown that C* is the value of C for which opportunity costs and trading costs are equal:

$(C*/2) \times R$   =   $(T/C*) \times F$

Solving this equation for C*:

$C*$   =   $[(2T \times F) / R]^{1/2}$

For our example, the target cash balance is:

$C*$   =   $[(2 \times \$240 \times \$1) / .10]^{1/2}$   =   $(4,800)^{1/2}$   =   $\$69.28$

The BAT model is simple to apply, but it has several deficiencies. The model is based on the assumption that cash disbursements are the same every day, and cash disbursements are known with certainty. To the extent that these assumptions are inconsistent with reality, the model may not be applicable for a particular firm.

**The Miller-Orr Model: A More General Approach:** The BAT model assumes certainty in the firm's cash flows; the Miller-Orr model allows for cash-flow variability. The essence of the Miller-Orr model is that the firm sets a lower limit (L) on cash holdings, based on the likelihood of a cash shortfall and the firm's willingness to tolerate the risk of a shortfall; then an upper limit (U*) and a target cash balance (C*) are determined by applying the model.

When the cash balance reaches U*, the firm returns to its target balance C* by investing (U* – C*) dollars in marketable securities. When the balance declines to L, the firm sells (C* – L) dollars of marketable securities in order to increase the cash balance to C*. As long as the firm's cash balance is between L and U*, no transactions are made.

Given L, the values of C* and U* which minimize expected total cost are determined as follows:

$$C^* = L + [(3/4 \times F \times \sigma^2)/R]^{1/3}$$

$$U^* = (3 \times C^*) - (2 \times L)$$

where F is the cost per transaction of buying and selling marketable securities, $\sigma^2$ is the variance of the firm's net cash flows per period, and R is the interest rate, per period, on marketable securities.

The average cash balance is determined as follows:

$$\text{Average cash balance} = [(4 \times C^*) - L]/3$$

Suppose that the daily variance of cash flows is $4, the daily interest rate is .02% (.0002), and that management has determined that a lower limit of $10 is desirable. Using the other data from the BAT model example in the previous section, we calculate C*, U*, and the average cash balance:

$$C^* = \$10 + [(3/4 \times \$1 \times \$4)/.0002]^{1/3} = \$34.66$$

$$U^* = (3 \times \$34.66) - (2 \times \$10) = \$83.98$$

$$\text{Average cash balance} = [(4 \times \$34.66) - \$10]/3 = \$42.88$$

## CONCEPT TEST

1.    The desire to take advantage of investment opportunities which might arise in the future is the _____ motive for holding cash. The need to hold cash as a financial reserve in the event of unanticipated increases in cash outflows or unanticipated decreases in cash inflows is the _____ motive.  Both of these motives can be satisfied by access to _____ and holding of _____ . Therefore, these might be referred to as motives for _____.

2.    The need to hold cash for regular disbursements and collections is the _____ motive.  An additional need to hold cash arises from the need to keep a _____, which is a minimum deposit required by a commercial bank as compensation for bank services.

3.    A firm which holds a cash balance in excess of the minimum balance required for transactions and compensating balances incurs a(n) _____ cost.  This cost is the interest income which the firm foregoes by holding cash rather than investing the cash.  This cost is a carrying cost, which (increases/decreases) with an increase in the cash balance.

4.    A firm whose cash balance is too low is subjected to the risk of being unable to meet required disbursements, which then requires the firm to either _____ or _____. The costs of holding too little cash are called _____ costs, or _____ costs.

5.    A firm with a (restrictive/flexible) working capital policy holds marketable securities to satisfy the transaction motive and the precautionary motive, while a firm with a (restrictive/flexible) policy relies on short-term borrowing to meet unanticipated cash requirements.  In the former case, the shortage costs are _____ costs, and in the latter case, the shortage costs are _____ expenses.

6.      A firm that holds a low cash balance incurs (high/low) shortage costs and (high/low) opportunity costs. As the cash balance increases, opportunity costs (increase/decrease) while shortage costs (increase/decrease). With high cash balances, opportunity costs are (high/low) and shortage costs are (high/low).

7.      The optimal cash balance, or target cash balance, is the cash balance which minimizes the sum of _____ and _____ costs.

8.      The amount of cash on a firm's financial statement is called the _____ balance or the _____ balance. The firm's bank balance is called the _____ balance or the _____ balance. The difference between the firm's available balance and its book balance is called _____.

9.      Cheques written by the firm reduce the _____ balance immediately, but do not affect the _____ balance until the cheque is actually presented to the firm's bank for payment. The difference in the balances is called _____ float.

10.     Cheques received increase the _____ balance but do not increase the _____ balance until payment is actually received by the bank. The difference is called _____ float.

11.     Net float is the sum of _____ float and _____ float. Float management involves speeding up _____ and delaying _____.

12.     Float can be broken down into three parts: _____ float is the time during which a cheque is in the mail; _____ float is the time between the receipt and deposit of a cheque; and, _____ float is the time required to clear the cheque through the banking system.

13.     The size of the float depends on both the dollar amount and the time delay involved. The total float is equal to _____ times _____. The average daily float is equal to _____ divided by _____. The average daily float can also be computed as _____ times _____.

14.     The cost of float is the _____ cost resulting from not being able to use the money.

15.     The most common approach used to accelerate collections is the _____. This approach reduces _____ float, because customers mail payment to a local post office, and eliminates _____ float.

16.     A second approach to accelerating collections is a _____ system, in which a firm's sales offices are used to receive and process cheques. Since customer payments are then deposited in local banks, this process reduces _____ float. Also, _____ float is reduced because cheques are mailed to local sales offices. Surplus funds are subsequently transferred to the firm's main bank, called the _____ bank. The fastest way to transfer funds to the firm's concentration bank is _____.

17.     Idle cash can be invested in _____, or _____, securities, which are securities with maturity of less than one year. The market for these securities is called the _____ market.

18.     Most firms limit their investments in money-market securities to those with maturity of _____. This strategy virtually eliminates _____ risk, which is the change in the value of an asset resulting from changes in interest rates. Firms also restrict their short-term investments to highly-rated securities with little or no _____ risk. That is, these securities have a very low probability that interest and principal will not be paid when due. Firms also prefer to invest in securities which are highly _____, or _____, meaning that they can be quickly sold without loss of value.

19. _____ is short-term, unsecured debt, issued by businesses, with maturities ranging from a few weeks to 270 days.

20. _____ are time deposits in banks. _____ are transactions involving the purchase of an instrument and a simultaneous agreement to sell it back at a higher price in the future.

21. In the BAT model, we assume that the cash balance is initially at C and declines to _____, at which time it is replenished to the level _____ by the sale of marketable securities. The average cash balance over the period is _____. The total opportunity cost is the _____ times the _____, or expressed algebraically, _____. The number of times that the cash balance is replenished during the year is equal to _____. The total trading cost for the year is equal to _____.

22. The BAT model identifies the cash balance (C*) which minimizes the total cost, which is the sum of the _____ cost and the _____ cost. Expressed algebraically: Total cost = _____ . C* is the value of C for which _____ costs and _____ costs are equal, and is computed as follows: C* = _____ .

23. In applying the Miller-Orr model, the firm sets a _____ limit (L) on cash holdings, and then an upper limit (U*) and a target cash balance (C*), which minimizes _____, and are determined as follows: C* _____ , U* _____ . The average cash balance is determined as follows: Average cash balance = _____ .

24. When the cash balance reaches U*, the firm returns to its target balance C* by investing _____ dollars in _____. When the balance declines to L, the firm sells _____ dollars of _____ in order to increase the cash balance to C*.

## ANSWERS TO CONCEPT TEST

1. speculative; precautionary; reserve borrowing ability; marketable securities; liquidity

2. transaction; compensating balance

3. opportunity; increases

4. sell marketable securities; borrow; shortage; adjustment

5. flexible; restrictive; trading; interest

6. high; low; increase; decrease; high; low

7. opportunity; shortage

8. book; ledger; available; collected; float

9. book; available; disbursement

10. book; available; collection

11.  disbursement; collection; collections; disbursements

12.  mail; processing; availability

13.  number of days delay; dollar amount of cheque; total float; total days; average daily receipts; weighted average delay

14.  opportunity

15.  lockbox; mail; processing

16.  concentration banking; availability; mail; concentration; wire transfer

17.  short-term; marketable; money

18.  90 days or less; interest-rate; default; marketable; liquid

19.  commercial paper

20.  certificates of deposit;  repurchase agreements

21.  zero; C; [(C + 0)/2]; average cash balance; interest rate on marketable securities; [(C/2) × R]; (T/C); [(T/C) × F]

22.  opportunity; trading; {[(C/2) × R] + [(T/C × F]}; opportunity; trading; $[\,(2T \times F)/R]^{1/2}$

23.  lower; expected total cost; $\{L + [(3/4 \times F \times \sigma^2)/R]^{1/3}\}$; [(3 × C*) – (2 × L)]; {[(4 × C*) – L]/3}

24.  (U* – C*); marketable securities; (C* – L); marketable securities

## PROBLEMS AND SOLUTIONS

### Problem 1

On a typical business day, a firm writes cheques for a total of $5,000.  On average, these cheques clear in eight days.  Simultaneously, the firm receives cheques whose total is $7,000.  On average, the cash is available in four days.  Calculate the disbursement float, the collection float, and the net float.  Interpret your answer.

**Solution:** The disbursement float is  (8 × $5,000)  =  $40,000. The collection float is   [4 × (–$7,000)]  =    – $28,000.  The net float is the sum of the disbursement float and the collection float: [$40,000 + (–$28,000)]    =  $12,000.

At any given time, the firm typically has disbursed cheques, which have not yet cleared, with a total value of $40,000.  That is, $40,000 is the available balance and the book balance is zero.  In addition, the firm has received cheques with a total value of $28,000, which are not yet available.  Therefore, the available balance is zero and the book balance is $28,000.  The firm's book balance is typically $12,000 less than its bank cash.

## Problem 2

A real estate firm receives 100 rental cheques a month. Of these, 70 are for $300 and 30 are for $200. The $300 cheques are delayed four days on average; the $200 cheques are delayed five days on average. Calculate the average daily collection float, and interpret your answer.

**Solution:** The total float during the month is: $(70 \times \$300 \times 4) + (30 \times \$200 \times 5) = \$114,000$. Assuming a 30-day month, the average daily float is: $\$114,000 / 30 = \$3,800$. On an average day, the firm has $3,800 in the mail or otherwise uncollected.

## Problem 3

Using the data from Problem 2, calculate the weighted average delay. Use the weighted average delay to calculate the average daily float.

**Solution:** Total monthly collections are: $(70 \times \$300) + (30 \times \$200) = \$27,000$. The weighted average delay is: $[(\$21,000/\$27,000) \times 4] + [(\$6,000/\$27,000) \times 5] = 4.2222$ days. Average daily receipts are $(\$27,000/30) = \$900$. The average daily float is: Average daily receipts $\times$ Weighted average delay $= \$900 \times 4.2222 = \$3,800$

This is the same as the result computed in Problem 2.

## Problem 4

A mail order company typically receives three cheques every month: one is for $1,500 and is delayed for 10 days; one is for $2,000 and is delayed for 17 days, and the last is for $1,200 and is delayed for 12 days. What is the total float and average daily float?

**Solution:**

Total float $= (\$1,500 \times 10) + (\$2,000 \times 17) + (\$1,200 \times 12) = \$63,400$

Assuming a 30-day month,

Average daily float $= \$63,400 / 30 = \$2,113.33$

## Problem 5

Gill Corporation is a fish tank manufacturer and writes $4,300 worth of cheques each day. These cheques clear in six days. Gill also receives cheques worth $5,900 each, although these cheques take five days to clear. What is Gill's disbursement float, collection float, and net float?

**Solution:** The disbursement float is $(6 \times \$4,300) = \$25,800$. The collection float is $(5 \times \$5,900) = \$29,500$. Net float is $\$25,800 - \$29,500 = -\$3,700$.

Note: Collection means that the firm is *not* collecting funds. So, when you calculate net float as the sum of disbursement and collection floats, you must reverse the sign for collection float.

## Problem 6

Suppose that, for the data of Problem 2, a bank has offered to operate a lockbox system which will reduce float by two days. The bank's fee is $200 per year, payable at the end of the year, and the annual interest rate is 9%. Calculate the net present value of this system.

**Solution:** If the weighted average delay is reduced from 4.2222 days to 2.2222 days, then:

Average daily float = Average daily receipts × Weighted average delay  = $900 × 2.2222 = $2,000

Therefore float is reduced by: ($3,800 – $2,000)  = (2 × $900)  =  $1,800

Since this $1,800 becomes available to the firm at the time that the lockbox system is instituted, the present value of the change is $1,800. This $1,800 is available to the firm as long as the lockbox system is in effect. The cost of maintaining the lockbox is $200 per year. The present value of the perpetuity is ($200/.09)  = $2,222.22. Therefore, the net present value of the lockbox system is ($1,800 – $2,222.22) = –$422.22, so that the system is unacceptable.

## Problem 7

Consider the data from Problems 2, 3, and 6. What is the maximum amount the firm would pay to reduce the float by two days?

**Solution:** The maximum fee the firm would pay is the amount such that the net present value of the lockbox system is zero. This is the amount such that the present value of the fee is equal to the present value of the system. To determine the maximum fee, solve the following equation:

Lockbox fee / .09  =  $1,800
Lockbox fee  =  $1,800 × .09  =  $162

If the firm pays $162 per year, the present value of the fee is ($162/09) = $1,800, and the net present value is zero.

## Problem 8

Your firm has an average receipt size of $100. A bank has approached you concerning a lockbox system that will decrease your collection float by three days. Your firm typically receives 10,000 cheques per day. The daily interest rate is .02%. The bank's fee for the lockbox service is $.05 for each cheque processed. Should the lockbox service be adopted?

**Solution:** Average daily collections are ($100 × 10,000) = $1 million. Speeding collections by three days will increase the firm's collected bank balance by (3 × $1 million) = $3 million, so the present value of the lockbox is $3 million.

The daily cost of the variable fee is ($.05 × 10,000) = $500. Since this is a perpetuity, the present value is ($500/.0002) = $2,500,000. The net present value of the service is ($3,000,000 – $2,500,000) = $500,000, so that the service should be adopted.

An alternative approach to computing the net present value is to first assume that the firm invests the $3 million collected balance at the daily rate of .02%. The daily interest earned is then $(.0002 \times \$3,000,000) = \$600$. Since the cost of the system is $500 per day, the daily net benefit is $100. The present value of this perpetuity is $(\$100/.0002) = \$500,000$.

## Problem 9

Suppose that the bank described in Problem 8 charges an annual fee of $5,000, payable at the end of the year, in addition to the variable fee; is the lockbox service still acceptable?

**Solution:** In order to compute the present value of the annual $5,000 fee, we first compute the annual interest rate as follows: $(1.0002)^{365} - 1 = .07572 = 7.572\%$

In order to maintain the benefit of the lockbox system, the $5,000 fee must be paid every year. Therefore, the present value of this perpetuity is $(\$5,000/.07572) = \$66,033$. The total present value of the costs is $(\$2,500,000 + \$66,033) = \$2,566,033$. The net present value is $(\$3,000,000 - \$2,566,033) = \$433,967$. The lockbox service is still acceptable.

## Problem 10

Suppose that, in addition to the fixed annual fee and the variable fee described in Problems 8 and 9, the bank requires that the firm maintain a compensating balance of $500,000. Should the lockbox service be adopted?

**Solution:** The $500,000 can be viewed as a reduction in the $3 million available cash calculated in Problem 8, so that the present value of the lockbox system is $2,500,000. Since the present value of the costs, as computed in the solution to Problem 9, is $2,566,033, the net present value of the service is −$66,033. The service should not be adopted.

## Problem 11

Given the bank fees identified in Problems 8 and 9, what compensating balance would leave the firm indifferent as to whether it adopts the lockbox service?

**Solution:** The firm will be indifferent if the present value of the cost of the lockbox service is exactly equal to the $3,000,000 present value computed in the solution to Problem 8. Since the present value of the costs, without the compensating balance, is $2,566,033, then the compensating balance which leaves the firm indifferent is $(\$3,000,000 - \$2,566,033) = \$433,967$. Given this figure, the bank might then negotiate the size of the compensating balance.

The firm would adopt the lockbox service only if the bank agreed to accept a compensating balance significantly below this figure. Otherwise, the lockbox service has little or no value to the firm.

## Problem 12

A company has all of its collections handled by a bank located in the same city as its home office. The bank requires a compensating balance of $100,000 and handles collections of $750,000 per day. The firm is considering a concentration banking system which would require total compensating balances of $450,000, but would accelerate collections by two days. The Treasury-bill rate is 6%. Should the company implement the new system?

**Solution:** The concentration banking system would increase the firm's collected bank balance by ($750,000 × 2) = $1,500,000, but an additional $350,000 would be required for compensating balances. The net result would be that ($1,500,000 − $350,000) = $1,150,000 can be invested at a 6% annual rate, providing net savings of ($1,150,000 × .06) = $69,000. Therefore, the concentration banking system should be implemented.

## Problem 13

Healy's Music Store requires a total of $1,000,000 cash for transactions during a year. Healy's fixed order cost is $25, and its annual interest rate is 20%. Using the BAT Model, determine the target cash balance for Healy's Music Store.

**Solution:**

$T$ = Cash needed = $1,000,000
$F$ = Fixed order cost = $25
$R$ = annual interest rate = 20%

Using the BAT Model, the target cash balance is:

$$C^* = [\,(2 \times \$1,000,000 \times \$25)\,/\,.20\,]^{\frac{1}{2}}$$

$$= \$250,000,000^{1/2} = \$15,811.39$$

According to the BAT Model, Healy's Music Store should maintain a cash balance of $15,811.39 because this is the balance which equalizes the opportunity and trading costs.

## Problem 14

Calculate Healy's opportunity cost, trading cost, and total cost for the cash balance determined in Problem 13.

**Solution:**

| | | |
|---|---|---|
| Average cash balance | = | $15,811 / 2 = $7,905.50 |
| Annual opportunity cost | = | $7,905.50 x 0.2 = $1,581.10 |
| Orders per year | = | $1,000,000 / $15,811 = 63.25 = 64 |
| Annual trading cost | = | 64 x $25 = $1,600 |
| Total holding cost | = | $1,581.10 + $1,600 = $3,181.10 |

## Problem 15

Try this one on your own. Your firm mails out 15,000 cheques, with a total value of $500,000, during a typical day. You have determined that if the cheques were mailed from Outer Mongolia, mail time would be increased by three days, on average. However, it would cost an extra $.10 per cheque in postage and handling. The daily interest rate is .00015. Should you adopt this method of delaying disbursements?

**Solution:** The firm could increase its disbursement float by $1.5 million.  Investing this amount generates $225 per day.  The extra cost would be $1,500 per day.  The firm should not adopt the plan.

## Problem 16

Given the following information, use the BAT model to calculate the target cash balance:

| | |
|---|---|
| Annual interest rate | 10% |
| Fixed order cost | $50 |
| Total cash needed | $ 2,500,000 |

**Solution:**  The target cash balance is:

$$C* \;=\; [(2T \times F)/R]^{1/2} \;=\; [(2 \times \$2,500,000 \times \$50)/.10]^{1/2} \;=\; [\$2,500,000,000]^{1/2} \;=\; \$50,000$$

## Problem 17

Calculate the opportunity cost, the trading costs, and the total cost for holding the target cash balance determined in Problem 16.

**Solution:**  The average cash balance is:  $(C + 0)/2 \;=\; \$50,000/2 \;=\; \$25,000$
The annual opportunity cost is:  $(C/2) \times R \;=\; \$25,000 \times .10 \;=\; \$2,500$
The number of orders during the year is:  $T/C \;=\; \$2,500,000/\$50,000 \;=\; 50$
The annual trading cost is:  $(T/C) \times F \;=\; 50 \times \$50 \;=\; \$2,500$
Total cost is the sum of the opportunity cost and the trading cost:  $(\$2,500 + \$2,500) = \$5,000$

The fact that the opportunity cost and the trading cost are equal is not coincidental.  The fact that this must always be true for the target cash balance identified by the BAT model can be demonstrated from the mathematical derivation of the model.

## Problem 18

Using the data given in Problem 16, calculate the opportunity cost, the trading costs, and the total cost assuming that a $25,000 cash balance is held.  Calculate the costs assuming that a $100,000 cash balance is held.

**Solution:**  If a $25,000 balance is held, the opportunity, trading, and total costs are $1,250, $5,000, and $6,250, respectively.  For a $100,000 balance, the costs are $5,000, $1,250, and $6,250 respectively.  Note that the total costs for both the $25,000 and $100,000 balances are higher than the total costs for the $50,000 balance as calculated in the previous problem.  This result is, of course, to be expected because the BAT model identifies the cash balance that minimizes the sum of these costs.

## Problem 19

Suppose that, for the data in Problem 16, the fixed order cost increased from $50 to $200.  How does this affect the target cash balance, and the costs computed in the solution to Problem 2?

**Solution:**  There are two approaches to computing the new target cash balance for this problem.  First, we can compute the solution directly by substituting the appropriate values in the equation for C*.  The alternative approach is to note that the value of F in this problem is four times the value in Problem 16.  Since F is in the numerator of the fraction, the value of the figure inside the square root sign is now four times its value in Problem 16.  Since we take the square root of this figure, the value of C* is twice the value in Problem 16, because the square root of four is two.  Consequently, the target cash balance here is $(2 \times \$50,000) = \$100,000$.

Since the target cash balance is double that of Problem 16, the opportunity cost is also double:  $(C/2) \times R = (\$100,000/2) \times .10 = \$5,000$.

It is not necessary to compute the trading costs, because the opportunity costs and the trading costs are equal when the firm holds a cash balance equal to C*.  Therefore, the trading costs are $5,000 and the total costs are $10,000.

This problem demonstrates the fact that there is a direct relationship between the fixed transaction cost of selling marketable securities and the target cash balance.  This is an intuitively reasonable result, because the increased cost of selling securities makes it more economical to hold larger cash balances.


## Problem 20

Suppose that, for the data in Problem 16, the interest rate decreased from 10% to 5%.  How does this affect the target cash balance?

**Solution:**  As in the solution to Problem 19, the result here can be computed directly.  Alternatively, we can take note of the fact that, since r is now half of its previous value, the fraction doubles in value.  Consequently, the target cash balance here is equal to the solution in Problem 16 times the square root of 2:  $\$50,000 \times 2^{1/2} = \$70,710.68$.

This solution demonstrates the inverse relationship between the interest rate and the target cash balance.  As the interest rate decreases, the target cash balance increases because the opportunity cost of holding additional cash decreases.  Similarly, as the interest rate increases, the target cash balance decreases because it becomes more expensive to hold larger balances.


## Problem 21

Suppose that the fixed cost, per transaction, to buy and sell marketable securities is $100, the daily interest rate is .03%, and the standard deviation of daily net cash flows is $50.  Management has set a lower limit of $200 on cash holdings.  Calculate the target cash balance, upper limit and average cash balance, using the Miller-Orr model.

**Solution:**  The variance of the daily cash flows is $\sigma^2 = (50)^2 = 2,500$. The target cash balance is:

$$C^* = L + [(3/4 \times F \times \sigma^2)/R]^{1/3} = \$200 + [(3/4 \times \$100 \times \$2,500)/.0003]^{1/3} = \$200 + \$855 = \$1,055$$

The upper limit is:  $U^* = (3 \times C^*) - (2 \times L) = (3 \times \$1,055) - (2 \times \$200) = \$2,765$

The average cash balance is:  $[(4 \times C^*) - L]/3 = [(4 \times \$1,055) - \$200]/3 = \$1,340$

When the cash balance reaches $U^* = \$2,765$, the firm returns to its target balance $C^* = 1,055$ by investing $(U^* - C^*) = \$1,710$ in marketable securities. When the balance declines to $L = \$200$, the firm sells $(C^* - L) = \$855$ of marketable securities in order to increase the cash balance to $C^* = \$1,055$.

# 20    Credit and Inventory Management

## CHAPTER HIGHLIGHTS

A firm may require cash on or before delivery in payment for its products, or it may decide to extend credit to its customers.  If credit is extended, then the firm must establish a credit policy involving three distinct components: the terms of sale, credit analysis, and collection policy.

## CREDIT AND RECEIVABLES

Granting credit to a customer results in the creation of an account receivable.  This process is referred to as either trade credit or consumer credit, depending on whether the customer is another business firm or an individual consumer.  Since approximately 15% of all of the assets of Canadian industrial firms are in the form of accounts receivable, credit management (or receivables management) is an important aspect of a firm's short-term financial policy.

**Components of Credit Policy:**  In managing its credit policy, a firm must establish its terms of sale, procedures for credit analysis, and its collection policy.  The firm's terms of sale consist of the following aspects of a credit sale: the credit period, the cash discount and discount period, and the type of credit instrument.  Credit analysis is the process of attempting to distinguish between customers who are likely and not likely to make payment on an account.  A firm's collection policy is the set of procedures the firm uses to collect payment on accounts.

**The Cash Flows from Granting Credit:**  A firm's accounts receivable period is the time period required for the firm to collect payment on a credit sale.  The sequence of events during the accounts receivable period is: (1) the credit sale is made; (2) the customer sends a cheque to the firm; (3) the firm deposits the cheque; and, (4) the firm's account is credited for the amount of the cheque.  In this chapter, we discuss the impact of the firm's credit policy on the accounts receivable period.

**The Investment in Receivables:**  Consider a firm with credit sales of approximately $5,000 per day, and an average collection period (ACP) of 40 days.  At any given time, the firm has not collected payment on the preceding 40 days' sales.  Consequently, at any given time, the firm's accounts receivable are equal to ($5,000 \times 40$) = $200,000.  In general:

   Accounts receivable  =  Average daily sales $\times$ ACP

A firm's credit policy has an impact on both average daily sales and the average collection period.  This means credit policy is a determinant of the level of the firm's investment in accounts receivable.

## TERMS OF THE SALE

The terms of sale involve: the credit period, the cash discount and discount period, and the type of credit instrument.

**Why Trade Credit Exists:**  In practice, trade credit helps overcome certain market imperfections.  If buyers and sellers have imperfect information, the buyer may prefer credit terms which give time to return defective products while the seller offering credit 'signals' potential customers that the product is high-quality. Also, any firm which grants credit lacks perfect information on the creditworthiness of the borrower, but a seller which has been granting trade credit to a purchaser likely has it already. Information advantages may allow the seller to offer more attractive and flexible credit terms. Finally, it may be cheaper to initialize credit from the seller than to set up a borrowing facility or to borrow in money markets.

**The Basic Form:** Credit terms might be quoted, for example, as *5/20, net 60*. This means a customer can take a 5% discount from the stated price if payment is made within 20 days of the invoice date (usually the shipping date or date of sale). Otherwise, the full amount of the sale is due within 60 days. A customer who makes a $2,000 purchase under these terms has the following alternatives: (1) pay [$2,000 × (1 − .05)] = $1,900 within 20 days; or, (2) pay $2,000 within 60 days.

**Credit Period:** The credit period is the length of the time before the customer is obligated to make payment. When a discount is offered, the credit period has two components. The first is the net credit period, which is the total amount of time the customer has to make payment. The second is the cash discount period, which is the time period during which the discount is available to the customer.

The invoice is the written statement of merchandise delivered to the buyer. The invoice date is the beginning of the credit period.

The firm must consider many factors when setting the *length of the credit period*. Since the seller's credit terms become the buyer's payable period, the buyer's inventory period and operating cycle are important considerations in setting the length of the credit period. Suppose Firm A's inventory period and accounts receivable period are 40 days and 30 days, respectively, so the operating cycle is 70 days. Firm B, however, provides a credit period of 70 days. Firm A could purchase inventory from Firm B on credit, sell the product to its customers, and collect payment in 70 days. Firm A can then use the proceeds from the sale of the product to pay the accounts payable to Firm B. In this scenario, Firm B has financed Firm A's entire operating cycle. Firm A would find a 70-day credit period desirable, and Firm B might attract additional business as a result. On the other hand, Firm B incurs an opportunity cost during the credit period. These considerations must be weighed by Firm B in determining its credit period.

Other factors which influence the length of a firm's credit period are:

1. *Perishability and collateral value.* Credit periods are shorter for perishable goods because they have rapid turnover and low collateral value.
2. *Consumer demand.* Successful products have more rapid turnover and shorter credit periods.
3. *Cost, profitability, and standardization.* Relatively inexpensive products, as well as standardized goods and raw materials, tend to have high turnover and short credit periods.
4. *Credit risk.* The greater the credit risk of the buyer, the shorter the credit period.
5. *The size of the account.* The credit period is shorter for small accounts, which are expensive to manage and less important to the seller.
6. *Competition.* Longer credit periods are sometimes offered to attract customers from competitors.
7. *Customer type.* A seller might have different credit periods for wholesale and retail customers.

A longer credit period is, in effect, a reduction in the price paid by the purchaser. Consequently, a longer credit period generally results in an increase in sales.

**Cash Discounts:** Cash discounts speed up collections of receivables because they provide an incentive to pay earlier. Discounts also provide firms with a way to effectively charge higher prices to credit customers, thus avoiding regulations prohibiting charging different prices for the same products.

Suppose we have a customer who routinely places a $100 order every month and pays the entire amount 60 days later. This customer is offered the alternative of paying within 10 days of the invoice date in exchange for a 3% discount. The alternative payment schedules are: (1) pay $97 in 10 days, or; (2) pay $100 in 60 days. Given these alternatives, the customer is actually obtaining $97 of financing for 50 days, from day 10 to day 60. The cost of the financing is the additional $3 which must be paid if payment is on day 60. The interest rate for this fifty-day period is ($3/$97) = .030928 = 3.0928%. Since there are (365/50) = 7.3 fifty-day periods in a year, the effective annual rate is:  EAR = $(1.030928)^{7.3} - 1$ = 0.24901 = 24.901%

A customer who doesn't take the discount is paying an effective annual rate of 24.901% to finance the $97 payment.

If the cash discount encourages customers to pay early, it will shorten the receivables period and generally reduce the firm's investment in receivables.

**An Example:**  A firm offers terms of net 30 and has an average collection period (ACP) of 30 days. If it offers terms of 2/15, net 30, then 40 % of the customers will pay in 10 days, and the remainder will pay on average in one month. If annual sales are $10 million before discounts, what will happen to the ACP and to the investment in receivables?

The new ACP will be:  ACP = .40 (10 days) + .60 (30 days) = 22 days. Average daily sales are $10 million/365 = $27,397.26 per day. Receivables will thus fall by $27,397.26 × 10 = $273,972.60.

**Credit Instruments:**  A credit instrument is an evidence of indebtedness. Most trade credit is offered on *open account*, which means the credit instrument is the invoice. The customer signs the invoice when the goods are received. Alternatively, the selling firm may require a *promissory note,* which is basically an IOU. This is not common, except when the order is large, there is no cash discount, and the credit risk is poor.

A *commercial draft* is a demand for payment sent to a customer's bank, along with shipping invoices. The buyer signs the draft before goods are shipped to the buyer. If the draft requires immediate payment, it is called a *sight draft*. If the bank 'accepts' the draft for future payment, it is called a *banker's acceptance* because the bank accepts responsibility for making payment. The banker's acceptance is then sent back to the seller of the goods, who can then sell this acceptance (at a discount) or keep it until payment is made.

A firm can also use a conditional sales contract as a credit instrument. In this case, the firm retains title to the goods until payment is completed, and payment is often made in instalments.

## ANALYZING CREDIT POLICY

**Credit Policy Effects:**  The decision regarding whether to grant credit depends on the following:

1. *Revenue effects.* Granting credit results in both a delay in revenue collections and an increase in total revenue.
2. *Cost effects.* Granting credit results in increased costs directly associated with the credit process and, if sales increase, increased variable costs.
3. *The cost of debt.* The cost of financing receivables must be considered.
4. *The probability of nonpayment.* Some buyers will default.
5. *The cash discount.* Some customers pay during the discount period.

**Evaluating a Proposed Credit Policy:** The relevant variables in analysing credit policy are:

| | | |
|---|---|---|
| P | = | Price per unit |
| v | = | Variable cost per unit |
| Q | = | Current quantity sold per month |
| Q′ | = | Quantity sold under new policy |
| R | = | Monthly required return |

**An Example:** Suppose that a firm is considering granting credit terms of net 30 days. Consider the following information regarding this decision:

| | | |
|---|---|---|
| P | = | $11 |
| v | = | $ 5 |
| Q | = | 100 |
| Q′ | = | 120 |
| R | = | 1% |

Should the firm grant credit terms of net 30 days to its customers?

If the firm does not extend credit:

Monthly sales are:  $P \times Q$  =  ($11 \times 100$)  =  $1,100

Monthly variable costs are:  $v \times Q$  =  ($5 \times 100$) = $500

The cash flow is:  Cash flow (old policy)  =  $(P - v) \times Q$  =  ($11 - $5) \times 100$  =  $600

If credit is granted, then:

Cash flow (new policy)  =  $(P - v) \times Q'$  =  ($11 - $5) \times 120$  =  $720

The incremental cash flow is defined as:

Incremental cash flow  =  Cash flow (new policy) – Cash flow (old policy)

$$= (P - v) \times (Q' - Q) = (\$11 - \$5) \times (120 - 100) = \$120$$

This incremental cash flow is in the form of a monthly annuity so that the present value of the annuity is:

$$PV = \frac{(P - v) \times (Q' - Q)}{R} = \frac{\$120}{.01} = \$12,000$$

The cost of the change in credit policy is the sum of two components. First, the variable cost of producing the additional units:

$$v(Q' - Q) = \$5 \times (120 - 100) = \$100$$

Second, the first month's sales that would be collected under the old policy are not collected until 30 days later under the new policy. Since collections are permanently delayed by 30 days, this cost is:

$$PQ = \$11 \times 100 = \$1,100$$

The sum of these costs is:

$$PQ + v(Q' - Q) = \$1,100 + \$100 = \$1,200$$

The net present value of the change in credit policy is:

$$NPV = -[PQ + v(Q' - Q)] + \frac{(P - v) \times (Q' - Q)}{R} = -\$1,200 + \$12,000 = \$10,800$$

Therefore, the change in credit policy to terms of net 30 days is beneficial in this example.

## OPTIMAL CREDIT POLICY

Firms must also consider the optimal amount of credit to be granted. In performing this analysis, the firm must consider two categories of costs: the carrying costs associated with granting credit and investing in accounts receivables, and the opportunity costs which result from a refusal to grant credit. The carrying costs include the required return on the investment in receivables, losses from bad debts, and the costs of managing credit and credit collections. The opportunity costs are the foregone profits from the lost sales if the firm denies credit. The optimal amount of credit minimizes the sum of the carrying costs plus the opportunity costs which is the total *credit cost curve*. This is depicted in the figure below.

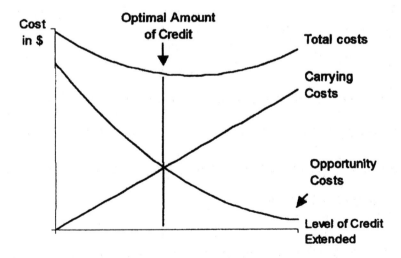

*Carrying costs* are the cash flows that must be incurred when credit is granted. They are positively related to the amount of credit extended. *Opportunity costs* are the lost sales from refusing credit. These costs go down when credit is granted.

In general, all other things being equal, it is likely that firms with (1) excess capacity, (2) low variable operating costs, and (3) repeat customers will extend credit more liberally than otherwise.

**Organizing the Credit Function:** Firms that grant credit may contract out all or part of the credit function to a factor, an insurance company or a capture finance subsidiary. Some firms buy credit insurance through an insurance company that covers up to a pre-set dollar limit for accounts. For example, exporters may qualify for credit insurance through the Export Development Corporation owned by the federal government. Setting up the credit function as a legal entity may allow more debt and save on borrowing costs.

## CREDIT ANALYSIS

Credit analysis is the process of estimating the probability that a customer will not pay, and then deciding whether to extend credit to that customer. The firm must first gather relevant information, and then determine the creditworthiness of the customer.

**When Should Credit be Granted?:** Consider a customer who purchases one unit on credit at a price of $P' = \$100$ per unit. The variable cost is \$70 per unit and the monthly required return is $r = 1\%$. Assume that this is a one-time sale and the customer pays in two months. The probability of default is $\pi = 25\%$. Should the firm grant credit to the new customer?

The net present value is the cost minus the present value of the cash inflow:

$$NPV = -v + \frac{(1 - \pi) \times P'}{(1 + R)^2} = -\$70 + \frac{\$75}{(1.01)^2} = \$3.52$$

Since the net present value is positive, the firm should extend credit to the new customer.

**Repeat Business:** In the preceding example, we assumed that the firm has no repeat business. In the next example, we analyze the credit decision under the following assumption about repeat business: A new customer who does not default on his first purchase will remain a customer indefinitely and will never default.

**An Example:** Assume the following data from the previous example: $P' = \$100$, $v = \$70$, and $\pi = 25\%$. Also, the firm's required return for a two-month period is 2%. Assuming that a customer who does not default will purchase one unit every other month forever, should the firm extend credit to a new customer?

The cost to the firm is the variable costs $v = \$70$. In two months, the customer will either default, or he will pay $P'$ = \$100 and purchase another unit. The probability that he will not default is $(1 - .25) = 75\%$ and the expected net cash inflow in two months is:

$$(1 - \pi) \times (P' - v) = .75 \times \$30 = \$22.50$$

The net present value of the decision to grant credit is:

$$NPV = -v + \frac{(1 - \pi) \times (P' - v)}{R} = -\$70 + \frac{\$22.50}{.02} = \$1,055$$

Since the net present value is positive, it is beneficial for the firm to extend credit to the new customer.

**Credit Information:** Useful information commonly used to assess creditworthiness can be obtained from financial statements, credit reports on the customer's payment history with other firms, banks, and the customer's payment history with the firm. Credit reports can be purchased from several sources in North America.

**Credit Evaluation and Scoring**: The traditional guidelines for assessing the probability of default are the five Cs of credit: *character* (willingness to pay), *capacity* (ability to pay), *capital* (financial reserves), *collateral*, and *conditions* (general business conditions). These criteria are applied in a subjective manner in determining creditworthiness.

Credit scoring is the process of computing a numerical rating as a guideline for assessing creditworthiness. Statistical procedures, called credit-scoring models, are used by some firms to forecast the probability that a customer will default. In general, credit is extended if the score is sufficiently high to indicate that the customer is likely to pay. Government regulations prohibit the denial of credit based on ethnic background, age, or gender.

Computerized scoring models employ a statistical technique called *multiple discriminant analysis* (MDA) to predict which customers will be good or bad accounts. MDA chooses a set of variables which best differentiate between good and bad credits with hindsight. For example, certain ratios like total asset turnover, gross profit margin, etc., may be the relevant variables for certain business customers used in the MDA. Statistic scoring models are more useful in consumer credit and not as popular with business customers because of the relatively smaller sample size in Canada than in the U.S.

## COLLECTION POLICY

Collection policy is the process of monitoring receivables and obtaining payment of overdue accounts.

**Monitoring Receivables:** Two of the tools which firms use to monitor outstanding accounts are the average collection period (ACP) and the aging schedule. The relationship between the ACP and the firm's credit terms indicate whether customers are generally paying accounts when due.

An aging schedule for a firm with credit terms of 2/10, net 30, might appear as follows:

| Age of account | Amount | Percent of total value of accounts receivable |
|---|---|---|
| 0 – 10 days | $400,000 | 40% |
| 11 – 30 days | 400,000 | 40 |
| 31 – 50 days | 100,000 | 10 |
| Over 50 days | 100,000 | 10 |

Since the terms require payment within 30 days, 80% of receivables are currently on time, but 20% of receivables are late. If this pattern is not typical or appropriate for the firm, then it is a signal that collection efforts should be intensified. Firms with seasonal sales find that the ACP changes during the year, and different aging schedules are typical at different times of the year.

**Collection Effort:** Collection effort generally involves a series of steps such as: (1) sending a delinquency letter, (2) calling the customer, (3) hiring a collection agency, and (4) initiating legal action.

## INVENTORY MANAGEMENT

For most Canadian manufacturing operations, inventory often exceeds 15% of assets and for retailers, inventory could represent more than 25% of assets. Since a firm's operating cycle consists of its inventory period and its receivables period, we discuss these two topics together.

**The Financial Manager and Inventory Policy:** Typically, other functional areas in addition to finance, such as purchasing, production, and marketing will normally share decision making authority.

**Inventory Types:** For a manufacturer, inventory can be classified as *raw material* (whatever the firm uses as a starting point in its production process), *work-in-progress* (unfinished product), and *finished goods* (products ready to ship and sell). Keep in mind that one company's raw materials could be another's finished goods. Furthermore, different types of inventory can be different in terms of their liquidity with work-in-progress being the most illiquid. Finally, demand for an inventory item that becomes part of another is referred to as derived or *dependent* demand whereas demand for finished goods is said to be *independent.*

**Inventory Costs:** *Carrying costs* represent all of the direct and opportunity costs of keeping inventory on hand such as *storage and tracking costs; insurance and taxes;* losses due to *obsolescence, deterioration or theft* and the *opportunity cost of capital* on the invested amount. The sum of these costs can range from 20 to 40% of inventory value per year. *Shortage costs* are associated with having inadequate inventory on hand and include *restocking costs* (costs of placing an order) and costs related to *safety reserves* (lost sales and loss of customer goodwill). The goal of inventory management is to minimize the sum of these carrying and shortage costs.

## INVENTORY MANAGEMENT TECHNIQUES

Cost minimization techniques include the simplistic to the very complex which are described below.

**The ABC Approach:** The idea is to divide inventory into groups which present portions of inventory value. For example, group A may constitute only 10% of inventory by count, but represent 50% of the value of inventory. Group A items are therefore monitored closely and inventory levels kept relatively low. At the other end, basic items such as nuts and bolts are grouped separately, and because these are crucial and inexpensive, large quantities are handled.

**The Economic Order Quantity (EOQ):** As illustrated in your text, inventory carrying costs rise as inventory levels increase, while, at the same time, restocking costs decrease. Restocking costs are increased when the firm holds a small quantity of inventory. Carrying costs are increased when there is a large quantity of inventory on hand. Total costs are the sum of the carrying and restocking costs.

With the EOQ model we attempt to specify the minimum total cost point Q*. This is not the actual cost of the inventory since the *total* amount of inventory a firm needs in a given year depends on sales. What we are determining is how much the firm should have on hand at any particular time or the order size it should place when it restocks its inventory.

**Total Costs and the EOQ:** For now we will assume that the firm's inventory is sold off at a steady rate until it hits zero and the firm replenishes its inventory back to some optimal level instantaneously. Suppose Q is the quantity of inventory ordered each time, then Q/2 would represent the average level of inventory. This is illustrated in Figure 20.6 on page 694 of your text.

Recall that carrying costs such as storage, insurance, obsolescence, etc., are normally directly proportional to inventory levels. If CC is the carrying costs per unit per year, the total carrying costs will be:

Total carrying costs  =  average inventory × carrying costs per unit

$$= (Q/2) \times CC$$

For now, let us also assume that, if we ignore safety reserves, the only shortage cost consists of restocking costs. These restocking costs (of placing an order) are normally fixed, so that if the firm orders Q units each time, then it will need to place T/Q orders, where T represents the firm's total unit sales per year. So, total restocking costs are:

Total restocking costs   =   fixed cost per order × number of orders   =   $F × (T/Q)$

Since the total costs with holding inventory are the sum of carrying and restocking costs, we have:

Total costs   =   carrying costs + restocking costs

=   $(Q/2) × CC$   +   $F × (T/Q)$

To find the precise cost-minimizing quality we can equate carrying costs with restocking costs and solve for Q*. The value of Q* is:

$Q*$   =   $[(2T \text{ x } F) / CC ]^{1/2}$

Where Q* is the economic order quantity (EOQ) which minimizes the total inventory cost.

**An Example:**  Suppose Fullfill Corporation starts out with 7,200 units of inventory. If weekly sales are 1,800 units (annual sales are 93,600 units) then after four weeks, all the inventory of 7,200 will be sold and another order of 7,200 will instantly replenish the company's inventory level. Carrying costs are $1.50 per unit per year while ordering costs are $100 per order. What are Fullfill's average level of inventory, total carrying and restocking costs, and the EOQ?

Since Q is 7,200 units, the average level of inventory is 7,200/2 = 3,600 units. The carrying costs are average inventory × carrying cost per unit, or, 3,600 × $1.50 = $5,400. The restocking costs are fixed costs per order × number of orders, or, $100 × (93,600/7,200) = $1,300 per year. Total costs are the sum of carrying and shortage costs, or, $5,400 + $1,300 = $6,700. The EOQ is:

$[ (2T \text{ x } F) / CC ]^{1/2}$   =   $[ 2 (93,600) (\$100) / \$1.50 ]^{1/2}$   =   3,532.7 or 3,533 units

**An Example:**  Given the EOQ for Fullfill Corporation, what are the carrying and restocking costs at Q*?

Carrying costs   =   (3,532.7/2)($1.5)   =   $2,649.53

Restocking costs   =   $100 × (93,600/3,532.7)   =   $2,649.53

Notice, we derived Q* by equating carrying and restocking costs.

**Safety Stocks:**  In reality, a firm reorders before its inventory goes to zero because it wants to minimize the risk of a stockout and when a firm does reorder, there will be some time lag before the order is replenished. Since a *safety stock* is the minimum level of inventory that a firm keeps on hand, inventories are reordered whenever the quantity falls to the safety stock level. Figure 20.7 on page 698 of your text illustrates how a safety stock is incorporated into the EOQ model.

**Reorder points:**  *Reorder points* are the inventory levels at which the firm will actually place its inventory orders. The result is a generalized EOQ in which the firm orders in advance of anticipated needs and also keeps a safety stock to guard against unforeseen fluctuations in demand and delivery times.

**An Example:** Suppose Fullfill Corporation, discussed earlier, wishes to hold a safety stock equal to seven days of sales. What is the safety stock and reorder point if the lead time required for the order to arrive is four days?

The safety stock is $7/365 \times 93,600 = 1,795$.

The reorder point is the lead time required $\times$ the daily usage plus the safety stock $= 4$ days $\times (93,600/365) + 1,795$ $= 1,025.75$ or $1,026$ units $+ 1,795 = 2,821$ units.

The figure below depicts the results for Fullfill Corporation when both the safety stock and reorder point are incorporated with the EOQ.

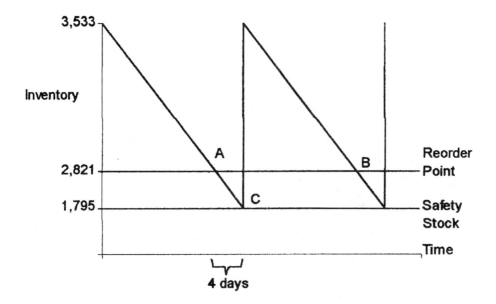

Fullfill will reorder at point A when the inventory level is 2,821 units. The order arrives four days later at point C when the minimum safety stock level is reached and the cycle continues thereafter.

**Materials Requirements Planning (MRP):** Computer-based systems for ordering and/or scheduling production of demand-dependent inventories allows a firm to schedule backward from finished goods inventories to the dependent nature of work-in-progress and raw materials inventories. It is particularly important for firms that use a variety of components are needed to create the finished product.

**Just-In-Time Inventory:** With JIT, the idea is that raw materials, parts, and other work-in-process should be delivered at the exact time they are needed on the factory floor so that the levels of inventory are minimized. Making JIT work requires extensive materials requirements planning so that all stages of production can be 'recoupled' and coordinated. There are no inventory buffers to fall back on to cover planning errors or equipment downtime.

## MORE ON CREDIT POLICY ANALYSIS (APPENDIX 20A)

We will evaluate two alternative approaches to the credit policy analysis described in the chapter. Then we will consider the impact of cash discounts and defaults on credit policy decisions.

**The One-Shot Approach:** This approach is based on computing the net present value of a change in credit policy under the assumption that the change is in effect for only one time period . Since the change is actually permanent, the NPV of the change is then computed by treating the one-period NPV as a perpetuity.  For the example in the chapter, the firm invests $(v \times Q') = (\$5 \times 120) = \$600$ in production costs today.  In addition, they forgo a net cash inflow of $[(P - v) \times Q] = [(\$11 - \$5) \times 100] = \$600$ which would be received this month under the existing credit policy.  Under the new credit policy, the firm then receives $(P \times Q') = (\$11 \times 120) = \$1,320$ cash inflow from payments 30 days later.  The present value of this inflow is $(\$1,320/1.01) = \$1306.9307$. The net present value of this transaction, if we regard this as a one-month change in policy, is:

$$NPV = \$1306.9307 - (\$600 + \$600) = \$106.9307$$

Since we can regard this NPV as repeating itself each month, the NPV of the change in credit policy is:

$$NPV = \$106.9307 + (\$106.9307/.01) = \$10,800$$

**The Accounts Receivable Approach:** The second approach is based on viewing the change in credit policy as an investment in accounts receivable.  The monthly carrying cost, or opportunity cost, of the investment in receivables is compared to the monthly net benefit resulting from the change in policy.  The firm's investment in accounts receivable is comprised of two parts.  The first part is the amount the firm would have received during the current month if the existing credit policy remained unchanged, which is $(PQ) = (\$11 \times 100) = \$1,100$.  The second part of the investment in receivables is the increase in the investment in receivables which results from the increase in sales.  The firm must invest $[v(Q' - Q)] = [\$5 \times (120 - 100)] = \$100$ in producing the additional quantity to be sold after the change in credit policy.  The total incremental investment in receivables is:

$$(PQ) + [v(Q' - Q)] = \$1,100 + \$100 = \$1,200$$

The required return on this investment for one month is:

$$\text{Carrying cost} = [(PQ) + v(Q' - Q)] \times R = \$1,200 \times .01 = \$12$$

The monthly benefit derived from the investment in receivables is:

$$(P - v) \times (Q' - Q) = (\$11 - \$5) \times (120 - 100) = \$120$$

The monthly net benefit is $(\$120 - \$12) = \$108$ and the net present value of the change in credit policy is $(\$108/.01)$ = \$10,800, as computed previously.

**Discounts and Default Risk:** In this section, we consider the impact of discounts and default risk on the credit decision.  The additional variables considered in this section are:

$\pi$ = Percentage of credit sales that go uncollected
$d$ = Percentage discount allowed for cash customers
$P'$ = Credit price

To clarify the analysis, we make two assumptions.  First, we assume a change in credit policy does not affect the firm's sales quantity, Q.  Second, we assume all customers buy on credit.

**An Example:** A company currently sells $Q = 50$ units of a product at a price $P = \$97$. The firm is considering a credit policy that allows customers 60 days to pay.  The price for credit customers will be $P' = \$100$, while the cash price will remain $97. The firm expects that the percentage of credit sales which will go uncollected is $\pi = 1\%$. Variable cost per unit is $v = \$70$ and the firm's required return for a two-month period is 2%. Should the firm adopt the new credit terms?

First, we compute the NPV of the change in credit terms. The cost of the change is the firm's investment in production costs plus the firm's foregone net cash inflow. However, since we have assumed here that Q and Q' are equal, we can simplify the calculation of this cost as follows:

$$(v \times Q) + [(P - v) \times Q] \;\; = \;\; P \times Q \;\; = \;\; \$97 \times 50 \;\; = \;\; \$4,850$$

To determine the net cash inflow from the change in credit policy, we first compute the monthly cash inflow for the current policy:

$$(P - v) \times Q \;\; = \;\; (\$97 - \$70) \times 50 \;\; = \;\; \$1,350$$

Next, compute the monthly cash inflow for the proposed policy. If all sales were collected, cash inflow would be $[(P' - v) \times Q]$. However, since $\pi$ is the percent of sales which are uncollected, then the percent of sales which are collected is $(1 - \pi)$, and the monthly cash inflow is:

$$[(1 - \pi)P' - v] \times Q \;\; = \;\; [(.99 \times \$100) - \$70] \times 50 \;\; = \;\; \$1,450$$

The net incremental cash flow is therefore ($1,450 - $1,350) = $100. This can also be computed as follows:

$$\text{Net incremental cash flow} \;\; = \;\; P' \times Q \times (d - \pi)$$
$$= \;\; \$100 \times 50 \times (.03 - .01) \;\; = \;\; \$100$$

The net present value of the change in credit policy is:

$$\text{NPV} \;\; = \;\; -(P \times Q) + \frac{P' \times Q \times (d - \pi)}{R} \;\; = \;\; -\$4,850 + \frac{\$100}{.02} \;\; = \;\; -\$4,850 + \$5,000 \;\; = \;\; \$150$$

Since the net present value of the change in credit policy is positive, the firm should make the change.

## CONCEPT TEST

1.    Granting credit to a customer results in the creation of a(n) _____ for the seller, and a(n) _____ for the buyer. This process is referred to as _____ credit if the customer is another business firm, or _____ credit if the customer is an individual consumer.

2.    Collectively, the credit period, the cash discount and discount period, and the type of credit instrument are the _____ .

3.    The process of attempting to distinguish between customers who are likely to make payment on an account and those who are not likely to make payment is referred to as _____ . The set of procedures the firm uses to collect payment on accounts is called the firm's _____ .

4. The time period required for the firm to collect payment on a credit sale is the firm's _____ or _____ . The firm's level of accounts receivable is equal to the product of the firm's _____ and the _____ . That is: Accounts receivable = _____ × _____

5. The length of the time period during which the customer is obligated to make payment is called the _____ period. When a discount is offered, this period has two components. The first is the _____ period, which is the total amount of time the customer has to make his payment. The second is the _____ period, which is the time period during which the discount is available to the customer.

6. The written statement of merchandise delivered to the buyer is the _____ . The beginning of the credit period is the _____ date.

7. Most trade credit is offered on open account, which means that the credit instrument is the _____ . Alternatively, the selling firm may require a(n) _____ , which is a basic IOU.

8. A(n) _____ draft is a demand for payment sent to a customer's bank. If the draft requires immediate payment, it is called a(n) _____ draft. Otherwise, if the bank 'accepts' the draft for future payment, it is called a(n) _____ .

9. A firm can also use a(n) _____ contract as a credit instrument. The firm retains title to the goods until payment is completed, and payment is often made in instalments.

10. When deciding whether to extend credit, the financial manager must compute the _____ of the change in credit terms. Assuming no discount period and a 30-day credit period, the incremental cash flow for a change in credit terms is : Incremental cash flow is _____ . Since this incremental cash flow is in the form of an annuity, the present value of the annuity is: PV = _____

11. The cost of the change in credit policy is the sum of two components. First, the variable cost of producing the additional units that will be sold with the new credit policy is equal to _____ . Second, the first month's sales that would be collected under the old policy are not collected until 30 days later under the new policy. Since collections are permanently delayed by 30 days, this cost is _____ . The sum of these costs is _____ .

12. The net present value of the change in credit policy is: NPV = _____

13. An additional issue which must be considered is the determination of the optimal amount of credit to be granted. In performing this analysis, the firm must consider two categories of costs: the _____ costs associated with granting credit and making the corresponding investment in accounts receivable, and the _____ costs which result from a refusal to grant credit. The optimal amount of credit minimizes the _____ of the _____ costs plus the _____ costs.

14. The traditional guidelines for assessing the probability that a customer will not pay are the 'five C's' of credit: (1) willingness to pay (i.e., _____ ); (2) ability to pay (i.e., _____ ); (3) financial reserves (i.e., _____ ); (4) general business conditions (i.e., _____ ); and (5) _____ .

15. The process of computing a numerical rating as a guideline for assessing creditworthiness is called _____ . Statistical procedures, called _____ , are used by some firms to forecast the probability that a customer will default.

16.   The process of monitoring receivables and obtaining payment of overdue accounts is referred to as _____ . Two of the tools which firms use to monitor outstanding accounts are the _____ period and the _____ schedule.

17.   _____ inventory is what the firm uses as a starting point in its production process; _____ represents products that are ready to sell, while _____ is classified as unfinished products.

18.   Storage and tracking costs are examples of _____ , while the costs of placing an order and costs related to safety reserves are called _____ .

19.   The basic idea behind the _____ is to divide inventory into groups which represent portions of inventory value.

20.   As inventory levels increase, carrying costs _____ while, at the same time, restocking costs _____ .

21.   Total inventory costs can be calculated by specifying total carrying costs, which are equal to _____ plus total restocking costs, which are equal to _____ .

22.   To find the precise _____ quantity we specify Q*, which represents the _____ . This can be computed using the following formula: _____ .

23.   The minimum level of inventory a firm keeps on hand is referred to as the _____ which minimizes the risk of a _____ and allows for the time lag before the inventory is _____ .

24.   The _____ can be calculated by multiplying the _____ which is the time it takes for the order to arrive, by the _____ and to this we add the _____ .

25.   Managing the Japanese based _____ method of minimizing inventory requires extensive _____ so that all stages can be '_____' and coordinated.


## ANSWERS TO CONCEPT TEST

1.   account receivable; account payable; trade; consumer

2.   terms of sale

3.   credit analysis; collection policy

4.   accounts receivable period; average collection period (ACP); average daily sales; average collection period; average daily sales; ACP

5.   credit; net credit; cash discount

6.   invoice; invoice

7.      invoice; promissory note

8.      commercial; sight; banker's acceptance

9.      conditional sales

10.     net present value; $[(P - v) \times (Q' - Q)]$; $[(P - v) \times (Q' - Q)]/R$

11.     $v(Q' - Q)$; $P \times Q$; $PQ + v(Q' - Q)$

12.     $-[PQ + v (Q' - Q)] + [(P - v) \times (Q' - Q)]/R$

13.     carrying; opportunity; sum; carrying; opportunity

14.     character; capacity; capital; conditions; collateral

15.     credit scoring; credit-scoring models

16.     collection; average collection; aging

17.     raw materials; finished goods; work-in-progress

18.     carrying costs; shortage costs

19.     ABC approach

20.     increase; decrease

21.     $(Q/2) \times CC$; $F \times (T/Q)$

22.     cost-minimizing; economic ordering quantity (EOQ); $[ (2T \times F) / CC ]^{1/2}$

23.     safety stock; stockout; replenished

24.     reorder point; lead time; daily usage; safety stock

25.     just-in-time; materials requirements planning; recoupled


## PROBLEMS AND SOLUTIONS


### Problem 1

Icarus Company (a well-known 'high flyer') manufactures suntan lotion. Its credit terms are 2/20, net 40. Suppose that a retailer purchases 10 cases of suntan lotion for $200 per case. If the retailer takes the full credit period to pay, how much should the retailer remit to Icarus? When should payment be made?

**Solution:**   If the retailer does not take the discount, then they must pay the net amount: ($200 × 10) = $2,000. Payment must be made within 40 days after the invoice date.  For a seasonal product such as this, the invoice date might be May 1, for example, regardless of whether the shipment is made prior to that date.  In this case, the $2,000 payment would be due within 40 days of the May 1 invoice date.

## Problem 2

For the data of Problem 1, when must the retailer pay in order to receive the discount offered by Icarus?  If the retailer takes the discount, how much should be remitted to Icarus?  If the retailer does not take advantage of the discount, how many days' credit do they receive?

**Solution:**  The retailer must pay within 20 days of the invoice date.  If, for example, the invoice is dated May 1, then the retailer must pay by May 21.  The discount is 2% in this example, so that the retailer must remit:

$$(1 - .02) \times \$200 \times 10 \ = \ \$1,960$$

If the retailer does not take advantage of the discount, they can  pay the net amount within 40 days, rather than 20 days, thus receiving 20 days credit.

## Problem 3

If the retailer in Problem 1 does not take the discount, what is the effective interest rate paid for trade credit?

**Solution:**  By not taking the discount, the customer is actually obtaining $1,960 of financing for 20 days, from day 20 to day 40.  The cost of  financing is the additional $40 which must be paid if payment is on day 40.  The interest rate for this 20-day period is ($40/$1,960) = .020408 = 2.0408%.  There are (365/20) = 18.25 twenty-day periods in a year.  The effective annual rate is: EAR = $(1.020408)^{18.25} - 1 = 1.44585 = 44.585\%$

A customer who does not take the discount is paying an effective annual rate of 44.585% for the financing of the $1,960 payment.

## Problem 4

Suppose that the Icarus Company described in Problem 1 finds that, historically, 80% of its customers take the discount.  What is the firm's average collection period?

**Solution:**  If we assume that all customers who take the discount pay on the twentieth day, while all customers who do not take the discount pay on the fortieth day, then the average collection period (ACP) is:
(.80 × 20 days) + (.20 × 40 days)  =  24 days.

## Problem 5

Suppose that the Icarus Company described in Problem 1 sells 600 cases of suntan lotion each month, at a price of $200 per case.  What is its average balance sheet amount in accounts receivable?

**Solution:** Icarus has average daily sales of [($200 × 600)/30] = $4,000.  The average collection period, as computed in the solution to Problem 4, is 24 days.  Therefore, the average level of accounts receivable is:
Average daily sales × ACP   =   $4,000 × 24  =  $96,000.

## Problem 6

Suppose that the Icarus Company described in Problem 1 has production costs equal to 80% of selling price.  What is the firm's average investment (i.e., its actual cost, as opposed to the balance sheet amount) in receivables?

**Solution:** The solution to Problem 5 indicates that average daily sales are $4,000.  Therefore, the daily investment in accounts receivable is (.80 × $4,000) = $3,200.  The average collection period is 24 days, as computed in Problem 4.  Therefore, the average investment in receivables is ($3,200 × 24) = $76,800.

## Problem 7

Daedulus Company has an average collection period of 30 days and an average level of accounts receivable of $600,000.  What are the firm's annual credit sales?  What is the receivables turnover ratio?

**Solution:** To solve this problem, we first note the following relationship:

Accounts receivable   =   Average daily credit sales × ACP

Solving for average daily credit sales, we have:

$600,000   =   Average daily credit sales  × 30 days
Average daily credit sales   =   $600,000/30   =   $20,000

Therefore, annual credit sales equal ($20,000 × 365) = $7,300,000.

The receivables turnover is: $7,300,000 / $600,000   =   12.17 days

## Problem 8

A firm offers credit terms of 3/15, net 60.  What effective annual interest rate does the firm earn when a customer does not take the discount?

**Solution:** Suppose the product costs $100.  The firm receives $97 if the discount is taken.  If the discount is not taken, then the firm receives $3, or ($3/$97) = 3.0928%, more.  This 3.0928% is earned by extending (60 − 15) = 45 additional days credit.  There are approximately (365/45) = 8 such periods per year.  The effective annual rate is therefore:  EAR   =   $(1.030928)^8 − 1$   =   .27593   =   27.593%

The EAR does not depend on the cost of the product since the 3.0928% would apply regardless of purchase price.

Note that the interest rate the firm earns is the same as the interest rate the customer pays by not taking the discount.

Consequently, from the customer's point of view it is generally not reasonable to pay an interest rate in excess of that which would be paid by financing the purchase through an alternative source.

## Problem 9

For each of the following credit terms, compute the effective annual rate:  1.5/20, net 45; 1/10, net 40

**Solution:**  For a 365-day year and terms of 1.5/20, net 45,  EAR $=$ $(1.015228)^{14.6} - 1$ $=$ $.24689$ $=$ $24.689\%$
For terms of 1/10, net 40, EAR $=$ $(1.010101)^{12.17} - 1$ $=$ $.1301$ $=$ $13.01\%$

## Problem 10

For each of the credit terms identified in Problems 8 and 9, determine whether a firm should take the discount or pay the net amount of the invoice.  Assume that the firm would have to borrow from a bank at a 15% annual interest rate in order to take advantage of the discount.

**Solution:**  For terms of 3/15, net 60, the firm would have to borrow 97% of the invoice amount in order to take advantage of the discount.  Interest on the loan would then accumulate at the rate of 1.5% per month, or approximately 2.25% for 45 days, at which time we assume that the firm would repay the bank loan. Let x represent the net amount, so that the bank loan is .97x and interest plus principal of $(.97x \times 1.0225) = .9918x$ is repaid to the bank after 45 days.  Since this is less than the net amount of the invoice, the firm is better off borrowing from the bank than paying the net amount.

In general, if the annualized effective rate is greater than the rate at which the firm borrows, the firm is better off borrowing from the bank in order to take advantage of the discount.  Therefore, for terms of 1.5/20, net 45, the firm should borrow in order to take the discount, but for terms of 1/10, net 40, the firm should pay the net amount.

## Problem 11

Krishna, Inc., is considering a new credit policy.  The current policy requires cash payment, while the new policy would extend credit for one month.  The following information has been collected:

|                         | Current policy | New policy |
|-------------------------|----------------|------------|
| Price per unit          | $50            | $50        |
| Cost per unit           | $40            | $40        |
| Sales per period, in units | 300         | 345        |

Also, the required return is 1.5% per month, and there will be no defaults.  Should Krishna make the change in credit policy?

**Solution:**  The relevant data for Krishna is:  $P = \$50$;   $v = \$40$; $Q = 300$;   $Q' = 345$;   $R = 1.5\%$

For the current policy:

Monthly sales are:  $P \times Q$ $=$ $(\$50 \times 300)$ $=$ $\$15,000$
Monthly variable costs are:  $v \times Q$ $=$ $(\$40 \times 300)$ $=$ $\$12,000$
The cash flow is:  Cash flow (old policy) $=$ $(P - v) \times Q$ $=$ $(\$50 - \$40) \times 300$ $=$ $\$3,000$

If credit is granted:  Cash flow (new policy)  $=$  $(P - v) \times Q'$  $=$  $($50 - $40) \times 345$  $=$  $3,450$

The incremental cash flow is: Cash flow (new policy) – Cash flow (old policy) = $(P - v) \times (Q' - Q)$ = ($50 – $40) $\times (345 - 300) = $450$

Since the incremental cash flow is in the form of a monthly annuity, the present value is:

$$PV \ = \ \frac{(P - v) \times (Q' - Q)}{R} \ = \ \frac{\$450}{.015} \ = \ \$30,000$$

The cost of the change in credit policy is the sum of two components. First, the variable cost of producing the additional units:  $v(Q' - Q) = $40 \times (345 - 300) = $1,800$

Second, since collections are permanently delayed by 30 days, the following cost is also incurred: $PQ = $50 \times 300 = $15,000$

The sum of these costs is:  $PQ + v(Q' - Q)$  $=$  $15,000 + $1,800$  $=$  $16,800$

The net present value of the change in credit policy is:

$$NPV \ = \ -[PQ + v(Q' - Q)] \ + \ \frac{(P - v)(Q' - Q)}{R} \ = \ -\$16,800 \ + \ \$30,000 \ = \ \$13,200$$

Therefore, the change in credit policy to terms of net 30 days is beneficial.

## Problem 12

Rita's Bakery is considering changing its credit policy by offering credit terms of net 30 days.  Given the information below, should they grant credit terms to their customers?

        P  =  $8
        v  =  $3
        Q  =  500
        Q' =  575
        R  =  5%

**Solution:**

 If Rita does not extend credit:

        Monthly sales  =  $8 x 500  =  $4,000
        Monthly variable costs  =  $3 x 500  =  $1,500
        Cash flow  =  $4,000 - $1,500  =  $2,500   or   ($8 - $3) x 500  =  $2,500

If credit is granted, the new cash flow is:

        ($8 - $3) x 575  =  $2,875

Incremental cash flow $=$ $2,875 - $2,500 $=$ $375

The present value of the incremental flow, treated as a monthly annuity is:

    PV $=$ $375 / .05 $=$ $7,500

The cost of the change in credit policy is the sum of the increase in variable costs plus the costs of delaying the collection period by 30 days.

    VC $=$ $3 (575 - 500) $=$ $225

    Cost of delayed collections $=$ $8 x 500 $=$ $4,000

    Total cost $=$ $225 + $4,000 $=$ $4,225

For Rita's Bakery, the NPV of changing its credit policy is:

    NPV    $=$    -$4,225 + $7,500 $=$ $3,275

The NPV is positive, so Rita's Bakery should change its credit policy to terms of net 30 days.

## Problem 13

Verify the calculation for Problem 11 by computing the net present value of the change in credit policy using the following alternative approach. First compute the NPV of the change under the assumption that the change is in effect for one time period only, and then treat the one-period NPV as a perpetuity.

**Solution:** The firm invests the following amount in production costs today: $(v \times Q') = ($40 \times 345) = $13,800$

Also, the firm foregoes the following net cash inflow, which would be received this month under the existing credit policy: $(P - v) \times Q = ($50 - $40) \times 300 = $3,000$

Under the new credit policy, the firm then receives the following cash inflow from payments 30 days later: $(P \times Q') = ($50 \times 345) = $17,250$

The present value of this inflow is $($17,250/1.015) = $16,995.0739$. The net present value of this transaction, if we regard this as a one-month change in policy, is: $16,995.0739 - ($13,800 + $3,000) = $195.0739$

Since this NPV actually repeats itself each month, the NPV of the change in credit policy is:   $195.0739 + ($195.0739/.015) = $13,200$

This is the same as the NPV computed in the solution to Problem 11.

## Problem 14

Verify the calculation for Problem 11 by computing the net present value of the change in credit policy using the following accounts receivable approach. Compare the opportunity cost of the investment in accounts receivable to the monthly net benefit resulting from the change in credit policy.

**Solution:** The firm's investment in accounts receivable is comprised of two parts. The first part is the amount the firm would have received during the current month if the existing credit policy remained unchanged:
$P \times Q = \$50 \times 300 = \$15,000$

The second part of the investment in receivables is the increase in the investment in receivables which results from the increase in sales:   $v + (Q' - Q) = \$40 \times (345 - 300) = \$1,800$

The total incremental investment in receivables is:   $(PQ) + [v(Q' - Q)] = \$15,000 + \$1,800 = \$16,800$

The required return on this investment for one month is:
Carrying costs $= [(PQ) + v(Q' - Q)] \times R = \$16,800 \times .015 = \$252$

The monthly benefit derived from the investment in receivables is:
$(P - v) \times (Q' - Q) = (\$50 - \$40) \times (345 - 300) = \$450$

The monthly net benefit is ($450 – $252) = $198.  The NPV of the change in credit policy is ($198/.015) =   $13,200.

## Problem 15

Brahma Company is considering a change in its credit policy.  The current policy requires cash payment, while the new policy would extend credit for one month.  The following information has been collected:

|                          | Current policy | New policy |
|--------------------------|:--------------:|:----------:|
| Price per unit           | $195           | $200       |
| Cost per unit            | $150           | $150       |
| Sales per period, in units | 1,000        | 1,000      |

Also, the required return is 1% per month, and all customers will buy on credit.  Brahma expects that 2% of its customers will default.  Should Brahma make the change in credit policy?

**Solution:** The relevant data for Brahma can be represented as follows:  $P = \$195$; $P' = \$200$; $v = \$150$; $Q = 1,000$; $R = 1.0\%$; $\pi = 2.0\%$; $d = 2.5\%$

The cost of the change is the firm's investment in production costs plus the firm's foregone net cash inflow.  Since the change in credit policy does not affect Q, this cost can be computed as follows:  $(v \times Q) + [(P - v) \times Q] = P \times Q = \$195 \times 1,000 = \$195,000.$

The monthly cash inflow for the current policy:  $(P - v) \times Q = (\$195 - \$150) \times 1,000 = \$45,000$
The monthly cash inflow for the proposed policy is:  $[(1 - \pi)P' - v] \times Q = [(.98 \times \$200) - \$150] \times 1,000 = \$46,000$

The net incremental cash flow is therefore ($46,000 – $45,000) = $1,000.  The net incremental cash flow can also be computed as follows:  $P' \times Q \times (d - \pi) = \$200 \times 1,000 \times (.025 - .020) = \$1,000$

The net present value of the change in credit policy is:

$$NPV = -(P \times Q) + [P' \times Q \times (d - \pi)] / R = -\$195,000 + \$1,000 - .10 = -\$95,000$$

Since the net present value of the change in credit policy is negative, the firm should not make the change.

**Problem 16**

Mary Kavanaugh is a manager at Witty Corporation and must decide whether to implement a new credit policy which would extend credit for one month. The current policy allows for cash sales only. If the required return is 2% per month, should Kavanaugh implement the change? Assume there are no defaults. The following information has been collected.

|                         | Current Policy | New Policy |
|-------------------------|:--------------:|:----------:|
| Price per unit          | $ 30           | $ 35       |
| Cost per unit           | 25             | 25         |
| Sales per period, in units | 450         | 525        |

**Solution:** For the current policy:

Monthly sales $= \$30 \times 450 = \$13,500$
Monthly variable costs $= \$25 \times 450 = \$11,250$
Cash flow (old policy) $= (\$30 - \$25) \times 450 = \$2,250$

If credit is granted: Cash flow (new policy) $= (\$35 - \$25) \times 525 = \$5,250$

The incremental cash flow is $\$5,250 - \$2,250 = \$3,000$. The present value is $\$3,000 / 0.02 = \$150,000$.

The cost of the change in policy is the increased variable cost plus the cost of the delayed payment. The increased variable cost is $\$25 \times (525 - 450) = \$1,875$. The cost of the delayed payment is $\$30 \times 450 = \$13,500$. The total cost of the change is $\$1,875 + \$13,500 = \$15,375$.

The NPV of the change in credit policy is $\$150,000 - \$15,375 = \$134,625$. The firm should change its policy.

**Problem 17**

A new customer, Mr. Hernandez, intends to purchase 200 units of a product from the Gooden-Carter Company, Inc. The price of the product is $500 per unit and the variable cost of producing the product is $350. Mr. Gooden must decide whether to extend credit to Mr. Hernandez for a one-month time period. Mr. Gooden has concluded that the probability of default is 30%, and the required return is 1% per month. Should Gooden-Carter extend credit to Mr. Hernandez? (Assume that this is a one-time sale and that Mr. Hernandez will not buy from Gooden-Carter if credit is not extended.)

**Solution:** The relevant data for this problem can be represented as follows: $P' = \$500$; $Q = 200$; $v = \$350$; $R = 1.0\%$; $\pi = 30.0\%$

The cost of granting credit to Mr. Hernandez is the variable cost of the product, which must be expended this month:
$v \times Q = \$350 \times 200 = \$70,000$

The cash inflow to Gooden-Carter in one month is: $(1 - \pi) \times P' \times Q = .70 \times \$500 \times 200 = \$70,000$

The net present value is:

$$NPV = -(v \times Q) + \frac{(1 - \pi) \times P' \times Q}{R} = -\$70,000 + \frac{\$70,000}{1.01} = -\$693.07$$

Since the net present value is negative, Gooden-Carter should not extend credit to the new customer.

## Problem 18

Muir Inc. sells Bunsen burners to high school chemistry labs.  If the company sells 125,000 burners annually and the carrying costs per unit and shortage costs are $0.95 and $55, respectively, what is the EOQ?  What is the total cost if Muir uses the EOQ?

**Solution:**

$$EOQ = [ (2 \times 125,000 \times \$55) / \$0.95 ]^{\frac{1}{2}} = 3,804.43 = 3,804$$

Total cost $= (3,804 / 2) \times \$0.95 + (125,000 / 3,804) \times \$55 = \$3,614.21$

## Problem 19

Consider the following additional information for Problem 17:  If Mr. Hernandez does not default, then he will continue to purchase 200 units each month for the foreseeable future.  Should Gooden-Carter extend credit to Mr. Hernandez?

**Solution:** The cost to Gooden-Carter of extending credit is still $70,000, as in the solution to Problem 17.  In one month, Mr. Hernandez will either default, or he will pay $(P' \times Q) = \$10,000$ and purchase an additional 200 units.  The probability that he will not default is $(1 - \pi) = 70\%$ and the expected net cash inflow in one month is:  $(1 - \pi) \times (P' - v) \times Q = .70 \times (\$500 - \$350) \times 200 = \$21,000$

The net present value of the decision to grant credit is:  NPV = -$70,000 + $21,000 / .01  =  $2,030,000. Since the net present value is positive, it is beneficial for the firm to extend credit to the new customer.

## Problem 20

Anna operates a bookstore where managing inventory is an important activity.  It costs her $50 to place an order, and her carrying costs are $1.50 per unit per year.  Anna's total sales per year are 400,000.  What is Anna's EOQ and the total cost of ordering the EOQ?

**Solution:**

$$EOQ = [ (2 \times 400,000 \times \$50) / \$1.50 ]^{\frac{1}{2}} = 5,163.98 = 5,164 \text{ units}$$

The cost of ordering the EOQ is:

Total cost  =  (5,164 / 2) x $1.50  +  (400,000 / 5,164) x $50  =  $3,873 + $3,873  =  $7,746

## Problem 21

Bajaba Inc., sells high quality hockey pucks and has an annual demand of 90,000 units.  The carrying costs are $0.60 per unit and the shortage costs are $30.  What is the EOQ?

**Solution:** EOQ   =       $[\,(\,2 \times 90{,}000 \times \$30) / \$0.60\,]^{1/2}$  =  3,000 units

## Problem 22

What is the total cost if Bajaba orders the EOQ?

**Solution:** Total Cost  =  $(Q/2) \times CC + F \times (T/Q)$  =  $(3{,}000/2) \times \$0.60 + \$30 \times (90{,}000/3{,}000)$ =  $900 + $900 = $1,800

## Problem 23

Suppose Bajaba meets a supplier who is willing to give a 1% discount on materials it normally sells for $1 per unit if orders were made in lot sizes of 6,000 units.  Should Bajaba purchase from this supplier?

**Solution:** Total Cost  =  $(6{,}000/2) \times \$0.60 + \$30 \times (90{,}000/6{,}000)$  -  $90{,}000 \times \$1.00 \times .01$  = $1,800 + $450 – $900  =  $1,350

Notice the total cost is reduced by the savings of the purchase price (the discount) so that Bajaha is better off ordering in lots of 6,000.

## Problem 24

Considering the original information for Bajaba in Problem 21, assume the lead-time of placing an order is six days.  Assume Bajaba is in business 360 days a year, and a seven-day safety stock is kept on hand.  On average, how many units are sold per day?  How much safety stock does Bajaba have on hand?

**Solution:**  On average, Bajaba sells 90,000/360 = 250 units per day, so the safety stock is $250 \times 7 = 1{,}750$ units.

## Problem 25

What is Bajaba's reorder point?

**Solution:** The reorder point is equal to the lead time × the daily usage + the safety stock = $(6 \times 250) + 1{,}750 = 3{,}250$ units.

## Problem 26

Suppose the EOQ of a firm is 1,000 units, the sales are 5,000 units per year, and the shortage costs are $500 per order.  What are the carrying costs in dollars per unit of inventory?

**Solution:** Solve the EOQ equation for the value of carrying costs (CC):

$$1,000 \; = \quad [(\,2 \times 1,000 \times \$500) \, / \, CC]^{1/2}$$

$$1,000,000 \quad = \quad \$1,000,000 \; CC$$

$$CC \quad = \quad \$1.00$$

## Problem 27

Cameron Ltd. needs 250,000 units per year.  The carrying costs per unit are $100, shortage costs are $200 per order and the safety stock is 8,000 units.  What is the EOQ?

**Solution:**   $EOQ \quad = \quad [\,(\,2 \times 250,000 \times \$200) \, / \, \$100\,]^{1/2} \quad = \quad 1,000 \text{ units}$

## Problem 28

What is the optimal number of orders Cameron should place each year?

**Solution:**  Number of orders  =  250,000/1,000 = 250 orders

## Problem 29

Assuming a 360-business day year and that the expected delivery time for Cameron is eight days, at what inventory level should the firm reorder?

**Solution:**  Reorder point  =  $8 \times (250,000/360) + 8,000 = 13,556$ units

## Problem 30

Fill out the following table for Cameron Ltd.

| Order Size | Q/2 | Q/2 x CC | T/Q | F x T/Q | Total Cost |
|---|---|---|---|---|---|
| 800 | | | | | |
| 1,000 | | | | | |
| 1,200 | | | | | |

**Solution:**

| Order Size | Q/2 | Q/2 x CC | T/Q | F x T/Q | Total Cost |
|---|---|---|---|---|---|
| 800 | 400 | $40,000 | 312.5 = 313 | $62,600 | $102,600 |
| 1,000 | 500 | 50,000 | 250 | 50,000 | 100,000 |
| 1,200 | 600 | 60,000 | 208.3 = 209 | 41,800 | 101,800 |

# 21        International Corporate Finance

## CHAPTER HIGHLIGHTS

The basic principles of corporate finance apply to international corporations just as they do to domestic corporations. That is, international corporations seek to invest in positive NPV projects and to arrange financing that creates value for shareholders. However, application of these principles in international finance is complicated by differences in foreign exchange, interest rates, accounting methods, tax rates, and government intervention.

## TERMINOLOGY

As in all specialized subject areas, international finance has a unique vocabulary. Some of the most important terms are defined in this section.

1.  **Belgian Dentist:** a stereotype of an investor who purchases Eurobonds because the income derived from these anonymous-bearer bonds is untraceable.
2.  **Cross rate:** the exchange rate between two currencies when both are quoted in a third currency.
3.  **Eurobond:** a bond issue denominated in a particular currency, sold simultaneously in several European countries, issued in bearer form.
4.  **Eurocurrency:** money deposited in financial institutions outside the country whose currency is involved. Eurodollars, the most important Eurocurrency, are American dollars deposited in banks outside the U.S. EuroCanadians are Canadian dollar bank deposits outside Canada.
5.  **Foreign bonds:** bonds issued by foreign borrowers in another country and denominated in the currency of the country where issued.
6.  **Gilts:** British and Irish government securities.
7.  **London Interbank Offered Rate (LIBOR):** the rate on overnight Eurodollar loans between major international banks. Interest rates on short-term debt of corporate and government borrowers are frequently based on this rate.
8.  **Swaps:** a currency swap is an agreement to exchange currencies; an interest rate swap is an exchange of a debt with a floating-rate payment for a debt with a fixed-rate payment (or vice versa).
9.  **Export Development Corporation (EDC):** a federal crown corporation which promotes Canadian exports by making loans to foreign purchasers.

## FOREIGN EXCHANGE MARKETS AND EXCHANGE RATES

The foreign exchange market is the world's largest financial market. It is strictly an over-the-counter market, consisting of a worldwide telecommunications network among traders in major commercial and investment banks around the world. Most of the trading takes place in a small number of major currencies, including the U.S. dollar, German Deutsche mark (DM), British pound sterling (£), Japanese yen (¥), Swiss franc (SF), and French franc (FF). Participants in the foreign exchange market include importers and exporters, portfolio managers, foreign exchange brokers, traders, and speculators.

**Exchange Rates:** An *exchange rate* is the price of one country's currency expressed in terms of the currency of another country. Thus the French franc (FF) might be quoted at FF 10/$1, indicating that it takes 10 francs to buy one dollar. A quote of units of foreign currency per dollar is called an *indirect quote* or *European quote*. A rate can also be quoted in terms of the number of American dollars required to buy one unit of foreign currency: for example, $.10/FF 1. This is a *direct quote* or *American quote*. The direct quote and the indirect quote are reciprocals of each other. In practice, almost all exchange rates are quoted in terms of U.S. dollars.

**Cross-Rates and Triangle Arbitrage:** Suppose the following exchange rates exist:

        French francs / German D-marks:  5
        French francs / U.S. dollars:        10
        German D-marks / U.S. dollars:     3

You could convert $1 into 3 marks. Next, convert 3 marks to 15 francs and then convert the francs to dollars. At the exchange rate of 10 francs to the dollar, you will have $1.50, or a 50% risk-free return! This outcome is, of course, impossible in an efficient market. This activity is referred to as *triangle arbitrage*. The data of this example are equivalent to two different prices for the dollar at the same point in time. The exchange rate for French francs is quoted here as FF 10/$1. The other two exchange rates are equivalent to an exchange rate of FF 15/$1. In other words, exchanging $1 for DM 3, and then exchanging DM 3 for [DM 3 × (FF 5/DM 1)] = FF 15 is equivalent to exchanging $1 for FF 15. The above triangle arbitrage is equivalent to selling $1 for FF 15, and then buying $1 for FF 10.

Since arbitrage opportunities do not exist in an efficient market, the above exchange rates cannot exist simultaneously. If $1 buys DM 3, and $1 buys FF 10, then the cross rate must be:

        (DM 3/$1) / (FF 10/$1)  =  DM 3 / FF 10  =  DM .3 / FF 1

**Types of Transactions:** Two basic kinds of transactions exist in the foreign exchange market. Spot trades involve agreement on the exchange rate today, called the *spot exchange rate*, for settlement in two business days. *Forward trades* involve agreement today on an exchange rate for settlement in the more distant future. The exchange rate in this case is the *forward exchange rate*, and settlement is typically one to 52 weeks in the future.

When a foreign currency is more expensive in the forward market than in the spot market, it is said to be selling at a *premium* relative to the dollar. For example, if the Japanese yen costs $.0075 in the spot market and $.0080 in the forward market, the Japanese yen is selling at a *premium* relative to the dollar. Equivalently, it is said that the dollar is selling at a *discount* relative to the Japanese yen.

As noted earlier, exchange rates are typically quoted in terms of U.S. dollars. That is, exchange rates are generally stated in terms of indirect quotes, which indicate the amount of the foreign currency per U.S. dollar. Throughout this chapter, we use indirect exchange rates in our discussion.

## PURCHASING POWER PARITY

In this section, we address the following two questions: (1) What are the factors which determine the level of the spot exchange rate? (2) What are the determinants of the rate of change in exchange rates? The concepts of *absolute purchasing power parity* and *relative purchasing power parity* provide part of the answer to these questions.

**Absolute Purchasing Power Parity:** Absolute purchasing power parity is based on the concept that a particular commodity must have the same price regardless of the currency used to purchase the commodity or the country in which it is purchased. For example, suppose that a litre of gasoline sells for $2 in Canada and for 30 French francs (FF 30) in France. If the exchange rate is FF 10/$1, then you could purchase a gallon of gasoline in Canada for $2, sell the gasoline in France for FF 30, and then exchange the 30 francs for $3. The profit for the transaction is $1. This transaction is analogous to the triangle arbitrage described in the previous section. The transaction is equivalent to buying and selling an asset (i.e., a gallon of gasoline) at two different prices (i.e., $2 in Canada, and FF 30, or $3, in France) at the same time.

As is true in the case of triangle arbitrage, the above scenario could not continue to exist; the stated prices and/or exchange rate would adjust in such a way as to eliminate the arbitrage profit for this transaction. This profit is eliminated if:

$$P_{FF} = S_0 \times P_{CDN}$$

where $P_{FF}$ is the current price of a commodity in France, $P_{CDN}$ is the current price in Canada, and $S_0$ is the spot exchange rate (i.e., the number of francs required to purchase one Canadian dollar). If, for example, the prices remain the same, then, in order for absolute purchasing power parity to prevail, $S_0$ must equal:

$$S_0 = P_{FF} / P_{CDN} = FF\ 30 / \$2 = FF15 / \$1$$

In the preceding example, we assumed that prices remained constant. In general, however, absolute purchasing power parity implies that both prices and exchange rates adjust. For instance, the profit opportunity indicated in the example would result in both increased demand for gasoline in Canada and increased supply in France, so that price would increase in Canada and decrease in France. In addition, the demand for francs would decrease and the demand for dollars would increase, thereby increasing the exchange rate.

The above argument is strictly accurate only if there are no shipping or other transactions costs, no barriers to trade, and commodities are identical in both countries. Clearly, these conditions are rarely met, so that, in general, we do not expect absolute purchasing power parity to apply precisely.

**Relative Purchasing Power Parity:** The concept of *relative purchasing power parity* provides the answer to the second question posed at the beginning of this section. That is, the rate of change in an exchange rate over time is determined by relative inflation rates in the two countries.

Suppose that the French franc / Canadian dollar exchange rate is FF 10 / $1. Further, assume that the expected inflation rates in France and Canada during the coming year are 9% and 0%, respectively. What is the expected exchange rate one year from now? Recall that the exchange rate is the number of francs required to purchase one dollar. Since prices in France are expected to increase by 9% during the coming year, while prices in Canada are expected to remain constant, then, by the end of the year, 9% more francs will be required to purchase one dollar. In other words, the exchange rate at the end of the year is expected to be (FF 10 × 1.09) = FF 10.9/ $1. It now takes more francs to buy one dollar because the higher inflation rate in France makes the franc worth relatively less.

If the expected inflation rate in Canada is 5%, rather than 0%, then, relative to prices in Canada, prices in France are expected to increase by (9% – 5%) = 4%. Therefore, the exchange rate at the end of the year is expected to be (FF 10 × 1.04) = FF 10.4 / $1.

To summarize this concept, we will use the following notation:

$S_0$ = Current spot exchange rate
$E[S_t]$ = Expected exchange rate in t periods
$h_{CDN}$ = Inflation rate in Canada
$h_{FC}$ = Inflation rate in foreign country

The expected percentage change in the exchange rate during the next year is represented as: $(E[S_1] - S_0)/S_0$. Relative purchasing power parity states that the expected change in the exchange rate is equal to the difference in the inflation rates:

$$\frac{E[S_1] - S_0}{S_0} = h_{FC} - h_{CDN}$$

This statement of relative purchasing power parity can be algebraically rearranged, as follows:

$$E[S_1] = S_0 \times [1 + (h_{FC} - h_{CDN})]$$

If the inflation rates remain constant for the next two years, then the above relationship could be applied to the second year, as follows:

$$E[S_2] = E[S_1] \times [1 + (h_{FC} - h_{CDN})]$$

Now, using the above, $E[S_2]$ can then be computed as follows:

$$E[S_2] = S_0 \times [1 + (h_{FC} - h_{CDN})^2]$$

Alternatively, $E[S_2]$ can be computed as follows:

$$E[S_2] = S_0 \times [1 + (h_{FC} - h_{CDN})]^2$$

$$= (FF\ 10/\$1) \times (1.04)^2 = FF\ 10.816/\$1$$

In general, for any time period t, relative purchasing power parity is stated as follows:

$$E[S_t] = S_0 \times [1 + (h_{FC} - h_{CDN})]^t$$

## INTEREST RATE PARITY, UNBIASED FORWARD RATES, AND THE INTERNATIONAL FISHER EFFECT

In this section, we investigate the relationship between spot exchange rates, forward exchange rates, and interest rates. The additional notation required in this section is:

$F_t$ = Forward exchange rate for settlement at time t
$R_{CDN}$ = Nominal risk-free interest rate in Canada
$R_{FC}$ = Nominal risk-free interest rate in foreign country

**Covered Interest Arbitrage:** An investor who makes an investment in a risk-free asset (i.e., Treasury bills) in Canada receives a return equal to $R_{CDN}$. On the other hand, an investor who makes an investment at the risk-free rate in a foreign country must first convert dollars to that foreign currency, invest in the risk-free asset, and then convert the foreign currency to dollars. Therefore, the return on this latter investment depends on not only the nominal risk-free interest rate in the foreign country, RFC, but also the spot exchange rate ($S_0$) and the forward exchange rate ($F_t$). Note that, if the exchange rate in effect in the future could not be established today, then the investment in the foreign country would not be risk-free; the actual return would depend on the spot exchange rate in effect at time t. Since the forward rate can be established today, the investment is risk-free, but the return is not the same as $R_{FC}$. If the actual rate on this investment differs from $R_{CDN}$, then an arbitrage opportunity exists.

We will use the following data to demonstrate these points:

$$
\begin{aligned}
S_0 &= FF\ 10.0\ /\ \$1 \\
F_1 &= FF\ 9.6\ /\ \$1 \\
R_{CDN} &= 9\% \\
R_{FF} &= 6\%
\end{aligned}
$$

An investor who invests \$1 in T-bills for one year will have, at the end of one year, ($\$1 \times 1.09$) = \$1.09. An investor who invests at the risk-free rate available in France proceeds as follows:

1.      Convert \$1 to ($\$1 \times S_0$)  =  [$\$1 \times (FF\ 10/\$1)$]  =  FF 10.

2.      Simultaneously, the investor enters into a forward agreement to convert dollars to francs at the forward rate $F_1$  =  FF 9.6/\$1.

3.      Invest FF 10 at the rate $R_{FF}$  =  6%, so that, at the end of one year, the investor has [$(FF\ 10) \times 1.06$] = FF 10.6.

4.      Convert FF 10.6 to dollars at the rate established in (2) above, so that the investor has [$(FF\ 10.6/\$1) / (FF\ 9.6/\$1)$]  =  \$1.10417.

Clearly, the investor prefers the latter investment; the actual rate of return is 10.417%, compared to $R_{CDN}$ = 9%.

The existence of the discrepancy in rates of return on risk-free investments gives rise to an arbitrage opportunity, referred to as *covered interest arbitrage*. Suppose a Canadian investor can borrow \$100,000 at $R_{CDN}$ = 9%, and invest the \$100,000 at the French risk-free rate, as described above. At the end of the year, the investor would repay ($\$100,000 \times 1.09$) = \$109,000 on the loan. On the other hand, the investor would have ($\$100,000 \times 1.10417$) = \$110,417 from the investment at the French risk-free rate. The arbitrage profit is ($\$110,417 - \$109,000$) = \$1,417.

**Interest Rate Parity (IRP):** In an efficient market, arbitrage opportunities, such as the covered interest arbitrage of the preceding example, do not exist. Therefore, the return for each of the risk-free investments must be the same. The return per dollar for the investment at the risk-free rate $R_{CDN}$ is [$\$1 \times (1 + R_{CDN})$]. The return per dollar for the investment in the foreign risk-free investment is:

$$[\ \$1 \times S_0 \times (1 + R_{FC})\ ] / F_1$$

The interest rate parity condition states that these two returns must be equal:

$$(1 + R_{CDN})  =  S_0 \times (1 + R_{FC}) / F_1$$

Alternatively, this can be rearranged algebraically, as follows:

$$F_1 / S_0 = (1 + R_{FC}) / (1 + R_{CDN})$$

Interest rate parity indicates that the relationship between the forward and spot exchange rates is a function of the relationship between foreign and domestic interest rates. An approximation to this statement of IRP can further clarify the relationship. This approximation states that the percentage forward premium or discount is equal to the difference between the foreign and domestic interest rates:

$$(F_1 - S_0) / S_0 = R_{FC} - R_{CDN}$$

This approximation is often algebraically rearranged as follows:

$$F_1 = S_0 \times [1 + (R_{FC} - R_{CDN})]$$

This statement can be extended to any number of time periods, t, as follows:

$$F_t = S_0 \times [1 + (R_{FC} - R_{CDN})]^t$$

**Forward Rates and Future Spot Rates:** The *unbiased forward rates* (UFR) condition is the statement that the forward rate ($F_1$) is equal to the expected future spot rate ($E[S_1]$):

$$F_1 = E[S_1]$$

UFR can also be stated for any number of time periods:

$$F_t = E[S_t]$$

Essentially, these statements indicate that the forward rate must be equal to the market consensus expectation regarding the future spot rate. UFR can also be thought of as a long-run average; that is, on average, the one-period forward rate for a particular currency is equal to the spot rate one period from now. Equivalent statements apply to the forward rate for any time period t.

**'Putting It All Together'** To this point, we have developed three basic relationships of international finance: absolute purchasing power parity (PPP), interest rate parity (IRP), and unbiased forward rates (UFR). These concepts can be stated as:

$$\text{PPP:} \quad E[S_1] = S_0 \times [1 + (h_{FC} - h_{CDN})]$$

$$\text{IRP:} \quad F_1 = S_0 \times [1 + (R_{FC} - R_{CDN})]$$

$$\text{UFR:} \quad F_1 = E[S_1]$$

$F_1$ is on the left side of both IRP and UFR. Therefore, the right-hand sides of these equations must be equal:

$$E[S_1] = S_0 \times [1 + (R_{FC} - R_{CDN})]$$

This statement is referred to as *uncovered interest parity* (UIP), which can be stated for t time periods as follows:

$$E[S_t] = S_0 \times [1 + (R_{FC} - R_{CDN})]^t$$

The right-hand sides of PPP and UIP must also be equal:

$$S_0 \times [1 + (h_{FC} - h_{CDN}) = S_0 \times [1 + (R_{FC} - R_{CDN})$$

This statement can be simplified as:

$$h_{FC} - h_{CDN} = R_{FC} - R_{CDN}$$

That is, the difference in foreign and domestic inflation rates is equal to the difference in foreign and domestic interest rates. This equation can be rearranged:

$$R_{CDN} - h_{CDN} = R_{FC} - h_{FC}$$

This statement is referred to as the *international Fisher effect* (IFE). It indicates that *real* interest rates in different countries are equal. In the absence of differences in attitudes toward risk from one country to another and barriers to the movement of money, the international Fisher effect is simply another implication of efficient markets. If the IFE did not apply to two countries, money would flow to the country with the higher real rate. This would increase values and lower returns in that country, while having the opposite effect in the country with the lower real rate.

## INTERNATIONAL CAPITAL BUDGETING

International capital budgeting decisions are made using the same net present value criterion used for domestic capital budgeting. The difference is that, for international capital budgeting decisions, we must compute the net present value in dollars even though cash flows are in another currency. Two equivalent approaches to accomplishing this objective are considered in this section: the *home currency approach* and the *foreign currency approach*. We will illustrate the two alternatives with the following example.

A firm is considering building a factory in Slobovia. The factory is a three-year project, which will cost 100 slobs (SL 100) to build and will produce after-tax cash inflows of SL 40 per year. The current spot exchange rate is SL 2 = \$1. The one-year risk-free rates for Canada and Slobovia are quoted at 5% and 3%, respectively, and the appropriate cost of capital for *dollar* cash flows is 10%.

**Method 1 - The Home Currency Approach:** To calculate the net present value using the home currency approach, first convert the SL cash flows to dollar flows, and then discount the dollar cash flows at the 10% cost of capital. In order to convert the foreign currency cash flows to dollar cash flows, we compute the expected future exchange rates, using the uncovered interest parity (UIP) relationship:

$$E[S_t] = S_0 \times [1 + (R_{FC} - R_{CDN})]^t$$

$$= (SL\ 2) \times [1 + (.03 - .05)]^t$$

$$= (SL\ 2) \times [1 + (-.02)]^t = (SL\ 2) \times (.98)^t$$

The expected spot exchange rates for years 1, 2, and 3 are presented in the following table:

| Year | Expected exchange rate |
|------|------------------------|
| 1 | $(SL\ 2) \times (.98)^1 = SL\ 1.9600$ |
| 2 | $(SL\ 2) \times (.98)^2 = SL\ 1.9208$ |
| 3 | $(SL\ 2) \times (.98)^3 = SL\ 1.8824$ |

These exchange rates are then used to convert cash flows to dollars:

| Year | Cash flow (in SL) | Expected exchange rate | Cash flow (in CDN $) |
|------|-------------------|------------------------|----------------------|
| 0 | -SL 100 | SL 2.0000 | -$50.0000 |
| 1 | SL  40 | SL 1.9600 | $20.4082 |
| 2 | SL  40 | SL 1.9208 | $20.8247 |
| 3 | SL  40 | SL 1.8824 | $21.2495 |

Using the 10% opportunity cost, the net present value of the investment in the new factory is +$1.7285.

**Method 2 - The Foreign Currency Approach:** The foreign currency approach requires that we discount the cash flows, measured in the foreign currency. The resulting net present value, measured in the foreign currency, is then converted to a dollar NPV. The foreign currency cash flows are not discounted at the firm's cost of capital. However, the cost of capital is converted to an appropriate rate for the foreign currency, using the international Fisher effect, before computing the net present value of the foreign currency cash flows.

The international Fisher effect indicates the difference in the nominal rates:

$$h_{FC}\ =\ h_{CDN}\ =\ R_{FC} - R_{CDN}\ =\ .03 - .05\ =\ -.02$$

Therefore, the firm's 10% cost of capital is reduced by 2%, to 8%. The net present value of the cash flows for the project, measured in the foreign currency, and discounted at 8%, is SL 3.0839. Using the spot exchange rate, this net present value is converted to dollars:

$$(SL\ 3.0839)\,/\,(SL\ 2/\$1)\ =\ \$1.5420$$

(Note that this net present value differs somewhat from the NPV obtained using the home currency approach. The reason for the difference is the approximation used in the previous section in deriving the international Fisher effect.)

**Unremitted Cash Flows:** A foreign subsidiary can remit funds to a parent via dividends, management fees for central services and royalties on the use of trade names and patents.

The example above assumes that the cash flows from the project are remitted to Canada as they are earned. However, in reality, this assumption is frequently not appropriate. First, foreign countries often place limitations on the ability of international firms to remit cash flows. Second, the issue of remittance is affected by foreign taxes. For example, tax incentives may make it advantageous for an international firm to reinvest foreign cash flows in the foreign country. Total taxes paid by a multinational firm may be affected by the timing of remittances. Therefore, the timing of remittances may alter the net present value of a foreign investment.

## FINANCING INTERNATIONAL PROJECTS

**The Cost of Capital for International Firms:**  The required return for international projects could be different from that of similar domestic projects if international financial markets were *segmented* (barriers preventing shareholders in Canada from holding foreign securities) and/or foreign political risk of expropriation, foreign exchange, and taxes existed.  Empirical evidence suggests that internationally diversified portfolios have a lower variance than purely domestic stock portfolios.  And, because investors are not fully diversified internationally, firms can benefit from a lower cost of capital for international projects which provide diversification services for the firm's shareholders.

**International Diversification and Investors:**  Financial engineering is aiding investors to overcome barriers and information costs.  As investors diversify globally, the cost of capital advantage to firms will likely decline.  For example, an *Index Participation* (IP) on the Standard & Poor's 500 Index is a vehicle for international diversification which gives the investor both liquidity and reduced trading costs.  Furthermore, recently, the maximum allowable foreign holding for Canadian pension funds was recently increased to 30%.

**Sources of Short and Intermediate Term Financing:**  For short and medium-term cash, Canadian multinationals can borrow from a charted bank at the Canadian rate or borrow EuroCanadian or Eurocurrency from a bank outside Canada.  These *Eurobanks* make loans and accept deposits in foreign currencies.  Loans are usually made on a floating rate basis, set at a fixed margin above LIBOR.

Under a *Note Issuance Facility* (NIF), a large borrower issues short-term notes with maturities ranging from three months to one year underwritten by a bank(s).  When banks sell NIFs to investors, the Euronotes issued are called *Euro-Commercial paper* (ECP), and unlike domestic commercial paper, the ECP issued in the unregulated Eurocredit market offers greater flexibility and possibly lower cost.

## EXCHANGE RATE RISK

*Exchange rate risk* is the risk of loss in value resulting from fluctuations in exchange rates over time.  The three categories of exchange rate risk, or exposure are: short-run exposure, long-run exposure, and translation exposure.

**Short-Run Exposure:**  Firms dealing in international trade are subject to exchange rate risk because they both make payments in foreign currencies and receive foreign currencies in payments.  Suppose the spot exchange rate for the Japanese yen is ¥ 125 / \$1 and that a company has receivables of ¥ 1,500,000 to be collected in 90 days. At the current exchange rate, the firm will be able to exchange ¥ 1,500,000 for [(¥ 1,500,000)/(¥ 125/\$1)] = \$12,000.  But, if the exchange rate in 90 days is ¥ 150 / \$1, the firm will receive only [(¥ 1,500,000) / (¥ 150/\$1)] = \$10,000.  Of course, it is also possible that the exchange rate will decrease during the next 90 days; this would result in an increase in the dollar value of the future payment.  The firm's exchange rate risk is the uncertainty associated with the dollar value of the future payment in the foreign currency.

Corresponding exchange rate risk is associated with an obligation to make a payment in a foreign currency at a future date.  In the example above, if the firm has payables of ¥ 1,500,000 due in 90 days, the increase in the exchange rate from ¥ 125 to ¥150 decreases the cost to the firm, measured in dollars.  Similarly, a decrease in the exchange rate increases the cost to the firm.

The forward market provides a means for hedging exchange rate risk. Suppose that, in the receivables example above, the 90-day forward rate is ¥ 140. The firm can eliminate exchange rate risk by purchasing a forward contract and promising to deliver yens for dollars. At the ¥ 140 forward exchange rate, the firm is certain to receive [(¥ 1,500,000)/(¥ 140/$1)] = $10,714.29 ninety days from now. That is, hedging in the forward contract means that,

when the firm receives the payment of ¥ 1,500,000 90 days from now, it will be able to exchange this sum for $10,714.29. This eliminates the risk associated with fluctuations in the exchange rate over the next 90 days.

Hedging is generally considered advantageous because, in an efficient market, exchange rate speculation is a zero NPV activity. That is, the UFR condition indicates that the forward rate is equal to the expected future spot rate so that, on average, there is no gain from speculating on the direction of the exchange rate. In addition, the costs of hedging are generally quite low.

**Long-Run Exposure:** Long-run exposure to exchange rate risk arises from, for example, a long-term commitment to purchase resources, such as labour or materials, in a foreign country. Since such commitments are denominated in the foreign currency, the dollar value of future payments is subject to exchange rate risk. In general, such long-run exposure to exchange rate risk can be hedged in the forward markets only to a limited extent, because forward contracts generally have maturities of one year or less. Protection against long-run exposure is generally accomplished by matching inflows and outflows in the foreign currency. Then, when changes in the exchange rate result in a decrease in the dollar value of the firm's inflows, these changes are offset by a decrease in the dollar value of the outflows. Exchange rate risk can also be hedged by obtaining financing in the country where the investment is to be made. The risk reduction occurs because changes in the value of the investment will be partially offset by changes in the value of the liabilities.

**Translation Exposure:** When a Canadian firm prepares its financial statements, the data for foreign operations must be translated into dollars. The major issues which arise from this process are: first, the determination of the appropriate exchange rate; and second, accounting for gains and losses from foreign currency translation. In the U.S., Financial Accounting Standards Board Statement Number 52 requires that all assets and liabilities be translated at current, rather than historical, exchange rates. Gains and losses from exchange rate fluctuations are carried as a separate item in the shareholder's equity portion of the balance sheet, but are not recognized on the income statement. In Canada, firms typically use the rules provided by the Canadian Institute of Chartered Accountants (CICA) rule 1650. This rule sets the guidelines for calculating the firm's translation exposure.

## CONCEPT TEST

1.      When the exchange rates for two currencies are quoted in a third currency, the exchange rate between the two currencies is a(n) _____ .

2.      A bond issue denominated in a particular currency, sold simultaneously in several European countries, issued in bearer form, is a(n) _____ .

3.      American money deposited in banks outside the U.S. is referred to as _____ .

4.      Bonds issued by foreign borrowers in another country and denominated in the currency of the country where issued are called _____ .

5.      The rate on overnight Eurodollar loans between major international banks is the _____ .

6.      An agreement to exchange currencies is a(n) _____ .

7.      An exchange of floating-rate debt for fixed-rate debt is a(n) _____ .

8.      The price of one country's currency expressed in terms of the currency of another country is a(n) _____ .  A quote of units of foreign currency per dollar is called a(n) _____ quote or _____ quote.  A rate can also be quoted in terms of the number of dollars required to buy one unit of foreign currency; this is a(n) _____ quote, or _____ quote.

9.      The simultaneous purchase and sale of the same asset (or similar assets) at different prices at the same time is called _____ .  Conversions among three currencies, in order to profit from discrepancies in spot exchange rates, is called _____ .  Such opportunities do not exist in a(n) _____ market.

10.     Spot trades involve agreement on the exchange rate today, called the _____ exchange rate, for settlement in _____ business days.  Forward trades involve agreement today on an exchange rate for settlement in the more distant future.  The exchange rate in this case is the _____ exchange rate. When a foreign currency is more expensive in the forward market than in the spot market, it is selling at a _____ relative to the dollar; equivalently, it is said that the dollar is selling at a _____ relative to the foreign currency.

11.     If a commodity has different prices when purchased with different currencies, this is a violation of the concept of _____ .  This scenario creates opportunities for _____ profits if the following three conditions are also met: (1) there are no _____ costs; (2) there are no barriers to _____ ; and (3) the commodities are _____ in both countries.

12.     In efficient markets, the opportunity for profits such as those just described cannot exist, so that the following condition applies:  $P_{FC} = $ _____ $\times$ _____ .  In an efficient market, any deviation from this condition results in adjustments in both _____ and _____ .

13.     The concept of relative purchasing power parity indicates that the rate of change in an exchange rate over time is determined by _____ in the two countries.  Relative purchasing power parity states that the expected change in the exchange rate is equal to the _____ , as indicated in the following equation: _____ = _____ .  This statement of relative purchasing power parity can be algebraically rearranged, as follows:  $E[S_1] = $ _____ .

14.     In general, for any time period t, relative purchasing power parity is stated as follows:  $E[S_t] = $ _____ .

15.     The rate of return on an investment in a risk-free asset in a foreign country depends not only on the minimal risk-free interest rate in the foreign country, but also on the _____ exchange rate and the _____ exchange rate.  If the actual rate on this investment differs from the risk-free rate in Canada, then an opportunity exists for a(n) _____ profit; the process of taking advantage of this opportunity is referred to as _____ .

16.     In an efficient market, such opportunities do not exist. The statement that these two returns must be equal is called the _____ condition, which is stated mathematically as follows:_____ = _____ .  This statement can be rearranged algebraically as follows:  $F_1/S_0 = $ _____ .

17.     An approximation of the above equation states that the percentage forward premium or discount is equal to the difference between the foreign and domestic interest rates:  _____ = _____ .

This approximation is often algebraically rearranged as follows:   $F_1 =$ _____ .   This statement an be extended to any number of time periods, t, as follows: $F_t =$ _____ .

18.    The statement that the forward rate is equal to the expected future spot rate is referred to as the _____ condition, which is stated mathematically as follows: _____ = _____ .   Essentially, this statement indicates that the forward rate must be equal to the _____ expectation regarding the _____ rate.

19.    The condition referred to as uncovered interest parity is stated as follows:   $E[S_1] =$ _____ . This condition can also be stated for t time periods as follows:   $E[S_t] =$ _____ .

20.    The international Fisher effect is derived by equating the right-hand sides of the PPP and UIP relationships, as follows: _____ = _____ .   This statement can be simplified as: $h_{FC} - h_{CDN} =$ _____ .   That is, the difference in foreign and domestic inflation rates is equal to the difference in foreign and domestic _____ .  This equation can be algebraically rearranged: $R_{CDN} - h_{CDN} =$ _____ .

21.    The international Fisher effect indicates that _____ in different countries are equal. In the absence of differences in attitudes toward risk from one country to another, and barriers to the movement of money, the international Fisher effect is an implication of _____ markets.

22.    International capital budgeting decisions are made using the _____ criterion.  The _____ approach requires that foreign currency cash flows are converted to dollar cash flows.  This conversion requires the calculation of _____ exchange rates, using the _____ relationship, as follows: $E[S_t] =$ _____ . The dollar cash flows are then discounted using the required rate of return for dollar cash flows.

23.    The _____ approach to international capital budgeting requires that we discount the cash flows, measured in terms of the _____ .  The resulting net present value is then converted to a net present value measured in _____ .  The foreign currency cash flows are not discounted at the firm's cost of capital. However, the cost of capital is converted to an appropriate rate for the foreign currency, using the _____ relationship.  This net present value is converted to dollars, using the _____ exchange rate.

24.    The risk of loss of value resulting from fluctuations in exchange rates over time is referred to as _____ risk.  Firms dealing in international trade are subject to exchange rate risk because they both make payments in foreign currencies and receive foreign currencies in payments.  Consequently, changes in exchange rates can result in losses; this is considered _____ exposure. For example, a firm which has receivables denominated in a foreign currency, experiences a(n) (increase/decrease) in the dollar value of the receivables when the exchange rate increases; the firm experiences a(n) (increase/decrease) in the dollar value of the receivables when the exchange rate decreases.  Similarly, a firm which has payables denominated in a foreign currency, experiences a(n) (increase/decrease) in the dollar value of the payables when the exchange rate increases.

25.    The _____ risk is the uncertainty associated with the dollar value of the future payment in the foreign currency.  A means of hedging exchange rate risk is provided by the _____ market.  The firm can eliminate exchange rate risk by _____ a forward contract and promising to deliver the foreign

currency in exchange for dollars.

26.   A long-term commitment to purchase resources, such as labour or materials, in a foreign country results in a _____ exposure to exchange rate risk.  Protection against such exposures is generally accomplished by _____ in the foreign currency.  When a Canadian firm prepares its financial statements, the information on foreign operations must be translated into dollars; this process results in _____ exposure.  The American Financial Accounting Standards Board Statement Number 52 requires that all assets and liabilities be translated at _____ exchange rates.  Gains and losses from exchange rate fluctuations are carried as a separate item in the _____ portion of the balance sheet, but are not recognized on the income statement.

## ANSWERS TO CONCEPT TEST

1.   cross rate

2.   Eurobond

3.   Eurodollars

4.   foreign bonds

5.   London Interbank Offered Rate

6.   currency swap

7.   interest rate swap

8.   exchange rate; indirect; European; direct; American

9.   arbitrage; triangle arbitrage; efficient

10.   spot; two; forward; premium; discount

11.   absolute purchasing power parity; arbitrage; transactions; trade; identical

12.   $S_0$; $P_{CDN}$; prices; exchange rates

13.   inflation rates; difference in the inflation rates; $[E(S1) - S_0] / S_0$; $(h_{FC} - h_{CDN})$; $S_0 \times [1 + (h_{FC} - h_{CDN})]$

14.   $S_0 \times [1 + (h_{FC} - h_{CDN})]^t$

15.   spot; forward; arbitrage; covered interest arbitrage

16.   interest rate parity; $\$1 \times (1 + R_{CDN})$; $S_0 \times (1 + R_{FC}) / F_1$; $(1 + R_{FC}) / (1 + R_{CDN})$

17.   $(F_1 - S_0) / S_0$ ; $(R_{FC} - R_{CDN})$; $S_0 \times [1 + (R_{FC} - R_{CDN})]$; $S_0 \times [1 + (R_{FC} - R_{CDN})]^t$

18.   unbiased forward rates; $F_t$; $E[S_t]$; market consensus; future spot

19.      $S_0 \times [1 + (R_{FC} - R_{CDN})]$; $S_0 \times [1 + (R_{FC} - R_{CDN})]^t$

20.      $S_0 \times [1 + (h_{FC} - h_{CDN})]$;  $S_0 \times [1 + (R_{FC} - R_{CDN})]$; $(R_{FC} - R_{CDN})$; interest rates; $(R_{FC} - h_{FC})$

21.      real interest rates; efficient

22.      net present value; home currency; expected future; uncovered interest parity; $S_0 \times [1 + (R_{FC} - R_{CDN})]^t$

23.      foreign currency; foreign currency; dollars; international Fisher effect; spot

24.      exchange rate; short-run; decrease; increase; decrease

25.      exchange rate; forward; purchasing

26.      long-run; matching inflows and outflows; translation; current; shareholders' equity

## PROBLEMS AND SOLUTIONS

### Problem 1

The direct exchange rate for German Deutsche marks is $.50/DM 1.  The direct exchange rate for British pounds is $1.50/£ 1.  If you have 1 Deutsche mark, how many pounds can you buy? (That is, what is the cross rate?)

**Solution:**  One Deutsche mark will buy $.50.  With $.50, you can buy 1/3 of a pound.  The cross rate is  M 3/£ 1.

### Problem 2

Suppose that, for the data in Problem 1, the cross rate is DM 3.3/£ 1, rather than the calculated result of DM 3/£ 1.  Describe the triangle arbitrage opportunity which would exist under these circumstances.

**Solution:**  Use the one Deutsche mark to purchase $.50, and then exchange the $.50 for £ (1/3).  At the cross rate of DM 3.3/£ 1, 1/3 pound can be exchanged for DM 1.1.  This results in an arbitrage profit of 10%.

### Problem 3

Suppose that, for the data in Problem 1, the cross rate is DM 2.7/£ 1.  Describe the triangle arbitrage opportunity which would exist under these circumstances.

**Solution:**  Exchange DM 1 for £ (1/2.7) = £ .37037, and then purchase £ .37037 × ($1.50/£ 1) = $.55556.  At the exchange rate of DM 2/$1, $.55556 can be exchanged for [$.55556 × (DM 2/$1)] = 1.1111 marks.  This result represents an arbitrage profit of 11.11%.

**Use the following data to solve Problems 4 to 7:**

The spot exchange rate for the British pound is $1.80/£ 1, and the 90-day forward rate is $1.75/£ 1. The spot rate and 90-day forward rate for the Swiss franc are $.80/SF 1, and $.75/SF 1, respectively. The spot rate and 90-day forward rate for the German Deutsche mark are $.65/DM 1, and $.70/DM 1, respectively.

## Problem 4

Compute the indirect exchange rate for each of the exchange rates quoted above. Which of these currencies are selling at a premium relative to the dollar? For which currencies is the dollar selling at a premium relative to the foreign currency?

**Solution:** The direct (or American) exchange rate is the number of dollars per unit of foreign currency; the exchange rates given above are quoted as direct exchange rates. The indirect exchange rate is the number of units of the foreign currency per dollar. To convert the direct spot exchange rate for the British pound to the indirect exchange rate, divide both sides of the direct exchange rate quote by 1.80: $1.80 / 1.80 = £ 1/1.80. So, $1.00 = £ .5556.

Therefore, the indirect exchange rate is £ 0.5556. In general, the indirect exchange rate is the reciprocal of the direct exchange rate. For the British pound, the 90-day direct exchange rate is (£ 1/1.75) = £ 0.5714. For the Swiss franc, the spot and 90-day forward rates are SF 1.2500 and SF 1.3333, respectively. For the Deutsche mark, the respective rates are DM 1.5385 and 1.4286.

The German Deutsche mark is more expensive in the future than it is today (i.e., $.70/DM 1 and $.65/DM 1, respectively), so the Deutsche mark is selling at a premium relative to the dollar. Equivalently, the dollar is selling at a discount relative to the Deutsche mark. On the other hand, the British pound is less expensive in the future than it is today (i.e., $1.75/£ 1 and $1.80/£ 1, respectively), so the pound is selling at a discount relative to the dollar. And, the dollar is selling at a premium relative to the pound. These latter conclusions also apply to the Swiss franc.

## Problem 5

What is the cross-rate, in the spot market, for pounds in terms of Deutsche marks? What is the cross-rate, in the spot market, for Deutsche marks in terms of pounds?

**Solution:** The spot rate for British pounds is £ 0.5556/$1; the spot rate for the Deutsche mark is DM 1.5385/$1. Therefore, £ 0.5556 and DM 1.5385 are equivalent, so that the cross-rate for pounds in terms of Deutsche marks is:
 £ 0.5556 / DM 1.5385  =  £ .3611 / DM 1.

The cross rate for pounds in terms of Deutsche marks is:  DM 1.5385 / £ 0.5556  =  DM 2.7691 / £ 1.

Note that the cross-rate for pounds in terms of Deutsche marks is simply the reciprocal of the cross-rate for Deutsche marks in terms of pounds.

## Problem 6

Suppose that the cross-rate for pounds in terms of Deutsche marks is actually £ .35/DM 1, rather than the result computed in the solution to Problem 5.  Describe the triangle arbitrage opportunity which would exist under these circumstances.

**Solution:**  Given the circumstances of this problem, the Deutsche mark is less expensive in terms of pounds than it is in terms of dollars.  Therefore, the triangle arbitrage opportunity requires purchasing Deutsche marks using pounds, and then selling Deutsche marks for dollars.  That is, buy Deutsche marks at the lower price and then sell Deutsche marks at the higher price.  Specifically, first convert $1 to £ 0.5556. Next, convert pounds to Deutsche marks:  £ .35 = DM 1.  So,  (£ 0.5556) / .35 = DM 1.5874.

Then convert DM 1.5874 to dollars:  DM 1.5385 = $1, and  (DM 1.5874) / 1.5385 = $1.0318.

Thus, $1 has been converted to $1.0318, using triangle arbitrage.

## Problem 7

Suppose that the cross-rate for pounds in terms of Deutsche marks is actually £ .37/DM 1, rather than the result computed in the solution to Problem 5.  Describe the triangle arbitrage opportunity which would exist under these circumstances.

**Solution:**  Now, the Deutsche mark is less expensive in terms of dollars than it is in terms of pounds.  Therefore, the triangle arbitrage opportunity requires purchasing Deutsche marks using dollars, and then selling Deutsche marks for pounds.  That is, buy Deutsche marks at the lower price and then sell Deutsche marks at the higher price.

Convert $1 to DM 1.5385.   Next, convert DM 1.5385 to pounds.   The cross-rate for Deutsche marks in terms of pounds is the reciprocal of the rate for pounds in terms of Deutsche marks:  DM (1/.37) / £ 1  =  DM 2.7027 / £ 1.

Therefore, DM 1.5385 are converted to [£ (1.5385/2.7027)] = £ 0.5692.  Pounds are now converted to dollars: £ 0.5692 = [$(.5692/.5556)] = $1.0245.

## Problem 8

An ounce of silver costs $5 in Canada  The exchange rate with Japan is ¥ 150 = $1. Is this an equilibrium situation: Suppose that a trader has $500 available; can the trader earn an arbitrage profit?

**Solution:**  The trader can purchase ($500/$5)  =  100 ounces of silver in Canada.  This can then be sold for (100 × ¥ 800)  =  ¥ 80,000 in Japan.  At an exchange rate of ¥ 150/$1, the trader can exchange ¥ 80,000 for (¥ 80,000 / (¥ 150/$1)]  =  533.33; the arbitrage profit is ($533.33 – $500) = $33.33.  This is not an equilibrium situation; it is a violation of the concept of absolute purchasing power parity.  The demand for silver in Canada will cause the dollar price of silver to increase and the supply of silver will cause the yen price to decrease in Japan.  Also, the exchange rate will increase due to the increased demand for dollars and the decreased demand for yen.

## Problem 9

Suppose that, for the data of Problem 8, the price of silver in Canada and Japan does not change.  What is the equilibrium exchange rate which is consistent with absolute purchasing power parity?

**Solution:** The condition for absolute purchasing power parity is: $P_{FC} = S_0 \times P_{CDN}$. Therefore, in order for absolute purchasing power parity to prevail, $S_0$ must equal: $S_0 = P_{FC} / P_{CDN} = ¥ 800 / \$5 = ¥ 160 / \$1$

## Problem 10

Suppose that, for the data in Problem 8, the price of silver in Japan is ¥ 700 per ounce. Describe the arbitrage profit opportunity for a trader with $500 available.

**Solution:** In this situation, the trader can exchange $500 for [$500 × (¥ 150/$1)] = ¥ 75,000. With ¥ 75,000, the trader can then purchase (75,000/700) = 107.1429 ounces of silver in Japan. He can sell the silver for ($5 × 107.1429) = $535.71, for an arbitrage profit of $35.71.

## Problem 11

The direct spot exchange rate for marks is $.50/DM 1 and the 90-day forward rate is $.51/DM 1. Is the mark selling at a premium or discount? Compute the indirect spot and forward rates.

**Solution:** The indirect rates are the reciprocal of the direct rates; therefore, the spot rate is DM (1/.50) = DM 2.0000 and the forward rate is DM 1.9608.

## Problem 12

Suppose that, in Problem 11, the Canadian 90-day risk-free rate is $R_{CDN} = 3\%$. What is the German risk-free rate, $R_G$?

**Solution:** From the interest rate parity condition:

$$F_1 / S_0 = (1 + R_G) / (1 + R_{CDN})$$

Substituting the known values and solving for $R_G$, we have:

$$1.9608 / 2.000 = (1 + R_G) / 1.03$$
$$2 \times (1 + R_G) = 1.9608 \times 1.03$$
$$1 + R_G = 1.009812$$
$$R_G = .009812$$

Therefore, the German risk-free rate is .9812%, or approximately 1%.

## Problem 13

In three years, the inflation rate in Canada is expected to be 4%, while in France it is expected to be 10%. The current exchange rate is $1 = FF 2.50. What is the expected spot exchange rate three years from now?

**Solution:** This can be calculated using relative purchasing power parity:

$$E[S_t] \; = \; S_0 \; x \; [h_{FF} - h_{CDN} ]^t \; = \; (FF \; 2.50 \, / \, \$1) \; x \; [1 + (.10 - .04)]^3$$

$$= (FF \; 2.50 \, / \$1) \; x \; (1.06)^3 \; = \; FF \; 2.978 \, / \, \$1$$

## Problem 14

Using the above spot rate and forward exchange rate, assume that a risk-free asset in Canada earns a 14% return, while in France the risk-free interest rate is 12%. Is there a covered interest arbitrage opportunity?

**Solution:** By investing $1 in a risk-free Canadian asset for three years, an investor will earn $1 x $(1.14)^3$ = $1.4815. By investing the same amount in a risk-free asset in France, the investor receives:

1. Convert $1: $1 x (FF 2.50 x $1)  =  FF 2.50
2. The investor may enter a forward agreement at a rate of $F_3$ = FF 2.978 / $1
3. Investing the FF 2.50, the investor will have [FF 2.50 x $(1.12)^3$]  =  FF 3.5123 at the end of three years
4. Converting the FF 3.5123 to dollars at the rate established above, the investor has [(FF 3.5123 / $1) / (FF 2.978 / $1) ]  =  $1.1794

There is a covered interest arbitrage opportunity, because the investor will prefer to earn 17.94% rather than the Canadian rate of 14%.

## Problem 15

The exchange rate for the French franc is $0.25 / 1FF and the rate for the British pound is $1.50 / £ 1. What is the cross rate for the French franc and the British pound?

**Solution:** With £1  you can buy $1.50.  With this you can then buy 6 FF.  The cross rate is therefore £1 / 6FF.

## Problem 16

If the actual cross rate were £1 / 5FF, how could an investor take advantage of an arbitrage opportunity?

**Solution:** Using £1, you could purchase $1.50 which could then be exchanged for 6 FF.  This represents an arbitrage profit of 20%.

## Problem 17

Suppose the Swiss inflation rate is forecasted to be 2% during the coming year and the United States rate over the same period will be 5%. The current exchange rate is $1.50 = SF 1. What is the expected spot exchange rate in one year?

**Solution:** From relative purchasing power parity:   $(E[S_1] - S_0) / S_0 = h_{FC} - h_{CDN}$

Since the exchange rates here are in terms of units of foreign currency per dollar, the relevant spot rate here is $S_0 = SF (1/1.50) = SF\ 2/3 = SF\ 0.66667$. Therefore, substituting into the relative purchasing power parity relationship:   $(E[S_1] - 2/3) / 0.6667 = .02 - .05$, and $E[S_1] = .64667$.

**Solution note**: You must remember to use the exchange rate expressed as units of foreign currency per dollar. The difference between the Swiss and the Canadian inflation rates is (–3%), so the price of a dollar, measured in terms of Swiss francs, will decrease by approximately 3%: $[(SF\ .66667) \times .97] = SF\ .64667$.

## Problem 18

The current yen/dollar exchange rate is   ¥ 150/\$1. The risk-free interest rate in Japan is 6% and in Canada is 8%. What is the expected spot exchange rate in one year?

**Solution:** From the interest rate parity condition:   $F_1 / S_0 = (1 + R_J) / (1 + R_{CDN})$

Substituting the known values and solving for $F_1$, we have: $F_1 / 150 = 1.06 / 1.08$. Therefore, the forward rate is ¥ 147.22/\$1.

## Problem 19

Suppose that, for the data Problem 18, the Canadian inflation rate is expected to be 4%.  What is the expected spot exchange rate in five years?

**Solution:**  Using the international Fisher effect, the Japanese inflation rate ($h_J$) can be determined as follows:

$$R_{CDN} - h_{CDN} = R_j - h_j$$
$$.08 - .04 = .06 - h_j$$
$$h_j = .02 = 2\%$$

The expected spot exchange rate five years from now is determined using the relative purchasing power parity relationship:

$$E[S_t] = S_0 \times [1 + (h_{FC} - h_{CDN})]^t$$

$$E[S_5] = S_0 \times [1 + (h_j - h_{CDN})]^5$$

$$= (¥\ 147.22) \times [1 + (.02 - .04)]^5 = ¥\ 133.08$$

**Use the following information to solve Problems 20 and 21.**

You have been asked to evaluate a proposed investment in the country of Westfield.  Westfield's home currency is the Sar, abbreviated SA. The current exchange rate is SA 2/$1. The inflation rate in Westfield is expected to be 10% higher than in Canada. The project will cost SA 1,000 and is expected to generate SA 300 per year for three years. The project will then be sold for an estimated SA 400. The appropriate discount rate for dollar flows of this risk level is 12%.

## Problem 20

What is the expected spot exchange rate at the end of the project's life?

**Solution:** The expected spot exchange rate is determined using the relative purchasing power parity relationship:

$$E[S_t] = S_0 \times [1 + (h_{FC} - h_{CDN})]^t$$
$$E[S_3] = S_0 \times [1 + (h_{FC} - h_{CDN})]^3$$
$$= (SA\ 2) \times [1.10]^3 = SA\ 2.662$$

## Problem 21

Use the home currency approach to compute the net present value of the proposed investment in dollars.

**Solution:** The expected spot exchange rates for years 1, 2, and 3 are presented in the following table:

| Year | Expected exchange rate |
|------|------------------------|
| 1 | $(SA\ 2) \times (1.10) = SA\ 2.200$ |
| 2 | $(SA\ 2) \times (1.10)^2 = SA\ 2.420$ |
| 3 | $(SA\ 2) \times (1.10)^3 = SA\ 2.662$ |

These exchange rates are then used to convert cash flows to dollars:

| Year | Cash flow (in SA) | Expected exchange rate | Cash flow (in $) |
|------|-------------------|------------------------|------------------|
| 0 | -SA 1,000 | SA 2.000 | -$500.0000 |
| 1 | SA   300 | SA 2.200 | $136.3636 |
| 2 | SA   300 | SA 2.420 | $123.9669 |
| 3 | SA   700 | SA 2.662 | $262.9602 |

At a 12% discount rate, the NPV in dollars is -$92.25.

# 22     <u>Leasing</u>

## CHAPTER HIGHLIGHTS

Leasing is a form of financing for businesses to use plant, property, equipment, and other assets. Our focus will be on long-term leases that are typically more than five years, which we will compare with the alternative of buying an asset financed by long-term debt.

## LEASES AND LEASE TYPES

A lease is a contracted agreement between the *lessee*, the user of the equipment, and the *lessor,* who is the owner. The lease agreement establishes the right of the lessee to use the asset by making periodic payments to the lessor.

**Leasing Versus Buying:** The decision to lease or to borrow and buy requires a comparison of alternative *financing* arrangements for the use of an asset. This implies that the capital budgeting decision has already been made.

When the leasing company purchases the asset from the manufacturer, the arrangement is called a *direct lease.* Here the leasing company arranges the financing, purchases the asset, and holds title to it. If a company leases its own assets from wholly-owned subsidiaries, the latter are referred to as *captive finance companies.*

**Operating Leases:** An operating or *service lease* is usually a short-term lease, meaning the life of the lease is less than the economic life of the asset. The lessor is responsible for insurance, taxes and upkeep. Operating leases are often cancellable on short notice, and the value of a cancellation clause depends on whether technological and/or economic conditions are likely to make the value of the asset to the lessee less than the value of the future lease payments under the lease.

**Financial Leases:** Payments made under a *financial lease* are usually sufficient to cover fully the lessor's cost of purchasing the asset and pay the lessor a return on the investment. Therefore, financial leases are typically a longer-term, fully amortized lease under which the lessee is responsible for the upkeep. These leases are usually noncancellable, at least not without a significant penalty. Two special types of financial leases include a *sale and lease back* arrangement and a *leveraged lease.*

**Sale and Lease Back Arrangements:** A *sale and lease back* arrangement occurs when a company sells an asset to another firm and simultaneously leases it back. In other words, the lessee receives cash from the sale of the asset and continues to use the asset. A sale and lease back is typically motivated by the realization of tax benefits.

**Leveraged Leases:** A *leveraged lease* is a tax-oriented lease involving three or more parties which at least include a lessee, a lessor, and a lender. The lessor usually puts up no more than 40 to 50% of the financing, is entitled to the lease payments but must pay interest to the lenders. The lenders supply the remaining financing but cannot turn to the lessor in case of a default. However, the lenders have a first lien on the asset and may actually receive the lease payments by deducting the principal and interest portion and then forwarding the remainder to the lessor.

Leveraged leases make sense when the lessee cannot fully use CCA and/or tax credits that come with owning the asset so that these benefits are passed on to the lessor. Of course, the lessor may return a portion of these tax benefits to the lessee in the form of lower lease costs.

# ACCOUNTING AND LEASES

Before 1979, lessees only had to report information on leasing activity in footnotes accompanying their financial statements. Thus, leasing was frequently called *off balance sheet financing*. This meant that firms could acquire a substantial number of assets with significant financial commitment via financial leases, yet not disclose the impact of this debt in their financial statements. To discourage companies from understating their financial leverage, the Canadian Institute of Chartered Accountants (CICA) implemented new rules for lease disclosure which meant that the present value of lease payments must be calculated and reported along with other liabilities of the lessee's balance sheet.

In order to determine whether a lease must be *capitalized* and appear in the balance sheet and declared as a financial lease, *one* of the following criteria must apply to the lease transaction:

1.      The lease transfers ownership of the property to the lessee by the end of the term of the lease.

2.      The lessee has an option to purchase the asset at a price below fair market value when the lease expires, commonly referred to as a bargain purchase option.

3.      The lease term is 75% or more of the estimated economic life of the asset.

4.      The present value of lease payments is at least 90% of the fair market value of the asset at the start of the lease.

# TAXES, CCRA, AND LEASES

Basically, Canada Customs and Revenue Agency (CCRA) requires that a lease be primarily for business purposes and not merely for tax avoidance. Normally, the lessee gets a tax deduction for the full lease payment. In a *Conditional Sales Agreement*, only the interest portion of the payment is deductible. If CCRA detects one or more of the following, including sale and lease backs, the lease will be disallowed:

1.      The lessee automatically acquires title after payment of a specified amount in the form of rentals,

2.      The lessee is required to buy the property from the lessor during or at the termination of the lease,

3.      The lessee has the right during (or at the expiration of) the lease to acquire the property at a price less than fair market value.

Current regulations allow lessors to deduct CCA from leasing income only and unused CCA tax shields cannot be passed along to other companies owned by the same parent holding campany.

# THE CASH FLOWS FROM LEASING

**The Incremental Cash Flows:** The following example illustrates the incremental after-tax cash flows from leasing instead of borrowing.

**An Example:**  Your firm needs 100 new machines to support a tremendous growth in sales.  Each machine can be purchased for $20,000 that will reduce operating costs on the existing equipment by $12,000 per machine per year, for the next five years.  The machines can be depreciated for tax purposes at CCA rate of 30% and are expected to have $1,000 residual value after five years.  Your firm has also contacted Welease Inc., which requires beginning of year lease payments of $5,000 per year for each machine over the five-year period.  With the lease, your firm is responsible for maintenance, insurance and operating expenses.  Your firm's tax rate is 40%.  What are the cash flow consequences of leasing instead of buying?  First compute the tax shield on CCA and the tax shield on the terminal loss that will occur in Year 5.

The schedule below shows the CCA and UCC schedule for one machine.  The half-year rule has been incorporated.

| Year | UCC | CCA | Tax Shield |
|------|------|------|------|
| 1 | $10,000 | $3,000 | $1,200 |
| 2 | 17,000 | 5,100 | 2,040 |
| 3 | 11,900 | 3,570 | 1,428 |
| 4 | 8,330 | 2,499 | 999.6 |
| 5 | 5,831 | 1,749.3 | 699.72 |
| 6 | 4,081.7 | | 1,232.68 |

In Year 5, the UCC balance after the sale is positive ($4,081.7 – $1,000) but there are no assets left in the pool because each of the machines are scrapped for $1,000 salvage.  This results in a terminal loss tax shield of $3,081.7 (.40) = $1,232.68.

To calculate the relevant cash flow for each of the next five years, a few points should be noted.  First, the $12,000 reductions of operating costs on the existing equipment will be realized whether the machines are leased or purchased and therefore, because these are not incremental, they must be ignored in the analysis.  Second, if the machine is leased there is a tax shield of $5,000 (.40) = $2,000 each year so that the after-tax cost is $3,000. However, because payments are made at the beginning of each period the tax shield will lag by one period.  In other words, the $2,000 tax shield will be realized at the end of each year.  Third, if the machines are leased, your firm cannot claim CCA for tax purposes.  This foregone tax shield represents an outflow for your firm.  Note: Unlike the payment shield the CCA tax shield has not been lagged for one period.  Finally, the initial investment of $20,000 per machine represents an inflow for your firm since by leasing them, this money does not have to be spent.  However, the salvage of $1,000 represents an outflow since this amount is forgone if the firm leases the machine. These points are summarized below.

| | | Year | | | | |
|---|---|---|---|---|---|---|
| | 0 | 1 | 2 | 3 | 4 | 5 |
| Investment | $20,000 | | | | | |
| Salvage | | | | | (1,000) | |
| Lease Payment | (5,000) | (5,000) (5,000) (5,000) | | (5,000) | | |
| Payment Shield | | 2,000 | 2,000 2,000 | | 2,000 | 2,000 |
| Forgone CCA Tax Shield | (1,200) | (2,040) | (1,428) | ( 999.6) | ( 699.72) | (1,232.68) |
| Total Cash Flow | $13,800 | (5,040) (4,428) (3,999.6) | | (3,699.72) | (232.68) | |

## LEASE OR BUY?

**A Preliminary Analysis:** Suppose your firm were to borrow $20,000 today and make after-tax payments equal to the cash flows shown above. What is the interest rate your firm is paying on this 'loan'? To find the unknown rate we solve the following equation:

$$0 = \$13,800 - \frac{\$5,040}{(1+i)} - \frac{\$4,428}{(1+i)^2} - \frac{\$3,999.6}{(1+i)^3} - \frac{\$3,699.72}{(1+i)^4} - \frac{\$232.68}{(1+i)^5}$$

The discount rate works out to 10.41%. In other words, your firm has arranged financing from Welease Inc., at an after-tax rate of 10.41%. This rate should be compared to the after-tax cost of the term loan that your firm could obtain from a financial institution.

**An Example:** Your firm has secured a five-year term loan from the Loyal bank at 14% interest rate. Should your firm lease or go with the bank?

Your firm should go with the bank because the after-tax interest rate would be .14 (1 − .4) = 8.4% which is less than the 10.41% implicit after-tax rate on the lease.

**Three Potential Pitfalls:** First, as we saw earlier, leasing would have been preferred to borrowing if the implicit rate on leasing was *lower* than the after-tax rate of borrowing. Normally, the higher the IRR, the better, but with this cash flow pattern, the IRR represents the rate we pay, so the *lower* the IRR the better. Second, a related pitfall is that we were calculating the advantage of leasing instead of borrowing, which is why a lower IRR from the cash flows of leasing is preferred over the after-tax borrowing rate. Third, some analysts mistakenly calculate the IRR of leasing by totally excluding the borrow-to-buy decision. This is incorrect because the incremental cash flows are misspecified because the CAA tax shields and salvage value are ignored.

**NPV Analysis:** Since we know that the relevant rate for evaluating a lease versus buy decision is the firm's after-tax borrowing cost, the NPV is simply discounting the cash flows in the above table   .14 (1 − .4) = 8.4%:

$$NPV = \$13,800 - \frac{\$5,040}{(1.084)} - \frac{\$4,428}{(1.084)^2} - \frac{\$3,999.6}{(1.084)^3} - \frac{\$3,699.72}{(1.084)^4} - \frac{\$232.68}{(1.084)^5}$$

The NPV of −$592.71 reinforces our decision earlier to buy and is often called the *net advantage to leasing* (NAL).

**A Misconception:** Some argue that the $20,000 your firm would borrow is not equivalent to the present value of after-tax interest plus principal repayments that are paid over five years. In fact, it can be shown that for any loan amortized over any given period, the present value of the after-tax interest plus principal repayments is always equal to the amount of the loan as long as the discount rate used is the loan rate after-tax. This is demonstrated in Problem 10 at the end of the chapter.

**An Example:** Suppose your firm was able to negotiate a lease payment of $4,000 per year. What is the IRR and NPV of the lease?

The table below shows the new calculations.

| | | | Year | | | |
|---|---|---|---|---|---|---|
| | 0 | 1 | 2 | 3 | 4 | 5 |
| Investment | $ 20,000 | | | | | |
| Salvage | | | | | (1,000) | |
| Lease Payment | (4,000) | (4,000) | (4,000) | (4,000) | (4,000) | |
| Payment Shield | | 1,600 | 1,600 | 1,600 | 1,600 | 1,600 |
| Forgone CCA Tax Shield | (1,200) | (2,040) | (1,428) | ( 999.6) | ( 699.72) | (1,232.68) |
| Total Cash Flow | $14,800 | (4,440) | (3,828) | (3,399.6) | (3,099.72) | (632.68) |

The IRR for leasing is 1.64% and the NPV using the after-tax loan rate of 8.4% is $2,109.75. Since the IRR is less than the after-tax cost of borrowing and the NPV is positive, your firm should now favour leasing over buying.

In the original example for your firm, since all of the machines were sold, the asset pool was closed with a resulting terminal loss. Suppose that your firm has other assets in the same class so that the unused UCC is depreciated from zero to infinity. In this case, we use the CCA tax shield formula developed earlier.

Install Equation Editor and double-click here to view equation.

While the formula looks formidable, the application is pretty straightforward. Notice the terms within the first set of brackets. These represent the present value of lease payment after-tax, taking into account the lag in the tax shields from the lease payments. The second set of brackets contains the familiar formula to compute the present value of infinite CCA tax savings, except that the sign preceding the formula is negative. This is because, by leasing, the tax savings are foregone. The third set of brackets contains the reduction in tax savings due to salvage for which, again, we reverse signs. The final term is the present value of salvage preceded by a negative sign, since it represents a forgone opportunity for leasing.

**An Example:**   Referring the original information provided for your firm, but assuming that there will be other machines in the assets class, what is your firm's NAL?

$$\text{NAL} = \$20,000 - \left[ \$5,000 + \$5,000(1.-.4)(\text{PVIFA8.4\%,4}) - \frac{\$5,000\,(.4)}{(1.084)^5} \right]$$
$$- \frac{(.4)\,(.3)\,(\$20,000)}{.084 + .3} \times \frac{1+.084/2}{1.084} + \frac{\$1,000\,(.3)\,(.4)}{.084+.3} \times \frac{1}{(1.084)^5} - \frac{\$1,000}{(1.084)^5}$$

$$= \$20,000 - \$13,512.31 - \$6,007.84 + \$208.79 - \$668.12 = \$20.52$$

With the full tax shield on CCA available instead of just the write-off in Year 5, the NAL increases from the original value of −$592.72 to +$20.52. Of course, if your firm acquires 100 machines, the NAL could be $2,052.

**A Leasing Paradox:** The cash flows from the lessor's perspective for Welease are presented below.

| | Year | | | | | |
|---|---|---|---|---|---|---|
| | 0 | 1 | 2 | 3 | 4 | 5 |
| Investment | $(20,000) | | | | | |
| Salvage | | | | | 1,000 | |
| Lease Payment | 5,000 | 5,000 | 5,000 | 5,000 | 5,000 | |
| Payment Shield | | (2,000) | (2,000) | (2,000) | (2,000) | (2,000) |
| CCA Tax Shield | 1,200 | 2,040 | 1,428 | 999.6 | 699.72 | 1,232.68 |
| Total Cash Flow | $(13,800) | 5,040 | 4,428 | 3,999.6 | 3,699.72 | 232.68 |

NAL   =  $592.71

The cash flows to Welease Inc. are exactly the opposite of the cash flows to your firm. The investment is an outflow today, the lease payments after taxes are reflected, and the benefit from the CCA tax shield is shown. This implies a zero-sum game where the positive NPV of one party (Welease, in our example) is the negative NPV of the other (your firm). In this case, Welease hopes that your firm will do the deal.

**Resolving the Paradox:** A lease contract is not a zero sum game, if the effective tax rates between the lessee and lessor differ. In this case, both sides may benefit. For example, the tax benefits of leasing and CCA tax shields can be shared between the two firms by setting the lease payments at the appropriate level and shareholders of both firms will benefit (CCRA will lose). The firm in the higher tax bracket should be the lessor in order to take advantage of CCA (especially in the early years) and debt financing, some of which are passed on to the lessee through lower lease payments.

### Reasons for Leasing

**Good Reasons:** First, *taxes* may be reduced by leasing because a potential tax shield that cannot be used by one firm can be transferred to another by leasing. Second, certain types of *uncertainty* may be reduced that may otherwise decrease the value of the firm. Transferring the uncertainty about the residual value insures the lessee and is especially valued in industries facing changes in technology and rapid obsolescence. Third, *transactions costs* such as those associated with changes in ownership can be lower for a lease contract than for buying an asset.

**Bad Reasons:** As mentioned earlier, *classification* of a lease as operating or financial (or capital) in nature may affect debt and profitability ratios, but this impact is not likely to fool anyone. The NPV gained or lost is far more important than the effect of the lease on a firm's financial statements. It is claimed that leasing provides *100% financing* whereas secured equipment loans require a downpayment. However, lease payments are often made in advance, and implicitly secured by assets of the firm.

Other reasons specific to a firm may motivate it to engage in leasing. For example, circumventing capital expenditure control systems, a liquidity crisis, application of unused capital losses, and so on, may be factors for companies to find leasing advantageous.

## CONCEPT TEST

1.      Leases are _____ agreements between the user of the asset, the _____ and the _____, the _____ of the asset.

2.      If the leasing company purchases the asset directly from the manufacturer, this is called a _____.
        However, a firm may lease its own assets from a wholly-owned subsidiary, sometimes also known as a
        _____.

3.      _____ are often cancellable on short notice and are short-term whereas _____ are fully
        amortized where the lessee is responsible for upkeep.

4.      Tax benefits and the need for liquidity may result in a _____ transaction where a company
        _____ an asset and _____ it back.

5.      Three parties or more are included in a _____ transaction where _____ benefits are shared
        between the lessee, lessor, and _____.

6.      The four criteria that determine whether a lease should be _____ include: the lease transfers
        ownership to the _____ by the end of the term; there is an _____ at a price below fair
        market value; the term of the lease is _____ or more than the estimated economic life of the assets;
        and that the present value of the _____ is at least 90% of the _____ of the asset.

7.      For tax purposes, normally the lease payment is fully _____ . However, in a _____ only the
        _____ portion of the payment is deductible.

8.      Lessors cannot use CCA deductions to increase _____.

9.      For the company leasing the asset, the incremental cash flows include the initial investment, an _
        (inflow/outflow); the salvage value, an (inflow/outflow); the lease payments, an (inflow/outflow) ;   the
        payment shield, an (inflow/outflow); and the foregone _____ , which is an (inflow/outflow) .

10.     The discount rate which makes the net advantage to leasing (NAL) equal to zero should be (higher/lower)
        _ than the after-tax rate on the loan for the NPV to be positive.  In other words, a _____ IRR from
        the cash flows of leasing is preferred over the after-tax borrowing rate.

11.     The appropriate discount rate for leasing is the _____ after tax.

12.     The present value of a loan adjusted for tax savings on interest is equal to the _____ if the discount
        rate is the loan rate _____ .

13.     If no other assets remain in the asset class when the pool is terminated, then the salvage value can result in
        taxes saved on a _____ or taxes paid on _____ income.

14.     A _____ refers to the notion that the positive NPV of the lessee is exactly equal to the _____
        NPV of the lessor. However, if the effective _____ of the lessee and lessor differ, then the lease
        contract need not be a _____ .

15.     Reduction in _____ , _____ and _____ are cited as good reasons for leasing, whereas
        accounting classification and 100% financing are considered to be bad reasons.

## ANSWERS TO CONCEPT TEST

1.       contracted; lessee; lessor; owner

2.       direct lease; captive finance company

3.       operating leases; financial leases

4.       sale and leaseback; sells; leases

5.       leveraged lease; tax; lender

6.       capitalized; lessee; option to purchase; 75%; lease payments; market value

7.       deductible; conditional sales agreement; interest

8.       operating losses

9.       inflow; outflow; outflow; inflow; CCA tax shield; outflow

10.      lower; lower

11.      loan rate

12.      loan; after-tax

13.      terminal loss; recaptured

14.      leasing paradox; negative; tax rates; zero-sum game

15.      taxes; uncertainty; transactions costs

## PROBLEMS AND SOLUTIONS

### The following information pertains to Problems 1 to 12

A & Sons Inc., is considering buying $80,000 worth of equipment, at a 20% discount from a wholesaler, financed by a 15%, five-year term loan from the Bank of Notreal. On the other hand, the equipment may be leased from Rigget Leasers Co., requiring beginning-of-year lease payments of $20,000 per year over the five-year period. The equipment can be depreciated at a CCA rate of 30%, worth $5,000 residual value at the end of the fifth year.

### Problem 1

If A & Sons are responsible for the upkeep of the equipment, what is the CCA tax shield on the equipment, assuming a tax rate of 40%?

## Solution:

| Year | UCC | CCA | Tax Shield |
|------|-----|-----|------------|
| 1 | $40,000 | $12,000 | $4,800 |
| 2 | 68,000 | 20,400 | 8,160 |
| 3 | 47,600 | 14,280 | 5,712 |
| 4 | 33,320 | 9,996 | 3,998.4 |
| 5 | 23,324 | 6,997.2 | 2,798.88 |
| 6 | 16,326.8 | | 4,530.72 (See Solution 2) |

## Problem 2

If there are no assets left in the equipment pool calculate the tax shield on the terminal loss in Year 5.

**Solution:** The UCC balance in Year 5, prior to the sale is $16,326.8 and is reduced by the residual value of $5,000 to give a terminal loss of $11,326.8.  The tax shield is $11,326.8 x .4   =   $4,530.72.

## Problem 3

Calculate the incremental cash flows for A & Sons.

**Solution:**

|  | | | | Year | | | |
|--|---|---|---|------|---|---|---|
|  | 0 | 1 | 2 | | 3 | 4 | 5 |
| Investment | $ 80,000 | | | | | | |
| Salvage | | | | | | (5,000) | |
| Lease Payment | (20,000) | (20,000) | (20,000) | | (20,000) | (20,000) | |
| Payment Shield | | 8,000 | 8,000 | 8,000 | 8,000 | 8,000 | |
| Forgone CCA Tax Shield | (4,800) | ( 8,160) | (5,712) | | ( 3,998.4) | ( 2,798.88) | (4,530.72) |
| Total Cash Flow | $55,200 | (20,160) | (17,712) | | (15,998.4) | (14,798.88) | (1,530.72) |

## Problem 4

Calculate the implicit IRR for leasing from the incremental cash flow in Problem 3.

**Solution:** The implicit IRR is the unknown discount rate for the net advantage of leasing when the NPV is equal to zero:

$$NPV = \$55,200 - \frac{\$20,160}{(1+i)} - \frac{\$17,712}{(1+i)^2} - \frac{\$15,998.4}{(1+i)^3} - \frac{\$14,798.88}{(1+i)^4} - \frac{\$1,530.72}{(1+i)^5}$$

The IRR for leasing is 10.73%.

## Problem 5

If the Bank of Notreal is charging 15% interest, should A & Sons lease or buy?

**Solution:** The after-tax interest rate will be $.15(1 - .4) = 9\%$ if the loan is taken. This is cheaper than the implicit IRR for leasing (10.73%). So, A & Sons should buy.

## Problem 6

What is the NPV of leasing?

**Solution:** Discounting the cash flows at 9% gives us the NPV:

$$NPV = \$55,200 - \frac{\$20,160}{(1.09)} - \frac{\$17,712}{(1.09)^2} - \frac{\$15,998.4}{(1.09)^3} - \frac{\$14,798.88}{(1.09)^4} - \frac{\$1,530.72}{(1.09)^5}$$

$$= -\$2,035.71$$

## Problem 7

Suppose there is other equipment in the asset pool. What is the NAL?

**Solution:**

$$NAL = \$80,000 - [\,\$20,000 + \$20,000\,(.60)\,(3.239720) - (\$20,000)\,(\,.6)/(1.09)^5\,] -$$

$$[(.4)(.3)(\$80,000)/(.09 + .3) \times (1.045/1.09)\,] + [\,\$5,000(.3)\,(.4)/(.09 + .3)$$

$$\times 1/(1.09)^5\,] - \$5,000/(1.09)^5 = \$3,073.62$$

## Problem 8

Why, and by how much, did the NAL change from negative in Problem 6 to a positive amount in Problem 7?

**Solution:** The NAL favoured leasing when A & Sons had other equipment in the asset pool which allowed for the full tax shield on CCA instead of the write-off in Year 5. The NAL changed by $5,109.33 (-$2,035.71 to $3,073.62).

## Problem 9

At what level of lease payments will A & Sons be indifferent towards leasing or buying? Assume that other equipment is in the pool so that the tax write-off in year 5 is ignored.

**Solution:** In the NAL equation used in the solution to Problem 7, we equate NAL to zero and solve for the unknown lease payments which equal $21,203.51 or approximately $21,204. At this level of payment, A & Sons will be indifferent between leasing and buying.

## Problem 10

Demonstrate that, if we use the after-tax loan rate as the appropriate discount rate, the present value after-tax cost of the loan is equal to the loan.  Set up a loan amortization table to arrive at your conclusion.

**Solution:**

| Period | Loan Payments (a) | Balance (b) | Interest (c) | Tax Shield (d) | After-Tax Payment (e) | Present value Equivalent (f) |
|--------|-------------------|-------------|--------------|----------------|------------------------|------------------------------|
| 1 | 23,865 | 80,000 | 12,000 | 4,800 | 19,065 | 17,491 |
| 2 | 23,865 | 68,135 | 10,220 | 4,088 | 19,777 | 16,646 |
| 3 | 23,865 | 54,490 | 8,174 | 3,270 | 20,595 | 15,903 |
| 4 | 23,865 | 38,799 | 5,820 | 2,328 | 21,537 | 15,257 |
| 5 | 23,865 | 20,752 | 3,113 | 1,245 | 22,620 | 14,701 |

a)  $80,000 / PVIFA (15\%,5) = \$80,000 / 3.352155 = \$23,865.24$
b)  Outstanding loan less amortized portion of the payment.  For example, amortized portion of Year 1 payment is $23,865 - $12,000 = $11,865.  Similarly, Year 2 portion of payment is $23,865 - $10,220 = $13,645.
c)  Loan balance times the interest rate of 15%
d)  Interest times the tax rate of 40%
e)  Payments less tax shield
f)  Discounted at the after-tax loan rate of 9%

The sum of all present value equivalents in the last column are equal to $79,998, which is equal to the loan of $80,000. (The $2 difference is due to rounding.)

## Problem 11

What are the cash flows from the lessor's perspective?

**Solution:**

| | Year | | | | | |
|---|---|---|---|---|---|---|
| | 0 | 1 | 2 | 3 | 4 | 5 |
| Investment | $(80,000) | | | | | |
| Salvage | | | | | 5,000 | |
| Lease Payment | 20,000 | 20,000 | 20,000 20,000 | 20,000 | | |
| Payment Shield | | (8,000) | (8,000) (8,000) | (8,000) | (8,000) | |
| CCA Tax Shield | 4,800 | 8,160 | 5,712 | 3,998.4 | 2,798.88 | 4,530.7 |
| Total Cash Flow | $(55,200) | 20,160 | 17,712  15,998.4 | 14,798.88 | 1,530.7 | |

NAL  =  $2,035.71

## Problem 12

What is the implicit rate of return for the lease company if you consider the lease payments and the investment in equipment, ignoring taxes?

**Solution:** The implicit return earned by Rigget Lease Co., can be found by solving for the interest rate in the following equation:      $80,000   =   $20,000   +   $20,000 x (PVIFA i%,4).   The solution is i  =  12.59%.

## Problem 13

Digital Manufacturing wishes to lease a microcomputer that costs $800,000 for lease payments of $210,000 per year, made in advance, for each of the next five years.  The equipment has a five-year useful life with no expected salvage value and a CCA rate of 30%.  The firm's marginal tax rate is 40%.  The after-tax cost of borrowing is 9%.  What is the present value of the foregone CCA tax shield if Digital decides to lease?

**Solution:** The foregone CCA tax shield is:

$$\frac{(\$800,000)\,(.4)\,(.3)}{.09\ +\ .3}\quad \times \quad \frac{1.045}{1.09}\quad =\quad \$235,992$$

## Problem 14

What is the present value of after-tax lease payments for Digital, if the tax shield on the payments lagged by one period?

**Solution:** The present value of the first payment is $210,000 plus the present value of the next four after-tax payments is $210,000 (.60) (PVIFA 9%,4)   =   $408,205 minus the present value of the lagged tax shield is $210,000 (.4) (PVIFA 9%,5)   =   $326,731. This adds up to $210,000  +  $408,205  -  $326,731 = $291,474.

## Problem 15

What is the net advantage of leasing for Digital?

**Solution:**   The NAL is $800,000  -  $291,474  -  $235,992  =  $272,534.  Digital should prefer leasing.

# 23        Mergers and Acquisitions

## CHAPTER HIGHLIGHTS

In principle, the decision to acquire another firm is a capital budgeting decision.  However, since the net present value of such an acquisition is difficult to measure, the subject of mergers and acquisitions warrants specific attention.

Mergers differ from ordinary investment decisions in at least four ways.  First, the value of a merger may depend on benefits, referred to as strategic fits and synergies.  Second, the accounting, tax, and legal aspects of a merger are complex.  Third, mergers often involve issues of corporate control (related to the conflict between managers and shareholders).  Finally, mergers are often 'unfriendly' transactions because management and/or shareholders of the sought-after firm do not want the firm to be acquired and may resort to defensive tactics.

## THE LEGAL FORMS OF ACQUISITIONS

The legal mechanism used by one firm to acquire another takes one of the following forms: (1) merger or consolidation, (2) stock acquisition, or (3) asset acquisition.  In discussing acquisitions, the acquiring firm is referred to as the *bidder*; the firm that is being bought is the *target firm;* and the cash or securities offered to the target firm is the *consideration*.

**Merger or Consolidation:**  A merger is the absorption of one firm by another; the acquiring firm retains its identity while the acquired firm ceases to exist. In a consolidation, an entirely new firm is created.  The shareholders of each firm exchange their shares for shares of the new firm.  Both the Canadian and Ontario Business Corporation Acts refer to combinations of firms as amalgamations.  We will use the general term merger to refer to any type of reorganization.

The primary advantage of a merger is its legal simplicity.  A disadvantage of a merger is the fact that the shareholders of each firm must vote to approve a merger; usually, a two-thirds majority is required for approval.

**Acquisition of Stock:**  Another way to acquire a firm is to buy the target firm's voting stock directly from shareholders.  This is most often accomplished through a tender offer.  This means the acquiring firm makes an offer directly to the shareholders of a firm to buy the firm's common stock.

A tender offer does not require a shareholder vote for approval; those wishing to keep their stock simply do not 'tender' their shares to the acquiring firm, and they thereby retain their ownership interest in the target firm.  A tender offer bypasses both the board of directors and the management of the target firm.  This is important because the management of the target firm may be opposed to the acquisition.  However, management's resistance can make this form of acquisition quite expensive.  Often, a minority of shareholders choose not to sell their shares, so that the firm is not completely absorbed; complete absorption requires a merger.  Many stock acquisitions are subsequently completed as a formal merger.

**Acquisition of Assets:**  A firm can acquire another firm by purchasing the assets of the target firm.  This procedure involves a costly legal transfer of title to the assets and must be approved by the shareholders of the selling firm.

**Acquisition Classifications:**  Acquisitions can be classified as *horizontal, vertical*, or *conglomerate*.  A horizontal acquisition involves two firms which compete in the same product market.  A vertical acquisition involves firms in different stages of the production process.  Conglomerate acquisitions involve firms in unrelated lines of business.

**A Note on Takeovers:**  A *takeover* is the transfer of control of a firm from one group to another.  The acquiring firm, or bidder, makes an offer to pay cash or securities in order to acquire the target firm.  A takeover can occur by acquisition (as described above), a *proxy contest*, or a *going-private transaction.*

A proxy authorizes another party to cast a shareholder's votes.  In a proxy contest, a group of dissident shareholders seeks to obtain enough proxies from the firm's existing shareholders to gain control of the board of directors.  In a going-private transaction, a small group of investors buys all of the firm's common stock.  The stock is then delisted, so that it no longer trades on a stock exchange.  Since a substantial portion of the financing for these transactions is generally obtained by borrowing, going-private transactions are often referred to as *leveraged buyouts* (LBOs).  The term *management buyout* is used when the bidding group includes existing management.

## TAXES AND ACQUISITIONS

The acquisition of one firm by another may or may not be a taxable transaction.

**Determinants of Tax Status:** The primary issue in determining the tax status of an acquisition is whether the shareholders of the acquired firm have sold their shares, resulting in a realized, taxable capital gain, or exchanged their shares for new shares of equal value. The former is a *taxable acquisition,* while the latter is a *tax-free acquisition.*  The general requirements for tax-free status are that the acquisition involves two Canadian corporations subject to corporate income tax and that there be continuity of equity interest.

For a taxable acquisition, the shareholders of the acquired firm have a realized, taxable capital gain equal to the difference between the price they receive for their shares and the initial purchase price of their stock.  In addition, the acquiring firm may elect to 'write-up' the value of the assets acquired, based on the cost of the acquisition. This has the advantage of increasing the firm's subsequent depreciation expenses.  However, such a write-up also requires that the firm treat the acquisition price of the asset as currently taxable income.

## ACCOUNTING FOR ACQUISITIONS

For accounting purposes, an acquisition is treated as either a purchase or a pooling of interests.

**The Purchase Method:** The *purchase accounting method* for an acquisition requires that the assets of the acquired firm be reported at fair market value on the financial statements of the acquiring firm.  The difference between the purchase price and the fair market value of the acquired assets is identified as 'goodwill' on the balance sheet of the acquiring firm.  The goodwill is amortized over a period of years, but this amortization is not a tax-deductible expense.  This means that the purchase accounting method results in lower reported net income than the pooling accounting method.  This, in turn has a negative effect on traditional accounting measures of performance, such as ROA and ROE.

**Pooling of Interests:**  With a *pooling of interests,* the balance sheets of the two firms are simply combined. Asset values are not adjusted to market value and, therefore, no goodwill is created.

**Which is Better: Purchase or Pooling of Interests?**  Income reported to shareholders after an acquisition is lower for the purchase method because the amortization of goodwill and the write-up of asset values result in higher depreciation expenses.  Neither of these considerations has any effect on the firm's taxable income.  Therefore, these alternative accounting treatments do not have any consequences for cash flow or net present value determinations.

## GAINS FROM ACQUISITION

In this section, we analyze the source of value derived from an acquisition.

**Synergy:** If Firm A (with value $V_A$) is acquiring Firm B (with value $V_B$), then the acquisition is beneficial to the shareholders of Firm A if:

$$V_{AB} > V_A + V_B$$

where $V_{AB}$ is the value of the combined firm.

The incremental net gain derived from the acquisition ($\Delta V$) is:

$$\Delta V \;=\; V_{AB} - (V_A + V_B)$$

If $\Delta V$ is positive, the acquisition is said to generate synergy.  In this case, the value of the whole ($V_{AB}$) is greater than the value of the sum of its parts ($V_A + V_B$).  Another way of looking at this relationship is to define the value of Firm B to Firm A as the sum of $\Delta V$ and $V_B$:

$$V^*_B \;=\; \Delta V + V_B$$

where $V^*_B$ is defined as the value of Firm B to Firm A.  If A and B are public companies, their values as separate companies can be observed in the marketplace.  Synergy exists when the cash flow for the combined firm is greater than the sum of the cash flows for the two firms as separate entities.  The gain from the merger is the present value of this difference in cash flows.

The incremental cash flow ($\Delta CF$) can be represented in terms of four components:

$$\Delta CF \;=\; \Delta EBIT + \Delta Depreciation - \Delta Tax - \Delta Capital\ Requirements$$

$$=\; \Delta Revenue - \Delta Cost - \Delta Tax - \Delta Capital\ Requirements$$

where the four components are the difference in revenues, costs, taxes, and capital requirements, respectively. Therefore, the synergy from an acquisition results from one or more of the following: (1) revenue enhancement, (2) cost reduction, (3) lower taxes, or (4) lower capital requirements.

**Revenue Enhancement:** Increased revenues may result from marketing gains, strategic benefits, and increases in market power.  Marketing gains are produced by more effective advertising, an improved distribution network, and a more balanced product mix.  Strategic benefits are the opportunities presented by options to enter and exploit new lines of business.  Finally, a merger may reduce competition, and thereby increase market power, allowing the company to increase prices and obtain monopoly profits.  Such mergers, of course, may run afoul of laws designed to limit takeovers that may limit market competition.  In general, there is little evidence that market power has been a major motivation for acquisitions.

**Cost Reductions:** Under some circumstances, larger firms operate more efficiently than two smaller firms.

Horizontal mergers sometimes generate 'economies of scale.' This means that the average production cost decreases following the merger. A vertical merger may allow a firm to save by more closely coordinating production and distribution; vertical mergers often allow for transfer of technology among different products. Economies may also be achieved when firms have complementary resources (e.g., one firm has excess production capacity and another has insufficient capacity). Some acquisitions also serve to remove inefficient management.

**Tax Gains:** Tax gains resulting from a merger may arise because of unused tax losses, unused debt capacity, surplus funds, or the ability to write-up the value of depreciable assets. A profitable firm may find it advantageous to acquire a firm that has *net operating losses* (NOL). The profitable firm can then use these losses to reduce taxes on current income. A firm with NOL can 'carry back' losses for three years and 'carry forward' losses for up to seven years. However, the benefit of an acquisition must be greater than the tax benefit the acquired firm could derive from its own losses. In addition, the tax credit may not be allowed if the primary purpose of the acquisition is to avoid taxes.

**Unused Debt Capacity:** Debt financing provides tax benefits because interest payments are tax deductible. Acquisition of a firm with a relatively low level of debt can be beneficial to the acquiring firm since the combined firm can then obtain additional debt financing. That is, the merged firm may be able to increase its debt capacity, thereby producing significant tax savings.

**Surplus Funds:** A firm with surplus funds may have motivation for acquiring another firm. The alternatives for a firm with surplus funds are the distribution of surplus funds as a dividend or the repurchase of some of the firm's outstanding shares. However, the former alternative increases shareholders' income taxes, while the latter may be illegal if the sole purpose is to avoid taxes. With an acquisition, no income taxes are paid by the shareholders of the acquiring firm.

**Changing Capital Requirements:** Reduced capital requirements might result from an acquisition if one of the merged firms has excess capacity while the other requires additional capacity in order to expand.

**Avoiding Mistakes:** In evaluating the profitability of an acquisition, an analyst must be aware of sources of potential errors. First, market values should be used to establish the value of an opportunity. Second, only cash flows that are incremental to the acquisition are relevant; the value of a target firm as a separate entity already reflects the value of its existing cash flows. Third, the discount rate used should reflect the risk associated with the incremental cash flows. The acquiring firm, for example, should not use its own cost of capital to value the cash flows of a firm to be acquired. Finally, acquisition generally involves significant fees and costs which are incremental expenses and therefore must not be ignored.

## SOME FINANCIAL SIDE EFFECTS OF ACQUISITIONS

Two important financial side effects associated with an acquisition are EPS growth and diversification. As we demonstrate in this section, neither of these effects has any impact on the value of the combined firm.

**EPS Growth:** Firm A has decided to acquire Firm B through an exchange of stock. Both firms are 100% equity. The following is some pre-merger information:

|                      | Firm A  | Firm B  |
|----------------------|---------|---------|
| Total earnings       | $100    | $200    |
| Shares outstanding   | 200     | 500     |
| Price per share      | $ 10    | $ 2     |

Firm B has a market value of ($2 × 500) = $1,000. To acquire Firm B, Firm A will have to give ($1,000/$10) = 100 shares to the shareholders of Firm B. The combined firm will have 300 shares outstanding.

Before the merger, earnings per share (EPS) for Firm A are ($100/200) = $ .50.  After the merger, the combined firm will have $300 in earnings and 300 shares, so EPS will be $1 per share, a 100% growth!  Of course, no real change has occurred.  Firm A has a higher value per share than does Firm B, so B's 500 shares are replaced with 100 shares of A.  Naturally, EPS rises, but this increase has no cash flow consequences, and, as a result, no impact on value.

**Diversification:**  Diversification is often cited as a benefit in mergers.  However, diversification by itself does not create value because the shareholders of the acquiring firm can accomplish the same thing by purchasing stock in the target firm.

To understand that a merger does not provide a diversification benefit to the shareholders of the acquiring firm, recall that variability of returns consists of unsystematic and systematic components.  Systematic variability cannot be eliminated by any form of diversification, including merger.  Unsystematic variability can be reduced by diversification.  However, an individual investor can achieve this diversification very inexpensively by purchasing shares of stock in different companies.

## THE COST OF AN ACQUISITION

The incremental net gain derived from a merger is:

$$\Delta V = V_{AB} - (V_A + V_B)$$

We  define the value of Firm B to Firm A as:

$$V^*_B = \Delta V + V_B$$

The net present value of a merger is:

$$NPV = V^*_B - \text{Cost to Firm A of the acquisition}$$

The NPV of the merger can be calculated from the following information for Firm A and Firm B:

|                    | Firm A   | Firm B   |
|--------------------|----------|----------|
| Price per share    | $   10   | $   5    |
| Number of shares   | 20       | 20       |
| Total market value | $  200   | $ 100    |

Both firms are all-equity firms.  The incremental net gain ($\Delta V$) is $80 and Firm B will agree to the acquisition at a price of $150.  The difference between the acquisition price and $V_B$ is referred to as the *merger premium*.  In this example, the merger premium is ($150 – $100) = $50.

To compute the net present value of the acquisition, we first compute the value of Firm B to Firm A.

$$V^*_B = \Delta V + V_B = \$80 + \$100 = \$180$$

Next, we determine the cost to Firm A of the acquisition.  Even though Firm B agrees to be acquired for $150, the cost of the acquisition to Firm A varies with the means of payment from Firm A to Firm B. The two methods of payment are a cash acquisition and a stock acquisition.

**Case I - Cash Acquisition:** If the cost of the acquisition is paid in cash, then the net present value is:

$$\text{NPV} = V^*_B - \text{Cost} = \$180 - \$150 = \$30$$

Since the net present value of the acquisition is positive, the acquisition is beneficial to the shareholders of Firm A. The value of the merged firm after the acquisition is equal to the value of the combined firm less the cash paid for Firm B:

$$V_{AB} = V_A + V^*_B - \text{Cost} = \$200 + \$180 - \$150 = \$230$$

After the merger, the value of the merged firm's stock will increase to $[(\$380 - \$150)/20] = \$11.50$ per share. The increase of $\$1.50$ per share above the price of Firm A stock is the net present value of $\$30$ on a per share basis, or $(\$30/20) = \$1.50$ per share gain.

**Case II - Stock Acquisition:** Suppose Firm A pays the $\$150$ acquisition cost by giving 15 shares of stock to the shareholders of Firm B. The cost appears to be $\$150$. However, this is an underestimate of the actual cost. After the merger, the value of the firm is:

$$V_{AB} = V_A + V_B + \Delta V = \$200 + \$100 + \$80 = \$380$$

The merged firm has $(20 + 15) = 35$ shares outstanding, the price per share is $(\$380/35) = \$10.857$. Therefore, the actual cost of the acquisition is $(15 \times \$10.857) = \$162.86$, and the net present value of the merger is:

$$\text{NPV} = V^*_B - \text{Cost} = \$180 - \$162.86 = \$17.14$$

Note that the $\$10.857$ per share value in this case is less than the $\$11.50$ value indicated above for a cash acquisition. The difference arises from the fact that a portion of the $\$30$ net present value for the cash acquisition now goes to the new shareholders. The 15 new shares of stock are each worth $(\$10.857 - \$10) = \$.857$ more than the pre-merger value of Firm A stock, for a total of $(15 \times \$.857) = \$12.86$ to the former shareholders of Firm B. That is, as indicated above, the shareholders of Firm B actually receive $\$162.86$ in this merger.

In a cash merger, the potential gains of the merger go entirely to the shareholders of the acquiring firm. When a merger is financed by an exchange of stock, the benefits are shared by the stockholders of both firms.

**Cash versus Common Stock:** The decision as to whether an acquisition should be financed with cash or stock depends on three factors. First, the use of stock means that the shareholders of the acquired firm will share in any gains from the merger; on the other hand, if the merger is unsuccessful, then the acquired firm's shareholders will share in the loss. Second, a cash acquisition is usually a taxable transaction; this consideration may result in a higher price for the target firm. Third, a cash acquisition does not affect control of the acquiring firm.

## DEFENSIVE TACTICS

Management of a target firm frequently resists takeover attempts.  This resistance may enable shareholders to subsequently receive a higher price for their shares.  On the other hand, management resistance to a takeover may be based largely, if not exclusively, on management's desire to protect its own interests.  The defensive tactics commonly used by the management of a target firm in order to resist takeovers are described below.

**The Control Block and the Corporate Charter:**  The *corporate charter* consists of the firm's articles of incorporation and the corporate bylaws.  These documents specify the firm's governance rules.  The charter can be amended to make acquisition difficult for the acquiring firm.  For example, the charter can be amended to require that an 80% majority of shareholders must vote to approve a merger.  Such a 'super majority' provision is in contrast to the usual two-thirds majority required for approval of a merger.  Another strategy is the 'staggering' of the election of board members so that only a few board members are elected at any one time.  This makes it more difficult to change the membership of the board quickly.

**Repurchase/Standstill Agreements:**  A *standstill agreement* specifies that the bidding firm will limit its holdings in the target firm.  Such agreements often precede a *targeted repurchase;* under this arrangement, the target firm buys back its own stock from the bidder.  Since this repurchase is usually at a premium above market price, the premium is viewed by critics as a bribe, and is frequently termed *greenmail.*

**Exclusionary Offers:**  In an *exclusionary self-tender*, the target firm offers to buy back its own stock, at a premium, from all shareholders except the bidder.  By excluding the bidder, the firm effectively transfers wealth to other shareholders by reducing the value of the bidder's stock.

**Poison Pills and Share Rights Plans:**  A *poison pill* is a procedure designed to force a bidder to negotiate with the management of a target firm, rather than acquire the firm by means of a tender offer.  Such procedures are sometimes called *share rights plans* (SRPs).  The potential target firm's shareholders receive share rights which entitle them to purchase shares of stock at a specified price.  This exercise price is substantially below the current market price of the firm's stock.  Normally, the rights cannot be exercised or sold.  However, the rights are 'triggered' when a tender offer is announced, or when an investor acquires 20% of the target firm's stock. At that point, the rights can be exercised.   This essentially allows shareholders of the target firm to purchase shares in the merged firm at 'bargain' prices.  This makes the takeover less attractive to potential buyers.

**Going Private and Leveraged Buyouts:**  A privately-owned firm is not subject to unfriendly takeovers.  A publicly-traded firm 'goes private' when a group, which usually includes the existing management, buys all of the firm's publicly held stock and takes it off the market.  Although such a buyout might be regarded as a takeover defence by the target firm's management, the target firm's shareholders view the buyout as a takeover itself.

## SOME EVIDENCE ON ACQUISITIONS

The impact of acquisitions on shareholder wealth has been extensively studied. Some empirical evidence regarding this issue is considered here.

There is little doubt that the shareholders of the acquired firm benefit substantially from an acquisition.  Excess returns for these shareholders are approximately 20% for mergers and 30% for tender offers.  Tender offers are typically made when a proposed friendly merger is rejected by the management of the target firm.  Subsequent tender offers must generally be at a higher price, resulting in the larger abnormal returns.

The gains to the shareholders of acquiring firms are difficult to measure. The best evidence suggests that these shareholders gain little, if anything, from an acquisition, and in fact, losses in value subsequent to merger announcements are not unusual. Some studies indicate that excess returns to shareholders of the acquiring firm average approximately 4% for tender offers and zero for mergers, while other studies indicate significant losses. These results seem to suggest that overvaluation of the target firm by the bidding firm is common. An alternative explanation of the evidence is that management is simply not pursuing the best interests of the shareholders in such cases.

## CONCEPT TEST

1.  The following terminology is often used when discussing acquisitions: the acquiring firm is referred to as the _____ ; the firm that is being sought is the _____ ; and, the cash or securities offered to the target firm is the _____ .

2.  Several different legal mechanisms are used by firms seeking to acquire other firms. The absorption of one firm by another, so that the acquiring firm retains its identity while the acquired firm ceases to exist, is called a(n) _____ . In a(n) _____ , an entirely new firm is created; the shareholders of each of the two firms involved exchange their shares for shares of the new firm. Another way to acquire a firm is to buy the target firm's voting stock directly from shareholders; this is generally accomplished through a process called a(n) _____ . A firm can also buy another firm by purchasing the _____ of the target firm.

3.  If the two firms compete in the same product market, the acquisition is called a(n) _____ acquisition. A reorganization of firms at different stages of the production process is a(n) _____ acquisition. Acquisitions involving firms in unrelated lines of business are called _____ acquisitions.

4.  The transfer of control of a firm from one group to another is called a(n) _____ ; the acquiring firm makes an offer to pay cash or securities in order to acquire the target firm. A takeover can occur by acquisition or in two other alternative ways. A proxy authorizes another party to _____ . In a(n) _____ contest, a group of dissident shareholders seeks to obtain enough proxies from the firm's existing shareholders in order to gain control of the board of directors. In a(n) _____ transaction, a small group of investors buys all of the firm's common stock; since a substantial portion of the financing for these transactions is generally obtained by borrowing, these transactions are often referred to as _____ . When the bidding group includes existing management, the term _____ is used.

5.  The acquisition of one firm by another may or may not be a taxable transaction. The primary issue in determining the tax status is whether the shareholders of the acquired firm have sold their shares, resulting in a realized _____ , or exchanged their shares for new shares of equal value. The former (is/is not) a taxable acquisition, while the latter (is/is not) a taxable acquisition.

6.  For accounting purposes, an acquisition is treated in one of two alternative ways. The _____ method requires that the assets of the acquired firm be reported at fair market value on the financial statements of the acquiring firm; the difference between the purchase price and the fair market value of the acquired assets is identified as _____ on the balance sheet of the acquiring firm. The second alternative treatment is a(n) _____ ; in this case, the balance sheets of the two firms are simply combined and asset values are not adjusted to market value.

7.      If Firm A (with value $V_A$) is acquiring Firm B (with value $V_B$), then the acquisition is beneficial to the stockholders of Firm A if: $V_{AB} >$ _____ ,where $V_{AB}$ is the value of the combined firm. The incremental net gain derived from the acquisition ($\Delta V$) is:      $\Delta V =$ _____ . If $\Delta V$ is positive, the acquisition is said to generate _____ . Another way of looking at this relationship is to define the value of Firm B to Firm A as the sum of $\Delta V$ and $V_B$. That is: $V^*_B =$ _____ , where $V^*_B$ is defined as the value of Firm B to Firm A.

8.      When the cash flow for the combined firm is greater than the sum of the cash flows for the two firms as separate entities, the acquisition is said to generate _____ . The gain from the merger is the present value of this difference in cash flows. The incremental cash flow ($\Delta CF$) can be represented in terms of four components: $\Delta CF = \Delta$ _____ $- \Delta$ _____ $- \Delta$ _____ $- \Delta$ _____ .
        Therefore, the synergy from an acquisition results from one or more of the following: (1) increase in _____ , (2) decrease in _____ , (3) decrease in _____ , or (4) decrease in _____ .

9.      The NPV of a merger is: _____ $-$ _____ . The difference between the acquisition price and $V_A$ is the _____ . The cost of the acquisition varies with the means of payment from Firm A to Firm B. The two methods of payment are a(n) _____ acquisition and a(n) _____ acquisition.

10.     If the cost of the acquisition is paid in cash, then the net present value is:  NPV = _____ $-$ _____ . The value of the merged firm after the acquisition is equal to the value of the combined firm less the cash paid for Firm B:  $V_{AB} =$ _____ $+$ _____ $-$ _____

11.     In a cash merger, the benefits of the merger go entirely to _____ . For a stock acquisition, a portion of the net present value for the cash acquisition goes to _____ . When a merger is financed by an exchange of stock, the benefits are shared by _____ .

12.     Several different defensive tactics are commonly used by the management of a target firm in order to resist takeovers. The firm's articles of incorporation and the corporate bylaws constitute the _____ ; these documents can be amended to make acquisition difficult for the acquiring firm by requiring that an 80% majority of shareholders must vote to approve a merger. An agreement which specifies that the bidding firm will limit its holdings in the target firm is called a(n) _____ agreement. Such agreements often precede a _____ ; under this arrangement, the target firm buys back its own stock from the bidder. The premium paid in such arrangements is viewed by critics as a bribe, and is frequently termed _____ . In a(n) _____ , the target firm offers to buy back its own stock, at a premium, from all shareholders except the bidder. A(n) _____ is a procedure designed to force a bidder to negotiate with the management of a target firm, rather than acquire the firm by means of a tender offer; such procedures are sometimes called _____ .


## ANSWERS TO CONCEPT TEST

1.      bidder; target firm; consideration

2.      merger; consolidation; tender offer; assets

3.      horizontal; vertical; conglomerate

4.      takeover; cast a shareholder's votes; proxy; going-private; leveraged buyouts; management buyout

5.      capital gain; is; is not

6.      purchase accounting; goodwill; pooling of interests

7.      $(V_A + V_B)$; $[V_{AB} - (V_A + V_B)]$; synergy; $(\Delta V + V_B)$

8.      synergy; revenues; cost; taxes; capital requirements; revenues; costs; taxes; capital requirements

9.      $V^*_B$; Cost to Firm A of the acquisition; merger premium; cash; stock

10.     $V^*_B$; Cost; $V_A$; $V^*_B$; Cost

11.     the shareholders of the acquiring firm; the new shareholders; the shareholders of both the acquiring and the acquired firm

12.     corporate charter; standstill; targeted repurchase; greenmail; exclusionary self-tender; poison pill; share rights plans

## PROBLEMS AND SOLUTIONS

### Problem 1

PMG Corporation wants to acquire JPH Corporation through a cash acquisition.  The incremental gain is $400, and JPH Corp. will agree to the acquisition at the price of $1,000.  Given the information below, what is the NPV of the acquisition?  What is the value of the merged firm after the acquisition?

|                    | PMG     | JPH   |
|--------------------|---------|-------|
| Price per share    | $  15   | $ 8   |
| Number of shares   | 120     | 100   |
| Total market value | $1,800  | $800  |

**Solution:** First, compute the net present value of the acquisition of JPH to MG:

$$V^*_{JPH}  =  \Delta V +  V_{JPH}  =  \$400 + \$800  =  \$1,200$$

With a cash acquisition, the cost to PMG Corp. is $1,000, making the NPV

$$NPV  =  V^*_{JPH} - Cost  =  \$1,200 - \$1,000  =  \$200$$

The NPV of the acquisition is positive, making it beneficial to PMG Corp.  The value of the merged firm is:

$$V_{PMG,JPH}  =  V_{PMG} + V^*_{JPH} - cost  =  \$1,800 + \$1,200 - \$1,000  =  \$2,000$$

## Problem 2

Suppose PMG Corporation decides to acquire JPH Corporation through an exchange of shares. How much will this cost? What is the NPV of the acquisition? Which type of acquisition would the shareholders of PMG Corporation prefer? Why?

**Solution:** To acquire JPH Corp., PMG Corp. will have to pay ($1,000 / $15) = 66 2/3 shares to the shareholders of JPH Corporation. After the merger, the value of the firm will be:

$$V_{PMG,JPH} \ = \ V_{PMG} + V_{JPH} + \Delta V \ = \ \$1,800 + \$800 + \$400 \ = \ \$3,000$$

The merged firm has (120 + 66 2/3) = 186 2/3 shares outstanding. Therefore, the price per share is $3,000 / 186 2/3 = $16.07, making the actual price of the acquisition (66 2/3 x $16.07) = $1,071.33. The NPV of the acquisition is

$$NPV \ = \ V*_{JPH} - Cost \ = \ \$1,200 - \$1,071.33 \ = \ \$128.67$$

In the cash acquisition, the value of PMG's stock increases to ($3,000 - $1,000) / 120 = $16.67 per share, a gain of 41.67 per share (which is the same as the NPV divided by the number of shares). With a stock acquisition, the new share price is $16.07, a gain of $1.07 per share, because some of the NPV of the merger goes to the shareholders of JPH. So, shareholders of PMG will prefer a cash acquisition because the merger gains go entirely to them.

**Use the following information to solve Problems 3 to 10. Firms A and B have no debt outstanding.**

|                     | Firm A   | Firm B   |
| ------------------- | -------- | -------- |
| Total earnings      | $3,500   | $1,400   |
| Shares outstanding  | 700      | 350      |
| Price per share     | $  50    | $  20    |

## Problem 3

Firm A is considering the acquisition of Firm B. Firm A has estimated that the value of the combined firm will be $43,000. Firm B has indicated that it would accept a cash purchase offer of $22 per share. Should Firm A proceed with the acquisition?

**Solution:** At $22 per share, Firm A is paying ($22 × 350) = $7,700 to acquire Firm B. The value of Firm A is: $V_A$ = $50 × 700 = $35,000. The value of Firm B is: $V_B$ = $20 × 350 = $7,000 . The incremental net gain derived from the merger is: $\Delta V = V_{AB} - (V_A + V_B) = \$43,000 - (\$35,000 + \$7,000) = \$1,000$. The value of Firm B to Firm A is: $V*_B = \Delta V + V_B = \$1,000 + \$7,000 = \$8,000$ .The net present value of the merger is: $NPV = V*_B - Cost$ to Firm A of the acquisition = $8,000 – $7,700 = $300 . Since the net present value is positive, the acquisition is beneficial to the shareholders of Firm A. Firm A should proceed with the acquisition.

## Problem 4

For the data of Problem 3, what is the synergy from the merger? What is the merger premium paid for the acquisition? Use the synergy and the premium to determine the net present value of the acquisition.

**Solution:** The synergy is equal to the value of the combined firm less the total value of the two separate firms: $\Delta V = V_{AB} - (V_A + V_B) = \$1,000$ as computed in the solution to Problem 3.

The merger premium is the difference between the acquisition price and $V_B$, the market value of the acquired firm: $(\$22 \times 350) - (\$20 \times 350) = \$700$. The net premium value can be computed as the synergy minus the merger premium, or $(\$1,000 - \$700) = \$300$, as indicated in Problem 3.


## Problem 5

For the data of Problem 3, what is the price of Firm A's stock after the merger?

**Solution:** The net present value of the merger is $300, so the stock will increase in value by $(\$300/700) = \$.43$ per share. The stock price will be $50.43. Note that, in the case of a cash acquisition, the net present value accrues to the shareholders of the acquiring firm.

This result can be computed in an alternative manner. The value of Firm A ($V_A$) is $35,000 prior to the merger. The value of the merged firm after the acquisition is: $V_{AB} = V_A + V^*_B - Cost = \$35,000 + (\$8,000 - \$7,700) = \$35,300$. The per share value is thus $(\$35,300/700) = \$50.43$, as previously calculated.


## Problem 6

For the data of Problem 3, what is the net present value of the merger if Firm A pays for the acquisition with common stock, based on the current market prices? What is the post-merger price of the stock?

**Solution:** Firm A will have to give $(\$22/\$50) = .44$ shares of its stock for every share of B, or $(.44 \times 350) = 154$ shares. This result is also equal to the cash price of the acquisition divided by the current market value of a share of Firm A stock: $(\$7,700/\$50) = 154$. The new firm will have a total of 854 shares outstanding. After the merger, the value of the firm is: $V_{AB} = V_A + V_B + \Delta V = \$35,000 + \$7,000 + \$1,000 = \$43,000$.

Consequently, the per share value is $(\$43,000/854) = \$50.3513$, and the actual cost of the acquisition is $(154 \times \$50.3513) = \$7,754.10$. the net present value of the merger is: $NPV = V^*_B - Cost = \$8,000 - \$7,754.10 = \$245.90$.


## Problem 7

For the data of Problem 6, what is the synergy from the merger? What is the merger premium paid for the acquisition? Use the synergy and the premium to determine the net present value of the acquisition. Why is the net present value lower for the acquisition through exchange of stock in Problem 4 compared to the acquisition for cash in Problem 3?

**Solution:** The synergy is $1,000, as indicated in Problem 4. The merger premium is the difference between the acquisition price and the market value of the acquired firm: $\$7,754.10 - (\$20 \times 350) = \$754.10$

The net present value is the synergy minus the merger premium, or $(\$1,000 - \$754.10) = \$245.90$. This NPV is $54.10 less than the $300 NPV of the acquisition for cash. When the acquisition is paid for with an exchange of stock, the shareholders of Firm B receive a proportionate part of the net present value of the acquisition: $(154/854) \times \$300 = \$54.10$.

This difference can also be viewed as the increment in the value of the shares of Firm A which is given to the shareholders of Firm B:  $(\$50.3513 - \$50) \times 154 = \$54.10$

## Problem 8

Problem 3 indicates that the shareholders of Firm B are willing to accept $7,700 for the acquisition.  How many shares of Firm A stock should Firm B shareholders receive so that they actually receive the $7,700 price?

**Solution:** In order for the Firm B shareholders to receive $7,700, they must receive stock which has a total value equal to $(\$7,700 / \$43,000) = .17907 = 17.907\%$ of the merged firm.  Therefore, the new shares issued must represent 17.907% of the outstanding shares of the merged firm.  This value is determined by solving for x in the following equation:

$$[x / (700 + x)] \quad = \quad .17907$$

The number of new shares which should be issued to the shareholders of Firm B is 152.691, so that the total number of shares outstanding will then be $(700 + 152.691) = 852.691$.  The price per share will be $(\$43,000/852.691) =$ $50.4386$.  The shareholders of Firm B receive 152.691 shares worth $50.4286, for a total value of $(152.69 \times \$50.4286) = \$7,700$.

## Problem 9

Suppose that, for the data in Problem 3, Firm A acquires Firm B in exchange for stock valued at $21 per share. How will this affect earnings per share for Firm A?

**Solution:**  The new firm will have total earnings of $4,900.   At $21 per share, Firm A will have to give $[(\$21/\$50) \times 350] = 147$ shares to the shareholders of Firm B, so that the new firm will have 847 shares outstanding.  EPS will be $(\$4,900/847) = \$5.785$ per share; this is an increase of $.785 from the pre-merger level of $5 per share.

## Problem 10

For the data of Problem 9, what is the price per share of the new firm if the market is 'fooled' by this earnings growth (i.e., if the P/E ratio does not change)?  What will the P/E ratio be if the market is not 'fooled?'

**Solution:**  Before the merger, Firm A had a P/E ratio of $(\$50/\$5) = 10$.  If the market is fooled, in the sense that this P/E ratio is unchanged after the merger, the stock will rise in value to $(10 \times \$5.785) = \$57.85$.

If the market is not fooled, then the P/E ratio will fall to $(\$43,000/\$4,900) = 8.776$, and the price per share will be $(8.776 \times \$5.785) = \$50.77$.  This result is also equal to the value of the firm divided by the number of shares: $(\$43,000/847) = \$50.77$.

## Problem 11

The following information is available for SMJH Corporation and BDA Corporation.

|                    | SMJH  | BDA   |
| ------------------ | ----- | ----- |
| Shares outstanding | 750   | 1,000 |
| Price per share    | $12   | $10   |

BDA would like to acquire SMJH. The value of the combined firm will have an estimated value of $22,000. BDA will accept a cash offer of $14 per share. Should BDA acquire SMJH?

**Solution:** BDA is paying 750 x $14  =  $10,500 to acquire SMJH. The value of BDA is 1,000 x $10  =  $10,000, and the value of SMJH is $12 x 750  =  $9,000. The net gain derived from the merger is $\Delta V$  =  $V_{AB}$  -  ($V_A$ - $V_B$)  =  $22,000  - ($10,000 + $9,000)  =  $3,000. The value of SMJH to BDA is $V^*_B$  =  $\Delta V$  +  $V_B$  = $3,000 + $9,000  =  $12,000. The NPV of the acquisition is $12,000 - $10,500  =  $1,500. BDA should acquire SMJH.

## Problem 12

What is the value of BDA's stock after the merger?

**Solution:** The NPV of the merger is $1,500, so the share price will increase by $1,500 / 1,000  = $1.50. The new share price will be $11.50.

## Problem 13

Blizzard Manufacturing, a producer of snow-removal equipment, is analysing the possible acquisition of Max Motors, a manufacturer of engine components. Blizzard forecasts that the purchase would result in incremental after-tax cash flows of $10,000 per year for the foreseeable future. Current market values of Blizzard and Max are $500,000 and $200,000, respectively. The opportunity cost of capital for the incremental cash flows is 20%. What is the synergy from the merger?

**Solution:**  The synergy is the present value of the perpetual annuity of $10,000 per year: $\Delta V = V_{AB} - (V_A + V_B) =$ ($10,000/.20) = $50,000. Therefore, Max's value to Blizzard is:  $V^*_B = \Delta V + V_B = $50,000 + $200,000 = $250,000.

## Problem 14

Suppose that, for the data of Problem 13, Blizzard is considering an offer of $220,000 cash for the acquisition of Max Motors. What is the merger premium for this acquisition? What is the net present value of the merger?

**Solution:** The merger premium is ($220,000 – $200,000) = $20,000. The net present value is the synergy minus the merger premium, or ($50,000 – $20,000) = $30,000. The net present value can also be determined as the difference between the value of the acquisition and the cost:  NPV = $V^*_B$ – Cost = $250,000 – $220,000 = $30,000.

## Problem 15

As an alternative to the $220,000 offer described in Problem 14, Blizzard is considering offering 25% of its stock to the shareholders of Max Motors.  What is the net present value of this offer?

**Solution:** The value of the combined company is:  $V_{AB} = V_A + V_B + \Delta V = \$500{,}000 + \$200{,}000 + \$50{,}000 = \$750{,}000$.  Twenty-five percent of the combined company is worth:  $.25 \times \$750{,}000 = \$187{,}500$

The net present value of this acquisition would be:  $NPV = V^*_B - Cost = \$250{,}000 - \$187{,}500 = \$62{,}500$

Blizzard would prefer to acquire Max Motors for 25% of the firm's stock rather than the $220,000 cash offer described in Problem 14.

**Use the following information to solve Problems 16 and 17:**

M. Wilson Company, Inc. ($ in thousands)

| | | | | |
|---|---|---|---|---|
| Current assets | $ 2,000 | Current liabilities | | $   600 |
| Fixed assets | 8,000 | Long-term debt | | 3,400 |
| | | Equity | | 6,000 |
| Total | $10,000 | Total | $10,000 | |

B. Buckner Company, Inc. ($ in thousands)

| | | | | |
|---|---|---|---|---|
| Current assets | $ 1,500 | Current liabilities | | $   750 |
| Fixed assets | 3,500 | Long-term debt | | 1,000 |
| | | Equity | | 3,250 |
| Total | $ 5,000 | Total | $ 5,000 | |

## Problem 16

Assume that the balance sheets above are in terms of book values.  Construct the balance sheet for M. Wilson Company, assuming that M. Wilson purchases B. Buckner, and the pooling of interests method of accounting is used.

## Solution:

With a pooling of interests, the balance sheets are added together, so the new balance sheet appears as follows:

M. Wilson Company, Inc. ($ in thousands)

| | | | | |
|---|---|---|---|---|
| Current assets | $ 3,500 | Current liabilities | | $ 1,350 |
| Fixed assets | 11,500 | Long-term debt | | 4,400 |
| | | Equity | | 9,250 |
| Total | $15,000 | Total | $15,000 | |

## Problem 17

Suppose that the fair market value of Buckner's fixed assets is $5,000, in contrast to the $3,500 book value shown.  Wilson pays $7,500 for Buckner and raises the needed funds through an issue of long-term debt.  Construct the balance sheet for M. Wilson Company, assuming that the purchase method of accounting is used.

**Solution:** Buckner's fair market value is $5,000 plus $1,500 in current assets, or $6,500 total. The ($7,500 – $6,500)

= $1,000 premium paid is goodwill.  Wilson's fixed assets would be $8,000 (the book value of Wilson's premerger fixed assets) plus $5,000 (the market value of Buckner's assets), or $13,000 total.   The balance sheet appears as follows:

| M. Wilson Company, Inc. ($ in thousands) | | | |
|---|---|---|---|
| Current assets | $ 3,500 | Current liabilities | $  1,350 |
| Fixed assets | 13,000 | Long-term debt | 10,150 |
| Goodwill | 1,000 | Equity | 6,000 |
| Total | $17,500 | Total | $ 17,500 |

Solution note: Buckner's assets are ($5,000 + $1,500) = $6,500.  Assuming that the current liabilities and long-term debt are shown at market value, the equity in Buckner is worth ($6,500 – $750 – $1,000) = $4,750.  Wilson pays a $1,000 premium, so the total amount of debt that Wilson must raise is ($4,750 + $1,000) = $5,750.  The total long-term debt after the merger is ($5,750 + $3,400 + $1,000) = $10,150, as shown.

# 24        Risk Management: An Introduction to Financial Engineering

## CHAPTER HIGHLIGHTS

Risk management is one of the most important aspects of modern financial management. In this chapter, we introduce you to some of the basic concepts associated with the field of risk management.

## HEDGING AND PRICE VOLATILITY

The term *hedging* refers to the reduction of a firm's exposure to either price or interest rate fluctuations. Alternatively, this process is also referred to as *immunization*. One aspect of the financial manager's job is to use existing financial instruments to create new ones that allow firms to hedge against specific risks. This process is called *financial engineering*. Corporate risk management frequently involves the use of *derivative securities* - securities that represent a claim to another financial asset. The process of financial engineering often involves creating new derivative securities or combining existing derivatives to accomplish the firm's hedging goals.

**Price Volatility - A Historical Perspective:** Although price changes have slowed down recently, volatility has greatly increased in three areas: interest rates, exchange rates, and commodity prices. Because of increased uncertainty about future interest rates, today's firms are less able to plan and predict future borrowing costs. Also, because global operations have become increasingly more important, exchange rates (and their volatility) play an increasingly important role in corporate finance. In addition, prices of various commodities have become more uncertain (for example, oil), increasing the need for risk management.

## MANAGING FINANCIAL RISK

Whether increased volatility in interest rates, exchange rates, and commodity prices affects a given firm depends on both the nature of the firm's operations and its financing. We discuss some of the relevant issues below.

**The Risk Profile:** A firm's *risk profile* shows the relationship between changes in the price of a particular good, service, or rate and changes in the firm's value. The concept is quite similar to the concept of a sensitivity analysis developed in Chapter 11.

**Reducing Risk Exposure:** Depending on the nature of the firm, fluctuations in the price of any good or service may have different effects on firm value. For example, an increase in the price of a raw material might mean an increase in cash flows for one firm but a decrease in cash flows for another firm. Both firms are subject to risk if prices change. Negotiations for an arrangement between the firms, however, can eliminate much of the risk.

For example, consider a firm that uses rice to make a popular brand of cereal. If the price of rice increases, the firm that raises and processes the rice will benefit; the firm that uses the rice in its cereal will lose. By signing a contract specifying that the rice producer will deliver a certain quantity of rice at a certain price, the cereal manufacturer has reduced (or eliminated) the uncertainty about the cost of rice. At the same time, the rice producer has eliminated uncertainty about the price they will receive for the processed rice.

**Hedging Short-Run Exposure:** Short-term price fluctuations due to unexpected events or shocks are referred to as *transitory* changes. Even though a business may be financially sound in the long run, these price fluctuations may force the firm into financial distress. Short-run financial risk is called *transactions exposure*. Various alternatives for managing this risk are discussed later in this chapter.

**Hedging Long-Term Exposure:** Some price fluctuations may reflect permanent changes due to a fundamental shift in the underlying economics of a business. Exposure to this type of risk is referred to as *economic exposure*. This type of risk is much more difficult to hedge than short-term exposure.

## HEDGING WITH FORWARD CONTRACTS

Forward contracts are among the oldest tools for risk management. In this section, we discuss how they can be used to hedge financial risk.

**Forward Contracts - The Basics:** A *forward contract* is a legal agreement between two parties in which they agree today on the price of an asset or product to be delivered at a future date. The delivery date of the goods is called the *settlement date*, and the agreed-upon price is the *forward price*. The *buyer* of the contract must take delivery and pay for the goods; the *seller* must make the delivery and accept payment for the goods. If prices increase before the delivery date, the buyer benefits. If prices decrease, the seller benefits.

**The Payoff Profile:** A *payoff profile* is a plot that depicts the gains and losses on a futures contract that result from unexpected price changes.

**Hedging with Forwards:** The basic idea is to use a risk profile to identify the firm's exposure to a given type of financial risk. Then, financial managers try to find a financial arrangement (for example, a forward contract) that has an offsetting payoff profile. Because the two payoff profiles exactly offset each other, the firm's cash flow will not be affected by changes in the underlying variable (interest rates, etc). This eliminates financial risk.

It is important to remember that, while hedging with forward contracts eliminates the risk associated with unfavourable price adjustments, it also eliminates any potential gain from favourable price adjustments. In a later section, we will discuss ways that a firm can hedge against only unfavourable price changes.

**Credit Risk:** Because no money changes hands until a forward contract is actually completed, there is a credit risk involved. The party on the losing end of the deal has an incentive to default on the agreement. Variations in forward contracts can reduce the risk of default by either party to the agreement.

## HEDGING WITH FUTURES CONTRACTS

Futures contracts are identical to forward contracts with one exception. With a forward contract, gains and losses are recognized only on the settlement date. With futures contracts, gains and losses to the buyer or seller are recognized on a daily basis. This daily settlement feature is referred to as *marking-to-market*. This daily settlement greatly reduces the default risk associated with forward contracts. Because of this, organized trading in futures contracts is much more common than in forward contracts.

**Trading in Futures:** Futures contracts for many items are routinely bought and sold around the world.  There are two main types of futures contracts: commodity futures, and financial futures.  The underlying asset in a commodity future is essentially anything except a financial asset.  The underlying asset in a financial future is any type of financial asset (stock, bond, etc.).

**Futures Exchanges:** Probably the largest futures exchange is the Chicago Board of Trade (CBOT).  Other major exchanges include the Chicago Mercantile Exchange (COMEX), the London International Financial Futures Exchange (LIFFE), the New York Futures Exchange (NYFE), and the Winnipeg Commodity Exchange (WPG).

**Hedging With Futures:** Essentially, a hedge created with futures contracts is conceptually the same as a hedge created with forward contracts.  The payoff profiles are drawn in the same way.  The only difference is that a firm hedging with futures must maintain an account with an investment dealer.  That account will be debited or credited each day as the contract is market to market.

Although there is a large variety of futures contracts available, many firms will not be able to find the precise hedging instrument they need.  So, firms typically use *cross-hedging*.  They buy contracts on a related, but not identical asset, to establish their hedge.

It should be noted that, in practice, futures contracts are very rarely held to maturity.  Firms usually sell and buy contracts, reversing their financial position before the contract matures.  In addition, firms wishing to hedge long-term contracts may need to roll over a series of short-term contracts.  This increases the risk to the firm.

## HEDGING WITH SWAP CONTRACTS

A *swap contract* is an agreement between two parties to exchange specified cash flows at specified intervals.  In essence, a swap contract is a series of forward contracts.  The major difference is that there are multiple exchanges, whereas forward contracts involve only one exchange.  The three major categories of swaps are: currency swaps, interest rate swaps, and commodity swaps.

**Currency Swaps:** In a *currency swap*, the two parties agree to exchange a specific amount of one currency for a specific amount of another currency at a specified future date.  For example, a Canadian firm doing business in France may want to use debt financing.  Because the cash flows related to the project in France are mostly in French francs, the firm may want to make its debt payments in French francs as well.  If the firm doesn't have good access to French capital markets, it may enter into a currency swap with a French firm that needs financing denominated in Canadian dollars.  The firms agree to exchange Canadian dollars for French francs at a fixed rate on a future date (or dates).  This eliminates the exposure to exchange rate changes for both firms.

**Interest Rate Swaps:** In an *interest rate swap,* firms typically exchange fixed-rate loans for floating-rate loans (and vice versa).  Frequently, interest rate swaps are combined with currency swaps.  Here, one firm will obtain fixed-rate financing in one currency and then swap it for floating-rate financing in another currency.  The floating rate loan is always based on some index, such as the one-year Treasury bill rate.

**Commodity Swaps:** A *commodity swap* is an agreement to exchange a specified quantity of some commodity at a specified future date.  This is the newest type of swap and, to date, the market for commodity swaps is relatively small compared to the other swap markets.

**The Swap Dealer:** Swap contracts are not traded on organized exchanges because, to date, the contracts are not sufficiently standardized. So, the *swap dealer* plays a major role in these transactions. When a firm enters into a swap contract, the dealer takes the opposite side of the agreement. Then, the dealer tries to find another party to establish an offsetting transaction. If this is not possible, dealers hedge their positions with futures contracts.

A dealer's contracts are detailed in a *swap book*. In general, dealers try to keep a balanced book (called a *matched book*) to limit their net exposure.

## HEDGING WITH OPTION CONTRACTS

An *option contract* differs from forward, futures and swap contracts in that the owner of the contract has the *right*, but *not* the *obligation*, to buy or sell an asset for a specified price at a specified date.

**Option Terminology:** The two types of options are puts and calls. The owner of a *call option* has the right to *buy* the underlying asset; the owner of a *put option* has the right to *sell* the asset. The fixed price at which the asset may be bought or sold is the *strike price* or *exercise price*. To actually buy or sell the underlying asset is referred to as *exercising* the option. The *expiration date* is the last date at which an option may be exercised.

**Options Versus Forwards:** There are two main differences between option contracts and forward contracts. First, as discussed above, the transaction associated with an option contract is only completed if the owner of the option chooses to exercise it. Second, when the buyer of an option obtains the right to purchase the underlying asset, that right is valuable. Consequently, the buyer of an option must pay for that right. The price paid is called the *option premium*. In a forward contract, on the other hand, no money changes hands until the transaction is completed.

**Option Payoff Profiles:** Study the option payoff profiles in your text. For a call option, the owner begins to make a profit when the price of the underlying asset rises above the strike price. From the seller's viewpoint, any gain to the owner of the option is a loss to the seller of the option. For a put option, the owner begins to make a profit when the price of the underlying falls below the strike price. Again, a gain to the buyer of a put option is a loss to the seller of the option.

**Option Hedging:** This works in essentially the same way as hedging with a forward or futures contract. The basic idea is to use options to create a payoff profile exactly the opposite of the cash flows expected. Because of the nature of options, firms can use option contracts to hedge against the downside risk caused by adverse price movements. At the same time, however, they can retain the potential for upside benefits if prices move in the desired direction.

**Hedging Commodity Price Risk with Options:** In addition to futures contracts for commodities, there are now options available on the same commodities. Usually, the options traded on commodities are really options on futures contracts; they are referred to as *futures options*. The owner of a futures call option receives a futures contract on the underlying commodity; in addition the owner receives the difference between the strike price on the option and the current futures price. This difference is paid in cash.

**Hedging Exchange Risk with Options:** Futures options are also available on foreign currencies. These allow firms to create additional hedges against exchange rate risk. Typically, firms wishing to hedge against adverse changes in the exchange rate do so by purchasing put options.

**Hedging Interest Rate Risk with Options:** There are a number of ways to use options to hedge against interest rate risk. One possibility is to buy a put option on a bond. This protects the firm in case interest rates increase. Firms can also buy call options on interest rates from a bank. These are called *interest rate caps*. If interest rates rise above an agreed-upon ceiling, the bank pays the cash difference between the actual payment and the interest rate ceiling. In contrast, a *floor* is a put option on an interest rate. Firms can buy a cap and sell a floor, creating a *collar*. If rates increase, the firm never pays above the ceiling price. If rates drop, though, the firm's rate will never be below the floor price. The result is that the firm knows its interest rate will always be between the floor and ceiling rates.

**Other Interest Rate Options:** There are two relatively new types of interest rate options. The *swaption* allows a firm to buy an option on an interest rate swap. This gives the firm the possibility to convert a floating-rate loan to a fixed-rate loan (or vice versa) at a future date. A *compound option* is an option on an option. The popularity of these financial instruments is growing.

## CONCEPT TEST

1.    The term hedging refers to the reduction of a firm's exposure to _____ or _____ fluctuation. This process is also referred to as _____ .

2.    The process of using existing financial instruments to create new ones that allow firms to hedge against specific risk is called _____ .

3.    Price changes have slowed down recently, but volatility has increased in the areas of _____ , _____ , and _____ .

4.    A firm's _____ shows the relationship between changes in the price of a particular good, service, or rate and changes in the firm's value.

5.    Short-term price fluctuations due to unexpected events or shocks are called _____ changes. Short-run financial risk due to these changes is called _____ .

6.    Exposure to price changes due to permanent changes in the underlying economics of a business are referred to as _____ . It is typically (more/less) difficult to hedge against this type of risk than against short-term exposure.

7.    A _____ is a legal agreement between two parties in which they agree today on the price of an asset or product to be delivered in the future. The date of delivery is the _____ , and the agreed upon price is the _____ . If prices increase before the delivery date, the (buyer/seller) benefits. If prices decrease, the (buyer/seller) benefits.

8.    Firms can use a _____ to identify their exposure to a given type of financial risk. Then, financial managers try to find a financial arrangement that has an _____ . The result is that the firm's cash flow (will/will not) be affected by changes in the underlying variable.

9.    Futures contracts are identical to forward contracts except that, with a forward contract, gains and losses are recognized on the _____ . With a futures contract, gains and losses are recognized on a ___

_____ basis. This is known as _____ . This feature _(increases/decreases)_ the default risk associated with the contracts.

10.    When firms cannot find the precise instrument they need to hedge against a particular type of risk, they buy contracts on a related asset. This is known as _____ .

11.    A _____ is an agreement between two parties to exchange specified cash flows at specified intervals. Essentially, this is a series of _____ . The main difference is that there are_____ exchanges, whereas _____ involve only one exchange.

12.    In a _____ , the parties exchange specified amounts of one currency for specified amounts of another. In an _____ , firms typically exchange fixed-rate loans for floating-rate loans (or vice versa.) In a _____ , firms agree to exchange specified quantities of a commodity at a future date.

13.    Since swap contracts aren't traded on organized exchanges, the _____ plays a major role in the transaction. The swap dealer takes the _____ side of the transaction and tries to find another party to take an _____ position. If this is not possible, the dealers hedge their position with _____ .

14.    A dealer's contracts are listed in a _____ . A balanced book is referred to as a _____ .

15.    An option gives the owner the _____ but not the _____ to buy or sell an asset for a specified _____ at a specified _____ .

16.    The two types of options are a _____ option, giving the owner the right to buy an asset, and a _____ option, giving the owner the right to sell an asset.

17.    The main difference between an option contract and a forward contract is that an option contract is only _____ if the owner of the option chooses to _____ the option. This choice has value to the owner. The price paid for the right to make this choice is called the _____ .

18.    Options can be used to hedge against changes in interest rates. The two main ways to do this are with _____ and _____ . If a firm buys a _____ and sells a _____ , then the interest rate paid will always be between the _____ and the _____ rates.

## ANSWERS TO CONCEPT TEST

1.    price; interest rate; immunization

2.    financial engineering

3.    interest rates; exchange rates; commodity prices

4.    risk profile

5.    transitory; transactions exposure

6.      economic exposure; more

7.      forward contract; settlement date; forward price; buyer; seller

8.      payoff profile; offsetting payoff profile; will not

9.      settlement date; daily; marking-to-market; decreases

10.     cross-hedging

11.     swap contract; forward contracts; multiple; forward contracts

12.     currency swap; interest rate swap; commodity swap

13.     swap dealer; opposite; offsetting; futures contracts

14.     swap book; matched book

15.     right; obligation; price; date

16.     call; put

17.     completed; exercise; option premium

18.     interest rate caps; floors; cap; floor; ceiling; floor

# 25            Options and Corporate Securities

## CHAPTER HIGHLIGHTS

Options such as the call provision on corporate debt have been described in previous chapters.  This chapter concerns the valuation of options in general.  In addition, we discuss the fact that corporate securities such as common stock and bonds can be thought of as options.  Consequently, we can gain additional insight into many financial problems and decisions by viewing them as options.  Warrants and convertible securities, which involve options issued by corporations to investors, are also discussed in this chapter.

## OPTIONS: THE BASICS

An option gives the owner of the option the right, but not the obligation, to buy or sell a certain asset at a fixed price (called the strike price or exercise price) during a specified period of time.  Options on stock and other assets are examples of *derivative securities*.  The value of an option is derived from the price and other features of the underlying assets.  The act of purchasing or selling the underlying asset, as specified in the option contract, is referred to as *exercising* the option.  The maturity date of the option is called the *expiration date*; the owner of the option cannot exercise the option after the expiration date.  An *American option* can be exercised anytime up to the expiration date.  A *European option* can be exercised only on the expiration date.  Options on stocks and bonds are traded on several exchanges, the largest of which is the Chicago Board Options Exchange (CBOE).  Option trading in Canada began in 1975 on the Montreal Exchange.  All options traded in Canada are cleared through Trans-Canada Options Inc.

**Puts and Calls:** A *call option* gives the owner of the option the right to *buy* a specified asset.  The most common call options are options on stocks.  For example, a call option to buy 100 shares of the Bank of Montreal (BOM) common stock for $30 per share can be purchased on the Montreal Exchange.  A *put option* gives the owner of the option the right to *sell* the underlying asset.  You might purchase a put option if you expect the value of the underlying stock to decline.

Suppose that, on October 1, an investor purchases a call option to buy 100 shares of BOM common stock: the expiration date is the third Friday in December; the exercise price is $30; the price of the option is quoted as $1½; the current market price of BOM stock is $27½.  How much does the investor pay for the option?  What is the investor's gain (or loss) if the price of BOM stock declines between October 1 and the third Friday in December?  What is the investor's gain (or loss) if the price of BOM stock increases?

The price of the option is $1½ per share, or a total cost of $150.  Trading takes place in *round lots* (multiples of 100 shares), so one option *contract* costs $1½ × 100 = $150.  If the price of BOM stock declines to $25, the investor would not exercise the option.  That is, he would not choose to purchase 100 shares of stock for $30 per share at a time when the market price of the stock is less than $30 per share.  When the market price of the stock is less than the exercise price of the call option, the option is said to be 'out of the money.'  If, on the expiration date, the market price of the stock is less than the exercise price of the option, then the option is worthless; the investor has lost $150 on the transaction, the purchase price of the option, because the option expired out of the money.

If the price of the stock exceeds the exercise price, then the option is 'in the money.'  For example, suppose that the price of the stock is $32¾ on the expiration date; the owner of the option could exercise the option for a profit.  The investor can exercise the option and purchase 100 shares of stock for ($30 × 100) = $3,000, and then immediately sell the shares for ($32.75 × 100) = $3,275.  The investor's profit is ($3,275 – $3,000) = $275, less the $150 purchase price of the option, for a net profit of ($275 – $150) = $125.

These transactions can also be viewed from the seller's perspective.  The seller, or writer, of the call option must sell the stock at the exercise price if the buyer exercises the option.  If the option expires out of the money, the writer keeps the purchase price of the option.  In the example above, the seller (writer) would have a profit of $150.  That is, the buyer's $150 loss is the seller's gain.

Now assume the price of the stock is $32¾ on the expiration date.  The writer of the option must sell 100 shares of BOM stock for ($30 × 100) = $3,000.  If the writer does not own the stock, he must buy it in the market for ($32¾ × 100) = $3,275.  His loss will be ($3,000 – $3,275) = $275.  This is partially offset by the $150 received for selling the option, so the actual loss is ($275 – $150) = $125.  Again the seller's loss is the same as the buyer's profit.

The size of the option writer's loss does not depend on whether he owns the stock.  Assuming the writer above owned the stock, he would be selling at $30 per share stock actually worth $32¾ per share.  In other words, the loss is still $275 (less the $150 received for selling the option).

**An Example:**  On October 1, an investor purchases a Times Mirror December 30 put, currently quoted at $3.  The market price of Times Mirror stock is $27½.  What is the investor's gain (or loss) if the price of Times Mirror stock declines between October 1 and the third Friday in December?  What is the investor's gain (or loss) if the price of Times Mirror stock increases?

A put is in the money if the market price is less than exercise price and is out of the money if market price exceeds the exercise price.  If the market price of Times Mirror stock is $25 on the expiration date, the investor will exercise the option.  That is, she will buy 100 shares in the market for ($25 × 100) = $2,500, and then sell the 100 shares to the writer of the call option for ($30 × 100) = $3,000.  The profit from this transaction is ($3,000 – $2,500) = $500.  Since the purchase price of the option is ($3 × 100) = $300, the investor's net profit is ($500 – $300) = $200.  The writer of the option incurs a loss of $500 when the put is exercised; he is obligated to purchase, for $3,000, stock with a market value of only $2,500.  This loss is partially offset by the $300 he received when he sold the option, so that his net profit is ($300 – $500) = –$200, or a $200 loss.

If the market price exceeds the exercise price, the put owner will not exercise the option.  If, for example, the market price is $32 on the expiration date, the owner of the option would not choose to exercise an option to sell, at $30 per share, stock which can be sold in the market for $32 per share.  Consequently, the option expires out of the money; the buyer of the option loses the $300 she paid to acquire the option, while the option writer has a net profit of $300.

## FUNDAMENTALS OF OPTION VALUATION

In this section, we introduce the basic factors that determine the value of an option.  Although the discussion focuses on call options, the basic principles discussed here also apply to put options.

**Value of a Call Option at Expiration:**  The following notation is used in the discussion of option valuation:

| | | |
|---|---|---|
| $S_1$ | = | Stock price at expiration (in one period) |
| $S_0$ | = | Stock price today |
| $C_1$ | = | Value of the call option on the expiration date (in one period) |
| $C_0$ | = | Value of the call option today |
| $E$ | = | Exercise price on the option |

The value of a call option on the expiration date ($C_1$) is zero if the stock price ($S_1$) is less than the exercise price (E). This statement can be written:

$$C_1 = 0 \text{ if } S_1 \le E$$

This relationship can also be stated as follows:

$$C_1 = 0 \text{ if } (S_1 - E) \le 0$$

A call option is in the money if $S_1 > E$. The value of a call option that is in the money at expiration is ($S_1 - E$). This relationship can be stated in either of the following ways:

$$C_1 = (S_1 - E) \text{ if } S_1 > E$$
$$C_1 = (S_1 - E) \text{ if } (S_1 - E) > 0$$

**An Example:** Suppose that the exercise price is $100. On the expiration date, the option is in the money if $S_1 >$ $100, and the value of the option is ($S_1 - \$100$). For example, if $S_1$ is $120, then the owner of the option can exercise it to buy the stock for $100, and then immediately sell the stock for $120, for a $20 gain. If $S_1 < \$100$ on the expiration date, the option is out of the money and has no value. The call cannot have a negative value because the owner of the call is not obligated to exercise the option.

**The Upper and Lower Bounds on a Call Option's Value:** Since a call option is simply the right to buy the stock, the option cannot be worth more than the stock. Therefore, the upper bound on the value of a call option can be expressed as follows:

$$C_0 \le S_0$$

The lower bound on the value of a call option depends on whether the option is in or out of the money. We established that the value of a call option at expiration is zero if the option is out of the money. However, prior to expiration, an out of the money option has a value greater than zero if the investor believes that the price of the stock might increase enough so that, at some time prior to expiration, the option is in the money. Therefore, the lower bound for the value of an out of the money call option, prior to the expiration date, can be written as:

$$C_0 \ge 0 \text{ if } (S_0 - E) < 0$$

A call that is in the money prior to expiration is worth at least the difference between the value of the stock and the exercise price of the call. Suppose the stock is selling for $80 and the option to buy the stock at $60 is selling for $15. You could buy the option for $15, exercise it by purchasing the stock for another $60, and then sell the stock for a guaranteed profit of $5. Consequently, the price of the call must be at least $20; at a lower price, the existence of arbitrage opportunities would immediately drive the price of the option higher. The price of the option generally exceeds the difference between the stock price and the exercise price due to the opportunity for additional profit if the price of the stock increases further prior to the expiration date. This relationship can be summarized as follows:

$$C_0 \ge (S_0 - E) \text{ if } (S_0 - E) \ge 0$$

The lower bound on the value of a call option is referred to as the *intrinsic value* of the option.

The upper bound on a call's value is given by the value of the stock ($C_0 \leq S_0$). The lower bound is either $S_0 - E$ or 0, whichever is larger.

**A Simple Model:**  To establish a precise value for a call option, we will initially assume that future stock prices can have only two possible values.

**An Example:**  Suppose a share of stock is currently selling for $100, and the risk-free rate ($R_f$) is 10%. Also assume that, one year from now, the stock price will be either $105 or $120. A call option with expiration in one year has an exercise price of $100. How much is the call worth today?

One year from now, the stock will be worth either $105 or $120. If you buy the option today, you will have either ($105 – $100) = $5 or ($120 – $100) = $20 one year from now. Suppose that, in addition to buying the option today, you also lend an amount equal to the present value of the exercise price: ($100/1.10) = $90.91. At the end of the year, you have $100 from the repayment of the loan and either $5 or $20 from the exercise of the option; the total return is either ($100 + $5) = $105 or ($100 + $20) = $120. Notice that the strategy of buying the option and lending $90.91 has the same possible future returns as does the strategy of simply buying the stock. Since the two strategies have the same future returns, they must have the same value today. Therefore, the value of the call option plus the present value of the exercise price must be the same as the price of the stock:

$$C_0 + \$90.91 \;=\; \$100$$

The value of the call option is $9.09. In general, this result can be written as:

$$C_0 \;+\; \frac{E}{(1 + R_F)} \;=\; S_0$$

$$C_0 \;=\; S_0 \;-\; \frac{E}{(1 + R_F)}$$

Although this result is based on the unrealistic assumption that the stock price will be one of only two possible values at the expiration date, it can be generalized to the case where the stock price at the expiration date will be any value greater than or equal to the exercise price of the option.

If the option expires in t time periods, then the value of the call option is:

$$C_0 \;=\; S_0 \;-\; \frac{E}{(1 + R_F)^t}$$

**Four Factors Determining Option Values:**  If we assume that a call option is certain to expire in the money, then the result of the previous section indicates that four factors determine the option's value. (If the option can expire out of the money, then a fifth factor influences the option's price; this fifth factor is discussed in the next section.) The four factors are:

1.      *The stock price.* As the price of the stock ($S_0$) increases, the value of the option increases.

2.      *The exercise price.* A higher exercise price (E) makes the option less valuable.

3.      *The time to expiration.* The value of the option decreases as the time to expiration (t) decreases. The longer the term to expiration, the greater the value of the option, because it provides the holder of the option a longer period of time during which to exercise.

4.      *The risk-free rate.* The value of the call increases as the risk-free rate ($R_f$) increases. The purchaser of a call option will pay the exercise price at some future date. The higher the interest rate, the lower the present value of this future amount. Thus, the higher the interest rate, the more the call option is worth.


## VALUING A CALL OPTION

In this section, we discuss the valuation of a call option under the more realistic assumption that the option might expire out of the money.  As in the previous section, we initially assume that only two future stock prices are possible.

**A Simple Model - Part II:**  In order to identify the factors which determine the value of an option which might expire out of the money, we first consider a modification of the example of the previous section.

**An Example:**  Assume again that the current price of the stock is $100, that the possible stock prices at the expiration of the option are $105 and $120, and that the risk-free rate is 10%.  A call option with an exercise price of $115 expires out of the money if the stock price is $105, and is in the money if the stock price is $120.  What is the value of the call option with an exercise price of $115?

To establish the value of this option, we develop a strategy of investing in the risk-free asset and purchasing call options which duplicate the possible returns resulting from owning the stock.

The strategy which duplicates the payoff on the stock is: invest ($105/1.10) = $95.45 in the risk-free asset, and buy three call options.  One year from now, the value of the investment in the risk-free asset is $105, which is the lower of the two possible stock prices.  If, one year from now, the stock price is $105, then the three call options are out of the money, and the total value of the investor's position is [$105 + (3 × $0)] = $105.  On the other hand, if the stock price is $120, then the call options are in the money, and the value of each call option is ($120 – $115) = $5. The total value of the investor's position is then [$105 + (3 × $5)] =  $120.  Therefore, the strategy of investing $95.45 in the risk-free asset and buying three call options has the same possible future returns as does the stock. Consequently, the current value of the two strategies must be the same:

$$(3 \times C_0) + \frac{\$105}{(1 + R_F)} = S_0$$

$$(3 \times C_0) + \frac{\$105}{(1.10)} = \$100$$

Solving for $C_0$, we find that the value of a call option is $1.52.

Option valuation is based on the fact that it is always possible to duplicate a stock's possible future returns with a combination of options and either lending or borrowing.  The required number of calls is equal to ($\Delta S/\Delta C$), where $\Delta S$ is the difference in possible future stock prices and $\Delta C$ is the difference in possible future option values.  In the above example, this fraction is equal to [($120 – $105)/($5 – $0)] = 3, indicating the purchase of three call options. The logic of this result is straightforward.  When the option is in the money, the options purchased must provide a return equal to the difference in possible stock prices; since one in-the-money option provides a return of $\Delta C$, the number of options required to provide a return of $\Delta S$ is ($\Delta S/\Delta C$).

**The Fifth Factor:** For an option which might expire out of the money, the fifth factor influencing the value of the option is the variability in the price of the underlying asset. The more variable the price of the underlying asset, the greater the value of the option. Imagine that you own a call on a riskless asset which is currently selling for $100 and will yield a 10% return for the year. What is the value of a call option to buy this asset for $120? Obviously, the value is zero because this asset can never be worth more than $110 during the year. If this asset's value were variable, however, then there would be a possibility that it would sell for more than $120, and the call would have value. The greater the variability, the greater the chance for profit, and consequently, the greater the value of the option.

**An Example:** Suppose the possible stock prices are $100 and $125, the risk-free rate is 10%, and the current price of the stock is $100. What is the value of a call option with an exercise price of $115?

The possible values of the option at the expiration date are: $0 and ($125 – $115) = $10. The investment strategy which duplicates the returns from an investment in the stock is as follows: invest ($100/1.10) = $90.91 in the risk-free asset, and purchase ($\Delta S/\Delta C$) = [($125 – $100)/($10 – $0)] = 2.5 call options. The value of a call option is the solution for $C_0$ in the following equation:

$$(2.5 \times C_0) \; + \; \frac{\$100}{(1 + R_F)} \; = \; S_0$$

$$(2.5 \times C_0) \; + \; \frac{\$100}{(1.10)} \; = \; \$100$$

The value of the call option is $3.64. In the example of the preceding section, the value of the option is $1.52. The value of an option which might expire out of the money increases when the possible stock prices are more variable.


## EQUITY AS A CALL OPTION ON THE FIRM'S ASSETS

The financial decision-making process can often be reformulated in terms of options. In this section, we view corporate securities as options on the value of the firm.

Suppose a firm has a single debt issue coming due in one year. At that time, the shareholders will have a choice. If the value of the firm ($V_1$) exceeds the face value of the debt ($B_1$), then the shareholders will pay off the debt and the stock will be worth $S_1 = (V_1 – B_1)$. By paying off the debt, the shareholders own the assets of the firm. However, if $V_1$ is less than $B_1$, then the shareholders will not exercise their option to acquire the firm's assets, and the bondholders will own the firm. The stock is worth zero in this case. Consequently, the equity in a firm with debt can be viewed as a call option on the assets of the firm. The bondholders' position can be described as follows: the bondholders own the firm and they have written a call option against the value of the firm, with an exercise price equal to the value of the debt. The value of the bonds is then equal to the value of the firm's assets less the value of the call option held by the shareholders.

**An Example:** A firm has a pure-discount $500 debt issue due in one year. The risk-free rate is 10%, and the current market value of the firm's assets is $475. One year from now, the value of the firm's assets will be either $525 or $550. What is the value today of the equity in the firm?

The firm's shareholders own a call option on the firm's assets. The exercise price of the option is $500. The value of their option is the current value of the underlying asset minus the present value of the exercise price:

$$C_0 = S_0 - \frac{E}{(1 + R_F)^t} = \$475 - \frac{\$500}{(1.10)} = \$20.45$$

Therefore, the firm's equity is worth $20.45.

The conclusion in this example can be verified by noting that the firm's debt is risk-free; therefore, the current value of the debt is ($500/1.10) = $454.55. Since the current value of the firm is $475, the value of the firm's equity is ($475 – $454.55) = $20.45.

## WARRANTS

A warrant gives the holder the right to buy common stock directly from the company at a fixed price during a specified time period. To the holder, a warrant is essentially a call option, although warrants usually have longer maturities. Typically, warrants are attached to the bond with which they are issued; however, some warrants are detachable, which means the warrants can be sold separately from the bond.

**The Difference Between Warrants and Call Options:** To the firm, a warrant is substantially different from a call option. A call option sold on the firm's stock is a private transaction between investors, in which the firm is not directly involved. In contrast, a warrant is a security issued by the firm. When a call option is exercised, existing stock merely changes hands, but when a warrant is exercised, the firm must issue new stock.

**Warrants and the Value of the Firm:** An example best illustrates the difference between warrants and calls; the following example also demonstrates the manner in which the exercise of a warrant affects the value of the issuing firm.

**An Example:** The Vinson Company is financed entirely with equity. The firm has assets valued at $9,000 and has 900 shares outstanding. Elizabeth and Steve Vinson each own 450 shares. Each has decided to sell a call option on 150 shares to Claire Vinson. The call option has an exercise price of $12. Now, suppose the company's assets increase in value to $13,500. Each share is now worth ($13,500/900) = $15. Claire will exercise her options by paying a total of ($12 × 300) = $3,600 to Steve and Elizabeth, and she will acquire a total of 300 shares. At this point, 900 shares are still outstanding and each share is still worth $15. Claire has made a profit of [300 × ($15 – $12)] = $900, but, from the corporation's point of view, no change has taken place. That is, the number of shares outstanding remains the same and no new financing becomes available to the firm.

Alternatively, suppose that Steve and Elizabeth have sold warrants entitling Claire to buy 300 shares at $12 per share. Assume again that the assets increase in value to $13,500 and the warrants are about to expire. The value of the firm can be thought of as either the value of its assets or the value of its equity, because the firm is financed entirely through equity. Since both the existing common stock and the warrants represent a claim on the firm's assets, prior to the expiration of the warrants, the total value is equal to the value of the common stock plus the value of the warrants.

If Claire exercises her warrants, the firm issues 300 new shares and receives ($12 × 300) = $3,600. The firm is now worth ($13,500 + $3,600) = $17,100 and 1,200 shares are outstanding. Each share is worth ($17,100/1,200) = $14.25. Claire's profit is [300 × ($14.25 – $12)] = $675, because she owns shares worth $14.25 for which she paid only $12. Immediately prior to the expiration of the warrants, the common stock is worth ($14.25 × 900) = $12,825 and the warrants are worth $675, for a total of $13,500. The reason the shares are worth $14.25, instead of $15, is that the warrants, which represent a direct claim on the firm's assets and cash flow, have value.

Even though the terms of the call and the warrant appear comparable, the consequences of the exercise of these options differ.  In the case of the call option, the value of the firm and the value of a share are unaffected by the exercise of the option.  Both before and after exercise, the firm has 900 shares outstanding, each share is worth $15 and the total value of the firm is $13,500.  Claire's profit is $900 since she exercises an option on each of 300 shares, and earns a $3 profit on each share.  On the other hand, when Claire exercises the warrant, 300 new shares are issued and the value of the firm increases by the $3,600 payment.  The exercise of the warrant changes the total number of shares from 900 to 1,200; the value of each share is $14.25, rather than $15; the value of the firm is $17,100 rather than $13,500.  Since each share is worth $14.25, Claire's profit on the exercise of the warrant is $675, compared to her $900 profit when she exercises the call.

The exercise of the warrants results in an increase in the number of shares, so that earnings per share will be diluted. Firms with a significant number of warrants outstanding report EPS in two ways: 'primary' (earnings divided by outstanding shares) and 'fully-diluted' (earnings divided by the number of shares that would be outstanding if all warrants were converted to stock).

## CONVERTIBLE BONDS

A convertible bond is a corporate bond that can be exchanged for a fixed number of shares of the firm's common stock, at the holder's option, at any time prior to the maturity of the bond.  A convertible preferred stock is similar to a convertible bond except that it has no maturity date.

**Features of a Convertible Bond:**  Consider a convertible subordinated debenture with a face value of $1,000 and a $50 *conversion price*.  The bondholder can exchange this bond for ($1,000/$50) = 20 shares of stock; that is, the *conversion ratio* is 20.  When a convertible bond is issued, the conversion price typically exceeds the stock price. The difference between the conversion price and the market value of the stock is called the *conversion premium*. If the market value of the firm's stock is $40, then the conversion premium is ($50 – $40) = $10.  The conversion premium is often expressed as a percent of the market value of the stock.  In this example, the conversion premium is ($10/$40) = .25 = 25% of the market value of the stock.

**Value of a Convertible Bond:**  The value of a convertible bond can be thought of in terms of its value as a bond and the value of the conversion feature.

The *straight bond value* is the price at which the bond would sell if it were not convertible.  A convertible sells at a price only slightly above its straight bond value when the conversion price greatly exceeds the stock price. The straight bond value is the present value of the coupon payments and the maturity value, and is therefore dependent on the appropriate discount rate for bonds with a given risk level.

The *conversion value* is the value of the bond if it were immediately converted into common stock.  That is, conversion value equals the conversion ratio times the current stock price.  The conversion value is another minimum value for a convertible bond since the bond cannot sell for less than its conversion value.  If the stock price exceeds conversion value, the value of the convertible bond depends primarily on the conversion value, because the conversion value is significantly greater than the straight bond value.  The minimum or 'floor' value of a convertible bond is either its straight bond value or its conversion value, whichever is higher.

The value of a convertible bond exceeds both the straight bond value and the conversion value because the holder has the right, but not the obligation, to convert.  Essentially, the bondholder has a call option that increases the value of the bond.  The option to wait has value, and it raises the value of the convertible bond over its floor value.  The total value of the convertible is equal to the sum of the floor value and the option value.

## REASONS FOR ISSUING WARRANTS AND CONVERTIBLES

A bond that is convertible or has warrants attached pays a lower coupon rate than does an identical straight bond. This interest saving is an apparent advantage to the issuing firm. Warrants and convertibles may also provide the firm with the opportunity to issue stock at a premium over current prices. This argument is based on the fact that the warrant or convertible is usually 'out of the money' initially, so that exercise will take place only if the stock price increases. These arguments seem to indicate that warrants and convertibles are 'no lose' propositions for the issuer. As explained below, this conclusion is incorrect.

**The 'Free Lunch' Story:**  Suppose that a firm can issue either straight subordinated debentures with a 13% coupon rate or convertible subordinated debentures, with a conversion price of $50, and a 10% coupon rate. The firm's common stock currently sells for $40 per share. If the stock declines in value, then the bonds will not be converted, and the firm will have succeeded in issuing debt at 10%, rather than 13%.

If the stock price increases, then conversion will occur, but the company will effectively be selling stock for $50 per share, or $10 more than the stock was worth at the time the convertible was issued. It *appears* that the convertible bond is preferable to either new common stock or straight debt as a source of long-term financing. However, the flaw in the above argument lies in the fact that we are comparing convertible-debt financing with each of the two alternatives only under the circumstances which make convertibles appear more attractive. That is, convertibles are preferable to straight-debt financing when the price of the stock declines, but not when the price increases; convertibles are preferable to common stock financing when the price of the stock increases, but not when the price decreases.

**The 'Expensive Lunch' Story:**  An argument can be constructed which *appears* to indicate that convertible securities are never the preferable alternative. For example, one could argue that, if the stock price declines subsequent to the issuing of the convertibles, then the firm would have been better off issuing common stock when its value was high. In comparison with common stock financing, a valuable opportunity is lost by issuing convertibles if the stock price subsequently declines.

Similarly, if the stock price subsequently rises, then the bondholders convert and reap some of the benefits of the company's success. The firm's existing shareholders would have been better off if the firm had issued straight debt, so that the gains to shareholders would not be diluted. In comparison with straight-debt financing, the existing shareholders are at a relative disadvantage when the firm issues convertibles and the stock price subsequently increases.

**A Reconciliation:**  Neither of the above analyses is correct. In an efficient market, issuing convertibles (or any other financial instrument) is a zero NPV transaction. From the perspective of the firm's existing shareholders, issuing convertibles is generally less desirable than issuing straight-debt and preferable to issuing stock if the company subsequently prospers. If the company does not fare as well, then the reverse is true. Of course, there is no way of knowing in advance whether stock price will increase or decrease, so it is not possible to determine which financing alternative is preferable.

## CONCEPT TEST

1.    An option gives the owner of the option the right, but not the obligation, to buy or sell a certain asset at a fixed price during a specified period of time. The asset specified in the option contract is referred to as the _____ asset. The price specified in the option contract is the _____ price or the _____ price. The act of purchasing or selling the underlying asset is referred to as _____ the option. The maturity date of the option is called the _____ date.

2.       A call option gives the owner of the option the right to (buy/sell) a specified asset. A put option gives the
         owner of the option the right to (buy/sell) a specified asset. The writer of an option is the individual who
         (buys/sells) the option. The writer of a call is obligated to (buy/sell) the stock if the buyer of the option
         chooses to exercise. The writer of a put is obligated to (buy/sell) the stock should the buyer of the put elect
         to exercise the option.

3.       A call is out of the money when the market price of the stock is (less/greater) than the exercise price of the
         call.  On the expiration date, a call is worthless if the market price of the stock is (less/greater) than the
         exercise price of the option. A call is in the money when the market price of the stock is (less/greater) than
         the exercise price of the call.

4.       A put is out of the money when the market price is (less/greater) than the exercise price and is in the money
         when the market price is (less/greater) than the exercise price. The owner of the put option will not exercise
         the option if the market price is (less/greater) than the exercise price.

5.       Because the profit earned by one party to an options contract is a loss to the other party, it is said that options
         represent a _____.

6.       If, on the expiration date, the stock price ($S_1$) is less than the exercise price (E) of a call option, then the value
         of the call ($C_1$) is _____. That is: $C_1 = $ _____ if _____. The value of a call option that
         is in the money at expiration is _____. That is:  $C_1 = $ _____ if _____

7.       The upper bound on the value of a call option prior to expiration ($C_0$) is _____. Prior to expiration,
         an out of the money call option has a value (less/greater) than _____ if the investor believes that the
         price of the stock might increase sufficiently so that, at some time prior to expiration, the option is in the
         money.  The lower bound for the value of an out of the money call option, prior to the expiration date, can
         be written as follows:  $C_0$ _____ if _____ $\geq 0$ .  A call that is in the money prior to expiration
         is worth at least the difference between the _____ and the _____.  That is: $C_0 \geq$ _____
         if _____ $\geq 0$

8.       Option valuation is based on the fact that it is always possible to duplicate a stock's possible future returns
         with a combination of options and either lending or borrowing.  When valuing call options, the required
         number of calls is equal to _____, where $\Delta S$ is the difference in _____ and $\Delta C$ is the difference
         in _____.  For a call option which is certain to expire in the money, the value of the option prior to
         expiration ($C_0$) is equal to the _____ minus the present value of the _____.  That is: $C_0 = $
         _____.

9.       For a call option which is certain to expire in the money, the following four factors determine the option's
         value: (1) _____; (2) _____; (3) _____; (4) _____.

10.      In order to establish the value of a call option which might expire out of the money, a strategy is developed
         which duplicates the possible _____ which result from owning _____. This strategy consists
         of investing in _____ and purchasing _____.  The value of the call option prior to expiration
         ($C_0$) is then determined by equating the _____ of the two strategies; that is, the total value of the
         _____ plus the present value of the _____ is equal to the _____.

11.  For an option which might expire out of the money, the fifth factor influencing the value of the option is the _____ in the price of the _____. The greater the _____, the greater the value of the option.

12.  The financial decision-making process can often be reformulated in terms of _____. The equity in a firm with debt can be viewed as a _____ option on _____. The bondholders own the firm and they have written a _____ option against the _____, with an exercise price equal to _____. The value of the bonds is then equal to the value of _____ less the value of _____ held by the shareholders.

13.  A warrant gives the holder the right to buy _____ from the issuing company at a fixed price during a specified time period. To the holder, a warrant is essentially a _____ option. Warrants are generally issued in combination with _____. To the firm, a warrant is substantially different from a call option. A _____ sold on the firm's stock is a private transaction between investors, while a _____ is a security issued by the firm. Existing stock merely changes hands when a _____ is exercised, but the firm must issue new stock when a _____ is exercised.

14.  In the case of the _____, the value of the firm and the value of a share are unaffected by the exercise of the option. Both the value of the firm and the value of a share are affected by the exercise of a _____; the value of the firm (increases/decreases) and the value of a share generally (increases/decreases).

15.  A convertible bond is a corporate bond that can be exchanged for a fixed number of _____ at any time prior to _____. The conversion ratio specifies the _____ into which the bond can be converted. The face value of the convertible bond divided by the conversion ratio is equal to the _____. When a convertible bond is issued, the conversion price is typically (less/greater) than the price of the firm's common stock. The difference between the conversion price and the market value of the stock is called the _____, which is often expressed as a percent of the _____.

16.  The value of a convertible bond can be thought of in terms of its value as a _____ and the value of the _____ feature. The straight bond value is the price at which the bond would sell if it were _____. The straight bond value is the _____ of the coupon payments and the maturity value, and is dependent on the appropriate _____ for bonds with a given risk level. The conversion value is the value of the bond if it were _____. The conversion value equals the _____ multiplied by the _____. The value of a convertible bond exceeds both the _____ and the _____.

17.  In an efficient market, issuing convertibles is a _____ transaction. From the perspective of the firm's existing shareholders, issuing convertibles is generally (more/less) desirable than issuing straight-debt and (more/less) desirable than issuing stock if the company subsequently prospers. If the company does not fare as well, then issuing convertibles is generally (more/less) desirable than issuing straight-debt and (more/less) desirable than issuing stock.

## ANSWERS TO CONCEPT TEST

1.  underlying; strike; exercise; exercising; expiration

2.  buy; sell; sells; sell; buy

3.  less; less; greater

4.      greater; less; less

5.      zero-sum game

6.      zero; zero; $S_1 \leq E$ or $(S_1-E) \leq 0$; $(S_1-E)$; $(S_1-E)$; $S_1 > E$ or $(S_1-E) > 0$

7.      the price of the stock; greater; zero; $\geq 0$; $(S_0-E)$; value of the stock; exercise price; $(S_0-E)$; $(S_0-E)$

8.      $\Delta S/\Delta C$; possible future stock prices; possible future option values; stock price; exercise price; $S_0-[E/(1+R_F)^t]$

9.      the stock price; the exercise price; the time to expiration; the risk-free rate

10.     future returns; the stock; risk-free assets; call options; current value; call options; exercise price; price of the stock

11.     variability; stock; variability

12.     options; call; the assets of the firm; call; value of the firm; the value of the firm's debt; the firm's assets; the call option

13.     common stock; call; privately placed debt; call option; warrant; call option; warrant

14.     call option; warrant; increases; decreases

15.     shares of the firm's common stock; maturity; number of shares; conversion price; greater; conversion premium; market value of the stock

16.     bond; convertibility; not convertible; present value; discount rate; converted into common stock; conversion ratio; current stock price; straight bond; conversion value

17.     zero–NPV; less; more; more; less


## PROBLEMS AND SOLUTIONS


## Problem 1

Common shares in Stone Company are currently trading at $25, and the risk-free rate is 12%. There is a call option that expires in one year with an exercise price of $30. How much should an investor pay for 100 calls today?

**Solution:** $C_0$ = $30 - $25 / 1.12 = $7.68

The cost of the call option for 100 shares is $7.68 x 100 = $768.

**Use the following information to solve Problems 2 to 6:**

The price of Walden Corporation common stock will be either $60 or $80 at the end of the year. A call option contract for the purchase of 100 shares of Walden stock has an expiration date in one year. The risk-free rate is 8%.

### Problem 2

Suppose the current price of Walden stock is $65 and the exercise price of the call is $70. What are the possible values of the call contract on the expiration date?

**Solution:** On the expiration date, Walden stock will be worth either $60 per share or $80 per share. That is, $S_1 = $60$ or $S_1 = $80$. If the stock is worth $60 per share, the option to buy at $70 is worthless; that is $C_1 = 0$ if $S_1 \leq E$. If the stock is worth $80 per share on the expiration date (i.e., $S_1 > E$), then the value of call option for one share of Walden stock is: $C_1 = S_1 - E = $80 - $70 = $10$.

Consequently, the value of a call option contract for 100 shares is ($10 \times 100) = $1,000$.

### Problem 3

For the data in Problem 2, what is the current value of the call contract?

**Solution**: If you buy the call, then, at the end of the year, you will have either $0 or $1,000. The number of options per share that must be purchased is equal to:

$$\frac{\Delta S}{\Delta C} = \frac{\$80 - \$60}{\$10 - \$0} = 2$$

A total of ($2 \times 100) = 200$ call options must be purchased.

The strategy which duplicates the returns from one share of stock is: invest $[\$60/(1 + R_f)] = (\$60/1.08) = \$55.56$ in the risk-free asset, and buy two call options. The current value of these two strategies must be the same:

$$(2 \times C_0) + \frac{\$60}{(1 + R_F)} = S_0$$

$$(2 \times C_0) + \frac{\$60}{(1.08)} = \$65$$

Solving this equation for $C_0$, the value of a call option for one share is $4.72; the value of the call option contract for 100 shares is ($4.72 \times 100) = $472$.

### Problem 4

Suppose the option described in Problem 2 has an exercise price of $50. What is the value of the call contract?

**Solution:** If the exercise price is $50, then the option is certain to expire in the money. If you buy a call option for one share of stock, then the return at the end of the year will be either ($60 - $50) = $10 or ($80 - $50) = $30. For an option which is certain to expire in the money, the number of options required for the strategy to replicate the returns for the stock is:

$$\frac{\Delta S}{\Delta C} = \frac{\$80 - \$60}{\$30 - \$10} = 1$$

In addition to buying the option today, you also lend an amount equal to the present value of the exercise price: ($50/1.08) = $46.30. The strategy of buying the option and lending $46.30 has the same possible future returns as does the strategy of simply buying the stock. Since the two strategies have the same future returns, they must have the same value today, as indicated in the following equation:

$$C_0 = S_0 - \frac{E}{(1 + R_F)} = \$65 - \$46.30 = \$18.70$$

The cost of the call option contract for 100 shares of Walden common stock is ($18.70 × 100) = $1,870.

## Problem 5

Suppose a call contract for 100 shares of Walden common stock, with an exercise price of $65, sells for $1,000. What is the current value of the stock?

**Solution:** The possible returns for a share of Walden stock are $80 and $60. The possible returns for a call option for one share of Walden stock are ($80 – $65) = $15 and $0. The number of options required for the strategy to replicate the returns for the stock is:

$$\frac{\Delta S}{\Delta C} = \frac{\$80 - \$60}{\$15 - \$0} = 1\ 1/3$$

To duplicate the returns for a call option for one share, invest the following amount in the risk-free asset:

$$\frac{\$60}{(1 + R_F)} = \frac{\$60}{1.08} = \$55.56$$

The strategy of buying the call options and investing at the risk-free rate has the same returns as does the strategy of buying the common stock. Therefore, the current value of these two strategies must be the same:

$$(1\ 1/3 \times C_0) + \frac{\$60}{(1 + R_F)} = S_0$$

$$(1\ 1/3 \times \$10) + \frac{\$60}{(1.08)} = S_0$$

Solving this equation for $S_0$, the current value of the stock is $68.89 per share.

## Problem 6

Calculate the value of the call if the current stock price is $50 and the exercise price is $70.

**Solution:**  The possible returns for a share of Walden stock are $80 and $60.  The possible returns for a call option for one share of Walden stock are ($80 – $70) = $10 and $0.  The number of options required for the strategy to replicate the returns for the stock is:

$$\frac{\Delta S}{\Delta C} = \frac{\$80 - \$60}{\$10 - \$0} = 2$$

To duplicate the returns for a call option for one share, invest the following amount in the risk-free asset:

$$\frac{\$60}{(1 + R_F)} = \frac{\$60}{1.08} = \$55.56$$

The current value of the two strategies must be the same:

$$(2 \times C_0) + \frac{\$60}{(1 + R_F)} = S_0$$

$$(2 \times C_0) + \frac{\$60}{(1.08)} = \$50$$

Solving this equation for $C_0$, the current value of the call option is (–$2.78) per share, or [(–$2.78 × 100] = (–$278).  Since an option cannot have a negative value, the call is worthless.

How can the option to buy a share of stock, that may be worth $80, for only $70 be worth nothing?  The inconsistency here arises from the fact that the current stock price cannot be $50.  You can borrow $50 at an 8% interest rate, and buy one share of stock.  Under the worst case scenario, the share will be worth $60, but you will have to repay only ($50 × 1.08) = $54 on the loan.  As a result, you would earn, at a minimum, a costless, riskless $6.  There is an arbitrage opportunity here because the return on the stock is always greater than the riskless 8% interest rate.  Therefore, the stock must sell for more than $50 per share.

## Problem 7

The common stock of Hanna Corporation is currently selling at $50 per share.  Assume that the continuously compounded interest rate is 10% and that the price of the Hanna stock is certain to increase at that rate.  What is the value of a call option to buy one share of Hanna stock for $40, if the expiration date is one year from today?

**Solution:**   If there is no uncertainty, then the value of Hanna stock one year from now will be: $50e^{.10} = $55.26.  The payoff on the option at that time is thus ($55.26 – $40) = $15.26.  The value of the call is the present value of the future payoff:   $15.26e^{-.10} = $13.81

## Problem 8

Calls on Barbera Corporation common stock are currently selling for $10; puts are selling for $8.  The exercise price is $80 and the expiration date of both options is in one year.  Barbera common stock is currently selling for $73 2/8 per share.  Suppose that an investor buys a put and holds it until the expiration date.  What is the profit (or loss) if the price of the stock, on the expiration date, is $65? $75? $80? $85? $95?  What is the maximum return possible?

**Solution:** If the price of the stock on the expiration date is $65, the investor will exercise the put, thereby selling the stock for $80. The gain on the exercise of the put is $(E - S_1) = (\$80 - \$65) = \$15$ since the investor can purchase a share in the market for $65 and sell the share for $80. Since the investor paid $8 to purchase the put, the net gain is $(\$15 - \$8) = \$7$.

If the price of the stock is $75 on the expiration date, the investor will exercise the put for a gain of $(E - S_1) = (\$80 - \$75) = \$5$. The net gain to the investor is $(\$5 - \$8) = -\$3$, or a net loss of $3. If the price of the stock is the same as the exercise price of the option, the investor will not exercise the option. If the investor did exercise the option, there would be no gain or loss on the transaction, which is the same result as if the option were discarded. The net loss would be the $8 purchase price of the option.

At a price of $85 or $95 (or at any stock price such that $E < S_1$), the investor will not exercise the option, so that the net loss is the $8 purchase price of the option. The maximum return the investor can earn is $80 per share, less the $8 price of the option. That is, if the market value of the stock declines to zero on the expiration date, the investor can sell, for $80, stock which has a value of $0.

## Problem 9

For the data in Problem 8, compute the gain (or loss) to the writer of the put if the price of the stock on the expiration date is $65? $75? $80? $85? $95? What is the maximum return the writer of the put can earn? What is the maximum possible loss for the writer of the put option?

**Solution:** If the price of the stock on the expiration date is $65, the buyer of the put will exercise the option, thereby selling the stock for $80. The writer of the put must therefore purchase, for $80, a share of stock with a market value of only $65; the gain on this transaction is $(\$65 - \$80) = -\$15$, or a loss of $15. The loss to the writer of the put is equal to the gain to the buyer of the put, as indicated by the solution to Problem 7. Since the writer of the put receives the $8 purchase price of the option, the net loss to writer $(-\$15 + \$8) = -\$7$. Again, since options are a 'zero-sum game,' the net loss to the writer is the same as the net gain to the buyer of the option.

If the price of the stock on the expiration date is $75, then the gain to the writer is $(\$75 - \$80) = -\$5$, or a loss of $5; the net gain is $(-\$5 + \$8) = \$3$.

Since the option will not be exercised if the price of the stock is $80 or more on the expiration date, the gain to the writer of the put is the $8 purchase price of the option.

The maximum return to the writer of the put is the $8 purchase price of the put. If the price of the stock falls to zero on the expiration date, the loss to the writer of the put is $(-\$80 + \$8) = \$72$.

## Problem 10

At the end of the year, a share of Dobrowolski Corporation, currently trading at $93, will be worth either $95 or $110. If a call expires at the end of the year and has an exercise price price of $90, what is the value of the call contract? The risk-free rate is 9.5%.

**Solution:** For one share, the return at year end will be either $5 or $20. The number of options required for the strategy to replicate the returns for the stock is:

$$\Delta S / \Delta C = (\$110 - \$95) / (\$20 - \$5) = 1$$

In addition to buying the option today, you could also lend the present value of the exercise price: $90 / 1.095 = $82.19. The two strategies have the same future returns, so the value of the call is

$$C_0 = S_0 - E / (1 + R_F)^t \quad \$93 - \$82.19 = \$10.81$$

The cost of the contract for 100 shares of Dobrowolski Corporation is $1,081.


## Problem 11

For the Barbera Corporation common stock described in Problem 8, assume that an investor buys a call and holds the call until the expiration date. What is the investor's profit (or loss) if the price of the stock, on the expiration date, is $65? $75? $80? $85? $95? What is the maximum return the investor can earn?

**Solution:** The value of the call option ($C_1$) is zero if the value of the stock is less than the exercise price of the option (i.e., if $S_1 \leq E$). Therefore, the investor's net loss is the $10 purchase price of the call for $S_1$ equal to $65, $75 or $80. If $S_1$ is $85 on the expiration date, the investor will exercise the option for a gain of $(S_1 - E) = (\$85 - \$80) = \$5$. The net gain is ($5 – $10) = –$5, or a net loss of $5. If $S_1$ is $95, the gain on the exercise of the option is $(S_1 - E) = (\$95 - \$80) = \$15$, and the net gain is ($15 – $10) = $5. In principle, there is no upper limit to the return on the call; the higher the price of the stock on the expiration date, the greater the net gain to the investor.


## Problem 12

For the data in Problems 8 and 10, compute the gain (or loss) to the writer of the call if the price of the stock, on the expiration date, is $65? $75? $80? $85? $95? What is the maximum return the writer of the call can earn? What is the maximum possible loss for the writer of the call option?

**Solution:** If the price of the stock on the expiration date is less than or equal to the exercise price (i.e., if $S_1 \leq E$), then the buyer of the call option will not exercise the option and the net gain to the writer of the option is the $10 purchase price. Note that this is the same as the loss to the buyer of the option, as indicated in Problem 9, because the writing of a call option is a zero-sum game.

The buyer of the call will exercise the option if the price of the stock is $85 on the expiration date, forcing the writer of the call to sell, for $80, a share of stock whose market value is $85. Therefore, the exercise of the option results in a $5 loss to the writer of the option; the net gain to the writer of the option is ($10 – $5) = $5. If the price of the stock is $95, the exercise of the option results in a $15 loss to the writer of the option, and a net gain of (–$15 + $10) = –$5, or a loss of $5.

The maximum return to the writer of the call is the $10 purchase price of the call. The writer earns this amount if $S_1 \leq E$, so that the call is not exercised. The maximum loss to the writer of the call is, theoretically, unlimited; as the price of the stock increases, the loss to the writer of the option increases.

## Problem 13

A firm has a pure-discount debt issue due in one year with a maturity value of $5,000. The risk-free rate is 11%, and the current market value of the firm's assets is $4,600. One year from now, the value of the firm's assets will be either $5,100 or $5,500. What is the value today of the equity in the firm? What is the value of the firm's debt?

**Solution:** The firm's shareholders own a call option on the firm's assets, with an exercise price of $5,000. The option is certain to expire in the money, since the value of the firm's assets will exceed the exercise price on the expiration date of the option. Consequently, the value of the option is equal to the current value of the underlying asset (i.e., the firm's total assets) minus the present value of the exercise price of the call option:

$$C_0 \; = \; S_0 \; - \; \frac{E}{(1 + R_t)} \; = \; \$4,600 \; - \; \frac{\$5,000}{(1.11)} \; = \; \$95.50$$

Therefore, the firm's equity is worth $95.50. The current value of the debt is ($5,000/1.11) = $4,504.50.


## Problem 14

From the data in Problem 13, suppose that the possible values of the firm's assets one year from now are $4,500 or $5,500. What is the value today of the equity in the firm? What is the value of the firm's debt? What is the interest rate on the firm's debt?

**Solution:** If, one year from now, the value of the firm's assets is $4,500, then the shareholders will elect to default on the firm's debt. That is, since the option is out of the money, the call option is worthless. On the other hand, if the value of the firm's assets is $5,500, then the value of the call option is $(S_1 - E) = (\$5,500 - \$5,000) = \$500$. The strategy which replicates the possible values of the underlying asset is an investment of ($4,500/1.11) = $4,054.05 in the risk-free asset and the purchase of an appropriate number of call options, computed as follows:

$$\frac{\Delta S}{\Delta C} \; = \; \frac{\$5,500 \; - \; \$4,500}{\$500 \; - \; \$0} \; = \; 2$$

The current value of the firm must be equal to the value of the two call options plus the present value of the investment in the risk-free asset: $\$4,600 \; = \; (2 \times C_0) + \$4,054.05$.

Solving for $C_0$, we find that the value of the firm's equity is $272.97. The value of the firm's debt is the total value of firm less the value of the equity:  $4,600 - 272.97 = $4,327.03$

The firm's debt has a maturity value of $5,000, so that the interest rate on the firm's debt is: ($5,000/$4,327.03) − 1 = .15553 = 15.553%


## Problem 15

A convertible bond issued by Erving Manufacturing, Inc., a manufacturer of medical supplies, has a face value of $1,000, a coupon interest rate of 12%, and matures in 18 years. Interest is paid annually. The Erving bond is rated BB; non-convertible, BB-rated corporate bonds currently yield 13%. At the holder's option, the bond can be exchanged for 16 shares of Erving common stock, which currently sells for $45 per share. What is the conversion ratio for the Erving Bond? What is the conversion price? What is the conversion premium?

**Solution:** The bond can be converted into 16 shares of common stock, so that the conversion ratio is 16. The conversion price is the face value of the bond divided by the conversion ratio: $1,000 / 16 = $62.5. The conversion premium is the difference between the conversion price and the market price of the common stock: ($62.50 – $45) = $17.50. The conversion premium as a percent of the market price is: ($17.50/$62.50) = .28 = 28%.

## Problem 16

Compute the straight bond value for the bond described in Problem 15.

**Solution:** The straight bond value of a convertible bond is the price at which the bond would sell if it were not convertible. As discussed earlier, the value of a bond is the present value of the future coupon interest payments plus the present value of the maturity value, which is computed as follows: PV = [$120 x PVIFA(13%,8)] + $1,000 / $(1.13)^{18}$ = ($120 × 6.839905) + ($1,000 × .1108123) = $931.60.

## Problem 17

Compute the conversion value for the Erving bond described in Problem 15. What is the floor value of the bond?

**Solution:** The conversion value is equal to the conversion ratio multiplied by the current price of the stock: 16 × $45 = $720.   The floor value of a convertible bond is the greater of the straight bond value and the conversion value; for the Erving bond, the floor value is $931.60.

## Problem 18

A bond with 10 detachable warrants has been offered for sale at a price of $1,000. The bond matures in 30 years and has an annual coupon payment of $100. Each warrant gives the owner the right to purchase five shares of stock at $15 per share. Ordinary bonds (i.e., bonds without warrants) of similar quality are priced to yield 14%. What is the value of a warrant?

**Solution:** If there were no warrants, the value of the bond would be the present value of the future coupon interest payments plus the present value of the $1,000 maturity value. Using the procedure described earlier, the value of the bond is $719.89. The total value of the warrants is ($1,000 – $719.89) = $280.11. Since there are ten warrants, each is worth $28.01.

## Problem 19

Using the data from Problem 18, determine the maximum current price of the firm's stock.

**Solution:** The straight bond value is $719.89. Each bond enables the owner to buy a total of 50 shares of stock for $15 per share. The minimum value of the warrants is [50 × (S – $15)]; the solution to Problem 18 indicates that the total value of the warrants is $280.11. Therefore, the current stock price is at most the value of S in the equation:
  50 × (S – $15) = $280.11.

Solving for S, we find that the current stock price is at most:   S = $15 + ($280.11/50) = $20.60.

## Problem 20

Tasha holds a convertible debenture in a firm with a $1,000 face value and a conversion price of $25. How many shares of stock can Tasha exchange the bond for? What is the conversion ratio? If the market value of the firm's stock is $18, what is the conversion premium?

**Solution:** Tasha can exchange the bonds for ($1,000/$25)   =   40 shares. The conversion ratio is 40. With a market value of $18 per share, the conversion premium is ($25-$18) = $7; expressed as a percent of the market value of the stock, the conversion premium is ($7 / $18)   =   38.89% of the market value of the stock.

## Problem 21

Billy Shakespeare holds a convertible debenture of the Globe Theatre, Inc. which has a face value of $1,000 and a conversion price of $20. Globe shares currently trade at $16.16. As a percentage, the How many shares can Shakespeare trade his bond for? What is the conversion premium?

**Solution:** Shakespeare can trade his bond for $1,000 / $20   =   50 shares of the Globe Theatre, Inc. The conversion ratio is 50 and the conversion premium is $20 - $16.16   =   $3.84. As a percentage, the premium is $3.84 / $16.16   =   0.2376   =   23.76%